THE BOXTREE A-Z OF tvSTARS

1992-93

BOXTREE

First published in the UK 1992 by
Boxtree Limited
36 Tavistock Street
London WC2E 7PB

10   9   8   7   6   5   4   3   2   1

© Boxtree Ltd 1992

Design by Paterson-Jones
Typesetting and reproduction by
Bookworm Typesetting, Manchester
Printed and bound in Great Britain by
Richard Clay Limited, Bungay, Suffolk

A catalogue record for this book is
available from the British Library

ISBN 1 85283 163 4

Publisher's Acknowledgements
Boxtree would like to thank all those who provided photographic
material for this edition, in particular, Channel Four, Granada
TV, Central TV, Yorkshire TV, BBC TV, Grundy TV, the ITV
Association and, of course, the many agents.

CONTENTS

FOREWORD

Welcome to *The Boxtree A-Z of TV Stars*, a new guide giving you the lowdown on 1,200 stars of the small screen. In the following pages, you will find details of the work and personal lives of actors, actresses, presenters and entertainers. Entries are listed alphabetically by surname and I have attempted to make each one as comprehensive as possible. Where a star's TV and film work is particularly extensive, I have omitted or cut down on theatre credits, for space reasons. I have done the same with film credits where TV ones are extensive. Below is a list of abbreviations used. Places mentioned are in the United Kingdom unless otherwise stated. Similarly, all theatres and drama schools are in London unless noted. Where television programmes have been made only for regional transmission, I have tried to specify the TV company. A list of addresses for agents, television companies and fan clubs is printed at the back of the book. I asked the stars to reveal their favourite television programmes, and many were glad to oblige. *Coronation Street* was far and away their No 1, reflecting the public's taste, but the American series *LA Law* and *Cheers* came in second and third. Finally, I would like to thank the stars and their agents, as well as television companies, the actors' union Equity and the British Film Institute Library, for their help in compiling this book. Special thanks, and love, to Deborah.

Anthony Hayward
EDITOR

Abbreviations used in this book.

ASM = assistant stage manager
b. = born
m. = married
d. = daughter
s. = son
(dec) = deceased
(dis) = marriage dissolved
(qv) = see under separate entry
RSC = Royal Shakespeare Company
RTS = Royal Television Society
SWET = Society of West End Theatres
BAFTA = British Academy of Film and Television Arts
SFTA = Society of Film and TV Arts (BAFTA's predecessor)

ABBOT, *russ*

Russ Abbot. Comedian/Entertainer/Actor. b. Chester, 18 September 1948. Formed the Black Abbots in 1965, before going solo. **Theatre:** *Russ Abbot's Madhouse; Little Me* (Prince of Wales Theatre); *One for the Road* (Lyric Theatre); *Russ Abbot and Friends; Russ Abbot's Palladium Madhouse* (London Palladium); *Russ Abbot's Summer Madhouse.* **TV:** *London Night Out; What's On Next?; Who Do You Do?; The Comedians; Bruce Forsyth's Big Night; Russ Abbot's Madhouse* (six series); *Des O'Connor Now; Live From Her Majesty's; Tarby and Friends; Wogan; The Bob Monkhouse Show; Live From the Palladium; The Russ Abbot Show; The Russ Abbot Christmas Show.* Winner, *TVTimes:* Funniest Man on Television award (five times). **Address:** c/o Mike Hughes Entertainments/Clifford Elson Publicity. m. Tricia; 1 d. Erika, 3 s. Richard, Gary, Christopher.

ACKLAND, *joss*

Joss Ackland. Actor. b. Kensington, West London, 29 February 1928. Trained at Central School of Speech and Drama. **Films:** *The Black Windmill; Great Expectations; Operation Daybreak; The Greek Tycoon; A Zed and Two Noughts; Lady Jane; To Kill a Priest; White Mischief; Lethal Weapon II; The Hunt for Red October; Six Columns In the Chronicle; To Forget Palermo; Object of Beauty.* **TV:** *The Crezz; Enemy At the Door; Tinker, Tailor, Soldier, Spy; Constance Kent; Shadowlands; Queenie; First and Last; The Man Who Lived At the Ritz; The Intercom Conspiracy; Never the Sinner; Jekyll & Hyde* (TV movie); *Ashenden; Agatha Christie's Miss Marple.* **Books:** *I Must Be In There Somewhere* (autobiography, 1990). **Address:** c/o ICM. m. Rosemary Kircaldy; 5 d. Melanie, Antonia, Penelope, Samantha, Kirsty, 2 s. Paul (dec), Toby.

ACTON, *dawn*

Dawn Jean Acton. Actress. b. Ashton-under-Lyne, Lancashire, 15 March 1977. Trained at Oldham Theatre Workshop. **TV:** Took over the role of Tracy Barlow in *Coronation Street* at the age of 11. **Address:** c/o Granada TV. Lives in Oldham. Pets: Cross jack russell called Skipper, goldfish called Herbert, Hamster called Clark, two parrots called Max and Freddie. Hobbies: Writing to pen-pals, meeting friends, watching TV and videos, playing electronic keyboard, reading magazines.

AGUTTER, *jenny*

Jenny Agutter. Actress. b. Taunton, Somerset, 20 December 1952. Trained at Elmhurst Ballet School. **Films:** *The Railway Children; The Eagle Has Landed; Equus; The Man In the Iron Mask.* **TV:** *Alexander Graham Bell; The Newcomers; The Railway Children; The Great Mr Dickens; The Wild Duck; The Cherry Orchard; The Snow Goose; The Ten Commandments; Omnibus: Shelley; A War of Children; A House In Regent Place; Kiss Me and Die; A Legacy; The Waiting Room; School Play; The Mayflower – Voyage of the Pilgrims; Beaulah Land; This Office Life; Love's Labour's Lost; Magnum; Silas Marner; Murder, She Wrote; The Twilight Zone; The Two Ronnies; The Equalizer; The Outsiders; Dear Jane; Not a Penny More, Not a Penny Less; Dear John; TECX; Boon; The Good Guys.* **Address:** c/o ICM. Lives in South Kensington, London. m. Johan Tham; 1 s. Jonathan.

AIRD, *holly*

Holly Aird. Actress. b. Aldershot, Hampshire, 18 May 1969. Trained at the Bush Davies Dance and Education School. **TV:** Miss Polly in *The History of Mr Polly* (aged 10); *The Flame Trees of Thika; The Tales of Beatrix Potter; The Muse Secrets; Spider's Webb; Seal Morning; TVTimes Star Family Challenge; Affairs of the Heart; Happy Valley; Inspector Morse; Hope It Rains; Soldier, Soldier; Agatha Christie's Miss Marple.* **Address:** c/o Hutton Management.

AITKEN, *maria*

Maria Aitken. Actress. b. Dublin, 12 September 1945. Theatre: Repertory theatre in Coventry, Manchester, Northampton and Cambridge; *Travesties* (RSC); *A Little Night Music*; *Blithe Spirit* (National Theatre); *Man of Destiny*. **Films:** *Some Girls Do; Mary Queen of Scots; Half Moon Street; A Fish Called Wanda*. **TV:** *Murder; The Gold Robbers; The Exiles; Manhunt; Counterstrike; Codename; Take Three Girls; The Regiment; The Three Marias; The Edwardians; Scotch On the Rocks; Moths; Quiet As a Nun; Company and Co; Private Lives* (own chat show); *Lizzie & Maria* (TV movie). **Address:** c/o Michael Whitehall. m. 1st Richard Durden (dis), 2nd actor Nigel Davenport (qv); 1 s. Jack.

ALAN, *ray*

Ray Alan. Ventriloquist/Presenter. b. Greenwich, south-east London, 18 September 1930. Aged 13, taught ukelele to George Formby while working as a call boy/lime boy at Lewisham Hippodrome, then became an impressionist and magician; won a talent competition as a ventriloquist, aged 18. **Theatre:** Toured with Laurel and Hardy; *Cinderella*. **TV:** *The Good Old Days; Check-Mates!; Britain By Jove!; Tich and Quackers; Ice Show* (presenter); *Where In the World* (presenter); *It's Your Word* (presenter); *Magic Circle* (presenter); *Bob Hope's Birthday Show; Cartoon Carnival; Three Little Words* (quiz show, host); *Bobby Davro's TV Weekly; A Gottle of Geer* (deviser-writer-presenter); *Starmakers* (deviser-writer-presenter). **Writer:** *Bootsy and Snudge; The Dave Allen Show; The Two Ronnies*. **Address:** c/o Peter Prichard. m. Barbie (dis).

ALDERTON, *john*

John Alderton. Actor. b. Gainsborough, Lincolnshire, 27 November 1940. **Theatre:** Repertory theatre in York. **Films:** *Zardoz*. **TV:** Dr Moon in *Emergency – Ward 10*; Bernard Hedges in *Please Sir!*; Thomas in *Upstairs, Downstairs; No, Honestly; The Wodehouse Playhouse; The Upchat Line*; title role in *Thomas and Sarah; Forever Green*. **Address:** c/o James Sharkey Associates. Lives in North London. m. 1st actress Jill Browne (dis), 2nd actress Pauline Collins (qv); 1 d. Catherine, 2 s. Nicholas, Richard.

ALDRED, *sophie*

Sophie Aldred. Actress/Presenter. b. Greenwich, London, 20 August 1962. Gained a BA Hons degree in drama from Manchester University; trained as a soprano at the Northern College of Music. **Theatre:** *The Silver Lake; The Good Person of Sezchuan; Theatre of Thelema; Underground Man; Hansel and Gretel* (opera); *Fiddler On the Roof; Cinderella*. **TV:** *Knowhow; Knock-Knock; Playbus* (storyteller/singer); *Jackanory* (storyteller); *Noel's Christmas Presents* (co-presenter); *Corners* (presenter/actress); Ace in *Doctor Who; Rainbow*. **Address:** c/o London Management.

ALEXANDER, *jean*

Jean Alexander. Actress. b. Liverpool, 24 February 1926. Library assistant for five years, before joining the Adelphi Guild Theatre in Macclesfield and touring Lancashire, Cheshire and Staffordshire. **Theatre:** Adelphi Guild Theatre; repertory theatre in Southport and York. **Films:** Christine Keeler's mother in *Scandal*. **TV:** *Deadline Midnight; Television Club; Top Secret; Jacks and Knaves; Z-Cars*; Hilda Ogden in *Coronation Street* (1964–87); *Boon*; Auntie Wainwright in *Last of the Summer Wine* (Christmas specials, 1988, 1989); *Woof!* **Books:** *The Other Side of the Street* (autobiography, 1989). Winner, Royal Television Society Best Performance award 1984–5, *TVTimes* Best Actress on TV award 1987. **Address:** c/o Joan Reddin. Single; lives in Southport.

ALEXANDER, maev

Maev Alexander. Actress. b. Glasgow, 3 February 1948. Trained at the Royal Scottish Academy of Music and Drama. **Theatre:** Perdita in *The Winter's Tale* (RSC); Frances in *Made In Bangkok.* **TV:** *Sutherland's Law; The Gentle Touch; Holding the Fort; Angels; A Leap In the Dark; Kids; Take the Stage; The Main Chance; This Man Craig; By the Sword Divided; Fools On the Hill; Scoop; That's Life* (newsdesk presenter). **Address:** c/o Peters Fraser & Dunlop. m. Simon Dunmore; 1 d. Alix.

ALEXANDER, peter

Peter Alexander. Actor. b. Midsomer Norton, Somerset, 15 October 1952. Trained at the Guildford School of Acting. **Theatre:** *Charley's Aunt; Twelfth Night; Joseph; Filomena; Good; Cabaret; A Christmas Carol; No Sex, Please – We're British* (London West End); *Beyond the Rainbow* (London West End); *The Canterbury Tales; Deep Blue Sea.* **TV:** *Family Man; Chessgame; Travelling Man; Winning Streak; Affairs of the Heart; Minder; Coronation Street; The Practice;* Phil Pearce in *Emmerdale Farm; All Creatures Great and Small; Medics; Singles.* **Address:** c/o Ruth Boyle Management. m. choreographer Penny Stevenson; 1 d. Emily, 1 s. Nicholas.

ALEXANDER, terence

Terence Alexander. Actor. b. London, 11 March 1923. **Theatre:** *Move Over, Mrs Markham; There Goes The Bride; Poor Bitos.* **Films:** *The League of Gentlemen; Magic Christian; Waterloo; Run a Crooked Mile; The Day of the Jackal; Internecine Affair; The Boy Who Never Was.* **TV:** *Codename; The Forsythe Saga; Unpleasantness At the Bellona Club; The Solarium; Flea In Her Ear; The Pallisers; Moody and Pegg; The Good Old Days; Churchill and the Generals; The Les Dawson Show; The Dick Emery Show; Devenish; Unity; Just Liz; Terry and June; Suntrap; The Jim Davidson Show; The Fall and Rise of Reginald Perrin; The Seven Dials Mystery;* Charlie Hungerford in *Bergerac; Crown Court; Strangers and Brothers; The New Statesman.* **Address:** c/o The Brunskill Management. m. 1st Juno, 2nd actress Jane Downs; 2 s. Nicholas, Marcus (both from 1st m.).

ALLDRIDGE, colin

Colin Alldridge. Actor/Singer. b. Bournemouth, 19 June 1965. Trained at The Drama Centre and the London Studio Centre. **Theatre:** *Spring Awakening; Romeo and Juliet; The Country Wife; Guys and Dolls* (all at The Drama Centre); *The Island; Billy Liar* (both at London Studio Centre); *Wild At Heart* (Riverside Studios). **TV:** *Press Gang;* PC Phil Young in *The Bill* (1989–91). **Address:** c/o CAM. Single; lives in London. Hobbies: Keeping fit, scuba-diving, water-skiing. **Favourite TV programme:** *The New Statesman.*

ALLEN, dave

David Tynan O'Mahony. Comedian. b. Tallaght, County Dublin, 6 July 1936. Nephew of poet Katharine Tynan. Worked as a journalist on the *Irish Independent* and *Drogheda Times,* then as a Red Coat at Butlin's in Skegness, before turning professional. **TV:** *Tonight With Dave Allen; The Val Doonican Show* (resident comedian); *The London Palladium Show* (compere); *The Dave Allen Show.* **Address:** c/o BBC TV. m. actress Judith Stott.

ALLEY, *kirstie*

Kirstie Alley. Actress. b. Wichita, Kansas, USA, 12 January 1955. **Films:** *One More Chance; Star Trek II: The Wrath of Khan; Blind Date; Champions; Runaway; Shoot To Kill; Deadly Pursuit; Look Who's Talking; Daddy's Home; Madhouse; Sibling Rivalry.* **TV:** *Two Heads; Highway Honeys; A Midsummer Night's Dream; A Bunny's Tale; Stark: Mirror Image* (all TV movies); *North and South, Book II* (mini-series); *Masquerade;* Rebecca Howe in *Cheers.* **Address:** c/o McCartt-Oreck-Barrett. m. actor Parker Stevenson.

ALTMAN, *john*

John Altman. Actor. b. Reading, Berkshire, 2 March 1952. Became a professional actor after graduating in photography. **Theatre:** *The Balcony; Dracula; Masque of the Red Death; Woyzeck.* **Films:** *Return of the Jedi; An American Werewolf In London; The Birth of The Beatles; Quadrophenia; The First Great Train Robbery; The John Lennon Story.* **TV:** *Going To Work; Life After Death; Remembrance; Lucky Jim; The Scarlet Pimpernel; Bouncing Back; Minder;* Nick Cotton in *EastEnders* (on and off, 1985-). **Address:** c/o ICM Duncan Heath Associates. m. Brigitte; 1 d. Rosanna.

ALVAREZ, *tony*

Tony Alvarez. Actor/Singer. b. Spain, 19 December 1956. **Theatre:** *Roberta; Evita* (both musicals). **Films:** *Fatty Finn; Starview; Oliver!; Nicholas and Alexander.* **TV:** *Two In the Bush;* Dr Tony Garcia in *The Young Doctors; Skyways; Prisoner: Cell Block H; Carson's Law; The Don Lane Show; The Mike Walsh Show; Ronnie Corbett Specials.* **Address:** c/o Richard Kent Management. m. Jamie. Hobbies: Squash, swimming, eating.

AMBROSE, *gladys*

Gladys Ambrose. Actress/Singer. b. Liverpool, 28 December 1930. **Theatre:** Started as a chorus dancer in *Joie de Vivre* (1949); comedy knockabout acrobatic act with husband Johannes for many years; experience on the trapeze and at foot juggling. **TV:** *Who Killed Julie Wallace?; Match of the Day; Guplin; The Brothers MacGregor; Bread;* Eddie Yeats' landlady and Mrs Hindle in *Coronation Street; Visiting Day; Bulman; Lonesome Road; The Les Dawson Show;* Julia Brogan in *Brookside.* **Address:** c/o Mersey Television. Lives in Liverpool. m. Johannes; 2 d. Janette, Wendy (The Votel Sisters). Hobbies: Walking, swimming, visiting museums, art galleries and stately homes, singing for various charities, writing pantomime scripts for own family productions. **Favourite TV programme:** *Open All Hours; Rising Damp;* anything with Ronnie Barker, David Jason or Thora Hird.

AMENTA, *jade*

Jade Amenta. Actress. b. Australia. Daughter of film director Pino Amenta. **TV:** Melissa Jarrett in *Neighbours* (1990-). **Address:** c/o Grundy Television.

AMORY, *peter*

Peter Amory. Actor. b. 2 November. Trained at RADA (won the Tree Prize). **Theatre:** Title role in *Fool*; *Psychosis Unclassified*; *Wait Until Dark*; *Busman's Honeymoon*. **TV:** *Boon*; *Running Wild* (two series); *Casualty*; *Chelworth*; *Inspector Morse*; *Gentlemen and Players*; *The Chief*; Chris Tate in *Emmerdale* (1989-). **Address:** c/o Daly Gagan Associates/Yorkshire Television.

ANDERSON, *jean*

Jean Anderson. Actress. b. Glasgow, 12 December 1908. Brought up in Guildford, Surrey. Played violin in the Guildford Orchestra before training at RADA. **Theatre:** Repertory theatre; *Martine*; *For Services Rendered* (both National Theatre); *Lent*; *The Dame of Sark*; *Hedda Gabler*; *Les Liaisons Dangereuses*. **Films:** *The Lady Vanishes*; *Half a Sixpence*; *A Town Like Alice*; *The Kidnappers*. **TV:** *Maigret*; *Dr Finlay's Casebook*; *Paul Temple*; *Kate*; *Jackanory*; *Bachelor Father*; *The Brothers*; *This Is Your Life*; *Little Women*; *Scoop*; *The Railway Children*; *Tenko*; *Paris*; *Agatha Christie's Miss Marple*; *The Good Doctor Bodkin Adams*; *Campion*; *Circles of Deceit*; *The House of Eliott*; *Keeping Up Appearances*; *The Good Guys*. **Address;** c/o The Brunskill Management. m. theatre director Peter Powell (dis); 1 d. theatrical agent Aude.

ANDREWS, *anthony*

Anthony Andrews. Actor. b. London, 12 January 1948. **Films:** *Operation Daybreak*; *The Holcroft Covenant*; *The Light Horsemen*. **TV:** *A Beast With Two Backs*; *Alma Mater*; *The Mating Machine*; *Dixon of Dock Green*; *Doomwatch*; *Woodstock*; *A Day Out*; *The Judge's Wife*; *Follyfoot*; *QB VII*; *Take Me High*; *Fortunes of Nigel*; *The Pallisers*; *The Duchess of Duke Street*; *David Copperfield*; *Upstairs, Downstairs*; *London Assurance*; *French Without Tears*; *The Country Wife*; *A Superstition*; *Much Ado About Nothing*; *Danger UXB*; *Romeo and Juliet*; Sebastian Flyte in *Brideshead Revisited* (winner, BAFTA Best Actor on TV award, 1981); *Love Boat*; *The Black Bayu*; *La Ronde*; *Ivanhoe*; *The Scarlet Pimpernel*; *Z for Zachariah*; *Sparkling Cyanide*; *Suspicion*; *A.D.*; *The Woman He Loved*; *Jekyll and Hyde*. **Address:** c/o Peters Fraser & Dunlop. m. former actress Georgina; 1 d. Jessica, 1 s. Joshua.

ANGERSON, *jeremy*

Jeremy Angerson. Actor. b. Australia. Took private acting lessons with Bruce Kerr. **Films:** *Struck By Lightning*; the Sparrow in *Sebastian and the Sparrow*. **TV:** *Mission Impossible*; Josh Anderson in *Neighbours* (1990-). **Address:** c/o Grundy Television.

ANHOLT, *tony*

Anthony Anholt. Actor. b. Singapore, 19 January 1941. Trained at the Royal Court Theatre in mask, mime, movement, drama and voice. **Theatre:** *The Importance of Being Earnest*; *Sleuth*; *Bedroom Farce*; *Amadeus*; *The Tempest*; *Boys In the Band*. **Films:** *Fear Is the Key*. **TV:** *Alice*; *Court Martial*; *Napoleon and Love*; *The Protectors*; *The Strauss Family*; *Marked Personal*; *A Family At War*; *Crown Court*; *The Sweeney*; *Jason King*; *Space 1999*; *Wilde Alliance*; *The Copyist*; *Terry and June*; *Triangle*; *The Kelly Monteith Show*; *The Fell Sergeant*; *Seasons*; *The Last Days of Pompeii*; *Juliet Bravo*; *The Late Nancy Irvine*; *Minder*; *Bulman*; *Howards' Way*; *Only Fools and Horses*; *At Any Time*; *Singles*. **Address:** c/o Roger Carey Management. 1 s. Christen.

ANNIS, *francesca*

Francesca Annis. Actress. b. London, 14 May 1944. Trained at the Corona Academy, first in ballet, then in drama. **Theatre:** *The Sun and the Wind;* Ophelia in *Hamlet.* **Films:** *Cleopatra; Run With the Wind; The Walking Stick; Penny Gold; Macbeth; Krull; Dune.* **TV:** *The Human Jungle; Heritage; Danger Man; Dr Finlay's Casebook; Great Expectations; View From the Bridge; The Family Is a Vicious Circle; Pin To See the Peepshow; Madame Bovary;* Lillie Langtry in *Lillie (TVTimes* Best Actress On TV award, 1978– 9); *Why Didn't They Ask Evans?; Coming Out of the Ice; The Secret Adversary; Partners In Crime; Inside Story; Onassis; Parnell and the Englishwoman; The Gravy Train Goes East; Performance: Absolute Hell.* **Address:** c/o ICM. 1 d. Charlotte (from relationship with photographer Patrick Wiseman).

ANTHONY, *lysette*

Lysette Anthony. Actress. b. London, 1963. **Films:** *Krull; Oliver Twist; Tug of Love; A Drop In the Ocean; The Emperor's New Clothes; In Search of Eileen; The Imposter of Baker Street; Without a Clue; 29 Days In February; The Lady and the Highwayman; A Ghost In Monte Carlo; The Pleasure Principle.* **TV:** *Ivanhoe* (TV movie); *Dombey and Son; Beauty and the Beast; Jemima Shore Investigates; Night Train To Murder; Auf Wiedersehen, Pet; Oliver Twist; Lovejoy; Three Up, Two Down; House On Kirov Street; The Bretts; Look Good, Feel Fantastic; Cosmopolitan; Home To Roost; Jack the Ripper* (TV movie); *Through the Looking Glass; Campion; Dark Shadows.* **Address:** c/o ICM Duncan Heath Associates. Lives in Los Angeles. m. artist Luke.

ARDEN, *mark*

Mark Arden. Actor. Also half of the double-act The Oblivion Boys. **Theatre:** *Hamlet; What the Butler Saw; Hobson's Choice; Romeo and Juliet; Aladdin; Cinderella; Godspell!; Joseph and the Amazing Technicolor Dreamcoat; Dirty Linen; Knots and Bumps; Rosencrantz and Guildenstern Are Dead* (Piccadilly Theatre); *Noises Off; Sleuth.* With The Oblivion Boys: *The Wow Show* (Wyndham's Theatre). **Films:** *Bearskin* (Channel Four film); *Trying To Connect You.* **TV:** *Romeo and Juliet; The Young Ones* (two series); *Carrott's Lib; Big Deal; Happy Families; The Black Adder; The Comic Strip Presents . . .; Little Armadillos; Money Talks; Checkpoint Chiswick; Inner City Fairy Tales; Girls On Top; This Is David Lander;* Fireman 'Vaseline' in *London's Burning; Lazarus and Dingwall; Bottom.* With The Oblivion Boys: *Saturday Live; The Tube; Loose Talk.* **Address:** c/o Mayer Management.

ARIS, *ben*

Benjamin Patrick Aris. Actor. b. Chelsea, London, 16 March 1937. Trained at the Arts Educational School. **TV:** *Muffin the Mule; Dr Jekyll and Mr Hyde; The Assassination Run; Cribb; To the Manor Born; Bergerac; By the Sword Divided; Video Stars; Hi-de-Hi!; Shine On Harvey Moon; Chance In a Million; Paradise Postponed; Star Quality; All In Good Faith; Call Me Mister; Slinger's Day; Executive Stress; The Kenny Everett Show; Hold the Dream; The Comic Strip Presents . . .; First of the Summer Wine; Agatha Christie's Poirot; Young Charlie Chaplin; Mr Majeika; You Rang, M'Lord?; No Job for a Lady; Hope It Rains; Further Up Pompeii; The Good Guys.* **Address:** c/o Barry Brown & Partner. Lives in London. m. Yemaiel; 1 d. Rachel, 1 s. Jonathan. Pets: Two cats. Hobbies: Music, ornithology, oenophily. **Favourite TV programme:** Any nature or wildlife subjects.

ARMSTRONG, *alun*

Alun Armstrong. Actor. b. 17 July 1946. **Films:** *The Duellists; A Bridge Too Far; Get Carter; The Fourteen; The French Lieutenant's Woman; Krull; No 1; The House; Billy the Kid and the Green Baize Vampire; White Roses; White Hunter, Black Heart; The Child Eater; American Friends; The Widow Maker; London Kills Me; Split Second; Patriot Games.* **TV:** *A Sharp Intake of Breath; Measure for Measure; Our Day Out; All Day On the Sands; The Stars Look Down; One In a Thousand; Days of Hope; Shooting the Chandelier; Only Make Believe; Get Lost; Nicholas Nickleby; Sharing Time; The Book Tower; Bulman; Joe Wilson Lives* (one-man show); *The Caucasian Chalk Circle; No 27; This Is David Lander; A Night On the Tyne; Breaking Rank; Sticky Wickets; Murder In Eden; Stanley and the Women;* Roy Grade in *Goodbye Cruel World.* **Address:** c/o Markham & Froggatt.

ARMSTRONG, *Fiona*

Fiona Armstrong. Newscaster. b. Preston, Lancashire, 28 November 1956. Reporter with Radio 210, in Reading, before moving to television. **TV:** BBC North West (reporter); Border TV (reporter and presenter); ITN (reporter and presenter). **Address:** c/o ITN. m. Rodney Potts.

ARMSTRONG, *pamela*

Pamela Armstrong. Presenter. b. Borneo, 25 August 1951. Presenter for Capital Radio, in London, before moving to television. **TV:** *London Today; Well Being;* ITN (newscaster); *Pamela Armstrong; Breakfast Time.* **Address:** c/o Jon Roseman Associates.

ARNOLD, *debbie*

Debbie Arnold. Actress. b. Sunderland, 14 June. **Theatre:** *Last of the Red Hot Lovers; The Sleeping Prince; The Lives of the Wives; Four In a Million; Women Behind Bars.* **Films:** *Valentino; Oliver Twist; Even Break.* **TV:** *Rockliffe's Babies; Once In a Lifetime; Miss Marple – Body In the Library; The Funny Side; Bootle Saddles; C.A.T.S. Eyes; The Two Ronnies; Minder; The Laughter Show; Don't Wait Up; The Bill; Ticket To Ride; Coronation Street; Up the Elephant and Round the Castle; The Citadel; Minder On the Orient Express;* Debbie in *Emmerdale;* Sylvia in *All Creatures Great and Small.* **Address:** c/o Mary Arnold Management. m. actor David Janson; 1 d. Ciara.

ARTHUR, *bea*

Bernice Frankel. Actress. b. New York, USA, 13 May 1926. Trained at the New School for Social Research's Dramatic Workshop, New York. **Theatre:** *Dog Beneath the Skin; Gas; Yerma; No Exit; Personal Appearance; Candlelight; Love Or Money; The Voice of the Turtle; The Taming of the Shrew; The Owl and the Pussycat; The Threepenny Opera; What's the Rush?; Nature's Way; Ulysses In Nighttown; Gay Divorcee; Fiddler On the Roof; Mame* (Tony award); *The Floating Light Bulb.* **Films:** *That Kind of Woman; Lovers and Other Strangers; Mame; History of the World – Part 1.* **TV:** *Once Upon a Time;* title role in *Maude* (Emmy award, 1977); *On the Air; Amanda's Place; My First Love* (TV movie); Dorothy in *The Golden Girls* (Emmy Best Comedy Actress award, 1988). **Address:** c/o William Morris Agency (USA). m. director Gene Saks (dis); 2 s. Matthew, Daniel.

ASH, *leslie*

Leslie Ash. Actress. Began career as a model, before turning to acting. **Theatre:** *The Bottom Drawer; Of Mice and Men; Cinderella; Paris Match* (Garrick Theatre); *Babes in the Wood; Robin Hood.* **Films:** *Rosie Dixon, Night Nurse; Quadrophenia; The Nutcracker; Curse of the Pink Panther; Shadey.* **TV:** *The Gentle Touch; Cupid Darts; Good Night and God Bless; World's End; Seconds Out; Shelley; La Ronde; Holding the Fort; Outside Edge; The Balance of Nature; The Happy Apple; The Two Ronnies; Four Track Live; The Tube* (co-presenter); *Murder – Ultimate Grounds for Divorce;* Fred in *C.A.T.S. Eyes; Sporting Chance; The Marksman; Home To Roost; Natural Causes; The Bill;* Deborah in *Men Behaving Badly; Haggard; Perfect Scoundrels; Love Hurts.* **Address:** c/o Hamper-Neafsey Associates. m. footballer Lee Chapman.

ASHER, *jane*

Jane Asher. Actress. b. London, 5 April 1946. Started acting, aged five, in the film *Mandy*. **Films:** *Alfie; Runners; Dreamchild; Paris By Night*. **TV:** *The Mill On the Floss; Love Story; Brideshead Revisited; Love Is Old, Love Is New; A Voyage Round My Father; East Lynne; Bright Smiler; The Mistress; Wish Me Luck; Still Life; Eats for Treats*. **Books:** *Jane Asher's Party Cakes; Jane Asher's Fancy Dress; Silent Nights for You and Your Baby; Jane Asher's Quick Party Cakes; The Moppy Stories; Easy Entertaining; Keep Your Baby Safe; Children's Parties; Calendar of Cakes; Eats for Treats*. **Address:** c/o Chatto and Linnit. Lives in London. m. artist Gerald Scarfe; 1 d. Katie, 2 s. Alexander, Rory. **Pets:** One dog, two cats, one hamster, three fish. Hobbies: Reading, cooking, skiing. **Favourite TV programme:** Good, exciting drama serials.

ASHLEY, *caroline*

Caroline Smith. Actress. b. Coatbridge, Lanarkshire, 4 March 1958. Trained at the Queen Margaret College Drama School, then taught drama, before acting professionally. **Theatre:** Perth Repertory; *Cinderella; Aladdin; Snow White and the Seven Dwarfs*. **TV:** Fiona Ryder (née Cunningham) in *Take the High Road* (1980-). **Address:** c/o Scottish Television. Single; lives in Glasgow.

ASHTON, *al*

Al Hunter. Actor/Writer. b. Liverpool. Trained at Manchester Polytechnic's School of Theatre. Writes under real name. **TV:** *Angels; Juliet Bravo; You Don't Have To Walk To Fly; Lytton's Diary; C.A.T.S. Eyes*; Colin Duma in *Brookside; Lost Empires; Constant Hot Water*; Ray Grice in *Crossroads; Rockliffe's Babies; The Bretts; Casualty; Surgical Spirit; Hard Cases; Flying High; Minder; Watching; Bergerac; Inspector Morse; The Endless Game; Alive and Kicking; Just; Devices and Desires; Birds of a Feather; Bread; She-Wolf of London*. As writer: *The Firm; EastEnders; Casualty; The Bill; Emmerdale; Streetwise; Alive and Kicking*. **Address:** c/o George Heathcote Management. Lives in London. m. Sue. Hobbies: 'Theatre, tennis, sex – but not necessarily in that order.' **Favourite TV programme:** 'Anything I'm in or have written.'

ASHTON, *john*

John Ashton. Actor. b. London, 29 November 1950. Trained at the Bristol Old Vic Theatre School. **Theatre:** *The Beggar's Opera; A Midsummer Night's Dream; The Bubble Band; Jesus Christ Superstar* (Palace Theatre); *The Caucasian Chalk Circle; The Threepenny Opera; Romeo and Juliet; Animal Farm; The Merchant of Venice; Absent Friends; Abigail's Party; Rosencrantz and Guildenstern Are Dead; The Taming of the Shrew; Macbeth; Who's Afraid of Virginia Woolf?; The Comedians; The Collector; One for the Road; Should Old Acquaintance...; Serious Money; City Sugar*. **Films:** *Possessions*. **TV:** *The Demolition Man; The Discovery of Animal Behaviour; Out of Court; Crimewatch; Grange Hill*; Det Insp Balfour in *Brookside*; Chief Supt Henderson in *Waterfront Beat*. **Address:** c/o Sarah Griffin Management. m. actress Serretta Wilson.

ASHWORTH, *dicken*

Dicken Ashworth. Actor. b. Todmorden, West Yorkshire, 18 July 1946. A teacher for four years, before becoming a professional actor. **Theatre:** Repertory theatre in Sheffield, Newcastle, Nottingham, Derby, Manchester and Richmond-upon-Thames. **Films:** *Tess; Krull; Chariots of Fire; Force 10 From Navarone; King of the Wind; The Biggest Bank Robbery*. **TV:** *Doctor Who; Blake's 7; Minder; C.A.T.S. Eyes; Flying Lady; The Chinese Detective; Return To Treasure Island*; Alan Partridge in *Brookside; The Two of Us; Scab; Making Out; Better Days; Nanny; We Are Seven; Keeping Up Appearances; The Bill; Inspector Morse*. **Address:** c/o Howes and Prior. Lives in London. m. set and costume designer Jane Ripley; 1 d. Tamasin.

ASNER, *ed*

Edward Asner. Actor. b. Kansas City, USA, 19 November 1926. **Films:** *Peter Gunn; The Slender Thread; Fort Apache; The Bronx; O'Hara's Wife.* **TV:** *Slattery's People; Profiles In Courage; The Fugitive; Ironside; The FBI; Medical Centre; Rich Man, Poor Man; Roots; The Gathering; A Case of Libel; Tender Is the Night;* title role in *Lou Grant;* Joe Danzig in *The Bronx Zoo.* Winner, seven Emmy awards and 1986 Anne Frank Human Rights Award. **Address:** c/o Gores/Fields Talent Agency. m. Nancy (sep); 2 d. Lisa, Kate, 1 s. Matthew.

ASPEL, *michael*

Michael Aspel. Presenter. b. London, 12 January 1933. Began career as an actor with BBC radio in Cardiff (1954), before becoming a BBC TV newsreader. **TV:** *Miss World; Crackerjack; Ask Aspel; Give Us a Clue; The Six O'Clock Show* (LWT); *Child's Play; Aspel & Company; This Is Your Life* (presenter); *BAFTA Awards; Trouble With the Fifties.* **Books:** *Polly Wants a Zebra; Hang On!* **Radio:** Own show, Capital Radio (1974–84), BBC Radio 2, LBC. Winner, Variety Club ITV Personality of the Year award and *TVTimes* Television Personality of the Year award. **Address:** c/o Bagenal Harvey Organisation. Lives in Surrey. m. actress Elizabeth Powell; 5 s. Gregory (dec), Richard, Edward (by previous m's), Patrick, Daniel, 1 d. Jane (by previous m.). Hobbies: Writing, swimming, boating, films, learning golf, various charities.

ATKINS, *eileen*

Eileen Atkins. Actress. b. Clapton, East London, 16 June 1934. Trained at Guildhall School of Music and Drama. **Theatre:** *The Killing of Sister George; The Cocktail Party; Vivat Vivat Regina; Suzanna Andler; Serjeant Musgrave's Dance; As You Like It; Heartbreak House; Thursday's Ladies; The Winter's Tale; Cymbeline; A Room of One's Own; Passion Play; Exclusive.* **Films:** *Equus; Let Him Have It.* **TV:** *The Letter Double Bill; The Heiress; Three Sisters; Olive; A Midsummer Night's Dream; The Duchess of Malfi; The Lady From the Sea; Electra; Omnibus: The Jean Rhys Women; She Fell Among Thieves; Sons and Lovers; Smiley's People; Titus Andronicus; Eden's End; Nellie's Version; Breaking Up; The Vision; The Burston Rebellion; A Room of One's Own.* **Address:** c/o ICM Duncan Heath Associates. m. Bill Shepherd.

ATKINSON, *rowan*

Rowan Atkinson. Actor. b. Newcastle upon Tyne, 6 January 1955. Trained as an electrical engineer but decided on a showbusiness career while at Queen's College, Oxford. **Theatre:** One-man show (London West End), national tour, world tour; *The Nerd; The Sneeze.* **Films:** *The Secret Policeman's Ball; Never Say Never Again; The Witches; Camden Town Boy.* **TV:** *Canned Laughter; Not the Nine O'Clock News; The Black Adder; Blackadder II; Blackadder III; Appointments of Dennis Jennings; Blackadder Goes Forth; Mr Bean; Bernard and the Genie.* Guest appearances: *The Innes Book of Records; The Lena Zavaroni Show; The Peter Cook Show.* Winner, Variety Club BBC Personality of the Year award (1980), BAFTA awards (1980, 1989). **Address:** c/o PBJ Management.

ATTENBOROUGH, *david*

David Attenborough. Broadcaster/Director/Writer. b. London, 8 May 1926. Worked for education book publishers, before joining the BBC as a trainee producer (1952). **TV:** *Zoo Quest;* controller of BBC2 (1965–8); director of BBC TV programmes (1969–72); *The Tribal Eye; Wildlife On One; Eastward With Attenborough; Life On Earth; The Living Planet.* **Books:** *Zoo Quest To Guiana; Zoo Quest for a Dragon; Zoo Quest In Paraguay; Quest In Paradise; Zoo Quest In Madagascar; Quest Under Capricorn; Tribal Eye; Life On Earth.* Winner, Society of Film and TV Arts special award (1961), Royal Television Society Silver Medal (1966), Society of Film and TV Arts Desmond Davis Award (1970). **Address:** c/o BBC TV. m. Jane; 1 d. Susan, 1 s. Robert.

AUBREY, james

James Aubrey. Actor. b. Klagenfurt, Austria, 1947. **Films:** Lord of the Flies; Home Before Midnight; Terror; Galileo; The Hunger; Forever Young; The Great Rock and Roll Swindle; The American Way; Cry Freedom; Buddy's Song. **TV:** All Who Sail In Her; A Bouquet of Barbed Wire; Another Bouquet; Danton's Death; St Joan; Infidelities; The Cleopatras; Tales of the Unexpected; Run Rabbit Run; Return of the Saint; Minder; The Sweeney; The Last Place On Earth; The Possessed; Shadow In a Landscape; Lytton's Diary; Lovejoy; Thin Air Eureka; The Mountain and the Molehill; The Final Frame (Channel Four film); Rockliffe's Folly; Mission Eureka; Rites of Passage; The Men's Room; TECX; Selling Hitler. **Address:** c/o Jeremy Conway.

AYRES, rosalind

Rosalind Ayres. Actress. b. Birmingham, 7 December 1946. **Films:** That'll Be the Day; The Slipper and the Rose. **TV:** Nearest and Dearest; Coronation Street; The Lovers; Home and Away (Granada TV series); Suspicion; General Hospital; Country Matters; Play for Today; 30-Minute Theatre; Shoulder To Shoulder; Within These Walls; Affairs of the Heart; Father Brown; Holding On; The House of Bernarda Alba; Hindle Wakes; Public Eye; Warship; Two's Company; Charades; The Limbo Connection; The Dick Emery Show; Rings On Their Fingers; Penmarric; The Gentle Touch; Agony; Psy-Warriors; Only When I Laugh; The Bounder; Jackanory; Father's Day; The Weather In the Streets; The Gay Lord Quex; Women of Durham; Nurses Do; Juliet Bravo; Who Dares Wins; New World; The Cat Brought It In; Mistress of Suspense. **Address:** c/o Michael Whitehall. m. actor Martin Jarvis (qv).

BADEL, sarah

Sarah Badel. Actress. b. London, 30 March 1943. **Films:** The Shooting Party; Not Without My Daughter. **TV:** The Visitors; Now Lies She There; Between the Wars; The Pallisers; Cold Comfort Farm; She; King Lear; Three Sisters; The Prime Minister's Daughter; Seven Faces of Woman; The Taming of the Shrew; Dear Brutus; Bavarian Night; Out of Order; Affairs of the Heart; The Irish RM; A Perfect Spy; The Cloning of Joanna May. **Address:** c/o Plunket Greene.

BAILEY, robin

Robin Bailey. Actor. b. Hucknall, Nottinghamshire, 5 October 1919. **Films:** Private Angelo; You Only Live Twice; The Four Feathers; Jane and the Lost City. **TV:** The $64,000 Question (compere); The Newcomers; The Pallisers; Upstairs, Downstairs; North and South; A Legacy; The Wild Duck; The Discharge of Trooper Lusby; Brett; Crown Court; I Didn't Know You Cared; Punch Revue; Took & Co; For Services Rendered; The Good Companions; Bognor; Cupid's Darts; If You Go Down In the Woods; Sorry, I'm a Stranger Here Myself; Janet; Tales From a Long Room; Potter; Sharing Time; Bleak House; Charters and Caldicott; Drummonds; Mozart; Return To the Broads; Rumpole of the Bailey; A Kind of Living; A Gentleman's Club; Number 27; Tinniswood Country; The Good Guys. **Address:** c/o Michael Whitehall. m. Patricia; 3 s. Nicholas, Simon, Justin.

BAIRSTOW, amanda

Amanda Bairstow. Actress. b. Bingley, West Yorkshire, 12 November 1960. Trained at the Italia Conti Academy. **Theatre:** Anything Goes; Firedragon; Lady Be Good; Rope; The Fantasticks; Noises Off; Borne In a Handbag; Why Not Stay for Breakfast?; Pride and Prejudice; Cinderella; Dick Whittington; Goldilocks and the Three Bears; The Wizard of Oz. **TV:** Lytton's Diary; Susan Denton in Coronation Street; Juliet Bravo; Cockles; Tears Before Bedtime; Play for Today: Only Children; Salad Days; The Bill. **Address:** c/o Adrian King Associates. Lives in North London.

BAKER, *cheryl*

Cheryl Baker. Presenter. b. Bethnal Green, London, 8 March 1955. Previously a singer with the groups CoCo and Bucks Fizz (1981 Eurovision Song Contest winners). **TV:** *The Six O'Clock Show* (LWT); *How Dare You; The Saturday Picture Show; Record Breakers; The Funny Side; Eggs and Baker; My Secret Desire.* **Address:** c/o Razzamatazz, Crofters, East Park Lane, Newchapel, Nr Lingfield, Surrey, tel (0342) 835359. Lives in Eltham, South London.

BAKER, *colin*

Colin Baker. Actor. b. London, 8 June 1943. Studied law before training at LAMDA. **Theatre:** *Hamlet; Macbeth; The Norman Conquests; Traitors; The Other House* (Mermaid Theatre); *The Price of Justice* (Mermaid Theatre); *Corpse; Deathtrap; Run for Your Wife* (Criterion Theatre); *Born In the Garden; Spider's Web; Privates On Parade; Time and Time Again.* **Films:** *A Clockwork Orange; Dangerous Davies; No Longer Alone.* **TV:** *Roads To Freedom;* Paul Merroney in *The Brothers; Cousin Bette; Hamlet; The Silver Sword; The Edwardians; War and Peace; Harriet's Back In Town; A Fall of Eagles; For Maddie With Love; Blake's 7; Swallows and Amazons Forever; The Brothers;* title role in *Doctor Who; Casualty.* **Address:** c/o Barry Burnett Organisation. m. 1st actress Liza Goddard (dis), 2nd Marion Wyatt Baker; 1 s. Jack (dec), 2 d. Lucy, Belinda.

BAKER, *danny*

Danny Baker. Presenter. b. Deptford, South London, 22 June 1957. Rock journalist before entering television. **TV:** *20th Century Box; The Six O'Clock Show* (LWT); *Danny Baker On ...; Six O'Clock Live* (LWT); *Win, Lose Or Draw.* **Address:** c/o Noel Gay Artists. m. Wendy; 1 d. Bonnie, 1 s. Sonny.

BAKER, *george*

George Baker. Actor/Writer. b. British Embassy, Varna, Bulgaria, 1 April 1931. **TV:** *The Fenn Street Gang; Bowler; Death of a Salesman; Medea; Candida; Rupert of Hentzau; I, Claudius; Died In the Wool/Opening Night/Vintage Murder/Colour Scheme; Goodbye Darling; Minder; Triangle; The Chinese Detective; Secret Adversary; Hart To Hart; Goodbye, Mr Chips; Dead Head; The Bird Fancier; Marjorie and Men; Time After Time; A Woman of Substance; If Tomorrow Comes; Coast To Coast; Room At the Bottom; Robin of Sherwood; Miss Marple At Bertram's Hotel; The Charmer; Verdi – Wolf To the Slaughter; Bergerac;* Inspector Wexford in *The Ruth Rendell Mysteries; No Job for a Lady.* **Address:** c/o ICM. Lives in West London. m. 1st designer Julia Squires (dec), 2nd actress Sally Home; 5 d. Charlie, Ellie (twins), Candy, Tessa (all from 1st m.), Sarah.

BAKER, *richard, OBE*

Richard Douglas James Baker. Presenter. b. Willesden, London, 15 June 1925. OBE, 1979. Played piano for Cambridge Footlights; an actor (1948–9) and teacher before joining the BBC. **Theatre:** *Richard Baker's Grand Tour To Melody; The Best of British; Music In My Life; Music Menagerie; Master Pieces* (writer). **TV:** BBC newsreader (1954–82); *Omnibus; The Proms; New Year's Day Concert From Vienna; Face the Music* (panellist); *Mary, Mungo and Midge* (narrator). **Radio:** BBC radio announcer (1951–4); *Melodies for You; Richard Baker Compares Notes; Music for a While; Mainly for Pleasure; Start the Week.* **Books:** *Mozart; Richard Baker's London.* Winner, Variety Club Radio Personality of the Year, 1984. **Address:** c/o Bagenal Harvey Organisation. Lives in Radlett, Hertfordshire. m. Margaret; 2 s. Andrew, James. Hobbies: Music, theatre, the sea.

BAKER, *tom*

Tom Baker. Actor. **Theatre:** *The Merchant of Venice; The Idiot; A Woman Killed With Kindness; The Rules of the Game* (all National Theatre Company); *Educating Rita* (RSC national tour); *Hedda Gabler.* **Films:** *Nicholas and Alexandra; The Canterbury Tales; Luther; Vault of Horror; The Mutations; Sinbad's Golden Voyage.* **TV:** Title role in *Doctor Who (1974–82); Hound of the Baskervilles; Robin Hood; The Life and Loves of a She-Devil; Selling Hitler; Medics.* **Address:** c/o Annette Stone Associates.

BALDWIN, *peter*

Peter Baldwin. Actor. b. Chichester, West Sussex, 1938. Trained at the Bristol Old Vic Theatre School. **Theatre:** Toured in repertory theatre with the West of England Theatre Company; *The Way of the World; The Browning Version; The Inspector Calls; Dance of Death; You Never Can Tell; Macbeth; Romeo and Juliet.* **TV:** *Bergerac; Agatha Christie's Miss Marple; Seven Deadly Sins;* Derek Wilton in *Coronation Street* (on and off 1976–87, regular 1988–); *Royal Variety Performance* (1989). **Address:** c/o Caroline Renton/Granada TV. Lives in North London and Manchester. m. actress Sarah Long (dec); 1 d. Julia, 1 s. Matthew. Hobbies: Collecting toy theatres.

BALL, *bobby*

Robert Harper. Comedian/Entertainer. b. Oldham, Lancashire, 28 January 1944. Half of the comedy duo Cannon & Ball, originally welders who sang semi-professionally as the Shirrell Brothers, then the Harper Brothers. **Theatre:** *You'll Do for Me.* **Films:** *The Boys In Blue.* **TV:** *Opportunity Knocks* (1968); *Royal Variety Performances; This Is Your Life* (subjects); *The Cannon & Ball Show* (1979–88); *Cannon & Ball's Casino* (hosts, quiz show); *Plaza Patrol* (sit-com). Winners, Variety Club Showbusiness Personalities of the Year award. **Address:** c/o International Artistes, Albert House, Albert Street, Chadderton, Oldham. Lives in Rochdale. m. 2nd Yvonne; 2 s. Robert, Darren, 1 d. Joanne. Hobbies: Reading the Bible and being with the family, writing books and poems, music – especially rock 'n' roll – fishing. **Favourite TV programme:** *Coronation Street.*

BALL, *johnny*

Johnny Ball. Presenter/Writer. b. Bristol, 23 May 1938. Was a Butlin's Red Coat and a comedian in Northern clubs and cabaret. **TV:** *Playschool; Play Away; Star Turn; Great Egg Race; Secret's Out; Cabbages and Kings; Think of a Number; Think Again.* **Video:** *You Are What You Eat.* **Books:** *Think of a Number; Think Box; Plays for Laughs; Second Thinks.* **Address:** c/o Arlington Enterprises. m. Dianne; 1 d. Zoe, 2 s. Nicholas, Daniel.

BANKS, *david*

David Banks. Actor. b. Hull, 24 September 1951. Drama degree from Manchester University; post-graduate course at Bristol Old Vic Theatre School. **Theatre:** *St Joan; The Merchant of Venice; Twelfth Night; Romeo and Juliet; Henry IV, Pt 1; The Jungle Book; The Circle; The Lion, The Witch and The Wardrobe; Woman In Mind; Falstaff; Macbeth; Doctor Who: The Ultimate Adventure; Aladdin; Gaslight.* As director: *Talking To John.* **Films:** *Talking To John* (as director). **TV:** *The Cuckoo Waltz; The Professionals; Keep it In the Family;* Cyberleader in *Doctor Who; Play for Today: Man of Letters; The Bill;* Graeme Curtis in *Brookside (1991–2); A Time To Dance.* **Books:** *Cybermen.* **Address:** c/o Shane Collins Associates. Lives in Islington, North London, with partner Maureen. Hobbies: T'ai chi, reading, cinema, restoring a farmhouse in France.

BANNEN, *ian*

Ian Bannen. Actor. b. Coatbridge, Lanarkshire, 29 June 1931. **Films:** *Private's Progress; Macbeth; The Flight of the Phoenix; Lock Up Your Daughters; Jane Eyre; The Mackintosh Man; Watcher In the Woods; Gandhi; Gorky Park; Eye of the Needle; Lamb; Defence of the Realm; Hope and Glory; The Gambler; Speaking of the Devil.* **TV:** *Jesus of Nazareth;* Jim Prideaux in *Tinker, Tailor, Soldier, Spy; Dr Jekyll and Mr Hyde; The Hard Word; Hart To Hart; Tickets for the Titanic; Bookie; On the Orient North; The Fifteen Streets; The Paris Deception; Uncle Vanya; Murder In Eden; The Common Pursuit; Ashenden; Arise and Go Now; The Treaty.* **Address:** c/o London Management. Lives in London and Arizona. m. Marilyn. Hobbies: Reading, swimming, photography, walking, music. **Favourite TV programme:** Any wildlife and nature programmes and operas.

BARBER, *glynis*

Glynis Barber. Actress. b. South Africa, 25 October. **Theatre:** *Hamlet; Ring Around the Moon; Rebecca; Once In a Lifetime; And Then There Were None; Table Manners; Summer Breeze.* **Films:** *Terror; Yesterday's Hero; Tangier; The Wicked Lady; The Hound of the Baskervilles; Dr Jekyll and Mr Hyde; The Edge of Sanity.* **TV:** *Blake's 7;* title role in *Jane; Lucky Jim; A Fine Romance; History of Mrs Polly; The Sandbaggers; The Voysey Inheritance; Visitors;* Makepeace in *Dempsey and Makepeace; Tales of the Unexpected.* **Address:** c/o Billy Marsh Associates.

BARKER, *ronnie, OBE*

Ronnie Barker. Actor/Comedian. b. Bedford, 25 September 1929. Retired from showbusiness in January 1988. **Films:** *The Cracksman; Doctor In Distress; And Father Came Too; The Bargee; A Home of Your Own; The Runaway Railway; The Man Outside; Futtock's End; Robin and Marian; Porridge; By the Sea.* **TV:** *The Walrus and the Carpenter; A Tale of Two Cities; Gaslight Theatre; Bruno; Barney Is My Darling; The Frost Report; Foreign Affairs; Before the Fringe; The Frost Programme; The Ronnie Barker Playhouse; Frost On Sunday; Hark At Barker; Charley's Aunt; Six Dates With Barker; The Two Ronnies; Porridge; A Midsummer Night's Dream; His Lordship Entertains; Seven of One; The Picnic; When We Are Married; Open All Hours; Going Straight.* **Radio:** *Floggits; The Navy Lark.* m. Joy Tubb; 1 d. Charlotte, 2 s. Larry, Adam.

BARKWORTH, *peter*

Peter Barkworth. Actor. b. Margate, Kent, 14 January 1929. Trained at RADA. **TV:** *The Power Game; Manhunt; Office Party; Asquith In Orbit; Rasputin; The Passenger; The Rivals of Sherlock Holmes; Dear Octopus; The Millionairess; Return Flight; Colditz; Who Sank the Lusitania?; Crown Matrimonial; Intent To Murder; Good Girl; Melissa; The Apple Cart; An Accident of Class and Sex; The Saturday Party; The Little Minister; The Five Pound Orange; Omnibus: Thomas Mann; The Country Party; Professional Foul; Secret Army; The Ragazza; Telford's Change; The Morecambe and Wise Christmas Show; Winston Churchill – The Wilderness Years; Tales of the Unexpected; The Secret Adversary; Reith; The Price; Late Starter; The Gospel According To St Matthew; The London Embassy; The Return of Sherlock Holmes.* **Address:** c/o Jonathan Altaras Associates.

BARLOW, *thelma*

Thelma Barlow. Actress. b. Middlesbrough, 19 June 1937. Worked for seven years as a secretary in Huddersfield and took speech and drama evening classes, appearing in amateur productions; turned professional, joining Joan Littlewood's Theatre Workshop, in East London. **Theatre:** Toured in rep with the West of England Theatre Company; repertory theatre in Liverpool, Birmingham and Nottingham; *I Am a Camera; The Way of the World* (Bristol Old Vic); London West End productions. **TV:** Classical serials such as *Vanity Fair;* Mavis Wilton (née Riley) in *Coronation Street* (1972-); *Royal Variety Performance* (1989). **Address:** c/o Granada TV. Lives in North Yorkshire and Manchester. m. designer Graham Barlow (dis); 2 s. Clive, James. Hobbies: Cookery, organic gardening, yoga.

BARNES, *carol*

Carol Barnes. Newscaster. b. Norwich, Norfolk, 13 September 1944. Public relations officer at the Royal Court Theatre, London, production manager of *Time Out* magazine and radio journalist with BBC and LBC (London independent news and information station), before moving to television. **TV:** Reporter and newscaster with ITN; *The Channel Four Daily* presenter (1989–91); *News At 5.40* presenter (1991–2); *Diana: Progress of a Princess*. **Address:** c/o ITN. Lives in Brighton. m. ITN cameraman Nigel Thomson; 1 d. Clare, 1 s. James.

BARNES, *dominique*

Dominique Barnes. Actress. b. Barnet, Hertfordshire, 21 June 1966. Trained at the Arts Educational School. **Films:** *Lubo's World; Bert Rigby, You're a Fool.* **TV:** *Father's Day; Return To Waterloo; Demons; Lytton's Diary; Queen of Hearts; Gems; Watching* (BBC play); *Brat Farrar; Jessie's Place; Hannay; All Creatures Great and Small; Rockliffe's Babies; Maigret; Bergerac; William Tell; The Bill; Casualty; Young, Gifted and Broke.* **Address:** c/o Spotlight.

BARNETT, *jeni*

Jeni Barnett. Presenter/Actress/Writer. b. East London, 24 March 1949. Trained at New College of Speech and Drama. **Theatre:** *Accidental Death of an Anarchist* (London West End). **TV:** *Cabbage Patch; Grapevine; Postbag* and *Pick of the Week (Good Morning Britain); Revolting Women; You and Me; Crying Out Loud; Six O'Clock Live* (LWT). **Address:** c/o Daly Gagan Associates/LWT. m. James Bywater; 1 d. Bethany Sue.

BARON, *lynda*

Lynda Baron. Actress. b. Manchester, 24 March. Trained in ballet at the Royal Academy of Dancing. **Theatre:** *Living for Pleasure; The Bedwinner; The Real Inspector Hound; Move Over, Mrs Markham; Not Now, Darling; Goodbye Charlie; Butterflies Are Free; Abigail's Party; Little Me; Stepping Out.* **Films:** *Trauma.* **TV:** *Play of the Month; Don't Forget To Write; Heartlands; Grundy; Z-Cars; KYTV; Open All Hours; Playhouse; Minder; The Cannon & Ball Show; Kelly; Plaza Patrol.* **Address:** c/o Peter Charlesworth. m. John M Lee; 1 d. Sarah, 1 s. Morgan.

BARR, *roseanne*

Roseanne Barr. Actress. b. Salt Lake City, Utah, USA, 3 November 1953. Performed in punk bars, biker bars and Unitarian Church coffee-house in spare time while working as a window-dresser and cocktail waitress. **Theatre:** Produced *Take Back the Mike*, a showcase for women performers at the University of Boulder; performed at The Comedy Store, Los Angeles. **Films:** Ruth Patchett in *She-Devil.* **TV:** *Funny; The Tonight Show; On Location: The Roseanne Barr Show* (two ACE awards); *Roseanne.* **Books:** *My Life As a Woman* (autobiography).

BARRACLOUGH, *roy*

Roy Barraclough. Actor. b. Preston, Lancashire, 12 July 1935. Worked as a draughtsman for 12 years, acting in amateur productions, before turning professional. **Theatre:** Falstaff in *Henry IV*; Henry VIII in *Manners Are a Thing of the Past*; Willie Loman in *Death of a Salesman*; *The Price*. **Films:** *The Slipper and the Rose*; *Car Trouble*. **TV:** *Castlehaven*; *Don't Touch Him, He Might Resent It*; *Nearest and Dearest*; *Never Mind the Quality, Feel the Width*; *Love Thy Neighbour*; *Pardon My Genie*; *Sez Les*; *Foxy Lady*; Butterfly Collector in *The Return of the Antelope*; *Lost Empires*; *T-Bag Strikes Again*; five speaking roles in *Coronation Street*, including Alec Gilroy (on and off 1973–5, regular 1986–); *Royal Variety Performance* (1989). **Address:** c/o Peter Graham Associates/Granada TV. Single. Pets: Terrier called Whisky. Hobbies: Good food, cooking.

BARRIE, *amanda*

Shirley Ann Broadbent. Actress. b. Ashton-under-Lyne, Lancashire, 14 September 1939. Began as a chorus girl, aged 14. **Theatre:** *Babes In the Wood*; *On the Brighter Side*; *See You Inside*; *A Public Mischief*; *Any Wednesday*; *Twelfth Night*; *Oh! Kay*; *Absurd Person Singular*; *Noises Off*; *Donkey's Years*; *Stepping Out* (all London West End); *Little By Little*; *The Beggar's Opera*; *Hobson's Choice*; *Cabaret*; *Up the 80s*; *The Cabinet Mole*. **Films:** *Carry On Cleo*; *I Gotta Horse*; *One of Our Dinosaurs Is Missing*. **TV:** *Running Wild*; *Double Your Money* (hostess); *The Bulldog Breed*; Hermia in *A Midsummer Night's Dream*; *Struggles*; *Are You Being Served?*; *Spooner's Patch*; *Sanctuary*; *L for Lester*; Alma Sedgewick in *Coronation Street (1981 and 1989–)*. **Address:** Peter Charlesworth. Lives in Covent Garden, London. m. actor and theatre director Robin Hunter (sep).

BARRON, *james*

James Barron. Actor. b. London, 24 December 1964. Son of actor Keith Barron (qv). Member of the National Youth Theatre, before training at The Drama Centre. **Theatre:** *The Bed Before Yesterday*; *King's Rhapsody* (national tour); *South Pacific* (national tour); *Kiss Me Kate*. **TV:** *West Country Tales* (two episodes while still at school); *Three Up, Two Down*; *Laura and Disorder*; *Shelley*; *On Her Majesty's National Service*; *The Endless Game*; *Home To Roost*. **Address:** c/o Lipson Tinker Associates. Lives in Twickenham, Middlesex. m. actress Shona Lindsay (qv).

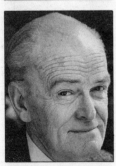

BARRON, *john*

John Barron. Actor. b. Marylebone, London, 24 December 1920. Trained at RADA. **TV:** *Emergency – Ward 10*; *The Beverly Hillbillies*; *The Saint*; *Department S*; *Doomwatch*; *All Gas and Gaiters*; *Ace of Wands*; *The Mind of J C Reeder*; *Spyder's Web*; *The Rivals of Sherlock Holmes*; *The Protectors*; *Crown Court*; *The Fosters*; CJ in *The Fall and Rise of Reginald Perrin*; *Victorian Scandals*; *The Foundation*; *Wodehouse Playhouse*; *Potter*; *The Taming of the Shrew*; *Bernie*; *Spooner's Patch*; *Shelley*; *The Glums*; *The Wizard of Crumm*; *The Gentle Touch*; *Yes Minister*; *Othello*; *To the Manor Born*; *Whoops Apocalypse*; *To Catch a King*; *Let's Parlez Francais*; *No Place Like Home*; *Kelly Monteith*; *Me & My Girl*; *Terry and June*; *Thirteen At Dinner*; *Duty Free*; *Don't Wait Up*; *Brush Strokes*. **Address:** c/o Green and Underwood. Lives in London. m. actress Jean Peart; 1 step-d. Hobbies: Fine wine.

BARRON, *keith*

Keith Barron. Actor. b. Mexborough, South Yorkshire, 8 August 1934. **Theatre:** Repertory theatre in Sheffield; Bristol Old Vic Theatre. **TV:** *The Odd Man*; *Lucky Jim*; *My Good Woman*; *A Family at War*; *Let's Get Away From It All*; title role in *Vote Vote Vote for Nigel Barton* and *Stand Up Nigel Barton*; *Telford's Change*; *Watching Me, Watching You*; *West Country Tales*; *Duty Free*; *Leaving*; *Room At the Bottom*; *Take Me Home*; *1996*; *Haggard*; *Plaza Patrol*; Guy Lofthouse in *The Good Guys*. **Address:** c/o Michael Whitehall. m. stage designer Mary Pickard; 1 s. actor James (qv).

BARRYMORE, michael

Michael Barrymore. Entertainer. b. Bermondsey, South London, 4 May 1952. **TV:** *The Royal Variety Performance; 40 Years On; Barrymore Special; Michael Barrymore's Saturday Night Out; Strike It Lucky* (game show, host); *Live From Her Majesty's; Get Set, Go; Russ Abbot's Madhouse; Barrymore.* **Radio:** *Barrymore Plus.* **Address:** c/o Norman Murray and Anne Chudleigh. m. Cheryl St Clair.

BATE, anthony

Anthony Bate. Actor. b. Stourbridge, Worcestershire. **TV:** *Grady; Ivanhoe; Intimate Strangers; Shades of Greene: Nobody's Conscience; Jubilee; Philby, Burgess and Maclean; Treasure Island; The Seagull; Crown Court; The Saint; The Avengers; Wilde Alliance; Englishman's Castle; Tinker, Tailor, Soldier, Spy; Crime and Punishment; Dalhousie's Luck; Network; 'Tis Pity She's a Whore; Leap In the Dark; Square Mile of Murder; Psy-Warriors; Fanny By Gaslight; Smiley's People; Golda; Shackleton; Grand Duo; Kisch-Kisch; Nellie's Version; Maybury; War and Remembrance; A Visit From Outer Space; Call Me Mister; Reykjavik – The Weekend That Changed the World; Game, Set & Match; Last Bus To Woodstock; Countdown To War; Agatha Christie's Poirot; Inspector Morse.* **Address:** c/o Al Parker. Lives in London. m. Diana; 2 s. Gavin, Mark.

BAXTER, lynsey

Lynsey Baxter. Actress. **Films:** *The French Lieutenant's Woman; The Pleasure Principle.* **TV:** *The Prime of Miss Jean Brodie; To the Lighthouse; Real Life; Succubus; Hedgehog Wedding; Starlings; Saracen; Golden Eye; Act of Will* (mini-series); *Chancer; Seduction – Ultimate Object of Desire; The Grass Arena; Zorro; Clarissa.* **Address:** c/o ICM Duncan Heath Associates.

BAXTER, stanley

Stanley Baxter. Actor/Comedian. b. Glasgow, 24 May 1928. **Theatre:** Glasgow Citizens' Theatre; *The Amorous Prawn; On the Brighter Side* (both London West End); *Phil the Fluter* (Palace Theatre); *What the Butler Saw* (Queen's Theatre); *Cinderella.* **Films:** *Geordie; Very Important Person; Crooks Anonymous; The Fast Lady; And Father Came Too; Joey Boy.* **TV:** *Shop Window; Garrison Theatre; Chelsea At Nine; Festival Fever; On the Bright Side; The Stanley Baxter Show; The Stanley Baxter Picture Show; Stanley Baxter's Christmas Box; Merrie Old Christmas; Stanley Baxter On Television; The Stanley Baxter Series; Stanley Baxter's Christmas Hamper; The Stanley Baxter Picture Annual; Mr Majeika; The Hogmanay Show.* **Address:** c/o David White Associates. m. Moira.

BAYLDON, geoffrey

Geoffrey Bayldon. Actor. b. Leeds, 7 January 1924. Trained at the Old Vic Theatre School. **TV:** *Z-Cars; Danton; Black Beauty; An Age of Kings; The Victorians; Nicholas Nickleby; Under Western Eyes;* title role in *Catweazle; The Avengers; The Saint; Devenish; Alice Through the Looking Glass; Edward VII; Tales of the Unexpected; The Trial of Lady Chatterley; Just Desserts;* the Crowman in *Worzel Gummidge; All Creatures Great and Small; Bergerac; Worzel Gummidge Down Under; Juliet Bravo; Hallelujah; There Comes a Time; This Office Life; Blott On the Landscape; All Passion Spent; Star Cops; Cause Célèbre; The Return of Sherlock Holmes; The Storyteller; Pisces Connection; The Chronicles of Narnia; Little Pig Robinson; Casualty; Campion.* **Address:** c/o Joy Jameson. Lives in Barnes, London. Hobbies: 'Watching the garden grow!'

BEACH, *ann*

Ann Beach. Actress. b. Wolverhampton, 7 June 1938. Trained at RADA. **TV:** *James and the Giant Peach; The Rag Trade; Steptoe and Son; This Year's Model; Brecht On Brecht; Fred Bassett* (voiceover)*; Jackanory; Rainbow; Nanny; Pilgrim's Way; Only When I Laugh; Tandoori Nights; The History of Mr Polly; Salad Days; Diary of a Nobody; The Vanishing Army; A Bit of a Life; Rising Damp; The Winslow Boy; Cranford; A Bouquet of Barbed Wire; The Widowing of Mrs Holroyd; The Great Glass Hive; The Government Inspector; Special Duties; Service Not Included; Villa Maroc; Rasputin;* title role in *Blodwen, Home From Rachel's Marriage; That Uncertain Feeling; Fresh Fields; Brookside; French Fields.* **Address:** c/o Barry Brown & Partner. Lives in North London. m. Francis Coleman; 2 d. actresses Charlotte (qv) and Lisa (Coleman). Hobbies: Music, art, travel.

BEACHAM, *stephanie*

Stephanie Beacham. Actress. b. Casablanca, 28 February. Trained at RADA. **Theatre:** National Theatre; RSC. **Films:** *The Games; Tam Lin; The Nightcomers; Dracula Today* (also titled *Dracula A.D. 1972); Bride of Fengriffen; Hoyst; The Confessional; Schizo; Inseminoid; The Wolves of Willoughby Chase.* **TV:** *The Queen's Traitor; The Saint; Love Story; Armchair Theatre; Public Eye; Callan; Jason King; Sentimental Education; Tales of Piccadilly; UFO; Marked Personal; Jane Eyre; Napoleon and Love; Prometheus; Hadleigh; Forget-Me-Not; The Old and the Young; Singular Life of Albert Nobbs; An Audience Called Edouard; Tenko; Sorrell & Son;* title role in *Connie;* Sable Colby in *The Colbys* and *Dynasty; To Be the Best* (mini-series). **Address:** c/o Peters Fraser & Dunlop.

BEADLE, *jeremy*

Jeremy Beadle. Presenter/Writer. b. Hackney, London, 12 April 1948. **TV:** *Game for a Laugh; Beadle's About; People Do the Funniest Things; Chain Letters; Born Lucky; Beadle's Box of Tricks; You've Been Framed!* As writer/consultant: *Lucky Numbers; Ultra Quiz; Pop the Question.* **Books:** *Today's the Day; Outlawed Inventions* (with Chris Winn); *Book of Lists* (contributor). **Address:** c/o MPC. m. Sue; 1 s. Leo, 3 d. Clare, Cassie, Bonnie.

BEAUMONT, *bill*, OBE

William Beaumont. Rugby commentator. b. Preston, Lancashire, 9 March 1952. Formerly a professional rugby player. **TV:** *A Question of Sport; Grandstand; Rugby Special.* **Address:** c/o John Hockey Associates. m. Hilary; 1 s. Daniel.

BEENY, *christopher*

Christopher Beeny. Actor. b. London, 7 July 1941. Danced with the Ballet Rambert at the age of six; trained at the Arts Educational School and RADA. **Theatre:** *Peter Pan; Stop the World, I Want To Get Off; The Long, The Short and The Tall; How the Other Half Loves; Local Affairs; One of Our Howls Is Missing; A Sting In the Tale; Boeing Boeing; Jack and the Beanstalk; Aladdin; Cinderella.* **Films:** *The Kidnappers; The Long Memory; Trouble In Store; Child's Play; Doctor In Distress.* **TV:** Lennie Grove in *The Grove Family* (from age of 12); *Dixon of Dock Green; Emergency – Ward 10; The Plane Makers; Armchair Theatre; Z-Cars; Softly, Softly;* Edward in *Upstairs, Downstairs; Miss Jones and Son; The Rag Trade; In Loving Memory; Playaway; Child's Play.* **Address:** c/o A.I.M. m. 1st (dis), 2nd singer Diana Kirkwood; 1 d. Joanne, 2 s. Richard (both from 1st m.), James.

BEGLEY, *ed, jr*

d Begley. Actor. b. Los Angeles, USA, 16 September 1949. Son of late actor Ed Begley. **Films:** *rivate Lessons; Cat People; She-Devil.* **TV:** *My Three Sons* (professional debut, aged 17); *Amateur ight At the Dixie Bar and Grill; A Shining Season; Riker; Rascals and Robbers – The Secret dventures of Tom Sawyer and Huck Finn; Tales of the Apple Dumpling Gang; Voyagers; Not Just nother Affair; Still the Beaver; An Uncommon Love; Insight; The Clearing House; Roman Holiday; pies, Lies and Naked Thighs; Not a Penny More, Not a Penny Less; In the Best Interest of the Child; oom 222; Roll Out; Happy Days; Quincy; M*A*S*H; Mary Hartman, Mary Hartman; Laverne and hirley; The Incredible Ida Early;* Dr Victor Ehrlich in *St Elsewhere* (three Emmy nominations). **Address:** o William Morris Agency (USA). m. Ingrid; 1 s. Nicholas, 1 d. Amanda.

BELL, *ann*

nn Bell. Actress. b. Wallasey, Cheshire, 29 April 1940. Trained at RADA. **Theatre:** Repertory theatre n Nottingham; Old Vic Theatre; *Say Who You Are* (Broadway); *Beware of the Dog; Othello.* **Films:** *ahrenheit 451; To Sir With Love; The Reckoning; Spectre; The Statue; Champions.* **TV:** *The Midnight amily; The Saint; Callan; Mr Rose; Public Eye; Frontier; The Baron; Danger Man; Melanie; Jane yre; Company of Five; Uncle Vanya; The Lost Boys; Very Like a Whale; Three Sisters; Ghost Sonata; acbeth; The Way of the World; The Ginger Man; War and Peace; For Whom the Bell Tolls; esurrection; An Unofficial Rose; Tenko; Tumbledown; Christabel; Double First; The Lost Boys; nspector Morse.* **Address:** c/o Julian Belfrage Associates. m. actor Robert Lang (qv); 1 d. Rebecca, 1 s. ohn.

BELL, *tom*

om Bell. Actor. b. Liverpool, 1932. Trained at Bradford Civic Theatre School. **TV:** *A Night Out; Cul de ac; No Trams To Lime Street; Angels Are So Few; Be Lucky; The Virginian; The Frighteners; Hedda abler; Straight On Till Morning; The Samaritan; A Man Without Friends; Sea Song; Death of an nformer; Horizon: Carl Jung; Play for Britain: The Proofing Season; Play for Today: Pope Pius XII; aversbridge; Holocaust; Out; Blue Peter: Duke of Wellington; Play for Today: Hester for Example: he South Bank Show: Roald Dahl; Words of Love; Love Story: Sweet Nothings; Sons and Lovers; ing's Royal; Reilly, Ace of Spies; Desert of Lies; Summer Lightning; The Detective; Unfinished usiness; Hidden Talents; The Rainbow; Chancer; Hope It Rains; Angels.* **Address:** c/o Hutton anagement. m. Lois Dane (dis); 1 s. Aran.

BELLAMY, *david*

avid Bellamy. Presenter/Writer. b. London, 18 January 1933. **TV:** *Life In Our Sea; Bellamy On otany; Bellamy's Britain; Animal Game; What On Earth Are We Doing?; Bellamy's Europe; Don't sk Me; It's Life; It's More Life; Botanic Man* (winner, *TVTimes* Special Award, 1978–9); *Looks atural; Bellamy On Heathland; Up a Gum Tree; Backyard Safari; Discovery; The End of the Rainbow how; Turning the Tide; Bellamy's Bird's Eye View; Bellamy's Hidden Country; Moa's Ark; Bellamy ides Again; The Four Great Seasons.* **Books:** *Bellamy On Botany; Bellamy's Britain; Bellamy's urope; Botanic Man; Botanic Safari; Half of Paradise; The Queen's Hidden Garden.* Writer of a allet, *Heritage.* Winner, BAFTA Richard Dimbleby Award, 1978. **Address:** c/o Jonathan Clowes. m. arine biologist Rosemary; 3 d. Henrietta, Brighid, Iseabal, 2 s. Rufus, Eoghain.

BELLINGHAM, *lynda*

nda Bellingham. Actress. b. Montreal, Canada, 31 May 1948. Moved to Britain as a child; trained at entral School of Speech and Drama. **Theatre:** Repertory theatre in Crewe, Coventry and Oxford; ordello; Norman, Is That You?; Noises Off; Salad Days; The Norman Conquests.* **Films:** *The Sweeney; tand Up Virgin Soldiers; Waterloo Bridge; Handicap; Heavy Metal.* **TV:** *Cottage To Let; Yes Honestly; econd Opinion; Don't Forget To Write; General Hospital; Angels; The Sweeney; Z-Cars; Hazell; The ink Medicine Show; Funny Man; Mackenzie; Doctor Who; All Creatures Great and Small; Second houghts.* TV commercials: Mum in the Oxo commercials. **Address:** c/o Saraband Associates. m. Nunzio eluso; 2 s. Michael, Robert.

BELLMAN, *gina*

Gina Bellman. Actress. b. Auckland, New Zealand, 10 July 1966. Gained a theatre studies A-level. **Theatre:** *The Rocky Horror Show.* **Films:** *King David.* **TV:** *Mussolini* (mini-series); *Sitting Targets; First Love* (play for Anglia TV's arts series *Folio); The Storyteller; Only Fools and Horses;* title role in *Blackeyes; Jim Henson's Greek Myths.* **Address:** c/o ICM Duncan Heath Associates.

BENEDICT, *dirk*

Dirk Niewoehner. Actor. b. Helena, Montana, USA, 1 March 1945. Trained at the John Fernald Academy of Dramatic Arts, Rochester, Michigan. **Theatre:** Seattle Repertory Company; *Abelard and Heloise; Butterflies Are Free; Hamlet.* **Films:** *Georgie, Georgia; SSSSSSS; W; Battlestar Galactica; Scavenger Hunt; Ruckus; Underground Aces; Body Slam.* **TV:** *Hawaii Five-O; Chopper One; Battlestar Galactica;* 'Faceman' in *The A-Team; Airwolf; Scruples; Trenchcoat In Paradise* (both TV movies). **Address:** c/o Michael Lewis/Gary Quinn, tel (0101) 213 552 9412. m. actress Toni Hudson.

BENJAMIN, *christopher*

Christopher Benjamin. Actor. b. Trowbridge, Wiltshire, 27 December 1934. Trained at RADA. **Theatre:** *A Severed Head; Maigret and the Lady; Arturo Ui; John Bull's Other Island; Nicholas Nickleby.* **Films:** *Brief Encounter.* **TV:** *Churchill's People; Private Affairs; The Forsyte Saga; Poldark; Doctor Who; Dick Turpin; Donkey's Years; Therese Racquin; We the Accused; It Takes a Worried Man; Holding the Fort; Nicholas Nickleby; Blott On the Landscape; The Return of Sherlock Holmes; Dempsey and Makepeace; Boon; The Diary of Anne Frank; The Miser; The Refuge; Yes, Prime Minister; The India Has Gone Fishing; Charlie the Kid; Anything More Would Be Greedy; Saracen; Campion; Haggard; Brass; Thatcher: The Final Days; Rumpole of the Bailey; Maigret.* **Address:** c/o Scott Marshall. Lives in North London. m. Anna Fox; 2 d. Kate, Emilia, 1 s. Sebastian.

BENJAMIN, *floella*

Floella Benjamin. Actress/Presenter/Producer/Writer. b. Trinidad, 23 September. **Theatre:** *Hair; Jesus Christ Superstar; The Black Mikado; The Husband In Law.* **Films:** *Black Joy.* **TV:** *Within These Walls; Crown Court; Doctor On the Go; Send In the Girls; Anansi; Angels;* Karen in *Mixed Blessings; Kids; Waterloo Sunset; The Ladies; Hole In Babylon; The Gentle Touch; Maybury; Bergerac; Strangers.* As presenter: *Playschool; What's Inside; Fast Forward; Play Away; Switch On To English; How Dare You; About Books; Lay On Five; Flo's Frolics (Breakfast Time); Daytime Live; A Houseful of Plants; Tree House; The Lord Mayor's Show; Playabout; Wish You Were Here ...?* **Address:** c/o Benjamin-Taylor Associates, 73 Palace Road, London SW2 3LB. Lives in South London. m. Keith Taylor; 1 s. Aston, 1 d. Alvina.

BENNETT, *alan*

Alan Bennett. Dramatist/Actor. b. Leeds, 9 May 1934. **Films:** *Parson's Pleasure; A Private Function; Prick Up Your Ears; A Handful of Dust; Little Dorrit.* **TV:** *On the Margin; An Evening With; A Day Out; Sunset Across the Bay; A Little Outing; A Visit From Miss Protheroe; Me, I'm Afraid of Virginia Woolf; Doris and Doreen; The Old Crowd; Afternoon Off; One Fine Day; All Day On the Sands; Our Winnie; A Woman of No Importance; Rolling Home; Marks; Say Something Happened; An Englishman Abroad; The Insurance Man; Talking Heads; 102 Boulevard Haussman; A Question of Attribution* (all as writer); *Sunday Night; Plato – The Drinking Party; Famous Gossips; Alice In Wonderland; The Merry Wives of Windsor; Fortunes of War; Selling Hitler* (all as actor); *Intensive Care* (actor-writer); *Poetry In Motion.* **Address:** c/o Chatto and Linnit.

BENNETT, hywel

Hywel Bennett. Actor/Director. b. Garnant, South Wales, 8 April 1944. Trained at RADA. **Theatre:** *Hamlet; Night Must Fall; Otherwise Engaged; Julius Caesar; Three Sisters; She Stoops To Conquer.* **Films:** *The Family Way; Twisted Nerve; The Virgin Soldiers; The Buttercup Chain; Loot; Percy; Endless Night; It's a 2 Feet 6 Inches Above the Ground World; Alice's Adventures In Wonderland; Murder Elite; War Zone.* **TV:** *Unman; Wittering; Zigo; A Month In the Country; The Idiot; Romeo and Juliet; Redcap; The Sweeney; Pennies From Heaven; Strangers; Malice Aforethought; Tinker, Tailor, Soldier, Spy; Artemis 81;* title role in *Shelley; The Critic; The Consultant; Absent Friends; Frankie and Johnnie;* title role in *The Return of Shelley; Twilight Zone.* **Address:** c/o James Sharkey Associates. m. TV presenter Cathy McGowan (dis); 1 d. Emma.

BENNETT, lennie

Mike Berry. Comedian/Presenter. b. Blackpool, Lancashire, 26 September 1938. Worked as a journalist on the *West Lancashire Evening Gazette* before entering showbusiness. **TV:** *The Good Old Days* (debut, 1966); *International Cabaret; The Lennie and Jerry Show; London Night Out; Rising Stars; Starburst; Punchlines* (host); *Bennett Bites Back; The Railway Carriage Game; All Star Secrets; The Kenny Everett Show; Lucky Ladders.* **Address:** c/o Alan Field, 11 Arden Road, Finchley, London N3 2AB, tel 081–346 7861. Lives in Blackpool. m. Margaret; 1 s. Tony.

BENNETT, tracie

Tracey Anne Bennett. Actress. b. Leigh, Lancashire, 17 June 1961. Trained at the Italia Conti Academy. **Theatre:** *Grease; Chicago; Educating Rita; Merrily We Roll Along; Carousel; Blood Brothers; Breezeblock Park; Putting On the Ritz.* **Films:** *Knights and Emeralds; Deep Red Instant Love; Shirley Valentine.* **TV:** *Going Out;* Sharon Gaskell in *Coronation Street; The Rector of Stiffkey; Shame; Knock-Knock; Relative Strangers; Boon; Black Silk; Unnatural Causes; The Refuge; The Ritz; The Bretts; Alas Smith and Jones; Brush Strokes;* Norma in *Making Out; Made In Heaven; The Ruth Rendell Mysteries;* Nikki in *Rich Tea & Sympathy; Joking Apart.* **Address:** c/o Annette Stone Associates. Single; lives in North London. Hobbies: Jazz, playing the piano, collecting Twenties dresses. **Favourite TV programme:** *Coronation Street; LA Law; I Love Lucy.*

BENSON, greg

Gregory Benson. Actor. b. Macksville, Sydney, 31 July 1967. Became a model at the age of 14 and appeared in TV commercials. **TV:** Matt Wilson in *Home and Away* (1988-). TV commercials: Nobby's Nuts; McDonald's; Coca-Cola; Pepsi-Cola; Wrigley; Levi jeans. **Address:** c/o Bedford & Pearce Management/Channel 7. Single; lives near Sydney.

BENTINCK, timothy

Timothy Charles Robert Noel Bentinck. Actor. b. Tasmania, 1 June 1953. Trained at Bristol Old Vic Theatre School. **Theatre:** *Hedda Gabler; The Beaux' Stratagem; Reluctant Heroes; Imaginary Wars In England; Pirates of Penzance; Boys From Hibernia; Bear; Henry IV.* **Films:** *North Sea Hijack; Pirates of Penzance; Success Is the Best Revenge; Winter Flight; The Year of the Comet.* **TV:** *Smuggler; Tales of the Unexpected; By the Sword Divided; Griffins; Boon; Tigers of Kumaon; Melba; Four Minute Mile; Three Up, Two Down; Square Deal; Made In Heaven.* **Radio:** David Archer in *The Archers* (1982-). Voice-overs for TV and film, including *A Tale of Two Cities* (TV). **Address:** c/o Noel Gay Artists. Lives in London. m. Judy; 2 s. William, Jasper. Hobbies: Songwriting, inventing, computers, house renovation, writing. **Favourite TV programme:** *GBH.*

BERNSEN, *corbin*

Corbin Bernsen. Actor. b. Hollywood, California, USA, 7 September 1954. Son of actress Jeanne Cooper. Degrees in theatre arts and playwrighting from the University of California Los Angeles. **Films:** *King Kong; S.O.B.; Hello Again; Eat My Dust!; Bert Rigby, You're a Fool; Major League; The Bank Manager; Disorganized Crime; Shattered.* **TV:** *Ryan's Hope; Another World; The Waltons; Breaking Point* (TV movie); *Police Story;* Arnie Becker in *LA Law.* **Address:** Agency for the Performing Arts. m. 1st actress Brenda Cooper (dis), 2nd actress Amanda Pays (qv); 1 s. Oliver.

BERTISH, *suzanne*

Suzanne Bertish. Actress. b. London, 7 August 1954. **Films:** *Hanover Street; The Hunger; Hearts of Fire.* **TV:** *The Limbo Connection; Are You Watching the Mummy?; Wings of Desire; Three Sisters; Maybury; The South Bank Show: The RSC On Tour; The Making of Nicholas Nickleby; The Life and Times of Nicholas Nickleby; To the Lighthouse; Freud; The Comedy of Errors; Rainy Day Women; Shine On Harvey Moon; The Lenny Henry Show; A Day In Summer.* **Address:** c/o Jeremy Conway.

BEVAN, *gillian*

Gillian Bevan. Actress. b. Stockport, Cheshire, 13 February. Trained at Central School of Speech and Drama. **Theatre:** Repertory theatre in Perth, Salisbury, Farnham and at Bristol Old Vic Theatre; three seasons with Alan Ayckbourn's theatre in Scarborough; founder-member of The Tight Assets Theatre Company; *Blood Brothers; Noel and Gertie; Ophelia; The School for Scandal; Follies* (London West End); *The Wizard of Oz; As You Like It* (both RSC). **TV:** *Sharon and Elsie; Coppers; Never the Twain; Lost Empires.* **Address:** c/o ICM Duncan Heath Associates.

BEWES, *rodney*

Rodney Bewes. Actor/Writer. b. Bingley, West Yorkshire, 27 November 1938. Trained at RADA. **Theatre:** Repertory theatre in Stockton-on-Tees, Hull, York, Watford, Eastbourne, Morecambe and Hastings; *A Night Out.* **Films:** *Billy Liar; Decline and Fall; Spring and Port Wine; Dance To Your Daddy; Whatever Happened To the Likely Lads?; The Spaceman and King Arthur; Saint Jack; Wildcats of St Trinian's; The Gothic Chimney.* **TV:** *The Likely Lads; Dear Mother . . . Love Albert* (also producer and co-writer); *Whatever Happened To the Likely Lads?; Love Story; Z-Cars; Albert; Jonah and the Whale; Just Liz; Camera Club; She Stoops To Conquer; 'Tis Pity She's a Whore; My Friend Dennis* (also writer). **Address:** c/o ICM Duncan Heath Associates. m. Daphne Black; 1 d. Daisy, 3 s. Joe, Tom, Billy (triplets).

BIGGINS, *christopher*

Christopher Biggins. Actor/Director. b. Oldham, Lancashire, 16 December 1948. Trained at Bristol Old Vic Theatre School. **Theatre:** Repertory theatre in Salisbury and Derby; RSC; *Winnie the Pooh; Beyond the Fringe; Touch of Spring; Side by Side By Sondheim;* directed at the Open Air Theatre, Regent's Park. **Films:** *Eskimo Nell; Applause; The Rocky Horror Picture Show; The Tempest; Massada.* **TV:** *Paul Temple; The Likely Lads;* Lukewarm in *Porridge; Man of Straw; Upstairs, Downstairs; Some Mothers Do 'Ave 'Em; Kidnapped; The Bronte Connection; Dancing Princess; Jackanory; Rentaghost; Watch This Space; Brendan Chase; Shoestring;* Nero in *I, Claudius;* Rev Ossie Whitworth in *Poldark; On Safari; Surprise, Surprise* (co-presenter); *Wife of the Week.* **Address:** c/o CDA.

BILGINER, *haluk*

Haluk Bilginer. Actor. b. Izmir, Turkey, 5 June 1954. Studied at the Turkish State Conservatoire and LAMDA. **Theatre:** *A Little Like Drowning; My Fair Lady; The Phantom of the Opera.* **Films:** *Half Moon Street; Children's Crusade; Ishtar.* **TV:** *Bergerac; Murder of a Moderate Man;* Mehmet Osman in *EastEnders; The Glory Boys.* **Address:** c/o Johnson's.

BIRD, *john*

John Bird. Actor/Director/Writer. b. Nottingham, 22 November 1936. Acted in and directed plays at Cambridge University. **Theatre:** Royal Court Theatre (assistant to director, later associate artistic director); *Habeas Corpus* (London West End). **Films:** *Take a Girl Like You; The Seven Per Cent Solution; Yellow Pages.* **TV:** *Not So Much a Programme, More a Way of Life; BBC3; Last Laugh; The Late Show; My Father Knew Lloyd George; A Series of Birds; With Bird Will Travel; John Bird/John Wells; Blue Remembered Hills; Shades of Greene; Timon of Athens; King Lear; The Falklands Factor; Marmalade Atkins; Blue Money; Oxbridge Blues; Travelling Man; A Very Peculiar Practice; Joint Account; Bejewelled; El C.I.D.* **Address:** c/o Chatto and Linnit.

BIRD, *norman*

Norman Bird. Actor. b. Coalville, Leicestershire, 30 October 1924. **Films:** *The Virgin and the Gypsy; Raging Moon; Young Winston; Ooh . . .You Are Awful; The Slipper and the Rose; The Medusa Touch; The Final Conflict; Queenie.* **TV:** *Worzel Gummidge; To Serve Them All My Days; A Voyage Round My Father; Yes Minister; The Ghost Downstairs; On Your Way, Riley; This Office Life; One By One; Lytton's Diary; The Practice; Ever Decreasing Circles; Woof!; After Henry; Second Thoughts; Stay Lucky.* **Address:** c/o London Management.

BIRDSALL, *jesse*

Jesse Birdsall. Actor. b. London, 13 February 1963. Trained at the Anna Scher Children's Theatre School. **Theatre:** *The Merry Wives of Windsor; Days of the Commune* (both with RSC); *Abide With Me; On the Spot.* **Films:** *Quadrophenia; Bloody Kids; Revolution; Shadey; Wish You Were Here; Getting It Right.* **TV:** *A Sudden Wrench; Remembrance; Jangles; Walter* (Channel Four film); *Who'll Be Mother?; Tales Out of School;* Pete in *Annika; Minder; We'll Support You Evermore; Honeymoon; Elvis;* Marty in *The Fear; Soldier, Soldier.* **Address:** c/o Jeremy Conway.

BLACK, *cilla*

Priscilla White. Presenter. b. Liverpool, 27 May 1943. A pop singer before becoming a TV presenter. **Films:** *Ferry Cross the Mersey; Work . . . Is a Four Letter Word.* **TV:** *Cilla; Cilla's World of Comedy* (situation comedy); *Surprise, Surprise; Blind Date; Cilla's Goodbye To the Eighties; Blind Date Wedding of the Year; The Best of Blind Date.* **Records:** *Anyone Who Had a Heart; You're My World; It's for You; You've Lost That Lovin' Feelin'; Love's Just a Broken Heart; Alfie; Surround Youself With Sorrow; Conversations; Something Tells Me (Something Is Gonna Happen Tonight)* (all Top 10 singles). Favourite Female TV Personality award, three consecutive years. **Address:** c/o Hindworth Management. m. manager Bobby Willis; 3 s. Robert, Benjamin, Jack.

BLACK, *isobel*

Isobel Black. Actress. b. Edinburgh, 15 December 1943. Granddaughter of actor Stuart Black; daughter of TV playwright Ian Stuart Black and actress Ann Brook. **Theatre:** Miranda in *The Tempest* (debut, Regent's Park Open Air Theatre, 1960); repertory theatre in Manchester and Edinburgh. **TV:** *My Three Angels; The Troubleshooters; Lower Largo Sequence; Redgauntlet; The Likely Lads; The White Bird Passes; Reid the Sheepstealer; Boswell for the Defence; Three Sisters; The Brief; Scotland's Story; The Tempest; The Hostage; Tygo Road; Pola Jones; Kate McIntyre.* **Address:** c/o LWA. m. TV executive James Gatward; 3 d. Annabel, Celia, Eloise.

BLACKMAN, *honor*

Honor Blackman. Actress. b. London, 22 August **Films:** *Fame Is the Spur; Daughter of Darkness; Diamond City; Breakaway; The Square Peg; A Matter of Who; Goldfinger; The Secret of My Success; Moment To Moment; Life At the Top; Twist of Sand; Shalako; The Struggle for Rome; The Last Grenade; Twinky; The Virgin and the Gypsy; Girl In the Dark; Something Big; To the Devil a Daughter; Summer Rain; The Cat and the Canary.* **TV:** *Four Just Men; Probation Officer; Man of Honour; Ghost Squad; Top Secret;* Cathy Gale in *The Avengers* (1962–4); *The Explorer; Visit From a Stranger; Out Damned Spot; The Movie Quiz; Wind of Change; Robin's Nest; Never the Twain; The Secret Adversary; Lace; The First Modern Olympics; Minder On the Orient Express; Doctor Who; William Tell; Voice of the Heart; The Upper Hand.* **Address:** c/o Michael Ladkin. 1 d. Lottie, 1 s. Barnaby.

BLAIR, *isla*

Isla Blair. Actress. b. South India, 29 September 1944. Trained at RADA. **Films:** *Indiana Jones and the Last Crusade.* **TV:** *The Liars; Present Laughter; The Dickie Henderson Show; The Avengers; The Saint; Department S; The Doctors; Jason King; The Three Princes; Space 1999; The Crezz; The Prime of Miss Jean Brodie; A Legacy; Quiller; When the Boat Comes In; Celebration; Wilde Alliance; Forgotten Love; Play of the Week: Songs; Only When I Laugh; Love Story; An Englishman's Castle; The History Man; Alexa; The Bounder; The Beggar's Opera; Crown Court; Six Centuries of Verse; Off Peak; Poppyland; Taggart; The Tennis Court; C.A.T.S. Eyes; King and Castle; Boogie Outlaws; Bookie; Treasure Island; Mother Love; Haggard; Advocates; Boon; The Good Guys.* **Address:** c/o Hutton Management. m. actor Julian Glover (qv); 1 s. Jamie.

BLAIR, *lionel*

Lionel Blair. Actor/Dancer/Presenter. b. Montreal, Canada, 12 December 1934. Child actor, before work as a dancer and choreographer. **Theatre:** *The Wizard of Oz* (debut, 1942); *Royal Variety Performance.* **TV:** *Give Us a Clue* (men's team captain, 1982-); *Name That Tune* (host). **Books:** *Stage Struck* (autobiography). **Address:** c/o Peter Charlesworth. Lives in West London. m. Susan; 2 s. Daniel, Matthew, 1 d. Lucy.

BLAKE, *christopher*

Christopher Blake. Actor. b. London, 23 August 1949. Trained at Central School of Speech and Drama. **Theatre:** *The Trials of Oscar Wilde.* **Films:** *Aces High.* **TV:** *Anne of Avonlea; Death Or Glory Boy; Love for Lydia; The Lost Boys; Mill On the Floss; Mixed Blessings; Alexa; That's My Boy; Love's Labour's Lost;* Tim Derby in *Brookside; The Lost Boys.* **Address:** c/o Ken McReddie. m. Wendy; 2 d. Charlotte, Louise, 1 s. Sean.

BLAKE, *susie*

ısie Blake. Actress. b. Highgate, North London. **Theatre:** *Godspell* (national tour); *The Rocky Horror how; The Bed Before Yesterday* (Lyric Theatre); *Cabinet Minister; Picture of Innocence; Exclusive arns* (London West End); *When Did You Last See Your Trousers?; Poor Nanny; Prin; Baby* (Library heatre, Manchester, and national tour). **TV:** *Comet Among the Stars; The Victoria Wood Show; Russ bbot's Madhouse; The Frankie Howerd Show;* Jackie in *Singles* (three series); *The Darling Buds of ay.* **Address:** c/o James Sharkey Associates. Lives in Surrey. m. actor Martin Potter; 1 s. Ben.

BLAKENEY, *gayle*

ayle Blakeney. Actress/Singer. b. Brisbane, Australia. **Theatre:** *Cinderella; Copelia; La Sylphide* (all allets). **TV:** *Happy Go Round; Saturday Jukebox; Wombat* (all as presenter); *The World Around Us;* ıristina Alessi in *Neighbours* (1990-). **Videos:** Promotional videos for pop group The Moniters, cluding *Singing In the Eighties.* **Address:** c/o Terry Blamey Management.

BLAKENEY, *gillian*

llian Blakeney. Actress/Singer. b. Brisbane, Australia. **Theatre:** *Cinderella; Copelia; La Sylphide* (all allets). **TV:** *Earth Patrol* (TV movie); *Happy Go Round; Saturday Jukebox; Wombat* (all as presenter); orld Around Us; Caroline Alessi in *Neighbours* (1990-). **Videos:** Promotional videos for pop group le Moniters, including *Singing In the Eighties.* **Address:** c/o Terry Blamey Management.

BLAKISTON, *caroline*

aroline Blakiston. Actress. b. London, 13 February 1933. Trained at RADA. **Theatre:** *A Midsummer ght's Dream; Look Back In Anger; King Lear; The Cocktail Party; Women All Over; Particular iendships; Les Parents Terribles; Division Belle; Everything In the Garden; The Real Inspector Hound; urderer.* **Films:** *The Idol; The Magic Christian; Sunday, Bloody Sunday; Yanks; Return of the Jedi. ':* *The Avengers; Emergency – Ward 10; The Saint; The Forsyte Saga; The Caesars; Wives and aughters; Saturday, Sunday, Monday; Kids; Raffles; The Racing Game; The Prince Regent; The allens; Crown Court; Private Schultz; Shoestring; Nanny; Brass; Charters and Caldicott; Mr Palfrey of estminster; Miss Marple; The Refuge.* **Address:** c/o Chatto and Linnit. m. actor Russell Hunter (qv), s); 1 s. Adam, 1 d. Charlotte.

BLANCH, *dennis*

ınnis Blanch. Actor. b. Barnet, Hertfordshire, 4 February 1947. Trained at Mountview Theatre hool, then toured in children's theatre, before going into repertory theatre. **Theatre:** Repertory eatre in Newcastle, Billingham, Exeter, Oldham and Manchester; *Cartoons; The Fantasticks; The inmaker; The Magician: The Lion In Winter; Confession of Murder.* **Films:** *The Spy Who Loved Me; rmission To Kill; The Eagle Has Landed; International Velvet.* **TV:** *Sunday Night Theatre; Fraud uad; Thriller; Van Der Valk; Villains; New Scotland Yard; The Sweeney; Dad's Army; No Honestly; arship; General Hospital; The Fenn Street Gang;* Det Con Willis in *The XYY Man* and *Strangers; erlock Holmes; The Naked Civil Servant; Upstairs Downstairs; Bulman; Give Us a Break; Grange l; Emmerdale Farm; One By One.* **Address:** c/o A.I.M. m. Carol Wilks; 1 s. David.

BLEASDALE, *alan*

Alan Bleasdale. Writer. b. Liverpool, 1946. Worked as a schoolteacher before becoming a full-tim writer. **Theatre:** *Fat Harold and the Last 26; The Party's Over; Down the Dock Road; It's a Madhouse Should Old Acquaintance...; Franny Scully's Christmas Stories; No More Sitting On the Old Schoo Bench; Pimples; Crackers; Having a Ball; Are You Lonesome Tonight?* (Phoenix Theatre); *On t Ledge.* **Films:** *No Surrender* (winner, Critics' Award, Toronto Film Festival, 1984). **TV:** *Early To Be Television Club; Watch Words; Scully's New Year's Eve; Play for Today: The Black Stuff; Play f Today: The Muscle Market; Boys From the Blackstuff* (winner, BAFTA, Critics' and Pye Televisio awards, 1983); *Scully; The Monocled Mutineer; GBH; Julie Walters & Friends.* **Address:** c/o Lemo Unna & Durbridge.

BLEASDALE, *ian*

Ian Bleasdale. Actor. **Theatre:** *Spend, Spend, Spend; September In the Rain* (national tour); *Talki To Planets.* **Films:** *To Be the Best.* **TV:** *Casualty; All Creatures Great and Small; Stay Lucky; Maki News; A Sense of Guilt; Boon; Hard Cases; Andy Capp; The Adventures of Sherlock Holmes; Flyi Lady; The Beiderbecke Affair; Brookside; First of the Summer Wine; Take the High Road; Brick Beautiful; The World of Eddie Weary; The Brittas Empire; Drop the Dead Donkey.* **Address:** c/o Bar Brown & Partner.

BLESSED, *brian*

Brian Blessed. Actor. b. Mexborough, South Yorkshire, 9 October 1937. Trained at the Bristol Old V Theatre School. **Films:** *Flash Gordon; High Road To China; Henry V; Robin Hood: Prince of Thieve* **TV:** *Z-Cars; Double Agent; Jackanory; Arthur of the Britons; Justice; Lorna and Ted; The Recruiti Officer; Boy Dominic; The Three Musketeers; Hadleigh; Public Eye; Brahms; Cold Comfort Farr Churchill's People; I, Claudius; The Aphrodite Inheritance; Tales of the Unexpected; The Little World Don Camillo; Lamb To the Slaughter; Space 1999; The Sweeney; Hound of the Baskervilles; T Master of Ballantrae; The Last Days of Pompeii; William the Conqueror; Treasure Island; War a Remembrance; Minder; Blackadder.* **Address:** c/o Vernon Conway. m. 1st actress Anne Bomann (di 2nd actress Hildegard Neil; 2 d. Catherine (from 1st m.), Rosalind.

BLETHYN, *brenda*

Brenda Blethyn. Actress. b. Ramsgate, Kent, 20 February 1946. Trained at the Guildford School Drama. **Theatre:** Bubble Theatre Company, London; *Tamburlaine the Great; Strife; Force of Hab The Double Dealer; The Fruits of Enlightenment; The Nativity; The Passion; Doomsday; Bedroo Farce; A Midsummer Night's Dream; The Guardsman; The Provoked Wife* (all National Theatre Steaming; Benefactors* (both London West End); **TV:** *King Lear; Henry VI; The Imitation Game; Ta of the Unexpected; Floating Off; Grown Ups; Sheppey; Alas Smith and Jones; Death of an Exp Witness; Chance In a Million; The Labours of Erica; The Richest Woman In the World* (mini-serie **Address:** c/o Ken McReddie.

BLOOM, *claire*

Claire Bloom. Actress. b. London, 15 February 1931. Trained at Guildhall School of Music and Dra and Central School of Speech and Drama. **TV:** *Cyrano de Bergerac; Caesar and Cleopatra; Romeo a Juliet; First Love; Victoria Regina; Mis-alliance* (all US); *Anna Karenina; Wuthering Heights; Imaginative Woman; The Legacy; Wessex Tales; In Praise of Love; Love for Lydia; The World of Em Dickinson; Henry VIII* (twice); *Hamlet* (twice); Lady Marchmain in *Brideshead Revisited; The Gh Writer; Separate Tables; Cymbeline; King John; Oedipus the King; Time and the Conways; Ellis Islar Shadowlands; Hold the Dream; Liberty; Anastasia; Women Writers; The Belle of Amherst; Intim Contact; Queenie* (TV movie). **Books:** *Limelight and After* (autobiography). **Address:** c/o Jere Conway. m. actor Rod Steiger (dis); 1 d. Anna.

BLUMENAU, *colin*

Colin Blumenau. Actor. b. London, 7 August 1956. Gained a degree in drama from the University of Hull. **Theatre:** *Altogether Now;* repertory theatre in Basingstoke, Salisbury, Exeter and Milford Haven; New End Theatre, London; Tricycle Theatre, London. **Films:** *Mendelssohn In Wales.* **TV:** *Jockey School; Andy Robson; The Bill.* **Address:** c/o London Management. m. Deborah O'Brien; 2 s. Dan, Jack.

BOARDMAN, *stan*

Stan Boardman. Comedian. b. Liverpool, 7 December. Operated a haulage business before winning a holiday-camp competition and turning professional as an entertainer. **Theatre:** Lowestoft summer season (1982); *Aladdin.* **TV:** *Opportunity Knocks; Celebrity Squares; Seaside Special; Runaround; The Comedians; The Video Entertainers; Success; The Railway Carriage Game; The Fame Game.* **Address:** c/o Bernard Lee Management. m. Vivienne; 1 d. TV presenter Andrea, 1 s. Paul.

BOHT, *jean*

Jean Boht. Actress. b. Bebington, Cheshire, 6 March 1936. Trained at Liverpool Playhouse. **Theatre:** *Meddle Not With Change; Eskimos Do it; Where Adam Stood; Cranford; Sons and Lovers; I Woke Up One Morning.* **Films:** *Distant Voices, Still Lives.* **TV:** *Juliet Bravo; Spyship; Funnyman; Boys From the Blackstuff; Scully;* Mrs Boswell in *Bread; The Cloning of Joanna May.* **Address:** c/o Peters Fraser & Dunlop. m. composer Carl Davis; 2 d. Hannah, Jessie.

BOLAM, *james*

James Bolam. Actor. b. Sunderland, 16 June 1938. Trained at Central School of Speech and Drama. **Theatre:** *Jeffrey Bernard Is Unwell.* **TV:** *Love On the Dole; Take Three Girls; The Rivals of Sherlock Holmes; Somerset Maugham;* Terry Collier in *The Likely Lads* (1965–9) and *Whatever Happened To the Likely Lads?* (1973); *The Protectors; Macbeth; The Philanthropist;* Jack Ford in *When the Boat Comes In* (four series); *Armchair Thriller: The Limbo Connection; As You Like It; Only When I Laugh* (four series); *Shades of Darkness;* Trevor Chaplain in *The Beiderbecke Affair, The Beiderbecke Tapes* and *The Beiderbecke Connection;* Nesbitt Gunn in *Room At the Bottom* (two series); title role in *Andy Capp; Executive Stress; Sticky Wickets; Second Thoughts.* **Address:** c/o Barry Burnett Organisation. m. actress Susan Jameson; 1 d. Lucy.

BOLAND, *eamon*

Eamon Denis Boland. Actor. b. Manchester, 15 July 1947. Trained at Bristol Old Vic Theatre School. **Theatre:** Repertory theatre in Manchester, Liverpool and Watford; *Masterpieces; Ambulance* (both at Royal Court Theatre); *Coming Clean* (Bush Theatre); Progress; *Funny Peculiar* (Garrick Theatre); *Why Me?* (London West End); *Of Mice and Men* (national tour). **Films:** *Business As Usual.* **TV:** *Raging Calm; Fox; Winter Sunlight; To Have and To Hold; Crossfire; Fell Tiger;* Clive in *Singles* (three series); *Coronation Street; The Bill; Kinsey; The Chief;* Tony Walker in *Casualty;* Dennis in *Hope It Rains.* **Address:** c/o Barry Brown & Partner. Lives in Lavenham, Suffolk. 1 d. Annie. **Hobbies:** Gardening, climbing, cards, cats. **Favourite TV programme:** None.

BOND, *philip*

Philip Bond. Actor. b. Burton-on-Trent, Staffordshire. **Films:** *I Want What I Want; Sleep Well, My Love.* **TV:** *The Onedin Line; The Barrier; Justice; Dial M for Murder; The Main Chance; Z-Cars; General Hospital; Warship; Snacker; Sister Dora; Children of the New Forest; Crown Court; An Englishman's Castle; Kids; The Sandbaggers; Hedda Gabler; Shoestring; Home Is the Sailor; Cold Warrior; Travellers By Night; Only Fools and Horses; Hilary; Bergerac; The Oldest Goose In the Business; Bowen; 63 Highmere Park; Forever Green.* **Address:** c/o Roger Carey Management.

BOOTH, *connie*

Connie Booth. Actress/Writer. **Films:** *Little Lord Fauntleroy; Romance With a Double Bass; The Revolutionaries; And Now for Something Completely Different; 84 Charing Cross Road; Hawks; High Spirits; American Friends.* **TV:** *Monty Python's Flying Circus;* Polly in *Fawlty Towers* (also co-writer); *The Deadly Game; Crown Court; Redundant Or The Wife's Revenge; Spaghetti Two Step; Worzel Gummidge; Why Didn't they Ask Evans?; The Unmade Bed; The Glittering Prizes; Readings From Dorothy Parker; Hello Comrades; The Story of Ruth; The Hound of the Baskervilles; Past Caring; Rocket To the Moon; Voice From the Gallows; The Return of Sherlock Holmes; Floodtide; Every Breath You Take; The Ronnie Corbett Show; The World of Eddie Weary; The Greater Good.* **Address:** c/o Kate Feast management. m. actor-writer John Cleese (dis).

BORGNINE, *ernest*

Ernest Borgnine. Actor. b. Hamden, Connecticut, USA, 2 January 1917. Trained at the Randall School of Dramatic Art. **Films:** *The Wild Bunch; The Poseidon Adventure; Bad Day At Black Rock; Marty* (winner, Best Actor Oscar, Cannes Film Festival Best Actor award, New York Film Critics' Award, National Board of Review Award, 1961); *Deadly Blessing.* **TV:** *Treasure Island; Blood Feud; The Dirty Dozen: The Next Mission; The Dirty Dozen III* (all TV movies); *McHale's Navy; Airwolf; Highway To Heaven.* **Address:** c/o Selected Artists Agency. m. Tova; 1 d. Nancy.

BOSSON, *barbara*

Barbara Bosson. Actress. b. Bellvernon, Pennsylvania, 1 November. Trained at Carnegie-Mellon University's drama school and the Pittsburgh Playhouse. **Films:** *Bullitt; Capricorn One; The Last Starfighter.* **TV:** *Richie Brockelman; Sunshine; McMillan and Wife; Owen Marshall; The Impatient Heart* (TV movie); *The Calendar Girl Murders* (TV movie); Capt C Z Stern in *Hooperman;* Fay Furillo in *Hill Street Blues* (nominated for Best TV Actress Emmy five times); Mayor Louise Plank in *Cop Rock.* **Address:** c/o Judy Schoen & Associates. m. TV writer-producer Steven Bochco; 1 s. Jesse, 1 d. Melissa.

BOSTOCK, *gerard*

Gerard Bostock. Actor. b. Liverpool, 22 May 1978. Trained in drama and singing. **TV:** *The Ginger Tree; Parnell and the Englishwoman; Children of the North; Bread;* Tony Dixon in *Brookside (1990-)* **Address:** c/o Lindsay Casting/Mersey Television. Single; lives in Liverpool. Hobbies: Drama, drawing. **Favourite TV programme:** *Brookside.*

BOVELL, *brian*

Brian Bovell. Actor. b. London, 26 October 1959. Acted with the Royal Court Youth Theatre Group.
Theatre: *Romeo and Juliet; One Fine Day; Sink Or Swim; Strange Fruit; Measure for Measure; The Caretaker; Bit of Business; Up for None; Macbeth; Othello; A Hero's Welcome; Where There Is Darkness* (British Theatre Association Best Supporting Actor award). **Films:** *Babylon; Burning an Illusion; Up High; Real Life; Playing Away.* **TV:** *Best of British; The Gentle Touch; Strangers; Bulman; The Hard Word; Driving Ambition; Miracles Take Longer; Casualty; Prospects.* **Address:** c/o Hope & Lyne.

BOWEN, *jim*

Jim Bowen. Comedian/Presenter. b. Heswall, Cheshire, 20 August 1937. Originally a dustbinman, labourer, driver and teacher; a deputy head in Morecambe, Lancashire, when he decided to become a comic. Turned professional, working in clubs and cabaret, after appearing on TV in *The Comedians* (1973). **TV:** *The Comedians; Muck and Brass* (acting debut); *Bullseye* (host, game show); *El C.I.D.* (acting himself). **Address:** c/o George Bartram Associates. Lives in Carnforth, Lancashire. m. Phyllis; 1 d. Susan, 1 s. Peter. Hobbies: Horse-riding, boating, tennis, driving. **Favourite TV programme:** *Emmerdale.*

BOWLER, *norman*

Norman Bowler. Actor. b. London, 1 August 1932. Trained at the City Literary Institute. **Theatre:** *The Caretaker* (New York); *Death Trap* (New Zealand); *Educating Rita* (tour). **Films:** *Tom Thumb; Naval Patrol; Von Ryan's Express; Julius Caesar.* **TV:** *Harpers West One; Deadline Midnight; The Ratcatchers; Letters From the Dead;* David Martin in *Park Ranger;* Det Chief Insp Harry Hawkins in *Softly, Softly; Jesus of Nazareth;* Sam Benson in *Crossroads;* Frank Tate in *Emmerdale* (1989-); *Some Other Spring* (TV movie). **Address:** c/o Rebecca Blond, 52 Shaftesbury Avenue, London W1V 7DE. Lives in Bristol. m. 1st (dis), 2nd Berjouhi (dis), 3rd Diane; 2 d. Caroline (from 1st m.), Tamara (from 2nd m.), 2 s. Joshua (from 1st m.), Simon (from 3rd m.). Pets: One cat. Hobbies: Sailing, painting, walking. **Favourite TV programme:** *Brideshead Revisited.*

BOWLES, *peter*

Peter Bowles. Actor. b. London, 16 October 1936. Trained at RADA. **Films:** *Blow Up; Charge of the Light Brigade; Laughter In the Dark; Eyewitness; A Day In the Death of Joe Egg; The Offence; For the Love of Benji; The Disappearance; Try This for Size.* **TV:** *The Avengers; The Saint; The Prisoner; Isadora; A Thinking Man As Hero; Shelley; Wittgenstein Brett; Napoleon and Love; Good Girl; Space 1999; The Survivors; Churchill's People; Only On Sunday; The Crezz; Vice Versa; I, Claudius; Flint; Prizewinners;* Mr Justice Featherstone in *Rumpole of the Bailey; To the Manor Born; Only When I Laugh; The Bounder; The Irish RM; Lytton's Diary* (also creator); *Executive Stress; Shadow On the Sun* (mini-series); *Perfect Scoundrels.* **Address:** c/o London Management. m. Susan; 1 d. Sasha, 2 s. Guy, Adam.

BOWN, *paul*

Paul Bown. Actor. b. Fenton, Staffordshire, 11 October 1957. Learned drama at art college. **Theatre:** Fringe theatre; *The Alchemist; The Gambler.* **Films:** *Morons From Outer Space; The Assam Garden; Underworld.* **TV:** *Play for Today: Staying Put; Coast To Coast* (TV movie); *Upline;* Malcolm in *Watching* (six series); *Reasonable Force; Mr Bean; Time Riders.* **Address:** c/o Burdett-Coutts Associates. m. Tracy; 1 s. Alfie.

BOXLEITNER, *bruce*

Bruce Boxleitner. Actor. b. Elgin, Illinois, USA, 12 May 1950. **Films:** *Tron; The Baltimore Bullet.* **TV:** *Happily Ever After; Passion Flower; Down the Long Hills; The Gambler; Gambler II; Angel In Green* (all TV movies); *The Mary Tyler Moore Show; Gunsmoke; How the West Was Won; The Macahans; Police Woman; Baretta; Bring 'Em Back Alive; Scarecrow & Mrs King; Kiss Me, Kill Me; East of Eden; Fly Away Home; The Last Convertible.* m. Kathryn Holcomb; 2 s. Sam, Lee.

BOYD, *tommy*

Tommy Boyd. Presenter. b. Syon Park, Middlesex, 14 December 1952. Worked for BBC Radio Brighton while training as an English teacher at Brighton College of Education, before becoming a stand-up comic at Butlin's, Bognor Regis, and a dolphin trainer at Brighton Dolphinarium. **TV:** *Magpie* (1977–80); *Jigsaw; Puzzle Trail; What's Happening; The Saturday Show; The Saturday Starship; Wide Awake Club; Children's ITV.* **Radio:** BBC Radio Brighton (presenter/producer); LBC (producer of *AM,* then a phone-in show presenter, winning the Variety Club's Independent Radio Personality of the Year award, 1980). **Address:** c/o MGA. m. Jayne; 1 s. Jack.

BOYLE, *tommy*

Tommy Boyle. Actor. b. Manchester, 3 May 1948. **TV:** *Fallen Hero; Over There: The Racing Game; The Professionals; Came the Rapper; From the Roots; The New Avengers; Summer Season; Benny Lynch; Beneath the News; The Wackers; Crown Court; Poor Girl; Raging Calm; Z-Cars* (as four different villains, then a detective inspector); *A Woman Sobbing; Mrs Podmore's Car; Home and Away* (Granada TV production); *Follyfoot; Slattery's Mounted Foot; Coronation Street* (as Frank Bradley, 1970, Phil Jennings, 1990–91); *Juliet Bravo;* Raymond in *Brookside; Strangers; Bulman; Travelling Man; All At No 20; The Bill; Brick Is Beautiful; Starlings; Hard Cases; Zatchi & Zatchi; William Tell; World In Action; Watching; Coasting; Waterfront Beat; House of Cards.* **Address:** c/o Shane Collins Associates. Lives in London. Hobbies: Golf.

BRACKNELL, *leah*

Leah Bracknell. Actress. b. London, 12 July 1964. Daughter of late assistant film director David Bracknell. **Theatre:** Joanna in *All Sewn Up;* Maria in *Out of the Valley;* Katie in *Flying Visit;* Marina in *Pericles;* Mephistophiles in *Doctor Faustus.* **Films:** *Savage Island.* **TV:** *The Chiffy Kids* (Children's Film & Television Foundation); *Dealers; The Cannon & Ball Show; The Bill; Wogan;* Zoe Tate in *Emmerdale* (1989-). Plus TV commercials. **Address:** c/o St James's Management/Yorkshire Television. 1 d. Lily. Hobbies: Reading, embroidery, travelling, eating.

BRADY, *moya*

Moya Brady. Actress. Trained at the Arts Educational School. **Theatre:** *The Red Devils; The Magic Olympica Games Show* (National Theatre); *Happy Days; Pig In a Poke* (both Royal Court Upstairs and national tours). **Films:** *Little Dorrit; Vroom; Life Is Sweet.* **TV:** Clare in *Road;* Ariadne in *Making Out* (three series). **Address:** c/o Richard Stone Partnership.

BRADY, *terence*

Terence Brady. Actor/Playwright. b. 13 March 1939. **Theatre:** *Beyond the Fringe; Present From the Corporation.* **Films:** *Baby Love; Foreign Exchange.* **TV:** Barty in *Pig In the Middle.* As writer: *Upstairs, Downstairs; No Honestly; Yes Honestly; Thomas and Sarah; Plays of Marriage; Take Three Girls; Pig In the Middle; Nanny; Oh Madeline!; Love With a Perfect Stranger; Father Matthew's Daughter.* **Address:** c/o Ian Lowe. m. actress-playwright Charlotte Bingham; 1 d. Candida, 1 s. Matthew.

BRAGG, *melvyn*

Melvyn Bragg. Presenter/Editor/Writer. b. Carlisle, Cumbria, 6 October 1939. LWT head of arts (1982-); Border TV chairman (1990-). **Theatre:** *Mardi Gras; The Hired Man; Orion.* **Films:** *Isadora; Jesus Christ Superstar; Clouds of Glory.* **TV:** *Monitor* (producer); *New Release; Writers' World; Take It Or Leave It* (all as editor); *In the Picture* (presenter); *Second House; Read All About It* (both as presenter/producer); *The South Bank Show* (presenter/editor, 1978-); *The Literary Island; Arts Review; A Time To Dance* (dramatisation). **Books:** Twelve novels, including *The Nerve, The Maid of Buttermere* and *A Time To Dance; A Christmas Child; Speak for England; Laurence Olivier; Rich – A Life of Richard Burton.* **Address:** c/o LWT. m. 1st Marie-Elisabeth (dec), 2nd TV producer Cate Haste; 2 d. Marie Elsa (from 1st m.), Alice, 1 s. Tom.

BRAILEY, *gil*

Gil Brailey. Actress. b. Liverpool. Trained at Central School of Speech and Drama. **Theatre:** *Late Nights; This Jockey Drives; A Short, Sharp Shock* (Royal Court Theatre); *Wednesday; Water Visitors; Sophia; The Sleeping Quarters; Last Summer In Chulimsk; Having a Ball; The Foursome; Kennedy's Children; Scully's Christmas Stories.* National Theatre: *Jews and Arabs; Plunder; A Double Dealer; When We Are Married; A Faire Quarrel; Plenty; The Passion.* **Films:** *Yanks; The Samaritans.* **TV:** *Harry's Game; Hold the Back Page; Home Video; Checkpoint Chiswick; Hard Cases; Casualty; Think About Science; Stay Lucky; The Adventures of Billy Webb* (two series). **Address:** c/o Tim Scott Personal Management.

BRANDON, *michael*

Michael Brandon. Actor/Writer/Director. b. Brooklyn, New York. **Theatre:** *Does a Tiger Wear a Necktie?* (Broadway); *Lady and the Clarinet.* **Films:** *Lovers and Other Strangers; Jennifer On My Mind; Four Flies; On Grey Velvet; Promises In the Dark; FM; Change of Seasons; Rich and Famous; Try This One for Size; The Care of Time.* **TV:** *The Red Badge of Courage; Queen of the Stardust Ballroom; James Dean; Red Alert* (all TV movies); *Visitors; Have a Nice Night; The Last Colt;* Dempsey in *Dempsey and Makepeace.* **Address:** c/o London Management.

BRANDRETH, *gyles*

Gyles Brandreth. Presenter. b. Wuppertal, Germany, 8 March 1948. **TV:** *Child of the Sixties; Call My Bluff; Puzzle Party; Chatterbox; Memories; Good Morning Britain* (TV-am); *The Time of Your Life; Connections; Babble; Tell the Truth; All Star Secrets; Catchword; Star Quality; The Railway Carriage Game; Discovering Gardens; Show Me; Countdown.* **Radio:** *A Rhyming Time; Funny Peculiar; Just a Minute; Gyles Brandreth's Puzzle Corner.* **Books:** Author of more than 50 children's books, plus biographies of Sir John Gielgud, Dan Leno and Harry Houdini. **Address:** c/o Jacque Evans Management. Lives in Chester. m. Michele; 1 s. Benet, 2 d. Saethryd, Aphra. Pets: Two cats. Hobbies: Chairman of the National Playing Fields Association. **Favourite TV programme:** *Countdown* (to be on); *Inspector Morse* (to watch).

BREMNER, *rory*

Rory Bremner. Actor/Writer. b. Edinburgh, 6 April 1961. Acted in revue and cabaret while at London University. **TV:** *It'll Be Alright On the Night; Spitting Image; Now Something Else; Rory Bremner.* **Radio:** *Week Ending; News Revue.* **Videos:** *The Best of Rory Bremner.* **Address:** c/o Richard Stone Partnership. Lives in Hampshire. m. artist Susan.

BRETT, *jeremy*

Jeremy Brett. Actor. b. Berkswell, Warwickshire, 3 November 1938. Trained at Central School of Speech and Drama. **TV:** *Affairs of the Heart; Ghost Story; Jennie; School for Scandal; A Legacy; Mother Love; The Picture of Dorian Gray; Love's Labour's Lost; Supernatural: Mr Nightingale; Rebecca; Seagull Island; On Approval; The Good Soldier; No 10; The Last Visitor; The Barretts of Wimpole Street; Morte d'Arthur; The Last Visitor; William Pitt the Younger;* title role in *The Adventures of Sherlock Holmes, The Return of Sherlock Holmes* and *The Casebook of Sherlock Holmes; Florence Nightingale; Deceptions;* Sherlock Holmes in *The Sign of Four, The Hound of the Baskervilles* and *Sherlock Holmes: Master Blackmailer.* **Address:** c/o William Morris Agency. m. 1st actress Anna Massey (dis), 2nd Joan; 1 d. Rebekah, 2 s. David, Caleb.

BRIDGES, *garey*

Garey Bridges. Actor. b. 11 August 1969. **Theatre:** *The Miracle Worker* (Byre Theatre, St Andrews, and Westminster Theatre). **TV:** *The Old Grey Whistle Test; The Hot Shoe Show; The Brides of Frankenstein; Rockliffe's Babies; Arcadia;* John in *The Bogeyman;* Winston in *Making News;* Terry in *Press Gang; Casualty;* Lloyd Tavernier in *EastEnders* (1990-). **Address:** c/o Sylvia Young Management.

BRIERS, *richard*

Richard Briers. Actor. b. Merton, Surrey, 14 January 1934. Trained at RADA. **Theatre:** Repertory theatre in Liverpool, Leatherhead and Coventry; *Present Laughter; Arsenic and Old Lace; Cat Among the Pigeons; Butley; Absurd Person Singular; Absent Friends; The Wild Duck; Middle-Aged Spread; Arms and the Man; Run for your Wife; Why Me?;* Malvolio in *Twelfth Night;* title role in *King Lear.* **Films:** *Fathom; All the Way Up; A Chorus of Disapproval; Henry V.* **TV:** *Brothers In Law; Marriage Lines;* Ben Travers farces; *The Norman Conquests; The Good Life; The Good Neighbours* (US); *The Other One; Goodbye Mr Kent; PQ17; Ever Decreasing Circles; The Aerodrome; All In Good Faith; Twelfth Night.* TV commercials: Nescafé; many voice-overs. **Address** c/o ICM. m. actress Ann Davies (qv); 2 d. Katy, Lucy.

BRIGGS, *johnny*

Johnny Briggs. Actor. b. Battersea, South London, 5 September 1935. Trained at the Italia Conti Academy from the age of 12. **Films:** *Carry On* films; *HMS Defiant.* **TV:** *The Planemakers; The Saint; Department 'S'; Private Eye; Softly, Softly; Z-Cars; Devil's Disciple; The Man With the Power; Do Me No Favours; Mogul; The Avengers; The Persuaders; Love Thy Neighbour; My Wife Next Door; Thick As Thieves; No Honestly; Yus My Dear;* Clifford Leyton in *Crossroads* (1973); Mike Baldwin in *Coronation Street* (1976-). Joint winner, with William Roache (qv) and Anne Kirkbride (qv), Pye Television Award, 1983. **Address:** Granada TV/Marina Martin Management. Lives in Stourbridge, Worcestershire, and Salford Quays. m. 1st Carole (dis), 2nd Christine; 1 s. Mark, 1 d. Karen (from 1st m.), 2 d. Jennifer, Stephanie, 2 s. Michael, Anthony (from 2nd m.).

BRITTON, *tony*

Tony Britton. Actor. b. Birmingham, 9 June 1924. Joined an amateur dramatics group while working in an estate agent's and an aircraft factory at Weston-super-Mare, then turned professional. **Theatre:** Repertory theatre in Weston-super-Mare and Manchester; RSC at Stratford-upon-Avon and the Old Vic Theatre; *Move Over, Mrs Markham; No, No, Nanette; The Dame of Sark; My Fair Lady* (national tour). **Films:** *There's a Girl In My Soup; Forbush and the Penguins; Sunday, Bloody Sunday; The Day of the Jackal; Nightwatch.* **TV:** *Romeo and Juliet; Six Proud Walkers; Melissa; Father, Dear Father; The Nearly Man; The Dame of Sark; Buffet; Robin's Nest* (four series); *Strangers and Brothers; Don't Wait Up.* **Address:** c/o ICM. m. 1st Ruth (dis), 2nd Danish sculptress Eve Birkefeldt (sep); 2 d. Cherry, TV presenter Fern (from 1st m.), 1 s. Jasper.

BROLIN, *james*

James Brolin. Actor/Writer/Director. **Films:** *Take Her, She's Mine; Goodbye Charlie; Pickup On South Street; Dear Brigitte; Von Ryan's Express; The Amityville Horror; High Risk; Beverly Hills Cowgirl Blues; Skyjacked.* **TV:** *Encounters* (TV movie); *Hold the Dream* (mini-series); *Bus Stop; The Monroes; Twelve O'Clock High; Marcus Welby, MD; Trapped; White Water Rebels; Cowboy; Hotel.* **Address:** c/o Triad Artists. m. 1st (dis), 2nd Jan Smithers; 2 s. Josh, Jess (from 1st m.).

BROOKE, *judy*

Judy Brooke. Actress. b. Leeds, 21 February 1970. Began professional career while at school and trained in violin, piano and singing. **Theatre:** *Our Day Out; The Amazing Dancing Bear; The Little Hotel On the Side; The Crucible; The Plotters of Cabbage Patch Corner.* **TV:** Yvonne in *The Beiderbecke Tapes* and *The Beiderbecke Connection; Living With AIDS; How To Be Cool; Coronation Street; All Creatures Great and Small; 4-Play: Goodbye and I Hope We Meet Again; The World of Eddie Weary; Coasting;* Paula Barker in *Emmerdale* (1991); child-abuse victim in a *World In Action* reconstruction; *Children's Ward; A Time To Dance.* **Radio:** *Benjamin Barrington Dancer; Derek's Destiny; Welcome Home; Coming From Together.* **Address:** Barbara Pemberton Associates. Single; lives in Leeds. Pets: Retriever spaniel called Ben and tropical fish.

BROOKE-TAYLOR, *tim*

Tim Brooke-Taylor. Actor/Writer. b. Buxton, Derbyshire, 17 July 1940. Began career in the Cambridge Footlights Revue. **Theatre:** *The Unvarnished Truth.* **Films:** *Twelve Plus One; The Statue; Willy Wonka and the Chocolate Factory.* **TV:** *The Ed Sullivan Show; The Jack Paar Show; At Last the 1948 Show; Marty; Broaden Your Mind; On the Braden Beat; His and Hers; The Rough With the Smooth; The Goodies; Hello Cheeky; Shades of Greene; Does the Team Think?; Me & My Girl; You Must Be the Husband.* **Radio:** *I'm Sorry I'll Read That Again; I'm Sorry I Haven't a Clue; Does the Team Think?; Loose Ends; The Fame Game.* **Records:** *Funky Gibbon; The New Goodies LP; The Goodies' Beastly Record; The Least Worst of Hello Cheeky; The Seedy Sounds of Hello Cheeky.* **Address:** c/o Jill Foster. Lives in Berkshire. m. Christine; 2 s. Ben, Edward.

BROOKS, *nikki*

Nicola Ashton. Actress/Singer. b. Nottingham, 29 June 1968. Trained at the Kaleidoscope Theatre Company, Julie Beech Stage School, Nottinghamshire, Morrison's School of Dance, and Hoofers Jazz Centre. **Theatre:** Principal dancer in *The Leslie Crowther Show; Mother Goose;* title role in *Cinderella; The Wizard of Oz; The Tempest; Just Girls; The Boy Friend; Snow White and the Seven Dwarfs; Dick Whittington; Annie.* **Films:** *Cresta Run; Bloody New Year.* **TV:** *Make Believe; The Secret Diary of Adrian Mole Aged 13¾; The Kid; The Marlows; The Fear;* Rosie Harding in *Crossroads; Inspector Morse; The Bill;* Hilandra in *Jupiter Moon; EastEnders.* **Records:** *Cheers To the Two of You* (EMI single). **Address:** c/o CCA. Single; lives in Hampstead, North London. Hobbies: Cinema, theatre, reading, travelling, exercise. **Favourite TV programme:** *LA Law.*

BROOKS, *ray*

Ray Brooks. Actor. b. Brighton, East Sussex, 20 April 1939. **Theatre:** Repertory theatre in Nottingham; *Backbone*. **Films:** *HMS Defiant; Play It Cool; Some People; The Knack . . .and how to get it; The Last Grenade*. **TV:** *Cathy Come Home; Gideon's Way; Taxi; Raging Moon; That Woman Is Wrecking Our Marriage; Death of an Expert Witness; Office Romances; Pennywise; Big Deal; Running Wild*; title role in *The World of Eddie Weary; Cine Memo* (narrator). **Address:** c/o Marmont Management. m. Sadie; 1 d. Emma, 2 s. William, Tom.

BROWN, *duggie*

Duggie Brown. Actor/Comedian. b. Rotherham, South Yorkshire, 7 August 1940. Brother of actress Lynne Perrie (qv). Played guitar with The Four Imps pop group, before turning professional as a comedian, then actor. **Theatre:** *The Price of Coal; Say Goodnight To Grandma; Cinderella; Dick Whittington; Robin Hood and Babes In the Wood; Aladdin*. **Films:** *For the Love of Ada; Kes*. **TV:** *The Good Old Days; The Comedians; Slattery's Mounted Foot; Leeds United; Say Goodnight To Grandma; Days of Hope; The Price of Coal; The House That Jack Built; Bring On the Girls; Take My Wife; Crown Court; The Enigma Files; The Cuckoo Waltz; The Glamour Girls; The Hard Word; Play for Today: The Combination; All Creatures Great and Small* (two roles); *The Bill; Minder*. **Address:** c/o ATS Casting. m. Jackie Ann; 1 d. Jacqueline.

BROWN, *faith*

Faith Brown. Singer/Impressionist/Actress. b. Liverpool, 28 May 1944. Sang with a Liverpool group at the age of 16, then formed The Carrolls vocal group with three of her four brothers, before going solo. **Theatre:** *Beauty Is the Business; Cinderella; My Fat Friend*. **TV:** *The David Frost Show; The Simon Dee Show; Lift Off* (all with The Carrolls); *Who Do You Do?; Songs That Stopped the Shows; For My Next Trick; Now Who Do You Do?; The Ken Dodd Show; The Faith Brown Awards; The Faith Brown Chat Show* (series); *The Mike Douglas Show* (USA); *Doctor Who* (straight acting debut, 1985); *QED* (host, one programme); plus many guest appearances. Awards: Speciality Act of the Year, 1980; *TVTimes* Funniest Woman On Television, 1980. **Address:** c/o Tony Lewis Entertainments/Clifford Elson Publicity. m. Len Wady; 1 d. Danielle. Hobbies: Fishing, cooking.

BROWN, *janet*

Janet Brown. Actress/Comedienne. b. Rutherglen, Glasgow. **Theatre:** *Mr Gillie*. **Films:** *Folly To Be Wise; Flood Tide; For Your Eyes Only*. **TV:** *Rainbow Room; Where Shall We Go?; Friends and Neighbours; Who Do You Do?; Mike Yarwood In Persons; Meet Janet Brown; Janet & Co*. **Books:** *Prime Mimicker* (autobiography). Winner, *TVTimes* Funniest Woman On TV award and Pye Colour TV award (both 1981). **Address:** c/o Bernard Lee Management. m. actor Peter Butterworth (dec); 1 d. Emma, 1 s. actor Tyler Butterworth (qv).

BROWN, *june*

June Brown. Actress. b. Suffolk. Trained at the Old Vic Theatre School. **Theatre:** *Macbeth; Hamlet; Twelfth Night* (RSC) *Fings Ain't What They Used To Be; The Lion In Winter; Claw; Wild Orchids; Dead Eyed Dicks; Equus; A Day for Ever; A View From the Bridge; Nightshade*. **Films:** *The Fourteen; Sherlock Holmes; Nijinski; The Hunchback of Notre Dame*. **TV:** *The Sweeney; Oranges and Lemons; Home and Away* (Granada TV series); *Churchill's People; South Riding; The Prince and the Pauper; Angels; The Duchess of Duke Street; Couples; Shining Pyramid; A Christmas Carol; Shadows; The Ladies; Letters Home; Now and Then; Young At Heart; The Bill; Minder; Lace; Relative Strangers*; Dot Cotton in *EastEnders* (1985-). **Address:** c/o Saraband Associates. Lives in Folkestone, Kent. m. 1st actor John Garley (dec), 2nd actor Robert Arnold; five children.

BROWN, *susan*

Susan Elisabeth Brown. Actress. b. Manchester, 6 May 1948. Trained at Rose Bruford College of Speech and Drama. **Theatre:** *Shirley; Downfall; Gibraltar Strait; Road* (Royal Court Theatre); *Back To Methuselah; The Vortex; The Beaux' Stratagem; A Woman of No Importance; The Way of the World; Roosters; By George!* **Films:** *The Year of the Bodyguard; Hope and Glory.* **TV:** *The Kids From 47A; The Duchess of Duke Street; Fanny By Gaslight;* Connie Clayton in *Coronation Street;* Helen in *Road;* Ruby in *Andy Capp; Loving Hazel;* Avril in *Making Out; Murder Weekend; The Bill; The Paradise Club; Prime Suspect; Nona; Absolute Hell; Prince* (TV movie). **Address:** c/o Barry Brown & Partner. Lives in London with Toby Whale. Pets: A cat called Lucy. Hobbies: Cooking.

BROWNE, *eithne*

Eithne Browne. Actress. b. Huyton, Liverpool, 25 November 1954. **Theatre:** *Dog Day Afternoon; The Odd Couple; Separate Tables; Business As Usual;* Mrs Johnstone in *Blood Brothers* (Lyric Theatre, London, and Leicester Haymarket); *Breezeblock Park; Stags and Hens* (Young Vic Theatre). **TV:** *Albion Market; The Practice;* Muriel Brand in *The Marksman;* Chrissy Rogers in *Brookside.* **Address:** c/o LWA. 1 s. Neil.

BROWNING, *michael*

Michael Browning. Actor. b. Ongar, Essex, 15 May 1930. Trained at RADA. **Theatre:** Rep in Windsor, Farnham, Oxford, Bromley, Leatherhead, Worthing and Northampton; season at Regent's Park Open Air Theatre; *Twelfth Night; Love's Labour's Lost; The Visit* (London West End). **TV:** *Airline; Take Three Women; Minder; The Bill; Emmerdale Farm; Crossroads; Miss Marple: Murder At the Vicarage; Coronation Street; Take the High Road.* **Address:** c/o Gary Trolan Management.

BRYAN, *dora*

Dora Bryan. Actress. b. Southport, 7 February 1923. **Theatre:** *The Merry Wives of Windsor; She Stoops To Conquer.* **Films:** *The Blue Lamp; A Taste of Honey; The Great St Trinian's Train Robbery; Apartment Zero.* **TV:** *Both Ends Meet; Triangle; Foxy Lady; Dora; Rookery Nook.* **Books:** *According To Dora.* **Address:** c/o James Sharkey Associates. m. William Lawton; 1 d. Georgina, 2 s. Daniel, William.

BUCHANAN, *beth*

Beth Buchanan. Actress. **Films:** *Newsfront; Cass; Fluteman; Fortress; The Third Wave.* **TV:** *Secret Valley; Island Trader; Zero Zero; A Country Practice* (five roles); *Five Mile Creek;* Nancy in *Runaway Island; Body Business* (mini-series); *The Haunted School; Last Frontier* (mini-series); *The Flying Doctors; Princess Kate* (TV movie); *All the Way; Home and Away; Hey Dad; Language Arts; GP; South Pacific Adventures* (four TV movies); Gemma Ramsay in *Neighbours* (1990-). **Address:** c/o International Casting Service/Grundy Television.

BUCHANAN, *neil*

Neil Buchanan. Presenter/Writer. b. Liverpool, 11 October 1961. Previously a musician and songwriter. **TV:** *Number 73; Motormouth; Motormouth 2; Art Attack* (also co-deviser). **Records:** *Marseille; Red, White and Slightly Blue* (both with group Marseille). **Address:** c/o Severn Management Services. m. Niki Woodcock; 1 d. Molly.

BULLMORE, *amelia*

Amelia Mary Bullmore. Actress. b. London, 31 January 1964. Trained at Manchester University's drama department. **Theatre:** *Ladies In the Lift; Breaking Rank; Under the Influence; Running Gags; Oh Yes We Can* (all with the Red Stockings Theatre Company, of which she was a founder-member); *Sweeney Todd; Summerfolk; The Red Balloon; Be-Bop-a-Lula* (Liverpool Playhouse and national tour); *The Threepenny Opera; A View From the Bridge; Romeo and Juliet.* **Films:** *The Wide Sargasso Sea* (Bristol Film Productions). **TV:** *The Other Side of Midnight;* Stephanie Barnes in *Coronation Street* (1990–91). **Radio:** *Villette; Ouzo In Ag Nik; Life With Lederer; Potato County; The Frightful Thing.* **Address:** c/o Barbara Pemberton Associates. Single; lives in Manchester. Hobbies: Swimming, cooking, writing, walking, drawing.

BULLOCH, *jeremy*

Jeremy Bulloch. Actor. b. Market Harborough, Leicestershire, 16 February 1945. Trained at the Corona Academy. **Theatre:** *Dangerous Obsession; I Love You; Mrs Patterson; What Every Woman Knows; Every Other Evening.* **Films:** *A French Mistress; Summer Holiday; The Virgin and the Gypsy; For Your Eyes Only; Octopussy; The Spy Who Loved Me; Mary Queen of Scots; The Empire Strikes Back; Return of the Jedi.* **TV:** *The Newcomers; Billy Bunter; The Chequered Flag; The Professionals; George and Mildred; Agony; Robin of Sherwood; Boon; After Henry; Casualty; Singles;* Commander Huxley in *The Bill.* **Address:** c/o Barry Brown & Partner. m. Maureen; 3 s. Christian, Jamie, Robbie.

BURDIS, *ray*

Raymond John Burdis. Actor. b. London, 23 August 1958. Trained at the Anna Scher Theatre School. **Theatre:** *Class Enemy.* **Films:** *Junket 89; Scum; Music Machine; Richard's Things; Gandhi; Harem.* As producer: *The Reflecting Skin; The Krays.* **TV:** *Mary's Wife; Ain't Many Angels; Alice; Seconds Out; Triangle; Diamonds; Going Out; Scene: It's Different for Boys; Scum; Now and Then* (two series); *The Baker Street Boys; The Gentle Touch; The Professionals; Minder; I Thought You'd Gone; Walrus: What's It Gonna Be?; West; Dream Stuffing; The Kit Curran Radio Show; C.A.T.S. Eyes; Three Up, Two Down; The Lenny Henry Show; Ties of Blood: Invitation To a Party; Everyman: John Lennon; God's Chosen Car Park; Murder At the Farm.* **Address:** c/o Anna Scher Theatre Management. Lives in Islington, North London. m. Jacqui; 1 d. Sky.

BURKE, *kathy*

Kathy Burke. Actress. b. 13 June 1964. Trained at the Anna Scher Theatre School. **Films:** *Scrubbers; Goodie Two Shoes; Expresso Splasho; Sacred Hearts; Straight To Hell; The Secret Policeman's Biggest Ball; Walker.* **TV:** *Educating Marmalade; The Falklands Factor; The Nation's Health; Love Kills; Funseekers; Eat the Rich; A Visitor From Outer Space; The Brief; Johnny Jarvis; No Problem; Round and Round; Bleak House; Caring; The History Trail: Plague and Fire; A Very Peculiar Practice; The Best Years of Your Life; Call Me Mister; Ladies In Charge; This Year's Model; French and Saunders; The Bill; Go With Scrote; South Atlantic Raiders;* Tina Bishop in *The Last Resort* and *One Hour With Jonathan Ross; Work Experience; Amongst Barbarians; Casualty.* Also a member of the alternative comedy act Raw Sex. **Address:** c/o Stephen Hatton Management.

BURNS, *gordon*

Gordon Burns. Presenter. b. Belfast, 10 June 1942. Worked as a journalist on the *East Antrim Times, Belfast Telegraph* and BBC radio in London, before moving into television. **TV:** Ulster Television (sports editor and presenter of *UTV Reports); The Gordon Burns Hour; Granada Reports; World In Action; Reports Politics* (Granada TV); *The Granada 500; The Krypton Factor; Irish Angle; A Way of Life; Password; Surprise, Surprise.* **Address:** c/o Granada TV. m. Sheelagh; 1 s. Tristun, 1 d. Anna.

BURROWS, *malandra*

Malandra Elizabeth Burrows. Actress. b. Woolton, Liverpool, 4 November 1965. Trained at the Mabel Fletcher Drama College, Liverpool. **Theatre:** *Dracula; Frankenstein; Snow White and the Seven Dwarfs; Cinderella;* Sally in *Cabaret.* **TV:** *Junior Showtime* (aged six); *New Faces* (winner, aged nine); *The Practice; Fell Tiger;* Sue and Lisa in *Brookside;* Kathy Tate (née Bates, formerly Merrick) in *Emmerdale* (1985-). **Records:** *Just This Side of Love* (1990). **Address:** c/o Yorkshire Television. Single; lives in Leeds. Hobbies: Horse-riding, travel.

BURTON, *amanda*

Amanda Burton. Actress. b. Londonderry, 10 October 1956. Trained at Manchester Polytechnic's School of Theatre. **Theatre:** Octagon Theatre, Bolton; Duke's Playhouse, Lancaster. **TV:** *The Mersey Pirate; My Father's House* (Open University); Heather Haversham in *Brookside;* Margaret Daly in *Boon; Summer School; Inspector Morse; A Casualty of War; Van Der Valk; Stay Lucky; Lovejoy.* **Address:** c/o ICM Duncan Heath Associates. m. photographer Sven Arnstein. Hobbies: Horse-riding, collecting watches.

BUSFIELD, *timothy*

Timothy Busfield. Actor. b. Lansing, Missouri, USA, 12 June 1957. Trained at Actors' Theater of Louisville; founded Fantasy Theater in Sacramento (1986). **Theatre:** *Richard II; A Tale Told, Getting Out* (European tour); *Mass Appeal; The Tempest; A Few Good Men* (Broadway). **Films:** *Stripes; Revenge of the Nerds; Revenge of the Nerds II; Field of Dreams.* **TV:** *Trapper John, MD; Reggie; Family Ties; Matlock; Paper Chase; Love American Style; After M*A*S*H;* Elliot in *thirtysomething.* **Address:** c/o Century Artists.

BUTTERWORTH, *tyler*

Tyler Butterworth. Actor. b. Redhill, Surrey, 6 February 1959. Son of actor Peter Butterworth and actress-comedienne Janet Brown (qv). **Films:** *Consuming Passions.* **TV:** *Two Gentlemen of Verona; Ties of Blood; Casualty; Bergerac; Murder of a Moderate Man; What the Butler Saw; Boon; Singles; Home To Roost; Mike & Angelo Iphegenia At Aulis; Rumpole of the Bailey;* Reverend Candy in *The Darling Buds of May.* **Address:** c/o James Sharkey Associates.

BYATT, *michelle*

Michelle Marie Byatt. Actress. b. Liverpool, 3 November 1970. Sister of actress Sharon and actor Paul (qv) Byatt. Trained at the Merseyside Dance and Drama Centre and the London Studio Centre. **Theatre:** *Piper Hamlyn; Yer Dancing?; Cinderella; All Flesh Is Grass; Innocent Mistress; Katie Krackernuts; Oliver!* **Films:** Jude in *Business as Usual.* **TV:** Nikki White in *Brookside* (1986-); *World In Action* (scene reconstructing classroom violence); *Fun Factory; Coasting.* TV commercials: *Allied Carpets; Clearasil.* **Address:** c/o Nigel Martin-Smith Personal Management/Mersey Television. Single; lives in Liverpool. Hobbies: Keep-fit, going out, meeting people, reading. **Favourite TV programme:** *Vic Reeves Big Night Out.*

BYATT, *paul*

Paul Byatt. Actor. b. Liverpool. Brother of actresses Michelle (qv) and Sharon Byatt. Trained at Liverpool Playhouse Youth Theatre. **Theatre:** Liverpool Playhouse; Liverpool Empire; New Brighton Floral Pavilion. **TV:** Mike Dixon in *Brookside* (1990-); *Big Chance.* **Address:** c/o Mersey Television.

BYGRAVES, *max*

Walter Bygraves. Entertainer. b. Rotherhithe, London, 16 October 1922. **Films:** *Skimpy In the Navy; Bless 'Em All; Tom Brown's Schooldays; Charley Moon; A Cry From the Streets; Bobbikins; Spare the Rod.* **TV:** *Max Bygraves; Max; Singalongamax; Max Rolls On; Side by Side; Family Fortunes* (presenter); *Max Bygraves – Singalongawaryears.* **Radio:** *Educating Archie.* **Records:** *Singaglong* LPs (awarded three platinum, 31 gold and 15 silver discs); *You Need Hands/Tulips From Amsterdam; Fings Ain't Wot They Used T'Be* (Top 10 singles). **Books:** *I Wanna Tell You a Story* (autobiography); *The Milkman's On His Way* (novel); *After Thoughts* (second volume of autobiography). **Address:** c/o Jennifer Maffini, 32 Stafford Mansions, Stafford Place, London SW1E 6NL, tel 071–828 4595. m. Gladys (Blossom); 2 d. Christine, Maxine, 1 s. Anthony.

BYRNE, *patsy*

Patsy Byrne. Actress. b. Ashford, Kent, 13 July. Gained a diploma in theatre arts; taught speech and drama. **Theatre:** Repertory theatre in Guildford and Coventry; *The Wesker Trilogy; Serjeant Musgrave's Dance; One Way Pendulum* (all English Stage Company, at Royal Court Theatre); *The Caucasian Chalk Circle; The Cherry Orchard; As You Like It* (RSC, Stratford-upon-Avon and Aldwych Theatre). **TV:** *Inspector Morse; A Taste for Death;* Nursie in *Blackadder II;* Mrs Stoneway in *Watching* (six series); *Think About Science: Our Pond; Adam Bede.* **Address:** c/o Crouch Associates. Lives in Guildford. m. Patrick Seccombe.

BYRNE, *peter*

Peter James Byrne. Actor/Director. b. London, 29 January 1928. Trained at the Italia Conti Academy. **Theatre:** *The Blue Lamp; Boeing Boeing; There's a Girl In My Soup; Deadly Nightcap; The Business of Murder.* National and overseas tours: *Boeing Boeing; Born In the Gardens; Move Over Mrs Markham; Sleuth; Nightcap; Underground; Run for Your Wife; The Unexpected Guest; A Murder Is Announced; Wait Until Dark; Jamaica Inn.* **Films:** *Large Rope; Reach for the Sky; Carry On Cabbie.* **TV:** *The Pattern of Marriage* (debut, 1953); *The New Canadians; Mutiny at Spithead;* Andy Crawford in *Dixon of Dock Green; Blake's 7; Cinderella Gang; Bluebirds; Bread.* **Address:** c/o Michael Ladkin Personal Management. Lives in London. m. 2nd Renee Helen. Hobbies: Squash, swimming, golf, travel. **Favourite TV programme:** *Cheers.*

BYRON, *kathleen*

Kathleen Byron. Actress. b. London, 11 January 1923. Trained at the Old Vic Theatre School; wartime work as a Ministry of Information censor. **Theatre:** *Pygmalion; Crown Matrimonial.* **Films:** *Black Narcissus; A Matter of Life and Death; Small Black Room; Prelude To Fame; Madness of the Heart; The Elephant Man; From a Far Country.* **TV:** *Emergency – Ward 10; The Avengers; Who Is Sylvia?; Countercrime; That Woman Is Wrecking Our Marriage; Emmerdale Farm; The Golden Bowl; Portrait of a Lady; Moonstone; Heidi; Tales of the Supernatural; The Professionals; Minder; General Hospital; Hedda Gabler; Together; Unity; Nancy Astor; Angels; Dearly Beloved; Gentlemen and Players; Casualty; Portrait of a Marriage; The Bill; Moon and Son.* Address: c/o L'Epine Smith & Carney Associates. m. writer Alaric Jacob; 1 d. Harriet, 1 s. Jasper.

CADELL, *simon*

Simon Cadell. Actor. b. London, 19 July 1950. Trained at Bristol Old Vic Theatre School. **Theatre:** Bristol Old Vic Company; *Don't Dress for Dinner* (Apollo Theatre). **TV:** *Hadleigh; Hine; Love Story; A Man From Haven; Love School; The Glittering Prizes; Wings; Space 1999; She Fell Among Thieves; Play for Today; Enemy At the Door; Edward and Mrs Simpson; Hi-de-Hi!; Minder; Bergerac; Blott On the Landscape; Life Without George; The Dog It Was That Died; A Wanted Man; Pride and Extreme Prejudice;* Dennis Duval in *Singles.* **Address:** c/o Caroline Renton. Lives in North London. m. Rebecca; 2 s. Patrick, Alec.

CAESAR, *johnny*

John Michael Caesar. Actor. b. South Shields, 30 October 1936. Worked as an engineer in Tyneside shipyards before turning professional as a guitarist in pop groups, then as an actor and stand-up comic. **Theatre:** *The Faith Brown Show; The Cannon & Ball Show.* **TV:** *The Stars Look Down; Coronation Street; Crown Court; The Practice; Truckers;* Bill Middleton in *Emmerdale* (1984-). **Records:** Composer of *Come Home, Rhondda Boy,* recorded by Tom Jones (1981). **Address:** c/o ATS Casting/Yorkshire Television. m. Dianne; 1 s. James. Hobbies: DIY, metal-detecting.

CAINE, *marti*

Marti Caine. Comedienne. b. Sheffield, South Yorkshire, 26 January 1945. Former photographic model; entered showbusiness aged 19 as singer, then compere. **Theatre:** *Voila* (cabaret extravaganza in Bophuthatswana); *Marti's Christmas Crackers;* Fanny Brice in *Funny Girl; Season's Greetings* (national tour); *An Evening With Marti* (one-woman show); *What About Luv;* the Red Queen in *Snow White and the Seven Dwarfs* (Strand Theatre). **Films:** *Birds of Paradise.* **TV:** *New Faces* (winner, 1975); *The Marti Caine Show; Marti; Royal Variety Show; Hilary* (situation comedy, two series); *This Is Your Life* (subject); *New Faces* (host, 1986–9); *Marti Caine.* **Books:** *A Coward's Chronicle* (1990). **Address:** c/o ICM. m. 1st Malcolm Stringer (dis), 2nd TV producer Kenneth Ives; 2 s. Lee, Max (from 1st m.). Hobbies: Gardening, music, films, interior decor.

CAINE, *michael*

Michael Caine. Actor. b. Bermondsey, South London, 14 March 1933. **Films:** *Zulu; The Ipcress File; Alfie; The Italian Job; Too Late the Hero; Get Carter; Kidnapped; The Black Windmill; The Marseilles Contract; Harry and Walter Go To New York; The Eagle Has Landed; A Bridge Too Far; Beyond the Poseidon Adventure; Ashanti; Deathtrap; The Hand; Escape To Victory; Educating Rita; The Honorary Consul; Blame It On Rio; The Holcroft Covenant; Water; Hannah and Her Sisters; Mona Lisa; The Fourth Protocol; Surrender; Jaws – The Revenge; Dirty Rotten Scoundrels; Bullseye.* **TV:** *The Compartment; The Playmates; Hobson's Choice; Funny Noises With Their Mouths; The Way With Reggie; Luck of the Draw; Hamlet; The Other Man; Jack the Ripper; Jekyll & Hyde.* **Address:** c/o ICM. m. 1st actress Patricia Haines, 2nd Shakira; 2 d. Dominique (from 1st m.), Natasha.

CALLARD, *beverley*

Beverley Callard. Actress. b. Leeds. Previously acted under the name Beverley Sowden. **Theatre:** Jaqui Coryton in *Hay Fever;* Liz and Rita in *Billy Liar;* Ada Figgins in *Hobson's Choice;* the Wicked Queen in *Snow White and the Seven Dwarfs.* **TV:** Angie Richards in *Emmerdale Farm; Dear Ladies; Hell's Bells; The Practice; Will You Love Me Tomorrow* (TV movie); *Coronation Street* (June Dewhurst 1984, Liz McDonald 1989-). **Address:** c/o Peter Graham Associates/Granada TV. Lives in Leeds. m. Steven; 1 d. Rebecca, 1 s. Joshua.

CALLOW, *simon*

Simon Callow. Actor/Director/Writer. b. London, 15 June 1949. Trained at The Dance Centre. **Theatre:** *Total Eclipse; Beastly Beatitudes of Balthazar B; The Relapse; On the Spot; Faust* (all London West End); *As You Like It; Galileo; Amadeus; Sisterly Feelings; Single Spies* (all National Theatre). As director: *Shirley Valentine* (London and New York); *Single Spies; Stevie Plays the Blues* (Los Angeles). **Films:** *Amadeus; The Good Father; A Room With a View; Maurice; Manifesto; Mr & Mrs Bridge; Postcards From the Edge* (all as actor); *At Freddy's; Ballad of the Sad Café* (both as director). **TV:** *Wings of Song; Instant Englishment Plus VAT; Man of Destiny; Deadhead; Chance In a Million; Handel; David Copperfield; Old Flames; Revolutionary; Witness; Performance: The Trials of Oz.* **Books:** *Shooting the Actor.* **Address:** c/o Marina Martin Management.

CALVERT, *jennifer*

Jennifer Calvert. Actress. b. Ontario, Canada, 7 December 1963. Settled in Britain in 1984; trained at RADA. **TV:** Cheryl Boyanowsky in *Brookside; Spatz; Come Home Charlie and Face Them.* **Address:** c/o Daly Gagan Associates. Lives in London. m. Matthew.

CAMPBELL, *gavin*

Gavin Campbell. Actor/Presenter. b. Letchworth, Hertfordshire, 17 March 1946. Trained at Central School of Speech and Drama; worked with Joan Littlewood's Theatre Workshop. **Theatre:** *When One Is Somebody.* **TV:** *Department S; Vendetta; Armchair Theatre; That's Life; Breakfast Time; Nationwide; London Plus; South-East At Six.* **Address:** c/o Jon Roseman Associates. m. Liz Hendry; 2 d. Holly, Hannah.

CAMPBELL, *joanne*

Joanne Campbell. Actress. b. Northampton, 8 February 1964. **TV:** *Parents and Teenagers* (Open University); *Night Kids; Copperfield Comedy and Co; All Electric Amusement Arcade; Dramarama; Me & My Girl; Home James!; Chalkface.* **Address:** c/o Evans and Reiss.

CAMPI, *marji*

Marji Campi. Actress. **Theatre:** *Rialto Prom; Go West Young Woman; The Wedding Ring; Double Double; They Made Their Excuses and Left; Back-Street Romeo; Marriage; Relative Strangers; Soaplights; All In Good Time.* **TV:** *I Wear a Very Big Hat; Pioneers of Social Change; Woyzeck; Within These Walls; What Now?; The Man From the Pru;* Dulcie Froggatt in *Coronation Street;* Betty Hunt in *Brookside;* Joyce in *Surgical Spirit.* **Address:** c/o LWA.

CANNON, *tommy*

Thomas Derbyshire. Comedian/Entertainer. b. Oldham, Lancashire, 27 June 1938. Half of the comedy duo Cannon & Ball, originally welders in an Oldham engineering factory who sang semi-professionally by night as the Shirrell Brothers, then the Harper Brothers, before changing their name to Cannon & Ball. **Theatre:** *You'll Do for Me.* **Films:** *The Boys In Blue.* **TV:** *Opportunity Knocks; Royal Variety Performances; This Is Your Life* (subjects); *The Cannon & Ball Show* (1979–88); *Cannon & Ball's Casino* (hosts, quiz show); *Plaza Patrol* (sit-com). Winners, Variety Club Showbusiness Personalities of the Year award. **Address:** c/o International Artistes, Albert House, Albert St., Chadderton, Oldham. Lives in York. m. Margaret (sep), lives with Hazel; 3 d. Janet, Julie (from 1st m.), Kelly-Anne (by Hazel). Hobbies: Horse-riding, golf, keep-fit. **Favourite TV programme:** *The Golden Girls.*

CAPRON, *brian*

Brian Capron. Actor. b. Woodbridge, Suffolk, 11 February 1949. Trained at LAMDA. **Films:** *The Chiffy Kids.* **TV:** *Murray; A Place To Hide;* Donald Worthington in *Coronation Street; Love Letters On Blue Paper; Carry On Laughing; Around the Corner; Steven Waldorf; Smiffs; Jack the Ripper; The Gentle Touch; Angels; Beryl's Lot; The Sweeney; Way Up To Heaven; Clubs; Henry Intervening; Grange Hill; Nelson; Just Liz; The Squad; Enemies of the State; Bergerac; Stanley Baxter's Christmas Hamper; Up the Elephant and Round the Castle;* Murray in *Full House; Never Say Die; The Bill; Minder; Casualty; Action Stations; Never Come Back; Uncle Jack; Moon and Son; Growing Pains.* **Address:** c/o Markham & Froggatt. Lives in Brighton. m. actress Janette Legge; 2 d. Lucy, Ellen.

CARBY, *fanny*

Fanny Carby. Actress. b. Sutton Coldfield, Warwickshire, 2 February. Trained at Joan Littlewood's Theatre Workshop. **Films:** *The Family Way; How I Won the War; Oh! What a Lovely War; Joe Egg; The Elephant Man; Bert Rigby, You're a Fool.* **TV:** *Not So Much a Programme, More a Way of Life; The History of Mr Polly; The Good Companions; Forgive Our Foolish Ways; Crossroads; Nearest and Dearest; Both Ends Meet; Who's Your Father?;* three series with Spike Milligan; *Angels; The Cost of Loving; Cockles; Juliet Bravo; Room At the Bottom; The Good Dr Bodkin Adams; David Copperfield; The Little Match Girl;* Amy Burton in *Coronation Street; Indiscreet; William Tell; The House Plant; Only Fools and Horses; In Sickness and In Health.* **Address:** c/o Barry Burnett Organisation. Hobbies: Gardening, antiques. Pets: A cat called Mrs Tiggy.

CAROLGEES, *bob*

Bob Carolgees. Comedian. b. Birmingham, 12 May 1948. **TV:** *Tiswas; 3–2–1; OTT; Hold Tight!; Saturday Stayback; Live From Her Majesty's; Look Who's Talking; Live From the Palladium; Seaside Special; Surprise, Surprise; Summertime; Concentration* (presenter). **Address:** c/o Tony West Entertainments. m. Alison; 1 d. Natalie, 1 s. Richard.

CARPENTER, *harry*

Harry Carpenter. Sports commentator. b. London, 17 October 1925. National newspaper journalist before entering television. **TV:** Commentator on boxing world heavyweight title fights and every Olympic Games since 1956; presenter of BBC Wimbledon lawn tennis coverage, Open golf championships and Oxford-Cambridge boat race. Author of three books on boxing. Winner, American Sportscasters' Association International Award, 1989. **Address:** c/o BBC TV. m. Phyllis; 1 s. Clive.

CARPENTER, *sue*

Susan Jane Carpenter. Newscaster. b. London, 17 May 1956. Sub-editor and newscaster in the Middle East, before returning to Britain. **TV:** *Breakfast Time; News After Noon;* ITN newscaster. Television and Radio Industries Club Newscaster of the Year, 1991. **Address:** c/o Jon Roseman Associates/ITN. Lives in London. Pets: A dog. Hobbies: Walking, cinema. **Favourite TV programme:** *LA Law.*

CARR, *jack*

Jack Carr. Actor. **Theatre:** *Wars of the Roses; Zack; Romeo and Juliet; Just a Kick In the Grass; The Taming of the Shrew; A Streetcar Named Desire; The White Devil; Shadow of a Gunman; An Enemy of the People.* **Films:** *Business As Usual; Suspect.* **TV:** *Death of an Expert Witness; Bleak House;* Tom Merrick in *Emmerdale Farm;* Tony Cunliffe in *Coronation Street; Private Practice; Snakes and Ladders; Tales of Sherwood Forest; Truckers; Making Out; Chancer; The Chief; Medics; The Bill; Never the Twain; Stay Lucky.* **Address:** c/o Barry Brown & Partner.

CARROLL, *diahann*

Diahann Carroll. Actress/Singer. b. New York, USA, 17 July 1935. Became a model at the age of 15, then studied drama at the High School of Music and Art, New York. **Theatre:** *House of Flowers; No Strings; Agnes of God.* **Films:** *Carmen Jones; Paris Blues; Porgy and Bess; Claudine.* **TV:** *Chance of a Lifetime* (talent show, won three weeks running); *Julia; Sister, Sister; Dynasty.* m. 1st Monte Kay, 2nd Fredde Glusman, 3rd Robert De Leon, 4th singer Vic Damone.

CARROTT, *jasper*

Robert Davies. Comedian. b. Birmingham, 14 March 1945. Started career in 1969 as club compere. **Films:** *Jane and the Lost City.* **TV:** *An Audience With Jasper Carrott; Half Hour With Jasper Carrott; The Unrecorded Jasper Carrott; Carrott Del Sol; Carrott's Lib* (BAFTA award, 1984); *Carrott Confidential; Canned Carrott; 24 Carrott Gold; Specially Selected Canned Carrott; Carrott's Commercial Breakdown (II).* **Records:** *Funky Moped/Magic Roundabout* (single); *Rabbits On and On; Carrott In Notts; The Best of Jasper Carrott; The Unrecorded Jasper Carrott; Beat the Carrott; Carrott's Lib; The Stun* (Carrott Tells All); *Cosmic Carrott* (LPs). Awarded three gold and three silver discs. **Address:** c/o BBC TV. m. Hazel; 3 d. Lucy, Jennifer, Hannah, 1 s. Jake.

CARSON, *frank, KSF*

Frank Carson. Comedian. b. Belfast, 6 November 1926. Knight of the Grand Cross of St Gregory. **TV:** *The Good Old Days; Opportunity Knocks; The Comedians; The Melting Pot; The Ballyskillen Opera House; Tiswas; This Is Your Life* (subject). **Address:** c/o Dorothy Solomon. m. Ruth; 1 d. Majella, 2 s. Tony, Aidan.

CARSON, *kevin*

Kevin Carson. Actor. b. Liverpool, 19 January 1974. **Theatre:** *No More Sitting On the Old School Bench; Game of Soldiers.* **TV:** *The Marksman;* Geoff Rogers in *Brookside.* **Address:** c/o Mersey Television.

CARTER, *lynda*

Lynda Carter. Actress/Singer/Dancer. b. Phoenix, Arizona, USA, 24 July 1951. A former Miss USA. **TV:** *Rita Hayworth – The Love Goddess* (TV movie); *Stillwatch;* Diana Prince in *Wonder Woman; Partners In Crime; Body and Soul; Born To Be Sold; The Muppet Show.* **Address:** c/o William Morris Agency (USA). m. 1st Ron Samuels (dis), 2nd Robert Altman; 1 s. James.

CARTERET, *anna*

Anna Carteret. Actress. b. Bangalore, India, 11 December 1942. **Films:** *Light Up the Sky; Dateline Diamonds; The Plank.* **TV:** *A Young Lady From London; The Ordeal of Richard Foverill; The Hon Bird; Mickey Dunne; The Reluctant Debutante; Riviera Police; The Saint; Constance; She Stoops To Conquer; Play for Today: The Pigeon Fancier; The Merchant of Venice; The Pallisers; The Glittering Prizes; Fathers and Families; Mother Song; Send In the Girls; The Man Who Liked Elephants; Crown Court; Little Mrs Perkins; None of Your Business; Change Partners; Being Normal;* Inspector Kate Longton in *Juliet Bravo; In the Pink; Make It Work; Raving Beauties; Everyone's a Winner; Heat of the Day; The Shell Seekers; Time To Talk; 01 for London; Cluedo; Women In Aids; Ashenden.* **Address:** c/o Peters Fraser & Dunlop. m. director Christopher Morahan; 2 d. Rebecca, Hattie.

CARTY, *todd*

Todd Carty. Actor. b. Ireland, 1963. Started appearing in TV commercials at the age of four. **Theatre:** Title role in *Lionel* (stage debut, New London Theatre, Drury Lane); *Dick Whittington.* **Films:** *Professor Popper's Problems; Please Sir!; The Gang's OK; The Magic Trip;* Oswyn in *Krull; What's In It for You; A Question of Balance; Serve Them Right; The Candy Show.* **TV:** *Z-Cars; Our Mutual Friend; Drummer; Headmaster; Focus On Britain; The Idle Bunch* (both for German TV); *We're Happy* (RTE, Ireland); Tucker in *Grange Hill;* title role in *Tucker's Luck; Aladdin; Scene In New York; The Jungle Creatures* (both as narrator); *Counter Intelligence;* Mark Fowler in *EastEnders* (1990–). **Radio:** *Les Miserables; The Three Loves of Ide Bliss; Wavelength; Midweek Jellybones.* **Address:** c/o John Redway and Associates/BBC Elstree Centre.

CASHMAN, *michael*

Michael Cashman. Actor/Writer. b. London, 17 December 1950. Began acting at the age of 12. **Theatre:** *Oliver!; Peter Pan; Zigger Zagger; Before Your Very Eyes; Bricks 'n' Mortar; The Chairs; Bent* (National Theatre). **Films:** *The Virgin Soldiers; Zee & Co; Unman.* **TV:** *Season's Greetings; Angels; The Sandbaggers; Waste; The World of J B Priestley; The Winning Streak; Doctor Who; The Life of Shakespeare; Nobody's Perfect; The Gentle Touch; Seven Deadly Virtues; Game for a Laugh; Bird of Prey; Dempsey and Makepeace;* Colin Russell in *EastEnders* (1986–8). **Address:** c/o Barry Burnett Organisation.

CASTLE, *john*

John Castle. Actor. b. Croydon, Surrey, 14 January 1940. **Films:** *The Lion In Winter; The Promise; Antony and Cleopatra; Man of La Mancha; Sarah; Eliza Fraser; Night Shift; Second Star To the Right.* **TV:** *Dead of Night; Pearcross Girls; Harlequinade; Town Without Pity; Fight Against Slavery; Ben Hall; I, Claudius; The Prime of Miss Jean Brodie; The Three Hostages; Eagle's Wing; Lost Empires; Inspector Morse.* **Address:** c/o Larry Dalzell Associates.

CASTLE, *roy*

Roy Castle. Entertainer/Actor. b. Scholes, nr Huddersfield, West Yorkshire. **Theatre:** *Singing In the Rain* (London Palladium). **Films:** *Dr Terror's House of Horrors; Dr Who and the Daleks; Carry On Up the Khyber; Legend of the Werewolf.* **TV:** *The Roy Castle Show; Roy Castle Beats Time; Record Breakers* (presenter); *Castle's Abroad.* **Radio:** *Castle's On the Air.* **Address:** c/o London Management. m. Fiona; 2 d. Julia, Antonia, 2 s. Daniel, Benjamin.

CAZENOVE, *christopher*

Christopher Cazenove. Actor. b. Winchester, Hampshire, 17 December 1945. Trained at Bristol Old Vic Theatre School. **Films:** *East of Elephant Rock; The Girl In Blue Velvet; Zulu Dawn; Heat and Dust; Mata Hari; The Fantasist; Souvenir; Hold My Hand, I'm Dying; The Lady and the Highwayman; Aces.* **TV:** *The Rivals of Sherlock Holmes;* Richard Gaunt in *The Regiment; The British Hero; Pathfinders; K Is for Killer; Affairs of the Heart; Jennie: Lady Randolph Churchill; Ladykillers; The Red Signal; Jenny's War; Dr Watson and the Darkwater Hall Mystery; The Duchess of Duke Street; Lou Grant; The Letter; Kane & Abel;* Ben Carrington in *Dynasty; Windmills of the Gods; Shades of Love; Tears In the Rain; Dangerous Love; Ticket To Ride; Lace 2; A Fine Romance; To Be the Best.* **Address:** c/o Michael Whitehall. m. actress Angharad Rees; 2 s. Linford, Rhys.

CHADBON, *tom*

Tom Chadbon. Actor. b. Luton, Bedfordshire, 27 February 1946. Trained at RADA. **Films:** *Tess; The Last of Linda Cleer; Dance With a Stranger; A Day In Summer.* **TV:** *The Brack Report; British Comedy Classics; Strangers and Brothers; Shine On Harvey Moon; Mitch; The Late Nancy Irving; Love Song; Bulman; Paradise Postponed; Floodtide; Crossfire; Doctor Who; Hard Cases; Wish Me Luck; Chancer; Devices and Desires; Sherlock Holmes and the Leading Lady* (mini-series); *The Bill; Thatcher: The Final Days.* **Address:** c/o London Management. m. Jane; 2 s. Dominic, Nicholas, 2 d. Amelia, Felicity.

CHADWICK, *cy*

Cy Chadwick. Actor. b. Leeds, 2 June 1969. **TV:** *The Book Tower* (aged 13); *How We Used To Live; On the Boat* (English-language series for German TV); Nick Bates in *Emmerdale* (1985-). Plus voice-overs for commercials. **Address:** c/o Tobias Management/Yorkshire Television. Single; lives in Leeds. Hobbies: Photography, listening to pop music.

CHALMERS, *judith*

Judith Chalmers. Presenter. b. Manchester, 10 October. **TV:** BBC TV announcer; *Come Dancing; After Noon Plus; Wish You Were Here ...?* (1973-); *This Is Your Life* (subject); *The Home Service* (also deviser); *Hot Property; Miss World; Miss United Kingdom;* royal film premières; The Derby; Royal Ascot. **Radio:** *Children's Hour* (aged 13); *Woman's Hour* (BBC Radio 4). *The Judith Chalmers Show* (BBC Radio 2). **Books:** *Wish You Were Here ...?; Judith Chalmers' 50 Best Holidays.* **Address:** c/o IMG. m. sports commentator Neil Durden-Smith; 1 d. Emma, 1 s. Mark.

CHARLESTON, *anne*

Anne Charleston. Actress. b. Melbourne, Australia. Drama lessons with actress Lorna Forbes. **Films:** *2,000 Weeks; Country Town; I Live With Me Dad.* **TV:** *The Shifting Heart; Bellbird; Antigone; Twenty Good Years; The Man of Destiny; Descent for Gossip; Homicide; The Sullivans; Division 4; Holiday Island; Cop Shop; Skyways; Matlock Police; Prisoner Cell Block H; Class of '75; The Two Way Mirror;* Elizabeth Macarther in *Possession;* Madge Bishop (née Ramsay, formerly Mitchell) in *Neighbours* (1985-). **Records:** *Old Fashioned Christmas* (single with Ian Smith, 1989). **Address:** c/o Melbourne Artists Management. Single; lives in Melbourne. 1 s. actor Nick (from a previous relationship with actor-singer David Ravenswood).

CHEGWIN, *keith*

Keith Chegwin. Presenter/Actor. b. Liverpool, 17 January 1957. Sang in Northern workingmen's clubs with a family trio from the age of 11; later sang with the pop group Kenny. **Theatre:** *The Good Old Bad Old Days; Tom Brown's Schooldays; Wally Scott Live.* **Films:** *Macbeth; Eggheads Robot; Elspeth's Double; Robin Hood Junior.* **TV:** *Junior Showtime; Swap Shop; Saturday Superstore; Cheggers Plays Pop; Wackers; Cheggers' Action Reports; Chegwin Checks It Out; The Ronnie Barker Show; The Liver Birds; The Chester Mystery Plays; My Old Man; Black Beauty; Armchair Theatre; Village Hall; Star Turn; All Star Record Breakers; Sky Star Search; Go Getters.* **Address:** c/o Dave Winslett Entertainments. m. TV presenter Maggie Philbin; 1 d. Rose.

CHERITON, *shirley*

Shirley Cheriton. Actress. b. London, 28 June 1955. Trained at the Italia Conti Academy. **Theatre:** *Goldilocks and the Three Bears; Pyjama Tops; Dick Whittington; The Monkey Walk; One for the Road; Robin Hood.* **TV:** *Crown Court; Within These Walls; The Cuckoo Waltz; Z-Cars; Bless This House; General Hospital; Angels; Hazell; Secombe With Music; The Final Frontier;* Debbie Wilkins in *EastEnders; Three Up, Two Down;* Miss Prescott in *Grace and Favour.* **Address:** c/o St James's Management. m. Howard Spinks (dis); 2 s. Mark, Adam.

CHILD, *jeremy*

Jeremy Child. Actor. b. Woking, Surrey, 20 September 1944. Trained at the Bristol Old Vic Theatre School. **TV:** *Take Three Girls; Coronation Street; Father, Dear Father; The Glittering Prizes; Wings; Robin's Nest; Winston Churchill – The Wilderness Years; Backs To the Land; Cork and Bottle; The Upchat Line; The Sweeney; Anna Karenina; Edward and Mrs Simpson; 'Tis Pity She's a Whore; When the Boat Comes In; Bird of Prey; Sapphire and Steel; Vice Versa; The Happy Apple; Minder; Bergerac; The Jewel In the Crown; Oxbridge Blues; Late Starter; Fairly Secret Army; Hart To Hart; First Among Equals; Game, Set & Match; Lovejoy; Perfect Scoundrels.* **Address:** c/o Richard Stone Partnership. m. 1st actress Deborah Grant (dis), 2nd Jan Todd (dis), 3rd Libby Morgan; 3 d. Melissa, Lenora, Eliza, 1 s. Alexander.

CHILDS, *tracey*

Tracey Childs. Actress. b. Chiswick, West London, 30 May 1963. Trained at Elmhurst Ballet School and Guildhall School of Music and Drama. **Theatre:** *The Hunchback of Notre Dame; Great Expectations – The Musical.* **TV:** *Upstairs, Downstairs; The Prime of Miss Jean Brodie; Sense and Sensibility; The Scarlet Pimpernel; A Married Man; Morgan's Boy; The Victoria Wood Show; Deceptions; The Happy Autumn Fields; Shades; A Talent for Murder; Flesh and Blood; The Devil's Crown: Prometheus; Cold Warrior; Dempsey and Makepeace; Howards' Way; The Shell Seekers.* **Address:** c/o Evans and Reiss.

CHITTELL, *christopher*

Christopher Chittell. Actor. b. 19 May. **Films:** *To Sir With Love; The Charge of the Light Brigade; Golden Rendezvous; Zulu Dawn.* **TV:** Eric Pollard in *Emmerdale* (1986–). **Address:** c/o Spotlight/ Yorkshire Television. m. Caroline: 1 s. Benjamin. 1 d. Rebecca.

CHRISTIAN, *peter*

Peter Christian. Actor. b. Liverpool, 14 August 1947. Worked as a builder and for the Forestry Commission and Liverpool docks, before backstage work for the David Lewis Theatre Group. **Theatre:** *Her Benny; Look Back In Anger; Son of Man;* Jesus in a nativity play; Zigger in *Zigger Zagger; Petty Life of the Bourgeois; Waiter; The Lover; Lost City Echoes; Can't Pay Won't Pay; Cloud Nine; Yellow Dwarf;* Sammy in *Blood Brothers* (Liverpool Playhouse and Lyric Theatre, London); *Stags and Hens* (Young Vic Theatre, London, and Nottingham Playhouse). **TV:** *Boys From the Blackstuff; Give Us A Break; Scully; The Brothers MacGregor; Travelling Man; Truckers;* Frank Blackburn, then Frank Rogers, in *Brookside.* **Address:** c/o Mersey Television.

CHRISTIE, *julie*

Julie Christie. Actress. b. Chukua, Assam, India, 14 April 1941. Trained at Central School of Speech and Drama. **Theatre:** Birmingham Rep; RSC; *Uncle Vanya* (New York). **Films:** *Crooks Anonymous; The Fast Lady; Billy Liar; Young Cassidy; Darling; Doctor Zhivago* (winner, Best Actress Oscar); *Fahrenheit 451; Far From the Madding Crowd; Tonite Let's All Make Love In London; Petulia; In Search of Gregory; The Go-Between; McCabe and Mrs Miller; Don't Look Now; Shampoo; Nashville; Demon Seed; Heaven Can Wait; Memoirs of a Survivor; The Roaring Forties; The Animals Film; The Return of the Soldier; Heat and Dust; The Gold Diggers; Power; Miss Mary; La Memoir Tatouée; The Control Room; Fools of Fortune; The Railway Station Man.* **TV:** *A for Andromeda; Fathers and Sons; Separate Tables; Dada Is Death.* **Address:** c/o ICM Duncan Heath Associates.

CLARKE, *jacqueline*

Jacqueline Clarke. Actress. b. Buckinghamshire, 13 February 1942. Trained at RADA. **TV:** *The Adventures of Don Quick; The Dave Allen Show; Thirty Minutes Worth; The Brighton Bell; Scott On; The Basil Brush Show; Battle of the Sexes; The Mike Yarwood Show; Rings On Their Fingers; Partners;* Sheila Barnes in *A Sharp Intake of Breath; The Critic; It's Different for Boys; The Young Ones; Only When I Laugh; The Kenny Everett Show; Chish 'n ' Fips; Slinger's Day; Little and Large; Maxwell's House.* **Address:** c/o Barry Burnett Organisation. Lives in Gloucestershire. m. 1st Peter Cartwright, 2nd actor Barrie Gosney; 1 d. Catherine-Anne. Pets: A labrador called Emma. Hobbies: Gardening, painting, walking. **Favourite TV programme:** Any gardening or nature programme.

CLARKE, *margi*

Margi Clarke. Actress. b. Liverpool, 1954. Sister of TV and film writer-director Frank Clarke. **Films:** Teresa in *Letter To Brezhnev; Loser Takes All; Blonde Fist.* **TV:** *What's On* (Granada TV, presenter); Queenie in *Making Out* (three series). **Address:** c/o Daly Gagan Associates. Lives in Wavertree, Liverpool, with artist Jamie Reid. m. (dis); 1 s. Lawrence.

CLAYTON, *edward*

Edward Clayton. Actor/Singer. b. Shelfield, Staffordshire, 9 October 1940. **Theatre:** *Our Day Out; Poppy; Comedians; Destiny;* Beadle in *Sweeney Todd; Trafford Tanzi.* **Films:** *Wilt; Whoops Apocalypse; Paris By Night; Prostitutes.* **TV:** Stan Harvey in *Crossroads; Tucker's Luck; Ladies In Charge; Reflections of Evil; Boy With the Transistor Radio; Travelling Light; Juliet Bravo;* Brian in *Eh Brian, It's a Whopper;* Robson in *First Among Equals; Rockliffe's Babies; A Sort of Innocence; The Bell Run; The Contract;* Arthur Parkinson in *Brookside;* Tom Casey in *Coronation Street; The Bill; First and Last; The Ruth Rendell Mysteries: The Best Man To Die; This Is David Harper; The Chief; Agatha Christie's Poirot; GBH; Perfect Scoundrels; Underbelly.* **Address:** c/o Sandra Griffin Management. m. Caroline; 3 d. Ella, Joby, Rosalie.

CLEESE, *john*

John Cleese. Actor/Writer. b. Weston-super-Mare, Somerset, 27 October 1939. Member of Cambridge Footlights Revue while at university. **Films:** *And Now for Something Completely Different; Monty Python and the Holy Grail; Monty Python's Life of Brian; Time Bandits; The Great Muppet Caper; The Meaning of Life; The Secret Policeman's Ball; Yellowbeard; Privates On Parade; Silverado; Clockwise; A Fish Called Wanda.* **TV:** *The Frost Report; The Frost Programme; At Last the 1948 Show; Monty Python's Flying Circus;* Basil Fawlty in *Fawlty Towers; Romance With a Double Bass; The Taming of the Shrew; The South Bank Show* (subject); *Cheers.* **Books:** *Families and How To Survive Them;* Winner, *TVTimes* Funniest Man On TV award, 1978–9. **Address:** c/o David Wilkinson. m. 1st actress Connie Booth (dis), 2nd film director Barbara Trentham; 2 d. Cynthia, Camilla.

CLIFTON, *bernie*

Bernie Clifton. Actor/Comedian/Entertainer. b. St Helens, Lancashire, 22 April. Began as half of vocal-comedy duo The Two Terry's; turned professional as a stand-up comedian after RAF service. **TV:** *The Good Old Days* (TV debut, 1971); *The Comedians; Crackerjack* (three series); *Royal Variety Show* (1979); *Bernie Clifton On Stage; Theatre Royal; The Children's Royal Variety Show; The Marti Caine Show; You Must Be Joking; The Jim Davidson Show; Des O'Connor Tonight; Big Top; Blankety Blank; All Star Secrets; 3-2-1; Bernie Clifton's Tricky Business.* **Radio:** *Bernie Clifton's Comedy Store; Three In a Row* (host, quiz show). **Address:** c/o Clifford Elson Publicity/Michael Vine Associates, 43 Cunliffe Rd, Blackpool. Lives in Derbyshire. Hobbies: Running (competed in London Marathon six times), flying micro-lite aircraft.

CLIVE, *john*

John Clive. Actor/Writer. b. London, 6 January 1938. Began acting as a child. **Films:** *Yellow Submarine* (voice of John Lennon); *The Italian Job.* **TV:** *Wear a Very Big Hat; Robert's Robots; Perils of Pendragon; How Green Was My Valley; Great Expectations; No Longer Alone; The Government Inspector; The Sweeney; Rising Damp; The Dick Emery Show; Leave It To Charlie; Tropic; The History of Mr Polly; The Nesbitts Are Coming; Some of Our Airmen Are No Longer Missing; A Dream of Alice; Lady Windermere's Fan; No Way Out; Bye Bye Baby.* **Books:** *KG200I; The Last Liberator; Ark; Barossa; Broken Wings; The Lion's Cage* (all novels). **Address:** c/o CCA. Lives in London and Liverpool. m. Carole Ann (dis); 1 d. Hannah, 1 s. Alexander. Hobbies: Cinema, theatre, football, boxing, walking. **Favourite TV programme:** *Hancock;* documentaries; old films.

COARD, *dennis*

Dennis Coard. Actor. Worked as an Australian Telecom engineer, before training at the Victorian College of the Arts, Australia. **Theatre:** *The Cherry Orchard; The Recruiting Officer; Our Country's Good; Dreams In an Empty City; Macbeth; Heart for the Future; See How They Run* (all Melbourne Theatre Company); *Marat/Sade; The Comedy of Errors; Our Country's Good* (all State Theatre Company of Southern Australia). **Films:** Noel McKenzie in *Return Home; Blowing Hot and Cold; Jigsaw.* **TV:** Palmer in *The Flying Doctors; Mission Impossible;* Michael Ross in *Home and Away* (1990-). **Address:** c/o The Actors' Agency/Channel 7. m. (dis).

COBURN, *norman*

Norman Coburn. Actor. b. Sydney, Australia, 6 March 1937. **Theatre:** *Twelfth Night; The Rivals; Hamlet; The Relapse; A Night In the Arms of Raeleen; White Nancy; Once In a Blue Moon; Hanging Together; Quartermains Terms; Plaza Suite; A Life In the Theatre; The Summer of the Seventeenth Doll;* title role in *Macbeth; Season's Greetings; Sons of Cain; Hamlet.* **Films:** *Circle of Deception; Oscar Wilde; Valiant Soldier.* **TV:** *Monitor; Compact; No Hiding Place; Dixon of Dock Green; The Professionals; Coronation Street; Step In the Right Direction; Coral Island; The Young Doctors; A Country Practice; 1915; Peach's Gold; Waterloo Station; Special Squad; Possession; Rafferty's Rules; Losing; Land of Hope; Five Mile Creek;* Donald Fisher in *Home and Away* (1988-). **Address:** c/o Australian Creative Management/Channel 7. m. (dis); 1 s. Troy, 1 d. actress Nana.

COCHRANE, *nicholas*

Nicholas Marc Cochrane. Actor. b. Cheadle, Cheshire, 16 December 1973. Discovered by Granada TV while still at school. **Theatre:** *Our Day Out* (Forum Theatre, Manchester). **TV:** Andy McDonald in *Coronation Street* (1989-). **Address:** c/o Peter Graham Associates/Granada TV. Single; lives in Cheadle. Pets: Cross-terrier called Jackson. Hobbies: Sport, driving.

COIA, *paul*

Paul Coia. Presenter. b. Glasgow, 19 June 1957. **TV:** First announcer heard on Channel Four (1982); *Preview; Pebble Mill At One; 6.55; Tricks of the Trade; The Spirit of Christmas; Doomsday Detectives; Rail Watch; A Song for Europe; Holiday '87; ITV Telethon* (Scottish host 1988, 1990); *The Birthday Show; Radio Industries Awards; The Paul Coia Show; European Special Olympics; Children In Need; Pick of the Week; Zig Zag; Catchword; Press Your Luck; The Garden Party; Spotlight* (Sky Movies). **Radio:** Presenter for ILR Glasgow station Radio Clyde (1977–82). (Winner, Scottish Radio Personality of the Year award, 1982.) **Address:** c/o Sara Cameron Management. Single; lives in Glasgow. Hobbies: Squash, reading, listening to music.

COLE, *george*

George Cole. Actor. b. Tooting, South London, 22 April 1925. **TV:** *The Informer; Blackmail; Vendetta; A Man of Our Times; The Sex Game; Out of the Unknown; Murder; Root of All Evil; The Gold Robbers; The Comic; The Right Prospectus; Menace; A Room In Town; UFO; The Ten Commandments; Madigan; Six Faces of a Man; Away From It All; Dial M for Murder; Village Hall; Affair of the Heart; The Sweeney; Quiller; Lloyd George Knew My Father; The Good Humoured Man; Don't Forget To Write; Losing Her; The Good Life; Return of The Saint; Getting In On Concorde; Minder; The Bounder; Blott On the Landscape; A Man of Our Times; Heggerty, Haggerty; Comrade Dad; Minder On the Orient Express; A Day To Remember; Natural Causes; Life After Life; Single Voices.* **Address:** c/o Joy Jameson. m. 2nd former actress Penny Morrell; 1 d. Tara, 1 s Toby.

COLE, *graham*

Graham Coleman Smith. Actor. b. Willesden, North London, 16 March 1952. Began in showbusiness as a Red Coat, then performed in chorus lines. **Theatre:** *Calamity Jane; Pygmalion; Glamorous Nights; Paddington Bear; Anne of Green Gables; Tom Foolery; California Suite; Abigail's Party; Jesus Christ Superstar; A Midsummer Night's Dream; Wait Until Dark; Cabaret; One Flew Over the Cuckoo's Nest; Boys In the Band; Murder At the Vicarage; The Hollow; Suddenly At Home.* **TV:** *The Kelly Monteith Show; The Kenny Everett Show; Doctor Who;* PC Tony Stamp in *The Bill.* **Address:** c/o Spotlight. Lives in Bromley, Kent. m. Cherry Anne; 1 s. Matthew, 1 d. Laura. Hobbies: Tennis, squash, aerobics, weight training, cars, driving anything. **Favourite TV programme:** *Steptoe and Son,* anything with Ronnie Barker, Tommy Cooper and nature programmes.

COLE, *julie dawn*

Julie Dawn Cole. Actress. b. Guildford, Surrey, 26 October 1957. Stage school, 1969–74. **Theatre:** *Dry Rot; The Browning Version; A Friend Indeed; Easy Virtue.* **Films:** *Willy Wonka and the Chocolate Factory; That Lucky Touch; Camille.* **TV:** *Angels; Poldark; Mill On the Floss; Tandoori Nights; Bergerac; Casualty; Up the Elephant and Round the Castle; Galloping Galaxies; EastEnders.* **Address:** c/o Barry Burnett Organisation. Lives in London. m. Nick Wilton; 1 d. Holly India. Pets: A standard Schnauzer called Shambles. Hobbies: 'Cycling with Holly, Shambles and Nick – not necessarily in that order!' **Favourite TV programme:** *GBH.*

COLEMAN, *charlotte*

Charlotte Coleman. Actress. Daughter of actress Ann Beach (qv); sister of actress Lisa Coleman. **Theatre:** *Cavalcade Tower Theatre; National Theatre.* **Films:** *Bearskin.* **TV:** *Two People;* Sue in *Worzel Gummidge* (four series); *Marmalade Atkins In Space; Marmalade Atkins* (two series); *Inappropriate Behaviour; Dark Angel; Oranges Are Not the Only Fruit; Sweet Nothing; Freddie and Max.* **Address:** c/o Kate Feast Management.

COLEMAN, *david*

David Coleman. Sports commentator. b. Alderley Edge, Cheshire, 26 April 1926. Previously a newspaper journalist, including job as editor of the *Cheshire County Express,* and radio reporter/commentator. **TV:** *Match of the Day; Grandstand; Sportsnight With Coleman; A Question of Sport;* football World Cups; Olympic Games. **Address:** c/o Bagenal Harvey Organisation. m. Barbara; 3 d. Anne, Mandy, Samantha, 3 s. David, Dean (twins), Michael.

COLEMAN, *jack*

Jack Coleman. Actor. b. Philadelphia, USA, 21 February 1958. Studied drama at Duke University, North Carolina, then attended the National Theatre Institute, Waterford, Connecticut. **Theatre:** *Grease; The Common Pursuit; Bouncers* (winner, Drama Critics' Circle Best Actor award, 1987). **TV:** Steven Carrington in *Dynasty*.

COLLINS, *joan*

Joan Collins. Actress. b. London, 23 May 1936. Trained at RADA. **Films:** *Alfie Darling; The Big Sleep; The Stud; The Bitch; Nutcracker; The Cartier Affair.* **TV:** *The Virginian; The Man From Uncle; The Persuaders; Fallen Angels; Mission Impossible; Space 1999; Police Woman; The Man Who Came To Dinner; Fallen Angels; The Bawdy Adventures of Tom Jones; Starsky and Hutch; Tales of the Unexpected; A Girl Can't Always Have Everything;* Alexis Colby Carrington in *Dynasty; The Making of a Male Model; Sins; Monte Carlo.* **Books:** *My Search for Love; Past Imperfect; Joan Collins' Beauty Book; Katy – A Fight for Life; Prime Time* (novel). **Address:** c/o Peter Charlesworth. m. 1st actor Maxwell Reed (dis), 2nd actor Anthony Newley (dis), 3rd film producer Ron Kass (dis), 4th Peter Holm (dis); 3 d. Tara, Sacha (from 2nd m.), Katyana (from 3rd m.).

COLLINS, *john*

John Christopher Dixon. Actor. b. London, 2 December 1942. Trained at RADA after winning Ivor Novello and Robert Donat scholarships. **Theatre:** Worked for 10 years with Spike Milligan as assistant director and actor in plays such as *Son of Oblomov* and *The Bed-Sitting Room;* appeared in Noel Coward's *Tonight at 8.30* in Austria and *Time and Time Again* in Sweden. **TV:** *Q* (Spike Milligan series); *A Family at War; Get Some In; Some Mothers Do 'Ave 'Em; Hammer House of Horror; Only Fools and Horses; Yes Minister; The Brittas Empire; Hi-de-Hi!; Only Fools and Horses; Chance In a Million; Rude Health;* Fairfax in *'Allo 'Allo!;* Jerry in *You Rang, M'Lord?* **Address:** c/o Evans & Reiss. Lives in Hatfield, Hertfordshire. m. Caryll; 1 d. Philippa, 1 s. Christopher. Pets: Two dogs, three cats. **Favourite TV Programme:** *The Epilogue.*

COLLINS, *lewis*

Lewis Collins. Actor. b. Birkenhead, Cheshire, 27 May 1946. Trained at LAMDA. **Theatre:** Repertory theatre; *City Sugar; The Threepenny Opera; Babes In the Wood; Cinderella; Troilus and Cressida; King Lear.* **Films:** *Who Dares Wins.* **TV:** *Warship; The New Avengers; The Cuckoo Waltz; The Professionals; Must Wear Tights; A Night On the Town; Jack the Ripper.* **Address:** c/o Spotlight. m. schoolteacher Michelle Larrett; 1 s. Oliver.

COLLINS, *matthew*

Matthew Collins. Presenter. b. 13 December 1960. Trained as a journalist in Cardiff. **TV:** *The Travel Show* (special assignments and independent traveller). Travel editor of *TVQuick* magazine. **Address:** c/o Arlington Enterprises. **Favourite TV programme:** *Newsnight.*

COLLINS, *pauline*

Pauline Collins. Actress. b. Exmouth, Devon, 3 September 1940. Granddaughter of opera singer Elaine Reid. Trained at Central School of Speech and Drama. **Theatre:** Repertory theatre in Windsor; *Passion Flower Hotel; The Happy Apple; The Importance of Being Earnest; The Night I Chased the Women With An Eel; Come As You Are; Judies; Engaged; Confusions;* title role in *Shirley Valentine* (London West End and Broadway). **Films:** Title role in *Shirley Valentine.* **TV:** *Emergency – Ward 10; Upstairs, Downstairs; No Honestly; Thomas and Sarah; Forever Green.* **Address:** c/o James Sharkey Associates. m. actor John Alderton (qv); 1 d. Catherine, 2 s. Nicholas, Richard.

COLTRANE, *robbie*

Robbie Coltrane. Actor. b. Rutherglen, Glasgow, 1950. **Films:** *Subway Riders; The Ghost Dance; Krull; Balham Gateway to the South; Revolution; Caravaggio; Mona Lisa; The Supergrass; Chinese Boxes; Defence of the Realm; The Fruit Machine; Slipstream; The Secret Policeman's Third Ball; Bert Rigby, You're a Fool; Danny Champion of the World; Let It Ride; Henry V; Nuns On the Run; Perfectly Normal; The Pope Must Die.* **TV:** *Alfresco; A Kick Up the Eighties; The Comic Strip Presents . . . Five Go Mad In Dorset; The Beat Generation; War; Summer School; Five Go Mad On Mescalin; Susie; Gino; Bullshitters; Laugh, I Nearly Paid My Licence Fee; Girls On Top; Saturday Night Live; Tutti Frutti; Miners' Strike; Midnight Breaks; Thompson; GLC; South Atlantic Raiders; The Robbie Coltrane Show; Mistero Buffo; Alive and Kicking* (TV movie). **Address:** c/o CDA.

COMAN, *gilly*

Gilly Coman. Actress. **Theatre:** *The Party's Over;* Carol in *Stags and Hens* (Young Vic Theatre); Bernadette in *Stags and Hens* (Library Theatre, Manchester); *Blood On the Dole; Ladies In Waiting; Aladdin; Dick Whittington; Having a Ball.* **TV:** Linda in *Emmerdale Farm; Boys From the Blackstuff; Gathering Seed; Scully;* Aveline in *Bread.* **Address:** c/o William Morris Agency.

CONDON, *james*

James Condon. Actor. b. Freemantle, Western Australia, 27 September 1923. Began as a radio actor in 1942; worked in Britain for BBC radio and TV (1949–51), before returning to Australia. **Films:** *The Stowaway; Tim; Hoodwink; The Boy Who Had Everything; Backstage.* **TV:** *1915; Bellamy; The Young Doctors; Sons and Daughters; Prisoner: Cell Block H; Neighbours; The Flying Doctors; Luke's Kingdom.* **Address:** c/o International Casting Service. m. 2nd actress Anne Haddy; 4 d. Elizabeth, Susan, Catherine, Mary Anne (from 1st m.).

CONNERY, *jason*

Jason Connery. Actor. b. London, 11 January 1963. Son of actor Sean Connery. **Theatre:** Repertory theatre in Perth; *Journey's End; The Three Musketeers; Lords of Discipline; Dream One; The Boy Who Had Everything; Tank Malling; Puss In Boots; La Venexiana; Bye Bye Baby; Casablanca Express.* **TV:** *The First Modern Olympics; Doctor Who;* title role in *Robin of Sherwood* (second series); *Serenade for Dead Lovers; The Train; The Secret Life of Ian Fleming.* **Address:** c/o Joy Jameson.

CONNOLLY, *billy*

Billy Connolly. Comedian. b. Glasgow, 24 November 1942. Member of The Humblebums folk du before becoming a stand-up comedian. **Theatre:** *Die Fledermaus; Red Runner; On Your Bike; Bee* in *Beastly Beatitudes of Balthazar B; Rebel Without a Clue.* **Films:** *Big Banana Feet; Absolution Blue Money; Water; Supergrass; The Big Guy.* **TV:** *Play for Today: The Elephant's Graveyard; A Audience With Billy Connolly; The Kenny Everett Video Show; The Kenny Everett Television Show; N the Nine O'Clock News; Minder; The Comic Strip Presents . . .; British Academy Awards* (co-presenter *Head of the Class* (US). **Videos:** *Billy Connolly Bites Your Bum; Hand Picked By Billy Connoll Billy and Albert.* **Address:** c/o John Reid Enterprises. m. 1st (dis), 2nd actress Pamela Stephenson; 3 Daisy, Amy, Scarlet.

CONTI, *tom*

Tom Conti. Actor. b. Paisley, Strathclyde, 22 November 1941. **Theatre:** *Savages; Other People; Th Black and White Minstrels; Don Juan; The Devil's Disciple; Whose Life Is It Anyway?* (London West En and Broadway); *They're Playing Our Song; Romantic Comedy.* **Films:** *Galileo; Flame; Eclipse; Fu Circle; The Duellists; The Wall; Merry Christmas, Mr Lawrence; Reuben, Reuben; American Dreame Saving Grace; Miracles; Heavenly Pursuits; Beyond Therapy; The Quick and the Dead; White Rose Shirley Valentine; The Siege of Venice.* **TV:** *Madame Bovary; The Glittering Prizes; The Norma Conquests; Treats; Blade On the Feather; The Beate Klarsfeld Story; Roman Holiday* (TV movie *Voices Within: The Lives of Truddi Chaw; Spooks.* **Address:** c/o Chatto and Linnit. m. Kara Wilson; 1 Nina.

CONWAY, *nick*

Nick Conway. Actor. b. Shrewsbury, 25 December 1962. Member of Manchester Youth Theatre for fiv years. **Theatre:** *Roll On Four O'Clock; Johnny Oil; Arrivederci Millwall; A Common Woman; Dressin Up; The Pied Piper; Breezeblock Park.* **TV:** *Keep On Running; Thank You Mrs Clinkscales; Bil* Boswell in *Bread; Bluebell; Starting Out; Sea View; Juliet Bravo; Going To Work; Miracles Tak Longer; The Brief; The Practice.* **Address:** c/o Hamper-Neafsey Associates.

CONWELL, *nula*

Nula Conwell. Actress. b. London, 24 May 1959. Trained at the Anna Scher Theatre Schoo **Theatre:** *Obsession.* **Films:** *Fords On Water; The Elephant Man; Red Saturday.* **TV:** *Magpie; Eric Syke Dinner At the Sporting Club; Out; Vanishing Army; Telford's Change; Only a Game; The Police; If On Going Out; Shoestring; Playhouse: A Silly Little Habit; Stars of the Roller State Disco; Roll Ov Beethoven; C.A.T.S. Eyes;* Maureen in *Only Fools and Horses; The Laughter Show; Home Cooking; Y In Mind;* Det Con Viv Martella in *The Bill* (1984-). **Address:** c/o Scott Marshall. Single; lives in Nor London. Hobbies: Circuit training, swimming, walking.

COOK, *sue*

Sue Cook. Presenter. b. Ruislip, Middlesex, 30 March 1949. Worked for Capital Radio and BBC Radi 1 and 4 before moving into television. **TV:** *Out of Court; Nationwide; Crimewatch; Children In Nee Childwatch; Daytime Live.* **Address:** c/o Curtis Brown. m. classical guitarist John Williams; 1 s. Charli 1 d. Megan.

COOMBS, *pat*

Pat Coombs. Actress. b. London, 27 August 1930. Trained at LAMDA, where she subsequently taught drama. **Films:** *Oooh ...You Are Awful; Adolf Hitler – My Part In His Downfall.* **TV:** *Lollipop Loves Mr Mole; Beggar My Neighbour; The Dick Emery Show; Don't Drink the Water; You're Only Young Twice* (four series); *This Is Your Life* (subject); *The Lady Is a Tramp* (two series); *Ragdolly Anna; And There's More; Mr Majeika; EastEnders; Roy's Raiders; An Actor's Life for Me.* **Radio:** Nola in *Hello Playmates.* **Address:** c/o Barry Burnett Organisation.

COPLEY, *paul*

Paul Copley. Actor/Writer. b. Denby Dale, 25 November 1944. Trained as an English and drama teacher; joined Leeds Playhouse as actor/teacher. **Theatre:** *For King and Country; German Skerries; Sisters; Whose Life Is It Anyway?; Making Noise Quietly; King Lear; Twelfth Night; Prin.* **Films:** *Alfie Darling; A Bridge Too Far; Zulu Dawn.* **TV:** *Cries From a Watchtower; After Julius; A Christmas Carol; Treasure Island; Dear Harriet; Secret Army; Strangers; Glad Day; Travellers; Mucking Out; The Turkey Who Lives on the Hill; Days of Hope; Trinity Tales; Some Enchanted Evening; Stepping Stones; Death of a Princess; The Bright Side; Silas Marner; Oedipus At Colonus; The Mistress; Our Geoff; Gruey; Testimony of a Child; War and Remembrance; Stay Lucky.* **Radio:** *Shakespeare In Africa.* **Address:** c/o Kate Feast Management. m. actress Natasha Pyne.

CORBETT, *matthew*

Matthew Corbett. Entertainer. b. Yorkshire, 28 March 1948. Son of Harry Corbett, creator of Sooty. Trained as an actor at Central School of Speech and Drama. **Theatre:** Repertory theatre in Bristol, York, Chelmsford, Dundee and Richmond-upon-Thames; *The Sooty Show.* **TV:** *Magpie; Rainbow; Matt and Gerry Ltd; The Sooty Show.* **Address:** c/o Vincent Shaw Associates. m. Sallie; 1 d. Tamsin, 2 s. Benjamin, Joe.

CORBETT, *ronnie*

Ronnie Corbett. Actor/Comedian. b. Edinburgh, 4 December 1930. **Films:** *Casino Royale; Some Will, Some Won't; The Rise and Rise of Michael Rimmer; No Sex, Please – We're British.* **TV:** *Crackerjack; The Dickie Henderson Show; Let Yourself Go; Art of Living; The Frost Report; No – That's Me Over Here; Frost On Sunday; The Corbett Follies; The Two Ronnies; Sorry!; Bruce and Ronnie.* **Address:** c/o International Artistes. m. Anne Hart; 2 d. Emma, Sophie.

CORNWELL, *judy*

Judy Cornwell. Actress/Author. b. London, 22 February 1942. **Films:** *Wuthering Heights; Devil's Lieutenant; Santa Claus; Cry Freedom.* **TV:** *The Younger Generation;* Feydeau farces; *Call Me Daddy; Relatively Speaking; Cork Moustache; Man of Straw; The Chinese Prime Minister; Night of the Tanks; Moody and Peg; London Assurance; Cranford; The Bonus; The Dick Emery Show; Touch of the Tiny Hacketts; Mill On the Floss; The Good Companions; Omnibus: The Brothers Grimm; A Case of Spirits; Jane Eyre; There Comes a Time; Play Acting; The Guest; Good Behaviour; Cake and Ale; December Rose; Paying Guests; Bergerac; Rumpole of the Bailey; Farrington of the FO; Strong Poison; Doctor Who; Boon; Van Der Valk; Keeping Up Appearances.* **Books:** *Cow and Cow Parsley; Fishcakes At the Ritz* (novels). **Address:** c/o Ken McReddie. m. John Parry; 1 s. Edward.

COSBY, *bill*

Bill Cosby. Actor/Comedian/Director/Writer. b. Philadelphia, 12 July 1938. Began career as a nightclub entertainer. **Films:** *Hickey and Boggs; Man and Boy; Uptown Saturday Night; Let's Do It Again; Mother Jugs and Speed; A Piece of the Action; California Suite; The Devil and Max Devlin; Bill Cosby Himself; Leonard: Part V; Ghost Dad.* **TV:** *I Spy* (Emmy award, 1969); *The First Bill Cosby Special; The Bill Cosby Special; The Second Bill Cosby Special; The Bill Cosby Show; Fat Albert; Fat Albert and the Cosby Kids; The Cosby Show; A Different World* (executive producer); *Cosby Salutes Alvin Ailey; To All My Friends On Shore* (TV movie); *Top Secret* (TV movie). **Books:** *Fatherhood; Time Flies; Love and Marriage.* **Address:** c/o William Morris Agency (USA). m. Camille; 1 s. Ennis, 4 d. Erika, Erinn, Ensa, Evin.

COSSINS, *james*

James Cossins. Actor. b. Beckenham, Kent, 4 December 1933. Trained at RADA (Silver Medal winner). **Theatre:** Repertory theatre; *Bonne Soupe; Celebration; She Stoops To Conquer; The Beggar's Opera; The Anniversary; Man and Superman; Stage Struck* (all London West End). **Films:** *How I Won the War; The Anniversary; A Dandy In Aspic; Scrooge; Privilege; The Lost Continent; Melody; Wuthering Heights; Otley; Villain; Young Winston; Hitler: The Last Ten Days; The Man With the Golden Gun; The Great Train Robbery; Sphinx; The Confessions of Felix Krull; Gandhi; The Masks of Death; A Fish Called Wanda; Grand Larceny.* **TV:** *Mad Jack; A Day Out; Dombey and Son; The Pickwick Papers; Some Mothers Do 'Ave 'Em; Marjorie and Men; S.W.A.L.K.; Rude Health; Miss Marple At Bertram's Hotel; Bergerac; Chelworth.* **Address:** c/o Julian Belfrage Associates.

COUNSELL, *elizabeth*

Elizabeth Counsell. Actress. b. Windsor, Berkshire, 7 June 1942. Parents, John Counsell and Mary Kerridge, ran the Theatre Royal, Windsor. **Theatre:** *As You Like It; Much Ado About Nothing; Dear Liar; Shakespeare's People; Jean Seberg; Present Laughter.* **TV:** *The Top Secret Life of Edgar Briggs; Song By Song By Hart; Partners; Executive Stress; Brush Strokes.* **Address:** c/o Daly Gagan Associates. m. actor David Simeon; 1 s. Leo.

COURTENAY, *margaret*

Margaret Courtenay. Actress. b. Cardiff, 14 November 1923. Trained at LAMDA. **Films:** *Isadora; Under Milk Wood; Royal Flash; The Mirror Crack'd; Duet for One.* **TV:** *The Expert; Z-Cars; Billy Liar; It Ain't Half Hot Mum; The Squirrels; Howerd Confessions; London Belongs To Me; Best of Friends; The Upchat Line; A Sharp Intake of Breath; Mind Your Language; Out; Fearless Frank; Rings On Their Fingers; The Old Curiosity Shop; Goodbye Darling; Good Companions; Only When I Laugh; Winston Churchill – The Wilderness Years; The Kelly Monteith Show; Tom, Dick and Harriet; The Morecambe and Wise Show; Fasting; Never the Twain; Fresh Fields; Moving House; The Stanley Baxter Show; Paradise Postponed; The Two Mrs Grenvilles; Executive Stress; The Two of Us; Don't Wait Up; Dandy Dick; Vanity Fair.* **Address:** c/o ICM Duncan Heath Associates. m. (dis); 1 s. Julian.

COURTENAY, *tom*

Tom Courtenay. Actor. b. Hull, East Yorkshire, 25 Feb 1937. Trained at RADA. **Theatre:** *Billy Liar; Andorra; Hamlet; She Stoops To Conquer; Otherwise Engaged* (New York); *The Dresser.* **Films:** *Loneliness of the Long Distance Runner; Private Potter; Billy Liar; King and Country; Operation Crossbow; King Rat; Doctor Zhivago; Night of the Generals; The Day the Fish Came Out; A Dandy In Aspic; Otley; One Day In the Life of Ivan Denisovich; Catch Me a Spy; The Dresser; Happy New Year; Leonard: Part VI; The Last Butterfly; Let Him Have It.* **TV:** *The Lads; Ghosts; Private Potter; I Heard the Owl Call My Name* (TV movie); *Jesus of Nazareth; Absent Friends; Chekhov In Yalta.* **Address:** c/o Michael Whitehall.

COWDEN, *lucinda*

Lucinda Cowden. Actress. Trained at the MTC Youth Theatre Workshop. **Theatre:** *Quick Eze Cafe; Who Killed Gloria Marshall?* (both at the MTC Youth Theatre Workshop); *Cain's Hand* (Nimrod Theatre); *Go Ask Alice; Comedia de l'Arte Mask & Mime.* **TV:** *Just Friends* (TV movie); *Handle With Care* (drama-documentary); Mandy Wright in *Prisoner: Cell Block H; P.S. I'm Pregnant* (TV movie); *Fish Are Safe;* Melanie Pearson in *Neighbours* (1987-); *The Power, The Passion.* **Address:** c/o Melbourne Artists Management.

COWPER, *nicola*

Nicola Cowper. Actress. b. Chelsea, London, 21 December 1967. Sister of actress twins Gerry and Jackie Cowper. Modelled and appeared in TV commercials up to the age of nine; trained at the Corona Academy. **Films:** Angie in *Winter Flight;* Lucy in *Dreamchild; Underworld; Lionheart; Journey To the Centre I; Journey To the Centre II.* **TV:** *Break In the Sun* (aged 12); *Minder; Home Video; The Burston Rebellion; S.W.A.L.K.;* Heather Golding in *The Practice; Night Voices;* Gina in *Streetwise; Inspector Morse.* **Address:** c/o Roger Carey Management. Lives in Twickenham, Middlesex.

COX, *doc*

Doc Cox. Presenter. b. Sheffield, South Yorkshire, 1 July 1946. Trained as a teacher, then became a BBC sound engineer. **TV:** *Nationwide; Look Stranger; Grapevine; Forty Minutes' Skiffle; Children In Need; Names & Games; Blankety Blank; Jim'll Fix It; That's Life!* (co-presenter, 1982-); *Going Live!; On Cue; Press Gang; Some of These Days; Snap.* **Radio:** *Top 20* (country-and-western show). **Address:** c/o Downes Presenters Agency. Single; lives in London. Pets: Three cats, called Watkins, Strat and Boogie. Hobbies: Collecting vintage records, playing guitar, banjo, washboard, piano and accordian, and performing with rock 'n' roll group Ivor's Jivers. **Favourite TV programme:** *Agatha Christie's Poirot.*

CRAIG, *andy*

Andrew Timm Craig. Presenter/Journalist. b. Cumbria, 5 December 1954. Presenter of *Simply Soul* on Metro Radio, Newcastle, before joining Tyne Tees Television in 1978. **TV:** *Northern Life* (Tyne Tees Television); *Central News; Good Morning Britain; Central Weekend Live; The Home Service; Hot Property; The Time, The Place; Head To Head* (TVS); *Searchline Special; This Morning; Sporting Triangles* (host); *Daytime Live; Late and Live* (Tyne Tees Television); *One False Move* (BSB Galaxy); *Brain Waves; That's History* (host). Producer: *Everyone's Problem,* ITV's first networked AIDS programme (1986); cartoon series *Coconuts; Late and Live.* **Address:** c/o Orbi-Tel, 3 The Coppice, Seer Green, Beaconsfield, Buckinghamshire HP9 2SH, tel (0494) 677054. Single; lives in Nottingham. Pets: Cats. Hobbies: Old cars and records.

CRAIG, *michael*

Michael Gregson. Actor. b. Poona, India, 27 January 1929. **Films:** *Eye Witness; The Silent Enemy; Doctor In Love; Mysterious Island; Payroll; A Pair of Briefs; Life for Ruth; The Iron Maiden; Captive City; Summer Flight; Of a Thousand Delights; Life At the Top; Modesty Blaise; Star; Royal Hunt of the Sun; Twinky; Country Dance; The Second Mrs Anderson; Vault of Horrors; A Town Called Bastard; Inn of the Damned; A Sporting Proposition; Port Essington; The Irishman; The Killing of Angel Street; Turkey Shoot; Stanley.* **TV:** *Emergency – Ward 10; St Joan; Spoiled; Daddy, Kiss It Better; Tiger Trap; The Talking Head; Husbands and Lovers; Second Time Around; The Emigrants; The Foundation; The Danedyke Mystery; The Timeless Land; Triangle; Doctor Who.* **Address:** c/o Chatto and Linnit. m. Susan; 1 d. Jessica, 2 s. Stephen, Michael.

CRAIG, *wendy*

Wendy Craig. Actress. b. Sacriston, Co Durham, 20 June 1934. Trained at Central School of Speech and Drama. **Theatre:** *George Dillon; The Sport of My Mad Mother; Ride a Cock Horse; I Love You Mrs Patterson; The Taming of the Shrew; The Constant Wife; Beyond Reasonable Doubt.* **Films:** *Room At the Top; The Mind Benders; The Servant; The Nanny; Just Like a Woman; I'll Never Forget What's 'is Name; Joseph Andrews.* **TV:** *Candida; Wings of a Dove; Not In Front of the Children; And Mother Makes Three; And Mother Makes Five; Butterflies; Nanny; Laura and Disorder.* Winner, BAFTA TV Drama Actress of the Year (1968), Variety Club TV Personality of the Year (BBC 1969, ITV 1973), *TVTimes* Funniest Woman On TV award (1972, 1973, 1974), BBC Woman of the Year (1984). **Address:** c/o Richard Hatton. m. musician/writer Jack Bentley; 2 s. Alaster, Ross.

CRANE, *andy*

Andy Crane. Presenter. b. Morecambe, Lancashire, 24 February 1964. Trained as a technical operator at Piccadilly Radio, Manchester, before becoming a presenter. **TV:** *Children's BBC.* **Radio:** Piccadilly Radio; Capital Radio; *History Lost and Found* (BBC schools radio). **Address:** c/o PVA.

CRANHAM, *kenneth*

Kenneth Cranham. Actor. b. Dunfermline, 12 December 1944. Trained at RADA. **TV:** *Coronation Street; Canterbury Tales; The Chauffeur and the Lady; Donkey's Years; Cribb; Butterflies Don't Count; La Ronde; The Caretaker; The Merchant of Venice; 'Tis Pity She's a Whore; Danger UXB; The Bell; Therese Raquin; Shine On Harvey Moon; Reilly – Ace of Spies; The Dumb Waiter; The Birthday Party; Lady Windermere's Fan; Normal Service; A Sort of Innocence; The Party; Normal Services; Inspector Morse; The Black and Blue Lamp; The Contractor; Boon; Master of the Marionettes; Just Another Secret; Rules of Engagement; Oranges Are Not the Only Fruit; El C.I.D.; TECX; Chimera; Van Der Valk; Casualty; Bergerac; Dunrulin; Young Indie; Murder Most Horrid.* **Address:** c/o Markham & Froggatt. m. actress Charlotte Cornwell (sep); 1 d. Nancy.

CRAVEN, *john*

John Craven. Presenter. b. Leeds, 16 August. Newspaper journalist in Yorkshire before entering radio as a newsreader. **TV:** *Sunday Break* (aged 16); *Look North; Points West; Search; Newsround* (presenter, 1972–9, then editor); *Multi-Coloured Swap Shop; Saturday Superstore; Breakthrough; Story Behind the Story; Country File.* **Address:** c/o Noel Gay Artists. m. Marilyn; 2 d. Emma, Victoria.

CRAWFORD, *michael*

Michael Patrick Smith. Actor/Singer. b. Salisbury, Wiltshire, 19 January 1942. Began acting as a child. **Theatre:** *Barnum; The Phantom of the Opera.* **Films:** *The Knack ...and How To Get It; A Funny Thing Happened On the Way To the Forum; The Jokers; How I Won the War; Hello, Dolly!; The Games; Hello-Goodbye; Condorman.* **TV:** *Billy Bunter; Probation Officer; Emergency – Ward 10; The Chequered Flag; The Guinea Pig; Police Surgeon; The Siege of Kilfaddy; The Seekers; Sir Francis Drake; Destiny; Still Life; Not So Much a Programme, More a Way of Life; The Move After Checkmate; The Three Barrelled Shotgun; The Policeman and the Cook; Some Mothers Do 'Ave 'Em; Sorry...; Chalk and Cheese; The South Bank Show; Save the Children With Michael Crawford.* **Address:** c/o ICM Duncan Heath Associates. m. Gabrielle (dis); 2 d. Emma, Lucy.

CRIBBINS, *bernard*

Bernard Cribbins. Actor. b. Oldham, Lancashire, 29 December 1928. **Theatre:** *Not Now, Darling; The Love Game; There Goes the Bride; Hiss and Boo; Run for Your Wife; Guys and Dolls.* **Films:** *Daleks – Invasion Earth 2150 A.D.; Casino Royale; Don't Raise the Bridge, Lower the River; Ghost of a Chance; The Undertaker; The Railway Children; Frenzy; The Water Babies.* **TV:** *Judgement Day; Cribbins; Comedy Playhouse; Val Doonican; Get the Drift; Children Singing; Jackanory; Patrick, Dear Patrick; The Good Old Days; The Wombles* (narrator); *Feydeau farces; Junkin; We Want To Sing; Fawlty Towers; Space 1999; Dangerous Davies* (TV movie); *Star Turn* (presenter); *Shillingbury Tales; Cuffy; Langley Bottom; High and Dry; When We Are Married.* **Address:** c/o Crouch Associates. m. Gillian McBarnet.

CRICKET, *jimmy*

Jimmy Cricket. Comedian. b. Cookstown, County Tyrone, 17 October 1945. Began as an entertainer for Butlin's and Pontins, and toured clubs. **TV:** *Children's Royal Variety Show; The Royal Variety Show; And There's More . . .* **Address:** c/o International Artistes. m. May; 3 s. Dale, Frank, Jamie, 1 d. Katy.

CROFT, *annabel*

Annabel Croft. Presenter/Actress. b. Kent, 12 July 1966. Brought up in Farnborough, Kent; former professional tennis player. **Theatre:** *Dick Whittington; Something's Afoot; Cinderella.* **TV:** *Cudmore's Call; Network 7; Treasure Hunt; The Interceptor.* **Address:** c/o Clifford Elson Publicity. Lives in London.

CRONIN, *paul*

Paul Cronin. Actor. b. Jamestown, Australia, 8 July 1938. **TV:** *The Sullivans; Solo One; Matlock Police; Matthew & Son; A Place To Call Home.* **Address:** 197 Cotham Road, Kew, Victoria 3103, Australia. m. Helen; 4 d. Jane, Katherine, Susanne, Juliana.

CROSBIE, *annette*

Annette Crosbie. Actress. b. Edinburgh, 12 February 1934. Trained at Bristol Old Vic Theatre School. **Theatre:** *Tramway Road; A Collier's Friday Night; Talk of the Devil; The Trojan War; Family Dance.* **Films:** *The Public Eye; The Slipper and the Rose.* **TV:** *Concussion; A Splinter of Ice;* Catherine of Aragon in *The Six Wives of Henry VIII; Separate Tables; Katharine Mansfield; The Boy Dave; Edward VII; Lillie; Jessie; Family Dance; Northern Lights; The Disappearance of Harry; Off Peak; Paradise Postponed; Beyond the Pale; Game, Set & Match;* Margaret Meldrew in *One Foot In the Grave.* **Radio:** *Clayhanger.* **Address:** c/o Julian Belfrage Associates. m. Michael Griffith; 1 s. Owen, 1 d. Selina.

CROWTHER, leslie

Leslie Crowther. Actor/Comedian. b. Nottingham, 6 February 1933. Son of stage actor Leslie Crowther Sr. **TV:** Hi Summer; Crackerjack; The Black and White Minstrel Show; Crowther Takes a Look; The Reluctant Romeo; Those Were the Days; The Saturday Crowd; The Leslie Crowther Show; Crowther's In Town; My Good Woman (situation comedy); Love and Marriage; Big Boy Now; Leslie Crowther's Scrapbook; Starburst; The Crowther Collection; The Royal Variety Performance; Bud 'n' Ches; The Price Is Right; Time of Your Life (subject); Spotlight On Leslie Crowther; Stars In Their Eyes; Birds of a Feather (acting himself). **Radio:** Variety Playhouse; Crowther's Crowd; Family Favourites; **Address:** c/o Billy Marsh Associates. m. Jean; 4 d. Lindsay, Elizabeth (twins), Caroline, Charlotte, 1 s. Nicholas.

CRYER, barry

Barry Cryer. Presenter/Comedian/Writer. b. Leeds, 23 March 1935. **Theatre:** Professional debut at Leeds City Varieties Theatre; Windmill Theatre. **TV:** Writer for Bob Hope, George Burns, The Two Ronnies, Morecambe and Wise, Tommy Cooper, Bruce Forsyth, Kenny Everett, Les Dawson, David Frost, Mike Yarwood, Rory Bremner, Jasper Carrott and Les Dennis. **Address:** c/o Roger Hancock. m. singer Terry Donovan; 3 s. Anthony, David, Robert, 1 d. Jacqueline.

CUKA, frances

Frances Cuka. Actress. b. London. Trained at Guildhall School of Music and Drama. **Theatre:** Jo in A Taste of Honey (London West End and Broadway); Waters of the Moon; Under Milk Wood; The Beggar's Opera; Sweet Bird of Youth; Same Time, Next Year. RSC: Twelfth Night; The Merchant of Venice; Troilus and Cressida; Silver Tassle; Silence; Travesties; Nicholas Nickleby. **Films:** Henry VIII and His Six Wives; Scrooge; Watcher In the Woods. **TV:** The Old Wives' Tale; Days In the Trees; Day of the Tortoise; Retreat; Point of Departure; Sense and Sensibility; Miss Nightingale; Within These Walls; Boy Dominic; One Day At a Time; Crown Court (two roles); Tea On St Pancras Station; The Beggar's Opera; Member of the Wedding; Girl Talk; Charlie Boy; Love Story; Henry IV, Pt II; Mary Lancaster in Crossroads; Maigret. **Address:** c/o Lou Coulson.

CULBERTSON, rod

Rod Culbertson. Actor. Trained at Central School of Speech and Drama. **Theatre:** Scribes; All Change; Stags and Hens; Macbeth; Katie Mulholland; Henry IV, Pt I; Yellow Rain; Death of a Salesman; The Bundle (RSC); Factory Birds (RSC); Hearing; A Tale of Two Cities; British Bulldog; Twelfth Night; The Third and Final Round; Strippers. **Films:** Spy Story; Porridge; SOS Titanic; Paul McCartney in The Birth of the Beatles. **TV:** Village Hall; Balcony; Hughie Fenwick in The Stars Look Down; The Sweeney; A Horseman Riding By; Play for Today: Bottles; After Julius; The Professionals; The World Cup: A Captain's Tale; Jamie Running; probation officer in Brookside; Courtney in William Tell; Taggart; Bust; No Further Cause for Concern; The Bill; Albert and the Lion; Bergerac; Casualty; Gas and Candles; Spender. **Address:** c/o Mary Arnold Management.

CUNLIFFE, jane

Jane Cunliffe. Actress. b. Oldham, Lancashire, 1 June 1962. Trained at the Manchester Polytechnic School of Theatre. **Theatre:** Passion Play. **TV:** Bulman; The Practice; Strike It Rich; Emmerdale Farm; Laura Gordon-Davies (née Wright) in Brookside (1987); Chateauvallon (voice dubbing); Francesca in Hollywood Sports; Shoot To Kill; Trouble In Mind. Plus TV commercials. **Address:** c/o London Management.

CURRY, *mark*

Mark Curry. Actor/Presenter. b. Stafford, 27 August 1961. **Theatre:** Pantomimes in Bridlington, Bath, Cambridge and Manchester; title role in *Billy Liar; Move Over, Mrs Markham.* **TV:** *Junior Showtime* (six years from the age of seven); *Sounding Brass; Stop-Watch; Get Set for Summer; The Saturday Picture Show; Make 'Em Laugh; Treasure Houses; All Star Record Breakers; Blue Peter; Bread.* **Address:** c/o Peter Graham Associates.

CUTHBERTSON, *iain*

Iain Cuthbertson. Actor. b. Glasgow, 4 January 1930. **TV:** *The Borderers; Z-Cars; The Duchess of Duke Street; Budgie; The Onedin Line; Tom Brown's Schooldays; Black Beauty; Sutherland's Law; Children of the Stones; The Ghosts of Motley Hall; Ripping Yarns; Caledonian Cascade; Danger UXB; The Voyage of Darwin; Doctor Who; The Casting of the Runes; Charles Endell Esquire; We the Accused; Happy Warrior; House With Green Shutters; Vice Versa; The Assam Garden; Lytton's Diary; Juliet Bravo; Hannay; Supergran; A Perfect Spy; First Among Equals; Smart Money; Heaven and Earth; Return of the Antelope; Bulman; Great Writers – Thomas Mann; The Venus De Milo Instead; Twist In the Tale; Minder; Campion; Shoot the Revolution; Naked Video; City Lights; Rab C Nesbitt; Inspector Morse.* **Address:** c/o Janet Welch Personal Management. m. actress Anne Kirsten.

DALE, *alan*

Alan Dale. Actor. b. Dunedin, New Zealand, 6 May 1947. Worked as a radio presenter before becoming a professional actor and moving to Australia. **Theatre:** *Macbeth; King Lear; The Knack . . .and How To Get It; Miss Julie; Applause;* James Bond in *The Secret Service Show.* **Films:** *The Applicant; Buffalo.* **TV:** *The Flying Angel; The McKenzie Affair; The Immigrants;* Jack Delamore in *Radio Waves* (all in New Zealand); Dr John Forrest in *The Young Doctors; Possession; The Far Country;* Jim Robinson in *Neighbours* (1985-). **Address:** c/o Melbourne Artists Management/Grundy Television. Lives in Melbourne. m. 1st Claire (dis), 2nd former Miss Australia Tracey Pearson; 2 s. Matthew, Simon (from 1st m.).

DALY, *tyne*

Ellen Tyne Daly. Actress. b. Madison, Wisconsin, USA, 21 February 1946. Daughter of actor James Daly and actress Hope Newell; sister of actor Timothy Daly. **Theatre:** *Gypsy* (winner, Tony Best Actress award, 1990). **Films:** *John and Mary; Angel Unchained; Play It As It Lays; The Enforcer; Telefon; Speedtrap; Zoot Suit; The Aviator; Movers and Shakers.* **TV:** *The Virginian; General Hospital; Quincy;* Mary Beth Lacey in *Cagney and Lacey* (four Emmy awards); *In Search of America; A Howling In the Woods; Heat of Anger; The Man Who Could Talk To Kids; Larry; The Entertainer; Better Late Than Never; Intimate Strangers; The Women's Room; A Matter of Life Or Death; Your Place Or Mine; Kids Like These; Stuck With Each Other* (all TV movies). **Address:** c/o Camden Artists. m. actor-director Georg Stanford Brown (sep); 3 d. Elisabeth, Kathryne, Alyxandra.

DANCE, *charles*

Charles Dance. Actor. b. Rednal, Worcestershire, 10 October 1946. **Theatre:** *The Beggar's Opera; The Taming of the Shrew; Saint Joan; Sleeping Beauty; Three Sisters;* title role in *Henry V* (RSC, London and US tour); title role in *Coriolanus* (RSC). **Films:** *For Your Eyes Only; Plenty; The Golden Child; Good Morning Babylon; Hidden City; White Mischief; Pascali's Island; China Moon.* **TV:** *The Fatal Spring; Edward VII; Dreams of Leaving; Nancy Astor; Frost In May; The Last Day; Rainy Day Women* (TV movie); *The Jewel In the Crown; The Secret Servant* (TV movie); *Thunder Rock; The McGuffin* (TV movie); *Out On a Limb* (TV movie); *First Born* (TV movie); *Goldeneye; The Phantom of the Opera* (mini-series). **Address:** c/o CDA. m. Joanna; 1 s. Oliver, 1 d. Rebecca.

DANEMAN, *paul*

Paul Daneman. Actor/Writer. b. London, 26 October 1925. Trained at RADA. **TV:** *A Glimpse of the Sea; Emma; Age of Kings; Danger Man; The Widowing of Mrs Holroyd; The Saint; Not In Front of the Children; Never a Cross Word; The Doll's House; Helen; Spy Trap; The Runaway; Love Story; Double Edge; Stay With Me Till Morning; Jessie; Partners; The Professionals; Tishoo; Affairs of the Heart* (as writer); *Two Gentlemen of Verona; Antigone; What Mad Pursuit; Hold the Dream; The Little Matchgirl; Roman Holiday; The Perfect Sky; Tears In the Rain; Fffizz; Rumpole of the Bailey; Till We Meet Again; Blore MP; GBH; Thatcher: The Final Days.* **Address:** c/o Chatto and Linnit. Lives in Putney, South London. m. 1st Susan (dis), 2nd Meredith; 2 d. Sophie, Flora. Pets: One dog, one cat. Hobbies: Painting, reading. **Favourite TV programme:** *Channel Four News.*

DANIELS, *martin*

Martin P Daniels. Entertainer. b. South Bank, Cleveland, 19 August 1963. **Theatre:** Summer seasons; pantomimes. **TV:** *Junior Royal Variety Performance* (three times); *Swap Shop; Saturday Superstore; Little and Large; 3-2-1; The Sooty Show; The Paul Daniels Magic Show; Russell Harty; Freetime; The Generation Game; Game for a Laugh; The Les Dennis Laughter Show.* **Address:** c/o Spotlight.

DANIELS, *paul*

Paul Daniels. Magician/Comedian. b. South Bank, Cleveland, 6 April 1938. Clerk, then ran a grocer's shop before becoming a professional entertainer. **TV:** *Opportunity Knocks; Be My Guest; Wheeltappers and Shunters Social Club; The Paul Daniels Show; Fall In the Stars; The Blackpool Bonanza; The Paul Daniels Magic Show* (winner, Montreux Golden Rose, 1985); *Odd One Out; Every Second Counts.* **Address:** c/o BBC TV. m. 1st (dis), 2nd assistant Debbie McGee; 3 s. Paul, entertainer Martin, Gary.

DANIELS, *pauline*

Pauline Ann Malam. Actress/Comedienne. b. Birkenhead, 30 June 1955. **Theatre:** Stand-up comedienne in workingmen's clubs; *Chicago; Comedians;* Rose in *Gypsy; Aladdin; The Battle of the Sexes;* title role in *Shirley Valentine.* **TV:** *The Comedians; Saturday Royal; Entertainment Express; All Cricket and Wellies; Mike Reid's Mates and Music; The Tom O'Connor Roadshow; Bread;* Maria Benson in *Brookside.* **Address:** c/o Ricky McCabe Entertainments. Lives in Whitby. m. David; 1 d. Sarah. Pets: A labrador called Pepper. Hobbies: Eating out, good wine, theatre, cinema.

DANIELS, *phil*

Phil Daniels. Actor. b. London, 25 October 1958. **Films:** *Breaking Glass; Quadrophenia; Scum; Zulu Dawn; The Class of Miss MacMichael; The Bride; Billy the Kid and the Green Baize Vampire.* **TV:** *Raven; Hanging Around; Jubilee; An Hour In the Life of . . .; Scum; The Country Wife; The Flockton Flyer; Four Idle Hands; A Midsummer Night's Dream; Nelson; Meantimes; Come To Mecca; The Pickwick Papers; Will You Love Me Tomorrow* (TV movie). **Address:** c/o Hope & Lyne.

DANN, *larry*

Larry Dann. Actor. b. London, 4 May 1941. A child star who entered films in the Forties, making his debut alongside Jean Simmons and Stewart Granger in *Adam and Evalyn*. Has been in more than 100 films, mostly as a child and usually appearing as an 'extra'. **Theatre:** *Oh! What a Lovely War; The Great American Backstage Musical; Leave Him To Heaven; Anyone for Denis?* **TV:** Sgt Alec Peters in *The Bill*. **Address:** c/o Howes and Prior/The Bill. Lives in Hampton Hill, Middlesex. m. Liz. Pets: One dog called Gimli, two cats called Bella and Merry, and goldfish. Hobbies: Cricket, golf, music.

DANSON, *ted*

Ted Danson. Actor. b. Flagstaff, Arizona, USA, 29 December 1947. Gained a drama degree from Carnegie-Mellon University; trained at the Actors' Institute. **Theatre:** *The Real Inspector Hound*. **Films:** *The Onion Field; Body Heat; Creepshow; Little Treasure; A Fine Mess; Just Between Friends; Three Men and a Baby; Cousins; Dad; Three Men and a Little Lady*. **TV:** *Somerset; Magnum;* barman Sam Malone in *Cheers* (Emmy nomination). TV movies: *The Women's Room; The Good Witch at Laurel Canyon; Cowboy; Something About Amelia* (Golden Globe Best Actor award, 1984); *Quarterback Princess; When the Bough Breaks* (also producer); *We Are the Children*. **Address:** c/o Creative Artists Agency. m. Casey; 2 d. Kate, Alexis.

DANVERS, *ivor*

Ivor Danvers. Actor. b. Westcliff-on-Sea, Essex. Trained at Central School of Speech and Drama. **Theatre:** *Robert and Elizabeth; Journey's End; The Mousetrap; The Norman Conquests* (all London West End); *Fings Ain't Wot They Used To Be; Irma La Douce; Afoot; Outside Edge; See How They Run; Middle-Aged Spread;* Noel in *Noel and Gertie* (English Theatre Company in Vienna); *A Touch of Danger* (Whitehall Theatre); *Me and My Girl* (Adelphi Theatre). As director: *The Man Who Came To Dinner; Plaza Suite*. **TV:** *Minder; Tenko; Terry and June; No Place Like Home; The World Walk; Dramarama: The World Walk; We're Going To Be All Right;* Gerald Urquhart in *Howards' Way* (six series). **Address:** c/o April Young. Lives in London. m. Henrietta; 1 d. singer Lindsey, 1 s. musician Tom. Hobbies: Golf, chess, bridge. **Favourite TV programme:** News and sport.

DARREN, *james*

James Darren. Actor. b. Philadelphia, USA, 8 June 1936. Trained by drama coach Stella Adler. **Films:** *Rumble On the Docks; Gidget; All the Young Men; The Lively Set; Diamond Head; The Guns of Navarone; Operation Madball; The Boss's Son*. **TV:** *Time Tunnel; City Beneath the Sea; The Lives of Jenny Dolan;* Officer Jim Corrigan in *T J Hooker*. **Address:** c/o Chasin Agency. m. 1st Gloria Terlitxky (dis), 2nd Evy; 3 s. James (from 1st m.), Christian, Anthony.

DAVENPORT, *nigel*

Nigel Davenport. Actor. b. Shelford, Cambridge, 23 May 1928. **Films:** *Life At the Top; A Man for All Seasons; Zulu Dawn; Chariots of Fire*. **TV:** *Breakdown; A Subject for Scandal and Concern; Point of Return; I Don't Like You; The Wrong Way Back; A Choice of Weapons; Until You Are Dead; Return To the Regiment; Double Stakes; To Bury Caesar; Gioconda Smile; Travelling Man; Guilty Party; Madame Bovary; The Picture of Dorian Gray; South Riding; The Applecart; Oil Strike North; Island of Dr Moreau; Romance; The Prince Regent; Much Ado About Nothing; The Ordeal of Dr Mud; Masadah; A Midsummer Night's Dream; Don't Rock the Boat; Bird of Prey; The Good Dr Bodkin Adams; The Biko Inquest; Howards' Way; Trainer*. **Address:** c/o Green and Underwood. m. 1st Helena (dis), 2nd actress Maria Aitken; 1 d. Laura, 2 s. Hugo (from 1st m.), Jack.

DAVEY, *bernard*

Bernard Davey. Weather presenter. b. Belfast, 29 March 1943. Joined Meteorological Office on leaving school in 1962. **TV:** BBC TV weather forecasts. **Address:** c/o BBC TV. m. Teresa; 1 s. Cormac, 2 d. Mica, Shauna.

DAVID, *joanna*

Joanna David. Actress. b. Lancaster, 1947. **TV:** *John Brown's Body; When Johnny Comes Marching Home; Sense and Sensibility; Last of the Mohicans; War and Peace; Colditz; Edwardians; Zodiac; Jenny; Rainbow; Ballet Shoes; Jane Austen; Omnibus; Softly, Softly; Within These Walls; The Duchess of Duke Street; Just William; Two's Company; Affront; Dancing Princesses; Rebecca; Lillie; Dominion Status; Ladykillers; Dear Brutus; No Need To Lie; Fame Is the Spur; Love Story; Jackanory; Agatha Christie; Red Signal; Lady's Maid's Bell; Rumpole of the Bailey; Brass; Anna Karenina; Tender Is the Night; Comrades; Murder At Lynch Cross; Paying Guests; First Among Equals; Treasure Houses; Agatha Christie's Miss Marple; The Emma Thompson Show; Hannay; Unexplained Laughter; Difficult People; Children of the North; Maigret; Inspector Morse.* **Address:** c/o Peter Browne Management.

DAVIDSON, *jim*

Jim Davidson. Actor/Comedian/Entertainer. b. Blackheath, South London, 13 December 1953. Appeared in Ralph Reader's Gang Show, aged 12. **TV:** *Gang Show; New Faces; What's On Next?; The Jim Davidson Show; Jim Davidson Special; Jim Davidson's Falklands Special; This Is Your Life* (subject, 1984); *Up the Elephant and Round the Castle; Home James!; Jim Davidson In Germany; Jim Davidson's Comedy Package; Stand Up Jim Davidson; Big Break* (host, game show). **Books:** *Too Risky; Jim Davidson Gets Hooked; Too Frisky.* Winner, *TVTimes* Funniest Man On Television award, 1980. **Address:** c/o International Artistes. m. 1st Susan (dis), 2nd Julie (dis), 3rd TV presenter Alison Holloway (dis), lives with Tracie Hilton; 1 d. Sarah (from 1st m.), 2 s. Cameron (from 2nd m.), Charlie (from relationship with Tracie Hilton). Hobbies: Fishing, football.

DAVIDSON, *ross*

Ross Davidson. Actor. b. Airdrie, 25 August 1949. PE teacher and international water-polo player before becoming a professional actor. **Theatre:** *Rosencrantz and Guildenstern Are Dead; The Importance of Being Earnest; Royal Hunt of the Sun; Animal Farm; Joseph; Godspell; Piaf; Guys and Dolls* (National Theatre); *The Merchant of Venice; Robin Hood* (both at the Young Vic Theatre); *Layers.* **Films:** *The Pirates of Penzance; Monty Python's The Meaning of Life; Paracelus.* **TV:** *The Stanley Baxter Show; Marco Baccer; Songs of Britain; Thingumyjig;* Andy O'Brien in *EastEnders; Rivals; Monkey Walk; Pob* (guest presenter); *Daytime Live* (presenter); *Run the Gauntlet* (presenter). **Address:** c/o Daly Gagan Associates.

DAVIES, *ann*

Ann Cuerton Davies. Actress. b. London, 25 November 1934. Trained at Liverpool Playhouse as a student, before becoming ASM, stage manager, then actress. **Theatre:** *Tons of Money; Sailor Beware!; The Lesson; The Marriage of Mr Mississippi; The Common Woman; A Midsummer Night's Dream/King Lear* (Renaissance Company world tour). **TV:** *Doctor Who; Within These Walls; Probation Officer; Poldark; Equal Terms The Nation's Health; Happy; A Voyage Round My Father; Widows; Love Is Not Enough; Shine On Harvey Moon; Paradise Postponed; Ever Decreasing Circles; The Specials.* **Address:** c/o Langford Associates. Lives in London. m. actor Richard Briers (qv); 2 d. Kate, Lucy. Pets: Mongrel called Fred. Hobbies: Studying for an Open University degree, weekly exercise class, swimming. **Favourite TV programme:** *House of Cards.*

DAVIES, *deddie*

Deddie Davies. Actress. b. Bridgend, 2 March 1938. Trained at RADA. **TV:** *You're Only Young Twice; The Gentle Touch; Father Charlie; Wentworth, BA; Partners In Crime; Murder At the Vicarage; Grange Hill; Metal Mickey; The Pickwick Papers; Solo; That's My Boy; Titus Andronicus; Chance In a Million; The Canterville Ghost; C.A.T.S. Eyes; My Husband and I; Trouble In Mind.* **Address:** c/o Amor Reeves. m. actor Paddy Ward.

DAVIES, *diana*

Diana Davies. Actress. b. Manchester, 20 July 1936. **Theatre:** *Dog Food Dan; Rose* (Duke of York's Theatre); *Babes In the Wood; Cinderella.* Doris in *A Family At War; The Liver Birds;* Norma Ford in *Coronation Street; Send In the Girls; Juliet Bravo; Enemy At the Door; Willie's Last Stand; Johnny Jarvis; Shoestring; How We Used To Live;* Caroline Bates in *Emmerdale; All Creatures Great and Small; Medics.* **Address:** c/o Lucinda Macdonald/Yorkshire Television. m. Peter (dis); 1 s. Stephen. Hobbies: Riding, bridge.

DAVIES, *dickie*

Richard Davies. Presenter. b. Wallasey, Cheshire, 30 April 1933. Began as entertainments purser on *Queen Mary* and *Queen Elizabeth I,* before entering television. **TV:** Southern Television (announcer/ newscaster); *World of Sport;* presenter of major ITV sports events, including the Olympic Games; Sportsmasters (presenter-producer). **Address:** c/o HTV West. Lives in Hampshire. m. Liz; 2 s. Daniel, Peter (twins).

DAVIES, *geoffrey*

Geoffrey Davies. Actor. b. Leeds, 15 December 1942. Commercial artist, then ASM, before training at RADA. **Theatre:** *Doctor In the House; Doctor In Love; No Sex, Please – We're British; Private Lives; Run for Your Wife; Season's Greetings; And Then There Were None* (Duke of York's Theatre and tour); *Doctor in Love; The Wizard of Oz.* **Films:** Lt Faversham in *Oh! What a Lovely War* (acting debut); *The Gap; Doctor In Trouble; Tales From the Crypt; Vault of Horror.* **TV:** *Kindly Leave the Raj;* Dick Stuart-Clarke in *Doctor In the House, Doctor At Large, Doctor In Charge, Doctor At Sea, Doctor On the Go, Doctor Down Under* (in Australia) and *Doctor At the Top; The Other 'Arf; Bergerac; The Bretts; The Labours of Erica* (two series). **Address:** c/o Barry Burnett Organisation. Lives in London. m. Ann; 1 d. actress Emma. Pets: Two King Charles cavaliers.

DAVIES, *martyn*

Martyn Paul Davies. Weather presenter. b. Bloxwich, West Midlands. Weather forecaster with the Meteorological Office before entering television. **TV:** Central Television (1983–4); BBC South (1984–9); ITV National Weather (1989-); *Coast To Coast* (TVS); LWT Weather (1990–91). **Address:** c/o International Weather Productions. Lives in Hampshire. m. Maggie; 1 s. Nathan, 1 d. Jordan. Pets: Fish in the garden. Hobbies: Cooking, films, squash. **Favourite TV programme:** *GBH; Newsnight.*

DAVIES, *windsor*

Windsor Davies. Actor. b. Canning Town, London, 28 August 1930. Miner, factory worker and teacher before becoming a professional actor. **Theatre:** *Run for Your Wife; Roll On Four O'Clock; Baron Hardup.* **TV:** *It Ain't Half Hot Mum; Never the Twain; Sporting Chance.* **Address:** c/o Peter Prichard. m. Lynne; 4 d. Jane, Sarah, Nancy, Beth, 1 s. Daniel.

DAVISON, *peter*

Peter Davison. Actor. b. London, 13 April 1951. Trained at Central School of Speech and Drama. **Theatre:** Nottingham Playhouse; Edinburgh Festival. **TV:** *The Tomorrow People; Love for Lydia; Print-Out; Once Upon a Time;* Tristan Farnham in *All Creatures Great and Small; Holding the Fort; Sink Or Swim; The Hitch-Hiker's Guide To the Galaxy;* title role in *Doctor Who; Anna of the Five Towns; A Very Peculiar Practice; Miss Marple; Campion.* Wrote TV theme music for *Mixed Blessings.* **Address:** c/o Jeremy Conway. m. actress Sandra Dickinson (qv); 1 d. Georgia.

DAVRO, *bobby*

Robert Christopher Nankeville. Comedian/Impressionist. b. Ashford, Middlesex, 13 September 1959. Entertained in pubs and clubs, before radio and TV work. **Theatre:** *Bobby Davro's All Laughter Spectacular; Cinderella.* **TV:** *Live From Her Majesty's; Copycats; The Bobby Davro TV Annual; Bobby Davro On the Box; Bobby Davro's TV Weekly; Davro's Sketch Pad; Davro.* **Address:** c/o Nick Thomas Enterprises. Single; lives in Staines, Middlesex, with Zoe Nicholas. Hobbies: Snooker, golf, fishing.

DAWN, *elizabeth*

Elizabeth Sylvia Butterfield. Actress. b. Leeds, 8 November 1939. Worked in a clothing factory, Woolworths, a shoe shop, and as a cinema usherette, singing in clubs by night. **Films:** *Who'd Be a Vet?* **TV:** Dot in *Larry Grayson Special; Z-Cars; Sam; Country Matters; Raging Calm; Mr Ellis Versus the People; The Greenhill Pals; Speech Day; Daft As a Brush; All Day On the Sands; Sunset Across the Bay; Kisses At Fifty; Leeds United; Crown Court;* Vera Duckworth in *Coronation Street* (1976-); *Royal Variety Performance* (1989). Plus TV commercials for director Alan Parker. **Records:** *I'll Be With You Soon* (single, with William Tarmey (qv), 1989). **Address:** c/o Granada TV. Lives near Manchester. m. Donald Ibbetson; 3 d. Dawn, Ann-Marie, Julie, 1 s. Graham.

DAWSON, *anna*

Anna Dawson. Actress. b. Bolton, Lancashire, 27 July. Trained at Elmhurst Ballet School and Central School of Speech and Drama. **Theatre:** Brian Rix Whitehall Theatre Company; Theatre of Laughter revue. **TV:** *The Benny Hill Show; The Morecambe and Wise Show; Life Begins At Forty; 3-2-1.* **Address:** c/o CDA. m. Black and White Minstrel John Boulter.

DAWSON, drew

Drew Dawson. Actor. b. Bridgeton, Glasgow, 22 October 1943. Trained at Glasgow RADA. **TV:** *Cousin Phyllis; The Game;* Jock McDonald in *Emmerdale.* **Address:** Ruth Boyle Management. m. (dis); 3 d. Jacqueline, Angie, Kate, 1 s. Myles.

DAWSON, les

Les Dawson. Comedian. b. Collyhurst, Manchester, 2 February 1934. Jazz pianist with Manchester band Cotton City Slickers, before working in clubs and pubs as a stand-up comedian. **TV:** *Opportunity Knocks; Jokers Wild; Stars On Sunday; Sez Les; Royal Command Performance; This Is Your Life* (subject); *Holiday With Strings; The Loner; Omnibus; Lulu; Looks Familiar; The Les Dawson Show; Dawson's Weekly; Blankety Blank* (presenter); *Performance: Nona.* **Books:** *The Spy Who Came; Smallpiece Guide To Male Liberation; British Book of Humour; A Time Before Genesis; Dawson Gives Up.* **Address:** Norman Murray & Ann Chudleigh. m. 1st Margaret (dec), 2nd Tracey; 2 d. Julie, Pamela, 1 s. Stuart (all from 1st m.).

DE LA TOUR, frances

Frances de la Tour. Actress. b. Bovingdon, Hertfordshire, 30 July 1944. Trained at The Drama Centre. **Theatre:** *The Relapse; A Midsummer Night's Dream* (both RSC); *Duet for One* (SWET, *Evening Standard* and Critics' Awards for Best Actress, 1981); *A Moon for the Misbegotten* (SWET Best Actress award, 1983); *St Joan;* title role in *Lillian Hellman; Three Sisters; King Lear.* **Films:** *Every Home Should Have One; Buttercup Chain; Country Dance; Our Miss Fred; To the Devil a Daughter; Wombling Free; Rising Damp* (Standard Best Actress award); *Loser Takes All.* **TV:** *Crimes of Passion; Play for Today;* Miss Jones in *Rising Damp; Cottage To Let; Flickers; Clem; A Kind of Loving; Skirmishes; Murder With Mirrors; Duet for One; Bejewelled.* **Address:** c/o James Sharkey Associates. 1 d. Tamasin, 1 s. Josh.

DEACON, brian

Brian Deacon. Actor. b. Oxford, 13 February 1949. Member of Oxford Youth Theatre; trained at Webber Douglas Academy. **Theatre:** Rep in Bristol, Coventry, Leicester, Soho Poly, Leeds, Edinburgh and Exeter; Ludlow Festival; *Antony and Cleopatra; Great and Small; As I Lay Dying; Madame Bovary; Exclusive Yarns.* **Films:** *The Triple Echo; Il Bacio; Vampyres; A Zed and Two Noughts; Jesus.* **TV:** *The Guardians; Love and Mr Lewisham; Thirty-Minute Theatre; What Shall We Do Next?; Full House; Public House; Sunday Night Theatre; Churchill's People; Good Girl; The Feathered Serpent; Ghosts; The Emigrants; Border Music; Lillie; Watching Me, Watching You; Inappropriate Behaviour; Henry VI, Parts I, II and III; Richard III; Bleak House; Separate Tables.* **Address:** c/o Kate Feast Management. m. actress Rula Lenska (dis); 1 d. Lara.

DEACON, eric

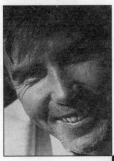

Eric Deacon. Actor. b. Oxford, 25 May 1960. Trained at Webber Douglas Academy. **Theatre:** *Hamlet; The Caretaker; Equus; Flashpoint; Relent; The Alchemist Revisited; Brotherhood; Small Craft Warning* (London West End). **Films:** *A Nous Le Petit Anglais (Those Little English Girls); One of the Lads; It Could Happen To You; Bitter; Yesterday's Hero; A Zed and Two Noughts.* **TV:** *Photograph; Postcards From Southsea; The Survivors; Penmarric; Minder; Secret Army; Spearhead; A Place Like Home; Dark Secret; Contract; King's Royal; Jackanory; Flashpoint; Only Children; Tess of the d'Urbervilles; The Caretaker; Operation Julie; Doctor Who; Dempsey and Makepeace; C.A.T.S. Eyes; London's Burning; Hard Cases; Casualty; Maigret; The Bill; Lovejoy; Stay Lucky.* **Address:** c/o Burdett-Coutts Associates. m. Laraine Joy; 2 s. Sam, Max.

DEAN, bill

Bill Dean. Actor. b. Liverpool, 3 September 1921. Worked in local government before becoming a comedian in pubs and clubs. **Theatre:** *Runway; Touched* (both Royal Court Theatre); RSC. **Films:** *Gumshoe; Kes; Family Life; Nightwatcher; Scum.* **TV:** *Oh No It's Selwyn Froggitt; Emmerdale Farm; Good Companions; When the Boat Comes In;* Harry Cross in *Brookside* (1983–90). **Address:** c/o Crouch Associates. m. (dec); 2 s. Peter, David, 1 d. Diane.

DEAN, letitia

Letitia Dean. Actress. b. Wild Hill, near Potters Bar, Hertfordshire, November 1967. Trained at the Sylvia Young Theatre School. **Theatre:** *Annie* (Victoria Palace Theatre); *Royal Variety Performance* (1982); *Grease.* **TV:** *Love Story* (BBC); *Tales Out of School;* Lucinda in *Grange Hill; Timmy and Vicky;* Dawn in *Brookside; Relative Strangers; The Bill;* Sharon Mitchell (née Watts) in *EastEnders* (1985-). **Records:** *Red Robin Rock/Goin' Fishing On Saturday Night; Bathsheba; EastEnders* singalong LP; *Something Outa Nothing* (with Paul Medford); *You Taught Me Everything I Know* (unreleased). **Address:** Downes Presenters Agency/Manager: Gordon Priestley, 29a Riding House Street, London W1P 7PG. Single; lives in London and Lincolnshire. Pets: Two dogs, shih-tzu Sydney and poodle Rocky. Hobbies: Country life. **Favourite TV programme:** *thirtysomething.*

DEAN, peter

Peter S Dean. Actor. b. Hoxton, East London, 2 May 1939. Formerly a market trader; trained at Mountview Theatre School. **Films:** *Murder By Decree; Sweet William; The Great Rock and Roll Swindle; Sherlock Holmes; The Fiendish Plot of Dr Fu Manchu.* **TV:** *Law and Order; Target; Shoestring; Minder, To Turn a Blind Eye; First Love; Shine On Harvey Moon; The Zoo; Coronation Street; Give Us a Break; One Man's Bent; Acceptable Levels; Big Deal;* Pete Beale in *EastEnders* (1985-). **Address:** c/o Howes and Prior/BBC Elstree Centre. m. 1st (dis), 2nd Jean; 1 d. Leah.

DELANEY, delvene

Delvene Delaney. Actress. b. Mackay, Australia, 26 August 1951. Trained at the National Theatre of Australia. **Films:** *End Play.* **TV:** Weather presenter in Brisbane; *The Paul Hogan Show; The Box,* Nurse Jojo Adams in *The Young Doctors; The Love Boat.* **Videos:** *The Beauty Cassette.* **Books:** *The Nine Month Calendar.* **Address:** c/o Showcast, Suite 4, 5 Alexander Street, PO Box 951, Crows Nest 2065, Australia. m. John Cornell; 1 d. Allira. Hobbies: Sewing, photography, bush-walking, photo-collage.

DELANY, pauline

Pauline Delany. Actress. b. Dublin, 8 June. Trained at the Brendan Smith Academy of Acting, Dublin. **Theatre:** Repertory theatre in Dublin and Britain; *The Poker Session; The Hostage; Richard III; The Saxon Shore; Juno and the Paycock.* **Films:** *The Young Cassidy; Percy; Brannigan; Rooney; Trenchcoat.* **TV:** *Public Eye; The Dead; The Achurch Letters; Crime of Passion; The Seagull; Playboy of the Western World; The Expert; The Avengers; Z-Cars; Fallen Hero; Mixed Blessings; Maybury; Touch of Evil; Shoestring; Dangerous Davies; The Mourning Thief; Late Starter; Bergerac; Beckett At 80; The Bill.* **Address:** c/o Daly Gagan Associates. m. Gerald Simpson; 1 d. Sarah.

DENCE, *maggie*

Maggie Dence. Actress. **Films:** *Wake In Fright; Play Faces; Best of Friends; Captain Invincible; Stanley.* **TV:** *Studio A; The Mavis Bramston Show; Homicide; I've Married a Bachelor; Skippy; The Linkmen; Dynasty; Australia A-Z; A Nice Day At the Office; Over There; Boney and the Emu Men; Mac and Merle;* Rose Sullivan in *The Sullivans; Doctor Down Under; Oracle; Tickled Pink; Trial By Marriage; A Town Like Alice; Kingswood Country; Skyways; Stress; Sporting Chance; Holiday Island; A Country Practice; Fire; Earthwatch; Prisoner: Cell Block H; For the Juniors; Kingswood Productions; Saturday Saturday; Blinky Bill; Winners – The Facts of Life; Willing & Abel; The Flying Doctors; Ned Kelly; Act of Betrayal; Eden's Lost; Rafferty's Rules; Swap Shop;* Dorothy Burke in *Neighbours* (1990-). **Address:** c/o International Casting Service.

DENCH, *dame judi, OBE*

Dame Judi Dench. Actress. b. York, 9 December 1934. Trained at Central School of Speech and Drama. **Films:** *A Handful of Dust; A Room With a View* (winner, BAFTA Best Supporting Actress in a Film award, 1987); *Henry V.* **TV:** *Hilda Lessways; Village Wooing; On Giant's Shoulders; Langrishe; Go Down; Macbeth; The Comedy of Errors; The Teachers; Z-Cars; The Age of Kings; Love Story; The Funambulists; Parade's End; Talking To a Stranger; The Morecambe and Wise Show; Love In a Cold Climate; Going Gently; The Cherry Orchard;* Laura in *A Fine Romance; Saigon – Year of the Cat; The Browning Version; Ghosts; Behaving Badly; Birthday; Performance: Absolute Hell;* Jean in *As Time Goes By.* Winner, *TVTimes* Funniest Female On TV award (1981–2), BAFTA Best Actress In a Comedy Series (1985). **Address:** c/o Julian Belfrage Associates. m. actor Michael Williams; 1 d. Tara.

DENISON, *michael, CBE*

Michael Denison. Actor. b. Doncaster, South Yorkshire, 1 November 1915. Trained at Webber Douglas Academy. **Films:** *Tilly of Bloomsbury; Hungry Hill; My Brother Jonathan; The Blind Goddess; The Glass Mountain; Landfall; The Franchise Affair; The Tall Headlines; Angels One Five; The Importance of Being Earnest; There Was a Young Lady; Contraband Spain; The Truth About Women; Faces In the Dark.* **TV:** *Boyd QC; Crown Court; The Generation Game; Private Schultz; Bedroom Farce; Blood Money; The Agatha Christie Hour: Red Signal; The Critic; The Week of the Scorpion; Marco Millions; Then Milestones; The Second Man; What's My Line?; Waiting for Gillian; Olympia; Rain On the Just; Who Goes Home; Funeral Games; Unexpectedly Vacant; The Provincial Lady; This Is Your Life* (subject); *Rumpole of the Bailey; Cold Warrior.* **Address:** c/o ICM. m. actress Dulcie Gray.

DENNIS, *les*

Les Dennis. Impressionist. b. Liverpool, 12 October 1954. Began career aged 14 in clubs. **Theatre:** Summer seasons; *Cinderella; Mother Goose; Babes In the Wood; Russ Abbot's Madhouse.* **TV:** *New Faces* (TV debut, winner of the talent show); *Who Do You Do?; The Comedians; Seaside Special; Live From Her Majesty's; Tarby and Friends; Russ Abbot's Madhouse; The Laughter Show* (three series, with comedy partner Dustin Gee, until his death in 1986); *Royal Variety Performance* (1984); *The Les Dennis Laughter Show; Family Fortunes* (host); *The Russ Abbot Show.* **Address:** c/o Mike Hughes Entertainments. m. Lynne; 1 s. Philip. Hobbies: Running, cinema, theatre.

DENNIS, *stefan*

Stefan Dennis. Actor/Singer. b. Melbourne, Australia. **Theatre:** Children's Arena Theatre; *New Balls, Please; The Deserter* (also as playwright); *Babes In the Wood* (Liverpool Empire). **Films:** *Thirst;* Robbie in *Dorrie May.* **TV:** *The Sullivans* (Tiger and two other roles); *Cop File; Cop Shop* (six roles); *Young Ramsey; Skyways; Prisoner: Cell Block H* (Peter Richards and two other roles); *Carson's Law; The Henderson Kids; Five Mile Creek; Twenty Good Years; Lawson's Mates; Here Comes Bucknickle; The Young Doctors;* Rick in *Infinity Limited; Home;* Doug in *The Flying Doctors;* Paul Robinson in *Neighbours* (1985-). **Records:** *Don't It Make you Feel Good; This Love Affair* (both singles). **Address:** c/o Probe One Enterprises. Lives in Melbourne. m. 1st (dec), 2nd model Roz Roy (sep).

DERBYSHIRE, *eileen*

Eileen Derbyshire. Actress. b. Urmston, Manchester, 6 October 1930. Took a teaching degree in speech and drama, trained at the Northern School of Music. **Theatre:** Assistant stage manager with Chorlton Rep; acted with the Century Theatre mobile company for two years; repertory theatre throughout Britain. **TV:** Emily Bishop (née Nugent) in *Coronation Street* (January 1961-); *Royal Variety Performance* (1989). **Radio:** Many plays from the age of 17. **Address:** c/o Granada TV. Lives in Cheshire. m. Thomas Holt; 1 s. Oliver. Hobbies: Reading literature, listening to opera, going to concerts, travelling.

DESMOND, *lorrae*, *MBE*

Lorrae Desmond. Actress/Entertainer. b. Mittagong, New South Wales, Australia, 2 October 1934. Trained as a singer. **TV:** *The Lorrae Desmond TV Show;* Shirley Gilroy (née Dean) in *A Country Practice.* Winner, three Logie awards, including Woman of the Year. **Address:** c/o Showcast, Suite 4, 5 Alexander Street, PO Box 951, Crows Nest 2065, Australia. m. (dis).

DEU, *amerjit*

Amerjit Deu. Actor. b. Punjab, India, 5 September 1960. Trained at the Webber Douglas Academy. **Theatre:** Tybalt in *Romeo and Juliet; The Clerical Outfitters; Trumpets and Raspberries; The Satanist; The Lion, The Witch and The Wardrobe;* Friar Laurence in *Romeo and Juliet; King Gawain and the Green Knight; Raj – An Indian Summer; Give Us a Job; Reckless Rupert; Hops; The Bald Prima Donna; The Game of the Few; Hansel and Gretel and Their Magic Cat.* **Films:** *Caught; Terminal Eye.* **TV:** *Playbus; Umbrella; Never the Twain.* Dr Singh in *EastEnders; Shadow of the Noose;* Sanjay in *Starting Out; Mysteries of the Dark Jungle; The Cloning of Joanna May.* **Address:** c/o A.I.M.

DEVANEY, *sue*

Sue Devaney. Actress/Singer. b. Ashton-under-Lyne, Lancashire, 2 July 1967. Trained at Oldham Theatre Workshop. **Theatre:** Ruby Birtle in *When We Are Married.* **TV:** Debbie Webster in *Coronation Street;* Rita Briggs in *Jonny Briggs; Exclusive Yarns;* Mad Bastard in *The Real Eddy English; About Face: Mrs Worthington's Daughter; Haggard; Spatz.* Half of funk duo Dunky Dobbers with actress Michelle Holmes (qv). **Address:** c/o Marmont Management. Single; lives in South London.

DEY, *susan*

Susan Dey. Actress. b. Pekin, Illinois, USA, 10 December 1952. A model at the age of 15, before becoming a professional actress. **Films:** *Skyjacked; First Love; Looker; Echo Park; That's Adequate.* **TV:** *The Partridge Family; Emerald Point NAS; Circle of Fear; Malibu; Barnaby Jones; Hawaii Five-O; Switch; Loves Me, Loves Me Not;* Grace Van Owen in *LA Law.* TV movies: *Cage Without a Key; Terror On the Beach; Mary Jane Harper Cried Last Night; Little Women; The Comeback Kid; The Gift of Life; Sunset Limousine; Angel In Green; A Place At the Table; Love Me Perfect.* **Address:** c/o International Creative Management. m. 1st theatrical agent Lenny Hirshan (dis), 2nd TV executive Bernard Sofronski; 1 d. Sarah.

DIAMOND, *anne*

Anne Diamond. Presenter. b. Birmingham, 8 September 1954. Joined the *Bridgwater Mercury* as arts and music correspondent (1975–7) and *Bournemouth Evening Echo* (1977–9), before moving into television. **TV:** *ATV Today; Central News; Nationwide;* BBC lunchtime newsreader; TV-am *(Good Morning Britain* and *Anne Diamond On Sunday); TV Weekly* (presenter); *The Time, The Place; This Morning; Six O'Clock Live* (all as guest presenter). **Address:** c/o TVS. m. TV executive Mike Hollingsworth; 3 s. Oliver, Jamie, Sebastian (dec).

DIBLEY, *janet*

Janet Dibley. Actress. b. Doncaster, South Yorkshire, 13 December 1958. Trained at the Rose Bruford College of Speech and Drama. **Theatre:** Repertory theatre at Leeds, Perth and Exeter; *Mr Cinders; Carousel; Twelfth Night; Figaro; Guys and Dolls; Cinderella* (National Theatre). **TV:** *A Brother's Tale; Foxy Lady; Lytton's Diary; The Two of Us.* **Address:** c/o Richard Stone Partnership.

DICKINSON, *sandra*

Sandra Dickinson. Actress. b. Washington DC, USA, 20 October. Trained at Central School of Speech and Drama. **Theatre:** Marilyn Monroe in *Legend; Barefoot In the Park.* **TV:** *The Tomorrow People; What's On Next?; Cover; The Hitch-Hiker's Guide To the Galaxy; Triangle; What Mad Pursuit; The Two Ronnies; The Clairvoyant; Eisenhower and Lutz.* **Address:** c/o Howes and Prior. m. actor Peter Davison (qv); 1 d. Georgia.

DICKSON, *nicolle*

Nicolle Dickson. Actress. b. Sydney, Australia, 1 January 1969. Trained at Lynda Keane Studios. **Theatre:** *The Wiz; Trouble In Nursery Rhyme Land;* title role in *Cinderella.* **Films:** Title role in *Jess* (Australian Film and Television School); *That's Democracy;* **TV:** *Willing & Abel;* Bobby Simpson in *Home and Away* (1988-). TV commercials: Coca-Cola; South Australian Insurance Policy; United Permanent. **Radio:** *A Cave Full of Dragons; Thinking About Animals; Learning English In Australia* (all educational plays). Winner, Logie Award for Best New Talent, 1988. **Address:** c/o Stacey Testro Management/Channel 7. Lives in Sydney. m. James Bell.

DIMBLEBY, *david*

David Dimbleby. Presenter. b. London, 28 October 1938. Son of broadcaster Richard Dimbleby; brother of presenter Jonathan Dimbleby. Chairman of the *Richmond & Twickenham Times.* **TV:** *Panorama; 24 Hours; People and Power; Yesterday's Men; Reporter At Large; Dimbleby Talk-In; Nationwide; This Week, Next Week; The White Tribe of Africa* (winner, Royal Television Society Supreme Documentary award, 1979); *An Ocean Apart;* BBC General Election results programmes. **Address:** c/o BBC TV. m. cookery writer Josceline; 2 d. Liza, Kate, 1 s. Henry.

DIMBLEBY, *jonathan*

Jonathan Dimbleby. Presenter. b. Aylesbury, Buckinghamshire, 31 July 1944. Son of broadcaster Richard Dimbleby; brother of presenter David Dimbleby. **TV:** BBC Bristol reporter (1969–70); *This Week* (1972–9); *TV Eye; Jonathan Dimbleby In South America; Jonathan Dimbleby In Evidence; The Police; The Bomb; The Eagle and the Bear; The Cold War Game; The American Dream; Four Years On – The Bomb; First Tuesday* (presenter and associate editor); *Jonathan Dimbleby On Sunday* (presenter and editor); *This Week; Witness* (series editor); *On the Record; Review of the Year.* **Radio:** BBC Bristol reporter; *The World At One; Any Questions.* **Books:** *Richard Dimbleby; The Palestinians.* Winner, BAFTA Richard Dimbleby Award. **Address:** c/o David Higham Associates. m. journalist/author Bel Mooney; 1 d. Kitty, 1 s. Daniel.

DINSDALE, *reece*

Reece Dinsdale. Actor. b. Normanton, West Yorkshire, 6 August 1959. Trained at Guildhall School of Music and Drama. **Theatre:** *Chips With Everything; As You Like It; Hobson's Choice; Beethoven's Tenth; Red Saturday; Observe the Sons of Ulster; Marching Towards the Somme; Woundings; Don Carlos; Old Year's Eve; Rhinoceros; Boys Means Business.* **Films:** *Winter Flight; A Private Function.* **TV:** *Knife Edge; Out On the Floor; The Secret Adversary; Partners In Crime; Threads; Glamour Night; Home To Roost; Robin of Sherwood; Bergerac; Coppers; The Storyteller; Fear Not; Take Me Home; The Attractions; Haggard; Young Catherine* (mini-series). **Address:** c/o Jeremy Conway.

DIVALL, *alistair*

Alistair Divall. Presenter. b. Lincoln, 10 January 1956. Turned to presenting after acting. **Theatre:** *Suddenly At Home; Relatively Speaking; Spring and Port Wine.* **TV:** *Oliver; Auf Wiedersehen, Pet; Girls On Top; Jenny's War; The South Bank Show* (all acting); ITV *Telethon;* Sky *Starsearch* judge; *Keynotes* (host, game show, four series); *First Cut.* **Address:** c/o Sara Cameron Management. Single; lives in St Albans, Hertfordshire. Hobbies: Music, playing hockey, sport in general.

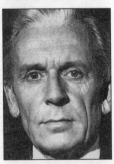

DOBIE, *alan*

Alan Dobie. Actor. b. Wombwell, South Yorkshire, 2 June 1932. Trained at Barnsley School of Art and Old Vic Theatre School. **TV:** *The Planemakers; Dance of Death; The Corsican Brothers; The Siege of Manchester; Why Aren't You Famous?; Conquest; Resurrection; Danton; Diamond Crack Diamond; The Troubleshooters; War and Peace; The Defector; For Services To Myself; Double Dare; Our Young Mr Wignall; A Collier's Friday Night; Eleanor Marks; Hard Times; Waxwork; Cribb; Death of Ivan Ilyich; Wobble To Death; The Detective Wore Silk Drawers; Madhatter's Holiday; Invitation To a Dynamite Party; Abra Cadaver; Hedda Gabler; Kessler; Gerican H; Master of the Game; House On Kirov Street; The Disputation; The Hospice.* **Address:** c/o Vernon Conway. m. 1st actress Rachel Roberts (dis), 2nd singer Maureen Scott; 2 d. Millie, Natasha, 1 s. Casey.

DOBSON, *anita*

Anita Dobson. Actress. b. London, 29 April 1949. Trained at the Webber Douglas Academy. **Theatre:** *Ardele; A Night In Old Peking;* title role in *Dick Whittington; Charley's Aunt; Budgie; Rough Crossing; My Lovely ...Shayna Maidel* (Ambasssadors Theatre); *Kvetch* (Garrick Theatre). **TV:** *What's Your Poison?; Play Away; Nanny; Partners In Crime; Up the Elephant and Round the Castle;* Angie Watts in *EastEnders; Split Ends; The World of Eddie Weary.* **Address:** c/o CAM.

DOBSON, *kevin*

Kevin Dobson. Actor. b. Queens, New York, USA, 18 March. Studied at the Neighbourhood Playhouse, New York. **Theatre:** *The Impossible Years.* **Films:** *Love Story; Midway; Klute; The French Connection.* **TV:** *Transplant; Orphan Train; Hard Hat and Legs; Reunion; Mark, I Love You* (all TV movies); *The Mod Squad;* Det Crocker in *Kojak; Shannon; Tales of the Unexpected; Knots Landing.* m. Susan; 1 d. Miriah, 2 s. Patrick, Shawn Kevin.

DOBSON, *wayne*

Wayne Dobson. Magician. b. Leicester. Became a member of the Magic Circle at the age of 16. Worked as a laboratory technician before turning professional as a magician. **TV:** *A Kind of Magic; Royal Variety Performance* (1989). **Address:** c/o Clifford Elson Publicity.

DODD, *ken, OBE*

Kenneth Arthur Dodd. Comedian. b. Knotty Ash, Liverpool, 8 November 1927. Self-taught entertainer and creator of the Diddymen; professional since 1954. **Theatre:** *Twelfth Night; Ha Ha – A Celebration of Laughter; Ken Dodd's Laughter Show* (summer and variety shows). **TV:** *The Ken Dodd Show; Doddy's Music Box; The Good Old Days; Super Trouper; Funny You Should Say That; Look Who's Talking; Ken Dodd's World of Laughter; Stars On Sunday; Ken Dodd's Showbiz; Ken Dodd At the London Palladium; This Is Your Life Special* (subject, 1990). **Radio:** *Pull the Other One.* **Records:** *Love Is Like a Violin; Tears; Happiness.* **Address:** c/o George Bartram Associates. Single; lives in Knotty Ash, Liverpool. Pets: Poodle called Doodle. Hobbies: Reading, relaxing. **Favourite TV programme:** *Coronation Street.*

DODWELL, *grant*

Grant Dodwell. Actor. b. Sydney, Australia, 2 July 1952. Trained at the National Institute of Dramatic Art. **Theatre:** *You're a Good Man, Charley Brown; Godspell; Everybody Makes Misteaks.* **Films:** *Goodbye Paradise.* **TV:** *Willing & Abel;* Dr Simon Bowen in *A Country Practice* (winner, four Logie awards); *Homicide; Glenview High; The Young Doctors; Patrol Boat.* **Address:** c/o Harry M Miller & Company Management, 153 Dowling Street, Kings Cross, New South Wales 2011, Australia. Hobbies: Sailing, fishing.

DONAT, *chris*

Christopher Donat. Presenter/Writer. b. Loughborough, Leicestershire, 15 March 1962. Gained law degree from Kent University and called to the Bar, before training at RADA. **Theatre:** Toured with three-man cabaret act 76a as actor and singer; appeared as alternative poet Lennie at The Comedy Store, London; appeared at 1985 Edinburgh Festival in *Pick of the Fringe.* **TV:** *Bergerac; Boon; No 73; Les Girls; Scruples* (small acting roles in each); *Jeopardy* (quiz show, host); *The Help Squad* (reporter and co-presenter); Anglia Television announcer and newsreader; narrated Channel Four film *Operation Dead End.* **Radio:** BBC World Service announcer and newsreader; occasional writer for Radio 4 satirical programme *Week Ending.* **Address:** c/o Downes Presenters Agency. Hobbies: playing saxophone and clarinet, tennis, swimming, singing, swing jazz, cooking.

DONOHOE, *amanda*

Amanda Donohoe. Actress. **Films:** *Castaway; Foreign Body; The Lair of the White Worm; The Rainbow; Diamond Skulls; Paper Mask.* **TV:** *An Affair In Mind* (TV movie); *Game, Set & Match; Laughter of God* (TV movie); C J Lamb in *LA Law.* **Address:** c/o Jonathan Altaras Associates.

DONOVAN, *terence*

Terence Donovan. Actor. **Films:** *Oliver!; The Getting of Wisdom; Breaker Morant; The Man From Snowy River; Emma's War.* **TV:** *No Hiding Place; Object Z; The Champions; Man In a Suitcase; Francis Durbridge Theatre; The Prisoner; Consider Your Verdict; Division 4; Love Story; Checker Cab Charlie; Rush; Last of the Australians; Homicide; Tandarra; Solo One; Hotel; Power Without Glory; The Outsiders; Going Home; Bellbird; Cop Shop; A Country Practice* (three times); *Prisoner: Cell Block H; Shoobie Doo; Sons and Daughters; Joe Wilson; Prime Time; Mike Willesee'e Australia; Errol Flynn; Australia Break; Mission Impossible; GP; The Flying Doctors; Flair;* Al Simpson in *Home and Away;* Doug Willis in *Neighbours.* **Address:** c/o Melbourne Artists Management. m. 1st actress Sue McIntosh (dis), 2nd Marlene; 2 s. actor/singer Jason Donovan (from 1st m.), Paul.

DORÉ, *edna*

Edna Doré. Actress. Trained at drama school attached to the Croydon Repertory Company. **Theatre:** *Peek-a-Boo;* Mrs Sowerberry in *Oliver!;* Mrs Crabtree in *Billy; The Crucible; Julius Caesar; Tales From Vienna Woods; The Cherry Orchard; The Country Wife; Don Quixote; A Midsummer Night's Dream; The Threepenny Opera; Three Sisters.* **Films:** *High Hopes.* **TV:** *Playschool* (writer and storyteller); *The Brothers; The Liver Birds; Doctor In the House; Doctor At Large; Open All Hours; Terry Scott; Roger Doesn't Live Here Anymore; Under the Skin; Reservation; Tenko; The Puppet Man; The Mysteries; The Bill; King of the Ghetto; Lizzie's Pictures; Casualty; Christabel; Hard Cases; Streets Apart;* Mo Butcher in *EastEnders* (1989–90); *Gas and Candles.* **Address:** c/o CDA. Lives in Barnes, south-west London. m. theatre director Alexander Doré; 1 s. Mike.

DOTRICE, *michele*

Michele Dotrice. Actress. b. Cleethorpes, Lincolnshire, 27 September 1948. Daughter of actor Roy Dotrice; sister of actress Karen Dotrice. Trained at the Corona Academy. **Theatre:** *Henry V; The Jew of Malta; Puntilla* (RSC); *Total Eclipse* (Royal Court Theatre); *The Servant of Two Masters* (Queen's Theatre); *Same Time, Next Year* (Prince of Wales Theatre); *The Male of the Species* (Piccadilly Theatre and Australia); *Private Lives* (Australia); *The Assassin; Richard III.* **Films:** *And Soon the Darkness; The Devil's Touch; Not Now Comrade.* **TV:** *Emma's Time; A Kind of Bonus; A Month In the Country;* Betty Spencer in *Some Mothers Do 'Ave 'Em; Three Sisters; The Sextet; On the Eve of Publication;* Catherine Winslow in *The Winslow Boy;* Lady Percy in *Henry IV, Pts I and II; Chintz; The Equalizer; Boon.* **Address:** c/o Eric Glass. m. actor Edward Woodward.

DOUGLAS, *angela*

Angela Douglas. Actress. b. Gerrards Cross, Buckinghamshire, 29 October 1940. **Theatre:** Repertory theatre in Worthing; *Anniversary Waltz* (London West End); *The Birthday Party; The First Mrs Frazer; The Scenario; The Seven Year Itch; Killing Jessica.* **Films:** *Feet of Clay; Cleopatra; Some People; It's All Happening; The Comedy Man; John Goldfarb; Please Come Home; Carry On Cowboy; Digby – The Biggest Dog In the World.* **TV:** *The Hard Knock; A Smashing Day; Wuthering Heights; Rosemary; The Dragon's Opponent; The Gentle Touch; Misterioso.* **Books:** *Swings and Roundabouts; Angela Douglas's Present Affairs* (both biographies). **Address:** c/o ICM. m. actor Kenneth More (dec).

DOUGLAS, su

Su Douglas. Actress. b. Nottingham, 8 November 1942. Trained at Aida Foster Stage School. **Theatre:** *A Dead Secret* (Piccadilly Theatre); *Oliver!* (twice); *Houseguest; A Sting In the Tale; Piaf; Don't Just Lie There, Say Something; Whodunnit?; Candida; The Elephant Man.* **Films:** *The Ghost Train Murder; Those Nice Americans; Funny Money; The Boys In Blue; Schhh!* **TV:** *Within These Walls; Triangle; Spotlight; Prospects; Chance In a Million; Mike Yarwood Spectacular; Rude Health; The Michael Barrymore Hour;* presented a cookery chat show for Channel TV; *The Weekend Starts Here* (HTV); Glenys Kinnock in *Campaign '87; Executive Stress; Rude Health; The Ruth Rendell Mysteries – A Sleeping Life; The Paradise Club; Never the Twain; Mr Bean.* **Address:** c/o A.I.M. m. actor Jack Douglas; 1 d. Sarah, 1 step-d. Deborah, 1 step-s. Craig.

DOVE, kate

Kate Dove. Actress. b. Portsmouth, Hampshire, 8 March 1947. Trained at Philippa Fawcett College of Education, London, and Triangle Theatre Workshop, New York. **Theatre:** *Relatively Thinking; Grace; A Life of Christ; Private Lives; Candida; Martha in Who's Afraid of Virginia Woolf?; The Importance of Being Earnest; Lady Macbeth; You Never Can Tell; Season's Greetings; The Real Thing; What the Butler Saw; The Provok'd Wife; A Midsummer Night's Dream; The Country Wife; The Plotters of Cabbage Patch Corner; Stagefright; Hamlet; The Unexpected Guest.* Playwright: *Colours; Gawain and the Green Knight; Hiawatha.* Director: British Council tours; *Hedda Gabler; Educating Rita.* **TV:** *Book Tower; Wipeout; Jackson Pace;* Elizabeth Feldmann in *Emmerdale.* **Address:** c/o Gillian Russell/Yorkshire Television. m. Alasdair Ramsay; 1 s. Michael Hales.

DOW, jonathan

Jonathan Bell Dow. Actor. b. Redditch, Worcestershire, 25 March 1965. Trained at the Guildhall School of Music and Drama. **TV:** *Piece of Cake; London's Burning; After the War; No Job for a Lady;* PC Barry Stringer in *The Bill.* **Address:** c/o The Bill Horne Partnership. Lives in London. m. actress Anne Healy. Pets: A spider. Hobbies: Theatre, art, cinema, swimming. **Favourite TV programme:** *Moviedrome.*

DRAKE, gabrielle

Gabrielle Drake. Actress. b. Lahore, Pakistan. Worked as an au pair in Paris before training at RADA. **Theatre:** *Tea Party; Jeeves; Noises Off; Court In the Act.* **Films:** *There's a Girl In My Soup; Au Pair Girls.* **TV:** Jill Hammond in *The Brothers; The Kelly Monteith Show;* Nicola Freeman in *Crossroads; The Importance of Being Earnest; No 10; Wellington.* TV commercials: Talking Pages. **Address:** c/o Peters Fraser & Dunlop. m. Louis De Wet.

DRINKWATER, carol

Carol Drinkwater. Actress. b. London, 22 April 1948. Trained at The Drama Centre. **Theatre:** Repertory Theatre in Birmingham and Leeds; National Theatre; Dublin, Edinburgh and Malvern Festivals; toured South East Asia, 1981. **Films:** *A Clockwork Orange; The Dawn Breakers; Mondo Candido; Queen Kong; Joseph Andrews; The Shout.* **TV:** *Public Eye; Bill Brand; Softly, Softly; The Sweeney; Raffles; Sam; A Bouquet of Barbed Wire; All Creatures Great and Small; Ladykillers; Tales of the Unexpected; Take the Stage; Chocky; The Haunted School; Captain James Cook.* **Address:** c/o London Management.

DRIVER, *betty*

Betty Driver. Actress. b. Leicester, 20 May 1920. Grew up in Manchester. Joined the Terence Byron Repertory Company aged nine; sang with bandleader Henry Hall. **Theatre:** *Mixed Bathing; Mr Tower of London; The Lovebirds; Pillar To Post; What a Racket.* **Films:** *Boots! Boots!; Penny Paradise; Let's Be Famous; Facing the Music.* **TV:** *Love On the Dole; Pardon the Expression;* Betty Turpin in *Coronation Street* (1969-); *This Is Your Life* (subject); *Royal Variety Performance* (1989). **Radio:** *Henry Hall's Guest Night; A Date With Betty.* **Records:** *The Sailor With the Navy Blue Eyes; MacNamara's Band; Pick the Petals of a Daisy; September In the Rain.* **Address:** c/o Granada TV. Lives near Altrincham, Cheshire. m. singer Wally Petersen (dis). Pets: Two boxer dogs, Totti and Polly, and one cat, Abby. Hobbies: Collecting antiques and paintings.

DRYER, *fred*

Fred Dryer. Actor. b. Los Angeles, California, USA, 6 June 1946. Trained with coach Nina Foch. **Films:** *Cannonball Run II: Death Before Dishonour.* **TV:** *Starmaker; Girl's Life; Force Seven; Something So Right; Kid From Nowhere* (all TV movies); CBS sports commentator; *Cheers; Lou Grant; Laverne and Shirley; Hunter.* **Address:** c/o William Morris Agency (USA). m. actress Tracy Vaccaro; 1 d. Caitlin.

DU SAUTOY, *carmen*

Carmen du Sautoy. Actress. b. London, 26 February 1952. **Theatre:** Repertory theatre in Nottingham, Crewe and Oxford; *Love's Labour's Lost; A Midsummer Night's Dream; Wary of the World; Once In a Lifetime* (all RSC); *Antony and Cleopatra; Macbeth; Candy Kisses;* Old Vic Theatre tour of USA; *Salome.* **Films:** *The Man With the Golden Gun; Our Miss Fred; Bert Rigby, You're a Fool.* **TV:** *The Citadel; The Barretts of Wimpole Street; Chessgame; Praying Mantis* (Channel Four film); *The South Bank Show; Lost Empires; Poor Little Rich Girl; Intercom Conspiracy; Bergerac; La Ronde; Boon.* **Address:** c/o ICM, Duncan Heath Associates. m. Charles Savage.

DUCE, *sharon*

Sharon Duce. Actress. b. Sheffield, South Yorkshire, 16 January 1950. **Theatre:** Repertory theatre in York, Scarborough and at Bristol Old Vic; *The Foursome; Touched; Tibetan Inroads; The Changeling; When I Was a Girl I Used To Scream and Shout.* **Films:** *Knots.* **TV:** *Renoir My Father; Helen, Woman for Today; Minder; The House That Jack Built; Funny Man; The Hard Word; Big Deal; Shooting Stars* (Channel Four film); *Misterioso.* **Address:** c/o Marmont Management. m. TV documentary-maker David Munro (dis), 2nd actor Dominic Guard; 1 s. William (from 2nd m.).

DUFFY, *patrick*

Patrick Duffy. Actor/Director. b. Townsend, Montana, USA, 17 March 1949. Studied drama while at University of Washington and sang with the Seattle Opera. **Theatre:** Seattle Repertory; 'A Contemporary Theater, Seattle; *Natural Affection;* San Diego Old Globe Shakespeare Company. **Films:** *Vamping* (also produced). **TV:** *The Stranger Who Looks Like Me; Hurricane* (both TV movies); *The Last of Mrs Lincoln; George Burns Comedy Week; Alice In Wonderland; Too Good To Be True; Charlie's Angels; Switch;* Mark Harris in *The Man From Atlantis; The Flight of the Enola Gay; 114 Going On 30; Leave Her To Heaven; Unholy Matrimony* (all TV movies); Bobby Ewing in *Dallas; Strong Medicine* (mini-series); *Hotel; Freedom Festival '89* (host); *Danielle Steele's Daddy* (TV movie). **Address:** c/o Writers & Artists Agency. Lives in San Fernando Valley, California. m. Carlyn; 2 s. Padraic, Conor.

DUNCAN, *peter*

Peter Duncan. Actor/Presenter. b. London, 3 May 1954. **Theatre:** Jim Hawkins in *Treasure Island* (Mermaid Theatre); title role in *Barnum*. **Films:** *Stardust; Mr Quilp; The Lifetaker; Flash Gordon.* **TV:** *Oranges and Lemons; Dragon's Opponent; John Halifax; Crown Court; Sam; Play for Today; Space 1999; Survivors; The Flockton Flyer; Robin Hood; Fathers and Families; King Cinder; General Hospital; Renoir – My Father; Warship; Fallen Hero; Family Affair; Sons and Lovers; Blue Peter; Duncan Dares; Teenage Health Freak.* **Address:** c/o Mark Hudson. m. Annie; 3 d. Lucy, Katie, Georgia.

DUNLOP, *lesley*

Lesley Dunlop. Actress. b. Newcastle-upon-Tyne, 10 March 1956. **Theatre:** *Other Worlds,* at the Royal Court Theatre, London; *Playing With Trains,* with the RSC. **Films:** *A Little Night Music; Tess; The Elephant Man; 13 At Dinner; Trick of the Light; The Monster Club.* **TV:** *A Drive In the Country; Walk With Destiny; South Riding; The Gathering Storm; The White Elephant; The Rose Garden; Penmarric; Black Beauty; Our Mutual Friend; Play for Love; Mates; The Red Shift; The Deadly Game; Waters of the Moon; Season's Greetings; Smuggler; Angels* (first series); *The Little Princess; Stanley;* Susie Q in *Doctor Who;* Sara in *Capstick's Law;* Zoe in *May To December.* **Address:** c/o Annette Stone Associates. m. actor Christopher Guard; 2 d. Daisy, Rosie.

DUTTINE, *john*

John Duttine. Actor. b. Barnsley, South Yorkshire, 15 March 1949. Trained at The Drama Centre. **TV:** *A Pin To See the Peepshow; Z-Cars; Holding On; Warship; Lord Peter Wimsey; Coronation Street; Spend, Spend, Spend; Jesus of Nazareth; Bery's Lot; Angels; Law Centre; Saturday, Sunday, Monday; The Devil's Crown; People Like Us; Wuthering Heights; Strangers; The Mallens; To Serve Them All My Days* (winner, *TVTimes* Best Actor On TV award, 1980–81); *Psy-Warriors; The Day of the Triffids; The Outsider; Tales of the Unexpected; Family Man; Shades of Darkness; The Intercessor; Love and Marriage; The Groundling and the Kite; Hamlet; A Woman of Substance; A Still, Small Shout; Lame Ducks; Long Live the King; Unnatural Causes; Lost Property; Master of the Marionettes; A Killing On the Exchange; Imaginary Friends.* **Address:** c/o A.I.M. m. 1 s. Oscar.

DYSART, *richard*

Richard A Dysart. Actor. b. Brighton, ME, USA, 30 March 1929. **Films:** *Petulia; The Lost Man; The Sporting Club; The Hospital; The Terminal Man; The Crazy World of Julius Vrooder; The Day of the Locust; The Hindenberg; Prophecy; Meteor; Being There; An Enemy of the People; The Thing; The Falcon and the Snowman; Mask; Warning; Signs; Pale Rider; Wall Street; Back To the Future Part III.* **TV:** *The Autobiography of Miss Jane Pittman; Blood and Orchids; First You Cry; Bogie; The Ordeal of Dr Mudd; Churchill and the Generals; The People Vs Jean Harris; A Bitter Harvest; The Last Days of General Patton; The Seal; Missing Children – A Mother's Story; Concealed Enemies; Malice In Wonderland; Day One* (all TV movies); *War and Remembrance; Jay Leno's Family Comedy Hour; Moving Target;* Leland McKenzie in *LA Law.* **Address:** c/o Writers & Artists Agency.

EAGLES, *leon*

Leon Eagles. Actor. b. Cardiff, 6 April 1932. Trained at RADA. **Theatre:** *A Small Family Business; King Lear; Antony and Cleopatra; Antigone; A View From the Bridge; Rosencrantz and Guildenstern Are Dead; Cowardy Custard; The Seagull; Relatively Speaking; The Secret Life; A Man for All Seasons; Richard; Rebecca.* **Films:** *Puppet On a Chain; Frenzy; Performance.* **TV:** *The Onedin Line;* Jensen in *The Jensen Code; Love for Lydia;* Kowajinski in *Dog's Ransom; The Famous Five; Secret Army; The Danedyke Mystery; Love In a Cold Climate; The Squad; Invasion; We'll Meet Again; Gulliver's Travels; Bergerac; The Fourth Arm; Operation Julie; C.A.T.S. Eyes; Chocky; David Copperfield; The Bill; Heading Home;* Dr Leon Hull in *Drummonds.* **Address:** c/o Langford Associates. Lives in London. m. Mary Preston; 1 d. Zillah. Hobbies: Music, cricket, food.

EARL, *vince*

Vince Earl. Actor. b. Birkenhead, Cheshire. Singer with the Vince Earl Talismen and the Vince Earl Attraction, before turning professional as a comedian and actor. **Theatre:** *Turn for the Worse.* **Films:** *No Surrender.* **TV:** *New Faces; The Comedians; The Video Entertainers; Starburst; The Jimmy Cricket Special; Boys From the Blackstuff;* Ron Dixon in *Brookside* (1990-). **Address:** c/o Mersey Television. Lives in Birkenhead. m. 2nd Irene; 2 s. Vince (from 1st m.), Stephen, 2 d. Nicole, Kimberley.

EASTER, *david*

David Easter. Actor/Musician. b. Eastleigh, Hampshire, 11 November 1959. Previously sang with a group and was an ASM, before performing in repertory theatre. **Theatre:** *The School for Scandal; The Front Page; A Midsummer Night's Dream; Grease; Godspell; Joseph and the Amazing Technicolor Dreamcoat; Piaf; The Rocky Horror Show; The Firedragon; Rockstar.* **Films:** *Give My Regards To Broad Street; The Music Machine.* **TV:** Pat Hancock in *Brookside; The Bill.* **Address:** c/o Susan Angel Associates.

EDDINGTON, *paul, CBE*

Paul Eddington. Actor. b. London, 18 June 1927. Trained at RADA. **Theatre:** Repertory theatre in Birmingham, Sheffield and Ipswich; *A Severed Head* (USA); *Absurd Person Singular; Donkey's Years; Ten Times Table; Middle-Aged Spread; Who's Afraid of Virginia Woolf?; Noises Off; Lovers Dancing; Forty Years On; Jumpers; HMS Pinafore* (Australian tour); *The Browning Version; Harlequinade; London Assurance.* **TV:** *Dixon of Dock Green; Special Branch; The Good Life; Yes Minister; Yes, Prime Minister; Let There Be Love; Outside Edge; Miss Marple.* **Address:** c/o ICM. m. actress Patricia Scott; 1 d. Gemma, 3 s. Toby, Hugo, Dominic.

EDMONDS, *noel*

Noel Edmonds. Presenter. b. London, 22 December 1948. Disc-jockey with Radio Luxembourg, then BBC Radio 1, before moving into television. **Theatre:** *Captain Beaky's Musical Christmas.* **TV:** *Top of the Pops; Z-Shed; Multi-Coloured Swap Shop; Come Dancing; Top Gear; Taking the Strain; Lucky Numbers; Juke Box Jury; The Late, Late Breakfast Show; Time of Your Life; Christmas With Noel; Telly Addicts; Whatever Next; The Saturday Roadshow; Foul Ups, Bleeps and Blunders* (USA); *Noel's House Party.* Winner, *TVTimes* Favourite Male TV Personality award, 1989. **Address:** c/o BBC TV. m. 1st Gill (dis), 2nd Helen; 2 d. Lorna, Charlotte.

EDMONDSON, *adrian*

Adrian Edmondson. Actor/Comedian. **Films:** *The Supergrass.* **TV:** *The Comic Strip Presents . . .; Girls On Top; Saturday Night Live; Honest, Decent and True; Happy Families; Hardwicke House; Filthy Rich and Catflap; French and Saunders; Bottom.* **Address:** c/o Jonathan Altaras Associates. m. actress/comedienne Jennifer Saunders; 2 d.

EDWARDS, *glynn*

Glynn Edwards. Actor. b. Malaya, 2 February 1931. Trained at Joan Littlewood's Theatre Workshop and Central School of Speech and Drama. **Theatre:** *The Quare Fellow; Macbeth; The Glass Menagerie.* **Films:** *Stick Up; The David Galaxy Affair; Red Monarch; Zulu; The Ipcress File; Under Milk Wood; Shaft In Africa; Get Carter.* **TV:** *The Newcomers; Spindo; The Main Chance; Man About the House; Dixon of Dock Green; The Paper Lads; Target; Rising Damp; The Fall and Rise of Reginald Perrin; Minder; History of Mr Polly; You're Only Young Twice; Shadow of Gunman; The Lucky Feller; Crown Court; The Harry Worth Show; Madame Bovary; Softly, Softly; Steptoe and Son; Sweet Sixteen; Minder On the Orient Express.* **Address:** c/o Joyce Edwards. m. 1st actress Yootha Joyce (dis), 2nd Christine Pilgrim (dis), 3rd Valerie; 1 s. Tom (from 2nd m.).

EGAN, *peter*

Peter Egan. Actor. b. London, 28 September 1946. Trained at RADA. **Theatre:** *The Rivals; Journey's End; What Every Woman Knows; Engaged; Rolls Hyphen Royce; You Never Can Tell; Arms and the Man.* **Films:** *The Hireling; Callan; Chariots of Fire; One Brief Summer; Hennessy.* **TV:** *Big Breadwinner Hog; Mother Love; The Inheritors; The Organisation; The Love School; The Deep Blue Sea;* Oscar Wilde in *Lillie; Reilly – Ace of Spies; The Dark Side of the Sun; The Kitchen; Prince Regent; Dear Brutus; Tales of the Unexpected; Thriller; The Greeks; Murder Mysteries; Arms and the Man; A Woman of Substance; Ever Decreasing Circles; Paradise Postponed; A Perfect Spy; Joint Account; The Ruth Rendell Mysteries: A New Lease of Death.* Winner, *TVTimes* Best Actor On TV award, 1986–7. **Address:** c/o James Sharkey Associates. m. Myra Frances; 1 d. Rebecca.

EIKENBERRY, *jill*

Jill Eikenberry. Actress. b. New Haven, Connecticut, USA, 21 January 1947. Trained at Yale University Drama School. **Theatre:** *All Over Town; Watch On the Rhine; Onward Victoria; Summer Brave; Moonchildren* (all Broadway). **Films:** *Between the Lines; The End of the World In Our Usual Bed In a Night Full of Rain; An Unmarried Woman; Butch and Sundance: The Early Days; Rich Kids; Hide In Plain Sight; Arthur; Grace Quigley; The Manhattan Project.* **TV:** *The Deadliest Season; Orphan Train; Swan Song; Uncommon Women and Others; Sessions; Kane & Abel; Assault and Matrimony; Family Sins; A Stoning In Fulham Country; My Boyfriend's Back; The Diane Martin Story; Hill Street Blues;* Ann Kelsey in *LA Law; The Best of Families; Destined To Live* (host/producer); *A Family Again.* **Address:** c/o STE Representation. m. actor Michael Tucker; 1 s. Max, 1 step-d. Alison.

ELDER, *michael*

Michael Elder. Actor. b. London, 30 April 1931. Trained at RADA. **Theatre:** Byre Theatre, St Andrews; Citizens' Theatre, Glasgow; Gateway Theatre, Edinburgh; Pitlochry Festival Theatre; Royal Lyceum Theatre, Edinburgh; Scottish Theatre Company; *Whalers* (one-man show, 1986 Edinburgh Festival, winner of a Fringe First award). **TV:** *Sam; Edward VII; Weir of Hermiston; Five Red Herrings; The Prime of Miss Jean Brodie;* Dr Wallace in *Take the High Road* (1980- , also scriptwriter and script editor). As writer: *The Walls of Jericho; King's Royal; Murder Not Proven.* **Address:** c/o Young Casting Agency/Scottish Television. m. actress Sheila Donald; 2 s. David, Simon.

ELÈS, *sandor*

Sandor Elès. Actor. b. Hungary, 15 June 1919. Trained at student theatre in Hungary and Bristol Old Vic Theatre School. **Theatre:** *Watch On the Rye* (National Theatre); *Whodunnit* (national tour). **TV:** Paul Ross in *Crossroads; The Treachery Game; Aubrey; The Seven Dials Mystery.* **Address:** c/o RKM.

ELLIOTT, *denholm*

Denholm Elliott. Actor. b. London, 31 May 1922. Trained at RADA. **Films:** *Station Six Sahara; Alfie; Robin and Marian; A Bridge Too Far; The Boys From Brazil; Zulu Dawn; The Sweeney; Cuba; Rising Damp; The Missionary; The Wicked Lady; Trading Places; A Private Function; Underworld; Defence of the Realm; A Room With a View; Maurice; September; Innocent Heroes; Return From the River Kwai; Indiana Jones and the Last Crusade; The Bangkok Hilton; Scorchers; Toy Soldiers; A Murder of Quality.* **TV:** *In Hiding; You're All Right, How Am I?; Gentle Folk; School Play; Donkey's Years; Blade On the Feather; Marco Polo; Sextet; Clayhanger; The Signalman; Bleak House; Hotel du Lac; Codename Kyril.* Winner, BAFTA Best Actor award, 1980. **Address:** c/o London Management. m. 1st Virginia McKenna (dis), 2nd Susan Robinson; 1 d. Jennifer, 1 s. Mark (from 2nd m.).

ELLIS, *janet*

Janet Michell Ellis. Actress/Presenter. b. Kent, 16 September 1955. Trained at Central School of Speech and Drama. **Theatre:** *Having a Ball; Cinderella; Alphabetical Order; The Misanthrope.* **TV:** *Jackanory Playhouse: Princess Griselda; Doctor Who; The Deceivers; April Fool; The Sweeney; Knock-Knock; ATV Playhouse* (all as actress); *Jigsaw* (presenter, four series); *Blue Peter* (presenter, 1983–7); *Open Air; Top Gear; The Motor Show; Parenting; The Motor Show* (all as presenter). TV commercials: Daz. **Radio:** *Janet's Bottom* (GLR, presenter). **Address:** c/o Arlington Enterprises. Lives in London. m. 1st Robin Bextor (dis), 2nd John Leach; 2 d. Sophie (from 1st m.), Martha, 1 s. Jack. Hobbies: Shopping, writing.

ELLIS, *peter*

Peter Ellis. Actor. b. Bristol, 30 May 1936. Trained at Central School of Speech and Drama. **Theatre:** Repertory theatre in Leeds, Sheffield, Nottingham and Birmingham; three years with the Old Vic Company; three years with the RSC; also worked with the Chichester Festival Company, Theatre Workshop and the Belt and Braces Company; *The Beggar's Opera; Trafford Tanzi; The Tulip Tree; Julius Caesar.* **Films:** *An American Werewolf In London; Agatha; Remembrance.* **TV:** *First Among Equals; The Outsider; How We Used To Live; In Two Minds; Edward and Mrs Simpson; Coronation Street; The Victoria Wood Show; Lytton's Diary;* Chief Supt Brownlow in *The Bill.* **Address:** c/o Lou Coulson. Lives in Bristol. m. (dis); 3 s. Christopher, Hugh, Charles. Hobbies: Gliding, walking, sailing.

ELLISON, *christopher*

Christopher Ellison. Actor. b. London, 16 December 1946. Trained as an artist at Camberwell School of Art, then as an actor at Studio '68. **Theatre:** RSC; *Once a Catholic; Oliver!* (both London West End). **Films:** *Buster.* **TV:** *The Professionals; Dempsey and Makepeace; The Gentle Touch; Strangers; Brond; Three Up, Two Down;* Det Insp Frank Burnside in *The Bill.* **Address:** c/o Barry Brown & Partner. m. actress Anita Joannou; 1 s. Louis.

ELLWOOD, *fionnuala*

Fionnuala Rachel Ellwood. Actress. b. Dublin, 3 July 1964. Trained at Rose Bruford College of Speech and Drama. **Theatre:** *Off the Road; Inside Out; Changa and the Journey;* London Bubble Theatre Company workshops dealing with special needs groups; *Arthur Awakes;* founder-member of Bexley Theatre Workshops. **TV:** *Scruples* (improvised sketches); *Families* (pilot programme); *World In Action* (voice-over); Lynn Whiteley in *Emmerdale; Seeking Susan; Thanks for Having Her; Prime Suspect.* **Radio:** *Billy Liar.* Plus drama workshops for deaf schools. **Address:** c/o MGA. Single; lives in London. Hobbies: Reading, embroidery, travel, cookery. **Favourite TV programme:** *Casualty.*

ELMALOGLOU, rebekah

Rebekah Elmaloglou. Actress. b. 23 January 1974. Trained at Lynda Keane Studios. **Theatre:** *The Sound of Music.* **Films:** *Five Times Dizzy; Mad Max: Beyond Thunderdome; Emma; 20:84.* **TV:** *The Adventures of Kythera; Damien Parer; The Trumplar Tree; Princess Kate; The Siege of Barton's Bathroom Ghost; A Country Practice; In Too Deep; Barlow and Chambels;* Sophie Simpson in *Home and Away* (1989-). **Address:** c/o Keane Management/Channel 7.

ELPHICK, michael

Michael Elphick. Actor. b. Chichester, West Sussex, 19 September 1946. Trained at Central School of Speech and Drama. **Films:** *The Elephant Man; Hitler; The Curse of the Pink Panther; Withnail & I; Privates On Parade; Gorky Park; Little Dorrit.* **TV:** *Parkin's Patch; Road To Freedom; Holding Forth; The Nearly Man; Holding On; Crown Court; This Year, Next Year; Blue Remembered Hills; The Sweeney; The One and Only Phyllis Dixey; The Knowledge; Wobble To Death; Private Schultz; Bloomfield; Chish 'n' Fips; Andy Robson; All the World's a Stage; Chains; Pocketful of Dreams; Don't Write To Mother; Supergran; Much Ado About Nothing; Jenny's War; CQ; Hitler's SS; Three Up, Two Down;* title role in *Boon; Pull the Other One; The Absolute Beginner's Guide To Cookery; Stanley and the Women.* **Address:** c/o ICM. Lives in Warwickshire. m. Julia; 1 d. Kate.

ELTON, ben

Ben Elton. Comedian/Writer. Has written for Rowan Atkinson, Rik Mayall, Lenny Henry, French and Saunders, and Adrian Edmondson. **Theatre:** *Gasping; Silly Cow* (both as writer, London West End). **TV:** *The Young Ones* (writer, BAFTA Best Comedy award, 1984); *Happy Families* (writer); *Filthy Rich and Catflap* (writer); *Blackadder* (four series, writer, with Richard Curtis, 1987 BAFTA Best Comedy award); *South of Watford* (presenter and co-writer); *Saturday Live; Friday Live; Wogan With Ben Elton; Ben Elton – The Man From Auntie; The Ben Elton Show.* **Books:** *Bachelor Boys* (*Young Ones* book); *Stark* (novel), *Gridlock* (novel). **Record:** *Motormouth* (LP). **Address:** c/o Jane McIntyre.

EMBERG, bella

Bella Emberg. Actress/Comedienne. b. Brighton, East Sussex, 16 September 1937. Stooged for Benny Hill, Frankie Howerd, Stanley Baxter and Les Dawson. **Theatre:** *Macbeth* (Ludlow Festival). **Films:** *History of the World–Part 1.* **TV:** *Take Three Girls; Softly, Softly; Pennies From Heaven; Testament of Youth; Robin's Nest; Russ Abbot's Madhouse; The Russ Abbot Show; Les Dennis's Laughter Show.* **Address:** c/o Clifford Elson Publicity.

EMERICK, louis

Louis Emerick Grant. Actor. b. Liverpool, 10 June 1953. **Theatre:** *Oh! What a Lovely War; The Lion, The Witch and The Wardrobe; The Resistible Rise of Arturo Ui; Hamlet; Playboy of the West Indies; Rent Party; Just Enough Rope; Night of Passion On Buttermoor Drive; Master Harold and the Boys.* **Films:** *The Fruit Machine.* **TV:** *Happy Families; The Practice; Albion Market; Home To Roost; Celebration; Floodtide; There Was an Old Woman; A View of Harry Clarke; Last of the Summer Wine; Coronation Street; Children's Ward; Ball-Trap On the Cote Sauvage;* Mick Johnson in *Brookside* (1989-). **Address:** c/o Tobias Management/Mersey Television. Lives in Manchester. m. Maureen; 2 d. Valerie, Zoe, 1 s. Louis. Pets: A cat called Tinker and two dogs called Jodie and Griffin. Hobbies: Sports, cinema, theatre. **Favourite TV programme:** *Hill Street Blues.*

EMERY, *ewen*

Ewen Emery. Actor. b. Edinburgh, 10 February 1960. Trained at Queen Margaret College Drama School, Edinburgh. **TV:** *Taggart; Shadow of the Stone; Extras; Bloodhunt; Strike It Rich; Take the High Road.* **Address:** c/o Ruth Tarko Agency.

ENFIELD, *harry*

Harry Enfield. Comedian/Writer. b. Sussex, 31 May 1961. Formed a double-act, Dusty and Dick, with friend Brian Elsley while studying politics at York University. **TV:** *Spitting Image* (scriptwriter and voice impersonator); *French and Saunders; Don't Miss Wax; The Tube; Filthy Rich and Catflap; The Lenny Henry Show; Girls On Top; Frocks On the Box; Comic Relief; Friday Live; Saturday Live; Norbert Smith – A Life* (starred in and co-wrote, with Geoffrey Perkins); *Harry Enfield's Television Programme; Men Behaving Badly; Gone To the Dogs.* **Address:** c/o PBJ Management.

ENGLISH, *arthur*

Arthur English. Actor. b. Aldershot, Hampshire, 9 May 1919. **Theatre:** *Royal Variety Performance;* revues; pantomimes; Chichester Festival; *On the Rocks; Die Fledermaus.* **Films:** *Are You Being Served?* **TV:** *Follyfoot; Copper's End; How's Your Father; Dixon of Dock Green; Crown Court; Doctor In the House; The Ghosts of Motley Hall; Are You Being Served?; Funny Man; Pygmalion; Never Say Die; In Sickness and In Health.* **Address:** c/o Patrick Freeman Management. m. 1st Ivy (dec), 2nd dancer Teresa Mann (dis); 1 s. Anthony (from 1st m.), 2 d. Ann (from 1st m.), Clare Louise.

ESHLEY, *norman*

Norman Eshley. Actor. b. Bristol, 30 May 1945. Trained at the Bristol Old Vic Theatre School. **Theatre:** *Romeo and Juliet; Hamlet; A Midsummer Night's Dream; Twelfth Night; Same Time, Next Year; Lady Chatterley's Lover.* **Films:** *The Immortal Story; Blind Terror; The Disappearance; Yanks.* **TV:** *Randall and Hopkirk (Deceased); Parkin's Patch; Bouncing Boy; Vienna 1900; The Onedin Line; The Skin Game; Windgate; Warship; The Duchess of Duke Street; I, Claudius; Supernatural; Secret Army; 1990; Justice; Thriller; The Strength of Gemini; Man About the House; And Mother Makes Five; Return of The Saint; The Sweeney; George and Mildred; Late Expectations; Maybury; The Professionals; The Outsider; Alun Jones in Brookside.* **Address:** c/o David White Associates. m. 1st actress/singer Millicent Martin (dis), 2nd Lynette Braid.

EVANS, *gillian*

Gillian Evans. Weather presenter. b. Australia, 25 May 1960. Came to London and joined ITN's press office in 1987 and trained as a weather presenter for ITN. **TV:** *Frost On Sunday; Good Morning Britain.* **Address:** c/o ITN. m. Nicholas Evans. Hobbies: Antiques, reading, aerobics, cinema, theatre.

EVERETT, *kenny*

Maurice Cole. Presenter. b. Seaforth, Liverpool, 25 December 1944. Previously a disc-jockey with Radio Luxembourg, pirate Radio London, BBC Radio 1 and Capital Radio. **Films:** *Captain Kremmen – The Movies; Blood Bath At the House of Horror;* **TV:** *Nice Time; The Kenny Everett Explosion; Making Whoopee; Ev; The Kenny Everett Video Show; The Kenny Everett Television Show; Brainstorm; That's Showbusiness; The Kenny Everett Show.* **Books:** *The Custard Stops At Hatfield* (autobiography). **Address:** c/o Jo Gurnett Management. m. former singer Audrey Middleton.

EYTLE, *tommy*

Tommy Eytle. Actor. **Theatre:** *Split Second* (Lyric Theatre, Hammersmith); *The Death of Bessie Smith; As Time Goes By; One More River; Toys In the Attic; South; Playboy of the West Indies* (all London West End); *Measure for Measure; The American Clock* (both with the National Theatre); *Leave Taking; A Blow To Bute Street; Take Back What's Yours; Ma Rainey's Black Bottom* (National Theatre). **Films:** *Day of the Fox; Elsa the Lioness; The Hi-jackers; Man Friday; Beyond the Sunrise; Blue Smoke, Red Mountains.* **TV:** *The Bill; Snakes and Ladders;* Jack in *Never Say Die;* Jules Tavernier in *EastEnders* (1990-). **Address:** c/o Crouch Associates/BBC Elstree Centre.

FAITH, *adam*

Terence Nelhams. Actor/Singer. b. Acton, West London, 23 June 1940. Previously worked in Pinewood Studios cutting room and as an assistant editor at Beaconsfield Studios while singing in the Working Men skiffle group. **Theatre:** *Night Must Fall; Alfie; Billy Liar; City Sugar* (Comedy Theatre); *Budgie.* **Films:** *Beat Girl* (US title *Wild for Kicks*); *Never Let Go; What a Whopper!; Mix Me a Person; Never Let Go; Stardust; McVicar; Foxes.* **TV:** *Oh Boy!* (TV debut); *Drumbeat; Boy Meets Girls; The Adam Faith Show;* title role in *Budgie; Video Video* (presenter); *Just Another Little Blues Song; Alfie; Minder On the Orient Express; Love Hurts.* **Records:** *What Do You Want; Poor Me* (both No 1 singles); *Adam; Beat Girl; Adam Faith; Faith Alive; The Best of Adam Faith; I Survive; 20 Golden Greats* (LPs). **Address:** c/o ICM Duncan Heath Associates.

FALK, *peter*

Peter Falk. Actor. b. New York, USA, 16 September 1927. **Films:** *It's a Mad, Mad, Mad, Mad World; The Great Muppet Caper; The Princess Bride.* **TV:** *Studio One; Kraft Theater; Alcoa Theater; NTA Play of the Week; Armstrong Circle Theater; Omnibus; Robert Montgomery Presents; Brenner; Deadline; Kraft Mystery Theater; Rendezvous; Sunday Showcase; The Untouchables; The Sacco-Vanzetti Story; The Dick Powell Show; The Danny Kaye Show; The Edie Adams Show; The Bob Hope Show; Chrysler Hour; The Trials of O'Brien; Columbo* (1971–77 and 1989, Emmy awards 1972, 1975, 1976); *A Step Out of Line; Griffen and Phoenix; A Love Story* (all TV movies); *The Million Dollar Incident; Brigadoon; A Hatful of Rain; Clue: Movies, Murder and Mystery.* m. 1st Alyce Mayo (dis), 2nd former beauty queen Shera Denes; 2 adopted d. Jackie, Kathy (from 1st m.).

FANCY, *brett*

Brett Fancy. Actor. b. Portsmouth, Hampshire, 4 January 1964. Trained at Guildhall School of Music and Drama (Gold Medal winner). **Theatre:** *The Scarlet Pimpernel; Cavalcade; Antony and Cleopatra; The Spirit of Jack Cade* (one-man Shakespeare show); *Single Spies; Oliver Twist.* **Films:** *Treasure Island.* **TV:** Steve Hood in *Rockliffe's Babies;* Sean Hooper in *Square Deal.* **Address:** c/o Jeremy Conway.

FARMER, *mark*

Mark Farmer. Actor. b. London, 22 May 1962. Trained at the Anna Scher Theatre School. **Theatre:** *The Wally; Undiscovered Country* (National Theatre); *And Miss Reardon Drinks a Little; The Bottom Drawer; The Hunchback of Notre Dame; Loot* (national tour). **Films:** *Memoirs of a Survivor; Mr Corbett's Ghost.* **TV:** *How Green Was My Valley; The World About Us; The Squad; Omnibus: Heinrich Boll; Scene; On Your Bike; Fancy Wanders; Grange Hill; You Must Believe; Triangle; Metal Mickey; Union Castle; Radio; Partners In Crime; Jury; David; Educating Marmalade; Jack and His Computer; Let There Be Love; Shine On Harvey Moon;* title role in *Johnny Jarvis;* John in *Relative Strangers; Minder; On Her Majesty's National Service;* Nigel Bentley in *Glorious Day* (TV movie). **Address:** c/o Anna Scher Theatre Management.

FERGUSSON, *jean*

Jean Fergusson. Actress. **Theatre:** *She Stoops To Conquer; The Odd Couple; Spider's Web; See How They Run; Death of a Salesman; Season's Greetings; It's a Bit Lively Outside; Suddenly At Home; Witness for the Prosecution; Last of the Summer Wine* (all national tours); *Breezeblock Park; On Golden Pond.* **TV:** Helen Ashcroft in *Coronation Street; A Woman of Substance; All Creatures Great and Small;* Caroline Herbert in *Crossroads;* Joyce Tibbs in *The Practice;* Marina in *Last of the Summer Wine.* **Address:** c/o Scott Marshall.

FINLAY, *frank*, CBE

Frank Finlay. Actor. b. Farnworth, Lancashire, 6 August 1926. Trained at RADA. Made CBE, 1984. **Films:** *The Three Musketeers; Return of the Soldier; King of the Wind.* **TV:** *Julius Caesar; Les Miserables; This Happy Breed; The Lie;* title role in *Casanova;* title role in *The Death of Adolf Hitler; Don Quixote; Candide; The Merchant of Venice; A Bouquet of Barbed Wire; Another Bouquet; 84 Charing Cross Road; Saturday, Sunday, Monday; Count Dracula; The Last Campaign; Betzi; Dear Brutus; Tales of the Unexpected; 1001 Nights; Aspects of Love; A Christmas Carol* (TV movie); *Arch of Triumph; In the Secret State; The Verdict On Erebus; Mountain of Diamonds; Encounters, The Other Side.* **Address:** c/o Al Parker. Lives in London. m. former actress and journalist Doreen Shepherd; 2 s. actor Stephen, actor Daniel, 1 d. actress Cathy.

FINNIGAN, *judy*

Judy Finnigan. Presenter. b. Manchester, 16 May 1948. **TV:** Joined Granada TV as a researcher; Anglia Television news reporter; Granada TV news reporter and presenter; *Reports Action; Flying Start; Scramble; Chalkface; ITV Telethon; This Morning* (co-presenter with husband Richard Madeley); *Classic Coronation Street.* **Address:** c/o Granada TV. m. 1st (dis), 2nd co-presenter Richard Madeley; 3 s. Tom, Dan (twins from 1st m.), Jack, 1 d. Chloe.

FIRTH, *colin*

Colin Firth. Actor. b. Grayshott, Hampshire, 10 September 1960. **Theatre:** *Another Country; Doctor's Dilemma.* **Films:** *Another Country; Dutch Girls; 1919; A Month In the Country; Apartment Zero; Valmont.* **TV:** *Camille* (TV movie); *Lost Empires; Tumbledown* (TV movie). **Address:** c/o Julian Belfrage Associates.

FIRTH, *peter*

Peter Firth. Actor. b. Bradford, West Yorkshire, October 1953. **Films:** *Brother Sun and Sister Moon; Aces High; Joseph Andrews; Equus; Tess; Letter To Brezhnev; Chain Reaction; Tree of Hands; Hunt for Red October; The Incident; The Pleasure Principle; Prisoner of Honour; The Perfect Husband.* **TV:** *The Double Deckers; The Flaxton Boys; Castlehaven; Home and Away* (Granada TV series); *The Sullens Sisters; Country Matters; The Simple Life; The Magistrate; The Protectors; Black Beauty; Arthur; Her Majesty's Pleasure; The Ballad of Ben Bagot; The Picture of Dorian Gray; Lady of the Camellias; The Flipside of Dominic Hyde; Another Flip for Dominic; The Aerodrome; Blood Royal; Northanger Abbey; The Way, The Truth, The Video; Murder In Eden; Children Crossing; The Laughter of God.* **Address:** c/o Markham & Froggatt.

FISH, *michael*

Michael Fish. Weather presenter. b. Eastbourne, East Sussex, 27 April 1944. Entered television after experience in the Meteorological Office. **TV:** BBC TV weather forecasts (1974-); *The Sky At Night.* **Address:** c/o BBC TV. m. Susan; 2 d. Alison, Nicola.

FISHER, *jeannie*

Jeannie Fisher. Actress. b. Glasgow, 18 February 1947. Trained at the Royal Scottish Academy of Music and Drama. **Theatre:** Began career as an understudy at the Royal Court Theatre, London; *Double Dealer; The Three Musketeers; Slag; Yarsdale* (1985 Edinburgh Festival); *Macbeth* (tour of India); *Whose Life Is It Anyway?; Blithe Spirit.* **TV:** *The Canterbury Tales; The Silver Sword; Adam Smith; Arthur of the Britons;* Morag Stewart in *Take the High Road.* **Address:** c/o Pat Lovett Agency/Scottish Television. Single; lives in London and Edinburgh. Hobbies: reading, going to the cinema and theatre.

FITZALAN, *marsha*

Marsha Fitzalan. Actress. b. Bonn, West Germany, 10 March. Daughter of the Duke of Norfolk. Trained at the Webber Douglas Academy. **Theatre:** *84 Charing Cross Road.* **Films:** *International Velvet; Anna Karenina; A Handful of Dust.* **TV:** *Pride and Prejudice; Shelley; The Duchess of Duke Street; Armchair Thriller; Something In Disguise; The Professionals; Diamonds; Upstairs, Downstairs; Dick Barton; Angels; Pygmalion; By the Sword Divided; The Comedy of Errors; Three Up, Two Down; Nancy Astor; The Wife's Revenge; Paradise Postponed; Brush Strokes; Inside Story; Hedgehog Wedding; The New Statesman; Soft Soap; Goldeneye* (TV movie). **Address:** c/o CDA. m. actor Patrick Ryecart; 1 s. Frederick, 2 d. Mariella, Jemima.

FITZ-SIMONS, *lesley*

Lesley Fitz-Simons. Actress. b. Glasgow, 23 Septembber 1961. **Theatre:** *The Merchant of Venice; The Kitchen; Mother Goose; Aladdin; Cinderella.* **TV:** BBC Schools; *The Standard; The Camerons; The Prime of Miss Jean Brodie; Playfair; Mendelssohn In Scotland; Annals of the Parish;* Ophelia in *Hamlet; Square Mile of Murder; House on the Hill; The Walls of Jericho; The Spaver Connection; Skin Deep; Funny You Should Say That;* Sheila Ramsay (née Lamont) in *Take the High Road* (1983-); *Play for Today: The Odd Job Man.* **Address:** Young Casting Agency/Scottish Television. m. Peter McIntyre.

FLEESHMAN, *david*

David Fleeshman. Actor. b. Leeds, 11 July 1952. **Theatre:** *Hedda Gabler; Are You Now Or Have You Ever Been; Having a Ball; Waiting for Godot; Milk and Honey; Serious Money; A Month In the Country; Guys and Dolls; Twelfth Night; Wild Oats; Carousel.* **Films:** *The Wall; The Nature of the Beast.* **TV:** Estate agent in *Coronation Street; Dear Enemy; The Practice; The Outsider;* Derek in *Boys From the Blackstuff;* Det Sgt Jones in *Edge of Darkness; Victorian Values; Bulman; One By One;* Frank Taylor in *Truckers; Soldier and Death; The Luddites; Blind Justice;* Gordon Knight in *After the War; Children's Ward;* Stanton in *Capstick's Law; The Ruth Rendell Mysteries; A Bit of a Do;* Charlie Aindow in *Emmerdale; Brookside.* **Address:** c/o RKM. m. actress Sue Jenkins (qv); 1 d. Emily, 1 s. Richard.

FLETCHER, *alexandra*

Alexandra Fletcher. Actress. **TV:** *Why Don't You...?; Cool Cube* (BSB): Jackie Dixon in *Brookside* (1990-). **Address:** c/o Mersey Television.

FLETCHER, *cyril*

Cyril Fletcher. Presenter. b. Watford, Hertfordshire, 25 June 1913. First made his name on radio and TV broadcasting his 'odd odes' in 1936. **Theatre:** London West End revues; London Palladium; pantomimes; summer shows. **TV:** *What's My Line?; That's Life!; Gardening Time* (Central Television); *Cyril Fletcher's TV Garden; Cyril Fletcher's Lifestyle Garden.* **Address:** c/o Central Television. m. actress Betty Astell; 1 d. actress/comedienne Gill Fletcher.

FLETCHER, *dexter*

Dexter Fletcher. Actor. b. North London. **Theatre:** *Summer Party; The Merry Wives of Windsor; The Knight of the Burning Pestle* (both RSC); *A Midsummer Night's Dream* (Glyndebourne); *Peter Pan; Twin Rivals; Henry IV; Hamlet; Henry VI; Derek* (all RSC); *Abbacadabra; Massage; A Midsummer Night's Dream.* **Films:** *Bugsy Malone; 4D Kids; Les Misérables; The Long Good Friday; The Elephant Man; The Bounty; Wings of Death;* Ned the Man in *Revolution;* Young Caravaggio in *Caravaggio; Lionheart; Gothic;* Tom in *The Raggedy Rawney; When the Whales Came; The Rachel Papers; The Mad Monkey; All Out.* **TV:** *Pig Ignorance; Didn't You Kill My Brother?; Across the Lake; The Bill; Boon; Working Week; Down and Out; Out of the Blue;* Spike in *Press Gang* (five series); *Murder Most Horrid; Re-Play: A Future In Fish.* **Address:** c/o Fletcher & Boyce. Lives in North London.

FLYNN, *barbara*

Barbara Flynn. Actress. b. Hastings, East Sussex, 5 August 1948. Trained at Guildhall School of Music and Drama (Gold Medal winner). **Theatre:** *The Philanderer; Plunder; Early Days; Tales From Hollywood; Antigone* (all National Theatre). **Films:** *Britannia Hospital.* **TV:** *Keep It In the Family; Second Chance; A Flight Fund; Murder Most English; Standing In for Henry; Bagthorpes;* Freda Ashton in *A Family At War; Afternoon Dancing; Love On a Gunboat; Maybury; No Visible Scar; The Last Song; Lucky Jim; Where Angels Fear; Barchester Towers; Open All Hours;* Jill Swinburne in *The Beiderbecke Affair, The Beiderbecke Tapes* and *The Beiderbecke Connection;* Dr Rose Marie in *A Very Peculiar Practice; Season's Greetings; Day To Remember; Inspector Morse; Benefactors; The Justice Game.* **Address:** c/o Markham & Froggatt. m. Jeremy Taylor.

FORBES, *natalie*

Natalie Forbes. Actress. b. Doncaster, South Yorkshire, **Theatre:** *Beyond the Rainbow; Outside Edge; The Best Little Whorehouse In Texas; The Collector; Insignificance.* **Films:** *Loss Adjustor; Napoleon and Josephine.* **TV:** *The Other 'Arf; Nanny; The Kelly Monteith Show; The Incredible Mr Tanner; Blood Money; The Gentle Touch; A Ferry Ride Away; Out On the Floor; Full House; Shadow of the Noose.* **Address:** c/o Susan Angel Associates.

FORD, *anna*

Anna Ford. Newscaster. b. Tewkesbury, Gloucestershire, 2 October 1943. Open University staff tutor in Belfast before moving into television. **TV:** *Reports Action* (reporter/researcher); *Man Alive; Tomorrow's World;* ITN newscaster; founder-member of TV-am (presenter of *Good Morning Britain); The Six O'Clock News* (BBC newsreader). Winner, TVTimes Most Popular Female TV Personality, 1978–9. **Address:** c/o Jo Gurnett Management. m. 1st Dr Alan Bittles (dis), 2nd cartoonist and Tatler editor Mark Boxer (dec); 2 d. Claire, Kate (both from 2nd m.).

FORSYTH, *brigit*

Brigit Forsyth. Actress. b. Edinburgh, 28 July. Trained at RADA. **Theatre:** *My Fat Friend; The Norman Conquests; Dusa; Fish, Stas and Vi; Effie's Burning.* **Films:** *The Wrong Side of the Blanket; The Roadbuilder; The Likely Lads; The Crystal Stone.* **TV:** *The Sinners; Adam Smith;* title role in *Holly; The Likely Lads; Graham's Gang; Whatever Happened To the Likely Lads?; I Told You So, Didn't I; The Visit; The Master of Ballantrae; My World; Jackanory; Playhouse: Henry; Glamour Girls; Holding the Fort; Tom, Dick and Harriet; Play for Today: Bizarre and Rummage; Sharon and Elsie; The Practice; Agatha Christie's Poirot; Running Wild; Stanley's Vision; Boon.* **Address:** c/o Jeremy Conway. m. TV director Brian Mills; 1 d. Zoe, 1 s. Ben.

FORSYTH, *bruce*

Bruce Forsyth. Entertainer/Presenter. b. Edmonton, North London, 22 February 1928. **Films:** *Star; Heironymous Merkin; Bedknobs and Broomsticks; The Magnificent Seven Deadly Sins.* **TV:** *Music Hall; Sunday Night At the London Palladium* (host); *The Bruce Forsyth Show; The Canterville Ghost; The Mating Game; The Generation Game; Bring On the Girls; The Muppet Show; Bruce and More Girls; The Entertainers; Bruce Forsyth's Big Night; Play Your Cards Right; Hollywood Or Bust; Slinger's Day* (situation comedy); *Sammy and Bruce; You Bet!; Bruce and Ronnie; Takeover Bid; Bruce Forsyth's Generation Game.* **Address:** c/o Billy Marsh Associates. Lives in Surrey. m. 1st Penny Calvert (dis), 2nd Anthea Redfern (dis), 3rd Wilnelia; 5 d. Deborah, singer Julie, Laura (from 1st m.), Charlotte, Louisa (from 2nd m.), 1 s. Jonathan.

FORSYTHE, *john*

John Forsythe. Actor. b. New Jersey, USA, 29 January 1918. Studied at the New York Actors' Studio. **Theatre:** *Mister Roberts; The Teahouse of the August Moon.* **Films:** *Destination Tokyo; And Justice for All; Goodbye and Amen; Madame X; In Cold Blood; Topaz; The Happy Endings; The Trouble With Harry; Scrooged.* **TV:** *World of Survival* (narrator); *Bachelor Father;* title role in *Charlie's Angels;* Blake Carrington in *Dynasty* (winner, Golden Globe Award for Best Performance In a TV Drama, 1983, 1984). **Address:** c/o Charter Management. m. Julie Warren; 1 s. Dall, 2 d. Page, Brooke.

FOSTER, *barry*

Barry Foster. Actor. b. Beeston, Nottinghamshire, 21 August. Trained at Central School of Speech and Drama. **Films:** *Ryan's Daughter; Frenzy; The Wild Geese; Heat and Dust; Maurice; King of the Wind.* **TV:** *Hamlet; Ghosts; Jack's Horrible Luck; Where the Difference Begins; Dan Dan the Charity Man; Mogul; The Soldier's Tale; A Taste of Honey;* title role in *Van Der Valk; Divorce His/Hers; Fall of Eagles; Old Times; Under Western Eyes; Wingate; The Three Hostages; A Family Affair; Random Moments In a May Garden; Rabbit-Pie Day; Smiley's People; A Woman Called Golda; How Many Miles To Babylon; Death of an Expert Witness; Woyzeck; After Pilkington; Hotel du Lac; Born In the Gardens; Inspector Morse; A Curious Suicide; The Free Frenchman.* **Address:** c/o Al Parker. Lives in Sussex. m. singer Judith Shergold; 2 d. Joanna, Miranda, 1 s. Jason.

FOWLDS, *derek*

Derek Fowlds. Actor. b. Balham, South London, 2 September 1937. Trained at RADA. **Films:** *Smashing Bird I Used To Know; Hotel Paradiso; Tower of Evil; Mistress Pamela; The 'Copter Kids.* **TV:** *The Basil Brush Show* (presenter); *Armchair 30: Captain Video's Story; Edward VII; Last of the Best Men; Captive Audience; The Doll; After That This; Miss Jones and Son; Clayhanger; Robin's Nest; Cribb; Strangers; Triangle; My Son, My Son; Yes Minister; Rings On Their Fingers; Intensive Care; Affairs of the Heart; Yes, Prime Minister; Rules of Enjoyment; Chancer; The Engagement; Die Kinder; Boon; Van Der Valk; Perfect Scoundrels.* **Address:** c/o CDA. m. (dis); 2 s. James, Jeremy.

FOWLER, *barry*, MBE

Henry James Fowler. Actor/Producer. b. Lambeth Walk, London, 10 December 1926. (MBE, 1970.) **Films:** *In Town Tonight; Champagne Charlie; Went the Day Well; Hue and Cry; I Believe In You; The Longest Day; Lawrence of Arabia; The Pickwick Papers; Ladies Who Do; The Prince and the Pauper; Chicago Joe and the Showgirl.* **TV:** Corporal Flogger Hoskins in *The Army Game; Our Man At St Mark's; Get This; Harry's Kingdom; Stalingrad; World's End; Dead Ernest; Entertainment Express; Dramarama; Me and the Girls; Scarecrow & Mrs King; Supergran; A Roller Next Year; Body Contact; Davro's Sketch Pad; In Sickness and In Health; The Bill.* TV commercials: Soap Sunlight; Asda; McVitie's biscuits; British Telecom; plus voice-overs. **Address:** c/o Essanay. Lives in London. m. Catherine. Hobbies: Tennis, toy collecting. **Favourite TV programme:** *Rab C Nesbitt.*

FOXWORTH, *robert*

Robert Foxworth. Actor. b. Huston, Texas, USA, 1 November 1941. Trained at Stratford University Contemporary Theater Workshop. **Theatre:** *The Crucible* (winner, *Theatre World* award); *Antony and Cleopatra.* **Films:** *Damien – Omen II; Airport '77; Treasure of Matecumba; The Black Marble; Prophecy.* **TV:** *The Questor Tapes; The FBI Versus Alvin Karpis; Mrs Sundance; The Devil's Daughter; The Memory of Eva Ryker; Act of Love; The Acts of Peter and Paul* (all TV movies); *Frankenstein; James Dean; It Happened At Lakewood Manor; Death Moon; Sadbird; The Storefront Lawyers; Hogan's Goat; Another Part of the Forest;* Chase Gioberti in *Falcon Crest.* **Address:** c/o International Creative Management. Lives with actress Elizabeth Montgomery; 1 s., 1 d.

FOY, *julie*

Julie Foy. Actress. b. Bolton, Lancashire, 5 May 1970. Trained at the College of Performing Arts, Salford. **Theatre:** Carol in *Our Day Out;* Jo in *A Taste of Honey;* Ruby Birtle in *When We Are Married.* **Films:** *Strapless.* **TV:** *Jossy's Giants* (two series while still at school); *Dramarama: Forever Young;* Gina Seddon in *Coronation Street* (1988); Deirdre in *How To Be Cool; 4-Play: Dawn and the Candidate; Press Gang; Missing Persons.* **Address:** c/o PBR Management. Single; lives in South London.

FRANCES, *cornelia*

Cornelia Frances. Actress. b. Liverpool, 7 April 1941. Trained at Guildhall School of Music and Drama, before emigrating to Australia. **Theatre:** *Look Back In Anger; Blythe Spirit; Boeing, Boeing.* **Films:** *Outbreak of Hostilities; All At Sea; Last Rites.* **TV:** Sister Grace Scott in *The Young Doctors;* Barbara Hamilton in *Sons and Daughters;* Morag Bellingham in *Home and Away.* **Address:** c/o Barbara Leane and Associates. m. Michael Eastland; 1 s. Lawrence.

FRANCES, *paula*

Paula Frances Muldoon. Actress. b. Liverpool, 7 September 1969. Trained at the Merseyside Dance and Drama Centre; took a theatre arts course at the Liverpool Theatre School. **Theatre:** Danced with Crazy Midnight Dancers international cabaret show on tour of Finland and Italy; *Once a Catholic; Charley's Aunt; The Passion; Chamber Music; The Matchgirls; Mime and Mask.* **TV:** Diana Spence in *Brookside* (1990-). **Address:** c/o Chiltern Casting. Single; lives in Liverpool. Pets: A cat called Bette. Hobbies: Teaching step aerobics and callanetics, going to the theatre and cinema. **Favourite TV programme:** *The Cosby Show; The Dame Edna Experience.*

FRANCIS, *clive*

Clive Francis. Actor. b. London, 1946. **Films:** *Inspector Clouseau; Villain; The Man Who Had Power Over Women; Clockwork Orange; Girl Stroke Boy.* **TV:** *David Copperfield; Poldark; Entertaining Mr Sloane; Masada; Bulman; The Rear Column; The Critic; The Far Pavilions; Dorothy L Sayers; As You Like It; Sherlock Holmes; Amy; Oedipus At Colonus; The Bretts; Quartermain's Terms; May To December; Yes, Prime Minister; Old Flames; The Piglet Files.* **Address:** c/o Ken McReddie.

FRANCIS, *jan*

Jan Francis. Actress. b. London, 5 August 1951. Trained as a dancer and performed with the Royal Ballet, before becoming an actress. **Theatre:** *The Farmer's Wife.* **Films:** *Dracula; Champions.* **TV:** *Hawkeye the Pathfinder; Anne of Green Gables; Lonely Man's Lover; Sutherland's Law; Village Hall; Looking for Clancy; The Launderette; Love's Labour's Lost; Rooms; London Assurance; The Duchess of Duke Street; Raffles; Premier; Secret Army; The Party of the First Part; The Racing Game; Ripping Yarns; Target; Casting the Runes; Play for Love; The Good Companions; Tales of the Unexpected; A Chance To Sit Down; Jackanory; The Corvini Inheritance;* Penny in *Just Good Friends;* Sally Hardcastle in *Stay Lucky.* **Address:** c/o Julian Belfrage Associates. m. Martin C Thurley.

FRANKAU, *nicholas*

Nicholas Frankau. Actor. b. Stockport, Cheshire, 16 July 1954. Trained at the Webber Douglas Academy. **Theatre:** *Peter Pan* (Shaftesbury Theatre). **Films:** *Plenty; Gunbus.* **TV:** *'Allo 'Allo!; Play for Today: The Last Term; I Remember Nelson; C.A.T.S. Eyes; Paradise Postponed.* **Address:** c/o Joyce Edwards.

FRANKLIN, *gretchen*

Gretchen Gordon Franklin. Actress. b. Covent Garden, London, 7 July 1911. **TV:** *Crossroads; I Didn't Know You Cared; Churchill's People; George and Mildred; Nicholas Nickleby; Some Mothers Do 'Ave 'Em; Lively Arts; Hazell; The Sweeney; The One and Only Phyllis Dixey; Rising Damp; Jackanory; Danger UXB; General Hospital; The Other One; Quatermass; Jekyll and Hyde; Fox; Potter; The Harry Worth Show; The Dick Emery Show; You're Only Young Twice; The Other 'Arf; The Kelly Monteith Show; Dead Earnest; Hallelujah; Maybury; Blackadder; In Loving Memory; Return To Waterloo; Victoria Wood;* Ethel Skinner in *EastEnders* (1985-). **Address:** c/o Barry Burnett Organisation. Lives in Barnes, south-west London. m. writer Caswell Garth (dec). Pets: Dog called Urney. Hobbies: Needlework, gardening, animals. **Favourite TV programme:** *Yes, Prime Minister.*

FRANKLYN, *sabina*

Sabina Franklyn. Actress. b. London, 15 September. Daughter of actor William Franklyn (qv). **Theatre:** *The Man Most Likely To ...; Charley's Aunt; Move Over, Mrs Markham; Duty Free* (London West End and National Theatre); *The Moving Finger; The Rivals.* **TV:** *Pride and Prejudice; Fawlty Towers; The Kelly Monteith Show; Strangers; Dave Allen Special; When the Boats Comes In; The Mike Yarwood Show; The Jim Davidson Show; Terry and June; Byron; Happy Ever After; Return of The Saint; Blake's 7; A Personal Tour; Keep It In the Family; Moving Finger; Full House; Miss Marple; The Worst Witch; All Creatures Great and Small.* **Address:** c/o Michael Ladkin Personal Management. m. John Challis.

FRANKLYN, *william*

William Franklyn. Actor. b. Kensington, West London, 22 September 1926. **Theatre:** *My Sister Eileen; Arsenic and Old Lace; The Love of Four Colonels; Deathtrap; In Praise of Love; Dead Ringer; Springtime for Henry; Guilty Conscience.* **Films:** *The Nutcracker.* **TV:** *Top Secret; No Wreath for the General; No Cloak, No Dagger; Paradise Island; What's On Next?; Master Spy; Steam Video Company; The Purple Twilight; Moon and Son.* TV commercials: Schweppes. **Address:** c/o Hobson's Personal Management. m. 1st actress Margot Johns (dis), 2nd actress Susanna Carroll; 3 d. actress Sabina (qv) (from 1st m.), Francesca, Melissa.

FRANKS, *philip*

Philip Franks. Actor. Former member of Oxford University Dramatic Society. **Theatre:** *Timon of Athens; Edward II; The Jungle Book; Heroes; Romeo and Juliet; Antony and Cleopatra; The Mad Woman of Chaillot; Much Ado About Nothing; Ivanov* (both Strand Theatre); *Seven Lears* (Crucible Theatre, Sheffield, Haymarket Theatre, Leicester, and Royal Court Theatre); *I Have Been Here Before; Victory.* RSC: *A Midsummer Night's Dream; Titus Andronicus; All's Well That Ends Well; Henry VI; The Winter's Tale; Peter Pan; Every Man In His Humour; The Art of Success; Worlds Apart;* title role in *Hamlet; The Comedy of Errors* (both national tours). **TV:** *To Serve Them All My Days; Love Is Old, Love Is New; Bleak House; The Murderers Among Us; Shadow of the Noose; The Green Man;* Charley in *The Darling Buds of May.* **Address:** c/o Richard Stone Partnership.

FRANZ, *dennis*

Dennis Franz. Actor. b. Chicago, Illinois, USA, 28 October. Member of the Organic Theater Company at Southern Illinois University. **Theatre:** *Bleacher Bums* (winner, Emmy award). **Films:** *Body Double; The Fury; Popeye; Blowout; Psycho II; Dressed To Kill; Remember My Name; A Fine Mess; A Perfect Couple.* **TV:** *Simon & Simon; Hunter; The A-Team; Hardcastle and McCormick; Riptide; T J Hooker; MacGruder and Loud; E.R.; Chicago Story; Bay City Blues; Deadly Messages;* Lieutenant Norman Buntz in *Hill Street Blues.* **Address:** c/o Gores/Fields Talent Agency.

FRASER, *liz*

Liz Fraser. Actress. b. London, 14 August 1935. Trained at the London School of Dramatic Art. **Films:** *Wonderful Things; I'm All Right, Jack; Two-Way Stretch; The Rebel; Double Bunk; Carry On Regardless; The Painted Smile; Live Now, Pay Later; The Americanisation of Emily; The Family Way; Dad's Army; Adventures of a Taxi Driver; Confessions of a Driving Instructor; Under the Doctor; Adventures of a Private Eye; Confessions From a Holiday Camp; Rosie Dixon, Night Nurse; Chicago Joe and the Showgirl; The Lady and the Highwayman.* **TV:** *Up the Junction; Sight Unseen; Rumpole of the Bailey; The Rockers; Robin's Nest; The Professionals; Shroud for a Nightingale; Fairly Secret Army; Hardwicke House; Miss Marple; Nemesis; Rude Health; Eskimos Do It; Capstick's Law; Streetwise; The Bill; Birds of a Feather.* **Address:** c/o AM Artists.

FREEMAN, *jane*

Jane Freeman. Actress. **Theatre:** Repertory theatre in York, Bournemouth, Dundee, Cardiff, Nottingham, Westcliff-on-Sea, Colchester, Leatherhead, Salisbury and Birmingham; *When We Are Married; Noises Off; Habeas Corpus; Situation Comedy* (all national tours); *The Importance of Being Earnest; Jack and the Beanstalk.* **Films:** *Who Dares Wins; Scrubbers; The Swimming Pool.* **TV:** *Diary of a Young Man; Crossroads; The Fishing Party; Within These Walls; Maybury; Ghost In the Water; Androcles and the Lion; Letty;* Mrs Kimble in *Silas Marner;* Helen in *A Taste of Honey; Hannah; Zigger Zagger; Lynsey;* Tully Applebottom in *Blackadder; The Hard Word;* Ivy in *Last of the Summer Wine.* **Address:** c/o Saraband Associates.

FREEMAN, *paul*

Paul Freeman. Actor. b. Barnet, Hertfordshire, 18 January 1943. Trained at the New College of Speech and Drama. **Theatre:** National Theatre; RSC; Royal Court Theatre. **Films:** *The Dogs of War; The Long Good Friday; Raiders of the Lost Ark; The Sender; Prisoner of Rio; Without a Clue; New Wine; Flight To Berlin; Shanghai Surprise; The Ronald Biggs Story; Sherlock and Me; The Last Island; Eminent Domain; A World Apart.* **TV:** *Winston Churchill – The Wilderness Years; Death of a Princess; Falcon Crest; Sins* (mini-series); *Yesterday's Dreams; Cagney and Lacey; Sakharov; Willie's Last Stand; The Index Goes Fishing; The Paris Paradox.* **Address:** c/o Ken McReddie. m. Maggie Scott; 1 d. Lucy.

FRENCH, *dawn*

Dawn French. Actress/Comedienne. Trained at Central School of Speech and Drama. Teamed up with Jennifer Saunders after a brief spell as a teacher. **Theatre:** *When I Was a Girl I Used To Scream and Shout; An Evening With French and Saunders; The Secret Policeman's Biggest Ball; Silly Cow.* **Films:** *Supergrass.* **TV:** *Five Go Mad In Dorset; Five Go Mad On Mescalin; Slags; Summer School; Private Enterprise; Consuela; Mr Jolly Lives Next Door; Bad News Tour; Strike; South Atlantic Raiders; GLC; Oxford; Spaghetti Hoops; Le Kiss* (all *The Comic Strip Presents . . .* TV films); *Girls On Top; Happy Families; French and Saunders; The Storyteller: Sapsorrow; Swank* (presenter); *Scoff* (presenter); *Ipso Facto; Murder Most Horrid.* **Books:** *French Knits; A Feast of French & Saunders.* **Address:** c/o Peters Fraser & Dunlop. m. comedian-actor Lenny Henry.

FRENCH, *victor*

Victor French. Actor. b. Santa Barbara, California, USA. Trained in New York with Uta Hagen and William Hickey. **TV:** *Little House On the Prairie; Gunsmoke; Get Smart; Bonanza; The Hero; Carter Country; Highway To Heaven.* **Address:** c/o David Shapira & Associates. m. 1st (dis), 2nd Julie Cobb (dis); 2 d. Lee Tracy, Lee Kelly (twins, from 1st m.), 1 s. Victor Allyn (from 2nd m.)

FREUD, *emma*

Emma Freud. Presenter. b. London, 25 January 1962. Daughter of MP Clement Freud. Drama degree from Bristol and London Universities, then worked as a journalist, composer, actress, singing telegram courier, magician's assistant and co-director of the Open Air Theatre, Regent's Park. **TV:** *Roundabout; The Six O'Clock Show* (LWT); *Pillowtalk* (Night Network); *Plunder; The Media Show; Drop the Dead Donkey* (acting herself). **Radio:** *Loose Ends.* **Address:** c/o Noel Gay Artists.

FRID, *amelia*

Amelia Frid. Actress. b. 30 July 1975. Russian. **Films:** *The Necromancer; Celia.* **TV:** Molly in *Adventures On Kythera;* Cody Willis in *Neighbours* (1990-). **Address:** c/o Maggie Jacques Promotions/Grundy Television.

FROST, *david*, OBE

David Paradine Frost. Presenter. b. Tenterden, Kent, 7 April 1939. **TV:** *This Week; Let's Twist On the Riviera; That Was the Week That Was; Not So Much a Programme, More a Way of Life; The Frost Report; The Frost Programme; The Wilson Interviews; At Last the 1948 Show* (producer); *No, That's Me Over Here* (producer); *David Frost Presents the Guinness Book of Records; The Beatles – Once Upon a Time; The Nixon Interviews; The Ordeal of Patty Hearst; The Remarkable Mrs Sanger* (both TV movies, producer); *Elvis – He Touched Their Lives; The Shah Speaks; Through the Keyhole;* founder-member of TV-am (presenter of *Good Morning Britain* and *David Frost On Sunday*); *The Next President.* **Address:** c/o David Paradine Productions, 115/123 Bayham Street, London NW1. m. actress Lynne Frederick (dis), Lady Carina Fitzalan-Howard; 3 s. Miles, Wilfred, George.

FRY, *stephen*

Stephen Fry. Actor/Comedian/Writer. b. Hampstead, North London, 24 August 1957. Member of Cambridge Footlights before turning professional. **Theatre:** *Me and My Girl; Latin; Bulldog Drummond* (all as playwright). **Films:** *The Good Father; A Handful of Dust; A Fish Called Wanda; The Secret Policeman's Third Ball.* **TV:** *Alfresco; The Young Ones; Alas Smith and Jones; Filthy Rich and Catflap; Blackadder II; The Crystal Cube; The Tube; Saturday Live; Whose Line Is it Anyway?; Blackadder Goes Forth; A Bit of Fry and Laurie; Grand Master Clash; Jeeves and Wooster; Old Flames; This Is David Lander.* **Radio:** *Loose Ends; Delve Special.* **Address:** c/o Noel Gay Artists.

FULLERTON, *fiona*

Fiona Fullerton. Actress. b. Kaduna, Nigeria, 10 October 1956. **Theatre:** *Cinderella* (London Palladium); *Something's Afoot* (Hong Kong); *Caught Napping; I Am a Camera; Barnardo* (Royalty Theatre); *The Beggar's Opera* (Lyric Theatre); *Gypsy; Camelot; The Boy Friend; The Royal Baccarat Scandal* (Chichester Festival and Haymarket Theatre Royal). **Films:** *Run Wild, Run Free* (aged 11); *Nicholas and Alexandra; Alice's Adventures In Wonderland; The Human Factor; A View To a Kill; A Ghost In Monte Carlo; A Girl Called Harry.* **TV:** *A Friend Indeed; Angels; Gaugin – The Savage; Lev Tolstoy; A Question of Faith; Strange But True; Hold the Dream; The Charmer; A Hazard of Hearts; Hemingway; A Taste for Death; Goldeneye; Shaka Zulu; To Be the Best.* **Address:** c/o London Management.

GAMBON, michael

Michael Gambon. Actor. b. Dublin, Ireland, 19 October 1940. **Theatre:** *Otherwise Engaged; The Norman Conquests; Just Between Ourselves; Zoo Story; Alice's Boys; Betrayal; Close of Play;* title role in *Galileo* (National Theatre); title role in *King Lear;* title role in *Antony and Cleopatra; Betrayal; Tales From Hollywood; A Chorus of Disapproval; Richard III; A View From the Bridge.* **Films:** *The Beast Must Die; Turtle Diary; Paris By Night; A Dry White Season; The Rachel Papers; The Cook, The Thief, His Wife and Her Lover; The Heat of the Day.* **TV:** *The Challengers; The Borderers; Eyeless In Gaza; The Seagull; The Other One; La Ronde; The Breadwinner; Ghosts; Oscar Wilde; The Holy Experiment; Absurd Person Singular; The Singing Detective; The Heat of the Day; Minder; The Storyteller; Jim Henson's Greek Myths;* title role in *Maigret.* **Address:** Larry Dalzell Associates.

GARDEN, graeme

Graeme Garden. Actor/Writer. b. Aberdeen, Grampian, 18 February 1943. Member of Cambridge Footlights Revue while at university. **TV:** *Twice a Fortnight; Broaden Your Mind; Doctor In the House* and *Doctor At Large* (co-writer); *Orson's Bag* (actor and writer); *The Goodies* (actor and co-writer); *Charlie's Climbing Tree; Tell the Truth; A Sense of the Past; Bodymatters* (presenter); *Astronauts* (co-writer). **Radio:** *I'm Sorry I'll Read That Again; I'm Sorry I Haven't a Clue* (both as writer). **Records:** *The In Betweenies/Father Christmas Do Not Touch Me; Funky Gibbon; Black Pudding Bertha; Nappy Love/Wild Thing; Make a Daft Noise for Christmas* (all with The Goodies). **Books:** *The Seventh Man; Skylighters; Very Silly Games.* **Address:** c/o Roger Hancock. m. Emma; 1 d. Sally, 2 s. John, Tom.

GARNER, james

James Garner. Actor. b. Oklahoma, USA, 7 April 1928. **Films:** *The Caine Mutiny Court Martial; Darby's Rangers; Marlowe; Support Your Local Sheriff; Dual At Diablo; Grand Prix; Victor/Victoria; The Fan; Murphy's Romance; Sunset.* **TV:** *Cheyenne; Maverick;* Jim Rockford in *The Rockford Files; Heart Sounds; Space; Promise.* **Address:** c/o International Creative Management. m. actress Lois Clarke; 1 d. Greta, 1 step-d. Kimberly.

GARWOOD, patricia

Patricia Garwood. Actress. b. Paignton, Devon, 28 January 1941. Trained at RADA. **Theatre:** *Woman In Mind; Letters Home; Come Back To the Five and Dime Jimmy Dean, Jimmy Dean; The Watcher; Sauce for the Goose; Steel Magnolias.* **Films:** *The Lavender Hill Mob* (aged nine). **TV:** *No Place Like Home; The Brack Report; Sherlock Holmes; C.A.T.S. Eyes; Lytton's Diary; Love and Marriage.* **Address:** c/o William Morris Agency. m. playwright Jeremy Paul; 4 d. Amanda, Tara, Sasha, Sophie.

GASCOIGNE, bamber

Bamber Gascoigne. Presenter. b. London, 24 January 1935. Scholarship to Yale School of Drama and later drama critic of *The Spectator* and *The Observer.* **TV:** *University Challenge* (quizmaster, 1962–87); *The Christians; Victorian Values; Man and Music; The Great Moghuls; Connoisseur* (quizmaster); *Brother Felix and the Virgin Saint.* **Books:** *World Theatre; The Great Moghuls; Treasures and Dynasties of China; Murgatreud's Empire; The Heyday; The Christians; Quest for the Golden Hare; How To Identify Prints.* **Address:** c/o Curtis Brown. m. Christina Ditchburn.

GASCOINE, *jill*

Jill Gascoine. Actress. b. Lambeth, South London, 11 April 1937. Trained at the Italia Conti Academy. **Theatre:** Repertory theatre in Nottingham, Dundee, Glasgow, Worthing, Hornchurch and Leicester; *42nd Street* (London West End). **Films:** *Pure Hell of St Trinian's; Confessions of a Pop Performer.* **TV:** *Dr Finlay's Casebook; Rooms; Plays for Britain; General Hospital; The Norman Wisdom Show; Three Kisses; Balzac; Z-Cars; Six Days of Justice; Dixon of Dock Green; Within These Walls; Holding On; Raffles; The Trigger; General Hospital; Justice; Peter Pan; Beryl's Lot; Softly, Softly; Oranges and Lemons; The Onedin Line; Rooms; The Gentle Touch; C.A.T.S. Eyes; Taggart; El C.I.D; Boon.* Winner, *TVTimes* Best Actress On TV award, 1984. **Address:** c/o Marina Martin Management. m. 2nd actor Alfred Molina (qv); 2 s. Sean, Adam.

GAUNT, *william*

William Gaunt. Actor. b. Pudsey, West Yorkshire, 3 April 1937. Child actor with Otley Little Theatre, then trained at RADA. **Theatre:** Dallas Theater Center, Texas; directed productions in Birmingham, Coventry and Cheltenham; artistic director, Liverpool Playhouse (1979–81); *Boys In the Band; The Flip Side; When Did You Last See Your Trousers?; Run for Your Wife* (all London West End). **Films:** *The Revolutionary.* **TV:** *54 Minute Theatre; Waiting for Wanda; Climate of Fear; Probation Officer; Harper's West One; Sergeant Cork; Softly, Softly; The Champions; Holly; The Saint; Cottage to Let; Nobody's House; The Foundation; Crown Court; Love and Marriage; No Place Like Home; Capstick's Law; Gentlemen's Club; Claire; Jury; Lucifer.* **Address:** c/o Julia MacDermot. m. actress Carolyn Lyster; 1 d. Tilly, 1 s. Albie.

GAYLE, *michelle*

Michelle Patricia Gayle. Actress. b. London, 2 February 1971. Trained at the Barbara Speake Stage School from the age of nine. **Theatre:** Title role in *Cinderella* (Theatre Royal, Stratford East); Susan in *Torn Apart.* **TV:** *The Biz; Splash!; No Adults Allowed;* Fiona Wilson in *Grange Hill;* Hattie Tavernier in *EastEnders* (1990-). **Address:** c/o CSM (Artistes)/BBC Elstree Centre. Single; lives in Wembley, Middlesex. Hobbies: Songwriting, singing, reading, listening to music. **Favourite TV programme:** *LA Law; thirtysomething.*

GEE-DARE, *vikki*

Vikki Gee-Dare. Actress/Sign-language interpreter. b. London, 29 November. Trained at Arts Educational School and Actors' Institute. **Theatre:** Lydia in *Children of a Lesser God* (RSC); Queenie in *This Happy Breed;* interpreted performances at the National Theatre, Soho Poly and Lyric, Hammersmith. **TV:** *The Two Ronnies; The Duchess of Duke Street; The Little Mermaid;* WPC Suzanne Ford in *The Bill.* **Address:** c/o Spotlight. Single. Hobbies: Reading, diving, theatre, cinema, country walks, looking around junk shops, listening to music, going out to dinner. **Favourite TV programme:** *Cheers; The Golden Girls; A Bit of a Do; Doctor Who; Lovejoy.*

GETTY, *estelle*

Estelle Getty. Actress. b. New York, USA, 25 July 1923. Trained at Herbert Berghof Studios. **Theatre:** *The Divorce of Judy and Jane; Widows and Children First; Table Settings; Demolition of Hannah Fay; Never Too Old; A Box of Tears; Hidden Corners; I Don't Know Why I'm Screaming; Under the Bridge; There's a Lonely Place; Light Up the Sky; Pocketful of Posies; Fits and Starts; Torch Song Trilogy; If I Knew What I Know Now ...So What?* (writer). **Films:** *Tootsie; The Chosen; Protocol; Mask; Mannequin.* **TV:** *No Man's Land; Victims for Victims; The Teresa Saldana Story; Copacabana* (all TV movies); *Cagney and Lacey; Nurse; Baker's Dozen; One of the Boys; Fantasy Island;* Sophia in *The Golden Girls* (Golden Globe Best Actress In a Comedy award). **Address:** c/o Harris & Goldberg Talent Agency. m. Arthur Gettleman; 2 s. Barry, Carl.

GHOSH, *shreela*

Shreela Ghosh. Actress. b. Shillong, India, 25 September 1962. Came to Britain aged 11. **Theatre:** *The Great Celestial Cow; Doolaly Days*. **Films:** *No Nationality, No Virginity*. **TV:** *The Jewel In the Crown; Pravina's Wedding; The Chinese Detective; The Prince and the Demons; Me & My Girl*; Naima Jeffery in *EastEnders* (1985–7). **Address:** c/o CDA. m. film director Jonathan Curling; 1 d. Shehnai (from a previous relatonship).

GIBSON, *richard*

Richard Gibson. Actor. b. Kampala, Uganda, 1 January 1954. Trained at Central School of Speech and Drama. **Theatre:** *In Praise of Love; Candida; French Without Tears; The Winslow Boy; Love's Labour's Lost; The Browning Version; The Scheming Lieutenant; 'Allo 'Allo!* (Prince of Wales Theatre and London Palladium). **Films:** *England Made Me; The Go-Between*. **TV:** *Tom Brown's Schooldays; The Children of the New Forest; Secret Diaries; Hadleigh; Wainwright's Law; Poldark; Penmarric; Prospects; The Key To Rebecca; Park Ranger; My Father's House; Four On Four; The Gate of Eden; Coral Island*; Herr Flick in *'Allo 'Allo!* **Address:** c/o Creative Talent Management.

GIELGUD, *sir john*

John Gielgud. Actor/Director. b. London, 14 April 1904. Great-nephew of actress Dame Ellen Terry. **Films:** *Julius Caesar; Saint Joan; Richard III; Becket; Murder On the Orient Express; Arthur; Gandhi; Plenty; Arthur 2*. **TV:** *A Day By the Sea; No Man's Land; The Cherry Orchard; Ivanov; The Mayfly and the Frog; Deliver Us From Evil; Edward VII; Tales of the Unexpected; Why Didn't They Ask Evans?; English Gardens; Brideshead Revisited; Parson's Pleasure; Inside the Third Reich; Vatican Pimpernel; The Far Pavilions; The Master of Ballantrae; Frankenstein; Camille; Romance On the Orient Express; War and Remembrance; A Man for All Seasons; Getting it Right; Summer's Lease; The Best of Friends*. **Books:** *Early Stages* (autobiography); *Stage Directions; Distinguished Company; An Actor and His Time*. **Address:** c/o ICM.

GILES, *annabel*

Annabel Claire Giles. Presenter. b. Griffithstown, Gwent, 20 May 1959. Temporary secretary for advertising agencies (1977–82), became a model (1982–6), then a TV presenter (1986–). **TV:** *Razzmatazz; Going Live!; Night Network; The Showbizz Show; Jameson Tonight* (Sky TV); *Help Squad; Posh Frocks and New Trousers* (two series); *Head Over Heels; The New Look* (acting role in film short); *Telethon '90; Blind Date; TV Weekly; 60something; This Morning*. Guest appearances: *Kilroy; The Time, The Place; The Cool Cube* (BSB); *Tell the Truth; Give Us a Clue; It'll Be Alright On the Night; Power Station* (BSB); *Comic Relief; Cluedo; You Bet!* **Address:** c/o Hamper-Neafsey Associates. Lives in London. m. rock musician Midge Ure (dis); 1 d. Molly. **Favourite TV programme:** *Brookside*.

GILLAN, *andrew*

Andrew Gillan. Actor. b. Glasgow, 7 February 1966. Trained at the Royal Scottish Academy of Music and Drama. **Theatre:** *The Gorbals Story; Vodka and Daisies; Greedy Giant; Mother Goose*. **TV:** *Taggart;* Tee Jay Wilson in *Take the High Road* (1990–92). **Commercial:** *The Phantom of the Opera* (German cinema). **Address:** c/o Pat Lovett Agency/Scottish Television. Single. Hobbies: Swimming, writing music, reading.

GILLESPIE, *robert*

Robert Gillespie. Actor/Director/Writer. b. Lille, France, 9 November 1933. Trained at RADA. **TV:** *The Black Brigand; Miss Em; Hotel Paradiso; The Queen and the Rebels; Maigret; Kipling; Crane; Danger Island; The Gamblers; Romeo and Juliet; The Drinking Party; Lord Peter Wimsey; Hugh and I; Mr Digby, Darling; New Scotland Yard; The Adventurers; Whatever Happened To the Likely Lads?; Freewheelers; Sadie, It's Cold Outside; The Good Life; Couples; Rising Damp; Warship; Rosie; Robin's Nest; It Ain't Half Hot Mum; George and Mildred; Angels; Butterflies; The Fall and Rise of Reginald Perrin; Agony; Mary's Wife; Secret Army; Keep It In the Family; I Woke Up One Morning; The Sweeney; The New Avengers; Van Der Valk; The Professionals; Return of The Saint; Sherlock Holmes; Blind Justice; Starting Out; Inmates; Heil Honey I'm Home.* **Address:** c/o William Morris Agency.

GILMORE, *susan*

Susan Gilmore. Actress. b. London, 24 November 1954. Trained at Bristol Old Vic Theatre School. **Theatre:** *The Beastly Beatitudes of Balthazar B.* **TV:** *Angels; Maelstrom; Howards' Way.* **Address:** c/o Joy Jameson. m. Daniel Topolski; 1 d. Emma.

GITTINS, *jeremy*

Phillip Jeremy Gittins. Actor. b. Manchester, 30 January 1956. Trained at Guildhall School of Music and Drama. **Theatre:** Rocky in *The Rocky Horror Show* (Comedy Theatre); *Mata Hari; Soft Shoe Shuffle; Asterix;* Frank N Furter in *The Rocky Horror Show; Not Later Than Six* (Young Vic Theatre); *Risky Kisses; Love All; Count Dracula; Company; A Slight Hangover.* **TV:** *Tenko; Doctor Who; The Kenny Everett Show; Andy Capp; The Kit Curran Show; Tales of the Unexpected; Radio Pictures; All In Good Faith; Fresh Fields; Wink Three Times; Terry and June; Matlock; Boon; Blackadder Goes Forth; Wish You Were Here...?; Lazarus and Dingwall; Keeping Up Appearances.* **Address:** c/o Barry Burnett Organisation. Lives in Kingston, Surrey. m. Sara; 1 d. Hayley. Hobbies: Playing the piano, cooking, squash. **Favourite TV programme:** *Coronation Street.*

GLAISTER, *gabrielle*

Gabrielle Glaister. Actress. b. Moreton-in-Marsh, Gloucestershire. Studied English and drama at Chichester College; member of the National Youth Theatre. **Theatre:** Repertory theatre; *Twelfth Night; The Caucasian Chalk Circle; Saved; Insignificance; The Rivals; Private Lives; Habeas Corpus;* title role in *Daisy Pulls It Off* (Globe Theatre); *Dandy Dick; Great Expectations* (Old Vic Theatre); *The Real Thing* (British Council international tour). **Films:** *The Class of Miss MacMichael.* **TV:** *The Ben Elton Show; The Franchise Affair; Casualty; Grange Hill; Rockliffe's Babies;* 'Bob' in *Blackadder II* and *Blackadder III; Happy Families; Jury; Jane Eyre; Have a Heart; Play Away; Houseparty; All At No 20; Wish Me Luck; London's Burning; Mitch; The Man From Auntie;* Patricia Farnham in *Brookside* (1990-). **Address:** c/o LWA/Mersey Television.

GLEN, *iain*

Iain Glen. Actor. b. Edinburgh, 24 June 1961. Trained at RADA (Bancroft Gold Medal winner). **Films:** Wallace in *Paris By Night;* John Hanning Speke in *Mountains of the Moon;* Larry Winters in *Silent Scream;* Willie Quinton in *Fools of Fortune.* **TV:** *Blood Hunt;* 'Sailor' in *Will You Love Me Tomorrow; The Picnic;* Carl Galton in *The Fear;* title role in *Adam Bede.* **Address:** c/o ICM Duncan Heath Associates.

GLESS, *sharon*

Sharon Gless. Actress. b. Los Angeles, California, USA, 31 May 1943. **Films:** *The Star Chamber.* **TV:** *Centennial* (mini-series); *The Longest Night; All My Darling Daughters; My Darling Daughters' Aniversary; The Immigrants; The Scream of Eagles; The Last Convertible; Hardhat and Legs; The Kids Who Knew Too Much; Moviola; The Miracle of Kathy Miller; Palms; Hobson's Choice; The Sky's The Limit; Letting Go; The Outside Woman* (all TV movies); *Marcus Welby, MD; Faraday and Co; Switch; Turnabout; House Calls;* Cagney in *Cagney and Lacey* (two Emmy awards); title role in *The Trials of Rosie O'Neill.* **Address:** c/o Creative Artists Agency.

GLOVER, *brian*

Brian Glover. Actor. b. Sheffield, South Yorkshire, 2 April 1934. Previously a teacher and professional wrestler. **Theatre:** *Much Ado About Nothing; The Passion* (National Theatre); *La Cage Aux Folles; The Resistible Rise of Arturo Ui.* **Films:** *Kes; Brannigan; O Lucky Man!; Quilp; Jabberwocky; Joseph Andrews; Trial By Combat; The Great Train Robbery; An American Werewolf In London; Britannia Hospital; Red Monarch; To Kill a Priest; Kafka.* **TV:** *Rank and File; The Frighteners; A Day Out; Speech Day; The Regiment; Porridge; Initiation; You'll Never Walk Alone; Dixon of Dock Green; Waiting At the Field Gate; The Wild Bunch; The Secret Army; Return of The Saint; Sounding Brass; Minder; Friday Night, Saturday Morning; Educating Marmalade Atkins; Foxy Lady; Campion; Bottom.* **Address:** c/o Felix de Wolfe. m. (dis); 1 d. Maxine, 1 s. Gus.

GLOVER, *julian*

Julian Glover. Actor. b. London, 27 March 1935. Trained at RADA. **Theatre:** RSC; *Habeas Corpus; Educating Rita; The Aspern Papers.* **Films:** *The Magus; Alfred the Great; The Last Grenade; The Rise and Rise of Michael Rimmer; The Adding Machine; Wuthering Heights; Hitler: The Last Ten Days; Luther; QB7; Dead Cert; Jacob and Esau; The Internecine Project; Quiller; The Brute; Search for Alexander; For Your Eyes Only; Heat and Dust; Kim; Cry Freedom; Indiana Jones and the Last Crusade; Treasure Island; King Ralph; Warburg, Man of Influence.* **TV:** *An Age of Kings; Henry VIII; Henry V; The Diary of Albie Sachs; Journals of Bridget; Hitler; Guerre en Pays Neutre; Nancy Astor; Ivanhoe; QED; Dombey and Son; By the Sword Divided; Wish Me Luck; Never the Sinner; Bergerac;* **Address:** c/o Jeremy Conway. m. actress Isla Blair; 1 s. Jamie.

GODDARD, *liza*

Liza Goddard. Actress. b. Smethwick, West Midlands, 20 January 1950. Trained at the Arts Educational School. **Theatre:** *Sign of the Times; No Sex, Please – We're British; One Fair Daughter; Three Sisters; See How They Run; Wife Begins At Forty.* **Films:** *Ooh You Are Awful; Wagner; Shostakovich.* **TV:** *Skippy the Bush Kangaroo; Take Three Girls; The Befrienders; Lady Windermere's Fan; Holding On; Yes Honestly; The Brothers; The Upchat Line; Queen of a Distant Country; Whodunnit?; Wodehouse Playhouse; Murder At the Wedding; The Plank; Pig In the Middle; Watch This Space; Brendon's Chase; Roll Over Beethoven; Doctor Who; Bergerac; Tales of the Unexpected; Just His Luck; Woof!; That's Love.* **Address:** c/o Barry Burnett Organisation. m. 1st actor Colin Baker (dis), 2nd singer Alvin Stardust (dis); 1 s. Thom (from 1st m.), 1 d. Sophie.

GODWIN, *christopher*

Christopher Godwin. Actor. b. Loughborough, Leicestershire, 5 August 1943. Started career in stage management. **Theatre:** *Ten Times Table; School for Scandal; Noises Off.* **Films:** *Porridge; Charlie Muffin; A Handful of Dust.* **TV:** *Don't Be Silly; Nice Work; Holding the Fort; Astronauts; The Other 'Arf; Nearly a Happy Ending; A Foggy Outlook; Return To Waterloo; Roll Over Beethoven; Return To Treasure Island; Ffizz; My Family and Other Animals; To Have and To Hold; Roger Doesn't Live Here Any More; Boon; Nice Work; Snakes and Ladders; The Chronicles of Narnia.* **Address:** c/o ICM. m. Christine; 2 s. Ben, Tom.

GOLDING, *leroy*

Leroy Golding. Actor. **Theatre:** *The Lost Fisherman.* **Films:** *Batman; A Dry White Season; Magic Moments.* **TV:** *A Site Better Off; The Bill; Loving Hazel;* policeman, then Celestine Tavernier (1990-), in *EastEnders.* **Address:** c/o Evans and Reiss.

GONSHAW, *francesca*

Francesca Gonshaw. Actress. b. London. Trained at the Academy of Live and Recorded Arts. **Theatre:** *The Ghost of Babock; Monty Cliff; You Should See Us Now; Sailors' Dreams; The Cat and the Canary; Dear Janet Rosenberg; Dear Mr Kooning; A Midsummer Night's Dream; Intimacy; Ghosts; Cyrano de Bergerac;* Ophelia in *Hamlet.* **Films:** *The Hound of the Baskervilles; Biggles; A Ghost In Monte Carlo; Only a Sap Trusts a Dame.* **TV:** *Shades; The Cleopatras; Gesualda; Crossroads; Sidni;* Maria in *'Allo 'Allo!; Cold Warrior; Farrington of the FO;* Amanda in *Howards' Way; Never Say Clever; She-Wolf of London.* **Address:** c/o GMM.

GOODALL, *caroline*

Caroline Goodall. Actress. b. London, 13 November 1959. Studied drama and English at Bristol University. **Theatre:** *Time and Time Again; Romeo and Juliet; Twelfth Night; While the Sun Shines; Daisy Pulls it Off; Tons of Money; Susan's Breasts* (Royal Court Theatre); *The Dare Kiss; Command Or Promise* (both National Theatre); *Richard III; Misalliance and Heresies* (RSC). **Films:** *Every Time We Say Goodbye.* **TV:** *The Moon Stallion; Gems; Remington Steele; Tales of the Unexpected; After the War.* **Address:** c/o James Sharkey Associates.

GOODMAN, *john*

John Goodman. Actor. b. St Louis, Missouri, USA, 20 June 1952. **Theatre:** *Big River* (Broadway). **Films:** *Eddie Macon's Run; The Survivors; Revenge of the Nerds; C.H.U.D.; Maria's Lovers; Sweet Dreams; The Big Easy; True Stories; Blind Date; Raising Arizona; The Wrong Guys; Burglar; Punchline; Everybody's All American; Sea of Love; Always; Stella; Arachnophobia; King Ralph; Barton Fink.* **TV:** *Heart of Steel; The Face of Rape; The Mystery of Moro Castle; Chiefs* (mini-series); *Roseanne.* **Address:** c/o The Gersh Agency.

GOODWIN, *harold*

Harold Goodwin. Actor. b. Wombwell, South Yorkshire, 22 October 1917. Trained at RADA. **Films:** *Dance Hall; Angels One Five; The Cruel Sea; The Dam Busters; A Kid for Two Farthings; Don't Raise the Bridge, Lower the River; Frankenstein Must Be Destroyed; Quest; The Hoverbug; All Creatures Great and Small; Jabberwocky; Spirits.* **TV:** *Rogue's Rock; Love Story; Oh No It's Selwyn Froggitt; Captain Varley Goes Home; The Onedin Line; The Dick Emery Show; The Crucible; A Brush With Mr Porter; On the Road; Eldorado; The Kamikaze Ground Staff Reunion Dinner; That's My Boy; A Voyage Round My Father; Angels; Juliet Bravo; The Gentle Touch; Shoreline; Minder; Bulman; It's Never Too Late; Casualty; Our Geoff; All Creatures Great and Small; Brush Strokes; Woof!; The Paradise Club.* **Address:** c/o Hilda Physick Agency. m. Beatrice.

GOODWIN, *trudie*

Trudie Goodwin. Actress. b. London, 13 November 1951. First professional work with the Theatre Centre, London, acting on two tours and directing another. **Theatre:** Repertory theatre in Nottingham, Worcester, Leicester; *The Beggar's Opera; Woomberang; Godspell.* **TV:** *Fox; The Gentle Touch; The Law Machine; Play for Today; Woodentop* (pilot programme for *The Bill*); WPC June Ackland in *The Bill* (1984-). **Address:** c/o Ellison Combe Associates. Lives in South London. m. actor Kit Jackson; 1 d. Jessica. Pets: One dog, two cats. Hobbies: Painting, gardening.

GOODYEAR, *julie*

Julie Goodyear. Actress. b. Bury, Lancashire, 29 March 1943. Trained as a shorthand typist, had office jobs, sold washing machines and did modelling work before acting. **Theatre:** ASM, then actress, in repertory theatre at Oldham Coliseum. **TV:** *Pardon the Expression; Scene At 6.30;* Bet Gilroy (née Lynch) in *Coronation Street* (1966 and 1970-); *The Dustbinmen; City '68; The War of Darkie Pilbeam; Nearest and Dearest; A Family At War; This Is Your Life* (subject); *How To Be Cool* (acting herself); *Royal Variety Performance* (1989). **Address:** c/o Granada TV. m. 1st Ray Sutcliffe (dis), 2nd businessman Tony Rudman (dis), 3rd businessman Richard Skrob (dis); 1 s. Gary (from 1st m.).

GORDON, *hannah*

Hannah Gordon. Actress. b. Edinburgh, 9 April 1941. Trained at Glasgow College of Dramatic Art. **TV:** *Great Expectations; David Copperfield; Middlemarch; Love Story; The Rat Catchers; Exiles; Hadleigh; Dr Finlay's Casebook; The Exiles; Heloise and Abelard; Scobie In September; Three Stories of Orkney; When the Bough Breaks; Brett; The Persuaders; The Protectors; Dear Octopus; Allergy; My Wife Next Door; Upstairs, Downstairs; What Every Woman Knows; Play of the Month: Waste; Telford's Change; Miss Morrison's Ghosts; The Morecambe and Wise Show; Goodbye, Mr Kent; The Gay Lord Quex; Good Behaviour; House of Hammer; Gardener's Calendar; Day After the Fair; My Family and Other Animals; Joint Account.* **Books:** *Woman At the Wheel.* **Address:** c/o Hutton Management. m. lighting cameraman Norman Warwick; 1 s. Ben.

GOUGH, *michael*

Michael Gough. Actor. b. Malaya, 1917. **Films:** *Anna Karenina; Women In Love; Julius Caesar; The Go-Between; Henry VIII and His Six Wives; The Boys From Brazil; Memed; The Dresser; Top Secret; Oxford Blues; A Christmas Carol; Out of Africa; Caravaggio; The Fourth Protocol; The Serpent and the Rainbow; Strapless; The Shell Seekers;* Alfred in *Batman.* **TV:** *Suez; Smiley's People; In Search of the Nile; Vincent the Dutchman; Shoulder To Shoulder; Fall of Eagles; George Sand; Shades of Greene; The Rivals of Sherlock Holmes; To the Lighthouse; The Citadel; Heartbreak Hotel; Unfinished Business; A Killing On the Exchange; Inspector Morse; Cariani and the Courtesan; After the War; The Case of the Late Pig; Campion; The Mountain and the Molehill; Blackeyes; Boon; Children of the North; The Good Guys.* **Address:** c/o Peters Fraser & Dunlop.

GRACE, *nickolas*

Nickolas A H Grace. Actor/Director. b. West Kirby, Liverpool, 21 November 1949. Trained at Central School of Speech and Drama. **Films:** *Heat and Dust; Lorca – Death of a Poet.* **TV:** *The Love School; The Anarchist; The Comedy of Errors; The Pink Medicine Show; Brideshead Revisited; Morte D'Arthur; Robin of Sherwood; The Master of Ballantrae; Huis Clos; Lace; The Last Place On Earth; Max Headroom; Napoleon and Josephine; Unreported Incident; The Man In the Brown Suit; Pursuit; Birds of a Feather; Cluedo; The Adventures of Sherlock Holmes; The Green Man; J'Accuse Mozart; Absolutely Fabulous; Lovejoy; Moon and Son; Tonight At 8.30; Sherlock Homes: The Master Blackmailer.* **Address:** c/o Hutton Management. Single; lives in London. Hobbies: Travel, cinema, riding, running, looking at sunsets. **Favourite TV programme:** *Brideshead Revisited; Hill Street Blues.*

GRANT, *deborah*

Deborah Grant. Actress. b. London, 22 February 1947. Trained at the Joyce Butler School of Dancing and Central School of Speech and Drama. **Theatre:** *Barnum; Bedroom Farce; Watch On the Rhine* (National Theatre). **TV:** *A Bouquet of Barbed Wire; Outside Edge; Mr Palfrey of Westminster; Victoria Wood As Seen On TV; Bergerac; Bulman; Room At the Bottom; Pulaski; Bread.* **Address:** c/o Larry Dalzell Associates. m. acttor Gregory Floy; 2 d. Melissa, Miranda.

GRANT, *russell*

Russell Grant. Astrologer. b. Hillingdon, Middlesex, 5 February 1952. **TV:** *Good Morning Britain; People Today.* **Books:** *Your Sun Signs; Your Year Ahead TVTimes Special.* **Address:** c/o Jacque Evans Management. Lives in Middlesex and Wales.

GRANTHAM, *leslie*

Leslie Grantham. Actor. b. Camberwell, South London, 30 April 1947. Trained at the Webber Douglas Academy. **Theatre:** *A Little Night Music; Lady Chatterley's Lover; Rick's Bar Casablanca.* **Films:** *Morons From Outer Space.* **TV:** *The Jewel In the Crown; Knock Back; Jake's End; Goodnight and God Bless; Doctor Who; I Thought You'd Gone; Bulman;* Den Watts in *EastEnders; Nightwatch; Winners and Losers; The Paradise Club;* Bob Grove in *The Lime Grove Story: The Grove Family; The Good Guys.* **Address:** c/o ICM. Live in London. m. actress. Jane Laurie; 1 s. Michael.

GRAY, *dulcie*, CBE

Dulcie Gray. Actress. b. Kuala Lumpur, Malaysia, 20 November 1920. Trained at the Webber Douglas Academy. **Theatre:** Sorel in *Hay Fever* (debut, Aberdeen, 1939); Teresa Browne in *The Living Room* (London West End). **TV:** Kate Harvey in *Howards' Way.* **Address:** c/o ICM. m. actor Michael Denison.

GRAY, *linda*

Linda Gray. Actress. b. Santa Monica, California, USA, 12 September 1942. Previously a model; trained with Charles Conrad's Acting Class. **Films:** *Haywire; The Two Worlds of Jenny Logan;* **TV:** *Marcus Welby, MD; All That Glitters; McCloud; Big Hawaii; Emergency;* Sue Ellen in *Dallas; Switch; Chimps* (TV movie); *Not In Front of the Children* (TV movie); *The Gambler* (TV movie); *Murder In Peyton Place* (TV movie); *The Body Human* (presenter); *The Loving Process* (presenter). **Address:** c/o International Creative Management. Lives in Canyon City, California. m. record producer Ed Thrasher (dis); 1 d. Kehly, 1 s. Jeff.

GRAY, *muriel*

Muriel Gray. Presenter. b. Glasgow, 30 August. Trained as an illustrator at Glasgow School of Art before entering television. **TV:** *The Tube; The Works; Casebook Scotland; Acropolis Now; The Hogmanay Show; Bliss; The Media Show; Frocks On the Box; Walkie Talkie; Art is Dead... Long Live TV!*. **Address:** c/o Gallus Besom Productions, Greenside House, 25 Greenside Place, Edinburgh EH1 3AA, tel 031–556 2429.

GREENE, *michele*

Michele Greene. Actress. b. Los Angeles, USA, 13 February 1962. Trained at the University of Southern California's Theater Arts Department. **Theatre:** *Dames At Sea; Once Upon a Mattress; The Shadow Box.* **TV:** *Laverne and Shirley; Highway To Heaven; Simon and Simon; Bay City Blues; Seduced* (TV movie); *Matlock; Perry Mason Returns;* Abby Perkins in *LA Law.* **Address:** c/o Gores/Fields Talent Agency.

GREENE, *sarah*

Sarah Greene. Presenter/Actress. b. London, 24 October. Started career as a child in films and commercials. **Theatre:** *The Swish of the Curtain.* **TV:** *Blue Peter; Eureka; Saturday Superstore; Going Live!; Life On One; Joy To the World; Posh Frocks and New Trousers.* **Address:** c/o Michael Ladkin. m. TV presenter Mike Smith.

GREENWOOD, *debbie*

Debra Greenwood. Presenter. b. Liverpool, 16 September 1959. Won the 1984 Miss Great Britain beauty contest, broadcast by the BBC, before becoming a TV presenter. **TV:** *Weekend; Scramble* (both for Granada TV); *Breakfast Time; Tricks of the Trade; Lifeline; First Class; The Tom O'Connor Road Show; International Eisteddfod; Children In Need; The Channel Four Daily: Streetwise; The Garden Party.* As an actress: *Cinderella; Pulaski; Hold the Back Page; Hello Mum.* **Radio:** *The Debbie Greenwood Show* (BBC Radio 2); *Start the Week* (guest presenter). **Address:** Downes Presenters Agency. Single; lives in London. Hobbies: Tennis, riding, weight training, eating out, cinema. **Favourite TV programme:** *Coronation Street.*

GREENWOOD, *richard*

Richard Peirse-Duncomb. Actor. Trained at the Royal Scottish Academy of Music and Drama. **Theatre:** *Witches of Traquair* (national tour). **TV:** *The Campbells; The Houseman's Tale;* Eric Ross-Gifford in *Take the High Road* (1987-); *Taggart.* **Address:** c/o Pat Lovett Agency/Scottish Television. Lives in Glasgow. m. actress Gillian McNeill.

GREGG, anne

Anne Gregg. Presenter. b. Belfast, 11 February 1940. Has been travel editor for *Radio Times, Living* and *Catalyst* magazines. **TV:** News and current affairs for Ulster Television and Anglia Television; *Folio* (Anglia Television arts series); *Holiday*. **Radio:** *Woman's Hour; In the Air*. **Address:** c/o BBC TV/Ken Wright, Quad Productions, 107 Nelson House, Dolphin Square, London SW1.

GREGSON, simon

Simon Alan Gregory. Actor. b. Wythenshawe, Manchester, 2 October 1974. Discovered by Granada TV while still at school. **TV:** Steve McDonald in *Coronation Street* (1989-). **Address:** c/o Langford Associates/Granada TV. Single; lives in Cheadle, Cheshire. Hobbies: Motorcycles. **Favourite TV programme:** *Coronation Street*.

GRIER, sheila

Sheila Grier. Actress. b. Glasgow, 11 February 1959. Trained at the Royal Scottish Academy of Music and Drama. **Theatre:** *Pals; Foodstuff; Babes In the Wood; Cinderella; Dick Whittington;* **TV:** *Take the High Road; The Odd Job Man; The End of the Line; Scotch and Wry; The United Shoelaces Show;* Sandra Maghie in *Brookside; Bookie; Shadow On the Earth; Taggart; Making Out; Emmerdale.* **Address:** c/o Felix de Wolfe.

GRIFFITHS, richard

Richard Griffiths. Actor. b. Cleveland, 31 July 1947. **Films:** *Superman II; Chariots of Fire; Britannia Hospital; Gandhi; Ragtime; Shanghai Surprise; The French Lieutenant's Woman; Greystoke – The Legend of Tarzan, Lord of the Apes; Gorky Park; A Private Function; Withnail & I; King Ralph; The Naked Gun; 2½.* **TV:** *The Cleopatras; Bergerac; Bird of Prey II; The World Cup – A Captain's Tale; Goldeneye; El C.I.D.* **Address:** c/o Michael Whitehall.

GRIFFITHS, sara

Sara Griffiths. Actress. b. Sheffield, South Yorkshire; brought up in Lancashire. Trained at Elmhurst School of Theatre Arts, Camberley, Surrey; took drama course with Andrew Neil and Graham Mitchell. **Theatre:** *Dick Whittington; Edith Grant* (Chichester Festival); *The Tempest* (Pendley Shakespeare Festival); *Cinderella; Jack and the Beanstalk; Two Gentlemen of Verona.* **TV:** *Late Expectations; Doctor Who;* Liz in *Gentlemen and Players* (two series); Clare in *Emmerdale Farm; Sisters; The Chief* (two series); *Kangaroo Valley; Van Der Valk; Rich Tea & Sympathy.* **Address:** c/o Carole James Management.

GROTH, michael

Michael Groth. Presenter. b. Ilkley, West Yorkshire, 28 October 1953. A professional musician for 12 years, singing, writing and playing guitar; performed with Blue Mink, Valentino and Trickster. Became a TV presenter in 1982, applying for a job on *That's Life!* while doing fill-in work in the BBC post room. **Theatre:** Title role in *Dick Whittington.* **TV:** *That's Life!* (1982–5); *Splash; Hearts of Gold; As It Happens; Four Square; ITV Telethon; Why On Earth?* Plus appearances on *Blankety Blank; What's My Line?; Whose Baby?; Wide Awake Club; Waterfront; Give Us a Clue; Jumble; PSI; Record Breakers; Sky Starsearch.* **Address:** c/o David Graham Management. Single; lives in Greenford, Middlesex. Hobbies: Music (writing, recording and producing). Runs a music production company with own recording studio. **Favourite TV programme:** *Coronation Street.*

GROUT, james

James Grout. Actor. b. London, 22 October 1927. Trained at RADA. **Theatre:** *Twelfth Night; Half a Sixpence* (London and Broadway). **TV:** *The First Lady; Diary of a Nobody; Born and Bred; All Creatures Great and Small; Z-Cars; Sister Dora; The Marriage Counsellor; Hymn for Jim; Jenny Can't Work Any Faster; Microbes and Men; Juliet Bravo; Honky Tonk Heroes; The Falklands Factor; Agatha Christie Hour; A Fine Romance; Reith; Stan's Last Game; The Bounder; Cockles; Box of Delights; Rachel and the Roarettes; The Beiderbecke Affair; Yes Minister; No Place Like Home; Murder of a Moderate Man; Bust; Ever Decreasing Circles; A Very Peculiar Practice; Inspector Morse; Vote for Them; After the War; Saracen; Mother Love; Late Expectations; Singles; Roy's Raiders; Titmuss Regained;* Judge Ollie Olliphant in *Rumpole of the Bailey.* **Address:** c/o Crouch Associates.

GUARD, christopher

Christopher Guard. Actor. b. London, 5 December 1953. **Theatre:** National Theatre; RSC; *Filumena* (London West End). **Films:** *A Little Night Music; Memoirs of a Survivor; Loophole; Lord of the Rings.* **TV:** Title role in *David Copperfield; Tom Brown's Schooldays; Vienna 1900; Wilfred and Eileen; My Cousin Rachel; A Woman of Substance; Return To Treasure Island; Blackeyes.* **Address:** c/o ICM Duncan Heath Associates. m. actress Lesley Dunlop; 2 d. Daisy, Rosie.

GUBBA, tony

Tony Gubba. Sports commentator. b. Manchester, 23 September 1943. National newspaper journalist before joining the BBC in the North West. **TV:** *Grandstand; Sportsnight; Match of the Day;* soccer World Cups; summer and winter Olympic Games. **Address:** c/o BBC TV. m. (dis); 2 d. Claire, Libby.

GUILLAUME, robert

Robert Guillaume. Actor/Producer. b. St Louis, Missouri, USA, 30 November. Studied classical singing at Washington University. **Theatre:** *Porgy and Bess; Fly Blackbird; Kwamina; Guys and Dolls;* title role in *The Phantom of the Opera* (Los Angeles). **Films:** *Seems Like Old Times; Wanted: Dead Or Alive.* **TV:** *Dinah; Mel and Susan Together; Rich Little's Washington Follies; Jim Nabors; All In the Family; Sanford and Son; Marcus Welby, MD;* Benson in *Soap;* title role in *Benson; Purlie; North and South* (mini-series); *The Kid With the Broken Halo; The Kid With the 200 IQ; Perry Mason: The Case of the Scandalous Scoundrel; The Robert Guillaume Show.* **Address:** c/o William Morris Agency (US). m. (dis); 3 children.

GUINNESS, *sir alec, CBE*

Alec Guinness. Actor. b. London, 2 April 1914. Advertising copy writer until winning a scholarship to the Fay Compton School of Dramatic Art. **Films:** *Great Expectations; Oliver Twist; Kind Hearts and Coronets; The Lavender Hill Mob; Father Brown; The Ladykillers; Bridge On the River Kwai* (Best Actor Oscar); *Dr Zhivago; Hotel Paradiso; Star Wars; The Empire Strikes Back; The Return of the Jedi; A Passage To India; Little Dorrit; A Handful of Dust; Kafka.* **TV:** *The Wicked Scheme of Jebel Jacks; Twelfth Night; Conversations At Night; Caesar and Cleopatra; Gift of Friendship; Tinker, Tailor, Soldier, Spy* (BAFTA Best Actor On TV award); *Lovesick; Edwin; Smiley's People* (BAFTA Best Actor On TV award); *Monsignor Quixote.* Winner, Special Oscar for services to films, 1982. **Address:** c/o London Management. m. Merula Salaman; 1 s. actor Matthew.

GUTHRIE, *gwyneth*

Gwyneth Guthrie. Actress. b. Ayr, 28 April 1937. Trained at the Royal Scottish academy of Music and Drama (James Bridie Silver Medal winner). **Theatre:** Perth Repertory; *For Love Or For Money;* poetry readings at the Edinburgh Festival; *Cinderella.* **Films:** *Privilege; Years Ahead.* **TV:** *Sutherland's Law; Hill O' The Red Fox; Degree of Uncertainty; The Lost Tribe; The Reunion; The Prime of Miss Jean Brodie; Something's Got To Give;* Mrs Mack in *Take the High Road* (1982-); *Now You See It.* **Radio:** *Scottish Children's Hour; Book At Bedtime* (storyteller); *The Misanthrope; The Opium Eater.* **Address:** c/o Scottish Television. Lives in Darvel, Ayrshire. m. John Borland; 3 d. Karen, Debbie, Olwen.

GUTTERIDGE, *lucy*

Lucy Gutteridge. Actress. b. London, 28 November 1956. Trained at Central School of Speech and Drama. **Theatre:** Repertory theatre in Norwich; *Nicholas Nickleby* (RSC, London and Broadway); *The Real Thing; A King of Alaska* (Los Angeles); *King Arthur* (opera, Buxton Theatre Festival). **Films:** *The Greek Tycoon; Little Gloria; Merlin and the Sword; Elephant's Child; Top Secret!; Fire In Eden.* **TV:** *The Hitchhiker; The Devil's Crown; The Marrying Kind; End of Season; Betzy; Renoir My Father; Tales of the Unexpected; Sweet Wine of Youth; Love In a Cold Climate; The Seven Dials Mystery; Nicholas Nickleby; A Christmas Carol* (TV movie); *Hitler's SS: Portrait of Evil* (TV movie); *The Trouble With Spies* (TV movie); *Edge of the Wind; Till We Meet Again; The Woman He Loved.* **Address:** c/o ICM. m. actor Andrew Hawkins (dis); 1 d. Isabella.

GUTTERIDGE, *reg*

Reg Gutteridge. Presenter/Commentator. b. London, 29 March 1924. Father Dick and Uncle Jack were boxing instructors. Reg boxed as an amateur, then turned to journalism, joining the *London Evening News in 1938.* **TV:** TV boxing commentator; commentary on six Olympic Games and greyhound racing; Home Box Office and ABC TV in USA; *10 Million* (co-presenter, consumer series). **Books:** *Let's Be Honest* (Jimmy Greaves biography); *Boxing – The Great Ones; The Big Punchers.* Regular contributor of the *Sunday Express* and *Boxing News.* Winner, Radio and TV Industries Club Sports Presenter of the Year award, *1991.* **Address:** c/o Bagenal Harvey Organisation. Lives in Barnet, Hertfordshire. m. Constance; 2 d. Sammi, Sally. Pets: Cats. Hobbies: Golf. **Favourite TV programme:** *Open All Hours; Only Fools and Horses.*

HACKETT, *claire*

Claire Hackett. Actress. Trained at RADA. **Theatre:** *Three Sisters; Steppenwolf; Tartuffe; The Father; Peer Gynt; All's Well That Ends Well* (all while at drama school); *Voyage of the Dawn Treader; Listen D'Yer Wanna Know a Secret?;* Viola in *Twelfth Night; Light of Day; Collier's Friday Night; The Public* (Theatre Royal, Stratford East); *After the Fall;* Stella in *A Streetcar Named Desire; Blue* (National Theatre Studio); Perdita in *The Winter's Tale;* Ophelia in *Hamlet.* **Films:** *Itch; A Nasty Story; Women at War;* Linda in *Dancin' Thru the Dark.* **TV:** *William Tell; 4-Play: Dawn and the Candidate.* **Address:** c/o Annette Stone Associates.

HADDY, *anne*

Anne Haddy. Actress. b. Quorn, South Australia, 5 October 1927. **Films:** *Newsfront.* **TV:** *Hunter; Homicide; Division 4; Matlock; Playschool; Dynasty; Over There; Lade and the Law; Crisis; The Evil Touch; Boney and the Bikeman; Behind the Legend; Boney and the Burial Tree; Seven Little Australians; Three Men of the City; Ben Hall; Boos and Cheers; Case for the Defence; Certain Women; Hunted; Chopper Squad; No Room To Move; Glenview High; A Place In the World; Prisoner: Cell Block H; Skyways; A Family Affair; A Town Like Alice; Cop Shop; Punishment; The Restless Years; 1915;* Rosie Palmer in *Sons and Daughters;* Helen Daniels in *Neighbours* (1985-); *The Private War of Lucinda Smith.* **Address:** c/o International Casting Service. Lives in Melbourne. m. 1st Max Dimmitt, 2nd actor James Condon; 1 d. Jane, 1 s. Tony (from 1st m.).

HAGMAN, *larry*

Larry Hagman. Actor. b. Fort Worth, Texas, USA, 21 September 1931. Son of actress Mary Martin. Trained at the Margo Jones Theater, Dallas. **Theatre:** *The Taming of the Shrew; South Pacific* ('extra', London West End); *God and Kate Murphy; The Nervous Set; The Warm Peninsula; The Beauty Part.* **Films:** *Fail Safe; Ensign Pulver and the Captain; The Group; In Harm's Way; Beware!; The Blob* (also as director); *The Cavern; Stardust; Three In the Cellar; Mother; Jugs and Speed; Harry and Tonto; The Eagle Has Landed; Superman; S.O.B.* **TV:** *The Edge of Night;* Major Anthony Nelson in *I Dream of Jeannie; The Good Life; Here We Go Again;* J R Ewing in *Dallas* (1978–91); *The President's Mistress; Last of the Good Guys; Battered; Deadly Encounter.* **Address:** c/o Sutton, Barth & Vennari. m. Maj Axelsson; 1 d. Kristina, 1 s. Preston.

HAILES, *gary*

Gary Hailes. Actor. b. North London, 4 November 1965. Trained at the Anna Scher Theatre School. **Theatre:** *Doctor On the boil; Aladdin; Jack and the Beanstalk.* **Films:** *Revolution.* **TV:** *Pinocchio; Nobody's Hero; Grange Hill; Contact; Born and Bred; Sorry; The Other One; Murder With Mirrors* (TV movie); Barry Clark in *EastEnders.* **Address:** c/o Fletcher & Bryce.

HALE, *gareth*

Gareth Hale. Comedian. b. London, 15 January 1953. Teacher before forming a double-act with Norman Pace. **TV:** *Pushing Up Daisies; Coming Next; The Young Ones; Live From the Palladium; Saturday Live* (host); *Just for Laughs; The Saturday Gang; The Management; Royal Variety Performance* (1987); *Hale & Pace* (winner, Golden Rose of Montreux, 1989). **Records:** *Hale & Pace Live In Concert* (LP). **Books:** *Falsies; The Hale & Pace Book of Writes and Rons* (both with Norman Pace). **Address:** c/o International Artistes. m. Deborah; 2 d. Sian, Cara.

HALLAM, *john*

John Hallam. Actor. b. Lisburn, 28 October 1942. Trained at RADA. **Theatre:** National Theatre; RSC. **Films:** *Hennessy; Love and Bullitts; Murphy's War; A Last Valley; Villain; Antony and Cleopatra; Burden of Proof; Nicholas and Alexandra; Flash Gordon; Dragon Slayer; Under Capricorn; Lifeforce; King David; Santa Claus.* **TV:** *Devil's Crown; The Regiment; Wings; Arnhem; The Story of an Escape; Cicero; The Pallisers; The Mallens; A.D.* (mini-series). **Address:** c/o ICM.

HAMEL, *veronica*

Veronica Hamel. Actress. b. Philadelphia, USA, 20 November 1943. Previously a model. **Theatre:** *The Big Knife; The Ballad of Boris K; Cactus Flower; The Miracle Worker.* **Films:** *Cannonball; Beyond the Poseidon Adventure; When Time Ran Out; A New Life.* **TV:** *The Rockford Files; Kojak; Dallas; Starsky and Hutch; Ski Lift; 79 Park Avenue; The Gathering; The Gathering II; Valley of the Dolls; Sessions; Kane & Abel; Twist of Fate; Hill Street Blues.* **Address:** c/o International Creative Management. m. actor Michael Irving (dis).

HAMILTON, *suzanna*

Suzanna Hamilton. Actress. b. 1960. Trained at the Anna Scher Theatre School and Central School of Speech and Drama. **Theatre:** *The Real Thing; The Oven Glove; My Sister In This House; Siblings.* **Films:** *Swallows and Amazons* (aged 12); *Wild Cats of St Trinian's; Tess; Brimstone and Treacle; Julia* in *1984; Wetherby; Out of Africa.* **TV:** *Wish Me Luck; Streetwise; Murder East, Murder West; The Ruth Rendell Mysteries: A New Lease of Death; Boon.* **Address:** c/o Julian Belfrage Associates.

HAMLIN, *harry*

Harry Hamlin. Actor. b. Pasadena, California, USA, 30 October 1951. Trained at Yale University. **Theatre:** American Conservatory Theater, San Francisco; *Hamlet; Faustus In Hell; Awake and Sing!* (Broadway). **Films:** *Movie Movie; King of the Mountains; Clash of the Titans; Making Love; Blue Skies Again.* **TV:** *Studs; Lonigan; Master of the Game; Space; Favorite Son; Laguna Heat* (TV movie); *Deceptions* (TV movie); *LA Law.* **Address:** c/o William Morris Agency (USA). m. actress Laura Johnson (sep); 1 s. Dimitri (from relationship with Ursula Andress).

HAMPTON, *meryl*

Meryl Hampton. Actress. b. Chester, 26 August 1952. Trained at Guildhall School of Music and Drama. **Theatre:** *Charley's Aunt; Equus; Joseph and the Technicolor Dreamcoat; Lucy; Harry Mixture; Lock Up Your Daughters; The Rivals; Love On the Dole; Under Milk Wood; Having a Ball; Season's Greetings; Breaking and Entering; In Dreams.* **TV:** *Softly, Softly; Knock for Knock; Letty; The GPs; Death of the Heart; Crossroads; Brookside; Casualty; First and Last; Listen To Me; The Harry Enfield Show; The Bill.* **Address:** c/o Sue Hammer Personal Management.

HANCOCK, *sheila*

Sheila Hancock. Actress. b. Blackgang, Isle of Wight, 22 February 1933. Trained at RADA. **Theatre:** Rep; Cyril Fletcher's concert party in Sandown; *Breath of Spring; One Over the Eight; The Anniversary; Fill the Stage With Happy Hours; Rattle of a Simple Man; Entertaining Mr Sloane* (New York); RSC; *What About Love?; Absurd Person Singular; The Deja Revue; The Bed Before Yesterday; Annie.* **Films:** *Light Up the Sky; The Girl On the Boat; Night Must Fall; Doctor In Love; Carry On Cleo; Take a Girl Like You; The Anniversary; Buster.* **TV:** *The Rag Trade; Entertaining Mr Sloane; The Bed Sit Girl; Mr Digby Darling; Horizontal Hold; The Mating Machine; Now Take My Wife; But Seriously – It's Sheila Hancock; God Our Help.* **Address:** c/o Jeremy Conway. m. 1st actor Alec Ross (dec), 2nd actor John Thaw; 2 d. Melanie (from 1st m.), Joanne, 1 step-d. Abigail.

HANN, *judith*

Judith Hann. Presenter. b. Littleover, Derbyshire, 8 September 1942. Gained a BSc in zoology at Durham University, then trained as a journalist with Westminster Press. **TV:** *Tomorrow's World.* **Books:** *But What About the Children?; Family Scientist; The Perfect Baby?; Judith Hann's Total Health Plan; The Food of Love; How Science Works.* Twice winner of the Glaxo Award for science writers. **Address:** c/o Dave Winslett Entertainments/BBC. m. John Exelby; 2 s. Daniel, Jake. Pets: Two dogs and one cat. Hobbies: Walking, reading, food. **Favourite TV programme:** *Tomorrow's World.*

HARDY, *robert*, CBE

Robert Hardy. Actor. b. Cheltenham, Gloucestershire, 29 October 1925. **TV:** *David Copperfield; The Troubleshooters; Age of Kings; Deronda; Elizabeth R; Manhunt; Edward VII; Churchill's People; Caesar and Claretta; Upstairs, Downstairs; The Duchess of Duke Street; Victorian Scandals; The Secret Agent; Bill Brand; The Peterloo Massacre; Supernatural; All Creatures Great and Small; Between the Covers; Twelfth Night; Speed King; Fothergill; Winston Churchill – The Wilderness Years; The Cleopatras; Gordon of Khartoum; The Far Pavilions; Jenny's War; Shades of Darkness; Death of the Heart; Paying Guests; Hot Metal; The Woman He Loved; Sherlock Holmes: The Master Blackmailer.* **Books:** *Longbow: A Social and Military History.* **Address:** c/o Chatto and Linnit. m. 1st (dis), 2nd actress Sally Cooper (dis); 2 d. actress Emma, Justine, 1 s. Paul.

HARGREAVES, *david*

David Hargreaves. Actor. b. New Mills, Derbyshire, 1940. A schoolteacher before taking a course at Central School of Speech and Drama. **TV:** *The XYY Man; Armchair Thriller; Strangers; Play for Today: Stronger Than the Sun; The House of Carridus; Sally Ann; The Professionals; Together; Juliet Bravo; Sorry, I'm a Stranger Here Myself; Science Workshop; Playschool; Forever Young; Shades of Darkness; A Brother's Tale; Bulman; Shine On Harvey Moon;* Derek Owen in *Albion Market; 1914 All Out; Closing Ranks; Truckers; No Further Cause for Concern; Casualty;* Colin in *Making Out; Hard Cases; Saracen; She's Madly In Love;* Arthur Scargill in *The Miners' Strike; TECX; The Conversion of St Paul; Kingdom Come; Keeper; Woof!; Josie; Bergerac; Thatcher: The Final Days.* **Address;** Richard Stone Partnership. m. actress Chloe Ashcroft.

HARRIS, *mel*

Mary Ellen Harris. Actress. b. Bethlehem, PA, USA, 1957. Worked as a model before becoming a professional actress in 1984. **Films:** *Wanted: Dead Or Alive; Cameron's Closet; K–9.* **TV:** *A Rags To Riches; Heart of the City; The Wizard;* Hope in *thirtysomething; Harry's Hong Kong; My Brother's Wife* (both TV movies). **Address:** c/o The Gersh Agency.

HARRIS, *rolf*

Rolf Harris. Presenter/Cartoonist/Singer. b. Perth, Australia, 30 March 1930. Won Australian radio talent competition in 1949; came to Britain as an art student in 1952. **Theatre:** *One Under the Eight; Talk of the Town; Royal Variety Performance.* **TV:** *Showcase; Rolf's Walkabout; Hey Presto; It's Rolf; The Rolf Harris Show; Rolf On Saturday, OK?; Cartoon Time; Rolf's Cartoon Club.* **Records:** *Tie Me Kangaroo Down Sport; Sun Arise; Two Little Boys* (all Top 10 singles). **Address:** c/o Billy Marsh Associates. m. sculptress Alwena Hughes; 1 d. Bindi.

HART, *tony*

Norman Anthony Hart. Presenter/Artist. b. Maidstone, Kent, 15 October 1925. Trained at Maidstone College of Art. **TV:** *Saturday Special; Playbox; In Town Tonight; Tich and Quackers* (unseen operator of Quackers); *Vision On; Take Hart* (SFTA Best Educational Children's TV Programme award, 1984); *Hartbeat.* **Books:** *Fun With Drawing; Fun With Art; Fun With Design; Fun With Picture Projects; Fun With Historical Projects; The Young Letterer; The Corporate Computer* (words by Norman Sanders); *Make It With Hart; Take Hart* project packs; *The Art Factory; Paint and Draw With Tony Hart.* **Address:** c/o Roc Renals, 10 Heatherway, Edgcumbe Park, Crowthorne, Berkshire RG11 6HG, tel (0344) 773638. Lives in Shamley Green, Surrey. m. Jean; 1 d. Carolyn. Hobbies: Cooking, photography.

HARTMAN, *kim*

Kim Hartman. Actress. b. London, 11 January 1955. Assistant stage manager at the Belgrade Theatre, Coventry, for a year before training at the Webber Douglas Academy. **Theatre:** Repertory theatre; *The Cherry Orchard; Billy Liar; Hobson's Choice; Hay Fever; 'Allo 'Allo!; Move Over, Mrs Markham* (Far and Middle East tours). **TV:** *Play for Today: The Peddlar; The Kelly Monteith Show;* Helga in *'Allo 'Allo!* **Radio:** *Lord Sky; Jamaica Inn.* **Address:** c/o Lou Coulson. m. John Nolan; 1 s. Tom, 1 d. Miranda.

HARVEY, *jan*

Jan Harvey. Actress. b. Penzance, Cornwall, 1 June 1947. **TV:** *Edward VII; Sam; Bill Brand; A Family Affair; Second Chance; A Different Drummer; The Old Men At the Zoo; Fell Tiger;* Jan Howard in *Howards' Way; Inspector Morse; Lovejoy.* **Address:** c/o The Brunskill Management.

HARVEY-WRIGHT, *peter*

Peter Harvey-Wright. Actor. b. Melbourne, Australia, 4 December 1946. Trained at Victoria College. **Theatre:** *HMS Pinafore; The Pearl Fishers; Return of Ulysses; Romeo and Juliet; Mother Courage.* **Films:** *Ground Zero; Ready Or Not; Below the Belt; Son of Alvin.* **TV:** *The Sullivans; Whose Baby?; Anzacs; The Flying Doctors; Special Squad; Carson's Law; Prisoner: Cell Block H; The Henderson Kids; Neighbours.* **Radio:** *Don't Get Off Your Bike.* **Address:** c/o Barry Michael Artists. m. Marijke; 1 d. Nicole, 1 s. Luke.

HASSELHOFF, *david*

David Hasselhoff. Actor. b. Baltimore, USA, 17 July 1952. Trained at the Academy of Dramatic Arts, New York, and California Institute of the Arts. **Films:** *Starcrash; Witchcraft.* **TV:** *Griffin and Phoenix; Semi Tough; After Hours – Getting To Know Us; The Cartier Affair; Bridge Across Time; Perry Mason: The Case of the Lady In the Lake* (all TV movies); *The Young and the Restless;* Michael Knight in *Knightrider;* Mitch Bucannon in *Baywatch.* **Records:** *Lovin' Feelings; Knight Rocker; Looking for Freedom.* Winner, Hispanic Award for Best TV Actor, 1985. **Address:** c/o Jan McCormack, 11342 Dona Lisa Drive, Studio City, California, 91604, USA. m. 1st Catherine Hickland (dis), 2nd Pamela Bach.

HAVERS, *nigel*

Nigel Havers. Actor. b. London, 6 November 1949. Son of former Attorney-General Sir Michael Havers. Trained at the Arts Educational School. **Films:** *Chariots of Fire; A Passage To India; Burke and Wills; The Whistle Blower; Empire of the Sun; Farewell To the King; Naked Under Capricorn; The Private War of Lucinda Smith; Sleepers.* **TV:** *Comet Among the Stars; Nicholas Nickleby; A Raging Calm; Upstairs, Downstairs; The Glittering Prizes; Pennies From Heaven; A Horseman Riding By; An Englishman's Castle; Coming Out; Goodbye Darling; Unity; Winston Churchill – The Wilderness Years; Nancy Astor; After the Party; Don't Wait Up; Strangers and Brothers; Star;* title role in *The Charmer; Hold the Dream; A Perfect Hero; The Good Guys.* **Radio:** Billy Owen in *The Dales.* **Address:** c/o Michael Whitehall. m. 1st Carolyn (dis), 2nd Polly; 1 d. Kate (from 1st m.).

HAWKINS, *carol*

Carol Anne Hawkins. Actress. b. Barnet, Hertfordshire, 31 January 1949. Trained at Corona Academy. **Films:** *Zeta One; When Dinosaurs Ruled the Earth; Bless This House; Carry On Behind; Carry On Abroad; Please Sir; Percy's Progress; Not Now Comrade.* **TV:** Sharon Spencer in *Please Sir* and *The Fenn Street Gang; The Two Ronnies; Mr Big; Porridge; Blake's 7; The Dick Emery Show; Leap In the Dark; Rings On Their Fingers; Together; Bloomfield; The Kelly Monteith Show; C.A.T.S. eyes; That's My Boy; Happy Families; See How They Run; God's Chosen Car Park; Relative Strangers; My Husband and I; All At No 20; Don't Wait Up; About Face;* Madge in *El C.I.D.; The Bill.* **Address:** c/o Darryl Brown Associates. m. Martyn Padbury. Pets: Two cats and a dog. Hobbies: Painting, writing, gardening.

HAWTHORNE, *nigel*

Nigel Hawthorne. Actor. b. Coventry, 5 April 1929. **Theatre:** *Privates On Parade; Otherwise Engaged; Tartuffe; The Magistrate; Across From the Garden of Allah; Hapgood; Shadowlands* (London and New York). **Films:** *Gandhi; History of the World – Part 1; Memoirs of a Survivor; Operation Shakespeare; Firefox; The Chain; King of the Wind.* **TV:** *Edward and Mrs Simpson; Destiny; The Knowledge; Jessie; The Schoolmistress; Rod of Iron; Marie Curie; The Sailor's Return; A Tale of Two Cities; Yes Minister* (winner, Broadcasting Press Guild award and BAFTA awards 1981, 1982); *The World Cup – A Captain's Tale; Mapp and Lucia; Jenny's War; The House; The Knowledge; Tartuffe; Yes, Prime Minister* (winner, BAFTA Best Light Entertainment awards 1986, 1987); *The Miser; The Shawl; Relatively Speaking; Flea Bites.* **Address:** c/o Ken McReddie.

HAYES, *geoffrey*

Geoffrey Hayes. Actor/Presenter. b. Stockport, Cheshire, 13 March 1942. Dye-tester in a cotton mill and British Rail booking clerk before becoming a professional actor; trained at the Royal Northern School of Music and Drama, Manchester. **Theatre:** Oldham Rep (scene shifter, then actor); repertory theatre in Liverpool, Dundee and Manchester. **TV:** *Z-Cars; Softly, Softly; Dixon of Dock Green; Rainbow* (presenter, 1973-). **Address:** c/o London Management.

HAYES, *melvyn*

Melvyn Hayes. Actor. b. London, 11 January 1935. Performed with the troupe Terry's Juveniles as a child. **Theatre:** *Absurd Person Singular; The Fantasticks; Spring and Port Wine; Toad of Toad Hall; Dick Whittington* (London Palladium); *Run for Your Wife; Wind In the Willows; The Dresser.* **Films:** *The Curse of Frankenstein; Violent Playground; No Trees In the Street; The Young Ones; Summer Holiday; Wonderful Life; King of the Wind.* **TV:** *Quatermass II; Oliver Twist; Billy Bunter; The Unloved; The Silver Sword; Jo's Boys; Sir Yellow; The Double Deckers; Potter's Picture Palace; It Ain't Half Hot Mum; SuperTed* (voice of Skeleton); *Sky Star Search* (resident judge). **Address:** c/o Howes and Prior. Lives in London and Gloucestershire. m. 1st (dis), 2nd actress Wendy Padbury (dis); 4 d. Sacha, Talla, Joanna, Charlotte, 1 s. Damian.

HAYES, *patricia*

Patricia Hayes. Actress. b. London, 22 December. Trained at RADA (Gold Medal winner). **Films:** *Hieronymous; Goodbye, Mr Chips; Carry On Again Doctor; Fragment of Fear; Love Thy Neighbour; The Never Ending Story; Little Dorrit; A Fish Called Wanda; The Last Island; The Fool.* **TV:** Title role in *Edna, The Inebriate Woman; Last of the Baskets; The Trouble With You, Lilian; On the Move; The Portland Millions; Till Death Us Do Part; London Belongs To Me; The Corn Is Green; The Tea Ladies; Spooner's Patch; Pat and Dandy; The Lady Is a Tramp; Cymbeline; Winter Sunlight; The Old Boy; Marjorie and Men; Mr Pye; Mrs Capper's Birthday; In Sickness and In Health; Our Lady Blue; Casualty.* **Address:** c/o Hazel de Leon. m. actor Valentine Brooke (dis); 2 d. Teresa, Gemma, 1 s. actor Richard O'Callaghan.

HAYGARTH, *tony*

Tony Haygarth. Actor. b. Liverpool, 4 February 1945. Worked as a psychiatric nurse before taking up acting full-time. **Theatre:** Repertory theatre; RSC; *Don Quixote* (National Theatre). **Films:** *Percy; Let's Get Laid; Dracula; Dick Turpin; SOS Titanic; The Human Factor; Caleb Williams; Britt; Ivanhoe; McVicar; A Private Function; Clockwise.* **TV:** *Last of the Summer Wine; Warrior Queen; Holocaust; The Beaux' Stratagem; I, Claudius; Rosie; Z-Cars; Shoestring; Kinvig; The Borgias; Dead Ernest; Lucky Jim; The Black Stuff; Two Gentlemen of Verona; The Caucasian Chalk Circle; The Insurance Man; The December Rose; Farrington of the FO; Hardwicke House; Making Out; El C.I.D.* **Address:** c/o Jeremy Conway.

HAYTON, *philip*

Philip Hayton. Newsreader. b. Keighley, West Yorkshire, 2 November 1947. Pirate disc-jockey before moving to BBC Radio Leeds. **TV:** BBC TV News reporter, Southern Africa correspondent (1980–83) and *One O'Clock News* presenter (1988-). **Address:** c/o BBC TV. m. Thelma; 1 s. James, 1 d. Julia.

HAYWARD, *mike*

Mike Hayward. Actor. **TV:** *Coronation Street; The Real Eddy English;* Alun Morgan in *Take the High Road* (1990-). **Address:** c/o Harbour & Coffey/Scottish Television. Lives in Wales. m. with children.

HAZLEGROVE, *jane*

Jane Hazlegrove. Actress. b. Manchester, 17 July 1968. **Theatre:** *The Princess and the Pauper; Whistle Down the Wind; The Silver Sword; The Crucible; Soapbox; Celebration; Power of Darkness; To Kill a Mockingbird; All In Good Time; Fangs.* **TV:** *Picture Friend; Lovebirds; Threads; Travelling Man;* Sue Clayton in *Coronation Street;* Debbie Taylor in *Albion Market; Who's Our Little Jenny Lind?; The Book Tower; How We Used To Live;* WPC Madeline Forest in *Waterfront Beat* (two series); *Made In Heaven;* Rosie in *Making Out* (two series); Alison Gibson in *Shooting Stars* (Channel Four film); Lisa Shepherd in *Families.* **Radio:** *Whistle Down the Wind; The Drowned Village; Charlie and the Chocolate Factory; Derek's Destiny; News of the World; Shaz, Daz, Gaz & Baz; China Doll; The Cure of the Terrible Oomphsktskt.* **Address:** c/o Barry Brown & Partner.

HEALY, *tim*

Timothy Healy. Actor. b. Newcastle upon Tyne, 29 January 1952. **TV:** *Coronation Street; The World Cup – A Captain's Tale; Emmerdale Farm; When the Boat Comes In; Crown Court; Minder; Auf Wiedersehen, Pet; A Kind of Living; A Perfect Spy; Tickle On the Tum; Flea Bites* (TV movie). **Address** c/o ICM Duncan Heath Associates.

HEINEY, *paul*

Paul Heiney. Presenter. b. Sheffield, South Yorkshire, 20 April 1949. **Films:** *Water.* **TV:** *That's Life!; The Big Time; In At the Deep End; The Travel Show; What On Earth Is Going On?; Trading Places; Food and Drink.* **Address:** c/o Jo Gurnett Management. m. broadcaster/writer Libby Purves; 1 s. Nicholas, 1 d. Rose.

HENDERSON, *don*

Don Henderson. Actor/Writer/Producer/Director. b. London, 10 November 1932. Amateur actor until joining RSC, aged 38. **TV:** *The Protectors; Warship; Poldark; New Scotland Yard; Softly, Softly; Dixon of Dock Green; The XYY Man; Van Der Valk; Crossroads; Play for Today: One Day at a Time; Crown Court; Strangers; Dick Turpin; The Onedin Line; Play for Today: Mavis; The Baker Street Boys; Me and My Town; Jemima Shore Investigates; Bottle Boys; Annika; Bulman; Dead Head; Knights of God; Henry's Leg; The Adventures of Polly Flint; Doctor Who; Hot Metal; Jumping the Queue; Making Out; Minder; Dempsey and Makepeace; Last of the Summer Wine; Maigret; Spelling It Out; The Paradise Club; Boon; Merlin of the Crystal Cave.* **Address:** c/o A.I.M. m. 1st Hilary (dec), 2nd actress Shirley Stelfox (qv); 1 d. Louise, 1 s. Ian (from 1st m.), 1 step-d. Helena.

HENRY, *lenny*

Lenny Henry. Comedian/Actor. b. Dudley, Worcestershire, 29 August 1958. **Films:** *The Millionaires Club; Lenny Henry Live and Unleashed; Double Take; The Secret Policeman's Third Ball; True Identity.* **TV:** *New Faces* (winner, aged 16); *The Black and White Minstrel Show; The Fosters; Tiswas; OTT; Three of a Kind; Saturday Live; Royal Variety Performance; Lenny Henry Tonite; The Lenny Henry Show; Coast To Coast; The Suicide Club; Just Like That!; The Comic Strip Presents ...: Oxford; Alive and Kicking* (TV movie); *Lenny Go Home; Bernard and the Genie; The South Bank Show: Lenny Henry Hunts the Funk* (subject). **Address:** c/o James Sharkey Assocs/Robert Luff (manager). m. comedienne-actress Dawn French.

HENSON, *nicky*

Nicky Henson. Actor. b. London, 12 May 1945. Trained at RADA as a stage manager. **Theatre:** *A Midsummer Night's Dream; The Taming of the Shrew; Noises Off;* RSC. **Films:** *Witchfinder General; Crooks and Coronets; There's a Girl In My Soup; All Coppers Are; The Love Ban; Penny Gold; Vampira; The Bawdy Adventures of Tom Jones; No 1 of the Secret Service.* **TV:** *Prometheus; Arthur; The Keith Michell Show; Shirley's World; Life of Balzac; Seagull Island; A Midsummer Night's Dream; Chains; Anyone for Denis?; Happy Apple; Driving Ambition; Absurd Person Singular; Tropical Moon Over Dorking; Season's Greetings; Love After Lunch; Thin Air; Star Trap* (TV movie); *Inspector Morse; Boon; The Green Man; Lovejoy.* **Address:** c/o Richard Stone Partnership. m. 1st actress Una Stubbs (dis), 2nd Marguerite Porter; 3 s. Christian, Joe, Keaton.

HEYLAND, rob

Rob Heyland. Actor. b. London, 2 April 1954. Trained at Central School of Speech and Drama. **Theatre:** *Trafford Tanzi; A Man for All Seasons; Funny Peculiar; Three Sisters; Romeo and Juliet* (RSC). **TV:** Donald Turner in *One By One; Murphy's Mob; Reilly – Ace of Spies; The Professionals; Charles & Diana: A Royal Love Story* (TV movie). **Address:** c/o CDA. m. Victoria; 3 d. Florence, Lily, Clemency, 1 s. Alfred.

HEYWOOD, jean

Jean Murray. Actress. b. Blyth, Northumberland, 15 July 1921. Librarian until married in 1945; joined Castle Theatre, Farnham, 1963, as acting wardrobe mistress and then actress. **Theatre:** Repertory theatre; Rose's mother in *Rose* (Duke of York's Theatre); Nurse in *The Father* (National Theatre). **TV:** Bella Seaton in *When the Boat Comes In;* Mrs Kay in *Our Day Out;* eccentric history professor in *A Very Peculiar Practice;* Dolly MacGregor in *The Brothers MacGregor;* Edith in *Missing Persons;* housekeeper Mrs Alton in *All Creatures Great and Small;* Mrs Calder in *The Specials; Spender.* **Address:** c/o Barry Burnett Organisation. Lives in Camberley, Surrey. m. Dr R B Heywood; 1 s. Bryon, 1 d. Carolyn. Hobbies: Making greetings cards, calligraphy, volunteer for scheme helping stroke victims, gardening.

HICKSON, joan

Joan Hickson. Actress. b. Kingsthorpe, Northampton, 5 August 1906. **Theatre:** *His Wife's Children* (debut, 1927); *The Tragic Muse* (London West End debut, 1928); *A Day In the Death of Joe Egg; Forget Me Not Lane; The Card; Bedroom Farce* (London and New York); *On the Razzle* (National Theatre). **Films:** *The Guinea Pig; Seven Days To Noon; Yanks; The Wicked Lady; Clockwise.* **TV:** *Nanny; Good Girl; Great Expectations; Poor Little Rich Girls; Time for Murder;* title role in *Agatha Christie's Miss Marple.* **Address:** c/o Plunket Greene.

HIGGINSON, huw

Huw Higginson. Actor. b. Hillingdon, Middlesex, 21 February 1964. **TV:** *Big Deal; How We Used To Live; Flood Tide; Defrosting the Fridge; Reaching Agreement;* PC George Garfield in *The Bill* (1989-). **Address:** Evans and Reiss/The Bill. Single; lives in Teddington, Middlesex. Pets: Dog and cat. Hobbies: Golf, cricket, snooker, pool, travel.

HIGHMORE, edward

Edward Thomas Highmore. Actor. b. Kingston-upon-Thames, Surrey, 3 April 1961. **Theatre:** *Bedroom Farce;* improvised play season at Pentameters Theatre; *The Merchant of Venice; Night Out; Crystal Clear; Rattle of a Simple Man; Mrs Warren's Profession; A Taste of Honey.* **TV:** *Doctor Who; Tripods;* Ernie in *Lame Ducks* (two series); Leo Howard in *Howards' Way* (five series). **Address:** c/o William Morris Agency. Lives in London with partner Sue Latimer. **Favourite TV programme:** *Hartbeat.*

HILL, *alex*

Alexander H A Hill. Weather presenter. b. Glasgow, 9 August 1954. Meteorologist before entering television. **TV:** *Scotland Today* (Scottish Television, 1981–4); *Motormouth; Children In Need; ITV Telethon; ITV National Weather* (1989-); *LWT Weather* (1990–91). **Address:** c/o International Weather Productions. Lives in Glasgow. m. Olive; 1 d. Sara-Jayne, 1 s. James. Pets: Four goldfish. Hobbies: Reading, music, football, gliding, chess. **Favourite TV programme:** *Hill Street Blues.*

HILL, *benny*

Alfred Hawthorne Hill. Comedian/Actor/Writer. b. Southampton, 21 January 1925. Worked as a weighbridge operator, milkman, army driver and drummer before turning professional as a comedian. **Theatre:** *Stars In Battledress; Paris By Night; Fine Fettle.* **Films:** *Light Up the Sky; Those Magnificent Men In Their Flying Machines; Chitty Chitty Bang Bang; The Italian Job; The Best of Benny Hill.* **TV:** *The Benny Hill Show; Omnibus: Benny Hill – Clown Imperial* (subject). Elected to TV Hall of Fame in *TVTimes* awards, 1978–9; winner, *TVTimes* Funniest Man On TV award, 1981–2. **Address:** c/o Richard Stone Partnership.

HILL, *bernard*

Bernard Hill. Actor. b. Manchester, 17 December 1944. **Films:** *The Chain; No Surrender; The Bounty; Bellman and True; Drowning By Numbers; Shirley Valentine; Mountains of the Moon.* **TV:** Yosser Hughes in *Boys From the Blackstuff; New World; The Burston Rebellion;* Lech Walesa in *Squaring the Circle* (Channel Four film). **Address:** c/o Julian Belfrage Associates.

HILL, *jimmy*

Jimmy Hill. Soccer presenter. b. Balham, South London, 22 July 1928. Professional footballer with Brentford and Fulham, and manager of Coventry City, before entering television (chairman of Fulham from 1987). **TV:** LWT head of sport (1968–73) and deputy controller of programmes (1971–3), appearing on *World of Sport* and *The Big Match; Match of the Day; Grandstand;* World Cup coverage. **Address:** c/o Bagenal Harvey Organisation. m. 1st Gloria (dis), 2nd Heather (dis); 2 d. Alison, Joanna (one from each marriage), 3 s. Duncan, Graham, Jamie (two from 1st m., one from 2nd m.).

HILL, *melanie*

Melanie Hill. Actress. Trained at RADA (Vanburgh Award winner). **Theatre:** *Under Milk Wood; Selfish Shellfish; Twelfth Night; Deathtrap; Dirty Linen; Breezeblock Park; Who Killed Hilda Murrell?; Fire In the Lake; Women Beware Women* (Royal Court Theatre); Aveline in *Bread.* **TV:** Hazel in *Auf Wiedersehen, Pet; Juliet Bravo; The Bill; A Night On the Tyne; Boon;* Aveline in *Bread;* Sue Hyles in *Spender.* **Address:** c/o Markham & Froggatt.

HILL, *rose*

Rose Hill. Actress. b. London, 5 June 1914. Trained at Guildhall School of Music and Drama. **Theatre:** *The Marriage of Figaro; The Beggar's Opera; Three Sisters; On the Razzle.* **Films:** *Heavens Above; For the Love of Ada; Every Good Home Should Have One; Footsteps.* **TV:** *Dixon of Dock Green; The Barber of Stamford Hill; Take a Sapphire; The Wild Geese; Benbow Was His Name; Three Sisters; Caring;* Fanny in *'Allo 'Allo!; Strangers; The Bill; Press GGang; Murder East, Murder West.* **Address:** c/o Richard Stone Partnership. m. J C Davis (dec); 1 s. John.

HINDLE, *madge*

Madge Hindle. Actress. b. Blackburn, Lancashire, 19 May 1938. **Theatre:** Repertory theatre; *Whodunnit?* (national tour); *Bare Necessities; Elsie and Norm's Macbeth* (national tour); *When We Are Married.* **Films:** *Nearest and Dearest.* **TV:** *On the Margin;* Lily in *Nearest and Dearest; Stan's Last Game; Intensive Care; Mr and Mrs Edgehill* (last three all *Play for Today* productions); Renee Roberts (née Bradshaw) in *Coronation Street; The Dick Emery Show; The Two Ronnies; The Cannon & Ball Show;* Mrs Schurer in *Lost Empires; Tickle On the Tum; First of the Summer Wine; Thank You for Having Her.* **Radio:** *A Proper Charlie.* **Address:** c/o Sandra Griffin Management. m. solicitor Michael Hindle; 2 d. TV presenter Charlotte, Frances.

HINES, *frazer*

Frazer Hines. Actor. b. Horsforth, West Yorkshire, 22 September 1944. Trained at the Marjorie Newbury School of Dancing, Harrogate (aged eight), and the Corona Academy (aged 10). **Theatre:** *Norman; The Good Woman of Szechuan; Happy Birthday; Boeing Boeing; Airs and Graces; On the Razzle; Hedda Gabler; Doctor In the House.* **Films:** *X the Unknown; The Weapon; Peril for the Guy; Salvage Gang; A King In New York; The Last Valley; Zeppelin.* **TV:** Jan in *The Silver Sword; Queen's Champion; Compact; Z-Cars;* Jamie in *Doctor Who; Smuggler's Cove; No Man's Land; Coronation Street; The Villains; Samson and Delilah; Seasons; Duty Free;* Joe Sugden in *Emmerdale* (1972-); *Country Challenge* (presenter). **Address:** c/o Peter Charlesworth/Yorkshire Television. Lives in Yorkshire. m. 1st actress Gemma Craven (dis), 2nd Liz Hobbs. Hobbies: Horse-riding.

HINSLIFF, *geoff*

Geoffrey Hinsliff. Actor. b. Leeds. Trained at RADA. **Theatre:** Many stage appearances, including performances at the Old Vic and Royal Court Theatres, and in London's West End. **Films:** *A Bridge Too Far; O Lucky Man!* **TV:** *Z-Cars; Softly, Softly; Striker; Accident;* George Fairchild in *Brass* (first series); Don Brennan in *Coronation Street* (1988-) (previously appeared in the serial in two other roles). **Radio:** Billy (lead role) in series *September Song* (1991). **Address:** c/o Spotlight/Granada TV. Lives in Essex. m. Judith; 2 d. Gabrielle, Sophie. Hobbies: Gardening.

HIRD, *thora*, OBE

Thora Hird, OBE. Actress. b. Morecambe, Lancashire, 28 May 1913. **Theatre:** *Flowers for the Living; Romeo and Juliet; No, No, Nanette.* **Films:** *The Entertainer; Over the Odds; A Kind of Loving; Term of Trial; Rattle of a Simple Man; Some Will, Some Won't; The Nightcomers.* **TV:** *Meet the Wife; The First Lady; Ours Is a Nice House; Flesh and Blood; The Hard Case; Albert Hope; The Bed; She Stoops To Conquer; Your Songs of Praise Choice; Thomas and Sarah; Me, I'm Afraid of Virginia Woolf; Afternoon Off; Intensive Care; In Loving Memory* (five series); *Hallelujah; Praise Be; Last of the Summer Wine; The Tailor of Gloucester; Talking Heads; A Cream Cracker Under the Settee* (winner, BAFTA Best Actress award). **Address:** c/o Felix de Wolfe. m. James Scott; 1 d. actress Janette Scott.

HODGE, *patricia*

atricia Hodge. Actress. b. Cleethorpes, Lincolnshire, 29 Septembber 1946. Trained at LAMDA (won veline Evans Award). **TV:** *The Naked Civil Servant; Softly, Softly; Jackanory Playhouse; Act of Rape; rimewriters; Target; Rumpole of the Bailey; The One and Only Phyllis Dixey; Edward and Mrs impson; Disraeli; The Professionals; Holding the Fort; The Other 'Arf; Rumpole's Return; Nanny; emima Shore Investigates; Rumpole and the Female Species; Hay Fever; The Death of the Heart; obin of Sherwood; OSS; The Adventures of Sherlock Holmes; Time for Murder; Hotel du Lac; The Life nd Loves of a She-Devil; Exclusive Yarns; Let's Face the Music of...; Inspector Morse; The Heat of the ay; The Shell Seekers; Goldeneye; Rich Tea & Sympathy; The Cloning of Joanna May.* **Address:** c/o ICM. ives in London. m. musician Peter Owen; 2 s.

HODGSON, *sharyn*

haryn Hodgson. Actress. b. Sydney, Australia, 25 August 1968. Trained at the Phillip Street Drama chool, Sydney, and the Peter Williams School of Dramatic Art. **Theatre:** *Home and Away* (British ur). **Films:** *Catch a Falling Star; Betty Cornell's Teenage Popularity Show; Metro Video Kids* (all for e Australian Film and Television School). **TV:** Leanne in *A Country Practice;* Carly Lucini (née Morris) Home and Away (1988–91). **Address:** c/o Australian Creative Management.

HOLDERNESS, *sue*

ue Holderness. Actress. b. Hampstead, North London, 28 May 1949. Trained at Central School of peech and Drama. **Theatre:** *Hay Fever; Edge of Darkness; When the Lights Go On Again; Duet for ne; Why Not Stay for Breakfast?; Our Kid* (one-woman show). **Films:** *That'll Be the Day; It Could appen To You.* **TV:** *Tightrope; Fly Into Danger; Bless This House; Lollipop Loves Mr Mole; Harriet's ack In Town; Four Idle Hands; Canned Laughter; The Sandbaggers; End of Part One; The New vengers; The Cleopatras; It Takes a Worried Man; Minder; The Brief; Only Fools and Horses; Dear hn; Lime Street; Long Live the King; Young, Gifted and Broke.* **Address:** c/o Peter Browne anagement. m. director Mark Piper; 1 d. Harriet, 1 s. Frederick.

HOLLAND, *jeffrey*

effrey Holland. Actor. b. West Midlands, 17 July 1946. **TV:** *Russ Abbot's Madhouse;* Spike in *Hi-de-Hi!; ou Rang, M'Lord.* **Address:** c/o London Management.

HOLLOWAY, *julian*

ulian Holloway. Actor. b. Watlington, Oxfordshire, 24 June 1944. Trained at RADA. **Theatre:** *All quare* (revue, London West End debut); *The Norman Conquests* (London West End); Professor Higgins Pygmalion (Cambridge Arts Festival). **Films:** *Loophole; The Spy's Wife, The Chairman's Wife* (both as -producer); *The Brute* (associate producer). **TV:** *Helen – A Woman of Today; The Importance of eing Earnest; Snooker; An Adventure In Bed; The New Avengers; The Sweeney; Rebecca; Minder; he Scarlet and the Black; Ellis Island; If Tomorrow Comes; My Darling Clementine.* **Address:** c/o chael Ladkin Personal Management. m. actress Zena Walker (dis).

HOLM, *ian*

Ian Holm. Actor. b. Essex. Trained at RADA. **Films:** *A Midsummer Night's Dream; Mary Queen of Scots; Young Winston; Juggernaut; Shout At the Devil; The Life of Christ; Man In the Iron Mask; Robin and Marian; The Holocaust; Alien; All Quiet On the Western Front; Time Bandits; Chariots of Fire; Return of the Soldier; Greystoke; Dance With a Stranger; Wetherby; Brazil; Laughterhouse; Dreamchild; Another Woman; Henry V; Hamlet; Kafka.* **TV:** *Frankenstein; Edward the Confessor; Omri's Burning; End of the Line; Dostoyefsky; Funny; The Freighteners; The Man From Heaven; Conjugal Rights; Oedipus; Napoleon and Love; Jubilee: Ramsey; Night School; Flayed; Mirage; The Misanthrope; The Bell; The Browning Version; Murder By the Book; Mr and Mrs Edgehill; Game, Set & Match; Uncle Vanya; Survival; The Lost Boys.* **Address:** c/o Julian Belfrage Associates.

HOLMES, *michelle*

Corinne Michelle Cunliffe. Actress. b. Rochdale, Lancashire, 1 January 1967. Trained at Oldham Theatre Workshop. Formed the funk group Dunky Dobbers with actress Sue Devaney (qv). **Theatre:** *Me Mam Sez; The Beauty Game; The Emperor's New Clothes;* Carol in *Road; In the Midnight Hour; Homeland; Translations; Mother Goose; Eight Miles High.* **Films:** Sue in *Rita, Sue and Bob Too; Once Upon a Time.* **TV:** *Juliet Bravo; In Loving Memory;* Susan Turner in *The Practice; Divided We Stand;* Jenny in *Damon & Debbie;* Tina Fowler in *Coronation Street.* **Address:** c/o PTA. Single; lives in Rochdale. Pets: Fish called Gavin. Hobbies: Singing, dancing, water-skiing, travelling. **Favourite TV programme:** 'None – don't watch much TV.'

HOLNESS, *bob*

Bob Holness. Presenter. b. Vryheid, Natal, South Africa, 12 November. Acting on stage and radio in South Africa before coming to Britain, where he became a TV and radio presenter. **TV:** *Take a Letter; World In Action; Junior Criss Cross Quiz; What the Papers Say; Today; Blockbusters* (quizmaster). **Radio:** *Late Night Extra; Top of the Form;* BBC World Service; *AM* (LBC). Winner, Variety Club Joint Independent Radio Personality of the Year (1979, 1984), *TVTimes* award (twice). **Address:** c/o Spotlight. Lives in Middlesex. m. Mary Rose; 2 d. Carol, Ros, 1 s. Jon.

HOPE, *jason*

Jason Hope. Actor. b. Liverpool, 5 March 1970. **Theatre:** Everyman Theatre and Neptune Theatre, Liverpool (as a child); *The Pied Piper of Hamelin; Romeo and Juliet; The Boy Friend;* Rick Morgan in *Soaplights.* **TV:** *20/20 Vision* (documentary); *The Beiderbecke Affair; Attachments;* Rod Corkhill in *Brookside* (1985-). **Address:** c/o Mersey Television.

HOPKINS, *anthony*

Anthony Hopkins. Actor. b. Port Talbot, West Glamorgan, 31 December 1937. Trained at RADA. **Films:** *Young Winston; Juggernaut; All Creatures Great and Small; A Bridge Too Far; The Elephant Man; The Bounty; 84 Charing Cross Road; A Chorus of Disapproval; Silence of the Lambs.* **TV:** *Three Sisters; A Flea In Her Ear; A Walk Through the Forest; Heritage and Its History; Danton; Dickens; Hearts and Flowers; Uncle Vanya; Poet Game; War and Peace; Dark Victory; The Lindbergh Kidnapping Case; The Hunchback of Notre Dame; A Married Man; Strangers and Brothers; Corridors of Power; Arch of Triumph; Mussolini and I; Hollywood Wives; Guilty Conscience; The Good Father; Guy Blunt; Across the Lake; Heartland; Great Expectations; To Be the Best.* **Address:** Jeremy Conway. m. 1st Petronella Barker (dis), 2nd Jennifer Lynton; 1 d. Abigail (from 1st m.).

HORDERN, sir michael, CBE

Michael Hordern. Actor. b. Berkhamsted, Hertfordshire, 3 October 1911. **Films:** *A Funny Thing Happened On the Way To the Forum; The Jokers; How I Won the War; Gandhi; Oliver Twist; The Missionary; Yellowbeard; Lady Jane Grey; The Fool.* **TV:** *Noah; Sir Jocelyn; The Minister Would Like a Word; The Tigers Are Burning; Nelson; The Dock Brief; What Shall We Tell Caroline?; The Browning Version; Tartuffe; Tall Stories; The Magistrate; Edward VII; Cakes and Ale; King Lear; A Christmas Carol; The Saints Go Marching In; Romeo and Juliet; Chester Mystery Plays; Shogun; The Tempest; The History Man; All's Well That Ends Well; You're Alright, How Am I?; Tales of the Unexpected; Trelawney of the Wells; Paradise Postponed; Scoop; Ending Up; The Green Man; Dream Gardens; Mistress of Suspense.* **Address:** c/o ICM. m. former actress Eve Mortimer; 1 d. Joanna.

HORNBY, clive

Clive Hornby. Actor. b. Liverpool, 20 October 1944. Trained as an acoountant; played drums for The Dennisons pop group; worked backstage at the Liverpool Playhouse; trained at LAMDA. **Theatre:** repertory theatre; *Candida; Oh! What a Lovely War; The Threepenny Opera; Macbeth; The Homecoming; How the Other Half Loves; An Inspector Calls; Present Laughter; The Recruiting Officer; After the Fall; The Glass Menagerie; See How They Run; Kennedy's Children; The Bed Before Yesterday; The Philanthropist.* **Films:** *No Longer Alone; Yanks.* **TV:** *Get Some In; Space 1999; Life At Stake; Minder;* Jack Sugden in *Emmerdale* (1980-). **Radio:** *The War Behind the Wire* (narrator). **Address:** c/o Vernon Conway/Yorkshire Television. m. 1st (dis), 2nd actress Helen Weir; 1 s. Thomas, 1 step-s. Daniel.

HORTON, peter

Peter Horton. Actor. Trained with Stella Adler, Lee Strassberg, Milton Katselas and Peggy Feury. **Films:** *Singles; The Men's Club; Where the River Runs Black; Children of the Corn; Split Image; Serial; Made To Black.* **TV:** Gary in *thirtysomething.* **Address:** c/o United Talent Agency. m. Michelle Pfeiffer (dis).

HOW, jane

Jane How. Actress. b. London, 21 December. Trained at Webber Douglas Academy. **Theatre:** *Return of A J Raffles; Crime and Punishment; Cavalcade; Oh, Kay!; Easy Virtue.* **Films:** *Gare au Male.* **TV:** *Doctor Who; General Hospital; The Return of A J Raffles; Warriors Return; Shuttlecock; The Killers; Don't Forget To Write; The Foundation; Cribb; The Spoils of War; Take Three Women; The Citadel; Seaview; The Kelly Monteith Show; Don't Wait Up; A.D.* (mini-series); Jan in *EastEnders; War and Remembrance* (mini-series); *Matlock; Made In Heaven.* **Address:** c/o James Sharkey Associates. m. actor Mark Burns; 1 s. Jack.

HOWARD, madeleine

Madeleine Howard. Actress. b. London, 15 March 1951. Trained at Guildhall School of Music and Drama (Comedy Prize winner). **Theatre:** Repertory theatre at the Crucible, Sheffield, the Marlowe, Canterbury, the Playhouse, Derby, the Phoenix, Leicester; Olivia in *Twelfth Night;* Yeelena in *Uncle Vanya;* Jessie in *Free for All;* Viola in *Twelfth Night;* Eve in *Garments;* Shirley in *Funny Peculiar;* Cordelia in *The Royal Fool;* Jo in *Doing Bird.* **Films:** *Daylight Robbery.* **TV:** Tricia Pope in *Gems; Howards' Way; The Bill; Strike It Rich; The Collectors;* Sarah Connolly in *Emmerdale* (1988-). Plus TV commercials. **Address:** c/o Royce Personal Management/Yorkshire Television. Single; lives in Yorkshire and Richmond-upon-Thames, Surrey. Hobbies: Reading.

HOWERD, *frankie*, OBE

Frankie Howerd. Actor/Comedian. b. York, 6 March 1922. **Theatre:** Bottom in *A Midsummer Night'* *Dream; Die Fledermaus.* **Films:** *The Ladykillers; Runaway Bus; Touch of the Sun; Jumping for Joy* *Further Up the Creek; The Great St Trinian's Train Robbery; Carry On Doctor; Carry On Jungle Boy; Up* *Pompeii; Up the Chastity Belt; Up the Front; Nightmare Park; Sgt Pepper's Lonely Hearts Club Band.* **TV:** *Comedy Playhouse; The Frankie Howerd Show; The David Frost Show; Cilla; Up Pompeii; Franci* *Howerd In Concert; The Frankie and Bruce Show; Francis Howerd's Tittertime; A Touch of the* *Casanovas; Up the Convicts; Oh Canada; The Howerd Confessions; HMS Pinafore; Then Churchill Said* *To Me; Trial By Jury; The Gong Show; Frankie Howerd On Campus; Further Up Pompeii* **Books:** *Trumps; On the Way I Lost It* (autobiography). **Address:** c/o Tessa Le Bars Management.

HOWMAN, *karl*

Karl Howman. Actor. b. London. **Theatre:** *Me and My Girl* (London West End). **Films:** *That'll Be the* *Day; Stardust; Porridge; Frankenstein; SOS Titanic; Babylon; The Long Good Friday; Party Party* **TV:** *The Prodigal Daughter; Shades of Greene; The Sweeney; Balcombe Street Siege; Hazell; People* *Like Us; Fox; The Flipside of Dominic Hyde; The Professionals; Minder; Shelley; A Fine Romance* *Oscar; Dempsey and Makepeace; Black Silk; Juliet Bravo; Ties of Blood; Upline; Boon; Brush* *Strokes; Saracen.* **Address:** c/o Noel Gay Artists.

HUDD, *roy*

Roy Hudd. Comedian/Actor. b. Croydon, Surrey, 16 May 1936. **Theatre:** *Oliver!; Underneath the Arches* *Roy Hudd's Very Own Music Hall; At the Palace; The Black and White Minstrel Show; Run for Your* *Wife; Cinderella; By Royal Command.* **Films:** *Blood Beast Terror; Up Pompeii; The Seven* *Magnificent Deadly Sins; Up the Chastity Belt; The Garnet Saga; An Acre of Seats In a Garden of* *Dreams; What'll You Have?; Up Marketing.* **TV:** *Not So Much a Programme, More a Way of Life; Hudd;* *The Illustrated Weekly Hudd; The Roy Hudd Show; Comedy Tonight; Up Sunday; Hold the Front Page;* *Show of the Week; Poor Christmas; The 607080 Show; Movie Memories; The Puppet Man; Halls of* *Fame; Hometown; Hazard a Guess; Chaplin the Kid.* **Radio:** *The News Huddlines; Huddwinks.* **Address:** c/o Aza Artistes. m. 1st Ann (dis), 2nd Deborah; 1 s. Max (from 1st m.).

HUGHES, *geoffrey*

Geoffrey Hughes. Actor. b. Liverpool, 2 February 1944. Began career with Newcastle University Theatre **Theatre:** *Rattle of a Simple Man; Run for Your Wife.* **Films:** *The Virgin Soldiers; The Bofors Gun; Till* *Death Us Do Part; The Man Who Had Power Over Women; Revenge; Adolf Hitler, My Part In His* *Downfall; Yellow Submarine* (voice of Paul McCartney). **TV:** *The Likely Lads; Z-Cars; Curry and Chips;* *Hoggs Back; The Mind of J G Reader; Shadows of Fear; Play for Today: The Pigeon Fancier; An Arrow* *for Little Audrey; No Honestly; Don't Drink the Water;* Eddie Yeats in *Coronation Street* (1975–83); *Mr* *Big; The Bright Side; Doctor Who; The Flying Lady; The Man From the Pru;* Dilk in *Making Out;* *Spender; Needle* (TV movie); *Coasting; Keeping Up Appearances; You Rang, M'Lord?* **Address:** c/o Richard Stone Partnership. Lives in Northamptonshire. m. Susan.

HUGHES, *nerys*

Nerys Hughes. Actress. b. Rhyl, Clwyd, 8 November 1941. Trained at Rose Bruford College of Speech and Drama. **TV:** *The Liver Birds; The Merchant of Venice; High Summer Seasons; Diary of a Young* *Man; How Green Was My Valley; Doctor Who; Jackanory; Play Away; Third Time Lucky; Alphabet Zoo,* title role in *District Nurse; Survival of the Fittest; Bazaar* (presenter). **Address:** c/o Barry Burnett Organisation. m. TV director Patrick Turley; 1 d. Mari-Claire, 1 s. Benjamin.

HULL, rod

Rodney Stephen Hull. Entertainer/Scriptwriter. b. Isle of Sheppey, Kent, 13 August 1935. **Theatre:** *Emu In Pantoland;* created, wrote and hosted first Children's Royal Variety Performance, 1981. **TV:** *Rod Hull and Emu; EBC; Emu's World; The Pink Windmill; Hamburgers* (USA); *Rod's TV Show* (Canada). **Books:** *The Reluctant Pote.* **Address:** c/o International Artistes. Lives in Rochester, Kent. m. 1st Sandra (dis), 2nd Cheryl; 3 d. Danielle, Debbie (from 1st m.), Amelia (from 2nd m.), 1 step-d. Catrina, 2 s. Toby, Oliver (from 2nd m.). Hobbies: Gardening, golf. **Favourite TV programme:** 'Hate TV.'

HUMPHRIES, barry

Barry Humphries. Actor/Comedian. b. Melbourne, Australia, 17 February 1934. Creator of Dame Edna Everage and Sir Les Patterson. **Theatre:** Union Theatre, Melbourne; Mermaid Theatre, London; *A Nice Night's Entertainment; Excuse I; A Load of Olde Stuffe; At Least you Can Say You've Seen It; Last Night of the Poms; An Evening's Intercourse With the Widely Liked Barry Humphries; Back With a Vengeance.* **Films:** *The Adventures of Barry McKenzie; Barry McKenzie Holds His Own; The Getting of Wisdom.* **TV:** *An Audience With Dame Edna; The Dame Edna Experience; The South Bank Show* (subject); *Single Voices: Sandy Come Home;* Rupert Murdoch in *Selling Hitler.* **Address:** c/o William Morris Agency. m. Dianne Millstead; 2 d. Tessa, Emily, 2 s. Oscar, Rupert.

HUNT, gareth

Gareth Hunt. Actor. b. London, 7 February 1943. Trained at the Webber Douglas Academy. **Theatre:** Repertory theatre in Ipswich, Bristol, Old Vic, Coventry, Royal Court Theatre and Watford; RSC; National Theatre; *Conduct Unbecoming; Alpha Beta; Deathtrap; Run for Your Wife; Man of the Moment* (London West End). **Films:** *Licence To Love and Kill; The World Is Full of Married Men; The House On Garibaldi Street; And the Walls Came Tumbling Down; Bloodbath At the House of Death; A Ghost In Monte Carlo.* **TV:** *Upstairs, Downstairs;* Gambit in *The New Avengers; That Beryl Marston...!; A Hazard of Hearts; Shaping Up; Doctor Who; Minder.* TV commercial: *Nescafé.* **Address:** c/o ICM. m. 1st Carol (dis), 2nd Anette; 2 s. Gareth (from 1st m.), Oliver-Leigh.

HUNTER, alan

Alan Hunter. Actor. b. Liverpool. **Theatre:** Royal Lyceum Theatre, Edinburgh. **TV:** *Crown Court; The Spoils of War; Bergerac; Hannay; Squadron; The Bill;* Greg Ryder in *Take the High Road* (1990-). **Address:** c/o PTA/Scottish Television. Lives in London and Glasgow. m. (dis).

HUNTER, russell

Russell Hunter. Actor. b. Glasgow, 18 February 1926. **Theatre:** Glasgow Unity Theatre at first Edinburgh Festival (debut, 1947); Old Vic Theatre; Open Air Theatre, Regent's Park; RSC; *Hochhuth's Soldiers; Lock Up Your Daughters.* **Films:** *The Gorbals Story; Callan.* **TV:** Lonely in *Callan; Mackenzie; The Standard; Five Red Herrings; Mind Your Language; Dickens of London; Rule Britannia; The Gaffer; Play for Tomorrow; The Dunroamin Uprising; Rab C Nesbitt; Lovejoy.* **Address:** c/o Marjorie Abel. m. actress Marjorie Thomson (qv) (dis), actress Caroline Blakiston (qv) (dis).

ILES, *jon*

Jon Iles. Actor. b. Ripon, North Yorkshire, 17 May 1954. Trained at the Rose Bruford College of Speech and Drama. **Theatre:** *Romeo and Juliet; Macbeth; The Winslow Boy* (all national tours); *Touch of Spring; Robin Redbreast Murder; Relatively Speaking;* Gatsby in *The Great Gatsby; Premier* (national tour). **Films:** *Those Glory, Glory Days.* **TV:** *To the Manor Born; Happy Endings; The Dick Emery Show; Bognor; Crown Court; Never the Twain; Fresh Fields;* DC Mike Dashwood in *The Bill.* **Address:** c/o Daly Gagan Associates/The Bill. Single; lives in London. Pets: Two dogs, German shepherd called Beef and rescued mongrel called Chips. Hobbies: Gym, writing, art and design. **Favourite TV programme:** *Vic Reeves Big Night Out.*

IMRIE, *celia*

Celia Imrie. Actress. b. Guildford, Surrey, 15 July 1952. **Theatre:** Royal Court Theatre; RSC world tour; *The Last Waltz; Particular Friendships; School for Wives; The Philanthropist; Yerma.* **Films:** *The Wicked Lady; Assassin; The House of Whipcord; Highlander; Death On the Nile.* **TV:** *Upstairs, Downstairs; Cloud Howe; To the Manor Born; Bergerac; The Nightmare Man; Shoestring; Victoria Wood As Seen On TV; Oranges Are Not the Only Fruit; The World of Eddie Weary; The New Statesman; The Darling Buds of May; Stay Lucky; Van Der Valk.* **Address:** c/o CDA.

INDRANI, *seeta*

Seeta Indrani. Actress. b. Brixton, South London. **Theatre:** *Cats* (London West End); *Orpheo ed Euridice* (Glyndebourne Opera); *Peter Pan; Poppy* (both RSC); *A City Event* (RSC); *Belisa; Jean Seberg* (National Theatre); *Midday Sun; The King and I* (London Palladium); *Fear and Loathing In the Holy Land; Henry IV, Pt I; The Caucasian Chalk Circle; Macbeth; Marlowe; Ishtar Descends; Flash Trash; Oedipus; Aida; Carmen.* **Films:** *The Nutcracker; Gunbus.* **TV:** *Timon of Athens; The Cleopatras; Omnibus; Here and Now; Rub a Dub Tub; Options; Tripods; Dido and Aeneas; C.A.T.S. Eyes; Dempsey and Makepeace;* Sita Sharma in *Albion Market; Damon & Debbie; Hunting the Squirrel; Into Music; Mathspy; Storytime;* WPC Norika Datta in *The Bill.* **Radio:** Anita Sharma in *Citizens.* **Address:** c/o Mayer Management. Lives in North London. Hobbies: Tending window-boxes.

INGLIS, *gordon*

Gordon Inglis. Presenter. b. Glasgow, 13 May 1962. **TV:** BBC video camera operator in Glasgow; *Breakout* (BBC Scotland); *The Disney Club.* **Radio:** *The Gordon Inglis Show* (BBC Radio Scotland). **Address:** c/o Sara Cameron Management. Single; lives in Glasgow. Hobbies: Listening to music.

INMAN, *john*

John Inman. Actor. b. Preston, Lancashire, 28 June 1935. **Theatre:** Repertory theatre; *Ann Veronica; Salad Days; Mother Goose; Pyjama Top.* **Films:** *Are You Being Served?* **TV:** Mr Humphries in *Are You Being Served?* and *Grace and Favour; Take a Letter Mr Jones; Odd Man Out; The Good Old Days; Top Secret; This Is Your Life.* Winner, 1976 BBC TV Personality of the Year award, 1976 *TVTimes* Funniest Man On Television award. **Address:** c/o Bill Robertson, W&J Theatrical Enterprises, 51a Oakwood Road, London NW11 6RJ, tel 081–458 1608.

INNOCENT, *harold*

Harold Harrison. Actor. b. Coventry, Warwickshire, 18 April 1936. Trained at Birmingham School of Drama. **TV:** *Alfred Hitchcock Presents; Gunsmoke; Adventures In Paradise; Ben Casey; Sea Hunt; The New Breed; The Barbara Stanwyck Show; Have Gun – Will Travel; Malice Aforethought; The Professionals; Crown Court; The Alan Bennett Plays; A Tale of Two Cities; The Further Adventures of Oliver Twist; For Services Rendered; Minder; Kessler; Wilfred and Eileen; East Lynne; Juliet Bravo; Porterhouse Blue; Inspector Morse; Hideaway; Paradise Postponed; The Canterville Ghost; Dead Entry; Rockliffe's Babies; The Two of Us; May To December; Thatcher: The Final Days; Maigret.* **Address:** c/o Susan Angel Associates. Single; lives in London. Hobbies: Music, conversation, food. **Favourite TV programmes:** *LA Law; Inspector Morse.*

IRVING, *jayne*

Jayne Irving. Presenter. b. Sheffield, South Yorkshire, 30 August 1956. Trained as a reporter on the *Doncaster Evening Post* (1977–80), before entering broadcasting. **Films:** *American Roulette.* **TV:** *Thames News* reporter (1982); TV-am reporter, newscaster, presenter (1983–9), including hosting *Good Morning Britain* and *After Nine; Open Air* presenter (1989–). **Radio:** Reporter-presenter with Sheffield ILR station Radio Hallam (1980–82); Independent Radio News reporter (1982). **Address:** c/o Downes Presenters Agency. Lives in London. m. TV director David Stewart. Hobbies: Horse-riding, swimming, working-out, cinema, theatre, literature, psychology, New Age medicine.

JACKSON, *warren*

Warren Ashley Jackson. Actor. b. Manchester, 24 November 1980. **TV:** Nicky Platt (formerly Tilsley) in *Coronation Street* (1980-). **Address:** c/o Granada TV. Lives in Manchester. Pets: A cat called Suki. Hobbies: Football, basketball, computer games. **Favourite TV programme:** *The Simpsons; Tom and Jerry; LA Law.*

JAMES, *clive*

Clive James. Presenter. b. Sydney, Australia, 1939. Television critic of *The Observer* (1972–6). **TV:** *The Clive James Show; Saturday Night People; Clive James On TV; Saturday Night Clive; Clive James On 1991.* **Books:** *The Crystal Bucket; Visions Before Midnight; Unreliable Memoirs* (autobiography). **Address:** c/o Peters Fraser & Dunlop.

JAMES, *geraldine*

Geraldine James. Actress. b. Maidenhead, Berkshire, 6 July 1950. Trained at The Drama Centre. **Theatre:** Rep at the Bush Theatre, Oxford Playhouse, the Royal Court Theatre and Bristol's Little Theatre; *Passion for Dracula; When I Was a Girl I Used To Scream and Shout; Cymbeline; The Merchant of Venice* (London West End and Broadway). **Films:** *Sweet William; Night Cruiser; Gandhi; The Wolves of Willoughby Chase; The Tall Guy; She's Been Away* (joint winner, Venice Film Festival Volpi Cup for Best Actress); *If Looks Could Kill; The Bridge.* **TV:** *The Sweeney; Dummy* (winner, Critics' Award for Best Actress, 1978); *The Jewel In the Crown; Blott On the Landscape; Echoes; 'Ex'* (TV movie); *Stanley and the Women.* **Address:** c/o Julian Belfrage Associates. m. Joseph Blatchley; 1 d. Eleanor.

JAMES, *john*

John James. Actor. b. Minneapolis, Minnesota, 18 April. Trained at the American Academy of Dramatic Arts. **Theatre:** *Butterflies Are Free; Suds*. **TV:** *Search for Tomorrow; The Love Boat; Fantasy Island;* Jeff Colby in *Dynasty* and *The Colbys*. **Address:** c/o William Morris Agency (USA). m. Denise Coward.

JAMESON, *louise*

Louise Jameson. Actress. b. Wanstead, East London, 20 April 1951. **Theatre:** *King Lear; Love's Labour's Lost; Summerfolk; Richard III; Passion Play; As You Like It; A Midsummer Night's Dream* (all RSC); *Sleeping Nightie* (Royal Court Theatre). **TV:** *Cider With Rosie; Z-Cars; The Omega Factor; Tenko; Boy Dominic; Bergerac; Emmerdale Farm; The Gentle Touch; The Secret Diary of Adrian Mole Aged 13¾; The Growing Pains of Adrian Mole; Casualty; The Bill; Rides*. **Address:** c/o Jeremy Conway. Lives with artist Martin Bedford; 2 s. Harry, Thomas.

JAMIESON, *charles*

Charles Reginald Wingate Jamieson. Actor. b. Rutherglen, Strathclyde, 12 March 1952. Studied drama at Texas Christian University. **Theatre:** *Mother Goose; Timephase; A Bed Full of Foreigners; Whose Life Is It Anyway?; Black Coffee; Joking Apart; Privates On Parade; Robinson Crusoe; Babes In the Wood; Twelfth Night; Sailor Beware; Tales of Toad Hall*. **Films:** *Fast Religion* (Royal College of Art). **TV:** *The Omega Factor;* Sargeant in *Blake's 7;* narrator of *Duel With an Teallach; Goodnight and Godbless;* Ruari Galbraith in *Take the High Road*. Plus numerous TV commercials. Narrator, *Early Cinema, Parts I and II* (British Film Institute). **Address:** c/o Joan Gray Personal Management. Lives in Ayrshire. m. Sally Ann Muir. Hobbies: Gardening, painting, horse-riding. **Favourite TV programme:** The news.

JANSON, *david*

David Janson. Actor. b. London, 30 March 1950. Trained at the Phildene Stage School from the age of nine. **Theatre:** *Oliver!; A Midsummer Night's Dream* (RSC); *Hanky Park; Roll On Four O'Clock; She Was Only an Admiral's Daughter; Out of the Crocodile; My Giddy Aunt; Season's Greetings; Taking Steps; The Rivals; Don't Start Without Me; Run for Your Wife*. **Films:** *A Hard Day's Night*. **TV:** *The Newcomers; Get Some In; Grundy; Don't Rock the Boat; Brush Strokes;* Hitler in *'Allo 'Allo!* **Address:** c/o Peter Graham Associates. m. actress Debbie Arnold (qv); 1 d. Ciara.

JARVIS, *martin*

Martin Jarvis. Actor. b. Cheltenham, Gloucestershire, 4 August 1941. Trained at RADA. **TV:** *The Forsyte Sage; Nicholas Nickleby; Little Women; Crimes of Passion; The Rivals of Sherlock Holmes; Doctor Who; The Pallisers; David Copperfield; Goodbye, Mr Chips; Softly, Softly; Zigger Zagger; She; Within These Walls; Charades; True Patriot; Rings On Their Fingers; Enemy At the Door; The Business of Murder; The Otterbury Incident; The Big One; Mr Palfrey of Westminster; Who Dares Wins; Let's Parlez Franglais; Just William's Christmas; Horizon; Survival; Juliet Bravo; The Black Tower; Make and Break; Rumpole of the Bailey; Chelworth; Des Res; The Life Revolution; Comic Relief; Coast To Coast; The South Bank Show; Inspector Morse; The Good Guys; Woof!* **Address:** c/o Michael Whitehall. m. actress Rosalind Ayres (qv); 2 s. Toby, Oliver.

JASON, *david*

David White. Actor. b. Edmonton, London, 2 February 1940. Brother of actor Arthur White. Amateur theatre while working as an electrician, then turned professional as an actor. **Theatre:** *South Sea Bubble;* repertory theatre; *Peter Pan; The Dick Emery Show; Not Now, Darling* (Middle and Far East tour). **Films:** *The Water Babies; The Odd Job; The B.F.G.* **TV:** Captain Fantastic in *Do Not Adjust Your Set; Hark At Barker; Six Dates With Barker; Doctor In the House; Doctor At Large; Doctor at Sea; The Top Secret Life of Edgar Briggs; Lucky Fella; A Sharp Intake of Breath; Porridge; Open All Hours;* Del in *Only Fools and Horses; Porterhouse Blue; A Bit of a Do;* Pop Larkin in *The Darling Buds of May; Amongst Barbarians.* Winner, BAFTA Best Light Entertainment Performance award, 1991. **Address:** c/o Richard Stone Partnership.

JAYSTON, *michael*

Michael Jayston. Actor. b. Nottingham, 29 October 1935. Trained at Guildhall School of Music and Drama. **Theatre:** Repertory theatre in Salisbury and Bristol; RSC; National Theatre. **Films:** *Cromwell; Nicholas and Alexandra; Follow Me; Bequest To the Nation; Tales That Witness Madness; Craze; The Internecine Project.* **TV:** *The Power Game; Mad Jack; Charles Dickens; Beethoven; Mr Rolls and Mr Royce; Jane Eyre; The Merchant of Venice; Quiller; King Lear; She Fell Among Thieves; The Last Romantic; Gossip From the Forest; Tinker, Tailor, Soldier, Spy; The Good Guys.* **Address:** c/o Michael Whitehall. m. Ann.

JEAVONS, *colin*

Colin Jeavons. Actor. b. Newport, Gwent, 20 October 1929. Trained at the Old Vic Theatre School. **Theatre:** Old Vic Theatre; *Cat On a Hot Tin Roof.* **Films:** *Caleb Williams; The French Lieutenant's Woman; Absolute Beginners.* **TV:** *Lucky Jim; Terrry Scott On ...;* Mr Shadrack in *Billy Liar; The Fuzz; Kinvig; Shoestring; Great Expectations; Jackanory; Ladykillers; The Hitch-Hiker's Guide To the Galaxy; Dear Heart; Travelling Man; Reilly – Ace of Spies; Atlantis; Travellers By Night; The Adventures of Sherlock Holmes; Charters and Caldicott; Fairly Secret Army; Sea of Faith; Bleak House; Squaring the Circle; Hitler's SS; Paradise Postponed; Prospects; Brat Farrar; Big Deal; The Return of Sherlock Holmes; Call Me Mister; Blackeyes; House of Cards; The House of Eliott; Sherlock Holmes: The Master Blackmailer.* **Address:** c/o ICM Duncan Heath Associates. m. Rosie; 2 s. Saul, Barney.

JEFFREY, *peter*

Peter Jeffrey. Actor. b. Bristol, Avon, 18 April 1929. **Theatre:** RSC; *Donkey's Years; For Services Rendered* (National Theatre). **Films:** *Becket; The Fixer; If ...; Ring of Bright Water; Anne of the Thousand Days; The Horsemen; The Odessa File; The Return of the Pink Panther; Midnight Express; Britannia Hospital; The Adventures of Baron Munchausen.* **TV:** *The Plane Makers; Triangle; Villette; The Atom Spies; Rifleman; For Services Rendered; Minder; All's Well That Ends Well; Boys and Girls Come Out To Play; Cakes and Ale; The Common; Destiny; London Belongs To Me; Porridge; Mr and Ms Bureaucrat; The Old Crowd; One By One; The Jewel In the Crown; Elizabeth R; By the Sword Divided; Nanny; Quartermaine's Terms; Chelworth.* **Address:** c/o London Management.

JEFFRIES, *lionel*

Lionel Jeffries. Actor/Director. b. London, 10 June 1926. Trained at RADA. **Films:** *The Colditz Story; Blue Murder At St Trinian's; Murder Ahoy; You Must Be Joking!; Arrividerci, Baby; Doctor At Large; The Spy With a Cold Nose; Journey To the Moon; Camelot; Chitty Chitty Bang Bang; Eyewitness; What Changed Charley Farthing?; The Railway Children; Who Slew Auntie Roo?; Baxter; The Amazing Mr Blunden; Royal Flash; The Water Babies; Wombling Free; Prisoner of Zenda; Ménage à Trois; Danny The Champion of the World; A Chorus of Disapproval.* **TV:** *Facts of Life; A Quick Double; Room At the Bottom; Cream In My Coffee; Shillingbury Tales; Father Charlie; Tom, Dick and Harriet; First and Last; Ending Up; Inspector Morse; Jekyll & Hyde; The Wild Duck; Rich Tea & Sympathy.* **Address:** c/o ICM. m. Eileen; 2 d. Martha, Elizabeth, 1 s. Timothy.

JENKINS, *sue*

Sue Jenkins. Actress. b. Liverpool. Trained at the Elliott-Clarke Theatre School, Liverpool. **Theatre:** Title role in *Educating Rita;* Viola in *Twelfth Night;* Desdemona in *Othello;* Beatrice in *The Changeling;* Nora in *The Plough and the Stars;* Doreen in *Having a Ball.* **TV:** *Z-Cars* (as a child); *How We Used To Live; The Beiderbecke Affair;* Gloria Todd in *Coronation Street; Coasting;* Jackie Corkhill in *Brookside* (1991-). **Address:** c/o Peter Graham Associates. m. actor David Fleeshman (qv); 1 d. Emily, 1 s. Richard.

JEPHCOTT, *dominic*

Dominic Jephcott. Actor. b. Coventry, Warwickshire, 28 July 1957. Trained at RADA. **Theatre:** *The Sons of Light; The Lorenzaccio Story; As You Like It; 'Tis Pity She's a Whore* (all RSC). **Films:** *Inseminoid; Good and Bad At Games; All Quiet On the Western Front; An American Dream.* **TV:** *Enemy At the Door; The Scarlet Pimpernel* (TV movie); Jonathan in *Hold the Dream; Napoleon and Josephine; Oliver Twist; Stalky & Co;* Reggie Brocklehurst in *The Jewel In the Crown; The Aerodrome;* Hobson in *The Beiderbecke Connection* and *The Beiderbecke Affair;* Magnus Strove in *Paradise Postponed; Great Writers: Proust; Claws; Rumpole of the Bailey; Stars In a Dark Night; Ticket To Ride; The Return of Sherlock Holmes; The Leading Lady; The Bill; Casualty; Stay Lucky; Family Album; Sam Saturday.* **Address:** c/o Markham & Froggatt.

JERRICHO, *paul*

Paul Jerricho. Actor. b. 18 November 1948. Trained at The Drama Centre. **Theatre:** *The Resistible Rise of Arturo Ui; Time and Time Again; The Bacchae; The Biko Inquest; A Man for All Seasons; As You Like It; The Taming of the Shrew; The Deep Blue Sea; Macbeth; Suspicions; Rough Crossing.* **Films:** *Force 10 From Navarone; The Empire Strikes Back; The Thirty-Nine Steps; Cry Freedom; Forced March.* **TV:** *Enemy At the Door; The Secret Army; Hay Fever; QED; Armchair Thriller; Ladykillers; Animal Behaviour; Doctor Who; The Biko Inquest; Triangle;* Danny Moorcock in *Emmerdale Farm; Grange Hill; Knights of God; Medicine Through Time;* Robert Hastings in *Howards' Way.* **Address:** c/o Darryl Brown Associates. Hobbies: Tennis, cycling, swimming, water-skiing, cricket, cooking, writing. **Favourite TV programme:** News and natural history programmes.

JEWEL, *jimmy*

Jimmy Jewel. Actor. b. Sheffield, South Yorkshire, 4 December 1912. On stage from the age of 10 and worked with comedian father (also Jimmy Jewel), then solo as a comedian, before teaming up with cousin Ben Warriss (1934–66). **Theatre:** *The Sunshine Boys; Comedians; Clown Jewels; Death of a Salesman; You Can't Take It With You;* National Theatre. **Films:** *Nearest and Dearest; The Krays; American Friends.* **TV:** Eli Pledge in *Nearest and Dearest; Thicker Than Water; Spring and Autumn; Funny Man; A Spanner In the Works; Oldest Goose In the Business; Missing Persons; One Foot In the Grave; Casualty.* Winner, Variety Club Special Award, 1985. **Address:** c/o Howes and Prior. m. Belle (dec); 1 s. Kerry, 1 adopted-d. Piper.

JOHNSON, *don*

Don Johnson. Actor. b. Flatt Creek, Missouri, USA, 15 December 1950. Won a drama scholarship to the University of Kansas, then went on to the American Conservatory Group in San Francisco. **Films:** *Sweetheart Dance; Ceasefire; Zacharias; Return To Macon Country; Dead-Bang.* **TV:** *The Rebels; From Here To Eternity; Elvis and Me; The Long Hot Summer; Revenge of the Stepford Wives;* Sonny Crocket in *Miami Vice.* Winner, Golden Globe Best Actor award. **Records:** *Heartbeat* (LP). **Address:** c/o Mike Belson, 50 Beverly Drive, Beverly Hills, California 90212, USA. m. 1st actress Melanie Griffith (dis); 2nd Melanie Griffith (remarried); 1 s. Jesse, 1 d. Dakota.

JOHNSTON, *sue*

Sue Johnston. Actress. b. Warrington, 7 December 1943. Trained at the Webber Douglas Academy. **Theatre:** Repertory theatre in Farnham, Salford, Lincoln, Manchester and Coventry; founder-member of the M6 theatre company; *To* (Edinburgh Festival, Octagon Theatre, Bolton, and national tour). **TV:** Mrs Chadwick in *Coronation Street*; Sheila Corkhill (formerly Grant) in *Brookside* (1982–90); Mum in *The Lime Grove Story: The Grove Family*; Barbara Grade in *Goodbye Cruel World*; *Medics*. **Books:** *Hold On To the Messy Times* (autobiography). **Address:** c/o Ken McReddie. m. (dis); 1 s. Joel.

JONES, *catherine zeta*

Catherine Zeta Jones. Actress. b. Swansea, West Glamorgan. **Theatre:** *The Pyjama Game* (national tour); *42nd Street*. **Films:** *Scheherazade*. **TV:** Mariette Larkin in *The Darling Buds of May*; *Out of the Blue*. **Address:** c/o ICM Duncan Heath Associates. Single; lives in Swansea.

JONES, *freddie*

Freddie Jones. Actor. b. Stoke-on-Trent, Staffordshire, 12 September 1927. Lab assistant before training at the Rose Bruford College. **Films:** *Marat/Sade*; *Deadfall*; *The Bliss of Mrs Blossom*; *Far From the Madding Crowd*; *Otley*; *Goodbye Gemini*; *Frankenstein Must Be Destroyed*; *The Man Who Haunted Himself*; *All Creatures Great and Small*; *The Elephant Man*; *Firefox*; *Young Sherlock Holmes*; *Krull*; *And the Ship Sailed*; *Dune*; *Firestarter*. **TV:** *Sword of Honour*; *Nana*; *Treasure Island*; *Cold Comfort Farm*; *Uncle Vanya*; *The Caesars*; *Germinal*; *Play for Today: Sorry . . .*; *Secret Orchards*; *Sweeney Todd*; *The Ghosts of Motley Hall*; *In Loving Memory*; *District Nurse*; *How To Be Cool*; *Tiny Revolutions*; *Vanity Fair*; *The Return of Sherlock Holmes*; *Inspector Morse*; *Adam Bede*. **Address:** c/o James Sharkey Associates. m. Jennifer Heslewood; 3 s. Toby, Rupert, Caspar.

JONES, *gareth ('Gaz Top')*

Gareth Jones. Presenter. b. Wales, 5 July 1961. **TV:** Presenter and producer for Music Box cable TV; *Get Fresh* (co-host, three series); *Children's ITV*; *Your Number's Up* (host, HTV game show); *APB*; presenter and producer for MTV Europe satellite TV; *Kellyvision* (co-host); *Pssst . . . The Really Useful Guide To Alcohol* (documentary series); *How 2* (two series); acting debut in Welsh Fourth Channel soap opera *Mwy Na Phapur Newydd*; presenter and producer of *The TCC Club* and *TCC On the Road* for the Children's Channel satellite TV. **Radio:** Own Saturday-morning show on BBC Radio Wales. **Address:** c/o Sara Cameron Management. Single; lives in London. Hobbies: Motorbikes, Space, playing guitar, listening to music.

JONES, *ken*

Ken Jones. Actor. b. Liverpool, 20 February 1930. Sign-writer and amateur actor before training at RADA. **Theatre:** *The Hostage* (Joan Littlewood's Theatre Workshop); *When the Wind Blows*. **Films:** *File of the Golden Goose*; *SWALK*; *Sherlock Holmes*; *No Surrender*. **TV:** *Z-Cars* (first episode); *Hunter's Walk*; *Go for Gold*; *The Liver Birds*; *The Life of Jesus*; *Germinal*; *Her Majesty's Pleasure*; *Last of the Baskets*; *The Wackers*; *The Squirrels*; *First Class Friend*; *Dead Earnest*; *Porridge*; *Seconds Out*; *Valentine Park*; *Boon*. **Address:** c/o David White Associates. m. actress/writer Sheila Fay.

JONES, *peter*

Peter Jones. Actor/Writer. b. Wem, Shropshire, 12 June 1920. **Theatre:** Thirty London West End plays. **Films:** Fifty films. **TV:** *The Rag Trade; Long Live the King; Beggar My Neighbour; Mr Digby Darling; Children of Dynmouth; One-Upmanship; Whoops Apocalypse; The Agatha Christie Hour; I Thought You'd Gone; Singles Weekend; Rumpole of the Bailey.* **Radio:** *Just a Minute; In All Directions; The Hitch-Hiker's Guide To the Galaxy.* **Address:** c/o Salopian Plays, 32 Acacia Road, London NW8 6AS. m. American actress/writer Jeri Sauvinet; 1 d. actress Selena Carey-Jones, 2 s. radio and TV producer Bill Dare, Charles. **Favourite TV programme:** *Channel Four News.*

JONES, *simon*

Simon Jones. Actor. b. Charlton Park, Wiltshire, 27 July 1950. **Theatre:** Repertory theatre in Bradford, Crewe and Derby; *Bloomsbury* (London West End debut); *Seven Days To Doomsday; The Carnation Gang; The Clandestine Marriage; The Browning Version; Wild Oats; Privates On Parade; Benefactors* (both RSC); *Candida; The Millionairess; Design for Living; The Real Thing; My Fair Lady.* **Films:** *Brazil; Monty Python's The Meaning of Life; Reds.* **TV:** *Newhart; Rock Follies; Victorian Scandals; Fothergill; The Kindness of Mrs Radcliffe; No Visible Scar; Muck and Brass;* Brideshead in *Brideshead Revisited;* Arthur Dent in *The Hitch-Hiker's Guide To the Galaxy; Blackadder II; Claws.* **Address:** c/o ICM Duncan Heath Associates. m. Nancy Lewis.

JONES, *steve*

David Stephen Vaughan Jones. Presenter. b. Crewe, Cheshire, 7 June 1945. Trained as a teacher and worked as a professional musician and ice-cream salesman before becoming a radio disc-jockey. **TV:** *Battle of the Comics; It's the Jones Boy; It's Friday; Sneak Preview; Steve Jones Illustrated; Watch This Space; Edinburgh Festival Show; Saturday Morning Show; The Steve Jones Game Show; Search for a Star; The Pyramid Game.* **Radio:** Disc-jockey with Radio Clyde (1973–8), LBC and BBC Radio 2 (1979-). Winner, Scottish Radio Personality award, 1977, Variety Club Independent Radio Personality, 1989. **Address:** c/o Bagenal Harvey Organisation. Lives in West London. m. Lolita (dec); 3 s. Marc, Jason, Oliver. Pets: A cat called Barney. Hobbies: Golf, cinema, tennis, cooking. **Favourite TV programme:** *Only Fools and Horses;* any live sport.

JONES, *sue*

Sue Jones. Actress. **Films:** *Blood Money; Dead Man's Float; Once Upon a Weekend; Mullaway; Evil Angels; Doing Time; Flynn.* **TV:** *Matlock; Division 4; Homicide; Bluey; The Box; The Sullivans; Cop Shop; Skyways; Holiday Island; Special Squad; Prime Time; The Flying Doctors; Bellbird; The Truckies; The Fast Lane; Sam's Luck Power Without Glory; House Rules; Home; Bandit; Inside Running; Rats; Boys From the Bush; The Tea Ladies; Love Thy Neighbour; Cash & Co; The Far Country; Skirts; M:any Are Called; Emerging; The Humpty Dumpty Man; Rainbow In the Rock; Preoccupied;* Pam Willis in *Neighbours* (1990-). **Address:** c/o Barbara Gange Management/Grundy Television.

JUDD, *lesley*

Lesley Judd. Presenter. b. London, 20 December 1946. Trained at the Arts Educational School. **Theatre:** *Half a Sixpence; Our Man Crichton; Twang!* (all as a dancer). **TV:** *Blue Peter; Micro-Live; Horizon; Pets In Particular; Holiday Talk; Dance Crazy; This Is Your Right; Let's Go Maths; Business Matters; Adventure Game; The Great Egg Race; Threads; Time To Talk.* **Address:** c/o Arlington Enterprises. m. A Relph; 1 d. Marta Carolina, 1 s. Henry Thomas.

JUNKIN, *john*

John Junkin. Actor/Writer. b. Ealing, West London, 29 January 1930. Joined Joan Littlewood's Theatre Workshop in 1960. **Films:** *A Hard Day's Night; Kaleidoscope; The Brass Target; Wombling Free; Rosie Dixon – Night Nurse; A Handful of Dust; Chicago Joe and the Showgirl.* **TV:** *Sam and Janet; Junkin* (four series); *Hello Cheeky; Marty; Looking for Clancy; Out; The Ravelled Thread; Dick Turpin; Penmarric; All for Love; Blott On the Landscape; 25 Years of Ronnie Scott's; Ask No Questions* (presenter); *Langley Bottom* (co-writer); *Mike Yarwood In Persons* (script editor); *All Creatures Great and Small; Shelley.* Programme associate/consultant: *Body Matters; Bob Says Opportunity Knocks; Bob's Full House; The $64,000 Question; Bob's Your Uncle.* **Address:** c/o London Management. m. Jennie; 1 d. Annabel.

KANE, *john*

John Kane. Actor/Writer. b. Dundee, Tay, 27 October 1945. Trained at Glasgow College of Dramatic Art. **Theatre:** RSC. **TV:** *Softly, Softly; Doctor Who; Doctor On the Go; Cymbeline; Love's Labour's Lost; The Seagull; Paradise Postponed* (all as actor); *Scott On...; Son of the Bride; Black Beauty; The Vamp; The Feathered Serpent; Four Idle Hands; Cloppa Castle; A Little Touch of Wisdom; Smuggler; Dick Turpin; Funny Ha-Ha; Terry and June; Happy Ever After; Never the Twain; Me & My Girl; All In Good Faith; The Return of Sherlock Holmes* (all as writer). **Address:** c/o ICM Duncan Heath Associates. m. Alison; 2 d. Alice, Susanna, 1 s. Simon.

KAY, *charles*

Charles Kay. Actor. b. Coventry, Warwickshire, 31 August 1930. Trained at RADA. **Theatre:** RSC; National Theatre; Old Vic Theatre. **Films:** *Hennessey; Nijinsky; Amadeus; Henry V.* **TV:** *The Duchess of Malfi; The Merchant of Venice; Sister Alice; Microbes and Men; Miss Nightingale; Fall of Eagles; Jenny; The Prodigal Daughter; Loyalties; I, Claudius; Countess Ilona; Target; The Devil's Crown; Minor Complications; Ladykillers; To Serve Them All My Days; A Visitor for Mr Hugh Peters; My Cousin Rachel; The White Guard; The Citadel; King John; Edge of Darkness; West of Paradise; Fortunes of War; London Embassy; Menace Unseen; Rumpole of the Bailey; A Quiet Conspiracy; Bomber Harris; Storyboard; Fiddlers Three; The Darling Buds of May; The Bill; The Return of Sherlock Holmes.* **Address:** c/o Marmont Management.

KAYE, *gorden*

Gorden Kaye. Actor. b. Huddersfield, West Yorkshire, 7 April 1941. **Theatre:** *Little Malcolm; As You Like It* (National Theatre); *Mother's Day; Sleak; Hobson's Choice; Sleeping Beauty; Better Times; 'Allo 'Allo!; Mother Goose.* **Films:** *Escape From the Dark* (aka *The Littlest Horse Thieves*); *Jaberwocky; The Waterloo Bridge Handicap; Porridge; Brazil.* **TV:** Bernard Butler in *Coronation Street; It Ain't Half Hot Mum; Are You Being Served?; The Growing Pains of PC Penrose; Shoestring; Oh Happy Band; The Foundation; All Creatures Great and Small; The Strange Affair of Adelaide Harris; God's Wonderful Railway; The Party's Over; Born and Bred; Fame Is the Spur; Codename Icarus; Rainy Day Women; Manfield Park; King John; Much Ado About Nothing; In the Secret State;* Rene Artois in *'Allo 'Allo!* **Address:** c/o Markham & Froggatt.

KEANE, *paul*

Paul Keane. Actor. b. Sydney, Australia. Trained at the National Institute of Dramatic Art. **Theatre:** *Romeo and Juliet; The Cherry Orchard.* **TV:** *Sons and Daughters;* Des Clarke in *Neighbours* (1985-). **Address:** c/o Lee Leslie Management/Grundy Television.

KEARNEY, *gillian*

Gillian Kearney. Actress. b. Liverpool, 9 May 1972. Attended the Liverpool Playhouse Youth Theatre. **Theatre:** *All Flesh Is Grass*; *'Yer Dancing?'*; *Katie Crackernuts* (all at the Liverpool Playhouse Youth Theatre); *Our Home In the West*. **Films:** Young Shirley in *Shirley Valentine*. **TV:** Debbie McGrath in *Brookside* and three-part spin-off *Damon & Debbie* (1987); Cassy in *The Final Frame* (Channel Four film); *Waterfront Beat*. **Address:** c/o Annette Stone Associates. Single; lives in Liverpool. Hobbies: Reading, dancing, swimming. **Favourite TV programme:** *Blackadder*.

KEAVENEY, *anna*

Anna Keaveney. Actress. b. Runcorn, Cheshire, 5 October 1949. Trained at Studio '68. **Theatre:** Repertory theatre in Oldham, Bolton, Pitlochry, Liverpool and at Glasgow Citizens' Theatre and Bristol Old Vic; *Once a Catholic* (Royal Court Theatre and Wyndham's); *Neaptide* (National Theatre); *Translations* (Hampstead Theatre and National Theatre); *Touched*; *Good Fun*. **Films:** *Shirley Valentine*. **TV:** *Within These Walls*; *Enemy At the Door*; *Widows*; Marie Jackson in *Brookside*; *Security* (Channel Four film); *Divided We Stand*; April Brooks in *Emmerdale*. **Address:** c/o Stephen Hatton Management.

KEEL, *howard*

Howard Keel. Actor/Singer. b. Gillespie, Illinois, USA, 13 April 1917. Previously an aircraft sales rep; began acting after winning a singing scholarship. **Theatre:** *No Strings*; *Carousel*; *Oklahoma!*; *South Pacific*; *Camelot*; *Kismet*; *Kiss Me Kate*. **Films:** *Seven Brides for Seven Brothers*; *Annie Get Your Gun*; *Calamity Jane*; *Showboat*. **TV:** Clayton Farlow in *Dallas*. **Address:** c/o Lew Sherrell Agency. m. 3rd Judy; 1 s. Gunnar, 3 d. Christina, Kaya (all from previous m.), Lesley (from 3rd m).

KEEN, *diane*

Diane Keen. Actress. b. London, 29 July 1946. Brought up in Kenya; returned to Britain aged 19. **Theatre:** Repertory theatre. **TV:** *Crossroads*; *Fall of Eagles*; *Softly, Softly*; *Public Eye*; *The Legend of Robin Hood*; *The Sweeney*; *The Feathered Serpent*; *Country Matters*; *Crown Court*; Fliss in *The Cuckoo Waltz*; *The Sandbaggers*; *Rings On Their Fingers*; *The Shillingbury Blowers*; *The Shillingbury Tales*; *The Reunion*; *The Morecambe and Wise Show*; *Bruce Meets the Girls*; *Foxy Lady*; *Oxbridge Blues*; *Killer Waiting*; *Sleeps Six*; *You Must Be the Husband*; *Jekyll & Hyde* (TV movie); *Three Go Round*; *The Ruth Rendell Mysteries*; *Key for Two*. TV commercials: Nescafé. **Address:** c/o Scott Marshall. m. Neil Zeiger; 1 d. Melissa.

KEITH, *penelope*

Penelope Keith. Actress. b. Sutton, Surrey, 2 April. Trained at the Webber Douglas Academy. **Films:** *The Hound of the Baskervilles*; *The Priest of Love*. **TV:** *Hadleigh*; *Six Shades of Black*; *Kate*; *The Pallisers*; *Two's Company*; *Jackanory*; *Saving It for Alvie*; *Private Lives*; *The Good Life*; *Private Lives*; *The Norman Conquests*; *The Morecambe and Wise Christmas Show*; *Much Ado About Nothing*; *Donkey's Years*; *On Approval*; *To the Manor Born*; *Spider's Web*; *Waters of the Moon*; *Sweet Sixteen*; *Capability Brown*; *Moving*; *Executive Stress*; *No Job for a Lady*; *What's My Line?* (presenter). Winner, *TVTimes* awards (1976, 1977, 1978, 1979, 1980), BAFTA Best Light Entertainment Performance award (1977), BAFTA Best TV Actress award (1978, 1979), Variety Club BBC TV Personality award (1979). **Address:** c/o London Management. m. Rodney Timson.

KEITH, *sheila*

Sheila Keith. Actress. b. Aberdeen, Grampian, 9 June 1920. Trained at the Webber Douglas Academy. **Theatre:** Repertory theatre in Liverpool, Coventry, Bristol and Leatherhead; *Present Laughter; Mame; Banana Ridge; Deathtrap.* **Films:** *Ooh You Are Awful; House of Whipcord; Frightmare; The Comeback; Clockwise.* **TV:** *David Copperfield; Moody and Peg; Ballet Shoes; Within These Walls; Angels; The Cedar Tree; The Pallisers; Jubilee; Roof Over My Head; Working Arrangements; Heartland; The Racing Game; Rings On Their Fingers; Swing, Swing Together; Agony; Bless Me Father; The Other 'Arf; Never the Twain; Fresh Fields.* **Address:** c/o David White Associates.

KELLY, *chris*

Chris Kelly. Presenter/Writer/Producer. b. Cuddington, Cheshire, 24 April 1940. **TV:** Anglia TV announcer and newsreader; Granada TV producer; *Sixth Form Challenge; Zoo Time; Anything You Can Do; Clapperboard; World In Action* (narrator); *Wish You Were Here...?; Friday Live; The Royal Film Performance; Folio; Fit for Living; The Royal Academy Summer Exhibition; I've Got a Secret; Never Too Early; Never Too Late; Cinema Scrapbook; Food and Drink; Zero Option* (writer); *The Telebook* (writer); *Soldier Soldier* (producer). **Address:** c/o Barry Burnett Organisation. m. Vivien; 1 d. Rebecca, 1 s. Nicholas.

KELLY, *david*

David Kelly. Actor. b. Dublin, Ireland, 11 July 1929. Trained at the Abbey Theatre School, Dublin. **Theatre:** Stage performances in Paris, Amsterdam, Oslo, Stockholm, Zurich and Berlin. **Films:** *The Red Monarch; The Jigsaw Man; Ann Devlin; Pirates.* **TV:** *Cowboys; The Gentle Touch; Strumpet City; Whoops Apocalypse; Robin's Nest; Oh! Brother; Fawlty Towers; Slinger's Day; 2point4 children.* **Address:** c/o Joy Jameson. m. actress Laurie Morton; 1 d. Miriam, 1 s. David.

KELLY, *henry*

Henry Kelly. Presenter. b. Dublin, Ireland, 17 April 1946. Newspaper reporter on the *Irish Times* before joining BBC Radio 4, then entering television. **TV:** *Game for a Laugh* (three series); *TV-am; Monkey Business; Scene '85, '86, '87, '88; Extra Time; Going for Gold; An Actor's Life for Me* (acting himself); *Big Decision.* **Radio:** *The World Tonight; Profile; Woman's Hour; Midweek.* **Books:** *How Stormont Fell.* **Address:** c/o 8 Sandy Road, London NW3 7EY. m. Marjorie; 1 d. Siobhan.

KELLY, *matthew*

Matthew Kelly. Actor/Presenter. b. Urmston, Manchester, 9 May 1950. **Theatre:** Repertory theatre; London West End. **Films:** *Gabrielle and the Doodleman.* **TV:** *The Bonus; Play for Today: Pickersgill People; The Rather Reassuring Programme; Funny Man; The Critic; Holding the Fort* (three series); *Game for a Laugh* (co-presenter, three series); *Madabout* (two series); *Quandaries; Relative Strangers* (two series); *The Sensible Show; Adventures of a Lifetime* (two series); *Kelly's Eye* (presenter); *You Bet!* (presenter). **Address:** c/o Stella Richards Management. m. Sarah; 1 d. Ruth, 1 s. Matthew.

KELLY, *sam*

Sam Kelly. Actor. b. Manchester, 19 December 1943. Trained at LAMDA. **Theatre:** Repertory theatre in St Andrews, Liverpool, Sheffield, Manchester, Coventry, Birmingham and Southampton; Young Vic Theatre; *'Allo 'Allo!* (London Palladium and national tour); *Run for Your Wife.* **TV:** *Emergency – Ward 10; The Liver Birds; Porridge; 'Allo 'Allo!; Who's Who; Grown Ups; Victoria Wood As Seen On TV; Boys From the Blackstuff; Now and Then; Coronation Street; Christabel; Will You Love Me Tomorrow* (TV movie); *Haggard; On the Up; Making Out; Inspector Morse; Stay Lucky.* **Address:** c/o Richard Stone Partnership.

KEMP, *ross*

Ross Kemp. Actor. Trained at the Webber Douglas Academy. **Theatre:** *Staircase; Fur Coat and No Knickers; The Wizard of Oz; Mr Punch; A Pin To See the Peep Show.* **TV:** *Playing Away; Claws;* Graham (Dolly Skilbeck's illegitimate son) in *Emmerdale Farm* (1985); *The Money Men; London's Burning; The Chief;* Grant Mitchell in *EastEnders* (1990-). **Address:** c/o Jonathan Altaras Associates.

KENDAL, *felicity*

Felicity Kendal. Actress. b. Birmingham, 25 September 1946. Daughter of travelling-actors. **Theatre:** *The Mayfly and the Frog;* Open Air Theatre, Regent's Park; *Kean; The Norman Conquests; Clouds; Amadeus; On the Razzle; The Second Mrs Tanqueray; Othello* (all National Theatre); *Made In Bangkok; Haggard; Much Ado About Nothing; Ivanov* (London *Evening Standard* Best Actress award, 1989); *The Real Thing Jumpers* (London West End *Tartuffe*). **Films:** *Shakespeare Wallah; The Seven Per Cent Solution; Valentino.* **TV:** *Crime of Passion; The Woodlanders; The Dolly Dialogues; Love Story; Edward VII; Home and Beauty; Cuckoo; Twelfth Night; The Good Life; Solo; The Mistress; Prisoners of Conscience.* **Address:** c/o Chatto and Linnit. m. 1st actor Drewe Henley (dis), 2nd Michael Rudman; 2 s. Charlie (from 1st m.), Jacob.

KENNEDY, *cheryl*

Cheryl Kennedy. Actress. b. Enfield, Middlesex, 29 April 1947. Trained at the Corona Stage Academy. **Theatre:** *Half a Sixpence; The Boy Friend; 1776; Time and Time Again; Absent Friends; Flowers for Algernon* (Queen's Theatre); *My Fair Lady* (USA); *Time and the Conways* (Old Vic Theatre); *What a Way To Run a Revolution* (Young Vic Theatre). **TV:** *The Cliff Richard Show; The Mike Yarwood Show; That's Life; Omnibus; Play for Today; Play of the Month; The Sweeney; Target; The Professionals; Brookside.* **Address:** c/o Larry Dalzell Associates. m. (dis); 2 d. Clarissa, Samantha.

KENNEDY, *kevin*

Kevin Patrick Kennedy. Actor. b. Manchester, 4 September 1961. Trained at Manchester Polytechnic School of Theatre. **Theatre:** *Ducking Out* (Greenwich Theatre and London West End); *Hamlet;* Runnicles in *No Sex, Please – We're British* (national tour). **TV:** 'Team helper' in *Cheggers Plays Pop; Dear Ladies; The Last Company Car; Keep On Running;* Curly Watts in *Coronation Street* (1982-); *Royal Variety Performance* (1989). **Radio:** *The Old Man Sleeps Alone; Metamorphosised Arkwright.* **Address:** c/o Saraband Associates/Granada TV. Lives in Manchester. m. Dawn (sep); 1 s. Ryan. Hobbies: Playing guitar, cinema, socialising, eating out, football, playing golf. **Favourite TV programme:** *Coronation Street; Dad's Army; Blackadder.*

KENNEDY, *sarah*

Sarah Kennedy. Presenter. b. Wallington, Surrey, 8 July 1950. Worked in radio in Singapore and Germany before joining BBC radio in London. **TV:** Southern TV; *Royale Progress; Animal Roadshow; Chipperfield Safari; Game for a Laugh* (three series); *60 Minutes; Daytime; Busman's Holiday; Animal Country.* **Radio:** *String Sound; Colour Supplement.* **Address:** c/o Bagenal Harvey Organisation.

KERCHEVAL, *ken*

Ken Kercheval. Actor. b. Wolcottville, Indiana, USA, 15 July 1936. **Theatre:** *Something About a Soldier; Fiddler On the Roof* (both Broadway). **TV:** *Enemy of the People* (TV movie); *Trapper John MD; Matlock; Love Boat; Hotel; Mike Hammer;* Cliff Barnes in *Dallas; Naked City; Secret Storm.* **Address:** c/o Triad Artists. m. 1st (dis), 2nd Ava Fox; 2 s. Aaron, Caleb, 1 d. Liza (from 1st m.).

KERRIGAN, *justine*

Justine Kerrigan. Actress. b. Liverpool, 5 December 1971. Granddaughter of actor Peter Kerrigan. **TV:** *Brookside* (Damon Grant's girlfriend, then Tracy Corkhill, 1985-). **Address:** c/o Mersey Television. m. computer operator Simon; 1 d. Holly.

KERSHAW, *noreen*

Noreen Kershaw. Actress. **Theatre:** Title role in *Shirley Valentine* (original production, Liverpool). **TV:** *Boys From the Blackstuff; Albion Market;* Kathy Roach in *Brookside;* Mrs Wilson in *Watching.* **Address:** c/o Ken McReddie.

KEY, *janet*

Janet Key. Actress. b. Bath, Avon, 10 July 1945. Trained at Bristol Old Vic Theatre School. **Films:** *Percy; I Don't Want To Be Born; 1984.* **TV:** *Pleased To Meet You; The Donati Conspiracy; Softly, Softly; Murder Must Advertise; Thriller; Napoleon and Love; Captain Rogers; Trial; The Sweeney; State of Emergency; Sutherland's Law; The Crezz; Cottage To Let; Cousin Bette; The Tenant of Wildfell Hall; Vanishing Army; Telford's Change; The Square Leopard; Kiss and Tell; Shoestring; Into Thin Air; Antony and Cleopatra; Flesh and Blood; Crown Court; You Don't Have To Walk To Fly; Amy; Cockles; Secrets; Demons; Roll Over Beethoven; Watching; Heart of the Country; Oliver's Ghost; Taggart; Big Deal; Running Wild; The Giftie; Making News.* **Address:** c/o Peter Browne Management. m. actor/writer Gawn Grainger; 1 d. Eliza, 1 s. Charlie.

KEYS, *richard*

Richard Keys. Presenter. b. Coventry, Warwickshire, 23 April 1957. Journalist on the Wolverhampton *Express & Star* and with Hayter's News and Sports Agency in Fleet Street, before entering radio, then television. **TV:** TV-am sports reporter, then presenter of *Good Morning Britain, After Nine, Saturday Sport* and *The Morning Programme; The Motor Show* (BBC); *Tour de France* (Channel Four); *Worldwide Soccer;* chief sports presenter on BSB, then Sky TV. **Radio:** Radio City (Liverpool) news journalist and sports reporter; Piccadilly Radio (Manchester) deputy newsroom editor and sports editor. **Address:** c/o IMG. Lives in Berkshire. m. Julia; 1 d. Jemma, 1 s. Joshua. Hobbies: Playing golf and watching all sports.

KILROY-SILK, *robert*

Robert Kilroy-Silk. Presenter. b. Birmingham, 18 May 1942. Labour MP (1974–86) before entering television. **TV:** *Day To Day; Kilroy!* **Address:** c/o BBC TV. m. Jan; 1 d. Natasha, 1 s. Dominic.

KING, *claire*

Claire King. Actress. b. Yorkshire, 10 January 1963. Trained at the Actors' Institute. Singer in rock groups Fidea and To Be Continued. **Theatre:** Nikki in *The Pleasure Principle.* **Films:** *Heart of Fire; Eat the Rich; The Cold Light of Day.* **TV:** *Alas Smith and Jones; Robbie Coltrane; Hale & Pace; Watch With Mother; Hot Metal; Starting Out; The Bill;* presenter of American pop programme *Shout;* Kim Tate in *Emmerdale* (1989-). Pop promotional videos: Zodiac Mindwarp; Elvis Costello; LA Mix. **Address:** c/o Heidi Cook Personal Management. Single; lives in Harrogate, North Yorkshire, and London. Hobbies: Horse racing, riding, cinema, swimming. **Favourite TV programme:** *Chancer.*

KINGSTON, *mark*

Mark Kingston. Actor. b. London, 18 April 1934. Trained at LAMDA. **Theatre:** Boscombe Hippodrome (debut, 1953); repertory theatre; *Caesar and Cleopatra* (Old Vic Theatre); Old Vic Theatre tours of Russia, Poland, Australia and New Zealand; *The Norman Conquests; The Cocktail Party; A Voyage Round My Father; Clouds; Educating Rita; Woman In Black.* **TV:** *United; Beryl's Lot; Time of My Life; Driving Ambition; Shine On Harvey Moon; No Job for a Lady; About Face.* **Address:** c/o CDA. m. Marigold Sharman.

KIRKBRIDE, *anne*

Anne Kirkbride. Actress. b. Oldham, Lancashire, 21 June 1954. Daughter of cartoonist Jack Kirkbride. Joined the Saddleworth Junior Players aged 11 and Oldham Rep on leaving school, as ASM, then actress. **Theatre:** Repertory theatre at Oldham Coliseum; stage-managed a charity performance of *Snow White.* **TV:** *Another Sunday and Sweet FA* (Jack Rosenthal play); Deirdre Barlow (née Hunt, formerly Langton) in *Coronation Street* (1972-). Joint winner, with William Roache (qv) and Johnny Briggs (qv), Pye Television Award, 1983. **Address:** c/o Granada TV. Single; lives in Withington, Cheshire. Pets: Two cats, Michael and Cass. Hobbies: Photography, gardening, reading, swimming, walking.

KITCHEN, *michael*

Michael Kitchen. Actor. b. Leicester, 31 October 1948. Trained at RADA. **TV:** *King Lear; The Brontes of Howarth; The Reporters* (Play for Today); *The Train; Country Matters; The Monkey's Paw; As Man and Wife; Affairs of Love; Savages; Young Stephen Hind; Enemy; A Divorce; The Four Beauties; Churchill's People; Fall of Eagles; The Misanthrope; The Long and the Short and the Tall; School Play; Caught On a Train; A Room for the Winter; Maybury; Ladykillers; The Best of Everything; Freud; Staying Put; Love Story; The Browning Version; The Comedy of Errors; Brimstone and Treacle; No Man's Land; Bedroom Farce; Love Song; The Justice Game; Island Gardens; Minder; Home Run; Benefactors; Ball-Trap On the Cote Sauvage; The Pied Piper; Stay Lucky; Inspector Morse; The Advocates; The Prodigal.* **Address:** c/o Markham & Froggatt.

KNOX, *barbara*

Barbara Knox. Actress. b. Oldham, Lancashire, 1938. Left school at 15 to work as a Post Office telegraphist, then in offices, shops and factories. After amateur theatre, joined Oldham Rep. **Theatre:** Oldham Coliseum and other repertory theatre. **Films:** *Goodbye, Mr Chips.* **TV:** *Emergency – Ward 10; Mrs Thursday; Never Mind the Quality, Feel the Width; The Dustbinmen; A Family At War;* Rita Fairclough (née Littlewood) in *Coronation Street* (1972-). **Radio:** Acted alongside Ken Dodd, Jimmy Tarbuck, Ray Alan, Mike Yarwood, Les Dawson, Freddie Davies. **Record:** *On the Street Where I Live* (LP, 1973). Winner, *TV Times* Best Actress award, 1989. **Address:** c/o Saraband Associates/Granada TV. Lives in Worcestershire. m. 1st Denis (dis), 2nd John Knox; 1 d. Maxine (from 1st m.).

KNOX-MAWER, *vanessa*

Vanessa Knox-Mawer. Actress. b. Fiji, 10 July. Daughter of broadcaster June Knox-Mawer. Member of the National Youth Theatre; trained at Central School of Speech and Drama. **Films:** *The Mysterious Stranger; Runners; Car Trouble.* **TV:** *Holding the Fort; Dear Enemy; Aspects of Love; Shelley; Alas Smith and Jones; It's Going To Be Alright; Drummonds;* Sarah in *Home James!* **Address:** c/o Peter Browne Management.

KOVE, *martin*

Martin Kove. Actor. b. Brooklyn, New York, USA, 6 March 1947. Began career at La Mama Theater, New York, then in repertory theatre. **Films:** *Where's Poppa?; Capone; Death Race 2000; Savages; The Four Deuces; Partners; First Blood II; The Karate Kid; Cry for the Stranger; The Sky Trap.* **TV:** *Code-R; The Edge of Night; The Optimist;* Isbecki in *Cagney and Lacey.* **Address:** c/o The Agency. m. Vivienne; 1 step-s. Sean Raymond.

LA RUE, *danny*

Daniel Patrick Carroll. Actor/Entertainer. b. Cork, Ireland, 26 July 1927. **Theatre:** *Cinderella; Come Spy With Me; Queen Passionella and the Sleeping Beauty; Danny At the Palace; Queen of Hearts; The Danny La Rue Show; The Exciting Adventures of Queen Daniella; Aladdin; Hello, Dolly!; Mother Goose.* **Films:** *Our Miss Fred.* **TV:** *The Good Old Days; Charley's Aunt; Queen of Hearts; A Night Out With Danny La Rue; Tonight With Danny La Rue; The Ladies I Love; Come Spy With Me; Danny At the Palace; Royal Variety Performance* (1969, 1972, 1978); *This Is Your Life* (subject, 1984). **Records:** *On Mother Kelly's Doorstep.* **Books:** *From Drags To Riches* (autobiography, 1987). Winner, Variety Club Showbusiness Personality of the Year award, 1969. **Address:** c/o Sonny Zahl Associates/Brian Shaw, 140 High Street, Cheshunt, Hertfordshire.

LALLY, *teri*

Teresa Lally. Actress. b. Coatbridge, Lanarkshire, 21 April 1961. Trained at Queen Margaret College Drama School. **Theatre:** *Cinderella* (twice); *Don't Tell the Wife; Never a Dull Moment; Babes In the Wood; Mother Goose; Dick Whittington; Merlin the Magnificent.* **Films:** *Restless Natives; Comfort and Joy.* **TV:** Carol Wilson (née McKay) in *Take the High Road; The Video Show; Cameron On Camera; Ready Or Not; Wheel of Fortune.* TV commercials: Bank of Scotland; William Low's. **Address:** c/o Scottish Television. m. Kenny Mackenzie (dis).

LAMAS, *lorenzo*

Lorenzo Lamas. Actor. b. Los Angeles, USA, 20 January 1958. Trained with the Film Actors' Workshop. **Films:** *Body Rock; Grease; Tilt; Take Down.* **TV:** *California Fever; Secrets of Midland Heights; Detour; Love Boat; Hotel; Switch; Sword of Justice;* Lance Cumson in *Falcon Crest.* **Address:** c/o Herb Nanas, 2128 Pico Boulevard, Santa Monica, California 9045, USA. m. 1st Victoria Hilbert (dis), 2nd Michele Smith (dis), 3rd Kathleen Kinmont; 1 d. Shayne, 1 s. Alvaro Joshua (both from 2nd m.).

LANCASHIRE, *sarah*

Sarah Lancashire. Actress. Daughter of TV scriptwriter Geoffrey Lancashire. Trained at Guildhall School of Music and Drama. **Theatre:** *Pacific Overtures; The Beauty Game;* Linda in *Blood Brothers* (Albery Theatre); title role in *Educating Rita.* **TV:** *Dramarama; Celebration; Watching; Bradley; My Secret Desire; About Face;* Wendy Farmer and Raquel Wolstenhulme (1991–) in *Coronation Street; Exam Conditions; The Bill.* **Address:** c/o Talent Artists. Lives in Oldham, Lancashire. m. music lecturer Gary Hargreaves; 2 s. Thomas, Matthew.

LANDEN, *dinsdale*

Dinsdale Landen. Actor. b. Margate, Kent, 4 September 1932. Trained at the Florence Moore School of Theatre, Hove, East Sussex. **Theatre:** *The Housemaster; Play On Love; The Philanthropist; Alphabetical Order; Plunder; The Merchant of Venice; Bodies; On the Razzle; Uncle Vanya; Thark; The Philanderer.* **Films:** *The Valiant; We Joined the Navy; Mosquito Squadron; Every Home Should Have One; Digby – The Biggest Dog In the World; Morons From Outer Space.* **TV:** Pip in *Great Expectations; The Canterbury Tales; The Mask of Janus; The Spies; Mickey Dunne; London Assurance;* title role in *Devenish; Fathers and Families; The Glittering Prizes; Pig In the Middle; Events In a Museum; This Office Life; Arms and the Man; Fight Against Slavery; Some Other Spring* (TV movie). **Address:** c/o ICM. m. actress Jennifer Daniel.

LANEUVILLE, *eric*

Eric G Laneuville. Actor/Director. b. New Orleans, USA, 14 July. Trained with UCLA Theatre Group. **Films:** *Love At First Bite; A Piece of the Action; A Force of One; Backroads.* **TV:** *Sacred Straight; The George McKenna Story; No Secrets* (all TV movies); Luther Hawkins in *St Elsewhere; Room 222; Hill Street Blues.* **Address:** c/o Twentieth Century Artists. m. (dis); 1 s. Sean.

LANG, *belinda*

Belinda Lang. Actress. b. London, 23 December 1955. **TV:** *Dear John; The Bretts; Bust; Stay Lucky; Inspector Alleyn; Second Thoughts.* **Address:** c/o Ken McReddie.

LANG, *robert*

Robert Lang. Actor/Director. b. Bristol, Avon, 24 September 1934. Trained at Bristol Old Vic Theatre School. **Theatre:** *Uncle Vanya; Dial M for Murder; Donkey's Years; The Medusa Touch; Rumpole and the Fascist Beast.* **Films:** *Savage Messiah; Night Watch.* **TV:** *An Age of Kings; Emergency – Ward 10; That Was the Week That Was; Not So Much a Programme, More a Way of Life; For Maddy With Love; 1990; The Rivals of Sherlock Holmes; The Brack Report; Edward 'G' - Like the Film Star; Bristol 600; Semmelweiss; The Microbe Hunter; King Lear; On the Edge of the Sand; Lady Windermere's Fan; The Father; Antigone; D'Ardenelle; The Birthday Party; Vanity Fair; The Contract; Parnell and the Englishwoman; To Each His Own; Ashenden; The Darling Buds of May.* **Address:** c/o Jvulian Belfrage Associates. m. actress Ann Bell; 1 d. Rebecca, 1 s. John.

LANGFORD, *bonnie*

Bonnie Langford. Actress/Dancer/Singer. b. Hampton Court, Surrey, 22 July 1964. Trained at Arts Educational School and Italia Conti Academy. **Theatre:** *Gone With the Wind; Gypsy; Cats; The Pirates of Penzance; Peter Pan – The Musical; Charlie Girl; Me and My Girl;* title role in *Cinderella.* **Films:** *Bugsy Malone; The Water Babies.* **TV:** *Opportunity Knocks* (joint winner, aged six); *Junior Showtime* (co-host); Violet Elizabeth in *Just William* (two series); *Lena and Bonnie* (with Lena Zavaroni); *Royal Variety Show* (three times); *The Saturday Starship; The Hot Shoe Show;* Melanie in *Doctor Who* (two series); *The Children's Royal Variety Show; A Royal Birthday Gala; Tonight At 8.30: A Family Album.* **Records:** *Just One Kiss* (single). **Address:** c/o Billy Marsh Associates. Lives in Twickenham, Middlesex.

LANGRISHE, *caroline*

Caroline Langrishe. Actress. b. London, 10 January 1958. Member of the National Youth Theatre; showgirl at the Hilton Hotel, London. **Films:** *Eagle's Wing; Hawks.* **TV:** *The Glittering Prizes; The Brothers; Anna Karenina; Wuthering Heights; The Flipside of Dominic Hyde;* Cosette in *Les Misérables* (TV movie); *Fortunes of War; Pulaski; Twelfth Night; The Return of Shelley; Boon; The Bill.* **Address:** c/o ICM Duncan Heath Associates. m. actor Patrick Drury; 2 d. Leonie, Rosalind.

LANSBURY, *angela*

Angela Lansbury. Actress. b. London, 16 October 1925. Trained at the Webber Douglas Academy, London, and Feagin Dramatic School, New York. **Films:** *The Picture of Dorian Gray; The Three Musketeers; Blue Hawaii; The Manchurian Candidate; Mr Buddwing; Dear Heart; The Greatest Story Ever Told; Harlow; The Amorous Adventures of Moll Flanders; Something for Everyone; Bedknobs and Broomsticks; Death On the Nile; The Mirror Crack'd; The Pirates of Penzance; The Company of Wolves.* **TV:** *The Lady Vanishes; Sweeney Todd; Little Gloria ...Happy At Last; Lace; The First Olympic Race; The Gift of Love; Rage of Angels: The Story Continues; Shootdown; Wings of the Water; The Shell Seekers;* Jessica Fletcher in *Murder, She Wrote.* **Address:** c/o William Morris Agency (USA). m. 1st Richard Cromwell, 2nd Peter Shaw; 1 s. Anthony, 1 step-s. David, 1 d. Deidre.

LARGE, *eddie*

Eddie Large. Comedian. b. Glasgow, 25 June 1942. Associate schoolboy footballer with Manchester City before teaming up with Syd Little (qv), first as a vocal duo and then as comedians. **Theatre:** London Palladium; summer seasons. **TV:** *Opportunity Knocks* (winners, 1971); *Crackerjack; Who Do You Do? Now Who Do You Do?; The David Nixon Show; Seaside Special; Wheeltappers and Shunters Social Club; The Little and Large Tellyshow; Little and Large; Disney Time.* **Address:** c/o Peter Prichard. m. Patsy Ann; 2 d. Alison, Samantha, 1 s. Ryan.

LATHAM, *bernard*

Bernard Latham. Actor. b. Manchester, 21 April 1951. Trained at Bristol Old Vic Theatre School. **Films:** *The Lovers; Boy Soldier.* **TV:** *The Practice; Carrott Del Sol; Tan Tro Nesa; The Danedyke Mystery; Crown Court; Fox; Coronation Street; Hard Times; Sally Ann; Flying Lady.* **Address:** c/o Michelle Braidman Associates. m. Jane; 1 d. Emily.

LATHAM, *philip*

Philip Latham. Actor. b. Leigh-on-Sea, Essex, 17 January. Trained at RADA. **Films:** *The Dam Busters.* **TV:** *Mogul; Maigret; When the Kissing Had To Stop; To Bury Caesar; Sergeant Cork; Poison Pen; The Campaign; A Month In the Country; Middlemarch; The Marquise; Justice; The Troubleshooters; Time-Lock; Whose Life Is It Anyway?; No Exit; Away From It All; The Caller; Is Nelly Dead?; Love Story; Good At Games; The Pallisers; The Cedar Tree; Murder of a Moderate Man; Killers; Lives of Our Own; Name for the Day; The Professionals; The Killers; Hammer House of Horror; Name for the Day; Nanny; No 10; Wellington; The Fourth Arm; Man From the Pru; Doctor Who; Jackanory Playhouse; Operation Democrat; Leaving; Tea In the Garden; From a Far Country: Pope John Paul II* (TV movie). **Address:** c/o Bryan Drew. m. Eve; 1 d. Amanda, 1 s. Andrew.

LAWLEY, *sue*

Sue Lawley. Presenter. b. Dudley, Worcestershire, 14 July 1946. Journalist with Thomson Regional Newspapers before joining the BBC in Plymouth. **TV:** *Nationwide; Tonight; General Election and Budget coverage; BBC newsreader; Wogan With Sue Lawley;* ITV interview programmes; *Arena: Desert Island Discs.* **Radio:** *Desert Island Discs.* **Address:** c/o Granada TV. m. David Ashby (dis); 1 d. Harriet, 1 s. Tom.

LAWRANCE, *debra*

Debra Lawrance. Actress. Trained at the National Institute of Dramatic Art, Australia. **Theatre:** *The Nowhere Land and the Topsy-Turvey Town; Middle-Aged Spread; First Born; No Sugar; Karamazov.* **Films:** *Before the Night Is Out; Flute Man; Silver City; Two Brothers Running; Evil Angels.* **TV:** *Glenview High; Ride On Stranger; Cop Shop; The Sullivans; Skyways; The Last Outlaw;* guest role, then Daphne, in *Prisoner: Cell Block H; I Can Jump Puddles; Bellamy; Holiday Island; Carson's Law; A Country Practice; Waterloo Station; The Keepers; Sons and Daughters;* Pat in *Fast Lane; How the World Really Runs; The Bear; Living With the Law; Skirts;* Pippa Ross (formerly Fletcher) in *Home and Away* (1990-). **Address:** c/o International Casting Service.

LAWRENCE, josie

Josie Lawrence. Actress/Entertainer. **Theatre:** *The Ragged Trousered Philanthropist; Bag; The Trial of Frankenstein; Accidental Death of an Anarchist; Cats; Carmen; Moll Flanders; A Little Hotel On the Side; Berlin Days, Hollywood Nights; Poppy; Valued Friends; Tatyana.* **Films:** *The American Way.* **TV:** *Rachel and the Roarettes; Campaign; Friday Night Live; Agatha Christie's Poirot; Norbert Smith – A Life; Jackson Pace; Whose Line Is It Anyway?; Rory Bremner; Alas Smith and Jones; Not With a Bang; Lucy in The Green Man; I Love Keith Allen; Josie; Lottie in Enchanted April; Picture Box; 40 Minutes: Boobs In Toyland.* **Radio:** *Hot Club de Paris; Brunch; Kaleidoscope; Ends of the Earth; Woman's Hour; Dodgy Accounts.* **Address:** c/o Richard Stone Partnership.

LAWRENCE, kelly

Kelly Lawrence. Actress. b. East London, 31 August 1966. Member of children's entertainment group Kids International, aged 14; trained at Boden Studios. **Theatre:** Children's Royal Variety Performances; *The Wizard of Oz; Anne of Green Gables; The Crucible.* **Films:** *Beelzebub* (National Film School). **TV:** *The Les Dawson Show; Dramarama; The Practice; Travelling Man;* Louise Todd in *Albion Market;* WPC Claire Brind in *The Bill.* **Address:** c/o Spotlight.

LAWRENCE, patricia

Patricia Lawrence. Actress. b. Andover, Hampshire, 19 November 1926. Trained at RADA (Bancroft Gold Medal winner). **Theatre:** *Heat of the Day; Funny Sunday/Sometime Never; West of Suez; Five Finger Exercise; Dead Ringer; Man of Mode; Across Oka; Restoration; Some Americans Abroad* (all London West End); RSC **Films:** *O Lucky Man!; The Beauty Adventure; Tom Jones; The Hireling; A Room With a View.* **TV:** *Intimate Strangers; Anna Karenina; Going Back; Our Mutual Friend; Love Story; Telford's Change; Turtle's Progress; To Serve Them All My Days; Barriers; Seven Faces of Woman; Staying On; Brimstone and Treacle; St Martin's Summer; Tenko; Paradise Postponed; Tenko Reunion; Vanity Fair; A Very Peculiar Practice; The Bill; They Never Slept.* **Address:** c/o David White Associates. m. Greville Poke; 2 s. Christopher, James.

LAWSON, charles

Charles Lawson. Actor. b. Belfast, 1959. Trained at Guildhall School of Music and Drama. **Theatre:** *Murderers* (National Theatre); *Henry VIII; Romeo and Juliet; The Comedy of Errors; The Shepherd's Tale* (all RSC); *Diary of a Hunger Striker; Gimme Shelter.* **Films:** *Ascendancy; SS; I Cannot Answer That Question; Wilt.* **TV:** *Harry's Game; Four Days In May; Joyce In June;* Trig in *The Firm; Crown Court; The Monocled Mutineer; Upline; Bread; Valentine Falls;* Jim McDonald in *Coronation Street.* **Address:** c/o Barry Brown & Partner/Granada TV. Lives in Stratford-upon-Avon. m. Susie; 1 d.

LAWSON, denis

Denis Lawson. Actor. b. 27 September 1947. **Theatre:** *Pal Joey* (Albery Theatre); *Mr Cinders; Lend Me a Tenor.* **Films:** *Star Wars; Providence; The Man In the Iron Mask; Local Hero.* **TV:** *Dead Head; That Uncertain Feeling; The Kit Curran Radio Show; Love After Lunch* (TV movie); *The Justice Game; One Way Out* (TV movie); *Bejewelled; El C.I.D.* **Address:** c/o James Sharkey Associates.

LAWSON, *leigh*

Leigh Lawson. Actor. b. Atherstone, Warwickshire, 21 July 1943. Trained at the Mountview Theatre School and RADA. **Theatre:** *The Cherry Orchard; The Second Mrs Tanqueray; From the Balcony; The Merchant of Venice.* **Films:** *Brother Sun, Sister Moon; Ghost Story; The God King; Percy's Progress; Love Among the Ruins; Golden Rendezvous; The Devil's Advocate; Tess; Sword and Fire; The Captain's Doll; Sword of the Valiant; Deadline Madrid; Madame Sousatzka.* **TV:** *Big Brother; Black Beauty; Trapped; Song of Songs; QB7; William; Thriller; The Duchess of Duke Street; Disraeli; Why Didn't They Ask Evans?; Murder Is Easy; Black Carrian; Journey Into the Shadows; Travelling Man; Lace; Queenie; Tears In the Rain; Voice of the Heart; I Accuse; Kinsey.* **Address:** c/o ICM Duncan Heath Associates. m. actress Twiggy Lawson; 2 s., 1 d.

LAWSON, *twiggy*

Twiggy Lawson. Actress. b. London, 19 September 1949. Model before becoming an actress. **Theatre:** *Captain Beaky's Musical Christmas; My One and Only* (Broadway). **Films:** *The Boy Friend; W; Shadow of Evil; There Goes the Bride; The Blues Brothers; The Doctors and the Devils; Club Paradise; Madame Sousatzka; Istanbul.* **TV:** *Twiggs; Twiggy; The Frontiers of Science; Bring On the Girls; Roller Coaster; The Muppet Show; Pygmalion; Jukebox; The Sun Child; The Little Match Girl; The Great Diamond Robbery; Charlie the Kid; The Young Charlie Chaplin; Betty.* **Records:** *The Boy Friend; Twiggy* (both LPs); *Here I Go Again* (Top 20 single). **Books:** *Twiggy* (autobiography); *Unlimited Twiggy.* **Address:** c/o London Management/Manager: Neville Shulman, 4 St George's House, 15 Hanover Square, London W1R 9AJ, tel 071–486 6363. m. actor Leigh Lawson; 1 d. Carly.

LAYTON, *george*

George Michael William Layton. Actor/Writer/Director. b. Bradford, West Yorkshire, 2 March 1943. Trained at RADA. **Films:** *Stand Up Virgin Soldiers.* **TV:** *The Likely Lads;* Dr Paul Collier in *Doctor In the House, Doctor At Large, Doctor In Charge* and *Doctor At the Top;* Bombardier Solomons in *It Ain't Half Hot Mum; The Sweeney; Minder; Pigeon Street; Robin's Nest; My Brother's Keeper.* Presenter: *That's Life* (first series); *Pass the Buck.* Writer: *Doctor In the house; Doctor at Large; Doctor In Charge; Doctor At the Top; That's Life; Robin's Nest; My Brother's Keeper* (with Jonathan Lynn); *Don't Wait Up* (creator); *Executive Stress* (creator). **Book:** *The Fib and Other Stories.* **Address:** c/o Barry Burnett Organisation. m. Moya; 3 d. Tris, Claudie (from 1st m.), Hannah, 1 s. Daniel. Pets: Chocolate labrador, tortoise. Hobbies: Tennis.

LE VELL, *michael*

Michael Turner. Actor. b. Manchester, 15 December 1964. Trained at Oldham Theatre Workshop. **Theatre:** *Kes; Joby; No More Sitting On the Old School Bench; Dick Whittington; Jack and the Beanstalk.* **TV:** *My Son, My Son; Fame Is the Spur; The Last Song; The Hard Word; A Brother's Tale; One By One;* Neil Grimshaw (1979), then Kevin Webster (1984–), in *Coronation Street; Royal Variety Performance* (1989). **Address:** c/o CAM/Granada TV. Lives in Saddleworth, West Yorkshire. m. actress Janette Beverley. Pets: Two German shepherd dogs, Goddess and Zak. Hobbies: Football, golf, squash. **Favourite TV programme:** *Duty Men.*

LEACH, *rosemary*

Rosemary Leach. Actress. b. Much Wenlock, Shropshire, 18 December 1935. Trained at RADA. **Films:** *Brief Encounter; A Room With a View.* **TV:** *Armchair Theatre; The Power Game; Germinal; Chariots of Fire; Roads To Freedom; On the Move; Jackanory; The Office Line; No That's Me Over Here; The Wild Duck; Cider With Rosie; Birthday; Now Look Here; When the Wheel Turns; Don Quixote; Hands; Bermondsey; When Day Is Done; Sadie It's Cold Outside; Tiptoe Through the Tulips; Dad; Six Women; Hindle Wakes; Disraeli; Just Between Ourselves; Life Begins At Forty; Hands; Tolstoy; The English In Love; Rumpole of the Bailey; All's Well That Ends Well; Othello; The Critic; The Jewel in the Crown; Swallows and Amazons; The Charmer; When We Are Married; Once In a Lifetime; Summer's Lease; Titmuss Regained.* **Address:** c/o William Morris Agency. m. Colin Starkey.

LEADER, *carol*

Carol Leader. Actress. b. Colchester, Essex, 10 November. **Theatre:** *Topokana Martyrs Day; Bazaar and Rummage; Whale Music.* **TV:** *Sally Ann; Playschool; Play Away; Flambards; Chockablock; Honky Tonk Heroes; Young At Heart; Out of Step; Getting On; Studio; Late Starter; Information World; First and Last.* **Address:** c/o Lou Coulson. m. Michael Maynard; 1 s. Jonathan.

LEBOR, *stanley*

Stanley Harvey Lebor. Actor. b. East Ham, London, 24 September 1934. Trained at RADA. **Films:** *Oh! What a Lovely War; A Bridge Too Far; The Medusa Touch; Flash Gordon; Gandhi; Superman IV; Personal Services.* **TV:** Marcus Berlin in *Coronation Street; The Naked Civil Servant; Ready When You Are, Mr McGill; Holocaust; The Flaxborough Crab; Exiles; The Bass Player and the Blonde; Hunting Tower; Minder; All the World's a Stage; Beyond the Pale; The Dig; Shoestring; Visitor From the Other Side; The Acts of Peter and Paul; Enemies of the State; The Baker Street Boys; Under the Hammer; Reilly – Ace of Spies; Paradise Postponed; Secret Army; Ever Decreasing Circles; 'Allo 'Allo!* **Address:** c/o Essanay. Lives in Canterbury, Kent. m. Jill Rodwell; 3 s. David, Thomas, Michael. **Pets:** Two cats. **Favourite TV programme:** *LA Law.*

LEHMAN, *valerie*

Valerie Lehman. Actress. **Theatre:** Mother in *Trafford Tanzi; Farewell Brisbane Ladies;* Mumma Morton in *Chicago; In Duty Bound; The Foreigner* (Elizabethan Theatre Trust); *Cake;* Eunice in *A Streetcard Named Desire; A Lie of the Mind; One Extra Dance Co* (Adelaide Festival); *A Touch of Silk; Who's Afraid of Virginia Woolf?; Coward; Prisoner: Cell Block H* (British tour). **Films:** *Kitty and the Bagman; Army Wives.* **TV:** Bea Smith in *Prisoner: Cell Block H* (1979-83, winner of three Logie awards, two years running for best lead actress in a series, once for most popular lead actress in a series); *A Fortunate Life; Bellbird Wives; Prime Time; The Flying Doctors; Army; Obsession; Power Without Glory; The Saturday Show; Parkinson; One To One.* **Address:** c/o London Management. m. 1st (dis), 2nd Charles Collins; 2 d., 1 s. (from 1st m.)

LENSKA, *rula*

Rula Lenska. Actress. b. St Neots, Huntingdonshire, 30 September 1947. Trained at the Webber Douglas Academy. **Theatre:** *Suddenly At Home; Flare Path; Forget Me Not Lane; A Midsummer Night's Dream; Secretary Bird; Candle In the Wind; Abel – Where Is Your Brother; Aladdin; Mr Fothergill's Murder; Conversations With a Stranger* (Old Vic Theatre); *Blithe Spirit.* **Films:** *Soft Beds, Hard Battles; Alfie Darling; Royal Flash.* **TV:** *Dixon of Dock Green; The Doctors; The Brothers; Edward VII; Special Branch; The Saint; The Seven Dials Mystery; Private Schultz; Take a Letter Mr Jones; To the Manor Born; Aubrey; Rock Follies; Minder; Boon; Design for Living;* Eva in *Family Pride; An Actor's Life for Me.* **Address:** c/o Vernon Conway. m. 1st actor Brian Deacon (dis), 2nd actor Dennis Waterman (sep); 1 d. Lara (from 1st m.).

LEUCHARS, *anne*

Anne Leuchars. Presenter. b. Kampala, Uganda, 2 August 1953. Newspaper reporter, feature writer and theatre critic (Coventry *Evening Telegraph* and Bristol *Evening Post*), before entering television. **TV:** *Points West* (BBC Bristol); *Report West; Report Extra* (both HTV West); *Lookaround; Mary Chipperfield and Friends* (both Border TV); *Central News;* ITN reporter and newscaster; *Big Business; Pieces of Parkin* (both Yorkshire Television); *Royal Review (This Morning).* **Address:** Jon Roseman Associates. Lives in London.

LEWIS, *alun*

Alun Lewis. Actor. **Films:** *Giro City; Smithfield;* Bobby Boyle in *Bowen; Experience Preferred But Not Essential.* **TV:** *Van Der Valk; Rumpole of the Bailey; A Woman's Place; Eustace and Hilda; Charley's Aunt; Crown Court; Angels; The Strange Affair of Adelaide Harris; Fearless Frank; New Girl In Town; Noah's Castle; Lifelike; The Professionals; Happy; Maybury; Minder; Findings On a Late Afternoon; Ennal's Point; The Falklands Factor; Jemima Shore Investigates; Just Another Blues Song; 92 Grosvenor Street; Boon II; The Choir;* Bobby Boyle in *Bowen* (third series); Tony Barclay in *Emmerdale Farm;* Daryl in *Birds of a Feather.* **Address:** c/o Annette Stone Associates.

LEWIS, *howard lew*

Howard Lew Lewis. Actor. b. London, 21 August 1939. Radio operator and computer programmer before training at the Half Moon Theatre. **Theatre:** *Jack and the Beanstalk; Robin Hood and the Babes In the Wood; A Hard Life; Dracula; Greyhound of the Baskervilles; Of Mice and Men; Insignificance; The Irresistible Rise of Arturo Ui; Golden Boy; Habeas Corpus.* **Films:** *Brazil; Robin Hood: Prince of Thieves.* **TV:** *Pulaski; Mr Pye; The Charmer; Corner House; The Two Ronnies; Open All Hours; Prospects; The Bill; F.L.I.P.; Jack and the Beanstalk; Maid Marion* (two series); *Chelmsford 123* (two series); *Brush Strokes* (five series); *Minder.* **Address:** c/o The Narrow Road Company. m. (dis.)

LEWIS, *martyn*

Martyn Lewis. Newsreader/Presenter. b. Swansea, West Glamorgan, 7 April 1945. **TV:** *BBC Belfast* reporter (1967–8); *HTV Wales* reporter/presenter (1968–70); ITN Northern correspondent, reporter and newscaster (1970–86); BBC TV News newscaster (1986-). Documentaries: *The Secret Hunters; MacGregor's Verdict; Fight Cancer; Songs of Praise.* **Videos:** *Battle for the Falklands* (ITN, producer/writer). **Books:** *And Finally; Cats In the News.* **Address:** c/o Roger Hancock.

LEWIS, *naomi*

Naomi Lewis. Actress. b. London, 24 March 1971. Trained at the Academy of Live and Recorded Arts. **Theatre:** *Jack the Ripper; Celebration;* title role in *Antigone;* Titania in *A Midsummer Night's Dream;* Miss Prism in *The Importance of Being Earnest; Under Milk Wood; Daisy Pulls It Off* (all at drama school); *Rosencrantz and Guildenstern Are Dead; Jack and the Giant; Cinderella.* **TV:** *Lost Empires;* Elsa Feldmann in *Emmerdale.* **Address:** c/o Tobias Management. Single; lives in London.

LILLICRAP, *christopher*

Christopher Lillicrap. Actor/Writer/Musician/Presenter. b. Plymouth, Devon, 14 February 1949. **Theatre:** Repertory theatre in Nottingham, Canterbury, Cheltenham and Theatre In Education. As writer: *Stop the Rot; Christmas Cat and the Pudding Pirates* (both with wife Jeanette Ranger). **TV:** *Playboard; Rose of Puddle Fratrum; The Bands Played On; Canned Laughter; Love Story; Follow the Star; King Robert of Sicily; Jackanory Playhouse; Chopsticks; Rainbow; We'll Tell You a Story; Clock On; Making the Most Of; Wondermaths; Flicks; Knock Knock; Busker.* **Address:** c/o Arlington Enterprises. m. actress Jeanette Ranger; 1 s. Dominic.

LINDEN, *jennie*

Jennie Linden. Actress. b. Worthing, West Sussex, 8 December 1939. Trained at Central School of Speech and Drama. **TV:** *For King and Country; Present Laughter; Lady Windermere's Fan; The Rivals; The Persuaders; His and Hers; Black Beauty; And No One Could Save Her; The Frighteners; My Last Duchess; Death of Sister Mary; The Visitors; Frame; His and Hers; Sister Mary; Little Lord Fauntleroy; Lillie; Dick Turpin; Breadwinner; Charlie Muffin; A Degree of Uncertainty; Jessie; Leap In the Dark; Our Mother's House; The Breadwinner; House On the Hill; Tales of the Unexpected; Low Key Lady On a High Speed Train; Missing From Home; Pepys; Sharing Time; Lytton's Diary; The Practice; Home James; Watching You, Watching Me; Menace Unseen; The Endless Game; Chancer; Lovejoy.* **Address:** c/o Creative Talent Management. m. Christopher Mann; 1 s. Rupert.

LINDSAY, *rachael*

Rachael Lindsay. Actress. b. Liverpool, 18 February 1972. Sister of actress/drama teacher Nikki Lindsay. **TV:** Sammy Daniels (née Rogers) in *Brookside.* **Address:** c/o Mersey Television. Single; lives in Liverpool. Pets: Two dogs, Yorkshire terriers Louie and Ziggy.

LINDSAY, *robert*

Robert Lindsay. Actor. b. Ilkeston, Derbyshire, 13 December 1949. Trained at RADA. **Theatre:** Repertory theatre; lead role in *Godspell;* Old Vic Theatre; *Me and My Girl* (London West End and Broadway). **Films:** *Bert Rigby, You're a Fool; Loser Takes All.* **TV:** *Letter From a Soldier; Get Some In* (two series); title role in *Citizen Smith* (four series); *Seconds Out; All's Well That Ends Well; A Midsummer Night's Dream; Twelfth Night; King Lear; Give Us a Break;* Michael Murray in *GBH;* Carter in *Nightingales; Prisoners of the Sun* (narrator). **Address:** c/o William Morris Agency. Lives in West London. m. actress Cheryl Hall (dis); 1 d. Sydney (from relationship with actress Diana Weston).

LINDSAY, *shona*

Shona Lindsay. Actress. b. Edinburgh, 4 December 1969. Trained at the Birmingham School of Speech and Drama. **Theatre:** Title role in *Annie* (national tour, aged 11); *Oliver!; Cat On a Hot Tin Roof; Alice In Wonderland; Once In a Lifetime; Hobson's Choice; The Enchanted Forest; King's Rhapsody; The Wicked World of Bel-Ami* (Theatre Royal, Stratford East); *Dick Whittington; Bernard Tropp's Unfinished Musical; Babes In the Wood; The Music of Andrew Lloyd Webber* (Prince Edward Theatre); Christine in *The Phantom of the Opera* (Her Majesty's Theatre). **TV:** Barbara Boyer in *The Secret Diary of Adrian Mole Aged 13¾* and *The Growing Pains of Adrian Mole; David Copperfield; Lizzie's Pictures; The Ritz;* Sara Briggs in *Crossroads.* **Record:** *Goodbye* (single, 1988). **Address:** c/o Eric Glass. Lives in Twickenham, Middlesex. m. actor James Barron (qv).

LIPMAN, *maureen*

Maureen Lipman. Actress. b. Hull, East Yorkshire, 10 May 1946. Trained at LAMDA. **Films:** *Up The Junction.* **TV:** *Up the Junction; Doctor At Large; The Lovers; Long Day's Journey Into Night; File It Under Fear; Crown Court; Rooms; The Evacuees; Couples; Rogue Male; The Sweeney; Bobby Bluesocks; Agony; Smiley's People; Last Night; Another Dissident; Codename; Dangerous Davies; The Knowledge; The Sporting Club Dinner; Jackanory Playhouse: The Witching Hour; Rolling Home; Outside Edge; Love's Labour's Lost; See How They Run; On Your Way Riley; Absurd Person Singular; Absent Friends; All At No 20* (winner, *TVTimes* Best Comedy Actress award); *About Face; Re: Joyce!* **Books:** *How Was It for You?; Something To Fall Back On; You Got an Ology?; Thank You for Having Me.* **Address:** c/o Hutton Management. Lives in North London. m. Jack Rosenthal; 1 d. Amy, 1 s. Adam.

LITTLE, *mark*

Mark Little. Actor. Trained at the National Institute of Dramatic Art. **Theatre:** *Love's Labour's Lost; Strife; The Caucasian Chalk Circle; The Fantasticks; Twelfth Night; A Chorus of Disapproval; Last Laugh; Le Joke; Facing Fanshawe; Stand Up for Christmas; Flabbadadabbada Daddy-o;* 1990 Edinburgh Festival. **Films:** *An Indecent Obsession; Short Changed; Starstruck; The Clinic; Once Upon a Weekend; Smoko; Wills and Bourke, The Untold Story; Evil Angels; Golden Braid; Nirvana Street Murder; What's the Big Idea?* **TV:** *Skyways; Cop Shop; The Sullivans; Waterfront; The Keepers; Infinity Limited; Carson's Law; The Flying Doctors; Rafferty's Rules; The Dunera Boys; A Matter of Convenience; The Great TV Game Show; Comedy Company;* Joe Mangel in *Neighbours* (1988-); *Countdown Revolution.* **Address:** c/o The Actors' Agency.

LITTLE, *syd*

Syd Little. Comedian. b. Blackpool, 19 December 1942. Guitarist and singer before teaming up with Eddie Large (qv), first as a vocal duo and then as comedians. **Theatre:** London Palladium; summer seasons. **TV:** *Opoportunity Knocks* (winners, 1971); *Crackerjack; Who Do You Do?; Now Who Do You Do?; The David Nixon Show; Seaside Special; Wheeltappers and Shunters Social Club; The Little and Large Tellyshow; Little and Large; Disney Time.* **Address:** c/o Peter Prichard. m. Sheree; 1 d. Donna, 1 s. Paul.

LLOYD, *kevin*

Kevin Reardon Lloyd. Actor. b. Derby, 28 March 1949. Trained at the East 15 Acting School. **Theatre:** *What the Butler Saw; Love Girl and the Innocent; Ducking Out; Stiff Options; The Foreigner; Playboy of the Western World.* **Films:** *Billy the Kid and the Green Baize Vampire; Link; Britannia Hospital; Trial By Combat.* **TV:** *Auf Wiedersehen, Pet; Dempsey and Makepeace; All In Good Faith; Andy Capp; Coronation Street; Z-Cars; Minder; Hazell; Bergerac; The Borgias; By the Sword Divided; Dear John; Boon;* Det Con 'Tosh' Lines in *The Bill.* **Address:** c/o Saraband Associates. Lives in Derby. m. Lesley; 2 d. Sophie, Poppy, 4 s. Mark, James, Henry, Edward, 1 adopted-d Eleanora. Pets: Two dogs, five rabbits, two banty hens. Hobbies: Football, cricket, rugby, tennis. **Favourite TV programme:** *Only Fools and Horses; Minder; The Bill.*

LLOYD, *siân*

Siân Mary Lloyd. Weather presenter. b. Maesteg, Mid Glamorgan, 3 July 1958. Began career with Cardiff independent radio station CBC as a presenter and trainee journalist, before entering television. **TV:** *Wales Today* (researcher, BBC Wales); S4C (Welsh Fourth Channel) news and weather presenter; WTN special shooting executive; *ITV National Weather* (presenter, 1990-); *LWT Weather* (1990–91). **Address:** c/o International Weather Producions/Knight Ayton Management, 70A Berwick Street, London W1V 3PE. Lives in Cardiff and Bath with partner Mark Cavendish. Hobbies: Cooking, theatre, cinema, swimming, chess, squash. **Favourite TV programme:** *Drop the Dead Donkey.*

LLOYD PACK, *roger*

Roger Lloyd Pack. Actor. b. London, 8 February 1944. Son of actor Charles Lloyd Pack. Trained at RADA. **Theatre:** *Kafka's Dick; Futurists; Yerma; Romersholm; Flea In Her Ear; The End* (writer-director). **Films:** *Prick Up Your Ears; Hamlet; The Virgin Soldiers; The Go-Between; 1984; The Cook, The Thief, His Wife and Her Lover; Object of Beauty; Wilt; American Friends.* **TV:** *One for the Road; Inspector Morse;* Trigger in *Only Fools and Horses; Making Good; Bouncing Back; Video Stars; The Brief; Made In Spain; The Contractor; Mr Bean; The Chief;* David Irving in *Selling Hitler; Stay Lucky; The Gravy Train Goes East; Boon; Archer's Goon.* **Address:** c/o Kate Feast Management. m. 1st (dis), 2nd Jehane Markham; 1 d. actress Emily Lloyd (from 1st m.), 3 s. Spencer, Hartley, Louis.

LOCKE, *philip*

Philip Locke. Actor b. Marylebone, London, 29 March 1928. Trained at RADA. **Theatre:** *The Knack... and How To Get It* (Royal Court Theatre); *Antony and Cleopatra* (RSC); *Amadeus* (National Theatre). **Films:** *Thunderball; Escape To Athena; Porridge; Hitler: The Last Ten Days; Ivanhoe; And the Ship Sailed On; The Inquiry; The Secret Garden; Stealing Heaven.* **TV:** *Doctor Who; Mill On the Floss; Oliver Twist; Dick Turpin; The Omega Factor; Codename Icarus; Connie; Antony and Cleopatra; A Night Out; She Fell Among Thieves; Pennies From Heaven; Butterflies; Don't Count; Dead Man's Kit; The Disappearance of Harry; Box of Delights; The Young Delinquent; Trelawney of the Wells; The Comic Strip Presents ...; Bergerac; Jekyll & Hyde; Saracen; Virtuoso; Agatha Christie's Poirot; Inspector Morse.* **Address:** c/o Jeremy Conway.

LOCKLEAR, *heather*

Heather Locklear. Actress. b. Los Angeles, USA, 25 September 1961. **Films:** *Swamp Thing.* **TV:** *City Killer; Jury Duty* (both TV movies); *T J Hooker;* Sammy Jo in *Dynasty.* **Address:** c/o International Creative Management. m. heavy-metal musician Tommy Lee.

LODGE, *david*

David William Frederick Lodge. Actor. b. Strood, Kent, 19 August 1921. **TV:** *Emergency – Ward 10; Sunday Night At the Prince of Wales; After Hours; United; Tottering Towers; Alexander the Great; The Reg Varney Revue; Carry On Laughing; Father Brown; Thriller; Barlow; Q6; Larry Grayson; Potter's Picture Palace; Q7; Lovely Couple; Q8; Murder At the Wedding; Q9; Beryl Reid and Friends; We the Accused; Worzel Gummidge; Spike Milligan; Superstars* (host); *The Kelly Monteith Show; Minder; Names and Games; Britain's Strongest Man; Super Teams; Junior Superstars; Superstars; International Superstars; Look Who's Talking.* **Books:** *Up the Ladder To Obscurity* (autobiography, 1986). **Address:** c/o CCA. Lives in Richmond-upon-Thames, Surrey. m. Lyn. Hobbies: Charity work. **Favourite TV programme:** *LA Law.*

LOE, *judy*

Judy Loe. Actress. b. Urmston, Manchester, 6 March 1947. Gained a BA in English and drama from Birmingham University. **Theatre:** *Hair; A Game Called Arthur; Illuminations; The World of J B Priestley; Middle-Aged Spread* (Lyric Theatre); *Class K; The Perfect Defence; No Sex, Please – We're British* (Strand Theatre). **TV:** *Ace of Wands; Man At the Top; General Hospital; Edward VII; Woodstock; Man of Straw; Z-Cars; Miss Jones and Son; The Upchat Line; Couples; Crown Court; Robin's Nest; Ripping Yarns; Heartland; Visitors for Andersons; When the Boat Comes In; The Home Front; Life After Death;* Pam in *Singles; Missing From Home; Yesterday's Dreams; The Chief; Eurocops.* **Address:** c/o Peters Fraser & Dunlop. Lives in West London. m. actor Richard Beckinsale (dec); 1 d. Kate. Engaged to film director Roy Battersby.

LOGAN, *phyllis*

Phyllis Logan. Actress. b. Paisley, 11 January 1956. Trained at the Royal Scottish Academy of Music and Drama. **Theatre:** *Threads; On the Edge; The Hired Man.* **Films:** *Another Time, Another Place* (winner, BAFTA Best Most Outstanding Newcomer award and *London Standard* Best Film Actress award); *Every Picture Tells a Story; The Chain; The Kitchen Toto; Out of Time; The Inquiry; Angry Earth.* **TV:** *The White Bird Passes; The Goodtime Girls; Off-Peak; Time and the Conways;* Lady Jane in *Lovejoy; The McGuffin; Bust; Hemingway; Defrosting the Fridge; And a Nightingale Sang; And the Cow Jumped Over the Moon; Effie's Burning.* **Address:** c/o CDA.

LONG, *shelley*

Shelley Long. Actress. b. Fort Wayne, Indiana, USA, 23 August 1949. Trained with Chicago Second City Improvisational Troupe. **Films:** *Hello Again; Outrageous Fortune; Night Shift; Caveman; The Money Pit.* **TV:** *The Cracker Factory; A Promise of Love* (both TV movies); *Cheers; Sorting It Out; M*A*S*H; Family; Love Boat.* **Address:** c/o William Morris Agency (USA). m. 2nd Bruce Tyson; 1 d. Juliana.

LONGTHORNE, *joe*

Joe Longthorne. Singer/Impressionist/Entertainer. b. Hull, East Yorkshire, 31 May 1957. Parents performed in travelling shows. **Theatre:** *Salute To the Superstars* (Drury Lane Theatre, Chicago, and Encore Theatre, Philadelphia); shows at London Palladium and Talk of the Town. **TV:** *Junior Showtime* (two years, from age of 14); *Search for a Star; 3–2–1; Des O'Connor Tonight; Live From the Palladium; Les Dennis's Laughter Show; Joe Longthorne Entertains; The Joe Longthorne Show* (three series); *Royal Variety Performance* (1989). **Records:** *The Joe Longthorne Songbook; Especially for You; The Joe Longthorne Christmas Album.* Winner, Variety Club Most Promising Artiste of the Year, 1982. **Address;** c/o Clifford Elson Publicity. Hobbies: Water-colour painting, cooking, tennis.

LONNEN, *ray*

Ray Lonnen. Actor. b. Bournemouth, 18 May 1940. Trained at the Hampshire School of Drama. **Theatre:** Guy Masterson in *Guys and Dolls; Wonderful Town; Murder By the Book; A Touch of Danger; Same Time, Next Year; Run for Your Wife; Hello, Dolly!* **Films:** *Zeppelin; Lady Caroline Lamb; Murder Elite; Maneaters.* **TV:** *Emergency – Ward 10; The Power Game; Honey Lane; The Troubleshooters; Pathfinders; General Hospital; Melissa; Crown Court; Z-Cars; Rooms; Jubilee; The Sandbaggers; The Gentle Touch; Hammer House of Horror; Glamour Girls;* title role in *Harry's Game; Tales of the Unexpected; The Brief; Murder Elite; Lovejoy; Yellowthread Street; Rich Tea & Sympathy; Singles.* **Address:** c/o Evans and Reiss. Lives in West London. m. actress Lyn Dalby (dis); 1 d. Amy, 2 s. Thomas, Rhys. Hobbies: Travel, playing tennis, cinema, listening to music.

LORD, *derek*

Derek Lord. Actor. b. Belfast. Trained at the Academy of Theatre Arts, Perth, Australia. **Theatre:** *The Admirable Crichton; King Lear* (both in Australia); *Juno and the Paycock; Jack and the Beanstalk.* **Films:** *The Black Windmill; Cal.* **TV:** *Billy;* Davie Sneddon in *Take the High Road* (1984-). **Address:** c/o Pat Lovett Agency/Scottish Television. Lives near Largs, on the Clyde coast. m. actress Lana McDonnell; 1 s. Barry.

LOTT, *barbara*

Barbara Lott. Actress. b. Richmond-upon-Thames, Surrey, 15 May 1920. Trained at RADA. **Theatre:** *Love for Love;* Arts Theatre seasons; *Major Barbara* (national tour); *Man and Superman; Richard II; King's Rhapsody* (national tour). **TV:** *Nightingale's Boys; Six Days of Justice; Ballet Shoes; The Survivors; Sexton Blake; Kids; Rings On Their Fingers; Sorry; Honeymoon.* **Address:** c/o Marmont Management. m. TV producer Stuart Latham.

LUCAS, *william*

William Lucas. Actor. b. Manchester, 14 April 1925. Trained at Bradford Civic Theatre. **Theatre:** Repertory theatre in Liverpool; *Amber for Anna; Ring of Jackals; Dual Marriageway.* **Films:** *Sons and Lovers; The Professionals; Payroll; Bitter Harvest.* **TV:** *Portrait of Alison; The Paragon; The Infamous John Friend; Rigoletto; A Flea Off Pepe; Champion Road; Flower of Evil; Mogul; Warship; Black Beauty; The Spoils of War; Doctor Who; The Two Ronnies; The New Adventures of Black Beauty; On the Up.* **Address:** c/o Michael Ladkin Personal Management. m. (dis); 2 s. Daniel, Thomas.

LUMLEY, *joanna*

Joanna Lumley. Actress. b. Srinagar, India, 1 May 1946. Previously a professional model. **Theatre:** *Othello; Private Lives; Noel & Gertie; Hedda Gabler.* **Films:** *The Girls Do; On Her Majesty's Secret Service; Tan Lin; The Breaking of Bumbo; Games Lovers Play; Trail of the Pink Panther; Curse of the Pink Panther; Shirley Valentine; A Ghost In Monte Carlo.* **TV:** *Release; The Mark II Wife; Two Girls; It's Awfully Bad for Your Eyes Darling; Satanic Rites of Dracula;* Elaine Perkins in *Coronation Street; The Protectors; General Hospital;* Purdey in *The New Avengers; That Was Tory;* Sapphire in *Sapphire and Steel; Oxbridge Blues; Steptoe and Son; Mistral's Daughter; The Glory Boys; The Weather In the Streets; A Perfect Hero; French and Saunders; Lovejoy.* **Address:** c/o Caroline Renton. m. 1st Jeremy Lloyd (dis), 2nd Stephen Barlow; 1 s. James.

LUNGHI, *cherie*

Cherie Lunghi. Actress. Trained at the Arts Educational School. **Films:** *Excalibur; King David; The Mission; To Kill a Priest.* **TV:** *Sign of Four; Praying Mantis* (Channel Four film); *Master of the Game; Tales of the Unexpected; Strangers and Brothers; Tales of the Klondyke; The Lady's Not for Burning; Harem; The Monocled Mutineer;* title role in *The Manageress* (two series); *The Man Who Lived At the Ritz.* **Address:** c/o ICM. 1 d. Nathalie (from previous relationship with film director Roland Joffe).

LYE, *jackie*

Jackie Lye. Actress. b. Newcastle upon Tyne, 25 July 1959. Trained at Central School of Speech and Drama. **TV:** Sandra in *Brush Strokes; Casualty; Mog; Hell's Bells; Fresh Fields; Tides of Laughter* (Channel Four film); *The Bill.* **Address:** c/o Janet Welch Personal Management.

LYNAM, *desmond*

Desmond Lynam. Sports presenter. b. Ennis, Co Clare, Ireland, 17 September 1942. **TV:** *Grandstand; Sports Review of the Year; Sunday Grandstand;* Olympics and World Cup coverage; *Match of the Day.* **Radio:** *Sport On 2; Sports Report; Today; Forces Chance; Treble Chance; Midweek.* **Address:** c/o BBC TV. m. (dis); 1 s. Patrick.

LYNDHURST, *nicholas*

Nicholas Lyndhurst. Actor. b. Emsworth, Hampshire, 21 April 1961. Trained at the Corona Stage Academy. **Theatre:** *The Foreigner* (Albery Theatre). **Films:** *Gun Bus.* **TV:** *Our Show* (co-presenter, as a child); *Anne of Avonlea; Heidi; The Prince and the Pauper; Going Straight; Butterflies;* Rodney in *Only Fools and Horses; Spearhead; To Serve Them All My Days;* Ashley in *The Two of Us; Slimming Down; The Piglet Files.* **Address:** c/o Chatto and Linnit.

LYNN, *jonathan*

Jonathan Lynn. Actor/Writer/Director. b. Bath, Avon, 3 April 1943. Began career with Cambridge Footlights Revue. **Theatre:** Artistic director, Cambridge Theatre Company, *1976–81;* *Loot* (Lyric Theatre); *A Little Hotel On the Side* (National Theatre); *Into the Night; Three Men and a Little Lady.* **Films:** *Mick's People* (director); *The Internecine Project* (writer); *Clue; Nuns On the Run* (both as writer-director). **TV:** *Doctor In the House; The Liver Birds; My Brother's Keeper* (also co-writer); *Barmitzvah Boy; She Fell Among Thieves; The Knowledge; Outside Edge; Diana; Suspicion; Yes Minister* (co-writer, winner of BAFTA Writer's Award, 1987); *Yes, Prime Minister;* (co-writer, winner of three BAFTA awards). **Books:** *A Proper Man; The Complete Yes Minister; Yes Prime Minister Vols I and II.* **Address:** c/o Julian Belfrage Associates. m. Rita Merkelis; 1 s. Edward.

MacARTHUR, *gordon*

Gordon MacArthur. Actor. b. Elgin, Morayshire, 7 November 1961. Trained at Guildhall School of Music and Drama. **Theatre:** Young Vic Theatre; Theatre of Comedy; *Treasure Island* (Edinburgh Festival). **TV:** *Boswell's London Journal; The Justice Game;* Rev Michael Ross in *Take the High Road.* **Address:** c/o Ruth Tarko Agency/Scottish Television. Single. Hobbies: Music, playing golf and the piano.

MacCORKINDALE, *simon*

Simon MacCorkindale. Actor/Writer/Director. b. Isle of Ely, 12 February 1952. Trained at Studio '68. **Theatre:** *The Merchant of Venice* (director); *The Importance of Being Oscar* (also director). **Films:** *Death On the Nile; Riddle of the Sands; The Sword and the Sorcerer; Falcon's Gold; Jaws 3-D; Stealing Heaven* (producer); *That Summer of White Roses* (writer-producer). **TV:** *The Pathfinders; Just William; The Skin Game; Jesus of Nazareth; I, Claudius; Romeo and Juliet; Beasts; Three Weeks; Out of Battle; Quatermass; Quatermass Conclusion; Cabo Blanco; The Dukes of Hazzard; Wilfred Owen; The Mannions of America; Manimal; Falcon Crest* (also as director); *Sincerely, Violet; Counterstroke* (also producer). **Address:** c/o James Sharkey Associates/Agency for the Performing Arts. m. 1st actress Fiona Fullerton (dis), 2nd actress Susan George.

MacDONALD, *james*

James MacDonald. Actor/Singer. b. Glasgow, 9 February 1931. Sang with folk group The Gaberlunzie, then turned solo, before becoming a professional actor. **Theatre:** *Breath of Scotland* (variety show); *Dick Whittington; Barons and Baddies;* **Films:** *Riff Raff; A Sense of Freedom.* **TV:** *United Kingdom; Murder Not Proven; Aliens; End of the Line; The Gift; Your Cheating Heart; House On the Hill; Sykes; Grey Granite;* Sergeant Murray in *Take the High Road.* **Address:** c/o Young Casting Agency/Scottish Television. Lives in Ayr. m. Ruby; 1 s. Cameron, 1 d. Joanne. Hobbies: Gardening.

MacLEOD, *tracey*

Tracey MacLeod. Presenter. b. Ipswich, Suffolk, 30 October 1960. Journalist before entering television. **TV:** *Wogan; Food and Drink; The Six O'Clock Show* (all as researcher); *Network 7* (first series as reporter, second series as producer/presenter); *The Late Show;* music specials on Paul McCartney, Elvis Costello and Eurythmics; *Edinburgh Nights* (Edinburgh Festival magazine programme); *Rapido* (voice-over); *The Booker Prize.* **Address:** c/o PBJ Management.

McANDREW, *deborah*

Deborah Louise McAndrew. Actress/Singer. b. Huddersfield, West Yorkshire, 11 October 1967. Appeared in school plays, wrote musical *Nativity Inn* aged 14, then trained at Manchester University's drama department. Sang with 18-piece big band Force 10 for two years and jazz quartet Something Else for seven years. **Theatre:** Hermia in *A Midsummer Night's Dream; The Accrington Pals; Happy End;* Kathe in *Woyzeck* (all at Manchester University). **TV:** Angie Freeman in *Coronation Street* (1990-). **Address:** c/o Barbara Pemberton Associates/Granada TV. Lives in Leeds. m. Tim. Hobbies: Choral singing, playing piano and guitar, painting, sewing. **Favourite TV programme:** *Inspector Morse;* Victoria Wood's shows.

McARDLE, *john*

John McArdle. Actor. b. Liverpool, 16 August 1949. Trained at the East 15 Acting School. **Theatre:** Repertory theatre in Liverpool, Oldham, Sheffield, Manchester and Cardiff; *To* (Octagon Theatre, Bolton, and national tour). **TV:** *Coronation Street* (two roles, including Det Con Meadows); *Charlie; Frankie and Johnny; How We Used To Live;* Billy Corkhill in *Brookside* (1985–90); *Underbelly.* **Address:** c/o Hope & Lyne. m. 1st (dis), 2nd actress Kathy Jamieson; 1 s. Justin (from 1st m.), 1 d. Katie.

McBURNEY, *judy*

Judy McBurney. Actress/Comedienne. b. Sydney, Australia, 19 May 1948. Studied acting, voice production, theatre and dancing in Sydney. **Theatre:** *Don't Just Lie There, Say Something; The Clown Who Lost His Circus.* **Films:** *Michael; First Time Round.* **TV:** Pixie in *Prisoner Cell Block H; The Young Doctors; A Country Practice; Seven Little Australians; Bellbird; Catwalk; Homicide; Division 4; The Spoiler; Ton-Up Trucking; The Box; No 96; Bluey; It Stands To Reason.* **Address:** RMK Management, 197 Walkeps Street, North Sydney, Australia.

McCALLUM, *david*

David McCallum. Actor. b. Glasgow, 19 September 1933. Trained at RADA. **Films:** *Hell Drivers; The Great Escape; The Greatest Story Ever Told; Mosquito Squadron; The Wind; The Watcher In the Woods.* **TV:** Ilya Kuryakin in *The Man From UNCLE; Colditz; The File On Devlin;* title role in *The Invisible Man;* Steel in *Sapphire and Steel; Teacher; Hauser's Memory;* Alan Breck in *Kidnapped; Frankenstein; The True Story Behind Enemy Lines; Freedom Fighters; She Waits; The Return of the Man From UNCLE; 92 Grosvenor Street; Wall of Tyranny; Hitchcock; The Return of Sam McCloud; Mother Love; The Man Who Lived At the Ritz; Trainer.* As director: *The Explorers: Charles Montague Doughty.* **Address:** c/o Daly Gagan Associates. m. 1st Jill Ireland (dis), 2nd Katherine Carpenter; 1 d. Sophie, 4 s. Paul, Jason (dec), Valentine, Peter.

McCALLUM, *eileen*, MBE

Eileen McCallum. Actress. b. Glasgow, 2 December 1936. Trained at the Royal Scottish Academy of Music and Drama (Gold Medal winner, 1959). **Theatre:** *Willie Rough; Kidnapped; The Thrie Estaites; The Miser; The Slab Boys.* **TV:** *Who Fought Alone?; Smeddum; Grey Granite; Sunset Song; Play for Today: Just Your Luck;* Jean Ross in *Garnock Way;* Isabel Blair in *Take the High Road* (1980-); *The Vision of Edwin Muir* (Channel Four film); *Just Another Saturday; Sweet Nothings; Baa Baa Black Sheep; The Scotched Earth Show; The Steamie; Taggart – The Movie.* **Radio:** *Scottish Children's Hour.* **Address:** c/o Young Casting Agency/Scottish Television. Lives in Edinburgh. m. Tom Fidelo; 3 s. Mark, Neal, Tim, 1 d. Sarah.

McCARDIE, *brian*

Brian McCardie. Actor. b. b. Bellshill, Glasgow, 22 January 1965. Trained at Rose Bruford College of Speech and Drama. **Theatre:** *Street Angels; Red Wind.* **TV:** PC Ronnie Barker in *Waterfront Beat;* Bunny McKinnon in *Forget About Me* (originally titled *Snow Queen* and broadcast as a Channel Four schools programme). **Address:** c/o Evans and Reiss.

McCASKILL, *ian*

Ian McCaskill. Weather presenter. b. Glasgow, 28 July 1938. Attended the Meteorological Office College before entering television. **TV:** BBC TV weather forecasts (1978-); Central Television weather forecasts (1982–3); *Birds of a Feather* (acting himself). **Address:** c/o BBC TV. m. Lesley; 2 d. Victoria, Kirsty.

McCLANAHAN, *rue*

Rue McClanahan. Actress. b. Healdton, Oklahoma, USA, 21 February 1934. **Theatre:** *Sticks and Bones; Jimmy Shine; California Suite; Who's Happy Now?* (winner, Obie award); *Crystal and Fox; Dylan; Dark Side of the Moon; Picnic.* **Films:** *They Might Be Giants; The People Next Door; The Pursuit of Happiness; Modern Love; Players.* **TV:** *Maude; Mama's Family; The Love Boat; Lou Grant;* Blanch in *The Golden Girls* (Emmy award, 1987); *Topper; Rainbow; The Great American; Traffic Jam; Word of Honor; The Day the Bubble Burst; The Little Match Girl; Liberace; The Man In the Brown Suit; Take My Daughters; Please; The Wickedest Witch; Let Me Hear You Whisper; The Dreamer of Oz; To the Heroes; Children of the Bride; To My Daughter* (all TV movies). **Address:** c/o International Creative Management. m. five times (dis); 1 s. Mark (from 1st m.).

McCOWEN, *alec*, CBE

Alec McCowen. Actor. b. Tunbridge Wells, Kent, 26 May 1925. Trained at RADA. **Theatre:** *St Mark's Gospel* (one-man show, London West End and Broadway); *Kipling; The Browning Version; Equus.* **Films:** *Loneliness of the Long Distance Runner; The Cool of the Day; The Agony and the Ecstasy; The Witches; Master of the Islands; Frenzy; Travels With My Aunt; Stevie; Hanover Street; Never Say Never Again; The Assam Garden; Personal Services; Cry Freedom.* **TV:** *All for Love; Private Lives; Family Dance; Twelfth Night; Mr Palfrey of Westminster.* **Address:** c/o Jeremy Conway.

McCOY, *sylvester*

Sylvester McCoy. Actor. b. Dunoon, Argyll, 20 August 1943. **Theatre:** *The Pied Piper; Twelfth Night* (National Theatre); *Antony and Cleopatra; The Caucasian Chalk Circle; Androcles and the Lion; The Tempest; Buster's Last Stand; Can't Pay, Won't Pay; Abracadabra; Pirates of Penzance; The Ken Campbell Road Show.* **Films:** *Fireworks; The Secret Policeman's Ball.* **TV:** *Big Jim and the Figaro Club; Jigsaw; Tiswas; Dramarama; Starstrider; Eureka; The Last Place On Earth;* title role in *Doctor Who.* **Address:** c/o Michael Ladkin Personal Management. m. Agnes; 2 s. Sam, Joe.

McDONALD, *sheena*

Sheena McDonald. Presenter. b. Dunfermline, Fife, 25 July 1954. Studied film at Bristol University before entering broadcasting. **TV:** *The Afternoon Show* (BBC Scotland); *Votes for Women; Scottish Eye; The World This Week; Right To Reply.* **Radio:** BBC Radio Scotland newreader, reporter, presenter and producer. **Address:** c/o Channel Four. Single; lives in Edinburgh.

McDONALD, *trevor*

Trevor McDonald. Newscaster. b. Trinidad, West Indies, 16 August 1939. Worked in radio and television in Trinidad, before joining BBC radio in London as a producer for the Caribbean Service and the World Service. **TV:** *Panorama; Dialogue* (both as interviewer, in Trinidad); ITN reporter (1973–80), diplomatic correspondent (1980–82), Channel Four News diplomatic correspondent and newscaster (1982–7); Channel Four News diplomatic editor (1987–9); *News At 5.40* newscaster (1989–90) and *News At Ten* newscaster (1990–). **Books:** Biographies of cricketers Viv Richards and Clive Lloyd. **Address:** c/o ITN. m. 1st Josephine (dis), 2nd Sabrina; 2 s. Tim, Jamie, 1 d. Joanne.

McKEOWN, *geråldine*

Geraldine McEwan. Actress. b. Old Windsor, Berkshire, 9 May 1932. **Theatre:** *The Entertainer; Dear Love; The Little Hut; Oh, Coward; On Approval; Look After Lulu; The Entertainer; The School for Scandal; Chez Nous;* member of National Theatre Company (1965–71, 1983–5); RSC. **Films:** *The Bawdy Adventures of Tom Jones; Escape From the Dark; Foreign Body; Henry V; Robin Hood: Prince of Thieves.* **TV:** *The Witch; Candida; Separate Tables; Pandora; Three Months Gone; The Magistrate; On Such a Night; We're Strangers Here; Hopcraft Into Europe; Dear Love; The Statue and the Rose; Fat;* title role in *The Prime of Miss Jean Brodie; Come Into the Garden Maude; L'Elégance; The Barchester Chronicles; Tears Before Bedtime; Mapp and Lucia; Oranges Are Not the Only Fruit.* **Address:** c/o Marmont Management. m. Hugh Cruttwell; 1 s. Greg, 1 d. Claudia.

McFADDEN, *steve*

Steve McFadden. Actor. Trained at RADA (winner, Derek Ware and Patrick Crane Awards). **Theatre:** *Entertaining Mr Sloane; Twelfth Night; The Threepenny Opera* (all while at RADA); title role in *The Ballad of Johnny Reece.* **Films:** *Rossinanti; Buster.* **TV:** Billy in *The Firm; Minder; Hard Cases; Vote for Them; The Bill; Pigmalion* (TV movie); *Saracen; Bergerac; All Change;* Phil Mitchell in *EastEnders* (1990–). **Address:** c/o Marina Martin Management/BBC Elstree Centre.

McGANN, *joe*

Joe McGann. Actor. b. Liverpool, 24 July 1958. Performed with the Liverpool Everyman Youth Theatre. **Theatre:** *West Side Story; Yakety Yak* (Half Moon and Astoria Theatres); Sammy in *Blood Brothers* (national tour); *Jack and the Beanstalk In the Wild West* (Young Vic Theatre); *The Canterbury Tales; The Resistible Rise of Arturo Ui;* Sky Masterson in *Guys and Dolls; The Long and the Short and the Tall* (national tour). **Films:** *No Surrender; Kiss Cross.* **TV:** *Johnny Jarvis; The Gentle Touch; The Brothers MacGregor;* O'Dowd in *Rockliffe's Babies; Boon; Casualty; Norbert Smith – A Life; The Chronicles of Narnia;* Charlie Burrows in *The Upper Hand.* **Address:** c/o Marina Martin Management. m. (dis).

McGANN, *mark*

Mark McGann. Actor. **Theatre:** Title role in *Lennon* (Everyman Theatre, Liverpool, and Astoria Theatre); title role in *Old King Cole; Brown Bitter, Wet Nellies and Scouse; Blood Red Roses; 1984; Yakety Yak* (Half Moon and Astoria Theatres); *True Romance;* Mickey in *Blood Brothers* (national tour); *Up On the Roof* (Plymouth, Donmar Warehouse and Apollo Theatre); *Comedians* (Young Vic Theatre); Sky Masterson in *Guys and Dolls.* **Films:** *No Surrender; Business As Usual; Abducted.* **TV:** *Moving On the Edge; Studio; Scully; Zastrozzi; Les Girls;* title role in *John and Yoko: A Love Story* (TV movie); Halliwell in *The Manageress; Yellowthread Street.* **Address:** c/o Marina Martin Management.

McGANN, *paul*

Paul McGann. Actor. b. Ireland. **Theatre:** *John Paul George Ringo...& Bert; Much Ado About Nothing;* title role in *Cain; Oi for England* (Royal Court Theatre); *Yakety Yak; The Genius; Loot* (Ambassadors Theatre); *The Seagull; A Lie of the Mind* (Royal Court Theatre). **Films:** *Tree of Hands; Streets of Yesterday; The Rainbow; Dealers; Withnail & I; Paper Mask; Afraid of the Dark.* **TV:** *Whistling Wally; Russian Night* title role in *Gaskin; Two Weeks In Winter; Give Us a Break;* Percy Toplis in *The Monocled Mutineer; The Importance of Being Earnest; Cariani and the Courtesan; Open Space;* Colin in *Drowning In the Shallow End* (TV movie). **Address:** c/o Marina Martin Management. Lives with Annie Milner; 1 s. Joe.

McGANN, *stephen*

Stephen McGann. Actor. **Theatre:** *Yakety Yak* (Half Moon and Astoria Theatres); *The Holiday; Serjeant Musgrave's Dance* (Old Vic Theatre); *Class K; Shamrocks and Crocodiles* (Liverpool Playhouse and National Theatre Studio); Wilfred Owen in *Not About Heroes* (national tour); *Loot; Up On the Roof* (Plymouth and national tour); Mickey in *Blood Brothers* (Albery Theatre). **Films:** *Business As Usual.* **TV:** *Missing From Home; Juliet Bravo; Bergerac; Brookside; Help!; Boon; Home Front; Stars In a Dark Night;* Bob in *Streetwise; Stay Lucky; The Strauss Dynasty.* **Address:** c/o Marina Martin Management.

McGEE, *henry*

Henry McGee. Actor. b. London, 14 May 1929. Trained at the Italia Conti Academy. **Theatre:** Repertory theatre in Britain and Australia; *Uproar In the House; The Man Most Likely To Be In London; Noises Off; The Cat and Canary; Run for Your Wife.* **Films:** *Holiday On the Buses; Adventures of a Taxi Driver; Carry On Emmanuelle; Revenge of the Pink Panther.* **TV:** *Paris 1900; The Worker; The Benny Hill Show; Doctor At Large; The Goodies; No, That's Me Over Here; Sykes; The Dick Emery Show; The Tommy Cooper Show; Up the Workers; Rising Damp; Let There Be Love.* **Address:** c/o CDA.

McINNERNY, *tim*

Tim McInnerny. Actor. b. Cheadle Hulme, Cheshire. **Films:** *Wetherby; Erik the Viking; August Saturday; Spaghetti Hoops.* **TV:** *Black Adder; Edge of Darkness; Blackadder II; The Adventures of Sherlock Holmes; Great Writers: Thomas Mann; Blackadder III; Anastasia: The Mystery of Anna* (TV movie); *A Very British Coup; Shadow of the Noose; Blackadder Goes Forth.* **Address:** c/o Hope & Lyne.

McKAY, *craig*

Craig McKay. Actor. b. Guiseley, West Yorkshire, 21 June 1973. **TV:** *The Book Tower; How We Used To Live;* Mark Hughes in *Emmerdale* (1988-). **Address:** c/o Regency Agency/Yorkshire Television. Single; lives in Guiseley, West Yorkshire. Hobbies: Playing badminton, squash, tennis, football and golf.

McKAY, *glenda*

Glenda Rose McKay. Actress. b. Leeds, 2 February 1971. Gained a theatre studies A-level. **Theatre:** Pepper in *Annie* (Grand Theatre, Leeds, 1983). **Films:** Gudrun in *The Rainbow.* **TV:** Rachel Hughes in *Emmerdale* (1988-); *Stargazers; The Krypton Factor Special.* **Address:** c/o Peter Graham Associates/Yorkshire Television. Single; lives in Harrogate with Mark Styles. Pets: Gerbil called Digby. Hobbies: 'Sport, eating out with boyfriend, visiting Mum and Dad.' **Favourite TV programme:** *Emmerdale.*

McKENZIE, *julia*

Julia McKenzie. Actress. b. Enfield, Middlesex, 17 February 1942. Trained at Guildhall School of Music and Drama. **Theatre:** *Guys and Dolls* (National Theatre); *Woman In Mind; Follies.* **Films:** *Shirley Valentine.* **TV:** *Ike: The War Years* (TV movie); *Andre Previn Meets Stephen Sondheim; Song By Song By Gershwin; The Two Ronnies; The John Curry Show; The Stanley Baxter Show; Maggie and Her; That Beryl Marston. . .!; Fame Is the Spur; Those Glory, Glory Days* (TV movie); *Dear Box No; Guilt On the Gingerbread; Fresh Fields; Blott On the Landscape; Absent Friends; Hotel du Lac; Julia and Company; French Fields; Adam Bede.* Winner, *TVTimes* Best Actress On TV award (1986) and Favourite Comedy Performance On TV award (1985, 1986, 1988). **Address:** c/o April Young. m. actor-director Jerry Harte.

McKERN, *leo*

Reginald McKern. Actor/Writer. b. Sydney, Australia, 16 March 1920. Trained as an electrical engineer and commercial artist in Australia; came to Britain in 1946. **Theatre:** *Rollo; Othello; A Man for All Seasons; Crime and Punishment; Uncle Vanya; Valpone.* **Films:** *Smarter Brother; The Omen; Candleshoe; Damien – Omen II; The Nativity; The House On Garibaldi Street; The Blue Lagoon; The French Lieutenant's Woman; Ladyhawke; The Chain; Travelling North.* **TV:** *The Prisoner; On the Eve of Publication; The Tea Party; The Caucasian Chalk Circle; Churchill's People; Shades of Greene; The Sun Is God; The Adventures of Sherlock Holmes;* title role in *Rumpole of the Bailey; Rumpole's Return; Country; Murder With Mirrors; Monsignor Quixote; The Master Builder.* **Address:** c/o Richard Hatton. m. actress Jane Holland; 2 d. actress Abigail, Harriet.

McLAUGHLIN, *lise-ann*

Lise-Ann McLaughlin. Actress. b. Dublin, Ireland, 24 June 1958. Began career acting at the Abbey Theatre, Dublin. **Theatre:** *Stephen D; The Way To Keep Him; Come and Go; City Sugar; A Midsummer Night's Dream; A Life; Nightshade; Our Town; The Importance of Being Earnest; Ourselves Alone* (Liverpool Playhouse and Royal Court Theatre); *Of Mice and Men; You Never Can Tell; Charley's Aunt.* **Films:** *Angel.* **TV:** *Miracles and Miss Langan; Passing Through; Teresa's Wedding; The Life of Sean O'Casey; A Life; Katie – The Year of the Child; Shadows On Our Skin; Easter 2016; Ties of Blood; Friends and Lovers; Invitation To a Party; Nobody's Property; We'll Meet Again; The Irish RM* (three series); *Dead Entry; Square Deal; Haggard.* Winner, *TVTimes* Most Promising Newcomer To Television Award, *1983.* **Address:** c/o Annette Stone Associates.

McLEOD, *shelagh*

Shelagh McLeod. Actress. b. Vancouver, Canada, 7 May. Trained at the Corona Stage Academy. **Theatre:** Royal Court Theatre; Stratford, Canada; *The Dresser; Love's Labour's Lost; Much Ado About Nothing.* **Films:** *Success; Lady Oscar; Indian Summer.* **TV:** *Cream In My Coffee; Keats; Camille; Street Think; Pygmalion; The Winning Streak.* **Address:** c/o James Sharkey Associates. m. James C Jordan.

McMAHON, *julian*

Julian Dana William McMahon. Actor. b. 27 July 1968. Worked as a florist, model and in an ice-cream shop, before training at the Stanislavsky School, Los Angeles, the Carenidi Acting School, Milan, and the Actors Centre, Sydney. **Theatre:** *Love Letters* (Sydney Opera House); *Home and Away* (British tour). **TV:** Kane Edmonds in *The Power, The Passion;* Ben Lucini in *Home and Away.* TV commercials: Pepsi-Cola; Levi jeans; Sprite; Clearasil; Speedo; Coca-Cola. **Address:** c/o Stacey Testro Management. Hobbies: Tennis, squash, horse-riding, skiing, water-skiing, T'ai Chi.

McMANUS, *mark*

Mark McManus. Actor. b. Hamilton, Lanarkshire, 1940. Began acting while living in Australia. **Theatre:** *The Passion; Larkrise To Candleford; The World Turned Upside Down; Herod; The Crucible* (all with National Theatre). **TV:** *Colditz; Crown Court; The Brothers; Sam; The Foundation; Target; The Albion Band; The Long, The Short and The Tall; Bull Week; Strangers; Union Castle; Two Percent;* title role in *Taggart* and *Taggart – The Movie.* **Address:** c/o ICM. m. Paulette; 1 d. Kate, 1 step-s. Christopher.

McNEILL, *gillian*

Gillian McNeill. Actress. b. Monifieth, Tay, 25 September 1965. Trained at the Royal Scottish Academy of Music and Drama. **Theatre:** *Aesop's Fables; The Skit* (both Theatre In Education productions); title role in *Snow White and the Seven Dwarfs.* **TV:** *The Houseman's Tale;* Lynne McNeil in *Take the High Road* (1987-). **Address:** c/o Ruth Tarko Agency/Scottish Television. Lives in Glasgow. m. actor Richard Greenwood.

McROBERTS, *briony*

Briony McRoberts. Actress. b. Welwyn Garden City, Hertfordshire, 10 February 1957. **Theatre:** *Much Ado About Nothing; Hay Fever; The Browning Version; Peter Pan; And Then There Were None; The Curse of the Baskervilles; Betzi; Charley's Aunt.* **Films:** *Captain Nemo and the Underwater City; The Pink Panther Strikes Again; Edge of Sanity.* **TV:** *Bachelor Father; Peter Pan; The Crezz; True Patriot; Malice Aforethought; Butterflies; Diamonds; The Professionals; Lucky Jim; Sink Or Swim; Strangers; Mr Palfrey of Westminster; Don't Wait Up; Brush Strokes; Fellow Traveller;* Carol in *EastEnders;* Sam Hagen in *Take the High Road* (1991-). **Address:** c/o William Morris Agency/Scottish Television. m. actor David Robb.

McSHANE, *ian*

Ian McShane. Actor. **Films:** *The Wild and the Willing; Sky West and Crooked; The Battle of Britain; If It's Tuesday It Must Be Belgium; Pussy Cat, I Love You; Tam Lin; Freelance; Villain; Sitting Target; The Last of Sheila; Ransom; Journey Into Fear; Yesterday's Hero; Exposed; Too Scared To Scream; Torchlight; Ordeal By Innocence.* **TV:** *What Would You Do?; Jesus of Nazareth; Roots; Shakespeare; Diamond Head; Disraeli; Dirty Money; The Pirate; The Letter; Marco Polo; Bare Essence; A.D.* (mini-series); *Evergreen* (mini-series); *War and Remembrance; Grand Larceny* (TV movie); *Lovejoy* (also co-producer); *The Grace Kelly Story* (TV movie); *The Great Escape; Dallas; Minder; Charlie the Kid; Columbo; Perry Mason; Survival* (narrator). **Address:** c/o ICM Duncan Heath Associates.

MACARTHUR, *edith*

Edith Macarthur. Actress. b. Ardrossan, Ayrshire. **Theatre:** Repertory theatre in Edinburgh, Perth, Glasgow and Bristol; RSC; London West End; *Marie of Scotland; The Thrie Estaites* (both Edinburgh Festival); *Hay Fever; Death of a Salesman; The Cherry Orchard; Daphne Laureola.* **TV:** *The Borderers; Sunset Song; Weir of Hermiston; Dr Finlay's Casebook; Five Women; Love Story; Heartland; The Sandbaggers;* Judith Sutherland in *Sutherland's Law;* Elizabeth Cunningham in *Take the High Road* (1980–87); *Menace Unseen; French Fields.* **Address:** c/o Larry Dalzell Associates.

MACKINTOSH, *andrew*

Andrew Neil Mackintosh. Actor/Musician. b. Pennsylvania, USA, 9 August 1960. Grew up in Scotland and trained at Webber Douglas Academy. A musician who composes, plays clarinet, saxophones, guitars, keyboards and drums, and is a musical director. **Theatre:** *Tosca; Macbeth; The Taming of the Shrew;* Bob Carlton's rock 'n' roll pantomimes at the Everyman Theatre, Liverpool; *Tess of the d'Urbervilles; Grease; Animal Farm; Cabaret.* **TV:** *Every Breath You Take; Coronation Street; Game, Set & Match; Agatha Christie's Poirot;* DS Alistair Greig in *The Bill.* **Address:** c/o Scott Marshall. Lives in London. m. Lucy Abercrombie; 2 d. Melissa, Ottilie. Hobbies: Food, wine and conversation, cricket, table tennis, playing games with Melissa. **Favourite TV programme:** *Cheers.*

MACNEE, *patrick*

Patrick Macnee. Actor. b. London, 6 February 1922. Trained at the Webber Douglas Academy of Dramatic Art. **Theatre:** *Little Women; Made In Heaven; The Grass Is Greener; House Guest; Killing Jessica.* **Films:** *Elusive Pimpernel; Battle of the River Plate; Les Girls; The Sea Wolves.* **TV:** Steed in *The Avengers; The New Avengers; Vintage Quiz; Empire; Lime Street; Where There's a Will.* **Address:** c/o London Management. m. 1st actress Barbara Douglas (dis), 2nd actress Catherine Woodville (dis); 1 d. Jennie, 1 s. Rupert (both from 1st m.).

MADELEY, *richard*

Richard Madeley. Presenter. b. Romford, Essex, 13 May 1956. Newspaper journalist and local radio producer before entering television. **TV:** Border Television reporter, 1978–80; Yorkshire Television reporter, 1980–82; Granada TV reporter and presenter (1982-); *Runway* (quiz show, host); *This Morning* (co-presenter, 1988-). **Address:** c/o Arlington Enterprises/Granada TV. m. co-presenter Judy Finnigan; 1 s. Jack, 1 d. Chloe, 2 step-s. Tom, Dan (twins).

MADOC, *philip*

Philip Madoc. Actor. b. Merthyr Tydfil, 5 July 1934. Worked as an interpreter before training at RADA. **Films:** *Operation Crossbow; High Wind In Jamaica; The Spy Who Came In From the Cold; The Quiller Memorandum; Circus of Blood; Private I; Doppelganger; Hellboats; A Bequest To the Nation; Soft Beds and Hard Battles; Operation Daybreak;* Trotsky in *Zina.* **TV:** *Manhunt; Last of the Mohicans; The Inheritors; A Bouquet of Barbed Wire; Another Bouquet; Target;* title role in *Lloyd George; If Tomorrow Comes* (TV movie); *Monte Carlo* (TV movie); *Fortunes of War; Court Case; A Very British Coup; First Born; Singles; Capital City.* **Address:** c/o Peter Browne Management. m. actress Ruth Madoc (dis); 1 d. Lowri, 1 s. Rhys.

MADOC, *ruth*

Ruth Madoc. Actress. b. Norwich, Norfolk, 16 April 1943. ASM with Nottingham Rep before training at RADA. **Theatre:** *Under Milk Wood; The Black and White Minstrels Show; Man From La Mancha* (Piccadilly Theatre); *Fiddler On the Roof;* title role in *Irma La Douce;* Letty in *Something's Afoot; Mixed Feelings; Nightclub Confidential;* Maria in *Twelfth Night* (Open Air Theatre, Regent's Park); *Babes in the Wood; Robinson Crusoe; Bless the Bride* (Sadlers Wells Theatre); *Touch and Go;* Rose in *gypsy* (national tour). **Films:** *Under Milk Wood; Fiddler On the Roof; The Prince and the Pauper.* **TV:** *Hunter's Walk; Leave It To Charlie; The Life and Times of David Lloyd George;* Gladys Pugh in *Hi-de-Hi!* **Address:** c/o Saraband Associates. m. 1st actor Philip Madoc (dis), 2nd manager John Jackson; 1 d. Lowri, 1 s. Rhys (both from 1st m.).

MAGILL, *ronald*

Ronald Magill. Actor/Director. b. Hull, East Yorkshire, 21 April 1920. Toured with Stars In Battledress concert party during Second World War, then joined the Arena travelling theatre company. **Theatre:** Actor and director at Nottingham Playhouse for nine years; *Death of a Salesman; The Browning Version;* translates Italian plays for production in Britain. **Films:** *Julius Caesar.* **TV:** Amos Brearly in *Emmerdale* (1972–92). **Address:** c/o Ken McReddie. Single; lives in South London.

MAGNUSSON, *magnus, Hon KBE*

Magnus Magnusson. Broadcaster/Writer. b. Reykjavik, Iceland, 12 October 1929. Family moved to Scotland when he was nine months old; reporter on the *Scottish Daily Express* and chief feature writer on *The Scotsman* before entering television. **TV:** *Tonight; Chronicle; Cause for Concern; Unsolved Mysteries; Checkpoint; Mainly Magnus; Mastermind; Living Legends; Vikings!; BC: The Archaeology of the Bible Lands.* **Books:** *BC: Archaeology of the Bible Lands; Introducing Archaeology; Viking Expansion Westwards; Landlord Or Tenant? – A View of Irish History; Magnus On the Move; Treasures of Scotland; Lindisfarne, The Cradle Island; Iceland Saga.* **Address:** c/o Rogers, Coleridge & White. m. journalist Mamie Baird; 3 d. Sally, Margaret, Anna, 1 s. Jon.

MALAHIDE, *patrick*

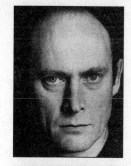

Patrick Malahide. Actor. b. Berkshire, 24 March 1945. Stage manager in St Andrews before becoming a professional actor. **Theatre:** Repertory theatre in Edinburgh, Birmingham, Manchester and Bristol; *Operation Bad Apple* (Royal Court Theatre). **Films:** *The Killing Fields; Comfort and Joy; A Month In the Country; December Bride.* **TV:** *Minder; Miss Julie; The One Game; Our Geoff; The Singing Detective; Lovejoy; Inspector Morse; Boon; Living With Dinosaurs; Children of the North; The Ruth Rendell Mysteries: Means of Evil.* **Address:** c/o Kate Feast Management. m. Rosie; 1 s. Liam, 1 d. Mairi.

MANDEL, *howie*

Howie Mandel. Actor/Comedian. b. Toronto, Canada, 29 November. Began as a stand-up comic at The Comedy Store, Los Angeles. **Films:** *A Fine Mess; Walk Like a Man.* **TV:** *Howie Mandel: Live From Carnegie Hall; The Tonight Show; Merv Griffin; Mike Douglas; HOBO Special; Bizarre;* Doctor Wayne Fiscus in *St Elsewhere.* **Address:** c/o William Morris Agency (USA). m. Terry; 1 d. Jackelyn.

MANETTI, *larry*

Larry Manetti. Actor. b. Pendleton, Oregon, 23 July. Trained with Sal Dano. **Films:** *Two Minute Warning.* **TV:** *Emergency; Chase; Switch; Black Sheep Squadron; Battlestar Galactica; The Duke; Ten Speed and Brown Shoe; Fantasy Island; Quincy; Barnaby Jones; Magnum PI; The Mob.* **Address:** c/o The Artists Group. m. actress Nancy; 1 s. Lorenzo.

MARINARO, *ed*

Ed Marinaro. Actor. b. New York, USA, 31 March. Played professional football with the Minnesota Vikings and the New York Jets; studied acting with coaches Milton Katselas and Warren Robertson. **Theatre:** *It Had To Be You.* **Films:** *Fingers.* **TV:** *Policewoman Centerfold* (TV movie); *Three Eyes; Born Beautiful;* Joe Coffey in *Hill Street Blues; Tonight's the Night; What If I'm Gay; Eischeid; Laverne and Shirley; Dynasty.* **Address:** c/o William Morris Agency (USA).

MARKS, *alfred*, OBE

Alfred Marks. Actor/Comedian. b. London, 28 January 1921. Worked as an engineer and auctioneer before turning professional on the variety stage. **Theatre:** *Where the Rainbow Ends; A Day In the Life of ...; Spring and Port Wine; The Young Visiters; Dead Silence; Don't Just Lie There, Say Something; The Entertainer; Twelfth Night; Zorba; The Sunshine Boys; Bus Stop; Fiddler On the Roof.* **Films:** *Desert Mice; There Was a Crooked Man; Weekend With Lulu; Frightened City; She'll Have To Go; Scream and Scream Again.* **TV:** *Don't Look Now; Alfred Marks Time; Paris 1900; Albert and Victoria; The Good Old Days; Looks Familiar; Opinions Unlimited; Funny Man; Maybury; The Olympian Way; Theatre Quiz* (presenter); *Sunday Night At the London Palladium* (compere). **Address:** c/o Barry Burnett organisation. m. actress Paddie Neil; 1 d. Danielle, 1 s. Gareth.

MAROT, *irene*

Irene Marot. Actress. b. Birkenhead, Cheshire. **Theatre:** *Audience; Morning Tiger; Miniatures; John Paul George Ringo &...Bert; Gigi; Last of the Red Hot Lovers; Who Killed Santa; Dracula* (national tour); *Passing Through; Top Girls; Scrap.* **Films:** *The Little Drummer Girl; Intimate Strangers; Further and Particular; Getting it Right.* **TV:** *The Nation's Health; Widows; Boon; The Chronicles of Narnia; Here Is the News; Mother Love;* D-D Dixon in *Brookside* (1990-). **Address:** c/o Lou Coulson/Mersey Television. Single; lives in London.

MARSDEN, *roy*

Roy Marsden. Actor. b. London, 25 June 1941. **TV:** *The Sandbaggers; Airline; Death of an Expert Witness; Goodbye, Mr Chips; Vanity Fair;* Det Chief Supt Adam Dalgliesh in *Shroud for a Nightingale, Cover Her Face* and *The Black Tower; Inside Story; Devices and Desires.* **Address:** c/o London Management. m. actress Polly Hemingway; 2 s. Joe, Bill.

MARSH, *reginald*

Reginald Marsh. Actor. b. London, 17 September 1926. **Theatre:** *Thark; The Death Is Announced* (actor-writer); *Relatively Speaking; Henry IV, Pt I; My Brother's Keeper; The Boundary; Bedroom Farce; The Last Gamble.* **Films:** *The Sicilians; Shadow of Fear; Jigsaw; Young Winston; The Day the Earth Caught Fire; Sky Pirates.* **TV:** Dave Smith in *Coronation Street; The Planemakers; The Man Who Came To Die* (actor-writer, TV version of *The Death Is Announced); Gazette; The Power Game; The Ratcatchers; Barlow; My Name Is Harry Worth; Whodunnit?; Bless This House; The Sweeney; Crown Court; The Good Life; Terry and June; Help!; Crossroads; Nye; Who Pays the Piper; George and Mildred.* **Books:** *Much More Than Murder.* **Address:** c/o Plunket Greene. m. former actress Rosemary Murray; 3 d. Kate, Rebecca and Alison (twins), 3 s. John, Adam, Alexander.

MARTIN, *derek*

Derek Martin. Actor. b. Bow, East London, 11 April 1933. Stuntman for five years before becoming a professional actor. **Films:** *Ragtime.* **TV:** *Paul Temple; The Sweeney; The Chinese Detective; Law and Order; The Bright Side; The Pickwick Papers; The Professionals; Hart To Hart; Minder; King and Castle; Dempsey and Makepeace.* **Address:** c/o JLM. 2 s. David, Jonathan (twins).

MARTIN, *jessica*

Jessica Martin. Actress/Comedienne. b. Fulham, London, 25 August 1962. Studied English and drama at London University. **Theatre:** *Me and My Girl* (London West End). **Films:** *Bert Rigby, You're a Fool; The Garden.* **TV:** *Spitting Image* (voice impersonator); *Copycats; Bobby Davro's TV Weekly; The Royal Variety Show; Saturday Live; Paul Nicholas and Friends; Doctor Who.* **Address:** c/o Saraband Associates.

MARTIN, *mel*

Mel Martin. Actress. **Theatre:** *Private Lives; Duet for One; The Importance of Being Earnest; The Devil's Disciple; The Skin Game; The Cherry Orchard; Lord Arthur Saville's Crime; Rules of the Game; Heartbreak House; Richard III; Il Candelaio; Much Ado About Nothing; The Rehearsal; A Streetcar Named Desire.* **Films:** *The Adventures of a Lady; Business As Usual; White Hunter, Black Heart.* **TV:** Violet Effingham in *The Pallisers; When We Are Married; Journey Into the Shadows; Persuasion; Playing With Fire; Lytton's Diary;* title role in *Love for Lydia; Melba;* Vivien Leigh in *Darlings of the Gods; Cover Her Face; Time and the Conways; Game, Set & Match; Inspector Morse; Summer Lease; Orpheus and Eurydice; Agatha Christie's Poirot;* Susan Lovejoy in *Lovejoy; The Men's Room; Hancock; Boon; The Big One.* **Address:** c/o Markham & Froggatt.

MATTHEWS, *francis*

Francis Matthews. Actor. b. York, 2 September 1930. **Theatre:** *Say Who You Are* (New York); *My Fair Lady; Noel and Gertie.* **Films:** *Hell Fire Club; Bhowani Junction; The Revenge of Frankenstein; Bitter Harvest; Murder Ahoy; The Intelligence Men; Moi, General de Gaulle.* **TV:** *Triton; St Ives; My Friend Charles; A Little Big Business; Tim Fraser; My Man Joe; Dark Island; Last Man Out;* title role in *Paul Temple; Roof Over My Head; Trinity Tales; Middlemen; Don't Forget To Write; Crowther Scrapbook; Crowther Collection; Crown Court; Tears Before Bedtime; The Gender Gap; The Marti Caine Show; The Morecambe and Wise Christmas Show; Ike: The War Years; Brat Farrar; The McGuffin; May We Borrow Your Husband?; Roman Holiday.* **Address:** c/o Barry Burnett Organisation. Lives in Esher, Surrey. m. actress Angela Browne; 3 s. Paul, Dominic, Damien.

MATTHEWS, *sally ann*

Sally Ann Matthews. Actress. b. Oldham, Lancashire, 19 September 1970. Trained at Oldham Theatre Workshop. **TV:** Jenny Bradley in *Coronation Street; The Lime Grove Story: The Grove Family.* **Address:** c/o Jeremy Conway. Single; lives in West Yorkshire.

MAUGHAN, *sharon*

Sharon Mughan. Actress. b. Liverpool, 22 June. **Films:** *Home Before Midnight.* **TV:** *Shabby Tiger; Dial M for Murder; The Main Chance; Huggy Bear; The Enigma Files; The Return of the Saint; The Flame Trees of Thika; Young Genius; Dombey and Son; By the Sword Divided; Inspector Morse; Hannay; Ticket To Ride; The Ruth Rendell Mysteries.* TV commercials; Nescafé Gold Blend. **Address:** c/o Lou Coulson. m. actor Trevor Eve; 1 d. Alice, 1 s. Jack.

MAXWELL, *lisa*

Lisa Maxwell. Singer/Dancer/Actress/Presenter. b. Elephant and Castle, South London, 24 November 1963. Trained at the Italia Conti Academy from the age of 11. **Theatre:** *Annie; Hotel Paradiso; Russ Abbot's Madhouse; Russ Abbot's Summer Madhouse.* **Films:** Kira in *The Dark Crystal;* Tracy in *Remembrance.* **TV:** *The Many Wives of Patrick* (debut, aged 11); *Ballet Shoes; A Place Like Home; Danger – Marmalade At Work; The Benny Hill Show; The Gender Trap; Radio; The Hello-Goodbye Man;* Zerlina in *Tripods; No Limits* (presenter); *The Bizz* (presenter); *Splash* (presenter); *Les Dennis's Laughter Show; The Joe Longthorne Show; Blankety Blank; Relative Strangers; The Satellite Show;* 'Janice' in *The Noel Edmonds Saturday Roadshow; The Russ Abbot Show; The Lisa Maxwell Show.* **Address:** c/o Mike Hughes Entertainments/Clifford Elson Publicity.

MAYALL, *rik*

Rik Mayall. Actor. b. Harlow, Essex. **Films:** *The Eye of the Needle; Shock Treatment; Couples and Robbers; Whoops Apocalypse; Mr Jolly Lives Next Door; More Bad News.* **TV:** *A Kick Up the 80s; The Young Ones; The Comic Strip Presents...; The Lenny Henry Show; Blackadder II; Happy Families; Jackanory; Saturday Night Live; Hardwicke House; French and Saunders; Filthy Rich and Catflap; Northern Lights;* Alan B'Stard in *The New Statesman; Jake's Journey; Grimm's Tales; Blackadder Goes Forth; Bottom; Love Hurts* (acting himself). **Address:** c/o The Brunskill Management. m. make-up artist Barbara; 1 d. Rosie, 1 s. Sid.

MAYRON, *melanie*

Melanie Mayron. Actress. b. Philadelphia, USA, 20 October 1952. Trained at the American Academy of Dramatic Arts. **Theatre:** *Godspell* (tour); *The Goodbye People; Gethsemane Springs; Crossing Delancey; Little Shiny Shoes* (as joint playwright and co-producer, with Catlin Adams). **Films:** *Harry and Tonto; The Great Smokey Roadblock; You Light Up My Life; Car Wash; Gable and Lombard; The Last of the Cowboys; Girl Friends* (Locarno Film Festival Best Actress award); *Heartbeeps; Missing; The Boss' Wife; Sticky Fingers* (as actress, co-writer and co-producer, with Catlin Adams); *Checking Out.* **TV:** *Rhoda; Lily Tomlin: Sold Out;* Melissa in *thirtysomething* (Emmy award, 1989); *Playing for Time; Will There Really Be a Morning?; Hustling; The Best Little Girl In the World; Wallenberg: A Hero's Story* (all TV movies).

MEAGHER, *ray*

Ray Meagher. Actor. Formerly a professional rugby player. **Films:** *Newsfront; Breaker Morant.* **TV:** *The Outsiders; The Restless Years; Glenview High; The Oracle; Roadhouse; One Day Miller; Prisoner: Cell Block H* (twice); *Cop Shop; Skyways; Secret Valley; Punishment; A Sporting Chance; Home Sweet Home; Holiday Island; Kingswood Country* (twice); *Bellamy; Sound; A Country Practice* (twice); *Noise Recycling; Waterloo Station; Keepers; Kings; Daily At Dawn; Five Mile Creek; Heads 'n' Tails; City West; Relatives; Mother and Son; Nationwide; A Fortunate Life; Colour In the Creek; Rafferty's Rules; Land of Hope; The Great Bookie Robbery; Five Times Dizzy; Vietnam; The Shiralee; Willing & Abel; True Believers; Spit MacPhee;* Alf Stewart in *Home and Away* (1988-). **Address:** c/o Lee Leslie Management/Channel 7. m. theatrical agent Lee Leslie.

MELIA, *michael*

Michael Melia. Actor. b. 1945. Son of boxer Joe Melia. **TV:** *There'll Almost Always Be an England; Village Hall; Kiss the Girls and Make Them Cry; Hazell; Fox; The Sweeney; Blake's 7; We the Accused; Diana; Doctor Who; Strangers; Maybury; The Chinese Detective; When the Boat Comes In; The Gentle Touch; A Christmas Present; Minder; Rumpole of the Bailey; Coronation Street; Collision Course; Travelling Man; Whoops Apocalypse; For 4 Tonight; The Hard Word; Dempsey and Makepeace; Big Deal; Bergerac; Campion; London's Burning; Inspector Morse; Reasonable Force; After Henry; The Bill; Room At the Bottom; Hollywood Sports; Here Is the News; Stay Lucky;* Eddie Royle in *EastEnders* (1990–91); title role in *In Suspicious Circumstances: The Freddie Mills Story.* **Address:** c/o Silvester Management. m. actress Celia Foxe; 1 d. Charlotte, 1 s. Thomas.

MELLINGER, *leonie*

Leonie Mellinger. Actress. b. Berlin, Germany, 24 June. Trained at Central School of Speech and Drama. **Theatre:** *The Winter's Tale* (RSC); *Titus Andronicus; The Cenci; Beached; Lady Macbeth.* **Films:** *Memoirs of a Survivor; Ghost Dance; Memed My Hawk; Zina; Partition; The Young Toscanini.* **TV:** *Sons and Lovers; Whale Music; Infidelities; Summer Lightning; Mr Palfrey of Westminster; Bergerac; Dead Head; Paradise Postponed; Small World; Hannay; The New Statesman; Frederick Forsyth Presents; Children Crossing; Stay Lucky; Maigret.* **Address:** c/o Peters Fraser & Dunlop. m. actor Robin Askwith.

MERCIER, *sheila*

Sheila Mercier. Actress. b. Hull, East Yorkshire, 1 January 1919. Sister of Brian Rix. WAAF adjutant in Fighter Command during World War Two. Trained at Stratford-upon-Avon College of Drama. **Theatre:** Debut with Donald Wolfit's touring company; Whitehall Theatre Company farces (1955–66). **TV:** *Six of Rix;* Annie Sugden in *Emmerdale* (1972-); *This Is Your Life* (subject, 1985). **Address:** c/o Peter Mercier, 36 Coastal Road, Angmering-on-Sea, East Preston, West Sussex BN16 1SJ/Yorkshire Television. Lives in West Sussex and Leeds. m. former actor Peter Mercier; 1 s. Nigel. Hobbies: Reading.

MICHELMORE, *cliff*

Cliff Michelmore. Presenter. b. Cowes, Isle of Wight, 11 December 1919. Started in radio with BFBS in Germany (1947–9); joined BBC to produce, direct and write for children's TV. **TV:** *Tonight; Panorama; 24 Hours; Our World; Holiday; space programmes; General Election programmes; Talkback; Wheelbase; Chance To Meet; Day By Day* (Southern Television); *Home On Sundays; Songs of Praise; Lifeline.* **Radio:** *Family Favourites.* **Address:** c/o BBC TV. Lives in Reigate, Surrey, and on the Isle of Wight. m. broadcaster Jean Metcalfe; 1 s. TV presenter Guy, 1 d. Jenny.

MIDDLEMISS, *philip*

Philip Middlemiss. Actor. b. Hartlepool, 1963. Trained at LAMDA. **Theatre:** *A Tale of Two Cities; Larkrise; A Christmas Carol; Pinocchio* (Theatre Royal, Stratford East); *Strippers; The Trackers of Oxyrhynchus* (both National Theatre tours). **TV:** *Ladies In Charge; Closing Ranks; Inspector Morse; Traffik; Christabel; The Bill;* PC Barry Smith in *Waterfront Beat;* Des Barnes in *Coronation Street* (1990-). **Address:** c/o Barry Brown & Partner/Granada TV. Single; lives in London and Manchester. Hobbies: Collecting videotapes, watching Liverpool FC.

MILES, *annie*

Anne Miller. Actress. b. Tynemouth, Tyneside, 5 May 1958. Trained at the Webber Douglas Academy. **Theatre:** *Dracula; The Hubble Bubble Band Show; The Taming of the Shrew; Return To the Forbidden Planet; Happy End;* title role in *Cinderella; Godspell; Grease; Glitterballs; The Taming of the Shrew* (all-woman version, Theatre Royal, Stratford East); *Pericles;* Alice in *Little Red Riding Hood* (both Theatre Royal, Stratford East); Linda in *Stags and Hens* (Young Vic Theatre); *The Rocky Horror Show; Wack and the Beanstalk; Cabaret* (Strand Theatre); Cindy Balsheesh in *Soaplights.* **TV:** *Sink Or Swim; The Lonely Hearts Kid; Auf Wiedersehen, Pet; The Optimist; Me & My Girl; All In Good Faith;* Sue Sullivan (née Harper) in *Brookside.* **Address:** c/o Jane Lehrer Associates. Single; lives in London. Hobbies: Keep-fit, piano.

MILES, *sarah*

Sarah Miles. Actress. b. 1943. Trained at RADA. **Theatre:** *Vivat! Vivat! Regina!; St Joan.* **Films:** *Term of Trial; The Ceremony; The Servants; Those Magnificent Men In Their Flying Machines; I Was Happy Here; The Blow-Up; Ryan's Daughter; Lady Caroline Lamb; The Hireling; The Man Who Loved Cat Dancing; Great Expectations; Pepita Jiminez; The Sailor Who Fell From Grace; The Big Sleep; Venom; Ordeal By Innocence; Steaming; D'Ardenelle; Hope and Glory; White Mischief; A Ghost In Monte Carlo.* **TV:** *Walter; Walter and June* (both TV movies); *Queenie* (TV movie); *Harem.* **Address:** c/o Marina Martin Management.

MILLER, *sam*

Sam Gary Miller. Actor. b. Saxmundham, Suffolk, 28 September 1962. Trained at the Arts Educational School. **Theatre:** *Chicago; My Fair Lady; Richard II; Richard III* (both at the Phoenix Theatre); *A Midsummer Night's Dream; Twelfth Night; The Swaggerer* (all at Regent's Park Theatre). **TV:** *Fortunes of War; To See Ourselves; Wish Me Luck; Campion; Boon; Piece of Cake; Casualty; Jack the Ripper; The Great Escape – The Final Chapter; Murder East, Murder West; Van Der Valk;* Sgt John Maitland in *The Bill.* **Address:** c/o Jeremy Conway. Single; lives in Islington, North London. Hobbies: Guitar playing, cinema, chess, squash, golf, renovating old VW Beetles, watching gangster films.

MILLIGAN, *spike*

Spike Milligan. Writer/Actor/Comedian. b. Ahmaddnagar, India, 16 April 1918. **Films:** *The Magic Christian; History of the World – Part 1.* **TV:** *Idiot's Weekly; A Show Called Fred; Son of Fred; Bookman; Monitor; Milligan At Large; Milligan's Wake; Muses With Milligan; The World of Beachcomber; Q5; Curry and Chips; The Other Spike; Oh In Colour; The Marty Feldman Comedy Machine; Milligan for All Seasons; The Last Turkey In the Shop Show; Q6; Melting Pot; Funniest TV Command In the World; Q7; The Best of British; Q8; Survival; Q9; Pirates of Penzance; There's a Lot of It About; Just Like That.* **Radio:** *Crazy People; The Goon Show; The Last Goon Show of All.* **Address:** c/o Norma Farnes. m. 1st June (dis), 2nd singer Patricia Ridgway (dec), 3rd Shelagh Sinclair; 3 d. Laura, Sile (from 1st m.), Jane (from 2nd m.), 1 s. Sean (from 1st m.).

MILLS, *adrian*

Paul Adrian Mills. Presenter/Actor. b. Uppingham, Oakham, Rutland, 16 July 1956. Acted with the National Youth Theatre of Great Britain (1973–7) and trained at the Rose Bruford College of Speech and Drama. **Theatre:** Performed at York Theatre Royal, Scarborough, the Liverpool Everyman, the Shaw Theatre, His Majesty's Theatre, Aberdeen, the Arts Theatre, Cambridge. **TV:** *Doctor Who; Minder; Play for Today; Brookside; That's My Boy; Fairly Secret Army; Storybook International; That's Life* (1985–90); *Breakfast Time* (1985–6); *South East News* (1985–6); *Facing Up To AIDS; Getaway; Lifeline; By Royal Appointment; Daytime UK* (1990-); *People Today.* **Address:** c/o Downes Presenters Agency. Single; lives in Southport, Lancashire. Hobbies: Cricket, tennis, cinema. **Favourite TV programme:** *Cheers.*

MILLS, *hayley*

Hayley Mills. Actress. b. London, 18 April 1946. Daughter of actor John Mills and actress Mary Hayley Bell. Trained at Elmhurst Ballet School. **Films:** *Tiger Bay; Polyanna; The Parent Trap; Whistle Down the Wind; Sky West and Crooked; The Family Way; Pretty Polly; Twisted Nerve; Take a Girl Like You; Endless Night; Mr What Changed Charley Farthing; The Diamond Hunters; Appointment With Death; Walk of Life.* **TV:** *Deadly Strangers; Only a Scream Away; Love Boat; The Flame Trees of Thika* (winner, *TVTimes* Best Actress On TV award, 1982); *Illusion of Life; Amazing Stories; Murder, She Wrote; Parent Trap II; Tales of the Unexpected; Good Morning Miss Bliss; Back Home; Parent Trap III; Parent Trap IV.* **Books:** *My God* (1988). **Address:** c/o Chatto and Linnit. m. (dis); 2 s. Crispian, Jason. Hobbies; Travel, reading, studying philosophy.

MILMOE, *caroline*

Caroline Milmoe. Actress. b. Manchester, 11 January 1963. Attended the Contact Youth Theatre, Manchester. **Theatre:** Mary McGregor in *The Prime of Miss Jean Brodie; The Winter's Tale* (RSC tour); *The Crucible* (RSC tour); *All My Sons; A View From the Bridge;* Hermia in *A Midsummer Night's Dream; Assuming the Role;* Jo in *A Taste of Honey.* **Films:** Melanie in *The Magic Toyshop;* Maid in *Without a Clue;* Girl in *The Fruit Machine;* Sonia in *The Final Warning* (US cable TV). **TV:** Sandra Lord in *The Practice;* Maureen Delaney in *Brick Is Beautiful;* Julie Jefferson in *Bread* (first two series); Cindy in *Valentine Park;* Maggie Troon in *Hot Metal; Celebration; The Bill* (two roles); Mary Durrant in *Agatha Christie's Poirot;* Lisa Horton in *Coronation Street.* **Address:** c/o Nigel Martin-Smith Personal Management.

MIRREN, *helen*

Helen Mirren. Actress. b. Southend, Essex. **Films:** *Caligula; The Long Good Friday; The Fiendish Plot of Dr Fu Manchu; Excalibur; Cal* (winner, Cannes Film Festival Best Actress award, 1984); *White Knights; Heavenly Pursuits; Mosquito Coast; The Cook, The Thief, His Wife and Her Lover; Where Angels Fear To Tread; The Gift.* **TV:** *Behind the Scenes; Cousin Bette; Miss Julie; Coffin for the Bride; Jackanory; Little Minister; The Changeling; Bellamira; The Apple Cart; The Philanthropist; Mussolini and Claretta Pietacci; The Collection; The Country Wife; As You Like It; Blue Remembered Hills; The Serpent Son; Quiz Kids; A Midsummer Night's Dream; Mrs Reinhart; After the Party; Cymbeline; Coming Through; Cause Célébre ; Red King, White Knight; Prime Suspect.* **Address:** c/o Al Parker. Lives in London and Los Angeles with Taylor Hackford.

MITCHELL, *warren*

Warren Mitchell. Actor. b. London, 14 January 1926. Trained at RADA. **Theatre:** *Death of a Salesman; The Caretaker* (both National Theatre); *The Homecoming.* **Films:** *Tommy the Toreador; Two Way Stretch; Sammy Lee; Carry On Cleo; Drop Dead Darling; Diamonds Before Breakfast; Assassination Bureau; Best House In London; Till Death Us Do Part; Moon Zero Two; Innocent Bystander; What Changed Charley Farthing; Jabberwocky; Stand Up Virgin Soldiers; Meetings With Remarkable Men; Knights and Emeralds; The Chain; Foreign Body; Incident on the Line.* **TV:** Alf Garnett in *Till Death Us Do Part* and *In Sickness and In Health; The Merchant of Venice; The Caretaker; Moss; Tickets for the Titanic;* Ivan Fox in *So You Think You've Got Troubles.* **Address:** c/o ICM. m. actress Constance Wake; 2 d. Rebecca, Anna, 1 s. Daniel.

MOLINA, *alfred*

Alfred Molina. Actor. b. London, 24 May 1953. **Films:** *Ladyhawke; No 1; Raiders of the Lost Ark; Letter To Brezhnev; Prick Up Your Ears; Manifesto; Not Without My Daughter.* **TV:** *Anyone for Denis?; Angels In the Annexe; C.A.T.S. Eyes; Blat; Casualty; Virtuoso; Apocalyptic Butterflies; The Accountant* (TV movie); *Drowning in the Shallow End* (TV movie); *El C.I.D.; Nativity Blues;* title role in *Hancock; Performance: The Trials of Oz; Ashenden; Angels.* **Address:** c/o Lou Coulson. m. actress Jill Gascoine; 2 step-s Sean, Adam.

MONKHOUSE, *bob*

Bob Monkhouse. Presenter/Comedian/Actor. b. Beckenham, Kent, 1 June 1928. Trained as a cartoon film animator with Gaumont British, before becoming the BBC's first contract comedian and forming a scriptwriting team with Denis Goodwin. **Theatre:** *Bob Monkhouse Startime; Aladdin; Come Blow Your Horn; Boys From Syracuse; The Gulls.* **Films:** *Carry On Sergeant; Dentist In the Chair; Weekend With Lulu; She'll Have a Go.* **TV:** *The Bob Monkhouse Comedy Hour; My Pal Bob; For Love Or Money; Candid Camera; Mad Movies; Sunday Night At the London Palladium; The Golden Shot; Quick On the Draw; Celebrity Square; I'm Bob – He's Dickie; Family Fortunes; The Bob Monkhouse Show; Bob's Full House; The $64,000 Question; Bob's Your Uncle.* **Address:** c/o Peter Prichard. m. 1st Elizabeth (dis), 2nd Jacqueline; 1 d. Abigail, 2 s. Gary, Simon.

MONTAGUE, *bruce*

Bruce Montague. Actor. b. Deal, Kent, 24 March 1939. Trained at RADA. **Theatre:** Repertory theatre in Birmingham; Old Vic Theatre; *Relative Strangers; The Chalk Garden; The Cabinet Mole; Ross* (Canada and Old Vic); *Last of the Red Hot Lovers; Two for the Seesaw; The Division Belle.* As writer: *Love Bites; 1793; A Touch of Menace.* **TV:** *Crane; Dimensions of Fear; The Saint; The Alpha Plan; Linkmen; Public Eye; The Thief of Baghdad; Lillie; For Maddie With Love;* Leonard in *Butterflies; Virginia Fly Is Drowning; The Concubine Cowboys; The Kelly Monteith Show; Whoops Apocalypse; Fairground; Sharon and Elsie; Fresh Fields; District Nurse; The Trial of Klaus Barbie; The Vision; Agenda for Murder; Olympus Force; The Vision; Agatha Christie's Poirot.* **Address:** c/o Peter Graham Associates. m. Barbara; 1 s. Sam, 1 d. Kate.

MONTEATH, *alec*

Alec Monteath. Actor. b. Doune, Perthshire, 22 May. Trained at the Royal Scottish Academy of Music and Drama. **Theatre:** *Othello;* Pitlochry Festival; *Brief Glory; Journey's End; Swansong; The Birthday Party; Battle Royal; Aladdin.* **TV:** Continuity announcer with Scottish Television and BBC Scotland; *The Omega Factor; Bothwell;* Dougal Lachlan in *Take the High Road* (1980-92). **Address:** c/o Scottish Television. Lives in Stirlingshire. m. actress Linna Skelton; 2 s. actor David, Alasdair.

MOORE, *brian*

Brian Moore. Soccer commentator. b. Benenden, Kent, 28 February 1932. Journalist with World Sports, *Exchange Telegraph* and *The Times,* before joining BBC Radio, then LWT. **TV:** *The Big Match; On the Ball; The Big Match Live; The Match; The London Match; The European Match* **Address:** c/o LWT. m. Betty; 2 s. Christopher, Simon.

MOORE, *roger*

Roger Moore. Actor. b. London, 14 October 1927. Trained at RADA. **Films:** *The Man Who Haunted Himself; Gold; Shout At the Devil; The Wild Geese; Escape From Athena; Live and Let Die; The Man With the Golden Gun; The Spy Who Loved Me; Moonraker; Octopussy; For Your Eyes Only; A View To a Kill; Bed and Breakfast; Bullseye.* **TV:** *Ivanhoe; The Alaskans; Maverick;* Simon Templar in *The Saint;* Lord Brett Sinclair in *The Persuaders.* **Address:** c/o ICM. m. 1st Doorn Van Steyn (dis), 2nd singer Dorothy Squires (dis), 3rd Luisa Mattioli; 2 s. Geoffrey, Christian, 1 d. Deborah.

MOORE, *william*

William Moore. Actor. b. Birmingham, 19 April. **Theatre:** Repertory theatre in Birmingham, Pitlochry and Swansea; taught at Bristol Old Vic Theatre School; *When We Are Married* (London West End). **TV:** *Z-Cars; Softly, Softly; Middlemarch; Dombey and Son; Better Than the Movies; Dad's Army; The Dick Emery Show; Charles Bravo; Scott On . . .; Coronation Street; The Rivals of Sherlock Holmes; South Riding; The Brontes; Sam; Love Story; The Cedar Tree; The Fenn Street Gang; No Honestly; Dick Turpin; Sorry; My Husband and I.* **Address:** c/o Joan Reddin. m. actress Mollie Sugden (qv); 2 s. Robert, Simon (twins).

MORGAN, *garfield*

Garfield Morgan. Actor. b. Birmingham, 19 April 1931. **Theatre:** Director of productions, Marlowe Theatre, Canterbury (1957–8) and Library Theatre, Manchester (1959–60); associate director, Northcott Theatre (1976–8) and Nottingham Playhouse (1978–80). **Films:** *The Pumpkin Eater; The Story of Private Pooley; Perfect Friday.* **TV:** *Softly, Softly; Spindoe; Judge Dee; Randall and Hopkirk (Deceased); Department S; Hadleigh; Dear Mother . . .Love Albert; The Sweeney; Shelley; One By One; The 19th Hole; No Job for a Lady; Lovejoy.* **Address:** c/o Michelle Braidman Associates. m. actress Dilys Laye (dis).

MORIARTY, *paul*

Paul Moriarty. Actor. b. London, 19 May 1946. **Theatre:** RSC; National Theatre; Royal Court Theatre; *The Contractor* (London West End). **Films:** *Quest for Love; The Chain.* **TV:** *Holly; Pelham; Coronation Street; Z-Cars; Minder; The Sweeney; Jackanory; Love Story; Troilus and Cressida; The Gentle Touch; Causualty; Saracen; The Paradise Club; Troublemakers.* **Address:** c/o Ken McReddie. m. Teresa; 1 d. Jessica, 1 s. Matthew.

MORLEY, *ken*

Ken Morley. Actor. Worked as a teacher, took a degree in English and drama at Manchester University, then went into acting. **Theatre:** *The Adventures of Mr Toad; Volpone; The Beaux' Stratagem* (Cambridge Theatre); *Insignificance; Comic Cuts; The Ragged Trousered Philanthropists; Dracula; Habeas Corpus; The Tax Exile; Pinocchio.* **Films:** *Alfie Darling; Little Dorrit.* **TV:** *The Fall and Rise of Reginald Perrin; Who Dares Wins; Quest; Bulman; The Return of the Antelope; All Passion Spent; Les Girls; The Management; Blind Justice; Chelmsford 123; Watching;* Flockenstuffen in *'Allo 'Allo!; You Rang, M'Lord?;* Reg Holdsworth in *Coronation Street* (1989-). **Address:** c/o ICM Duncan Heath Associates/Granada TV. m. Sue; 1 s. Roger.

MORRIS, *beth*

Beth Morris. Actress. b. Goirseinon, West Glamorgan, 19 July 1949. Trained at the Cardiff College of Music and Drama. **Theatre:** Repertory theatre in Northampton, Bristol and Birmingham; RSC; *Man and Superman; Banana Ridge; Travesties; Passion of Dracula; Mrs Brabofskie's Academy.* **TV:** *Play of the Week; Play of the Month; Jude the Obscure; Minder; Z-Cars; Softly, Softly; I, Claudius; David Copperfield; Ballroom; District Nurse* (two series); *Better Days; We Are Seven.* **Address:** c/o Ken McReddie.

MORRIS, *jonathon*

Jonathon Morris. Actor. b. Urmston, Manchester, 20 July 1960. Trained at Bristol Old Vic Theatre School. **Theatre:** *La Cage Aux Folles; As You Like It; The Cherry Orchard; Candida; Wuthering Heights; Tess of the d'Urbervilles; Rain From Heaven; Diary of a Somebody; Semi Monde.* **TV:** *Beau Geste; Bread; The Consultant; The Prisoner of Zenda; That Beryl Marston...!; Ties of Blood; Jackanory; The Agatha Christie Hour; The Practice; Bingo; Hell's Bells.* **Address:** c/o ICM Duncan Heath Associates.

MORRIS, *mike*

Mike Morris. Presenter. b. Harrow, Middlesex, 26 June 1947. Journalist with the *Surrey Comet,* Sydney-based news agency AAP Reuters (as bulletins editor) *and* United Newspapers (as sports reporter, then sports editor), before entering television. **TV:** Thames Television sub-editor and reporter; TV-am sports presenter and host of *The Saturday Morning Show,* before becoming a presenter of *Good Morning Britain* (1987-). **Address:** c/o TV-am. m. Alison; 2 d. Sarah, Helen.

MORRISSEY, *neil*

Neil Morrissey. Actor. b. Stafford, 4 July 1962. Trained at Guildhall School of Music and Drama. **Theatre:** *Daughter In Law.* **Films:** *Playing Away.* **TV:** *The Bounty; Juliet Bravo; Rocky in Boon; Travellers By Night; Pulaski; William Tell.* **Address:** c/o ICM. m. actress Amanda Noar (sep); 1 s. Sam.

MORSE, *david*

David Morse. Actor. b. Hamilton, Massachusetts, USA, 11 October. **Theatre:** Boston Repertory Company; Circle Repertory Company, New York; *Of Mice and Men* (Los Angeles, Logie Award-winner). **TV:** *Family Business; Prototype; Shattered Vows; St Elsewhere; Personal Foul; Six Against the Rock; The Best Kept Secret; Down Payment of Murder.* **Address:** c/o Yvette Bikoff Agency. m. actress Susan Wheeler Duff. Hobbies: Oil painting, drawing, running, charity work.

MOSES, *billy*

Billy Moses. Actor. b. Los Angeles, USA, 11 November 1959. **Films:** *Choices.* **TV:** Cole Gioberti in *Falcon Crest; Love Boat; Glitter; Finder of the Lost Loves; Battle of the Network Stars.* **Address:** c/o Leading Artists.

MOSLEY, *bryan*

Bryan Mosley. Actor/Director. b. Leeds, 25 August 1931. Trained at the Northern Theatre School; also stunt fighter and arranger in films. **TV:** *Skyport; Little Doris; The Front Room; The High Game; The Rise and Fall of Nellie Brown; The Planemakers; The Saint; Z-Cars; The Avengers; Adam Adamant; Bent; No Hiding Place;* Denis Rutledge in *Crossroads; The Villains; The Men From Room 13; Doctor Who; It's a Square World; The Worker; The Clitheroe Kid; Queenie's Castle;* Alf Roberts in *Coronation Street* (1961 and 1968-); *Royal Variety Performance* (1989). **Address:** c/o Granada TV. Lives near Shipley, West Yorkshire, and Salford. m. Norma; 3 d. Jacqueline, Simone, Helen, 3 s. Jonathan, Bernard, Leonard. Hobbies: Travel, painting, drawing, photography, films, reading, walking. **Favourite TV programme:** *Wildlife On One.*

MOSLEY, *roger é*

Roger E Mosley. Actor. b. Los Angeles, USA. Champion wrestler while at college and a founder member of the Watts Repertory Company. **Films:** *Semi-Tough; Leadbelly; The Greatest; Stay Hungry; K-God.* **TV:** *Attica; I Know Why the Caged Bird Sings; The Jericho Mile; Love Boat;* TC in *Magnum PI.* **Address:** c/o Aimee Entertainment, 13743 Victory Boulevard, Van Nuys, California 91401, USA. m. 1st (dis); 5 children.

MUIR, *frank*, CBE

Frank Muir. Scriptwriter/Performer. b. Broadstairs, Kent, 5 February 1920. **TV:** *And So To Bentley; Whack-O!; The Seven Faces of Jim* (as scriptwriter, all with Denis Norden); *Sound of Laughter; Call My Bluff; How To Be an Alien; We Have Ways of Making You Laugh;* BBC assistant head of comedy (1964–7); LWT head of light entertainment (1968–9); *TV Heaven.* **Radio:** *Take It From Here; Bedtime With Braden* (as scriptwriter, both with Denis Norden); *My Word!; My Music.* **Books:** *Call My Bluff; Upon My Word!; The Frank Muir Book; What-a-Mess* series; *Take My Word for It; Frank Muir Goes Into . . .* series; *The Glums; Frank Muir On Children; Oh My Word!; The Book of Comedy Sketches; The Oxford Book of Humorous Prose.* **Address:** c/o April Young. m. Polly; 1 d. Sally, 1 s. James. Hobbies: Collecting books, staring into space.

MULLIGAN, *richard*

Richard Mulligan. Actor. b. New York, USA, 13 November 1932. Started career as a playwright, was mistaken for an actor at a Miami theatre and landed the role of Andy Mayo in *Beyond the Horizon.* **Films:** *The Mixed Up Files of Mrs Basil E Frankweiler; Irish Whiskey; Rebellion; One Potato, Two Potato; The Group; The Big Bus; Little Big Man; Scavenger; Hunt; S.O.B.; The Trail of the Pink Panther; Meatballs Part II; Teachers; Micki and Maude; Doin' Time; The Heavenly Kid; A Fine Mess; Quicksilver.* **TV:** *Having Babies; Poker Alice; The Hero; The Diana Rigg Show;* Burt in *Soap* (winner, Emmy Best Comedy Actor award, 1980); *Harvey; The Public Incident;* title role in *Reggie;* Harry in *Empty Nest* (winner, Best Comedy Actor award, 1989); *Highway To Heaven.* m. 1st Patricia Jones (dis), 2nd Joan Hackett (dis), 3rd Leonore Stevens.

MULVILLE, *jimmy*

Jimmy Mulville. Actor. b. Liverpool. Former member of Cambridge Footlights Revue. **Theatre:** *An Evening Without* (national tour, Edinburgh Festival and Australian tour); *Totally Foxed; Big In Brazil* (Old Vic Theatre); *Who Dares Wins* (national tours); *Valued Friends.* **Films:** *Morons From Outer Space.* **TV:** *The Steam Video Company; Who Dares Wins* (also as writer); *Chelmsford 123* (also as writer); Donald Redfern in *That's Love* (four series); Philip in *GBH.* As presenter: *Acropolis Now; The Hogmanay Show; Babylon 2; Just for Laughs; Going Loco; Holiday '92.* **Address:** c/o Mayer Management.

MURDEN, *karen*

Karen Murden. Actress. b. Nottingham, 24 April 1970. Joined the Central Junior Television Workshop at the age of 13. **Theatre:** *On the Beach; The Gallopers; A Collier's Tuesday Tea; Roses of Eyam; The Boy Friend; Cabaret; Bugsy Malone* (all with the Central Junior Television Workshop). **TV:** *Your Mother Wouldn't Like It* (two series); *Hardwicke House;* Beverley Grice in *Crossroads;* Sheila in *Tales of Sherwood Forest;* Sarah Robbins in *Jupiter Moon* (BSB, 1990); Irene Carter in *EastEnders.* **Address:** c/o Spotlight. Lives in North London with dancer Nick Davion.

MURPHY, *brian*

Brian Murphy. Actor. b. Ventnor, Isle of Wight, 25 September 1933. Trained at RADA and worked with Joan Littlewood's Theatre Workshop. **Theatre:** *On Your Way, Riley!;* RSC. **Films:** *Sparrers Can't Sing; San Ferry Anne; Diary of a Nobody; Just Like a Woman.* **TV:** George Roper in *Man About the House* and *George and Mildred; The Incredible Mr Tanner; L for Lester; Lame Ducks; All In Good Faith.* **Radio:** Ernest in *Citizens.* **Address:** c/o Saraband Associates. m. Carole; 2 s. Trevor, Kevin.

MURRAY, *bryan*

Bryan Murray. Actor. b. Dublin, Ireland, 13 July 1949. Trained at the Abbey Theatre School, Dublin. **Theatre:** Abbey Theatre Company (also as director and co-writer of two musicals); National Theatre Company; RSC; *Catchpenny Twist; Nashville New York; Blood Brothers; Miss Firecracker Contest.* **TV:** *Rifleman; Shepherd's Life; GBS; Oscar; Strumpet City; Bread Or Blood; I'm a Dreamer Montreal; Year of the French; The Irish RM; The Franchise Affair; Bread; Final Run; Encore; Perfect Scoundrels.* **Address:** Peters Fraser & Dunlop. m. actress Angela Harding (sep); 1 d. Laura.

NAIL, *jimmy*

Jimmy Nail. Actor. **Films:** *Morons From Outer Space; Master of the Game; Robinson Crusoe; The Dream Demon; Just Ask for Diamond; Danny the Champion of the World.* **TV:** Geordie in *Shoot for the Sun;* Oz in *Auf Wiedersehen, Pet; Blott On the Landscape; Minder; Wallenberg: A Hero's Story* (TV movie); *Spyship;* Freddie Spender in *Spender* (also co-creator, with Ian La Frenais, two series). **Address:** ICM Duncan Heath Associates.

NALLON, *steve*

Steve Nallon. Impressionist. b. Leeds. Gained a degree in English and drama. **Theatre:** Edinburgh Festival Fringe; *The Cloggies; Mrs Thatcher's Star Spangled Cabinet; Maggie and the Wolf; The Carnival of the Animals; Greenpeace Gala* (Royal Albert Hall); *A Cook's Tour* (Shaftesbury Theatre); *The Secret Policeman's Third Ball* (London Palladium); *Night of 100 Stars* (Adelphi Theatre); *The Secret Policeman's Biggest Ball* (Cambridge Theatre). **TV:** *Spitting Image* (voice impersonator and puppeteer); *World In Action; Bullseye Christmas Special; The New Statesman; Ten Glorious Years; Live From the Palladium; Face To Face; Frankie and Johnny* (TV movie); *The James Whale Show; The South Bank Show; Arena; The Late Show; Staggering Stories.* **Records:** *Spit In Your Ear; Great Golden Gobs; No Clause 28.* **Address:** c/o Eric Glass.

NETTLES, *john*

John Nettles. Actor. b. St Austell, Cornwall, 1948. Took part in dramatic society productions while at Southampton University. **Theatre:** Royal Court Theatre; RSC; *The Hollow Crown* (US tour); *The Relapse; La Ronde.* **TV:** *The Liver Birds* (four series); Ian Mackenzie in *A Family At War; Black Beauty; Play for Today: Findings On a Late Night; The Merchant of Venice;* Jim Bergerac in *Bergerac* (1982-). **Address:** c/o Saraband Associates. Lives in Jersey. m. Joyce (dis); 1 d. Emma.

NEWMAN, *nanette*

Nanette Newman. Actress/Presenter/Author. b. Northampton. Trained at the Italia Conti Academy and RADA. **Films:** *The L-Shaped Room; The Whisperers; The Wrong Box; The Love Ban; Man At the Top; The Stepford Wives; The Raging Moon; International Velvet.* **TV:** *Prometheus; The Fun Food Factory; London Scene; Stay With Me Till Morning; Let There Be Love;* title role in *Jessie; Late Expectations; The Endless Game.* **Books:** *The Root Children; Fun Food Feasts; My Granny Was a Frightful Bore; The Cat Lover's Coffee-Table Book; The Dog Lover's Coffee-Table Book; The Cat and Mouse Love Story; The Christmas Cookbook; Bad Baby; ABC Book; 123 Book; Cooking for Friends.* **Address:** Chatto and Linnit. Lives in Surrey. m. film director/screenwriter Bryan Forbes; 2 d. Sarah, Emma. Pets: Cats and dogs. Hobbies: Needlepoint.

NICHOLAS, *paul*

aul Nicholas. Actor/Singer. b. Peterborough, Cambridgeshire, 3 December 1945. Former rock 'n' roll
iano player. **Theatre:** Hair; Jesus Christ Superstar; Pirates of Penzance; Charlie Girl. **Films:** Canabis;
lind Terror; Whatever Happened To Jack and Jill?; Stardust; Three for All; Tommy; Lisztomania;
ergeant Pepper's Lonely Hearts Club Band; The World Is Full of Married Men; Yesterday's Hero; Alice;
he Jazz Singer; Nutcracker; Invitation To a Wedding. **TV:** Z-Cars; Early Struggles; Paul; Golden Sea
wallow of Knokke; Season of the Witch; Three Up, Two Down; Chips; Ladykillers; The Boys From
panema; A Little Rococo; Starburst; Just Good Friends; Doubting Thomas; The Royal Variety
erformance; Bust; Paul Nicholas and Friends; Close To Home. **Address:** c/o Billy Marsh Associates.
n. Linzi; 2 d. Natasha, Carmen, 2 s. Oscar, Alexander.

NICHOLLS, *sue*

The Hon Susan Frances Harmar-Nicholls. Actress. b. Walsall, Staffordshire, 23 November 1943.
aughter of former Tory MP Lord Harmar-Nicholls. Trained at RADA. **Films:** Expresso Splasho!; The
ightingale Saga. **TV:** Marilyn Gates in Crossroads; Not On Your Nellie; Jangles; Rentaghost; Pipkin's;
ycoon; The Duchess of Duke Street; Solo; Wodehouse Playhouse; Doctor On the Go; Heartland; Village
all; The Professionals; Up the Elephant and Round the Castle; The Fall and Rise of Reginald Perrin;
udrey Roberts (née Potter) in Coronation Street (1979-); Royal Variety Performance (1989). **Records:**
Where Will You Be; All the Way To Heaven. **Address:** c/o Barry Brown & Partner/Granada TV. Lives
n London and Manchester with actor Mark Eden. Hobbies: Swimming, singing and sitting doing
othing. **Favourite TV programme:** Neighbours; Dad's Army; 'anything that makes me laugh.'

NICHOLSON, *mavis*

Mavis Nicholson. Presenter/Interviewer. b. Briton Ferry, 19 October 1930. Advertising copywriter before
becoming a freelance journalist. **TV:** Mavis; Happy Returns; Mavis – Wanting To Know; Other People's
Children; Volunteers; Medical Express; Good After Noon; Afternoon Plus; The Garden Party; Mavis
Catches Up With...; Relatively Speaking; Third Wave With Mavis Nicholson. **Address:** c/o BBC TV. m.
ournalist Geoffrey Nicholson; 3 s. Steve, Lewis, Harry.

NIMMO, *derek*

Derek Nimmo. Actor. b. Liverpool, 19 September 1933. **Theatre:** The Amorous Prawn; Duel of Angels;
Charlie Girl; A Friend Indeed; See How They Run (all London West End). **Films:** One of Our Dinosaurs Is
Missing. **TV:** All Gas and Gaiters; Oh Brother!; Oh Father!; My Hon Mrs; Sorry I'm Single; Life Begins
At Forty; Third Time Lucky; Hell's Bells; Neighbours. **Address:** c/o Barry Burnett Organisation. m.
Patricia; 1 d. Amanda, 2 s. Timothy, Piers.

NORDEN, *denis, CBE*

Denis Norden. Broadcaster/Writer. b. Hackney, London, 6 February 1922. A theatre manager before
writing for troops shows while in the RAF, then becoming a scriptwriter for variety shows and teaming
up with Frank Muir (1947–64) to write for TV and radio. **Films:** Bueno Sera, Mrs Campbell; Every
Home Should Have One; The Water Babies (all as writer). **TV:** And So To Bentley; Whack-O!; The
Seven Faces of Jim; Brothers-In-Law; The Glums (all as writer, with Frank Muir); The Name's the
Same; How To Be an Alien (both as writer); Looks Familiar; It'll Be Alright On the Night; With
Hilarious Consequences; Ten Years of Alright On the Night; 21 Years of Laughter; In On the Act; Pick of
the Pilots; Denis Norden's Laughter File; Worst of Alright On the Night (all as writer-presenter).
Address: c/o April Young. m. Avril; 1 d. TV producer Maggie (Norden), 1 s. Nick.

NORMAN, *barry*

Barry Norman. Presenter/Writer. b. London, 21 August 1933. Son of film producer Les Norman. Journalist with the *Daily Mail* before becoming a freelance TV reviewer. **TV:** *Late Night Line-Up; Film* series; *The Hollywood Greats; Omnibus; The British Greats; Barry Norman In Chicago; Barry Norman's Hong Kong; Barry Norman On Broadway; Barry Norman's London Season; Barry Norman In Celebrity City; The Rank Charm School; Films of the Year.* **Books:** *End Product; A Series of Defeats; To Nick a Good Body; The Hollywood Greats; The Movie Greats; Have a Nice Day; Sticky Wicket; The Film Greats; Talking Pictures: The Story of Hollywood.* Winner, BAFTA Richard Dimbleby Award, 1980 **Address:** c/o Curtis Brown. m. Diana; 2 d. Samantha, Emma.

NUNN, *judy*

Judy Nunn. Actress. Daughter of actress Nancy Nunn. **Theatre:** *Guinness Book of Records* (revue); *Goodbye Charlie; The Hollow; Gaslight* (all London West End); *Blithe Spirit; Man and Superman; The Winter's Tale; A Bedful of Foreigners; Rattle of a Simple Man; The Taming of the Shrew; Hay Fever; The Norman Conquests; The Human Voice* (one-woman show) **Films:** *Hostage; The Box; Song of Norway.* **TV:** *The Onedin Line; Z-Cars; The Befrienders;* Irene Fisher in *Sons and Daughters; A Country Practice;* Vicki Stafford in *The Box; Skyways; Mother and Son; Prisoner: Cell Block H; Bit Part; The Newman Shame; The Land We Love; Yes What;* Ailsa Stewart (née Hogan) in *Home and Away* (1988-). As writer: *Possession; Neighbours.* **Books:** Children's books; *The Glitter Game* (novel). **Address:** c/o June Cann Management/Channel 7. m. actor Bruce Venables.

OBERMAN, *claire*

Claire Oberman. Actress. b. Holland, 1956. Brought up in New Zealand. Trained at the National Drama School, Wellington. **Theatre:** *Lovers and Vagabonds* (also writer, one-woman show); *The Taming of the Shrew; Twelfth Night; Kennedy's Children; Pygmalion; Time and Time Again; Just Between Ourselves; The Merchant of Venice* (all in New Zealand); *Boeing Boeing; Rose; Move Over, Mrs Markham* (all in Britain). **Films:** *Goodbye Pork Pie* (New Zealand, winner of Best Film Actress award); *The Beautiful End of the World* (Germany). **TV:** *Hunter's Gold; Moynihan; Joe and Koro; Mortimer's Patch* (all in New Zealand); Kate Norris in *Tenko; Hi-de-Hi!; Bottle Boys; The Two Ronnies; Paradise Postponed; Ladies Night; Fortunes of War;* Sandy Savage in *Gentlemen and Players; Matlock; To Be the Best.* **Address:** c/o Barry Burnett Organisation.

O'BRIEN, *peter*

Peter O'Brien. Actor. b. Murray Bridge, Australia, 25 March 1960. Trained at St Martin Youth Theatre. **Theatre:** *Romeo and Juliet; The Bear; Runaways.* **Films:** *The Mortal Coil.* **TV:** *Starting Out; Carson's Law; Prisoner: Cell Block H; The Henderson Kids;* Shane in *Neighbours;* Dr Sam Patterson in *The Flying Doctors; Performance: The Trials of Oz.* **Address:** c/o Hamper-Neafsey Associates.

O'BRIEN, *richard*

Richard O'Brien. Actor. b. Cheltenham, Gloucestershire, 25 March 1942. Brought up in New Zealand. **Theatre:** *Gulliver's Travels; Hair; Jesus Christ Superstar; The Unseen Hand; The Hostage; The Tooth of Crime; They Used to Star In Movies; Eastwood Ho!; The News.* As writer: *The Rocky Horror Show; T. Zee; Disaster; Top People.* **Films:** *Carry On Cowboy; The Fighting Prince of Donegal; The Odd Job Man; Flash Gordon; Shock Treatment; Revolution.* **TV:** *A Hymn for Jim; Robin of Sherwood; The Crystal Maze.* **Address:** c/o Chatto and Linnit. m. Jane Elizabeth Moss-O'Brien; 2 s. Linus, Joshua, 1 d. Amelia.

O'BRIEN, simon

Simon O'Brien. Actor/Presenter. b. Garston, Liverpool, 19 June 1965. **Theatre:** Kav in Willy Russell's *Stags and Hens; Prisoners; Shelter,* at the National Theatre Studio. **Films:** Kav in Willy Russell's *Dancin' Thru the Dark* (film version of *Stags and Hens).* **TV:** Damon Grant in *Brookside* (1982–7) and three-part spin-off serial *Damon & Debbie* (1987); *Night Network; I Can Do That; Move It; Fraggle Rock* (all as presenter); *Young, Gifted and Broke; Standing Room Only* (presenter). **Address:** c/o Annette Stone Associates. Single.

O'CALLAGHAN, tony

Tony O'Callaghan. Actor. b. London, 16 June 1956. Trained at The Drama Centre. **Theatre:** *Can You Hear Me At the Back?; Rose; Waiting for Gillian; The Dresser; Bérénice; The Importance of Being Earnest; Time and Time Again; The Phantom of the Opera; The Long and the Short and the Tall; My Brother's Keeper; J M Synge Trilogy; Statements After an Arrest; The Cradle Will Rock; Up 'n' Under; Sweet As a Nut; Abigail's Party* (national tour). **TV:** *Jockey School; Murphy's Mob; Me & My Girl; Terry and June; Dempsey and Makepeace; Three Up, Two Down; Hannay; The Bill; The Upper Hand; A Safe House; Children of the North.* **Address:** c/o The Bill Horne Partnership.

O'CONNOR, des

Des O'Connor. Entertainer/Presenter. b. Stepney, East London, 12 January 1932. **TV:** *Spot the Tune; Sunday Night At the London Palladium; For Love Or Money; The Des O'Connor Show; Des O'Connor Now; Des O'Connor Tonight.* **Records:** *Careless Hands; I Pretend; 1–2–3 O'Leary; Dick-a-Dum-Dum (King's Road); Loneliness; I'll Go On Hoping; The Tips of My Fingers; The Skye Boat Song.* LPs: *I Pretend; With Love; Sing a Favourite Song; Just for You; Des O'Connor Now; True Love Ways.* **Books:** *Somebody Laughed* (autobiography). Winner, *TVTimes* Favourite Male TV Personality, 1969, 1970, 1971, 1972, 1973. **Address:** c/o IMG/Clifford Elson Publicity. Lives in London. m. 1st Phyllis (dis), 2nd actress Gillian Vaughan, 3rd Jay (sep); 4 d. Karen (from 1st m.), Tracey, Samantha (from 2nd m.), Cristina Eva (from 3rd m.). Hobbies: Golf.

O'CONNOR, tom

Tom O'Connor. Comedian/Presenter. b. Bootle, Merseyside, 31 October 1939. Originally a maths and music teacher, entertaining in clubs by night; turned professional in 1974. **Theatre:** Summer seasons and pantomimes. **TV:** *The Comedians; Opportunity Knocks* (won three times); *Wednesday At Eight; London Night Out; The Tom O'Connor Show; Royal Variety Performance* (1976); *This Is Your Life* (subject, 1977); *Tom O'Connor At the Casino; The Tom O'Connor Roadshow; Zodiac; Name That Tune; Gambit; Password; I've Got a Secret; A Question of Entertainment; Cross Wits.* **Books:** *Tom O'Connor's Book of Liverpool Humour.* **Address:** c/o Clifford Elson Publicity. Lives in Berkshire. m. Pat; 3 d. Ann, Frances, Helen; 1 s. Stephen. Hobbies: Golf, snooker, football.

ODDIE, bill

William Oddie. Actor/Writer. b. Rochdale, Lancashire, 7 July 1941. Member of Cambridge Footlights revue while at university. **TV:** *That Was the Week That Was; Twice a Fortnight; Broaden Your Mind; We Have Ways of Making You Laugh; Galton and Simpson Playhouse; The Goodies; Saturday Banana* (presenter); *From the Top; Fax; Oddie In Paradise; Titmuss Regained.* **Records:** *The In Betweenies; Father Christmas Do Not Touch Me; Funky Gibbon; Black Pudding Bertha; Nappy Love/Wild Thing; Make a Daft Noise for Christmas* (all singles with The Goodies). **Address:** c/o London Management. m. 1st (dis), 2nd Laura Beaumont; 3 d. Kate, Bonnie (from 1st m.), Rosie.

OGILVY, *ian*

Ian Ogilvy. Actor. b. Woking, Surrey, 30 September 1943. Worked backstage at the Royal Court Theatre before training at RADA. **Theatre:** Repertory theatre in Colchester, Canterbury and Northampton; *The Waltz of the Toreadors; The Millionairess.* **Films:** *Stranger In the House; The Sorcerers; Witchfinder General; The Invincible Six; Waterloo; Wuthering Heights; Fengriffin; No Sex, Please – We're British.* **TV:** *The Liars; Upstairs, Downstairs; Affairs of the Heart; A Walk With Destiny;* title role in *The Return of The Saint; Tom, Dick and Harriet; Design for Living; Horses; Anna Karenina; Menace Unseen Maigret* (TV movie). Winner, *TVTimes* Most Compulsive Character award, 1978–9. **Address:** c/o Michael Whitehall. m. former model Diane; 1 step-d. Emma, 1 s. Titus.

O'MARA, *kate*

Kate O'Mara. Actress. b. Leicester, 10 August 1939. Trained at the Aida Foster School; worked as a speech therapist. **Films:** *The Nativity; Whose Child Am I?; The Tamarind Seed; The Horror of Frankenstein; The Vampire Lovers; Cannon To Cordoba; The Desperados; The Limbo Line; Corruption; Promenade; Great Catherine; An Unknown Friend.* **TV:** *No Hiding Place; Weaver's Green; Court Martial; Don Quick; Danger Man; It's Not Me, It's Them; Hereward the Wake; Never a Cross Word; Honey Lane; Codename; Paul Temple; Jason King; Pathfinders; The Troubleshooters; The Champions; Z-Cars; The Saint; The Protectors; Spy Trap; The Brothers; The Main Chance; The Plank; The Morecambe and Wise Show; The Two Ronnies; The Return of The Saint; Triangle; Dynasty; Howards Way.* **Address:** c/o Michael Ladkin. m. actor Jeremy Young (dis); 1 s. Dickon.

ORCHARD, *nick*

Nicholas Shaun Orchard. Actor. b. Bristol, 1 July 1957. Worked in stage management at Bristol Old Vic Theatre, then trained at Birmingham School of Drama. **Theatre:** *Flibberty and the Penguin; Oliver!; Satyricon; Piaf; Once a Catholic; Aladdin; Romeo and Juliet/Twelfth Night; Submariners; Romantic Comedy; Loot.* **TV:** *Out Of the Past: Village of War; Maths Counts; The Brief; Look and Read: Badger Girl* (all *BBC Schools*); *In the Secret State; Timeless Tales;* Gavin in *EastEnders; Going To Work: Pressure of Work; Customer Care (Open College); Beadle's About; Casualty; The Rita Rudner Show;* Gary Lipman in *Emmerdale;* Mr Thomas in *Coronation Street.* **Address;** c/o Darryl Brown Associates. Lives in London. m. Cazz Scattergood; 1 s. Oliver. Pets: A dog called Finn. **Favourite TV programme:** *Coronation Street; Hard News; Newsnight.*

O'SHEA, *kevin*

Kevin O'Shea. Actor. b. Enfield, Middlesex, 7 March 1952. Trained with the National Youth Theatre and at the Bristol Old Vic Theatre School. **Theatre:** *A Midsummer Night's Dream; The Bundle; Frozen Assets; Much Ado About Nothing; Troilus and Cressida; Romeo and Juliet; The Way of the World* (all RSC); *The Lion In Winter; Equus; The Caretaker; Robin Redbreast; Kill Is a Four-Letter Word; Butley; Macbeth; Romeo and Juliet.* **Films:** *SOS Titanic; Black Joy; Woman On a Roof; Inseminoid; Dirty Dozen III.* **TV:** *Thank You Comrades; We Think the World of You; Spearhead; The Professionals; The Gentle Touch; The Scarlet Pimpernel; The Kelly Monteith Show; Shadow of the Noose; Secret Army;* Max Hargreaves in *Grange Hill.* **Address;** c/o CAM. Lives in London. m. Cristina. Hobbies: Qualified glider pilot, film-making. **Favourite TV programme:** *The Sweeney.*

OSOBA, *tony*

Tony Osoba. Actor. Trained at Royal Scottish Academy of Music and Drama. **Theatre:** RSC. **Films:** *Porridge.* **TV:** *Charles Endell Esquire;* McLaren in *Porridge;* Det Con Chas Jarvis in *Dempsey and Makepeace; The Flame Trees of Thika; Snakes and Ladders; Reunion; The Professionals; Gruey; Treasure Island; The Cleopatras; Churchill's People; Brookside; Bergerac; Minder; Doctor Who; The Bill; Umbrella* (storyteller); Peter Ingram in *Coronation Street* (1990); Freddie in *Making News.* **Address:** c/o Barry Brown & Partner. Lives in London. m. Hobbies: Golf, tennis, running a classic car (E-Type Jaguar), travel, collecting old toys. **Favourite TV programme:** Most sports programmes, travel, historical and wildlife documentaries, old black-and-white films, news and current affairs programmes, investigative-reporting programmes; *Cheers.*

O'SULLIVAN, richard

Richard O'Sullivan. Actor. b. Chiswick, West London, 7 May 1944. Started acting professionally as a child; trained at Corona Stage Academy. **Theatre:** *The Government Inspector; Boeing Boeing; Cinderella* (London Palladium); *Run for Your Wife* (Criterion Theatre). **Films:** *Jacqueline; Stranger's Hand; Dangerous Exile; Cleopatra; Father, Dear Father; Man About the House.* **TV:** Title role in *Little Lord Fauntleroy* (aged 12); *Doctor At Large; Doctor In Charge; Father, Dear Father; Alcock and Gander; Man About the House; Robin's Nest;* title role in *Dick Turpin; Me & My Girl; The Giftie; Trouble In Mind.* **Address:** c/o Al Mitchell Associates. m. model Diane Terry (dis); 1 s. James (from relationship with actress Tessa Wyatt).

OWEN, bill, MBE

Bill Owen. Actor/Writer. b. Acton Green, West London, 14 March 1914. **Films:** *Perfect Strangers; The Way To the Stars; School for Secrets; When the Bough Breaks; Daybreak; Dancing With Crime; Easy Money; My Brother's Keeper; Holiday Camp; Once a Jolly Swagman; The Girl Who Couldn't Quite; Hotel Sahara; Carve Her Name With Pride; Carry On Cabby; Georgy Girl; O Lucky Man!; In Celebration; The Comeback; Laughterhouse; Singleton's Pluck.* As writer: *Lysette; Breakout; Matchgirls; Fruits of Philosophy.* **TV:** *Three Piece Suite; The Challengers; The Quiet Half-Hour; 17 Said Push Off; The Likely Lads; Taxi; Treasure Island; Coppers End; Coronation Street;* Compo in *Last of the Summer Wine; Brideshead Revisited; Passing Through; Tales of the Unexpected.* **Address:** c/o Richard Stone Partnership. m. former actress Kathie; 1 s. Tom, 1 step-d. Kathie.

OWEN, nicholas

Nicholas Owen. Newscaster. b. London, 10 February 1947. **TV:** BBC TV; ITN *Channel Four News* business correspondent, then presenter of news programmes on ITV and Channel Four. **Address:** c/o ITN. m. Brenda; 1 d. Rebecca, 1 s. Anthony, 1 step-d. Justine, 1 step-s. Daniel.

OWEN, nick

Nicholas Owen. Presenter. b. Berkhamsted, Hertfordshire, 1 November 1947. Journalist in newspapers *(Doncaster Evening Post* and *Birmingham Post)* and local radio (BBC Radio Birmingham), before entering television. **TV:** ATV/Central Television news and sports presenter (1978–83); TV-am sports presenter, then presenter of *Good Morning Britain* (1983–6); *Midweek Sport Special; Sporting Triangles* (quiz show, host); ITV athletics, ice skating and royal premieres; *Hitman; Thames Sport Special* (Thames Television); *Sportsworld Extra.* **Address:** c/o Severn Management Services. m. Jill; 3 s. Andrew, Timothy, Christopher, 1 d. Jenny.

OWEN, sid

David Owen. Actor. b. London. **Films:** Young Ned in *Revolution.* **TV:** *Oliver Twist; Metal Mickey; Shackleton; Bottle Boys; Jury; Everybody Here; No Adults Allowed; Timmy and Vicky; Give Us a Break; Winter Break; William Tell;* Ricky Butcher in *EastEnders* (1988-). **Address:** c/o Fletcher & Boyce. Single; lives in London. Pets: One cat.

OXENBERG, *catherine*

Catherine Oxenberg. Actress. b. New York, USA, 22 September 1962. Daughter of Princess Elisabeth of Yugoslavia. Previously a model; studied acting with Stanley Zaraff in New York. **TV:** Lady Diana Spencer in *The Royal Romance of Charles and Diana* (TV movie); *Love Boat; Cover Up; Crazy Like a Fox;* Amanda Bedford in *Dynasty; Saturday Night Live; Roman Holiday; Swimsuit.* **Address:** c/o ICM.

PACE, *norman*

Norman Pace. Comedian. b. Dudley, Worcestershire, 17 February 1953. Worked as a teacher before forming a double-act with Gareth Hale and turning professional as an entertainer. **TV:** *Pushing Up Daisies; Coming Next; The Young Ones; Live From the Palladium; Saturday Live* (host); *Just for Laughs; The Saturday Gang; The Management; Hale & Pace* (winner, Golden Rose of Montreux, 1989). **Books:** *Falsies; The Hale & Pace Book of Writes and Rons* (both with Gareth Hale). **Records:** *Hale & Pace Live In Concert* (LP, with Gareth Hale). **Address:** c/o International Artistes. m. Beverley; 2 s. Liam, Charlie, 1 d. Holly.

PACKER, *suzanne*

Suzanne Jackson. Actress. b. Cardiff, 1962. Sister of athlete Colin Jackson. Attended the National Youth Theatre of Wales and took a BA in theatre and drama at the University of Warwick; trained at the Webber Douglas Academy. **Theatre:** *Our Country's Good; The Recruiting Officer; A Hero's Welcome* (all Royal Court Theatre); *Carmen Jones; Lady Be Good; Porgy and Bess* (Glyndebourne Festival Opera, at the Queen Elizabeth Hall); *The Little Shop of Horrors; Fat Pig; A Blow To Bute Street; Dreams With Teeth; Power of Darkness; Playboy of the West Indies; To Kill a Mockingbird.* **TV:** *Bowen;* Josie Johnson in *Brookside* (1990–91). **Address:** c/o Kerry Gardner Management. Single; lives in London. Hobbies: Swimming, yoga, reading, watching sport.

PAGETT, *nicola*

Nicola Pagett. Actress. b. Cairo, Egypt, 15 June 1945. Brought up in Hong Kong. Trained at RADA. **Theatre:** *Widower's Houses* (Royal Court Theatre); *Voyage Round My Father; The Ride Across Lake Constance; A Family and a Fortune; Gaslight; Yahoo; Old Times* (Los Angeles). **Films:** *The Viking Queen; Anne of the Thousand Days; There's a Girl In My Soup; Operation Daybreak; Frankenstein; Seven Men At Daybreak; Oliver's Story; Privates On Parade; All of You.* **TV:** *Barlow At Large; The Persuaders; Upstairs, Downstairs; The Rivals of Sherlock Holmes; Napoleon; The Sweeney; French Without Tears; Anna Karenina; War and Peace; Aren't We All; Love Story; Scoop; A Bit of a Do* (two series); *Shadow of the Sun.* **Address:** c/o James Sharkey Associates. Lives in Richmond-upon-Thames, Surrey. m. writer Graham Swannell; 1 d. Eve.

PALIN, *michael*

Michael Palin. Actor/Writer. b. Sheffield, South Yorkshire, 5 May 1943. **Films:** *And Now for Something Completely Different; Monty Python and the Holy Grail; Jabberwocky; Monty Python's Life of Brian; Monty Python Live At the Hollywood Bowl; Time Bandits* (also as writer); *The Missionary* (also as writer); *Monty Python's The Meaning of Life* (also as writer); *A Private Function; Brazil; The Dress; A Fish Called Wanda; American Friends.* **TV:** *Do Not Adjust Your Set; Complete and Utter History of Britain; Monty Python's Flying Circus; Ripping Yarns; Three Men In a Boat; Tomkinson's Schooldays; Confessions of a Train Spotter; East of Ipswich* (TV movie); *Number 27* (writer); *Around the World In 80 Days* (presenter); Jim Nelson in *GBH.* **Address:** c/o Mayday Management. Lives in North London. m. Helen; 1 d. Rachel, 2 s. Thomas, William.

PALMER, *geoffrey*

Geoffrey Palmer. Actor. b. London, 4 June 1927. Started career as trainee assistant stage manager at the Q Theatre. **Theatre:** *St Joan; Tishoo; A Friend Indeed; The Mask of Moriarty; Kafka's Dick; Piano.* **Films:** *O Lucky Man!; The Outsider; Retribution; The Honorary Consul; A Zed and Two Noughts; Clockwise; A Fish Called Wanda; Hawks.* **TV:** *The Fall and Rise of Reginald Perrin; The Houseboy; Butterflies; Fawlty Towers; A Midsummer Night's Dream; The Last Song; Absurd Person Singular; Radio Pictures; Fairly Secret Army; Hot Metal; The Insurance Man; Season's Greetings; After the War; Christabel; Executive Stress; Inspector Morse; Bergerac; A Question of Attribution* (TV movie); Lionel in *As Time Goes By.* **Radio:** *Little Secrets; Keys; The Riddle of the Sands.* **Address:** c/o Marmont Management. m. Sally; 1 s. Charles, 1 d. Harriet.

PALMER, *toni*

Toni Palmer. Actress. b. London, 17 September 1932. Trained as a dancer. **Theatre:** *Saturday Night and Sunday Morning; Fings Ain't Wot They Used To Be; Steaming; Sweeney Todd; The Phantom of the Opera.* **Films:** *The French Lieutenant's Woman; Personal Services; The Doctor and the Devils; Smashing Time.* **TV:** *The Rag Trade; Within These Walls; Take My Wife; The Confederacy of Wives; Russ Abbot's Madhouse; King and Castle; West End Tales; The Kelly Monteith Show; The Cuckoo Sister; Only Fools and Horses; Mog!; Ellis Island; Hi-de-Hi!; The Bill.* **Address:** c/o Barry Brown & Partner.

PARFITT, *judy*

Judy Parfitt. Actress. b. Sheffield, South Yorkshire, 7 November. **Films:** *Hide and Seek; Hamlet; Galileo; Saturday, Sunday, Monday; Champions; Street Dreams; Mr Pyg; Maurice; Getting It Right; Diamond Skulls.* **TV:** *Girl In a Bird Cage; Jackson's Wharf; Bullseye; Sentimental Agent; Odd Man; Villette; Edith Nesbitt; The Sufragettes; Edward G; Daughters of the Late Colonel; The Edwardians; Malice Aforethought; Pride and Prejudice; Death of a Princess; Secret Orchards; Grand Duo; Redundant – Or the Wife's Revenge; The Jewel In the Crown; Bon Voyage; The Charmer; The Charmings.* **Address:** c/o Jeremy Conway.

PARKIN, *leonard*

Leonard Parkin. Presenter. b. Thurnscoe, Yorkshire, 2 June 1929. Started as a reporter on the *Wakefield Express, Yorkshire Observer, Bradford Telegraph & Argus* and *Yorkshire Evening News;* joined BBC radio newsreel and TV news in 1954. **TV:** BBC correspondent in Canada (1960), Washington (1963–65); *Panorama; 24 Hours;* ITN reporter and newscaster from 1967; ITN General Election programmes; *Pieces of Parkin* (Yorkshire Television). **Address:** c/o Yorkshire Television. m. Barbara; 1 s. Jeremy.

PARKINSON, *michael*

Michael Parkinson. Presenter. b. Cudworth, South Yorkshire, 28 March 1935. Previously a newspaper journalist. **TV:** *Scene* (Granada TV); *Granada In the North; World In Action; What the Papers Say; 24 Hours;* executive producer, LWT sports documentaries; *Cinema; Teabreak; Where In the World; Sports Arena; Movie Quiz; Parkinson;* founder-member of TV-am (presenter of *Good Morning Britain*); *Give Us a Clue; All Star Secrets; Parkinson One To One; Parky; The Help Squad.* **Radio:** *Desert Island Discs.* **Books:** *Football Daft; Cricket Mad; A Pictorial History of Westerns; Sporting Fever; Best: An Intimate Biography; Bats In the Pavilion; A To Z of Soccer; The Woofits; Parkinson's Lore; The Best of Parkinson.* **Address:** c/o IMG. Lives in Bray, Berkshire. m. TV presenter Mary Parkinson; 3 s. Andrew, Nicholas, Michael. Hobbies: Golf, cricket.

PARRY, *ken*

Ken Parry. Actor. b. Wigan, Lancashire, 20 June 1930. **Theatre:** *The Kitchen; Amadeus; Macbeth; Noises Off.* **Films:** *Tom Jones; The Liquidators; The Taming of the Shrew; Two Times Two; A Whole Lot of Trouble; Start the Revolution Without Me; Spring and Port Wine; Come Play With Me; What's Up Nurse; Life Force; Dardinelle; Lisztomania; The Rainbow Thief.* **TV;** *Z-Cars* (as 13 different villains); *The Sweeney; Crossroads; A Midsummer Night's Dream; The Merchant of Venice; Coronation Street; Horne Aplenty; Never Say Die; Hazell; The Big Sleep; Vice Versa; King's Royal; Filthy Rich and Catflap; The Young Ones; The Kelly Monteith Show; Blott On the Landscape; Children's Ward* (four series); *Saracen.* **Address:** c/o PBR Management. Single; lives in London. Pets: A cat called Tammy. Hobbies: Clairvoyance, old films and orchestral music.

PARSONS, *nicholas*

Nicholas Parsons. Presenter/Actor. b. Grantham, Lincolnshire, 10 October 1928. Engineering apprenticeship at Clydebank before attending Glasgow University; began as an impressionist before turning to acting. **Theatre:** *Boeing Boeing; Say Who You Are; Uproar In the House; Why Not Stay for Breakfast?* **Films:** Sixties film comedies. **TV:** *Straight man to Arthur Haynes for 10 years; The Benny Hill Show; Sale of the Century; Alphabet Quiz* (Night Network); *Laughlines* (BSB). **Address:** c/o Billy Marsh Associates. m. actress Denise Bryer (dis); 1 d. Suzy, 1 s. Justin.

PASCO, *richard, CBE*

Richard Pasco. Actor. b. Barnes, London, 18 July 1926. Made CBE, 1977. Trained at Central School of Speech and Drama (Gold Medal winner). **Films:** *Room At the Top; Yesterday's Enemy; The Gorgon; Rasputin; Hot Enought for June; The Watcher In the Woods; Wagner.* **TV:** *Henry Irving; Dial M for Murder; Traveller Without Luggage; Ivanov; The Three Musketeers; As You Like It; Julius Caesar; The Chief Mourner; The British In Love; Sweet Wine of Youth; The Poisoned Gift; Trouble With Gregory; Philby; Siegfried Idyll; The Emergency Channel; John Donne; Disraeli; Ghosts; Savages; The Houseboy; Timon of Athens; Let's Run Away To Africa; Pythons On the Mountain; Sorrell & Son; Arch of Triumph; Drummonds; Hannay; The Man From the Pru.* **Address:** c/o Michael Whitehall. m. 1st Greta Watson (dis), 2nd actress Barbara Leigh-Hunt; 1 s. William (from 1st m.).

PASKE, *ashley*

Ashley Paske. Actor. b. Wollongong, Australia. **TV:** *Robin Hood* (pantomime); *Kids' News* (reporter-presenter); *The Boy On the Roof; A Country Practice;* Marty Bryant in *Richmond Hill; Ridgey Didge* (presenter); Matt Robinson in *Neighbours* (1989-). TV commercials: Coca-Cola. **Address:** c/o June Cann Management.

PAUL, *andrew*

Paul Andrew Herman. Actor. b. London, 17 March 1961. Trained at the Anna Scher Theatre School. **Theatre:** *Dracula; Cider With Rosie; If You Want To Know What Heaven's Like You'll Be There Soon; Groping for Words; Remember Me; When Your Bottle's Gone In SE1; Grease; Shout Across the River.* **Films:** *The Pirates of Penzance; Scum; Bellman and True.* **TV:** *Help: The Setbacks; Tripper's Day; Barnet; Timmy and Vicky; Out of Tune; Time of My Life; Out; Going Out; Mrs Capper's Birthday; Slinger's Day; Gentlemen and Players; Sizzler; Vote for Hitler; After Image; Vote for Them; Inspector Morse; Missing Persons;* PC Dave Quinnan in *The Bill.* **Address:** c/o Scott Marshall. Lives in London. m. Laura; 2 s. Ben, Nicholas. Hobbies: Reading, cinema, music, golf, football, cricket (all sport). **Favourite TV programme:** *Only Fools and Horses; LA Law.*

PAXMAN, *jeremy*

Jeremy Paxman. Presenter. b. Leeds, 11 May 1950. Journalist in Northern Ireland (1974–7), before entering television. **Films:** *Called To Account – How Roberto Calvi Died.* **TV:** *Tonight; Panorama; London Plus; Six O'Clock News; Breakfast Time; Newsnight; The Bear Next Door; Did You See . . .?* Winner, Royal Television Society International Current Affairs award, 1984. **Books:** *A Higher Form of Killing; Through the Volcanoes; Friends In High Places.* **Address:** c/o BBC TV.

PAYS, *amanda*

Amanda Pays. Actress. b. London, 6 June 1959. A model before turning professional as an actress. **Films:** *The Kindred; Oxford Blues; Off Limits; The Leviathan.* **TV:** *The Cold Room* (Home Box Office); *A.D.* (mini-series); *Max Headroom; The Pretenders; Minder On the Orient Express; Mr and Mrs Edgehill; LA Law.* **Address:** c/o International Creative Management. m. actor Corbin Bernsen (qv); 1 s. Oliver.

PENHALIGON, *susan*

Susan Penhaligon. Actress. b. Manila, Philippines. Brought up in England; trained at the Webber Douglas Academy. **Theatre:** Repertory theatre in Worthing, Manchester, Guildford, Brighton and Bromley; title role in *Romeo and Juliet.* **Films:** *No Sex, Please – We're British; The Land That Time Forgot; Nasty Habits; Under Milk Wood; Leopard In the Snow; Private Road; Patrick.* **TV:** *Public Eye; Country Matters; A Bouquet of Barbed Wire; Fearless Frank; The Taming of the Shrew; A Fine Romance; A Kind of Loving; Heather Ann; Remington Steele; A Kind of Living* (presenter); *Heart of the Country; Bergerac; Trouble In Mind.* **Address:** c/o Jeremy Conway. m. 1st Nicholas Loukes (dis), 2nd TV documentary director David Munro (dis), 3rd actor Duncan Preston (dis); 1 s. Truan (from 2nd m.).

PENROSE, *tricia*

Tricia Penrose. Actress. b. Liverpool, 9 April 1970. Trained at Elliott-Clarke School. **Theatre:** *Bye, Bye, Birdie; Macbeth.* **Films:** *Vroom; Cresta Run; Dancin' Thru the Dark.* **TV:** Ruth and WPC Emma Reid in *Brookside; Help!; Albion Market; Boon;* Julie in *How To Be Cool; Split Ends;* title role in *Katy's Story; Tydi Bywyd yn Boen! (Isn't Life a Pain!)* (TV movie); *Shooting Stars* (Channel Four film); *Medics; Coasting;* Louise in *Emmerdale;* hotel receptionist in *Coronation Street.* TV commercials: Mates; National Savings Bank; Heart of England Building Society; Argos; Dairy Crunch; McDonald's; Halifax Building Society. **Address:** c/o TAM Management. Single; lives in Liverpool.

PEPPARD, *george*

George Peppard. Actor. b. Detroit, Michigan, 1 October 1928. **Films:** *Breakfast At Tiffany's; How the West Was Won; The Victors; The Carpetbaggers; The Third Day; Operation Crossbow; The Blue Max; Tobruk; Rough Night In Jericho; P.J.; House of Cards; Newman's Law; Damnation Alley; Five Days From Home* (also producer-director-writer); *Your Ticket Is No Longer Valid; Battle Beyond the Stars; Race To the Yankee Zephyr; From Hell To Victory; Silence Like Glass.* **TV:** *Banacek; The A-Team; Little Moon of Alban; Suspicion; US Steel Hour. Alfred Hitchcock Presents; Matinee Theatre; Alcoa-Goodyear Playhouse; Studio One; Hallmark Hall of Fame; The Bravos; Doctors' Hospital; The Story of Dr Sam Sheppard; Crisis In Mid-Air; Torn Between Two Lovers; Man Against the Mob.* **Address:** c/o David Shapira & Associates.

PERLMAN, *rhea*

Rhea Perlman. Actress. b. Brooklyn, New York, USA, 31 March 1948. Gained degree in drama. **Films:** *Love Child; My Little Pony* (voice); *Enid Is Sleeping.* **TV:** *Funny, You Don't Look 200; Two Daddies* (voice); *Taxi;* Carla in *Cheers* (Emmy Best Supporting Actress award, 1984, 1985, 1986, 1989); *I Want To Keep My Baby!; Stalk the Wild Child; Having Babies II; Intimate Strangers; Mary Jane Harper Cried Last Night; Like Normal People; Drop-Out Father; The Ratings Game; Dangerous Affection; A Family Again.* **Address;** c/o Triad Artists. m. actor-director Danny DeVito; 2 d. Lucie, Gracie.

PERRIE, *lynne*

Jean Dudley. Actress/Singer. b. Rotherham, South Yorkshire, 7 April 1931. Sister of actor-comedian Duggie Brown (qv). Trained as a dispenser at Boots chemist, then worked in a stocking factory, before singing with a dance band. **Theatre:** Singer-comedienne in clubs in Britain, France, Germany, America and South Africa, including shows with Sacha Distel, the Rolling Stones and The Beatles. **Films:** Mother in *Kes; Yanks.* **TV:** *Slattery's Mounted Foot; Leeds United; Follyfoot; Mrs Petty; Queenie's Castle; The Intruder; Crown Court; It Was a Good Story, Don't Knock It;* Ivy Brennan (née Tilsley) in *Coronation Street (1971-); Royal Variety Performance* (1989); *Fight Cancer* (co-presenter). **Address:** c/o Granada TV. Lives in Maltby, South Yorkshire, and Manchester. m. Derrick Barksby; 1 s. Stephen. Hobbies: Horse and greyhound racing.

PERTWEE, *bill*

William Desmond Pertwee. Actor/Comedian. b. Amersham, Buckinghamshire, 21 July 1926. Brother of actors Jon (qv) and Michael. Started as a stooge for Jon Pertwee, Beryl Reid, Charlie Chester, Ted Ray and Jimmy James. **Theatre:** *There Goes the Bride; See How They Run; Run for Your Wife.* **Films:** *The Seven Magnificent Deadly Sins; Psychomania; Carry On Loving; Dad's Army; Action; Confessions of a Pop Performer; What's Up Nurse; See How They Run.* **TV:** *Dad's Army; Jackanory; Sykes; Billy Liar; Frost Weekly; The Larry Grayson Show; Pierrots; Tom, Dick and Harriet; Chance In a Million; Halls of Fame; Super Troupers; By Royal Command; Spytrap; Pob; You Rang, M'Lord?* **Radio:** *Beyond Our Ken; Round the Horn.* **Books:** *Promenades and Pierrots; Dad's Army: The Making of a Television Legend.* **Address:** c/o Richard Stone Partnership. m. Marion; 1 s. Jonathan.

PERTWEE, *jon*

John Pertwee. Actor/Comedian. b. London, 7 July 1919. Son of playwright Roland; brother of actors Bill (qv) and Michael. Trained at RADA. **Films:** *Carry On Cleo, Cowboy* and *Screaming; Ladies Who Do; I Gotta Horse; You Must Be Joking; A Funny Thing Happened On the Way To the Forum; The Ugly Duckling; The House That Dripped Blood; Mr Drake's Duck; One of Our Dinosaurs Is Missing; There's a Girl In My Soup; Oh Clarence; March of the Desert; Adventures of a Private Eye; The Boys In Blue.* **TV:** *Three of a Kind;* title role in *Doctor Who; Whodunnit?; Jackanory; The Goodies;* title role in *Worzel Gummidge* and *Worzel Gummidge Down Under; The Curious Case of Santa Claus; The Five Doctors; Do You Know the Milky Way?* **Address:** c/o London Management. m. 1st actress Jean Marsh (dis), 2nd Ingeborg Rhosea; 1 d. Dariel, 1 s. actor Sean (both from 2nd m.).

PETTIFER, *julian*

Julian Pettifer. Presenter. b. Malmesbury, Wiltshire, 21 July 1935. **TV:** Southern Television reporter; *Tonight; 24 Hours; Panorma* (both as war correspondent); *90 South; War Without End; Millionaire; Vietnam – The Other World; The Regiment; The Country Game; World About Us; The China Programme; The History of Civil Aviation; Nature Watch; Diamonds In the Sky; The Living Isles; World Safari; Only One Earth; Automania; Busman's Holiday* (quiz show, host); *Africawatch; Missionaries; Safari UK; Biteback; See for Yourself – A Biteback Special; Defenders of the Wild.* **Address:** c/o Curtis Brown.

PHILBIN, *maggie*

Maggie Philbin. Presenter. b. Manchester, 23 June 1955. Gained a degree in English and drama. **TV:** Multi Coloured Swap Shop; The Show Me Show; Ticket To Ride; Tomorrow's World; The Saturday Picture Show; The Quest; Hospital Watch; Bodymatters Roadshow; This Morning. **Books:** The Maggie Philbin Good-Looking Book. **Address:** c/o Dave Winslett Entertainments. m. TV presenter Keith Chegwin; 1 d. Rose.

PHILLIPS, *siân*

Siân Phillips. Actress. b. Carmarthenshire, 14 May 1934. Trained at RADA (Gold Medal winner). **TV:** The Quiet Man; Platanov; Lady Windermere's Fan; The Man Outside; Shoulder To Shoulder; Jennie; Jackanory; The Shadow; How Green Was My Valley; I, Claudius; The Achurch Letters; Heartbreak House; Boudicea; Off To Philadelphia In the Morning; The Oresteia; Crime and Punishment; Tinker, Tailor, Soldier, Spy; Winston Churchill – The Wilderness Years; Smiley's People; Barriers; Language and Landscape; George Borrow; The Two Mrs Grenvilles; Murder On the Exchange; Vanity Fair; I'd Like To Teach the World To Sing; Snow Spider; Shadow of the Noose; Perfect Scoundrels; Emlyn's Moon. **Books:** Siân Phillips Needlepoint. **Address:** c/o Saraband Associates. m. 1st actor Peter O'Toole (dis), 2nd Robin Sachs; 2 d. Kate, Pat (both from 1st m.).

PICKLES, *carolyn*

Carolyn Pickles. Actress. b. Halifax, West Yorkshire, 8 February 1952. Daughter of Judge Pickles. **Films:** Tess; Elephant Man; The Mirror Crack'd; Champions. **TV:** The Cost of Loving; Partisans; A Shepherd's Life; Bless Me, Father; Virginia Fly Is Drowning; Lace; The Gentle Touch; Willie's Last Stand; We'll Meet Again; Mr Right; Love Story; Whose Child; Letting the Birds Go Free; East Lynne; Miracles Take Longer; Juliet Bravo; Bulman; Bluebell; The Victoria Wood Show; The Enemy Within; Leaving Home; Blair; May To December; Bread Or Blood; Through the Dragon's Eye; Leopard; Chancer; Det Chief Insp Kim Reid in The Bill (1990-); The Yellow Wallpaper. **Address:** c/o Jeremy Conway. Lives in North London. m.; 2 d. Lucy Jane, Hettie, 2 step-s. Tod, Theo. Pets: One cat. Hobbies: Four children and the occasional play, film, swim, sauna or doodle.

PICKUP, *ronald*

Ronald Alfred Pickup. Actor. b. Chester, 6 June 1940. Trained at RADA. **Films:** The Day of the Jackal; Zulu Dawn; Never Say Never Again; The Mission. **TV:** Roses of Eyam; Dragon's Opponent; All Good Men; Jennie; Long Day's Journey Into Night; Mahler; Fight Against Slavery; King Lear; Ghost Trio; Henry VIII; Memories; England's Green and Pleasant Land; Omnibus: The Life of Giuseppe Verdi; The Letter; Ivanhoe; Wagner; From a Far Country: Pope John Paul III; Einstein; Waters of the Moon; Orwell On Jura; Puccini; Fortunes of War; Bergerac; Chekhov In Yalta; Deathlock; The Hiding Place; Jekyll & Hyde; Inspector Morse; Performance: Absolute Hell; A Time To Dance; El C.I.D. **Address:** c/o London Management. Lives in London. m. Laus; 1 s. Simon, 1 d. Rachel. Hobbies: Listening to music, walking, reading. **Favourite TV programme:** Coronation Street.

PIGG, *alexandra*

Sandra McKibbin. Actress. b. Liverpool. **Films:** Letter To Brezhnev; Strapless. **TV:** Petra Taylor in Brookside; Smart Money; Making Out; Murder East, Murder West. **Address:** c/o ICM Duncan Heath Associates.

PIGOTT-SMITH, *tim*

Tim Pigott-Smith. Actor. b. Rugby, Warwickshire, 13 May 1946. Trained at the Bristol Old Vic Theatr School. **Films:** *Aces High; Joseph Andrews; Sweet William; The Day Christ Died; Clash of the Titans Escape To Victory; Richard's Things.* **TV:** *Hamlet; Antony and Cleopatra; The Regiment; Doctor Who The Glittering Prizes; North and South; Wings; Eustace and Hilda; Measure for Measure; Henry IV, Pa I; No, Mama, No; 'Tis Pity She's a Whore; Hannah; I Remember Nelson; Fame is the Spur; Winston Churchill – The Wilderness Years; The Hunchback of Notre Dame; The Jewel In the Crown* (winne BAFTA, Broadcasting Press Guild and *TVTimes* Best Actor awards, 1984); *State of Emergency; Dead Man's Folly; Challenge; Life Story; The Secret Case of Sherlock;* title role in *The Chief; The Lost Boy* **Address:** c/o Michael Whitehall. m. Pamela Miles; 1 s. Tom.

PILGER, *john*

John Pilger. Journalist/Documentary-maker. b. Sydney, Australia, October 1939. **TV:** *World In Action Midweek; Pilger; Pilger In Australia; Personal Report – Pilger; Do You Remember Vietnam?; Year Zer – The Silent Death of Cambodia; The Mexicans; Cambodia – Year One; Heroes; The Truth Game; Th Last Day* (play); *The Outsiders; Frontline: The Search for Truth In Wartime; Nicaragua; Burp! Pepsi Coke In the Ice-Cold War; The Secret Country: The First Australians Fight Back; Japan: Behind th Mask; The Last Dream; Cambodia – Year Ten; Cambodia – Year Ten Update; Cambodia – Th Betrayal.* Winner, BAFTA Richard Dimbleby Award, 1991. **Address:** c/o Central Television, 4 Charlotte Street, London W1. Lives in South London. m. 1st journalist Scarth Flett (dis), 2nd journali Yvonne Roberts; 1 s. Sam (from 1st m.), 1 d. Zoe.

PINDER, *steven*

Steven Pinder. Actor. b. Whalley, Lancashire, 30 March 1963. Trained at The Drama Centre **Theatre:** *Deathwatch* (Edinburgh Festival); *Iphegenia; Macbeth; The Miser; The Quest for the Rose an the Ring; Dick Whittington; Up 'n' Under;* Malcolm in *Watching* (national tour). **TV:** *Foxy Lady; Crow Court* (twice, as Paul Freeman and PC Charnley); *Now and Then; Scotch and Wry; C.A.T.S. Eyes;* Ro Lambert in *Crossroads* (1985–8); Tony in *Hollywood Sports;* Max Farnham in *Brookside* (1990-). T commercials: Harp lager; VAG-Audi; Northern Ireland Electricity Board; Bank Contact; Bonus Prim **Address:** c/o David Graham Management/Mersey Television. Lives in north-west London. m. Taj; 1 c Pets: Dog called Westie. **Favourite TV programme:** *The New Statesman.*

PINNER, *steven*

Steven Pinner. Actor. b. Maidstone, Kent, 28 December 1961. Trained at Guildhall School of Music ar Drama. **Theatre:** Toured Middle and Far East with Derek Nimmo's Intercontinental Hote Entertainment Company; RSC at Stratford-upon-Avon (1985). **Films:** *Link.* **TV:** *The Life and Times John Wycliffe; The Eye of the Yemanger;* Jonathan Gordon-Davies in *Brookside.* **Address:** c/o Shar Collins Associates.

PIPER, *jacki*

Jacki Crump. Actress. b. Birmingham, 3 August 1948. Trained at Birmingham Theatre Schoo **Theatre:** *Charley's Aunt; The Birthday Party; Billy Liar; The Tempest; Boeing Boeing; Move Ove Mrs Markham; The Happy Apple; The Secretary Bird; Big Bad Mouse; No Sex, Please – We British; Run for Your Wife; Hobson's Choice.* **Films:** *Carry On Matron; Carry On At Your Convenienc Carry On Loving; Carry On Up the Jungle; Doctor In Trouble; The Man Who Haunted Himself; The Lo Ban; Mr Love.* **TV:** *The Kelly Monteith Show; Rough With the Smooth; The Fall and Rise of Reginal Perrin; Thriller; Men of Affairs; Don't Dilly Dally; Hogg's Back; The Bill.* **Address:** c/o Langfo Associates. Lives in London. m. Douglas Barrell; 2 s. Nick, Tim. Pets: Two cats. Hobbies: Tennis, musi hall, reading, art (watercolours). **Favourite TV programme:** *GBH.*

PITTS, tony

Tony Pitts. Actor. b. Sheffield, South Yorkshire, 10 October 1962. Trained as a ballet dancer and a boxer, becoming schoolboy light middleweight champion; formed a contemporary dance group. **Theatre:** Arthur in *Billy Liar*; Finn in *Oi for England* (national tour). **Films:** Alan Wright in *Looks and Smiles*. **TV:** *Bingo*; *Welcome To the Times*; *Rainy Day Women*; Archie Brooks in *Emmerdale* (1985-). **Address:** c/o Susan Angel Associates/Yorkshire Television. Hobbies: Playing football, riding motorcycle.

PLANER, nigel

Nigel Planer. Actor/Writer. b. London, 22 February 1955. Trained at LAMDA. **Theatre:** Co-founder of the Comic Strip, London, and comedian at the original Comedy Store. **Films:** *Yellowbeard*; *Brazil*; *Supergrass*; *Eat the Rich*. **TV:** *Shine On Harvey Moon* (three series); *The Young Ones* (two series); *The Comic Strip Presents...*; *Roll Over Beethoven* (two series); *King and Castle*; *Filthy Rich and Catflap*; *Number 27*; *Blackeyes*; *Frankenstein's Baby*; *Nicholas Craig – The Naked Actor*; *The Return of The Magic Roundabout*. As writer: Creator of Neil in *The Young Ones*. **Records:** *Hole In My Shoe*. **Books:** *Neil's Book of the Dead*; *The Comic Strip* (both as co-author), *A Good Enough Dad*. **Address:** c/o Peters Fraser & Dunlop.

PLATER, alan

Alan Plater. Writer. b. Jarrow-on-Tyne, Tyne & Wear, 15 April 1935. **Films:** *The Virgin and the Gypsy*; *Juggernaut*; *It Shouldn't Happen To a Vet*; *Priest of Love*. **TV:** *Oh No It's Selwyn Froggitt*; *The Beiderbecke Affair*, *Tapes* and *Connection* (all original series); *The Stars Look Down*; *Flambards*; *The Barchester Chronicles*; *Fortunes of War*; *A Day In Summer*; *A Very British Coup*; *Misterioso* (all dramatisations); *Z-Cars*; *Crane*; *Softly, Softly*; *Cribb*; *The Adventures of Sherlock Holmes*; *Miss Marple*; *Maigret* (all contributions); *The Referees*; *Christabel*; *The Crystal Spirit – Orwell On Jura* (all plays and TV movies). Winner, Royal Television Society Writer's Award (1984–5), BAFTA Writer's Award (1988). **Address:** c/o Alexandra Cann. m. 2nd Shirley Rubinstein; 2 s. Stephen, David, 1 d. Janet (all from 1st m.), 3 step-s. Peter, John, Paul.

POLLARD, su

Su Pollard. Actress. b. Nottingham, 7 November 1949. Started acting as an amateur with the Co-operative Arts Theatre while working as a secretary at the Nottingham Co-op. **Theatre:** *Desert Song*; *Rose Marie*; *Godspell*; *Oh, Mr Porter*; *Big Sin City*; *Grease*; *Not Now, Darling*; *One of the Family*; *Philately Will Get You Nowhere*; *Goldilocks*; *Aladdin*; *Hi-de-Hi!*; *Don't Dress for Dinner*; sang with all-girl group Midnight News. **TV:** *Summer Royal*; *The Comedians*; *A Silver Jubilee*; *Clock-on*; *Three Up, Two Down*; *We're Going Places*; *Get Set for Summer*; Peggy in *Hi-de-Hi!*; *You Rang M'Lord?* **Address:** c/o Noel Gay Artists. m. teacher Peter Keogh.

POLYCARPOU, peter

Peter Polycarpou. Actor. b. Brighton, East Sussex (of Greek-Cypriot parents). **Theatre:** *Jesus Christ Superstar*; title role in *Snoopy*; *You're a Good Man Charlie Brown*; *Godspell*; *Grease*; *The Front Page*; *Sexual Perversity In Chicago*; *Antony and Cleopatra*; *Much Ado About Nothing*; *The Taming of the Shrew*; *Les Misérables* (Barbican and Palace Theatres); Aaron in *Titus Andronicus*; Calymath in *The Jew of Malta*; Micha in *A Question of Geography* (all RSC); *Miss Saigon* (Theatre Royal, Drury Lane); Heathcliff in *Wuthering Heights*; title role in *The Phantom of the Opera* (Her Majesty's Theatre). **TV:** *Hammer House of Horror*; *Dancers*; *The Last Days of Pompeii*; *The Professionals*; Diego Armado in *Jupiter Moon* (BSB); *Capital City*; Chris in *Birds of a Feather*; *Rich Tea & Sympathy*. **Address:** c/o Eric Glass.

PORTEOUS, *shane*

Shane Porteous. Actor. b. Coleraine, Victoria, Australia, 17 August 1942. Studied art at Queensland University and worked as a book designer, illustrator and animator. **Theatre:** *Rosencrantz and Guildenstern Are Dead; Hamlet; Major Barbara; Death of a Salesman; King Oedipus; Love's Labour's Lost.* **Films:** *Scobie Malone; Puzzle; Round the Bend; Burning Man.* **TV:** *Taming of the Shrew; Chopper Squad; The Sullivans;* Dr Terence Elliot in *A Country Practice.* **Address:** c/o June Cann Management. m. Jennifer; 2 d. Fiona, Polly, 1 s. Benjamin.

POSTLETHWAITE, *pete*

Pete Postlethwaite. Actor. **Theatre:** *Elizabeth I; Cromwell; The Recruiting Officer; Troilus and Cressida; Timon of Athens; The Duchess of Malfi; Breezeblock Park; Coriolanus; The Bofors Gun; Richard III; Henry V; Cyrano de Bergerac; The Taming of the Shrew; King Lear; Macbeth; Funny Peculiar; The Fair Maid of the West; A Midsummer Night's Dream; Every Man and His Humour; Richard III; The Good Person of Szechuan.* **Films:** *Distant Voices; A Private Function; The Dressmaker; To Kill a Priest; Treasure Island; Hamlet; Aliens III; Last of the Mohicans; Waterland.* **TV:** *Thwum; A Day Out; The Muscle Market; Watching* (BBC play); *Coast To Coast; Blind Justice; Tumbledown; Tales of Sherwood; No 27; They Never Slept; Debut On Two: Box of Swan; Needle; Zorro – The Marked Man; Boon; El C.I.D.; The Bill.* **Address:** c/o Markham & Froggatt.

POTTER, *dennis*

Dennis Christopher George Potter. Playwright. b. 17 May 1935. Joined the BBC as a current affairs journalist in 1959, then wrote for national newspapers, before success as a playwright. **Films:** *Pennies From Heaven; Brimstone and Treacle; Gorky Park; Dreamchild; Track 29.* **TV:** *Vote Vote Vote for Nigel Barton* (SFTA award); *Stand Up Nigel Barton; Where the Buffalo Roam; A Beast With Two Backs; Son of Man; Traitor; Paper Roses; Casanova; Follow the Yellow Brick Road; Only Make Believe; Joe's Ark; Schmoedipus; Late Call; Brimstone and Treacle; Double Dare Where Adam Stood; Pennies From Heaven* (BAFTA award); *Blue Remembered Hills* (BAFTA award); *Blade On the Feather; Rain On the Roof; Cream In My Coffee* (Prix Italia); *Tender Is the Night; The Singing Detective; Visitors; Blackeyes.* **Address:** c/o BBC TV. m. Margaret Morgan; 1 s., 2 d.

POWELL, *jenny*

Jennifer Powell. Presenter. b. Ilford, Essex, 8 April 1968. Trained at the Italia Conti Academy. **TV:** *No Limits; Top of the Pops; Two By Two; UP24.* **Radio:** Metro FM (Newcastle upon Tyne ILR station). **Address:** c/o Arlington Enterprises.

POWELL, *robert*

Robert Powell. Actor. b. Salford, Lancashire, 1 June 1944. **Films:** *The Italian Job; Secrets; Running Scared; The Asphyx; Asylum; Mahler; Tommy; Beyond Good and Evil; The Four Feathers; The Thirty-Nine Steps; Harlequin; Jane Austen In Manhattan; The Survivor; The Jigsaw Man; Imperative; D'Annunzio; The Sign of Command; Long Conversation With a Bird.* **TV:** *Sentimental Education; Jude the Obscure; Mrs Warren's Profession; Mr Rolls & Mr Royce; The Caucasian Chalk Circle; Looking for Clancy;* title role in *Jesus of Nazareth; Pygmalion; Shaka Zulu;* title role in *Hannay; The Jasper Carrott Show; The First Circle; Merlin of the Crystal Cave.* Winner, *TVTimes* Best Actor On TV award, 1978. **Address:** c/o ICM Duncan Heath Associates. m. Barbara; 1 s. Barnaby, 1 d. Katherine.

POWLEY, mark

Mark Chelmer Powley. Actor. b. Chelmsford, Essex, 4 October 1963. Brought up in Swindon, Wiltshire. Trained at LAMDA. **Theatre:** Angelo in *Piaf;* pantomime in Colchester; *Street Trash* (National Theatre Studio). **Films:** *Time Warp Terror; Bloody New Year; Sherlock Holmes and the Leading Lady.* **TV:** *Victoria Wood; Rockliffe's Babies; Bergerac;* PC Ken Melvin in *The Bill;* Ray Burnside in *Moon and Son.* **Address:** c/o CCA. Lives in London. m. ex-dancer Janis Jaffa. Hobbies: Golf, scuba-diving, cricket. **Favourite TV programme:** *Hill Street Blues.*

PRAED, michael

Michael Praed. Actor. b. Gloucestershire, 1 April 1960. Trained at Guildhall School of Music and Drama. **Theatre:** Title role in *The Pirates of Penzance* (London West End); *Abbacadabara; The Three Musketeers* (Broadway). **TV:** *The Gentle Touch; The Professionals; Rothko; Video Entertainers;* title role in *Robin of Sherwood; Dynasty.* **Address:** c/o ICM Duncan Heath Associates.

PRESLEY, priscilla

Priscilla Beaulieu Presley. Actress. b. Brooklyn, New York, USA, 24 May 1945. Studied acting with Milton Katselas. **Films:** *Naked Gun.* **TV:** *Comeback;* Jenna Wade in *Dallas.* **Address:** c/o William Morris Agency (USA). m. singer Elvis Presley (dis); 1 d. Lisa Marie, 1 s. Navarone (from relationship with Marco Garibaldi).

PRINGLE, bryan

Bryan Pringle. Actor. b. Glascote, Staffordshire, 19 January 1935. Trained at RADA. **TV:** *The Dustbinmen; Diary of a Nobody; The Good Companions; Love Story; Oedipus At Colonus; Paradise Postponed; Radical Chambers; Auf Wiedersehen, Pet; Ladies' Night; Hardwicke House; What the Butler Saw; The Oldest Goose In the Business; Leaving Home; The Storyteller: A Story Short; The Management; Blind Justice; Casualty; King and Castle; Les Girls; Flying Lady; My Kingdom for a Horse; All Creatures Great and Small; Inspector Morse; After Henry; Capstick's Law; A Night On the Tyne; Wish Me Luck; Crimestrike; Alfonso Bonzo; Coracle A Box of Swan; Perfect Scoundrels; Rumpole of the Bailey; Prime Suspect; Raise the Hispanic; Boon; Young Indie; Roots; Ollie's Prison.* **Address:** c/o Markham & Froggatt. m. actress Anne Jameson; 1 d. Kate, 1 s. Craster.

PROTHEROE, brian

Brian Protheroe. Actor. b. Salisbury, Wiltshire, 16 June 1944. Technician in a pathological laboratory, then played in a folk group, before acting. **Theatre:** *Larkrise To Candleford; The Beggar's Opera; Pericles; Othello; Pump Boys and Dinettes; Macbeth; The Gift; Little Love; Our Own Kind; The Sound of Music; The Winter's Tale.* **Films:** *Superman; A Nightingale Sang In Berkeley Square.* **TV:** *Two People; Strangers; Leave Him To Heaven; The Perfect House; Cover; The Quiet Days of Mrs Stafford; Bavarian Nights; Henry VI; Richard III; Spider's Web; Titus Andronicus; Reilly – Ace of Spies; King and Castle; To Have and To Hold; Every Breath You Take;* Miles Beaufort in *Gentlemen and Players; Not a Penny More, Not a Penny Less; Shrinks.* **Records:** *Pinball* (Top 30 single); *Pinball; Pickup; I/You* (all LPs). **Address:** c/o Marmont Management. 1 s. Billy, 1 d. Rosie (by partner Gilly).

PRYCE, *jonathan*

Jonathan Pryce. Actor. b. Holywell, Clwyd, 1 June 1947. Trained at RADA. **Theatre:** *Comedians* (London and Broadway, Tony award 1977); *Hamlet; Measure for Measure; The Seagull; Macbeth; Uncle Vanya; Miss Saigon.* **Films:** *Voyage of the Damned; The Day Christ Died; Peter and Paul; Breaking Glass; Loophole; Murder Is Easy; Something Wicked This Way Comes; The Ploughman's Lunch; Brazil; The Doctor and the Devils; Haunted Honeymoon; Jumpin' Jack Flash; Man On Fire; Consuming Passions; Baron Munchausen; The Rachel Papers.* **TV:** *Daft As a Brush; Playthings; Bill Brand; Comedians; Partisans; Spasms; Glad Day; For Tea On Sunday; Timon of Athens; The Caretaker; Roger Doesn't Live Here Any More; School for Clowns; Praying Mantis; Martin Luther – Heretic; The Man From the Pru; Selling Hitler.* **Address:** c/o James Sharkey Associates.

QUAYLE, *anna*

Anna Quayle. Actress. b. Birmingham, 6 October 1937. Daughter of actor-producer Douglas Quayle. Trained at RADA. **Films:** *Casino Royale; Chitty Chitty Bang Bang; Eskimo Nell; Three for All; The Seven Percent Solution; Adventures of a Private Eye; Never Take Yes for an Answer; Adventures of a Plumber's Mate; SOS Titanic; The Towers of Babel.* **TV:** *Tempo International; The Avengers; Beauty Operators; Up the Chastity Belt; Grub Street; A Degree of Frost; What's My Line?; The Queen and the Robot; The Georgian House; Aquarius; James and the Giant Peach; In the Looking Glass; What a Performance; Arena; The Light Princess; Brideshead Revisited; Henry V; Sakharov; The People From the Forest; Father Charlie; Never the Twain; Marjorie and Men; Mapp and Lucia; Lytton's Diary; Grange Hill.* **Address:** c/o CDA. m. Donald Baker; 1 d. Katy.

QUAYLE, *john*

John Quayle. Actor. b. London, 21 December 1938. Trained at RADA. **Theatre:** Repertory theatre; *Habeas Corpus; When We Are Married; Watch On the Rhine; Noises Off; Life Begins At Forty; Run for Your Life.* **Films:** *Privates On Parade.* **TV:** *Upstairs, Downstairs; Jumbo Spencer; The King's Dragon; Nanny; Pig In the Middle; Jane; This Office Life; Charles & Diana: A Royal Love Story* (TV movie); *Marjorie and Men; Farrington of the FO* (two series); *Terry and June; Tricky Business; The 19th Hole.* **Address:** c/o Barry Burnett Organisation. m. Petronella.

QUICK, *diana*

Diana Quick. Actress. b. Kent, 23 November 1946. **Films:** *Nicholas and Alexandra; A Private Enterprise; The Duellists; The Big Sleep; Ordeal By Innocence; 1919; Max Mon Amour; Vroom; Wilt.* **TV:** *The Playground; Christ Recrucified; Complete and Utter History of Britain; Hamlet; Hopcraft Into Europe; Napoleon and Love; Bedtime Story: The Sleeping Beauty; Mr Garrick and Mrs Woffington; Holding On; The Three Hostages; The Odd Job; Word for Word; At Last It's Friday; Julia Flyte in Brideshead Revisited; The Woman In White; It's My Pleasure; Dorothy Parker; Friday Night, Saturday Morning* (host, USA); *Phantom of the Opera; Chekhov in Yalta; Cariani and the Courtesans; Kimberley Carlisle; Minder; Flesh and Blood; The Justice Game; Frederick Forsyth Presents; Smith and Jones; The Orchid House; Clarissa.* **Address:** c/o Julian Belfrage Associates.

QUILLEY, *denis*

Denis Quilley. Actor. b. London, 26 December 1927. **Theatre:** Debut with Birmingham Rep (1945); *Death Trap; Sweeney Todd; Antony and Cleopatra; La Cage aux Folles; The White Devil* (National Theatre). **Films:** *Life At the Top; Anne of the Thousand Days; Murder On the Orient Express; Evil Under the Sun; King David; Privates On Parade; Memed; Foreign Body; Mister Johnson.* **TV:** *Timeslip; Dixon of Dock Green; Clayhanger; Murder In the Cathedral; The Crucible; Honky-Tonk Heroes; Gladstone In No 10; The Bretts; After the War; The Interrogation of John; George Rudge in Rich Tea & Sympathy; Family Album.* **Address:** c/o Bernard Hunter Associates. Lives in North London. m. Stella Chapman; 2 d. Sarah, Joanna, 2 s. Stephen (dec), David. Pets: Flat-coat retrievers.

QUIRKE, *pauline*

Pauline Quirke. Actress. b. London, 8 July 1959. Acted since childhood; trained at Anna Scher Theatre School. **Theatre:** *A Tale of Three Cities.* **Films:** *The Elephant Man; Getting It Right; The Return of the Soldier; QED; Little Dorrit; Still Lives.* **TV:** *Dixon of Dock Green* (aged 10); *Kids About Town; Days of Hope; You Must Be Joking; Eleanor; Jenny Can't Work Any Faster; Pauline's Quirkes; The Duchess of Duke Street; You Can't Be Serious; Lovely Couple; Pauline's People; Crown Court; The Further Adventures of Oliver Twist; Ain't Many Angels; A Name for the Day; Baby Talk; The Story of the Treasure Seekers; Life After Death; Angels;* Veronica in *Shine On Harvey Moon; Girls On Top; Hardwicke House;* Sharon in *Birds of a Feather; Very Big Very Soon; Rockliffe's Babies; Casualty.* **Address:** c/o Noel Gay Artists.

RACHINS, *alan*

Alan Rachins. Actor. b. Boston, Massachussetts, USA, 3 October 1942. Gained a degree in film production from Empire State College. **Theatre:** *After the Rain; Hadrian VII; Oh Calcutta!* **Films:** *Always.* **TV:** *Paris; Mistress; Hart To Hart; The Fall Guy; Hill Street Blues;* Douglas Brackman in *LA Law.* **Address:** c/o Agency for the Performing Arts. m. actress Joanna Frank; 1 s. Robby.

RANTZEN, *esther*

Esther Rantzen. Presenter. b. Berkhamsted, Hertfordshire, 22 June 1940. Began career in radio studio management, TV research and production. **TV:** *Braden's Week* (researcher-reporter); *That's Life!* (presenter-producer, 1973-); *That's Family Life!; The Big Time* (reporter-producer); *Children In Need; Drug Watch; Hearts of Gold; Childline.* **Address:** c/o Noel Gay Artists. m. TV producer-writer Desmond Wilcox; 2 d. Emily, Rebecca, 1 s. Joshua.

RASHAD, *phylicia*

Phylicia Ayers-Allen. Actress. b. Houston, Texas, USA, 19 June. Trained with the Negro Ensemble Company. **Theatre:** *The Wiz; Dream Girls; Ain't Supposed To Die a Natural Death; Duplex.* **TV:** *One Life To Live; The Cosby Show;* title roel in *Zora.* **Address:** c/o Artists Agency. m. sportscaster Ahmad Rashad; 1 s. William (from previous m.), 1 d. Condola.

RASHBROOK, *stephen*

Stephen Rashbrook. Actor. b. Essex, 2 July 1958. Trained at Guildhall School of Music and Drama. **Theatre:** Sebastian in *Twelfth Night; Othello; Julius Caesar; The Knight of the Burning Pestle; The Merry Wives of Windsor; Peter Pan* (all RSC); *Nicholas Nickleby* (RSC, London and New York); Player Queen in *Hamlet; Forty Years On* (both London West End); *A Private Treason; Talk of the Devil; Knots and Bumps; The Sound of Music; Robert and Elizabeth.* **Films:** *The Fool; Foreign Body.* **TV:** *Nicholas Nickleby; Grange Hill; 'Allo 'Allo!; Androcles and the Lion; Partners In Crime; Bergerac; Move Over Darling* (documentary); *Wogan;* Rev Tony Charlton in *Emmerdale* (1990–91). **Radio:** *The Way We Live Now; The Ascent of F6; Morning Story; Kaleidoscope.* **Address:** c/o Nina Quick Associates. Lives in Essex. m. Elaine; 1 s. Oliver, 1 d. Sophie.

RASHLEIGH, *andy*

Andy Rashleigh. Actor/Writer. b. East London, 23 January 1949. Trained at Bretton Hall College of Education; taught drama in London and Jamaica for six years. **Films:** *The Ploughman's Lunch; Acceptable Levels; Ends and Means.* **TV:** *Life for Christine; Brideshead Revisited; Juliet Bravo; Mitch; Dear Ladies; Strangers;* PC Woodhouse in *Coronation Street; Crown Court; The Adventures of Sherlock Holmes; The Practice; The South Bank Bank Show: Hawksmoor;* Colin Arnold in *Albion Market; The Bill; Dramarama; Gems;* Chef in *Crossroads; Panorama;* Ted Sharp in *Emmerdale; Making Out; Hale & Pace;* DS Pryde in *EastEnders;* Eliot Creasy in *Jupiter Moon* (BSB); *Minder.* As writer: *Crossroads.* **Radio:** *The Archers* (as writer). **Address:** c/o Michelle Braidman Associates. Lives in London with Maggie Wilkinson.

RATCLIFF, *sandy*

Sandy Ratcliff. Actress. b. London, 2 October 1950. Trained as a designer/pattern cutter and photographic model before acting. **Theatre:** *Lucky Strike; Chorus Girls; The Workshop.* **Films:** *Family Life; Yesterday's Hero.* **TV:** *Cork and Bottle; Shelley; Target; Shoestring; Cast Off; Danger UXB; Hazell; Couples; The Sweeney; Minder;* Sue Osman in *EastEnders; Maigret.* **Address:** c/o Markham & Froggatt. m. photographer Peter Wright (dis); 1 s. William.

RATZENBERGER, *john*

John Ratzenberger. Actor. b. Bridgeport, Connecticut, USA, 6 April 1947. Member of the Sacred Heart University's drama club. **Films:** *The Ritz; Valentino; Hanover Street; Yanks; A Bridge Too Far; Superman; Superman II; Ragtime; The Empire Strikes Back; Ghandi; The Bitch.* **TV:** *House II; Time Stalkers;* Cliff Calvin in *Cheers; Small World.* **Address:** c/o The Agency. m. Georgia; 1 s. James.

RAVENS, *jan*

Jan Ravens. Actress. b. Bebington, Cheshire, 14 May 1958. Trained as a drama teacher at Cambridge University; member of Cambridge Footlights Revue. **Theatre:** *Ha Bloody Ha; Loitering Within Tent; The Sloane Ranger Revue* (Windsor and London West End); *The Relapse; The End of the World Show; The History of Tom Jones; Twelfth Night.* **TV:** *Just Amazing; Getting Into Shape; Carrott's Lib; The Lenny Henry Show; The Kenny Everett Show; Friday People; Carrott Election Confidential; Farrington o· the FO; All In Good Faith; Saturday Live; C.A.T.S. Eyes; Spitting Image* (voice impersonator); *No Frills, Whose Line Is It Anyway?; KYTV; Smith and Jones; Alexei Sayle's Stuff; An Actor's Life for Me; One Foot In the Grave.* **Address:** c/o Barry Burnett Organisation. m. composer-performer Steve Brown; 1 s. Alfie.

RAVENSCROFT, *christopher*

Christopher Ravenscroft. Actor. Trained at Bristol Old Vic Theatre School. **Theatre:** Repertory theatre in Farnham, Hornchurch, Salisbury, Liverpool and Manchester; *Twelfth Night* (Renaissance Theatre Company); *Richard III; Crimes In Hot Countries; Henry V; Julius Caesar; Nicholas Nickleby; Twelfth Night; Baal* (all RSC); *Bent; A Severed Head.* **TV:** *Henry V; Twelfth Night; Pericles; The forth Arm; Nicholas Nickleby; The Hound of the Baskervilles; Gossip From the Forest; World In Action* (narrator); police sergeant in *Coronation Street; Crown Court;* Det Insp Burden in *The Ruth Rendell Mysteries.* **Address:** c/o RKM.

RAWLE, jeff

Jeff Rawle. Actor/Writer. b. Birmingham, 20 July 1951. Worked at Sheffield Playhouse before training at LAMDA. **Theatre:** *Equus; Bent; The Arbor; The Elephant Man; Queerfolk; Releevo.* **Films:** *Baal; A Hitch In Time; Correction, Please; Rating Notman; Duchamp; Crystal Gazing; Awayday; Laughterhouse; The Doctor and the Devils.* **TV:** Title role in *Billy Liar; The Water Maiden; Play for Today: Death of a Young Man; Love On the Dole; Wilde Alliance; Singles; Juliet Bravo; Claire; Bergerac; Singles Weekend; Doctor Who; Country and Irish; Remington Steele; Call Me Mister; Fortunes of War; Boon; Run for the Lifeboat; South of the Border; Vote for Them; The Gift; Beyond the Pale; The Bill; A Perfect Hero; This Is David Lander;* George in *Drop the Dead Donkey;* AIDS counsellor in *EastEnders.* **Address:** c/o Annette Stone Associates.

RAYNER, claire

Claire Rayner. Agony aunt. b. London, 22 January 1931. Trained as a nurse and midwife before entering broadcasting. **TV:** *Pebble Mill; Kitchen Garden; Claire Rayner's Casebook; After Nine* (TV-AM). **Radio:** *Woman's Hour; Schools; Today; Contact; The Michael Aspel Show;* Capital Radio. **Address:** c/o TV-am. m. Desmond Rayner; 1 d. Amanda, 2 s. Adam, Jason.

REDDIN, jacqueline

Jacqueline Reddin. Actress. b. Dublin, Ireland, 1956. Trained at Bristol Old Vic Theatre School. **Theatre:** *City Sugar; The Boy Friend; Knots and Bumps; Relatively Speaking; This Happy Breed* (national tour); *Grease* (Astoria Theatre); *Dick Whittington* (London Palladium); title role in *Cinderella; Table Manners.* **TV:** *Play for Today: Brencham People; The Duchess of Duke Street; The Professionals; Return of The Saint;* Maggie in *Emmerdale Farm; Minder; Florence Nightingale; Tickle On the Tum; Hold Tight; Hale & Pace.* **Address:** c/o Hamper-Neafsey Associates. Lives with singer Maynard Williams; 1 d. Jemma, 1 s. Luke.

REDFERN, michael

Michael Ian Redfern. Actor. b. Isleworth, Middlesex, 30 March 1943. Trained at the Corona Academy. **TV:** *The Newcomers; United; Out; Muck and Brass; Hi-de-Hi!; Maybury; The Gentle Touch; The Young Ones; Carrott's Lib; Never the Twain; Minder; Three Up, Two Down; The New Statesman; Terry and June; Comrade Dad; The Bill; Sorry; Girls On Top; Relative Strangers; Filthy Rich and Catflap; Alas Smith and Jones; The 19th Hole; Boon; Charles de Gaulle; In Sickness and In Health; London's Burning; Hope It Rains; Michael Winner's True Crimes; Bottom.* TV commercials: Dad in Oxo campaign. **Address:** c/o Darryl Brown Associates. Lives in Fetcham, Surrey, with partner Carol; 1 s. Ashley. Pets: Two golden retrievers called Fudge and Mushroom, and two cats called Dale and Woodstock. Hobbies: Golf, football, swimming. **Favourite TV programme:** *Cheers.*

REDING, nick

Nick Reding. Actor. b. London, 31 August 1962. Began career as a stage hand. **Theatre:** *Easter; The Seagull; The Earth Divided; A Christmas Carol;* acted in and co-directed four productions for the Elephant Walk Children's Theatre Company. **Films:** *Real Life; Captive; Heroine.* **TV:** *Last Summer's Child; Stalky & Co; Henry IV, Pt III; Richard III; Play for Today: The Remainder Man; Love and Marriage: Dearly Beloved; Oscar Wilde; Paradise Postponed; Chance In a Million; The Monocled Mutineer; District Nurse; My Family and Other Animals;* lawyer in *EastEnders;* PC Ramsey in *The Bill;* Haki in *The Final Frame* (Channel Four film); *Minder; The House of Eliott; The Count of Solar* (TV movie). **Address:** c/o William Morris Agency.

REES, *roger*

Roger Rees. Actor. b. Aberystwyth, Dyfed, 5 May 1944. Trained as an artist and painted sets at Wimbledon Rep before becoming a professional actor. **Theatre:** *Hindle Wakes; The Taming of the Shrew* (RSC, London and Broadway, winner of Tony Best Actor award); title role in *Nicholas Nickleby* (London and Broadway, Tony Best Actor award 1981); *Masquerade; The Real Thing* (Strand Theatre); *Hamlet* (RSC); *Love's Labour's Lost; Archangels Don't Play Pinball; Hapgood.* As director: *Turkey Time; Julius Caesar; John Bull.* **Films:** *Star 80; If Looks Could Kill.* **TV:** *Place of Peace; Under Western Eyes; A Bouquet of Barbed Wire; Saigon – Year of the Cat; Imaginary Friends; Nicholas Nickleby; A Christmas Carol* (TV movie); *The Comedy of Errors; Macbeth; The Voysey Inheritance; The Ebony Tower; Singles; Cheers.* **Address:** c/o ICM Duncan Heath Associates.

REGALBUTO, *joe*

Joe Regalbuto. Actor. b. Brooklyn, New York, 14 August 1949. Trained at the Academy of Dramatic Arts. **Films:** *Missing; Lassiter; Star Chamber; Six Weeks; The Sicilian; Raw Deal.* **TV:** *The Associates; Barney Miller; Mork and Mindy; Betrayal of Trust; Knots Landing; Our House; J J Starbuck; Ace Crawford; Private Eye; Divorce Wars; You the Jury;* Norman Tuttle in *Street Hawk.* **Address:** c/o Triad Artists. m. Rosemary; 2 s. Nicholas, Michael, 1 d. Gina.

REGAN, *brian*

Brian Regan. Actor. b. Liverpool, 2 October 1957. Apprentice footballer with Liverpool football club; assistant stage manager, then stage manager, at Liverpool Playhouse, before becoming a professional actor. **Theatre:** *Stags and Hens; Hamlet; Blood On the Dole.* **TV:** Stevie King in *Murphy's Mob;* Terry Sullivan in *Brookside* (1982-). **Address:** c/o Mersey Television. m. Lisa; 1 d. Ashley.

REID, *beryl*

Beryl Reid. Actress. b. Hereford, 17 June 1920. **Films:** *The Belles of St Trinian's; Star!; The Killing of Sister George.* **TV:** *Vic's Grill; Henry Hall's Guest Night; A-Z; Most Likely Girl; The Beryl Reid Show; Man O' Brass; Comedy Playhouse; Wooster; Mrs Capper's Birthday; Beryl Reid; The Frog; The Rivals; Father, Dear Father; The Goodies; The Good Old Days; Alcock and Gander; Wink To Me Only; Smike; The Apple Cart; When We Are Married; Flint; Tinker, Tailor, Soldier, Spy; Beryl Reid Special; Does the Team Think?; Get Up and Go; Doctor Who; Smiley's People; Minder; Late Starter; The Growing Pains of Adrian Mole; A Perfect Spy; The Beiderbecke Tapes.* **Books:** *So Much Love* (autobiography). **Address:** c/o James Sharkey Associates/Robert Luff. Lives in Middlesex. m. 1st Bill Worsley (dis), 2nd musician Derek Franklin (dis).

REID, *mike*

Michael Reid. Actor/Comedian. b. London, 19 January 1940. Formerly a coalman and lorry driver, performing as a stand-up comic in pubs by night. **TV:** *The Saint; The Baron* (both as an 'extra'); *The Comedians; Runaround* (presenter); *Yus, My Dear; Big Deal;* Frank Butcher in *EastEnders* (1988-). **Records:** *The Ugly Duckling.* **Address:** c/o Tony Lewis Entertainments/BBC Elstree Centre. Lives in Essex. m. 2nd Shirley; 2 s. Mark (dec), Michael, 2 step-children.

REISER, *paul*

Paul Reiser. Actor. **Films:** *Skeeball Blues; The Marrying Man; Crazy People; Beverly Hills Cop; Beverly Hills Cop II; Cross My Heart; Aliens; Diner.* **TV:** *The Tower; My Two Dads.* **Address:** c/o United Talent Agency.

REITEL, *enn*

Enn Reitel. Actor. b. Forfar, Tay, 21 June 1950. Trained at Central School of Speech and Drama. **Theatre:** *Me and My Girl* (Adelphi Theatre). **TV:** *The Further Adventures of Lucky Jim; The Misfits; The Optimist; The Kelly Monteith Show; Mog; Spitting Image* (voice impersonator); *Round the Bend* (voice); *One Foot In the Grave.* **Address:** c/o Roger Carey Management.

RHYS JONES, *griff*

Griff Rhys Jones. Actor/Writer. b. Cardiff, 16 November 1953. **Theatre:** *Charley's Aunt* (Aldwych Theatre); *Single Weekend; Roots of Racism; Thark; The Wind In the Willows* (National Theatre). **Films:** *Morons From Outer Space; Wilt.* **TV:** *Not the Nine O'Clock News; Alas Smith and Jones; The Best of Smith and Jones; 'Ex'* (TV movie). **Address:** c/o TalkBack.

RICE, *anneka*

Annie Rice. Presenter. b. Cowbridge, South Glamorgan, 4 October 1958. Worked in Hong Kong in radio, on TV as a newscaster and producer (TVB), and as editor of a children's book about Hong Kong (1979–82). **TV:** *CBTV; Treasure Hunt; Sporting Chance; Show Business; Family Trees; Wish You Were Here ...?; Name and Games; Driving Force; World Circus Championships; Good Morning Britain; Challenge Anneka* (also co-deviser); *The Other Side of Christmas; Holiday; Challenge Anneka Special Report; Play It Safe!* **Address:** c/o BBC TV. m. theatre producer Nick Allott; 2 s.

RICHARD, *eric*

Eric Richard. Actor. b. Margate, Kent, 27 June 1940. **Theatre:** Repertory theatre in Nottingham, Liverpool, Sheffield, Birmingham and Manchester; Royal Court Theatre. **TV:** *The Onedin Line; Shoestring; Mitch; Angels; Juliet Bravo; Home Sweet Home; Made In Britain; Games Without Frontiers; Shogun; Victoria Wood As Seen On TV;* Sgt Bob Cryer in *The Bill.* **Address:** c/o Peters Fraser & Dunlop/The Bill. m. Cristine; 1 s. Richard, 1 d. Frances.

RICHARD, *wendy*

Wendy Richard. Actress. b. Middlesbrough, Cleveland, 20 July 1946. Trained at the Italia Conti Academy. **Theatre:** *No Sex, Please – We're British.* **Films:** *Doctor In Clover; Bless This House; On the Buses; Gumshoe; Are You Being Served?.* **TV:** Joyce Harker in *The Newcomers;* Doreen in *On the Buses; Harpers West One; The Arthur Haynes Show; Dixon of Dock Green; Danger Man; No Hiding Place; Joe Nobody; The Making of Jericho; Z-Cars; Please Sir!; The Fenn Street Gang; Not On Your Nellie; Hugh and I; Both Ends Meet; Spooner's Patch; Dad's Army; West Country Tales;* Miss Brahms in *Are You Being Served?* and *Grace and Favour;* Pauline Fowler in *EastEnders* (1985-). **Address:** c/o David White Associates/BBC Elstree Centre. Lives in London. m. 1st Leonard Black (dis), 2nd Will Thorpe (dis), 3rd Paul Glorney.

RICHARDS, *stan*

Stanley Richardson. Actor. b. Barnsley, South Yorkshire, 8 December 1930. Worked as a Ministry of Labour clerk on leaving school, entered showbusiness as a dance-band pianist, formed comedy and musical quartet Melody Maniacs, then became a solo entertainer. **Theatre:** Eddie Waters in *Comedians* (Theatre Royal, York, 1979). **Films:** *Yanks; Agatha.* **TV:** *Play for Today: The Price of Coal; Play of the Week: Stepping Out; Coronation Street; The Cuckoo Waltz; Crown Court; All Creatures Great and Small; Last of the Summer Wine;* Seth Armstrong in *Emmerdale* (1977-). **Address:** c/o ATS Casting/Yorkshire Television. Lives in Barnsley. m. Susan; 3 s. Alan, Keith, Irvin, 3 d. Joan, Dawn, June. Pets: A dog called Smokey. Hobbies: Work. **Favourite TV programme:** 'Anything of quality.'

RICHARDSON, *ian*

Ian Richardson. Actor. b. Edinburgh, 7 April 1934. **Films:** *A Midsummer Night's Dream; The Darwin Adventure; Brazil; Whoops Apocalypse; The Fourth Protocol; Cry Freedom; Burning Secret; Pursuit.* **TV:** *As You Like It; All's Well That Ends Well; The Canterbury Tales; Sorry...; A Voyage Round My Father; Civilisation; Eyeless In Gaza; Danton's Death; Ike: The War Years; Churchill's Generals; Charlie Muffin; Private Schulz; Passing Through; A Cotswold Death; We Never Make Mistakes; The Woman In White; The Hound of the Baskervilles; The Sign of Four; The Master of Ballantrae; Mistral's Daughter; Slimming Down; Mountbatten; Six Centuries of Verse; Monsignor Quixote; Star Quality; Blunt; Porterhouse Blue; The Devil's Disciple; Troubles; The Winslow Boy; The Gravy Train; House of Cards; The Gravy Train Goes East.* **Address:** c/o London Management.

RICHARDSON, *joely*

Joely Richardson. actress. b. London, 9 January 1965. Daughter of director Tony Richardson and actress Vanessa Redgrave. **Films:** *Wetherby; Drowning By Numbers; Shining Through.* **TV:** *Body Contact; Behaving Badly; Heading Home; The Storyteller.* **Address:** c/o ICM Duncan Heath Associates.

RICHARDSON, *miranda*

Miranda Richardson. Actress. **Films:** *Dance With a Stranger; The Innocent; Underworld; Empire of the Sun; Dream of a Mad Monkey.* **TV:** *Blackadder II; After Pilkington; Blackadder III; Smith and Jones; Ball-Trap On the Cote Sauvage; Die Kinder (The Children); Blackadder Goes Forth; Redemption; The Storyteller; Performance: Old Times; Snapshots.* **Address:** c/o Kerry Gardner Management.

RICHARDSON, *natasha*

Natasha Richardson. Actress. b. London, 11 May 1963. **Theatre:** *High Society.* **Films:** *Every Picture Tells a Story; In the Secret State; Gothic; Patty; Fatman and Little Boy; The Handmaid's Tale; The Comfort of Strangers.* **TV:** *The Adventures of Sherlock Holmes; The Copper Beeches; Ghosts; A Month In the Country.* **Address:** c/o Hutton Management.

RIDLEY, *joanne*

Joanne Ridley. Actress. b. London, 23 March 1970. Trained at the Arts Educational School and Guildhall School of Music and Drama. **Theatre:** *Spookhouse; Intermezzo; The Lady From the Sea.* **Films:** *The World Is Full of Married Men* (aged six). **TV:** *A Question of Guilt; Mackenzie;* Samantha Harrap in *Me and My Girl;* Natasha in *Streetwise.* **Address:** Elaine Murphy Associates. Single; lives in Islington, London. Hobbies: Yoga, shiatsu, reading, swimming, photography, music, dancing, travelling to faraway places, eating exotic food. **Favourite TV programme:** *Life On Earth;* anything about the planet we live on and the creatures on it.

RIGG, *diana*

Diana Rigg. Actress. **Theatre:** RSC; National Theatre; *Follies.* **Films:** *A Midsummer Night's Dream; The Assassination Bureau; On Her Majesty's Secret Service; Hospital; Theatre of Blood; A Little Night Music; Evil Under the Sun; A Hazard of Hearts.* **TV:** Emma Peel in *The Avengers; Diana* (USA); *Bleak House; Mother Love.* **Address:** c/o Jonathan Altaras Associates.

RINGHAM, *john*

John Ringham. Actor. b. Cheltenham, Gloucestershire, 10 February. Worked as an assistant stage manager before becoming a professional actor. **Theatre:** Repertory theatre; London West End; National Theatre. **TV:** *Age of Kings; Just Good Friends; Woof!; The Piglet Files; The Darling Buds of May.* **Address:** c/o Joseph and Wagg. m. Hedwig Felizitas; 2 d. Jessica, Hannah, 2 s. Max, Ben.

RIPPON, *angela*

Angela Rippon. Presenter. b. Plymouth, Devon, 12 October 1944. Newspaper journalist before entering TV. **TV:** *Spotlight South West* (BBC Plymouth); *Open House; Westward Reports; Young Eyes; Generation Three; The Silent Valley* (all Westward TV); BBC TV News reporter and newsreader (1973–81); *The Morecambe and Wise Christmas Show; The Eurovision Song Contest;* 1979 General Election (BBC); founder-member of TV-am (presenter of *Good Morning Britain*); *Live From London; The Don Lane Show; Angela Rippon Meets ...; The Antiques Roadshow; People In Power; In the Country; Top Gear; The Rippon Reports; Come Dancing; Masterteam; What's My Line?; The Entertainers; Crufts '92.* **Address:** c/o IMG. Lives in London and Tavistock, Devon. m. Chris Dare (sep). Pets: A dog called Benson and a horse called Extra Time. Hobbies: Horse-riding, theatre.

RITCHIE, *kate*

Kate Ritchie. Actress. b. Sydney, Australia. **Theatre:** *Annie; The Sound of Music; Carousel; Say It With Music.* **TV:** Molly in *Cyclone Tracy* (mini-series); Sally Keating in *Home and Away* (1988-). **Address:** c/o Channel 7.

RIX, *debbie*

Debbie Rix. Presenter. b. 28 April. Began as a researcher and production assistant for BBC radio. **TV:** BBC Bristol reporter; *Breakfast Time* newsreader; *Making Waves; Game for a Laugh; Fax; Trans World Sport.* **Address:** c/o IMG. Lives in East Sussex and London. m. Tony; 1 d. Charlotte.

ROACH, *pat*

Pat Roach. Actor. b. Birmingham, 13 May. **Films:** *Adventures of the Spaceman and King Arthur; Clash of the Titans; Red Sonja; A Clockwork Orange; Barry Lyndon; Conan the Destroyer; Rising Damp; Raiders of the Lost Ark; Indiana Jones and the Temple of Doom; Never Say Never Again; Willow; Indiana Jones and the Last Crusade; Return of the Musketeers; Superman III; Robin Hood: Prince of Thieves.* **TV:** *Auf Wiedersehen, Pet; The Last Place On Earth; Minder; Bullseye; Three Wishes for Jamie; Hazell; Gangsters; Juliet Bravo; Tiswas; The Lenny and Jerry Show; We Love TV; The Saturday Show; The Jim Davidson Show; Harry's Kingdom; Coasting.* **Address:** c/o Peter Charlesworth.

ROACHE, *william*

William Roache. Actor. b. Ilkeston, Derbyshire, 25 April 1932. Went into acting after five years in the Royal Welsh Fusiliers. **Theatre:** Repertory theatre in Clacton, Nottingham and Oldham. **Films:** *Behind the Mask; His and Hers; The Queen's Guards.* **TV:** *Knight Errant; Skyport; The Bulldog Breed; Marking Time;* Ken Barlow in *Coronation Street* (1960-). Joint winner, with Anne Kirkbride (qv) and Johnny Briggs (qv), Pye Television Award, 1983. **Address:** c/o Granada TV. Lives in Wilmslow, Cheshire. m. 1st actress Anna Cropper (dis), 2nd actress Sara McEwen; 2 s. actor Linus (from 1st m.), William, 2 d. Verity, Edwina (dec). Hobbies: Playing golf.

ROBB, *david*

David Robb. Actor. b. London, 23 August 1947. Trained at Central School of Speech and Drama. **Films:** *The Four Feathers; The Deceivers.* **TV:** *Crown Court; The Glittering Prizes; I, Claudius; French Without Tears; The Winslow Boy; Wings; Wuthering Heights; Hess; Romeo and Juliet; The Caledonian Cascade; Hamlet; Hazell; Out; The Legend of King Arthur; The Flame Trees of Thika; Forgive Our Foolish Ways; Fanny By Gaslight; Ivanhoe; Charles & Diana: A Royal Love Story; Morte d'Arthur; The Last Days of Pompeii; Wallenberg: A Hero's Story; Off-Peak; First Among Equals; Dreams Lost, Dreams Found; Wall of Tyranny; The Man Who Lived At the Ritz; Flight To Istanbul; Taggart; Parnell and the Englishwoman; To Be the Best; Up the Garden Path; Some Other Spring; Strathblair.* **Address:** c/o William Morris Agency. m. actress Briony McRoberts (qv).

ROBB, *natalie*

Natalie Robb. Actress/Singer. b. Bellshill, Glasgow, 3 December 1974. Attended Glasgow Youth Theatre. **Theatre:** Glasgow Mayfest; *Grease; Oliver!; Big Al; The Wiz.* **Films:** *Facts of Life.* **TV:** *Young Entertainer of the Year* (winner, 1988); *Going Live!; But Can You Do It On TV?; Dreams and Recollections; Return Journey; Taggart;* Trish McDonald in *Take the High Road* (1990-). **Records:** *Girls, Girls, Girls.* **Address:** c/o JR Management/Scottish Television.

ROBBIE, *sue*

Susan Jennifer Robinson. Presenter. b. London, 5 July 1949. Taught English and worked as an air stewardess before entering TV. **TV:** Granada TV announcer; *First Post; Hold Tight!; Sneak Preview; Weekend; Children's ITV; Cartoon Crackers; Connections; Names and Games; TX; Ark Royal – The Rock Show; Video Active; The Dodo Club; Breakfast Time; Showreel 87; The Dodo Christmas Club; ITV Telethon; 01- for London; Pick of the Week; Emergency (This Morning); Consumer File* (TSW, 1989-); *Streetwise (The Channel Four Daily); Business South West* (TSW). Voice-overs: *Your Living Body; The Micro At Work; Chemistry In Action.* **Address:** c/o Arlington Enterprises. Single; lives in Congleton, Cheshire. Hobbies: Walking, cinema, theatre, personal growth/self-awareness, spirituality and New Age issues. **Favourite TV programme:** *thirtysomething.*

ROBERTS, *ben*

Ben Roberts. Actor. b. Bangor, 1 July 1950. **TV:** *Tales of Sherwood Forest;* Chief Insp Derek Conway in *The Bill* (1989-). **Address:** Spotlight/The Bill. Lives in Nottingham. m. Helen; 1 s. Joe. Pets: An old cat called Henry. Hobbies: Doing up old cars.

ROBERTS, *ivor*

Ivor Roberts. Actor. b. Nottingham, 19 July 1925. **Theatre:** *Objections To Sex and Violence; The Unvarnished Truth; The Government Inspector; Pravda; The Attractions.* **Films:** *The Sailor's Return; Hopscotch; Sweet William; Another Country; Portrait of Evil; Personal Services; We Think the World of You.* **TV:** *Secret Army; Bergerac; Sam; Born and Bred; Dombey and Son; Yes Minister; Minder; Sorry; The New Statesman; Coronation Street; The Bretts; Shadow of the Noose; Snow; Better Days; We Are Seven; The 19th Hole; You Rang, M'Lord?* **Address:** c/o Howes and Prior. m. Iris; 1 d. Melanie.

ROBINSON, *anne*

Anne Robinson. Presenter. b. Crosby, Liverpool, 26 September. Journalist with *The Sunday Times,* then the *Daily Mirror.* **TV:** *Breakfast Time* (TV critic); *Points of View; Just Questions.* **Radio:** *The Anne Robinson Show.* **Address:** c/o IMG. m. journalist John Penrose; 1 d. Emma.

ROBINSON, *jancis*

Jancis Robinson. Presenter/Writer. b. Cumbria, 22 April 1950. Edited monthly wine and spirit tra
journal, before joining *The Sunday Times* as wine correspondent in 1980, then the London *Eveni*
Standard in 1987 and was awarded the Master of Wine. **TV:** *The Wine Programme; The Dump; Jan*
Robinson Meets. **Books:** *Jancis Robinson's Food and Wine Adventures.* **Address:** c/o Curtis Brown.
Nick Lander; 1 d. Julia, 1 s. William.

ROBINSON, *robert*

Robert Robinson. Presenter. b. Liverpool, 17 December 1927. **TV:** *Picture Parade; Points of View; A*
the Family; All Our Yesterdays; Call My Bluff; The Fifties; Brain of Britain; Robinson's Travels; T
Book Programme; The Book Game; Word for Word; Robinson Country; Behind the Headline
Robinson Cruising; B Traven. **Books:** *Conspiracy; Landscape of Dead Dons; Inside Robert Robinso*
The Dog Chairman; Everyman Book of Light Verse; Bad Dreams (novel); *Prescriptions of a P*
Doctor's Clerk. **Address:** c/o BBC TV. m. Josephine; 2 d. Lucy, Suzy, 1 s. Nicholas.

ROBINSON, *tony*

Tony Robinson. Actor/Writer. b. London, 15 August 1946. **TV:** *Who Dares Wins; Black Adde*
Blackadder II; Blackadder III; Blackadder Goes Forth; Bergerac; Maid Marian and Her Merry Me
(also writer); *Stay Tooned* (presenter); *House of Payne; Teenage Health Freak; Blood and Hon*
(storyteller). **Address:** c/o Kate Feast Management.

ROBSON, *linda*

Linda Robson. Actress. Trained at the Anna Scher Theatre School. **Films:** *Absolution.* **TV:** *Jackano*
Playhouse (aged 12); *Pauline's Quirkes; Within These Walls; Mary's Wife; Ain't Many Angles; The Goo*
Neighbour; If Only; Cribb; Going Out; Agony; The Other 'Arf; The Case of the Middle Aged Wife
Chains; Harry's Game; L for Lester; Up the Elephant and Round the Castle; Maggie Moon in *Shine O*
Harvey Moon; Lizzie's Pictures; Elphida; Bad Boys; Thin Air; South of the Border; The Bil
Underground; Tracey in *Birds of a Feather.* **Address:** c/o Noel Gay Artists.

RODGERS, *anton*

Anton Rodgers. Actor/Director. b. Wisbech, Cambridgeshire, 10 January 1933. Acted as a child; traine
at the Italia Conti Academy and LAMDA. **Theatre:** *Carmen; Great Expectations; The Winslow Boy* (a
as a child); *The Boy Friend; Songbook; St Joan; Two Into One; Windy City; Passion Play.* **Films**
Rotten To the Core; The Man Who Haunted Himself; Scrooge; The Fourth Protocol. **TV:** *Ukridge; Th*
Elusive Pimpernel; The Organisation; Zodiac; Rumpole of the Bailey; Lillie; The Flaxboroug
Chronicles; Fresh Fields; Comeback; Talking Takes Two; Murder By Mirrors (TV movie); *Pictures*
Sharing Time; French Fields; After the War; 4-Play: Goodbye and I Hope We Meet Again; May T
December. **Address:** c/o Michael Whitehall. m. 1st Morna, 2nd actress Elizabeth Garvie; 1 d. Thalia, 4 s
Adam (both from 1st m.), Barnaby, Dominic, Luke.

RODRIGUES, *tania*

Tania Maria Rodrigues. Actress. b. Hong Kong (Indian), 10 September 1965. Trained at The Drama Studio. Speaks English, Cantonese and French. **Theatre:** *Everyman; Magic Land; Swan With the Golden Wings; Castles In the Air; The Institutue; Robin Hood.* **Films:** *Before the Wedding.* **TV:** *The Real Eddy English; Oranges Are Not the Only Fruit; Lovejoy; Dancing In the Dark;* Joanne Khan in *Coronation Street; Short and Curlies: A Nice Arrangement.* **Radio:** *Dora.* Plus TV commercials. **Address:** c/o Actorum. Lives in London. m. Matthew Marsh. Hobbies: Aromatherapy, swimming, having fun. **Favourite TV programme:** *GBH.*

ROËVES, *maurice*

Maurice Roëves. Actor/Director/Writer. b. Sunderland, Tyne & Wear, 19 March 1937. Trained at the Royal College of Drama, Glasgow. **Films:** *The Fighting Prince of Donegal; Ulysses; Oh! What a Lovely War; Young Winston; A Day At the Beach; The Eagle Has Landed; Transfusion; When Eight Bells Toll; SOS Titanic; Escape To Victory; Hidden Agenda; The Big Man.* **TV:** *The Sweeney; Target; Oil Strike North; Danger UXB; Twelfth Night; Inside the Third Reich; Heather Ann; Magnum PI; Remington Steele; The Quest; Lytton's Diary; Bergerac; Tutti Frutti; Unreported Incident; Bookie; North and South Book II; Movie of the Month; Days of Our Lives; Father, Son 'n' Holy Terror* (as writer); *Jake and the Fat Man; Hunter; Middle for Diddle* (as writer); *El C.I.D; Rumpole of the Bailey; Spender.* **Address:** c/o ICM Duncan Heath Associates. m. Annie (sep); 1 d. Sarah.

ROGERS, *jean*

Jean Rogers. Actress. b. Perivale, Middlesex, 2 February 1942. Trained at Guildhall School of Music and Drama. **Theatre:** *Perchance To Dream; Dancing Years; Little Brother, Little Sister; The Room; Mother Goose; Cinderella.* **TV:** Nurse Rogers in *Emergency – Ward 10;* Julie Shepherd in *Crossroads; Here's Harry; Charge; Comedy Playhouse; Callan; George and Mildred; General Hospital; Watch* (presenter); *Calendar* (presenter, Yorkshire TV regional news magazine); Dolly Skilbeck (née Arcaster) in *Emmerdale* (1980–91). **Radio:** More than 1,500 broadcasts; *Listen With Mother; Poetry Corner; Children's Hour.* **Address:** c/o Daly Gagan Associates. m. 1st Terry Moakes (dis), 2nd TV assistant director Philip Hartley; 1 d. Justine, 1 s. Jeremy, four step-d. Pam, Zoe, Lucy, Jody. Hobbies: Cooking, wine-making, gardening, badminton, yoga.

ROGERS, *katharine*

Katharine Rogers. Actress. b. London, 21 December 1960. Performed with Anna Scher's Children's Theatre (aged 15); trained at RADA. **Theatre:** *A Midsummer Night's Dream; Romeo and Juliet; Camille; The Party; Today; Golden Girls; Red Noses; The Castle; Crimes In Hot Countries* (all RSC); *This Green and Pleasant Land; Women At War; Linda's; Camberwell Beauty; And All Things Nice; Twelfth Night; The Oedipus Plays; fugue; The Seagull; Yerma; Our Town; Action Replay; The Piggy Bank; The Barker Poems; The Possibilities* (both as actress and founder-diretgor of Not The RSC). **Films:** *Quadrophenia.* **TV:** *Bloody Kids; The Magnificent One; Johnny Jarvis; Only Yesterday;* Firewoman Josie Ingham in *London's Burning.* **Address:** c/o Hope & Lyne. Single; lives in North London.

ROGERS, *ted*

Ted Rogers. Comedian/Presenter. b. Kennington, South London, 20 July 1935. Worked as a clerk, did national service, then became a Butlin's Red Coat, before touring in revues. **Theatre:** *Cinderella;* variety performances on same bill as Tom Jones, Engelbert Humperdinck, Jack Jones, Andy Williams, Perry Como, Lena Horne, Bing Crosby and Shirley Bassey; *Aladdin; Goldilocks and the Three Bears; Snow White and the Seven Dwarfs; Dick Whittington.* **TV:** *Billy Cotton's Band Show* (debut, 1963); *And So To Ted; Sunday Night At the London Palladium; Royal Variety Show; 3–2–1* (presenter, nine series); *Ted On the Spot; This Is Your Life* (subject, 1986). **Address:** c/o Clifford Elson Publicity. m. 1st Margie (dis), 2nd Marion; 3 d. Dena, Fenella (from 1st m.), Canna, 1 s. Danny.

ROSE, *clifford*

Clifford Rose. Actor. b. Hamnish, Herefordshire. **TV:** *The Roads To Freedom; Callan; Elizabeth R; The Lady From the Sea; Buccaneer; Strife; The Pallisers; How Green Was My Valley; Devil's Crown; Richard II;* Kessler in *Secret Army* and *Kessler; The Cold Room; A Married Man; Strangers and Brothers; Reilly – Ace of Spies; Oxbridge Blues; Love's Labour's Lost; One By One; The Mozart Inquest; Oedipus the King; Fortunes of War; Gentlemen and Players; Inspector Morse; Agatha Christie's Poirot; The Gibralta Inquest; War and Remembrance; GBH.* **Radio:** *Volpone; Henry IV; Macbeth; Tom Jones; Summer at Apendorf; Murder At the Red October; XPD; The Confidential Clerk; Scenes From an Execution* **Address:** c/o ICM. Lives in London. m. actress Celia Ryder; 1 d. Alison, 1 s. Jonathan. Hobbies: Travel gardening, music, languages. **Favourite TV programme:** *GBH.*

ROSENTHAL, *jim*

Jim Rosenthal. Sports presenter. b. Oxford, 6 November. Journalist with the *Oxford Mail* and *Times* then with BBC radio, before entering television. **TV:** *Saint & Greavsie; World of Sport; The Big Match Live; The London Match;* 1982 and 1986 *World Cup;* ITV athletics coverage; ITV boxing commentaries **Address:** c/o LWT/John Hockey Associates. m. Chrissy.

ROSS, *jonathan*

Jonathan Ross. Presenter. b. London, 17 November 1960. Researcher for TV game shows before becoming a presenter. **TV:** *Have Words; George Michael; The Last Resort; The Incredibly Strange Film Show; One Hour With Jonathan Ross; Tonight With Jonathan Ross; British Comedy Awards 1991* **Radio:** *Drug Alert.* **Address:** c/o Channel Four Television/Gary Farrow, Jonathan Ross Enterprises, Suite 3, 15 Clanricarde Gardens, London W2 4JJ, tel 071-727 6251. Lives in North London. m. Jane; 1 d Betty Kitten.

ROSS, *nick*

Nick Ross. Presenter. b. London, 7 August 1947. **TV:** *In Question; Scene Around Six* (both BBC Northern Ireland); *Man Alive Report; Out of Court; The Editors; Play for Today; Portrait of a 'Terrorist' Fair Comment; Did You See . . .?; Sixty Minutes; Horizon; Breakfast Time; Crimewatch UK; Watchdog A Week In Politics; Crimestoppers.* As producer: *The Fix; The Cure; Man Alive: The Biggest Epidemic Our Times.* As director: *Out of Court.* **Radio:** *Round-up Reports; Speaking Personally* (both BBC Northern Ireland); *The Price of Violence; Newsdesk; The World At One; The World This Weekend; The World Tonight; PM; Time for Action; Checkpoint; You the Jury; Any Questions; Call Nick Ross.* **Address:** c/o Jon Roseman Associates/BBC TV. m. Sarah; 3 s. Adam, Sam, Jack.

ROSSINGTON, *norman*

Norman Rossington. Actor. b. Liverpool, 24 December 1928. Acted as an amateur while working as a office boy at Liverpool docks, then trained at Bristol Old Vic Theatre School. **Theatre:** *In the Red; Midsummer Night's Dream* (Old Vic Theatre US tour, 1954); *Guys and Dolls.* **Films:** *Saturday Night and Sunday Morning; The Longest Day; A Hard Day's Night; Double Trouble; Tobruk; The Charge of the Light Brigade; Digby – The Biggest Dog In the World; Man In the Wilderness; Young Winston* **TV:** *Tracy and Me; The Army Game; Our House; Curry and Chips; The Misfit; Roads To Freedom; The Search for the Nile; Casanova; Hamlet; Lenin; Hunter's Walk; Crime of Passion; Comedy Playhouse Armchair Theatre; Village Hall; Budgie; Follow That Dog; Spooner's Patch; Big Jim and the Figaro Club.* **Address:** c/o Collis Management, 182 Trevelyan Road, London SW17 9LW, tel 081-767 0196.

ROTHWELL, *alan*

Alan Rothwell. Actor. b. Oldham, Lancashire, 9 February 1937. Trained at RADA. **Theatre:** *Otherwise Engaged; Bodies; Clouds; The Mating Game; A Delicate Balance; Bent; Guys and Dolls; Who's Afraid of Virginia Woolf?; Educating Rita; The Real Thing; The Pretty Lady; Brother Eichmann.* **Films:** *Two Living, One Dead; Linda; Nothing But the Best; Zeppelin.* **TV:** David Barlow in *Coronation Street* (1960–68); *Top Secret; Z-Cars; Hickory House; Daisy, Daisy; Picture Box* (presenter-writer-producer); *The Lie; Crown Court;* Nicholas Black in *Brookside; Angel Voices; All Creatures Great and Small; Children's Ward; How We Used To Live; Conspiracy of Cells; The Fool of the World and the Flying Ship; Sherlock Holmes: The Master Blackmailer.* **Radio:** Jimmy Grange in *The Archers.* **Address:** c/o Tobias Management. m. Maureen; 2 s. Toby, Ben.

ROUTLEDGE, *patricia*

Patricia Routledge. Actress. b. Birkenhead, Cheshire, 17 February. Trained at Bristol Old Vic Theatre School. **TV:** *Hobson's Choice; Victoria Regina; Z-Cars; Samson and Delilah; Sense and Sensibility; Tartuffe; David Copperfield; Nicholas Nickleby; Steptoe and Son; Jubilee: Plain Jane; The Cost of Loving; Crown Court; The Imitation Game; A Visit From Miss Protheroe; Green Forms; The Years Between; Doris and Doreen; A Woman of No Importance; The Beggar's Opera; The Two Ronnies; Victoria Wood As Seen On TV; Home Video; Marjorie and Men; When We Are Married; Tales of the Unexpected; Lady of Letters; Sophia and Constance; Talking Heads: A Lady of Letters; Five To Eleven; Let's Face the Music; First and Last; Missing Persons;* Hyacinth in *Keeping Up Appearances.* **Address:** c/o Marmont Management. Single; lives in Kensington, London.

ROWLANDS, *patsy*

Patsy Rowlands. Actress. b. London, 19 January 1934. Trained at Guildhall School of Music and Drama. **Films:** *A Kind of Loving; Carry On Again Doctor; Carry On Loving; Alice's Adventures In Wonderland; Bless This House; Please Sir!; Carry On Girls; Joseph Andrews; Tess; Little Lord Fauntleroy.* **TV:** *The Gamblers; In Loving Memory; Public Eye; Pinky; Arthur Through the Looking Glass; Pere Goriot; Inside George Webley; Imperial Palace; Kate; Bless This House; Follow That Dog; The Squirrels; Kinvig; Ladies; The History of Mr Polly; Juliet Bravo; Hallelujah; George and Mildred; Robin's Nest; Carry On Laughing; Mooncat and Company; The Little Princess; Charlie the Kid; Crimestrike; Rainbow; My Son, My Son; One By One; When We Are Married; Imaginary Friends.* **Address:** c/o Saraband Associates. m. Malcolm Sircom (dis); 1 s. Alan.

ROYLE, *carol*

Carol Royle. Actress. b. Blackpool, Lancashire, 10 February 1954. Daughter of actor Derek Royle and film make-up artist Jane Royle; sister of actress Amanda Royle. Trained at Central School of Speech and Drama. **Theatre:** *Come Blow Your Horn; The Breadwinner; Relatively Speaking* (RSC); *Hamlet* (winner, London Drama Critics Most Promising Actress award); *Troilus and Cressida; A Midsummer Night's Dream.* **Films:** *Tuxedo Warrior; Deadline.* **TV:** *The Cedar Tree; Blake's 7; The Professionals; Waxwork; Heartland; Girl Talk; The Racing Game; Possibilities; Shades of Darkness: Feet Foremost; The Outsider; Judgement Day; Bergerac; When the Walls Come Tumbling Down; Oxbridge Blues; A Still Small Shout; Ladies In Charge; Hedgehog Wedding; Life Without George; The London Embassy; Blackeyes.* **Address;** c/o Hutton Management. m. Julian Spear; 1 s. Taran.

RUSHTON, *willie*

William Rushton. Actor/Writer/Comedian. b. London, 18 August 1937. Previously a cartoonist and co-founder of *Private Eye.* **Theatre:** *The Private Eye Revue; Pass the Butler.* **Films:** *Flight of the Doves; Those Magnificent Men In Their Flying Machines; The Bliss of Mrs Blossom; Adventures of a Private Eye.* **TV:** *That Was the Week That Was; Not So Much a Programme, More a Way of Life; Don't Just Sit There; Up Sunday; Jackanory; Grubstreet; When Santa Rode the Prairie; Dawson and Friends; You Can Make It; Those Wonderful TV Times; Ask a Silly Answer; Open House; Star Turn Challenge; I'm Sorry, I Haven't a Clue; Wake Up Wizzy; The Day of the Grocer; Does the Team Think?; The Cobblers of Umbridge; The Kenny Everett Show.* **Address:** c/o Roger Hancock. m. actress Arlene Dorgan; 1 s. Tobias, 2 step-s. Matthew, Sam.

RUTTER, *barrie*

Barrie Rutter. Actor. b. Hull, East Yorkshire, 12 December 1946. Former member of the National Youth Theatre. **Theatre:** *Apprentices* (winner, London Critics Most Promising Actor award); repertory theatre in Nottingham; RSC; National Theatre. **Films:** *Porridge.* **TV:** *Apprentices; The Saint; Queenie's Castle; Our Kid; Bavarian Nights; Astronauts; The Oresteia; The Big H; Way Up Stream; The South Bank Show: Great Writers; Countdown To War.* **Address:** c/o Michelle Braidman Associates. m. author and university lecturer Dr Carol Rutter; 2 d. Briony, Rowan.

RYAN, *helen*

Helen Ryan. Actress. b. Liverpool, 16 June 1938. Trained at RADA. **Theatre:** *Madras House; The Cherry Orchard* (both National Theatre); *Terra Nova; Making Noise Quietly; Lettice and Lovage.* **Films:** *The Elephant Man.* **TV:** *Edward VII; Hannah; My Father's House; C.A.T.S. Eyes.* **Radio:** *A Room With a View.* **Address:** c/o Joyce Edwards. m. Guy Slater (dis); 1 s. Daniel, 1 d. Rebecca.

SACHS, *andrew*

Andrew Sachs. Actor/Writer/Narrator. b. Berlin, Germany, 7 April 1930. **Films:** *Romance With a Double Bass; Revenge of the Pink Panther; History of the World – Part 1.* **TV:** Manuel in *Fawlty Towers; James and the Giant Peach; Krek Bristle; Took & Co; Crown Court; Rising Damp; The Dawson Watch; Lovely Couple; The Tempest; The History of Mr Polly; This Is Your Life* (subject); *Dead Earnest; Play It Again; The Discovery of Animal Behaviour; The World About Us; The Natural World; Rainbow Safari; It'll All Be Over In Half An Hour; There Comes a Time; The Galactic Garden; Points of View; Architecture At the Crossroads; You Gotta Have Heart; When In Spain; Assert Yourself; Berliners; Bergerac; Supersense.* **Address:** c/o Richard Stone Partnership. m. actress Melody Lang; 1 d. Kate, 2 s. TV and radio presenter John, William.

SALEM, *pamela*

Pamela Salem. Actress. b. Bombay, India, 22 January. Trained at Central School of Speech and Drama. **Theatre:** *The Secretary Bird; Linden Tree; Night Cap; The Constant Wife; Phoenix Too Frequent; Romantic Comedy.* **Films:** *The Bitch;* Miss Moneypenny in *Never Say Never Again; Train To Murder; After Darkness; Salome; Succubus; God's Outlaw.* **TV:** *Jason King; The Onedin Line; Doctor Who; Blake's 7; Carnforth Practice; Sons and Daughters of Tomorrow; Into the Labyrinth; Seagull Island; Buccaneer; The Consultant; Tripods; Magnum PI; The Professionals; General Hospital; Crown Court; Strangers; All Creatures Great and Small; Lytton's Diary; Howards' Way; Boon; Ever Decreasing Circles;* Joanne in *EastEnders; French Fields; The Chain; El C.I.D; Fish In the Sky; The Paradise Club.* **Address:** c/o Burdett-Coutts Associates. m. actor Michael O'Hagan.

SALIH, *nejdet*

Nejdet Salih. Actor. b. London, 23 December 1958. Trained at Mountview Theatre School. **Theatre:** *Old Tyme Music Hall.* **TV:** *The Brief; Auf Wiedersehen, Pet; West;* Ali Osman in *EastEnders.* **Address:** c/o Ken McReddie. m. Sue; 1 d. Sophia.

SALLIS, *peter*

Peter Sallis. Actor. b. Twickenham, Middlesex, 1 February 1921. Trained at RADA. **Films:** *The Mouse On the Moon; The VIPs; Anastasia.* **TV:** *Into the Dark; How To Murder Your Wife; The Big Eat; Public Eye; Spider's Web; The Moonstone; The Diary of Samuel Pepys; Barlow; The Pallisers; Softly, Softly; The Flaxborough Chronicles; Yanks Go Home; A Crowded Room; Leave It To Charlie; Daedelus Equations; Cleggy in Last of the Summer Wine; Murder Most English; Raffles; The Obelisk; Across a Crowded Room; You're Not Watching Me Mummy; She Loves Me; Tales of the Unexpected; Ladykillers; The Kamikaze Ground Staff's Reunion Dinner; Strangers and Brothers; Mountain Men; Lucy Walker; The Bretts; The New Statesman; Come Home Charlie and Face Them.* **Address:** c/o ICM Duncan Heath Associates. m. actress Elaine Usher (divorced and remarried); 1 s. Crispian.

SALTHOUSE, *john*

John Salthouse. Actor/Writer. b. London, 16 June 1951. Professional footballer before training at LAMDA. **Theatre:** *Man Is Man; Abigail's Party; Ten Times Table; Red Saturday.* With National Theatre: *The Long Voyage Home; The Iceman Cometh; Dispatches; The Shoemaker's Holiday.* **Films:** *A Bridge Too Far; An American Werewolf In London; Give My Regards To Broad Street; Prick Up Your Ears.* **TV:** *Man Above Men; Not Quite Cricket; The Bill; Abigail's Party; Glamour Night; Making Out; The Ruth Rendell Mysteries: From Doon With Death.* **Address:** c/o PTA. m. actress Heather Tobias; 1 s. William.

SANDERSON, *joan*

Joan Sanderson. Actress. b. Bristol, Avon, 24 November 1912. Trained at RADA. **Theatre:** *See How They Run* (Whitehall Theatre); *When We Are Married* (National Theatre); *Anyone for Denis?* (Whitehall Theatre). **Films:** *Please Sir!; The Muppet Movie; Prick Up Your Ears.* **TV:** *All Gas and Gaiters; Well, Anyway . . .;* Miss Ewell in *Please Sir!; Upstairs, Downstairs; Jubilee; The Ghosts of Motley Hall; Rising Damp; Ripping Yarns; Fawlty Towers; Mixed Blessings; How's Your Father?; Barriers; The Janet Brown Show; The Kelly Monteith Show; The Other 'Arf; All for Love; Play for Today: Intensive Care; House of Withering Death; Anyone for Denis?; Me & My Girl; Faint Hearted Feminist; East of Ipswich; Full House;* Mother in *After Henry; The Emma Thompson Show; Land of Hope and Gloria.* **Radio:** Mother in *After Henry.* **Address;** c/o Bryan Drew. m. Gregory Scott.

SAUNDERS, *jennifer*

Jennifer Saunders. Actress/Comedienne. b. Sleaford, Lincolnshire, 12 July 1958. Trained at Central School of Speech and Drama, where she met and teamed up with Dawn French, touring in cabaret, starting at the Comedy Store, London. **Theatre:** *An Evening With French and Saunders* (also co-directed); *The Secret Policeman's Biggest Ball.* **Films:** *The Comic Strip Presents . . . : Supergrass.* **TV:** *Five Go Mad In Dorset; Five Go Mad On Mescalin; Slags; Summer School; Private Enterprise; Consuela; Mr Jolly Lives Next Door; Bad News Tour; Strike; South Atlantic Raiders; G.L.C.; Oxford; Spaghetti Hoops; Le Kiss* (all *The Comic Strip Presents . . .* productions); *Girls On Top; Happy Families; French and Saunders; The Storyteller: Sapsorrow.* **Books:** *A Feast of French & Saunders.* **Address:** c/o Peters Fraser & Dunlop. m. Adrian Edmondson; 2 d.

SAVAGE, *fred*

Fred Savage. Actor. b. Highland Park, Illinois, USA, 9 July 1976. **Films:** *The Boy Who Could Fly; The Princess Bride; Vice Versa; Little Monsters; The Wizard.* **TV:** *Convicted: A Mother's Story; Video Madness; Run Til You Fall* (all TV movies); Kevin in *The Wonder Years; Runaway Ralph; The Twilight Zone.*

SAVALAS, *telly*

Telly Savalas. Actor. b. Garden City, New York, USA, 21 January 1925. **Films:** *The Birdman of Alcatraz; The Slender Thread; Beau Geste; The Dirty Dozen; The Dirty Dozen III; On Her Majesty's Secret Service; The Border.* **TV:** Title role in *Kojak; The Equalizer; J J Starbuck; Alice In Wonderland.* **Address:** c/o International Creative Management. m. 4th Julie; 3 d. Christina, Candace, Ariana, 2 s. Nicholas, Christian.

SAVILE, *sir jimmy*

James Savile. Presenter. b. Leeds, 3 October 1926. Knighted, 1990. Worked as a miner and managed a dance-hall, before entering showbusiness. **TV:** *Savile's Travels; Top of the Pops; Jim'll Fix It.* **Books:** *As It Happens* (autobiography); *Love Is an Uphill Thing; God'll Fix It.* **Address:** c/o BBC TV/National Spinal Injuries Centre, Stoke Mandeville Hospital, Mandeville Road, Aylesbury, Buckinghamshire HP21 8AL.

SAWALHA, *julia*

Julia Sawalha. Actress. b. London. Trained at the Italia Conti Academy. **Theatre:** *Voyage of the Dawntreader; The Silver Chair; Peter Pan.* **Films:** Chrissy in *Buddy's Song.* **TV:** *Absolutely Fabulous; Casualty; El C.I.D;* Lynda in *Press Gang; How Others See Us; The Outing; Inspector Morse; Spatz; The Keeper; Ghost Train* (guest presenter); *Second Thoughts.* **Address:** c/o A.I.M.

SAYLE, *alexei*

Alexei Sayle. Actor/Comedian. b. Liverpool, 7 August 1952. Attended Southport and Chelsea Schools of Art. **Films:** *Gorky Park; The Bride; Supergrass; Whoops Apocalypse; Love Child; Indiana Jones and the Last Crusade; Reckless Kelly.* **TV:** *OTT; The Young Ones; Whoops Apocalypse; Give Us a Break; Upline; Doctor Who; The Caucasian Chalk Circle; Les Girls; City Tails; Didn't You Kill My Brother?; Love Child; The Strike; Comic Roots; Alexei Sayle's Stuff; Spaghetti Hoops; Le Kiss; Night Voice; 4-Play: Itch; Small World; Selling Hitler; The Gravy Train Goes East.* Writer: *The Young Ones; Arena: The History of the Ford Cortina; Great Bus Journeys of the World; Comic Roots; Didn't You Kill My Brother?* **Address:** c/o Mayer Management. Lives in London. m. Linda. Pets: Cat called Dexter. **Favourite TV programme:** Tour de France cycling coverage.

SCALES, *prunella*

Prunella Scales. Actress. b. Sutton Abinger, Surrey, 22 June 1932. Trained at the Old Vic Theatre School and with Uta Hagen in New York. **Theatre:** *When We Are Married; Single Spies; Queen Victoria: Evening At Osborne.* **Films:** *The Hound of the Baskervilles; The Boys From Brazil; Wagner; The Wicked Lady; Hobson's Choice; The Lonely Passion of Judith Hearne; A Chorus of Disapproval.* **TV:** Eileen Hughes in *Coronation Street; Marriage Lines;* Sybil Fawlty in *Fawlty Towers; Target; Bergerac; Jackanory; Queen Victoria: Evening at Osborne; Never the Twain; Slimming Down; Mapp & Lucia; Beyond the Pale;* Sarah in *After Henry; Kennet and Avon* (presenter); Elizabeth II in *A Question of Attribution* (TV movie). **Address:** c/o Jeremy Conway. Lives in South London. m. actor Timothy West; 2 s. actor Samuel, Joseph.

SCANNELL, *tony*

ony Scannell. Actor. b. Kinsale, Co Cork, Ireland, 14 August 1945. After leaving the RAF, trained at the ast 15 Acting School and Theatre Workshop. **Theatre:** Work in repertory theatre and at the National heatre; *The Plough and the Stars; A Streetcar Named Desire* (both as director). **Films:** *Flash Gordon; lue Money; Cheap Perfume.* **TV:** *The Gentle Touch; Cribb; All the Fun of the Fair; Little Lord ountleroy; Up the Elephant; Flying Lady;* Det Sgt Ted Roach in *The Bill.* **Address:** c/o ICM. Lives in ondon. m. (dis); 1 s. Sean. Hobbies: Golf, music, cycling.

SCHMID, *kristian*

ristian Schmid. Actor. b. Australia, 28 November 1974. Trained at the Actors' Training Studio. **heatre:** *Mother Goose* (Britain). **TV:** Todd Landers in *Neighbours* (1988-). **Address:** c/o Grundy elevision. Single; lives in Geelong and Melbourne.

SCHOFIELD, *phillip*

hillip Schofield. Presenter. b. Oldham, Lancashire, 1 April 1962. Emigrated to New Zealand with his arents, where he entered television. **Theatre:** *Joseph and the Amazing Technicolor Dreamcoat* (London est End). **TV:** *Shazam; Music Awards* (both in New Zealand); *Children's BBC; Saturday Superstore; ake Two; Newsround; Royal Variety Performance; Going Live!; Schofield's Europe; Children In Need eport; Disney Time.* **Radio:** Capital Radio; BBC Radio 1. **Address:** c/o James Grant Management.

SCOTT, *brough*

rough Scott. Racing presenter. b. London, 12 December 1942. Professional National Hunt jockey 1962–71), before entering television. **TV:** *Something To Brighten the Morning; The Derby Stakes; The hallenge of the Sexes; Sporting Chance; Thames Sport;* ITV racing coverage; Channel 4 Racing. **ooks:** *The World of Flat Racing; On and Off the Rails.* **Address:** c/o LWT/Racing Post, 120 Coombe ane, Raynes Park, London SW20 0BA. m. former British skier Susie McInnes; 2 d. Sophie, Tessa, 2 s. harlie, Jamie.

SCOTT, *mike*

Michael Scott. Presenter. b. London, 8 December 1932. Began career as a stagehand with the Festival allet, before joining the Rank Organisation as a production trainee, then Granada TV as a floor nanager, then director. **TV:** *Scene At 6.30; Cinema; World In Action; Granada* TV programme controller 1979–87); *The Time, The Place.* **Address:** c/o Thames Television. m. Sylvia; 1 d. Julia.

SCOTT, *terry*

Terry Scott. Actor/Comedian. b. Watford, Hertfordshire, 4 May 1927. **Theatre:** Repertory theatre Grange-over-Sands; *Great Scott, It's Maynard* (with Bill Maynard); *The Mating Game; A Bedfu. Foreigners.* **Films:** *The Bridal Path; Carry On Up the Khyber; Carry On Camping; Carry On Hei Carry On Up the Jungle; Carry On Loving; Carry On Matron; Bless This House.* **TV:** *Hugh and I; Gnomes of Dulwich; The Scott On ...; Panto; The Good Old Days; Son of the Bride; Happy Ever Afi Terry and June.* **Address:** c/o Richard Stone Partnership. Lives in Surrey. m. 1st (dis), 2nd former ba dancer Margaret Pollen; 4 d. Sarah, Nicola, Lindsay, Alexandra.

SEAGROVE, *jenny*

Jenny Seagrove. Actress. b. Kuala Lumpur. **Theatre:** *Jane Eyre.* **Films:** *Local Hero; Savage Islands Shocking Accident; Moonlighting; To Hell and Back In Time for Breakfast; Tattoo; Appointment V Death; A Chorus of Disapproval; The Guardian.* **TV:** *The Brack Report; The Woman In White; Dia Crown Court; Three Men In a Boat; A Woman of Substance; Mask of the Devil; Hold the Dream; Sign of Four; In Like Flynn; Killer; Lucy Walker; Mountain Men; The Betrothed; Magic Moments; So Other Spring* (TV movie); *The Eye of the Beholder; Sherlock Holmes and the Incident At Victoria Fa* **Address:** c/o London Management.

SECOMBE, *sir harry, CBE*

Harry Secombe. Presenter/Comedian. b. Swansea, West Glamorgan, 8 September 1921. Made a CBE 1963; knighted in 1981. **Films:** *Helter Skelter; Penny Points To Paradise; Down Among the Z M. Forces Sweetheart; Svengali Jet Storm; Davy; Oliver!; The Bed-Sitting Room; Song of Norw Rhubarb; Doctor In Trouble; The Magnificent Seven Deadly Sins; Sunstruck.* **TV:** *The Harry Secom Show; Secombe and Friends; Sing a Song of Secombe; Fall In the Stars; Have a Harry Christmas; H. a Harry Birthday; Harry Secombe's World of Music; Easter Story; Captain Beaky and His Ba Secombe With Music; Highway.* **Radio:** *Variety Bandbox; Welsh Rarebit; Educating Archie; The Go Show.* **Address:** c/o 46 St James's Place, London SW1. Lives in Surrey. m. Myra; 2 d. Jennifer, Katy s. actor Andrew, David.

SEED, *graham*

Graham Seed. Actor. b. London, 12 July 1950. Trained at RADA. **Theatre:** Repertory theatre Manchester; Chichester Festival; Mole in *Toad of Toad Hall;* Gerald in *Me and My Girl; Tons of Mor* (national tour). **TV:** *I, Claudius; Who's Who; Brideshead Revisited; Bergerac; Edward VII; CAB; Go and Bad At Games* (Channel Four film); *Crossroads; Ashenden; The Upper Hand.* **Radio:** *Summ Lightning;* Nigel Pargetter in *The Archers.* **Address:** c/o Saraband Associates. m. Clare Colvin; 1 Nicola, 1 s. Toby.

SELBY, *david*

David Selby. Actor. b. Morgantown, West Virginia, USA, 5 February 1941. **Films:** *Rich and Famous; the Sandbox; Super Cops; Rich Kids; Raise the Titanic.* **TV:** *Dark Shadows; The Waltons; Kojak; Fam Washington Behind Closed Doors; Flamingo Road; Knightrider;* Richard Channing in *Falcon Cre* **Address:** c/o William Morris Agency (USA). m. Chip; 1 s. Todd, 2 d. Brooke, Amanda.

SELBY, *tony*

Tony Selby. Actor. b. Lambeth, London, 26 February 1938. Trained at the Italia Conti Academy. **Films:** The Queen's Guards; Press for Time; Witchfinder General; Alfie; Villain; Before Winter Comes; Adolf Hitler – My Part In His Downfall; Nobody Ordered Love. **TV:** The Changeling; A Tap On the Shoulder; Three Clear Sundays; Up the Junction; Silent Song; Another Day, Another Dollar, A Night Out; The Devil a Monk Would Be; The Hard Word; The Gentleman Caller; The Inquisitors; Present Laughter; The Informer; The Break; Ace of Wands; A Touch of the Tiny Hackets; Get Some In; Cockles; Antigone; Hideaway; Glitz in Doctor Who; The Good Life; The Sweeney; Minder; Lady Is a Tramp; C.A.T.S. Eyes; Bergerac; Casualty; The 19th Hole; Lovejoy; Love Hurts. **Address:** c/o A.I.M. m. 1st (dis), 2nd Gina Sellers; 1 d. Samantha, 1 s. Matthew (both from 1st m.).

SELLECK, *tom*

Tom Selleck. Actor. b. Detroit, Michigan, USA, 29 January 1945. Studied drama at Valley College. **Films:** Myra Breckenridge; High Road To China; Lassiter; Three Men and a Baby; An Innocent Man; Quigley Down Under. **TV:** The Young and the Restless; The Rockford Files; title role in Magnum PI. **Address:** McCartt-Oreck-Barrett. m. 1st Jacki Ray (dis), 2nd actress Jilly Mack; 1 step-s. Kevin (from 1st m.), 1 d. Hannah.

SERLE, *chris*

Chris Serle. Presenter. b. Bristol, Avon, 13 July 1943. Began career as an actor with Bristol Old Vic Theatre, before entering radio and television. **TV:** That's Life!; In At the Deep End; Medical Express; Sixty Minutes; Windmill; People; Wordpower; The Computer Programme; Greek Language and People; Friday Now. **Radio:** Petticoat Line; Brain of Britain; Late Night Extra (all as producer). **Address:** c/o Curtis Brown/BBC TV. m. Anna; 2 s. Harry, Jack.

SEYMOUR, *jane*

Joyce Frankenberg. Actress. b. Hillingdon, Middlesex, 15 February 1951. Former dancer with the London Festival Ballet (aged 13). **Films:** Oh! What a Lovely War; Young Winston; Live and Let Die; Battlestar Galactica. **TV:** The Strauss Family; The Pathfinders; The Onedin Line; The Double Deckers; Frankenstein: The True Story; The Leather Funnel; The Hanged Man; Our Mutual Friend; King David; Captains and Kings; Benny and Barney; Las Vegas Undercover; Seventh Avenue; Killer On Board; Seventh Avenue; The Four Feathers; The Awakening Land; Love's Dark Ride; Dallas Cowboys; East of Eden; The Haunting Passion; Jamaica Inn; The Sun Also Rises; The Dark Mirror; Obsessed With a Married Woman; Crossings; War and Remembrance; The Woman He Loved; Onassis; Jack the Ripper; The French Revolution. **Address:** c/o London Management.

SHABAN, *nabil*

Nabil Shaban. Actor. b. Jordan, 1953. Crippled from birth with brittle bones and confined to a wheelchair. Formed the Graeae Theatre Company of Disabled Performers with Richard Tomlinson in 1980. **Films:** The Dwarf in Born of Fire; City of Joy; Deptford Graffiti. **TV:** Handicapped Person In the Community; The Breakthrough; Reports Action (wrote and presented appeal for the International Year of Disabled People); Walter; The Skin Horse (wrote and starred, winning RTS award for most innovative documentary of 1983); Where There's Life . . . (guest); Sil in Doctor Who; Bandung File; South of the Border; Raspberry Ripple. **Radio:** The Birth of Jesus (writer-narrator, cowboy musical version of the Nativity); Was the Cross (writer-narrator); six-part BBC World Service series on Mahatma Gandhi in Reflections series (writer-presenter). **Address:** c/o A.I.M.

SHAKESBY, *patricia*

Patricia Shakesby. Actress. b. Cottingham, East Yorkshire, 6 November 1942. **Theatre:** Repertory theatre; *The Real Inspector Hound*; *Night of the Iguana*; *Suddenly At Home* (all London West End); *Romeo and Juliet*; *Hamlet*; *Troilus and Cressida*; *Love Girl and the Innocent*; *La Ronde* (all RSC). **TV:** Susan Cunningham in *Coronation Street*; *Z-Cars*; *Saturday While Sunday*; *War and Peace*; *Crime and Punishment*; *Late Starter*; *Sapphire and Steel*; *Yes Minister*; *The Pity of It All*; *Flowering Cherry*; Poll Urquhart in *Howards' Way*. **Address:** c/o Roger Carey Management. m. (dis).

SHANE, *paul*

Paul Shane. Actor. b. Rotherham, South Yorkshire, 19 June 1940. An amateur stand-up comic in Northern clubs while working as a miner, before turning professional. **Theatre:** *Hi-de-Hi!* **TV:** *Sounding Brass*; *Turtle's Progress*; *Muck and Brass*; *The Generation Game*; *Coronation Street*; Ted Bovis in *Hi-de-Hi!*; *This Is Your Life* (subject); *You Rang, M'Lord*; *Very Big Very Soon*. **Address:** c/o ATS Casting. m. Dory; 3 d. Janice, Andrea, Gillian.

SHANNON, *johnny*

John Shannon. Actor. b. Lambeth, South London, 29 July 1932. **TV:** *The Gold Robbers*; *Dixon of Dock Green*; *Z-Cars*; *Budgie*; *The Operation*; *Go for Gold*; *The Donati Conspiracy*; *Never Mind the Quality Feel the Width*; *Beryl's Lot*; *The XYY Man*; *The Sweeney*; *Old Dog With New Tricks*; *Pursuit*; *The Other One*; *The Losers*; *Hazell and the Greasy Gunners*; *Fawlty Towers*; *The Enigma File*; *Minder*; *Secret Army*; *Tales of the Unexpected: Man At the Top*; *Angels*; *The Chinese Detective*; *The Professionals*; *Union Castle*; *The Boy Who Won the Pools*; *Watch All Night*; *Give Us a Break*; *Keep It In the Family*; *Big Deal*; *Supergran*; *The Bright Side*; *Keeping Score*; *Queenie*; *Coast To Coast*; *Bust*; *High Street Blues*; Alfie Phillips in *EastEnders*. **Address:** c/o Chatto and Linnit. Lives in Bexleyheath, Kent. m. Rose; 1 s. Gary, 1 d. Terry. Hobbies: Boxing, horse-racing.

SHARP, *andrew*

Andrew Sharp. Actor. b. Sydney, Australia, 26 May 1953. **Theatre:** Artful Dodger in *Oliver!*; Brad Majors in *The Rocky Horror Show*; *Hamlet*; *As You Like It* (all in Australia); *Beyond the Rainbow*; *Stage Struck*; *Deathtrap*; *Men* (all London West End). **Films:** *Summer of Secrets*; *Buddies*; *Undercover*. **TV:** *Shannon's Mob*; *Homicide*; *Bobby Dazzler*; *Tenko*; *Taurus Rising*; *Glass Babies*; *Sword of Honour*; Andrew Baxter in *the Young Doctors*. **Address:** c/o International Casting Service.

SHARPE, *lesley-anne*

Lesley-Anne Maria Sharpe. Actress. b. Liverpool, 28 December 1964. Trained at Liverpool Theatre School and Arts Educational School. **Theatre:** *Annie* (Victoria Palace Theatre); *Stars of Tomorrow*; *Babes In the Wood*; title role in *The Snow Queen*; *Jack and the Beanstalk*; Brenda in *Watching* (Octagon Theatre, Bolton, and national tour); *Tracey and the Troyboy*. **TV:** *Boys From the Blackstuff*; Dawn Finney in *Brookside*; Carol in *Coronation Street*; *Albion Market*; Harriet Mills in *What Now?*; Debbie Yates in *Boon* (second series); *Harry Enfield Show*; Joey's girlfriend in *Bread*; *The Bill*; Marie Jenson in *EastEnders*. **Address:** c/o Elaine Murphy Associates. Single; lives in Tottenham, North London. Hobbies: Watching Everton FC, football in general, British motorbikes, going to ballet. **Favourite TV programme:** *Match of the Day*.

SHARROCK, *ian*

Ian Sharrock. Actor. b. Harrogate, North Yorkshire, 20 December 1959. Trained at the Corona Academy from the age of 11. **Theatre:** Max in *Lend Me a Tenor;* Harry Thunder in *Wild Oats* (opening production at the West Yorkshire Playhouse); *Relatively Speaking; Mixed Blessings.* **Films:** *Candleshoe.* **TV:** Title role in *Smike; Peter Pan;* Rhodes in *Scum; Play for Love: Games;* Jackie Merrick in *Emmerdale Farm* (1980–89); *She-Wolf of London.* **Address:** c/o Susan Angel Associates. Lives in Chelmsford, Essex. m. Pamela; 1 d. Natalie, 1 s. William. Pets: Labrador cross called Barney, cats called Tom and Billy. Hobbies: Golf. **Favourite TV programme:** *The World About Us.*

SHATNER, *william*

William Shatner. Actor/Director. b. Montreal, Canada, 22 March 1931. Studied law at university. **Theatre:** Repertory theatre; Stratford Shakespeare Festival, Ontario. **Films:** *Star Trek – The Motion Picture; Star Trek II: The Wrath of Khan; Star Trek III: The Search for Spock; Star Trek IV: The Voyage Home; Star Trek V: The Final Frontier; Star Trek VI: The Undiscovered Country; The Brothers Karamazov; The Intruder; The Outrage; Big Bad Mama; Judgement At Nuremberg; Airplane II.* **TV:** Captain Kirk in *Star Trek; Go Ask Alice; The Horror At 37,000 Feet; Beachwood and Rawhide; Saturday Night Live; Barbary Coast;* title role in *T J Hooker.* m. 1st Gloria Ranel, 2nd Marcy Lafferty; 3 d. Leslie, Lisabeth, Melanie (all from 1st m.).

SHAW, *martin*

Martin Shaw. Actor. b. Birmingham, 21 January 1945. Worked as a sales clerk, before training at LAMDA. **Theatre:** *Are You Lonesome Tonight?* (Phoenix Theatre and Australia). **Films:** *Macbeth; The Golden Voyage of Sinbad; Operation Daybreak; Ladder of Swords.* **TV:** *Travelling Light; Doctor At Large; Villains; Hamlet; Achilles Heel; Helen – A Woman of Today; Love's Labour's Lost; The Explorers; Electra; Spice Island Farewell; Z-Cars; Sutherland's Law; Beasts; Buddyboy; The Duchess of Duke Street; Our Kid; Exiles; The New Avengers;* Doyle in *The Professionals;* Jack Butcher in *Cream In My Coffee; Face Lift; East Lynne; The Hound of the Baskervilles;* Captain Scott in *The Last Place On Earth; The Most Dangerous Man In the World; Who Bombed Birmingham?* **Address:** c/o Hutton Management. m. Maggie; 2 s. Luke, Joe, 2 d. Sophie, Kate.

SHELLEY, *cindy*

Cindy Shelley. Actress. b. Barnet, Hertfordshire, 23 March 1960. Trained at New School of Speech and Drama. **Theatre:** *A Taste of Honey; Magic.* **TV:** *Going To Work; Cockles; Long Live the Babe; Tenko; Tenko Reunion;* Abby Howard in *Howards' Way.* **Address:** c/o The Brunskill Management. m. Philip; 1 d. Hannah.

SHEPHERD, *jack*

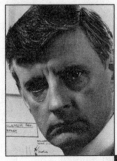

Jack Shepherd. Actor/Director/Writer. b. Leeds, 29 October 1940. Trained at The Drama Centre. **TV:** *Full House; Bill Brand; Through the Night; Mr and Mrs Bureaucrat; The Devil's Crown; The Killing; Nina; Underdog; Sons and Lovers; A Room for the Winter; The Mysteries; Hard Travelling; The Holy City; Escape From Sobibor; Scoop; Bulman; The Party; Pastoral Care; The Hospice; Cracking Up; Body Contact; Blind Justice; A Day In Summer; The Murderers Are Among Us; The Act; Omnibus: Vincent Van Gogh; Crimestrike; Nobody Here But Us Chickens; Ball-Trap On the Cote Sauvage; Simon Wiesenthal – A Murderer Among Us; Misterioso; Woman At War; Shoot To Kill; Tales From Hollywood.* **Address:** c/o Markham & Froggatt. m. 1st Judy Harland (dis), 2nd Ann Scott; 1 d. Jan, 1 s. Jake (from 1st m.), 2 twin d. Victoria, Catherine, 1 s. Ben (all from 2nd m.).

SHERIDAN, *dinah*

Dinah Sheridan. Actress. b. Hampstead Garden Suburb, North London, 17 September 1920. Trained at the Italia Conti Academy. **Theatre:** *Where the Rainbow Ends.* **Films:** *Irish and Proud of It; Full Speed Ahead; Salute John Citizen; For You Alone; Hills of Donegal; Calling Paul Temple; The Story of Shirley Yorke; Paul Temple's Triumph; Where No Vultures Fly; Genevieve; The Railway Children; The Mirror Crack'd.* **TV:** *Picture Page* (first regular BBC TV broadcast, October 1936); *Gallows Glorious; Winning Streak; Don't Wait Up; Keeping Up Appearances.* **Address:** c/o ICM. m. 1st actor Jimmy Hanley (dis), 2nd film producer-director John Davis (dis), 3rd John Merivale (dec); 1 d. actress-TV presenter Jenny Hanley.

SIKKING, *james b*

James B Sikking. Actor. b. Los Angeles, USA, 5 March 1934. Gained a BA in theatre arts from University of California Los Angeles. **Theatre:** *The Big Knife.* **Films:** *The Terminal Man; Outland; Von Ryan's Express; Scorpio; The Magnificent Seven; The Electric Horseman; Ordinary People; Star Chamber; Star Trek III: The Search for Spock; Soul Man.* **TV:** *Charlie's Angels; The Incredible Hulk; Starsky and Hutch; M*A*S*H; Turnabout; General Hospital;* Lieutenant Howard Hunter in *Hill Street Blues; Dress Grey.* TV movies: *The Jesse Owens Story; First Steps; Bay Coven.* **Address:** c/o McCartt-Oreck-Barrett. m. Florine; 1 s. Andrew, 1 d. Emily.

SILVERA, *carmen*

Carmen Silvera. Actress. b. Toronto, Canada, 2 June. Trained at LAMDA (winner Bronze, Silver and Gold Medals). **Theatre:** *Serious Change; Let's Get a Divorce; Torrents of Spring; People Are Living There; On the Rocks; Waters of the Moon; Hobson's Choice; A Coat of Varnish* (all London West End); *'Allo 'Allo!* **TV:** *Z-Cars;* Camilla Hope in *Compact; Beggar My Neighbour; New Scotland Yard; Sergeant Cork; Doctor Who; Dad's Army; Two Women; Within These Walls; The Gentle Touch; Before Water Lilies; Lillie; Whoops Apocalypse; Maggie and Her; Tales of the Unexpected;* Edith Artois in *'Allo 'Allo!* **Address:** c/o Barry Burnett Organisation. Lives in London. m. (dis). Hobbies: Travel, watching athletics, golf, tennis, painting, reading, cooking. **Favourite TV programme:** Most wildlife programmes; *Coronation Street; Agatha Christie's Poirot.*

SIMS, *joan*

Joan Sims. Actress. b. Laindon, Essex, 9 May 1930. Trained at RADA. **Films:** *Colonel March Investigates; The Belles of St Trinian's; Doctor In Clover; Doctor In Trouble; The Magnificent Seven Deadly Sins; The Garnett Saga; Not Now, Darling;* 24 *Carry On* films; *Love Among the Ruins; One of Our Dinosaurs Is Missing; Don't Just Lie There, Say Something!* **TV:** *Carry On Christmas; Till Death Us Do Part; The Way of the World; The Dick Emery Show; Sykes; The Howerd Confessions; The Two Ronnies; Lord Tramp; East Lynne; Your Move; Born and Bred; Worzel Gummidge; In Loving Memory; Ladykillers; Virginia Fly Is Drowning; Waters of the Moon; Crown Court; Poor Little Rich Girls; Cockles; A Murder Is Announced; Hay Fever; Deceptions; Farrington of the FO; Tickle On the Tum; Simon and the Witch; Only Fools and Horses; The Victoria Wood Show; On the Up.* **Address:** c/o MGA.

SINDEN, *donald, CBE*

Donald Sinden. Actor. b. Plymouth, Devon, 9 October 1923. Brother of actor Leon Sinden (qv). Trained at the Webber Douglas Academy. **Films:** *The Cruel Sea; Doctor In the House; The Beachcomber; Eyewitness; Doctor At Large; The Captain's Table; Operation Bullshine; Your Money Or Your Wife; Twice Round the Daffodils; Mix Me a Person; Decline and Fall; Villain; Rentadick; The National Health; The Day of the Jackal; The Island At the Top of the World.* **TV:** *Bullet In the Ballet; Our Man From St Mark's; The Organisation; Two's Company; Discovering English Churches; All's Well That Ends Well; Present Laughter; Never the Twain; The Rivals.* **Books:** *A Touch of the Memoirs; Laughter In the Second Act* (autobiographies); *The English Country Church.* **Address:** c/o Michael Whitehall. m. Diana Mahony; 2 s. actors Jeremy (qv), Marc (qv).

SINDEN, *jeremy*

Jeremy Mahony Sinden. Actor/Producer/Director. b. London, 14 June 1950. Son of actor Donald Sinden (qv); brother of actor Marc Sinden (qv). Trained at LAMDA (won the Forsyth Award). **TV:** *The Expert; The Sweeney; Crossroads; Danger UXB; For Maddie With Love; Brideshead Revisited; Number Ten; Holding the Fort; Never the Twain; Squadron; The Far Pavilions; Chance In a Million; Fairly Secret Army; Lytton's Diary; Mountbatten – The Last Viceroy; Three Up, Two Down; Robin of Sherwood; All at No 20; Bergerac; Fortunes of War; The Management; After the War; Square Deal; Don't Wait Up.* **Address:** c/o ICM. Lives in London. m. Delia Lindsay; 2 d. Kezia, Harriet. Pets: Dog, goldfish, snails. Hobbies: Croquet, tennis, long-distance walking, driving, train travel, photography, tree-climbing. **Favourite TV programme:** *Around the World in 80 Days.*

SINDEN, *leon*

Leon Fuller Sinden. Actor. b. Ditchling, East Sussex, 20 July 1927. Brother of actor Donald Sinden (qv). Began career in MESA, a Brighton-based ENSA group, in 1941. **Theatre:** *Pygmalion; Romanoff and Juliet; The Spider's Web; Brides On March; Ross* (Haymarket Theatre); Stratford-upon-Avon RSC season; *Semi-Detached* (Broadway); seven seasons with the Pitlochry Festival Theatre Company; *Entertaining Mr Sloane; London Assurance* (Broadway); *Relapse; Charley's Aunt; Jamie the Sax; Macbeth; Mr Gillie; The Wallace.* **TV:** Uncle Roderick in *Scoop; Rebecca; Assassination Run; Taggart;* Mr Carradine in *Take the High Road.* **Address:** Tel 081–209 0660 (London) or (0738) 26466 (Perth). Single; lives in London and Perth. Pets: Three-legged cat. Hobbies: Auctions, holidays, music. **Favourite TV programme:** Opera and archaeology programmes.

SINDEN, *marc*

Marcus Sinden. Actor. b. London, 9 May 1954. Son of actor Donald Sinden (qv); brother of actor Jeremy Sinden (qv). Trained at Bristol Old Vic Theatre School. **Films:** *Clash of Loyalties; The Wicked Lady; White Nights; Manges d'Hommes.* **TV:** *Dick Turpin; If you Go Down To the Woods Today; Bergerac; Home Front; Strange But True; Crossroads; Magnum PI; All At No 20; Never the Twain; Rumpole of the Bailey; Wolf To the Slaughter; Fiddlers Green; Oratory; The Country Boy.* **Address:** c/o Jo Gilbert's Associates. m. Joanne; 1 s. Henry, 1 d. Bridie.

SINER, *guy*

Guy Siner. Actor. b. New York City, USA, 16 October 1947. Trained at the Webber Douglas Academy. **Theatre:** *Cowardy Custard; Off the Peg; Nickleby and Me; Biograph Girl; Toad of Toad Hall; The Frogs; Wealth; 'Allo 'Allo!* Tours: *Blithe Spirit; The Master Builder; The Relapse; An Inspector Calls; Uncle Vanya; The Sunshine Boys; Barefoot In the Park; How the Other Half Loves; Noel and Gertie; Peg O' My Heart.* Regional: *Out of Bounds; Off the Peg; Joseph; Habeas Corpus; Black Comedy; Comedy of Errors; Party Piece.* **TV:** *I Claudius; Life At Stake; Secret Army; Softly, Softly, Z-Cars; Doctor Who;* Gruber in *'Allo 'Allo!;* Noel Coward in *You Rang, M'Lord?* **Radio:** *When In Germany* (presenter). Winner, Rodney Millington Award, 1971. **Address:** c/o Barry Burnett Organisation. Lives in London. **Favourite TV programme:** *Cheers.*

SINGLETON, *valerie*

Valerie Singleton. Presenter. b. Hitchin, Hertfordshire, 9 April 1937. Won scholarship to RADA, acted in repertory theatre and worked on TV advertising magazines, before joining BBC TV as an announcer. **TV:** *Blue Peter; Blue Peter Special Assignments; Blue Peter Royal Safari; Val Meets the VIPs; Nationwide; Tonight; The Money Programme.* **Radio:** *PM.* **Address:** c/o Arlington Enterprises.

SISSONS, *peter*

Peter Sissons. Newsreader. b. Liverpool, 17 July 1942. **TV:** ITN (1964–89) as trainee, general reporter, foreign correspondent, news editor, industrial editor, presenter of *News At One* and presenter and associate editor of *Channel Four News;* BBC TV as presenter of *The Six O'Clock News* and *Question Time.* **Address:** c/o BBC TV. m. Sylvia; 1 d. Kate, 2 s. Jonathan, Michael.

SLATTERY, *tony*

Tony Slattery. Presenter/Actor/Comedian. b. London. **TV:** *Saturday Stayback; TX; Behind the Bike Sheds* (writer); *Boon; Whose Line Is It Anyway?; Saturday Night At the Movies; David Harper; Drowning In the Shallow End; S & M; That's Love.* **Address:** c/o Noel Gay Artists.

SMITH, *ian*

Ian Smith. Actor. b. Melbourne, Australia. **Theatre:** *The Desert Song; The Student Prince; The Mikado; Pirates of Penzance; Trial By Jury; The Gondoliers; The Merry Widow; Orpheus In the Underworld; Camelot; Fiddler On the Roof; My Fair Lady; Robert and Elizabeth; Breakfast With Julia; Caroline; The Heretic; The Winslow Boy; The Servant; The Grotto; Dirty Dick's.* **TV:** *Homicide; Division 4;* Constable Russell in *Bellbird; Matlock Police; Ryan; The Sullivans; Cop Shop; Skyways; Power Without Glory; I Can Jump Puddles; Rush;* Ted Douglas in *Prisoner: Cell Block H* (also as associate producer and a writer); Harold Bishop in *Neighbours* (1986- also as a writer). **Records:** *Old Fashioned Christmas* (single with Anne Charleston, 1989). **Address:** c/o Grundy Television. Lives in Elsternwick, Melbourne. m. Gail.

SMITH, *mel*

Mel Smith. Actor/Director. b. London, 3 December 1952. **Films:** *Slayground; Bullshot; No 1; Morons From Outer Space; The Princess Bride; The Wolves of Willoughby Chase; The Tall Man* (director); *Wilt; Lame Ducks.* **TV:** *Not the Nine O'Clock News; Alas Smith and Jones; Minder; Muck and Brass; The Best of Smith and Jones.* **Address:** c/o TalkBack.

SMITH, *mike*

Mike Smith. Presenter. b. Hornchurch, Essex, 23 April 1955. Began career in hospital radio, before moving to Capital Radio and BBC Radio 1, then entering television. **TV:** *Greatest Hits; CBTV; Breakfast Time; Family Tree; The Late, Late Breakfast Show; Speak Out; Live Aid; The Royal Tournament; Motor Fair; Airport 86 – Live; Secret's Out; The Montreux Rock Restival; First AIDS; Driving Force; Wogan* (guest presenter); *Transit; Family; Trick Or Treat; That's Showbusiness; No Kidding.* Winner, Sony Awards DJ of the Year (1986, 1987), Variety Club Radio Personality of the Year (1987). **Address:** c/o ICM Duncan Heath Associates. m. TV presenter Sarah Greene.

SMITH, ray

Ray Smith. Actor. b. Trealaw, Mid Glamorgan, 1 May 1936. **Theatre:** *Hamlet; Woyzeck; What the Butler Saw; Pygmalion; The Dresser; No Man's Land.* **Films:** *The Painted Smile; Under Milk Wood; Operation Daybreak; Rogue Male; Masada.* **TV:** *Shadows of Heroes; Stella; Company of Five; Callan; A Family At War; Six Days of Justice; Public Eye; Sam; Country Matters; Second City Firsts; Like I've Never Been Gone; Colditz; Little Lord Fauntleroy; The Sailor's Return; Rooms; Enemy At the Door; The Mayor's Charity; The Story Behind the Sands; End of Season; Hills of Heaven; The Mill On the Floss; The Atom Spies; The Beast; Warrior Queen; Target; Question of Guilt; Lloyd George; Juliet Bravo; We'll Meet Again; Constance Kent; Dempsey and Makepeace.* Winner, Sony Awards Best Actor, 1986. **Address:** c/o Felix de Wolfe. m. Gale (dis); 1 d. Branwen, 1 s. Justin.

SMITS, jimmy

Jimmy Smits. Actor. b. Manhattan, New York, USA, 9 July 1955. Gained a masters degree in theatre from Cornell University. **Theatre:** *Hamlet; Little Victories; Buck; The Ballad of Soapy Smith.* **Films:** *Running Scared; The Believers; Old Gringo; Vital Signs; Fires Within; Switch.* **TV:** *Miami Vice; The Other Side of the Border* (narrator); *Rockabye; Glitz; The Highwayman; Dangerous Affection* (all TV movies); Victor Sifuentes in *LA Law.* **Address:** c/o Creative Artists Agency. m.; 2 children, Taina, Joaquin.

SNOW, jon

Jonathan Snow. Newscaster. b. Ardingly, Sussex, 28 September 1947. Began career as a radio reporter for LBC/IRN (1973–6). **TV:** ITN as reporter (1976–83), Washington correspondent (1983–6), diplomatic correspondent (1986–9) and *Channel Four News* presenter (1989-). Awards: Monte Carlo Festival Golden Nymph, 1979; Royal Television Society Journalist of the Year, 1980; Valiant for Truth Award, 1982; Royal Television Society International News award, 1982; Royal Television Society Home News award, 1990 *(Channel Four News* coverage of Kegworth air disaster*).* **Address:** c/o ITN. Lives with partner Madeleine Colvin; 2 d. Leila, Freila. Pets: Two cats, two rabbits. Hobbies: Holidays in Cape Cod, France, playing the piano, painting. **Favourite TV programme:** *Newsnight.*

SNOWDEN, jane

Jane Snowden. Actress. b. York, 31 January 1965. **Theatre:** Juliet in *Romeo and Juliet* (National Youth Theatre). **Films:** *The Frog Prince* (acting debut). **TV:** *All Passion Spent; A Very Peculiar Practice; The Pyrates; Gaudy Night;* Emily in *Wish Me Luck.* **Address:** c/o ICM Duncan Heath Associates. m. actor James Simmons.

SPALL, timothy

Timothy Spall. Actor. b. London, 27 February 1957. Trained at RADA (Bancroft Gold Medal winner). **Theatre:** *The Merry Wives of Windsor; Nicholas Nickleby; Three Sisters* (all RSC). **Films:** *Quadrophenia; Remembrance; The Missionary; The Bride; Predator; Gothic; The Nihilist's Double Vision; Robinson Crusoe; To Kill a Priest; White Hunter, Black Heart; 1871; The Sheltering Sky; Life Is Sweet; Young Indie.* **TV:** *Vanishing Army; The Brylcream Boys; Three Sisters; The Cherry Orchard; A Cotswold Death; Home Sweet Home; Guest of the Nation; SOS Titanic; Auf Wiedersehen, Pet; Dutch Girls; Arena: Night Moves; Great Writers: Dostoyevsky; Body Contact; Stolen; Broke; Performance: Nona; Murder Most Horrid; Boon; Roots; Benjamin and Zephaniah; Not Mozart.* **Address:** c/o Markham & Froggatt. m. Shane; 2 d. Pascale, Mercedes, 1 s. Rafe.

SPENCE, *fiona*

Fiona Spence. Actress. b. Kent, 1949. Worked in Montreal, Canada, as a hostess for the Australia Pavillion at the Canadian Expo, moved to London and then to Australia, where she worked in the trav industry, before becoming a professional actress at the age of 27. **Theatre:** *Prisoner: Cell Block* (British tour). **TV:** Prison officer Vera Bennett in *Prisoner: Cell Block H; Women of the Sun; Hom Hurly Burly;* Celia Stewart in *Home and Away* (1988–90). **Address:** c/o Peter Graham Associate Single; lives in Melbourne.

SPENDLOVE, *rob*

Rob Spendlove. Actor. b. London, 1 May 1953. Studied drama at Middlesex Polytechnic, then a teache before setting up his own theatre company, touring London schools. **Theatre:** Fringe theatre; reperto theatre. **Films:** *Tai-Pan.* **TV:** *Strangers;* Roger Huntington in *Brookside; Lizzie's Pictures; Winds War; Queenie;* Rick Sneaden in *Closing Ranks; That's Love; Hard Cases;* Det Chris Tierney in *TEC Lovejoy; El C.I.D.* **Address:** c/o Julian Belfrage Associates. m. actress Sandy Hendrickse.

SPIERS, *judi*

Judi Spiers. Presenter. b. Plymouth, Devon, 15 March 1953. Trained at Rose Bruford College of Spee and Drama, qualifying as a teacher, before entering television as a presenter. **TV:** Westward T announcer; *Summer Scene; Down the Line; Gus Honeybun; Spytrap; Today South West* (TSW); *Wha Ahead; Mister TSW; Judi; Judi Goes On Holiday; Best of Spirits; Bazaar; Daytime Live; Children Need; ITV Telethon; Scavenger Hunt; The Noel Edmonds Roadshow; Pebble Mill.* **Address:** c/o Arlingto Enterprises.

SPRIGGS, *elizabeth*

Elizabeth Spriggs. Actress. b. Buxton, Derbyshire, 18 September 1929. Previously trained for opera Royal School of Music. **Theatre:** *Hamlet; Romeo and Juliet; A Delicate Balance; London Assurance (c RSC); Blithe Spirit; Tales from the Vienna Woods; The Country Wife; Macbeth; Love Letters On Bl Paper* (all National Theatre). **Films:** *Work Is a 4-Letter Word; Richard's Things; Lady Chatterley Lover; An Unsuitable Job for a Woman.* **TV:** *Black and Blue; Village Hall; Victorian Scandals; T Glittering Prizes; Prometheus; The Expert; Abel's Will; Wings of a Dove; The Dybuk; Julius Caesa Fox; Tales of the Unexpected; The Cause; We, the Accused; The Kindness of Mrs Radcliffe; Bogno Cribb; Shine On Harvey Moon; Frost In May; The Haunting of Cassie Palmer; Watching.* **Address** c/o Harbour & Coffey. m. musician Murry Manson; 1 d. Wendy.

ST CLEMENT, *pam*

Pamela St Clement. Actress. b. Harrow-on-the-Hill, Middlesex, 12 May 1942. Trained at Rose Brufor College, London, and Rolle College, Devon. **TV:** *The Tripods; Indelible Evidence: Gaslight; His ar Hers; Orson Welles' Great Mysteries; Thomas and Sarah; The Onedin Line; The Fenn Street Gang; Vc Der Valk; Follyfoot; All Our Saturdays; Within These Walls; Enemy At the Door; Matilda's Englan Shall I See You Now?; A Horseman Riding By; Bottle Boys; Emmerdale Farm; C.A.T.S. Eyes; Minde Shoestring; Private Schultz; Together; Not for the Likes of Us; The Nation's Health; Angels; We'll Me Again; Ladykillers; The Chinese Detective; The Clergyman's Daughter; Struggle; King;* Pat Butcher (ne Wicks) in *EastEnders.* **Address;** c/o Saraband Associates. Lives in Hertfordshire and Norfolk. m. Andre Gordon (dis).

STABLEFORD, *howard*

Howard Stableford. Presenter/Reporter. b. Poynton, Cheshire, 12 April 1959. Worked for BBC Radio Lancashire and Northampton, before moving into television. **TV:** *Jigsaw; Puzzle Trail; Beat the Teacher; Newsround; Tomorrow's World* (1985-). **Address:** c/o Dave Winslett Entertainments. Lives in Kingston-upon-Thames, Surrey. m. Lizanne. Pets: Two cats, called Preston and KC ('After our home towns – KC being short for Kansas City). Hobbies: Running, motorbikes, squash, scuba-diving. **Favourite TV programme:** Anything to do with current affairs or sport.

STACY, *neil*

Neil Stacy. Actor. b. Stowupland, Suffolk, 15 May 1941. Performed with Oxford University's Dramatic Society. **Theatre:** *The Second Mrs Tanqueray* (National Theatre); *A Patriot for Me; Holiday Snap* (Theatre of Comedy); *Canaries Sometimes Sing* (Albery Theatre); *Blithe Spirit.* **TV:** *War and Peace; Man Outside; Dead of Night; Colditz; Barlow At Large; The Pallisers; Mr Garrick and Mrs Woffington; The Way of the World; Law Centre; Return of The Saint; Crown Court; The Standard; Strangers; Quatermass; To Serve Them All My Days; Nanny; Shackleton; The Fourth Arm; Strangers and Brothers; Duty Free; Cold Warrior; Three Up, Two Down; Rumpole of the Bailey; Haggard.* **Address:** c/o Michael Whitehall.

STAFF, *kathy*

Kathy Staff. Actress. b. Dukinfield, Cheshire, 12 July 1928. Began career with a touring theatre company in Scotland. **Theatre:** Repertory theatre; *Two Into One; When We Are Married* (both Theatre of Comedy); *The Rivals* (national tour). **Films:** *A Kind of Loving; The Dresser; The Family Way; Camille; Little Dorrit.* **TV:** *Castlehaven; Within These Walls; Hadleigh;* Vera Hopkins in *Coronation Street; Sez Les; Separate Tables; The Benny Hill Show;* Winnie Purvis in *Emmerdale Farm;* Doris Luke in *Crossroads;* Mrs Blewett in *Open All Hours;* Nora Batty in *Last of the Summer Wine.* **Address:** c/o London Management. m. John; 2 d. Katherine, Susan.

STALLARD, *margaret*

Margaret Stallard. Actress. b. Birmingham, 30 April 1929. Trained at LAMDA. **TV:** *Emmerdale Farm; Juliet Bravo; Grange Hill; Last of the Summer Wine; Lovejoy; Divided We Stand;* Mrs Babbit in *Crossroads.* **Address:** c/o Actors Alliance. m. musician John Davis; 3 d. Caroline, Deborah, twins, Miranda and 1 s. Benjamin.

STANDING, *john*

Sir John Leon (fourth baronet). Actor. b. London, 16 August 1934. Son of actress Kay Hammond. Previously studied at art school. **Films:** *The Wild and the Willing; Psychopath; The Legacy; Elephant Man; The Sea Wolves; Privates On Parade; Invitation To The Wedding.* **TV:** *Arms and the Man; The First Churchills; Charley's Aunt; Love Story; Tartuffe; The Dirtiest Soldier; Rogue Male; The Sinking of HMS Victoria; Home and Beauty; Ms Or Jill and Jack; Nanny's Boy; The Relapse; The Other 'Arf; All the World's a Stage; Tinker, Tailor, Soldier, Spy; The Young Visiters; Waterloo; Hart To Hart; To Catch a King; Lime Street; LA Law; Chameleons; The Endless Game; Spooks; Night of the Fox.* **Address:** c/o James Sharkey Associates. m. actress Jill Melford (dis), 2nd Sarah Forbes; 2 s. Alexander (from 1st m.), Archie, 2 d. India, Octavia.

STARKE, *michael*

Michael Starke. Actor. b. Liverpool. Worked as a dustbinman, then fronted a comedy showband that toured Liverpool, Newcastle and Scotland. **Theatre:** *Cavern of Dreams; Jack and the Beanstalk;* Sammy in *Blood Brothers; One for the Road; The Resistible Rise of Arturo Ui; Dick Whittington; The Taming of the Shrew; She Stoops To Conquer; Aladdin; Hamlet; Three Sisters; The Winter's Tale; No Holds Bard; Be-Bop-a-Lula.* **Films:** *No Surrender; Distant Voices, Still Lives.* **TV:** *Boys From the Blackstuff; Tripods;* Sinbad in *Brookside; Watching.* **Address:** c/o Tobias Management/Mersey Television.

STEADMAN, *alison*

Alison Steadman. Actress. b. Liverpool, 26 August 1946. **Films:** *Champions; No 1; A Private Function; Clockwise; Stormy Monday; The Adventures of Baron Munchausen; The Short and Curlies; Shirley Valentine; Wilt; Life Is Sweet.* **TV:** *Nuts In May; Through the Night; Our Flesh and Blood; Abigail's Party; Pasmore; P'tang Yang Kipperbang* (Channel Four film); *The Muscle Market; Tartuffe; Nature In Focus; Coming Through; The Caucasian Chalk Circle; The Singing Detective; The Finding; Virtuoso; A Small Mourning; Newshounds; 1000 Nights; Gone To the Dogs; Selling Hitler.* **Address:** c/o Peters Fraser & Dunlop.

STEED, *maggie*

Maggie Steed. Actress. **Films:** *Babylon; Intimate Contact.* **TV:** *Fox; The History Man; Clapper; Claw; Shine On Harvey Moon; Charlie* (TV movie); *Van Der Valk.* **Address:** c/o Marina Martin Management.

STELFOX, *shirley*

Shirley Stelfox. Actress. b. 11 April 1941. **Theatre:** *King Lear; Three Sisters; Macbeth; Not Now Darling; Toad of Toad Hall; Cavalcade; Trumpets and Raspberries; Hobson's Choice.* **Films:** *1984;* Shirley in *Personal Services.* **TV:** *Hobson's Choice; A Pin for the Peepshow; Owen MD; General Hospital; Between the Wars; Wicked Women; The Liars; Crown Court; Coronation Street; Strangers; Monica Swaine; S.W.A.L.K.; Bootle Saddles; Knights of God;* Madge Richmond in *Brookside; Radical Chambers; Bergerac; King and Castle;* Carol May in *Making Out* (three series); *Stay Lucky; Voice; Keeping Up Appearances.* **Address:** c/o A.I.M. m. 2nd actor Don Henderson (qv), 1 d. Helena (from 1st m.), 1 step-d. Louise, 1 step-s. Ian.

STENNETT, *stan*, MBE

Stan Stennett. Actor. b. Pencoed, Mid Glamorgan, 30 July 1927. **Films:** *Possessions.* **TV:** *Stan At Ease; Road Show; The Good Old Days; Those Wonderful TV Times; The Golden Shot; Celebrity Squares; Whose Baby?; Top Town; Leeds United; What a Performance; Cries From a Watchtower; 1,2,3;* Sid Hooper in *Crossroads.* **Radio:** *Welsh Rarebit; Show Band; The Black and White Minstrel Show.* **Address:** c/o George Bartram Associates. Lives in South Wales. m. Elizabeth; 2 s. Roger, Ceri. Hobbies: Flying his own aircraft, golf and soccer.

STEPHENSON, *nicola*

Nicola Stephenson. Actress. b. Oldham, Lancashire, 5 July 1971. Trained at Oldham Theatre Workshop. **Theatre:** Co-founded The Old School Stage Society, performing at Oldham Coliseum, The Green Room, Manchester, the Edinburgh Festival and the National Students' Drama Festival. **TV:** *Jossy's Giants; The Rainbow; Children's Ward; Family Tree; Medics; The Final Frame* (Channel Four film); Margaret Clemence in *Brookside* (1990-). **Address:** c/o Mersey Television.

STEPHENSON, *pamela*

Pamela Stephenson. Actress/Comedienne. b. Auckland, New Zealand, 4 December. Grew up in Australia. Trained at National Institute of Dramatic Art, Australia. **Theatre:** *Small But Perfectly Formed; Naughty Night Nurses Without Panties Down Under No 2; Shocking Behaviour.* **Films:** *Stand Up Virgin Soldiers; The Comeback; History of the World – Part 1; The Secret Policeman's Other Ball; Superman III; Scandalous; Bloodbath At the House of Death; Finders Keepers.* **TV:** *Within These Walls; Space 1999; The New Avengers; Target; Hazell; The Professionals; Funny Man; Man From the South; Behind the Scenes With...; Not the Nine O'Clock News; Move Over Darling; Lost Empires; Saturday Night Live.* **Address:** c/o John Reid Enterprises. m. 1st actor Nicholas Ball (dis), 2nd comedian Billy Connolly (qv); 3 d. Daisy, Amy, Scarlett Layla.

STEVENSON, *juliet*

Juliet Stevenson. Actress. Trained at RADA (Gold Bancroft Medal winner). **Theatre:** *The Tempest; The Taming of the Shrew; Antony and Cleopatra; Once In a Lifetime; Henry IV, Pts I and II; Money; A Midsummer Night's Dream; Measure for Measure; Troilus and Cressida; As You Like It; Les Liaisons Dangereuses* (all RSC); *Other Worlds; Yerma; The Trackers of Oxyrhynchus; On the Verge; Hedda Gabler; Burn This; Death and the Maiden.* **Films:** *Drowning By Numbers; Ladder of Swords; Truly Madly Deeply* (winner, London *Evening Standard* Film Awards Best Actress, 1991). **TV:** *Maybury;* Barbara Mallen in *The Mallens; Bazarre and Rummage; Freud; Antigone; Oedipus At Colonus; Life Story; Stanley; Out of Love; Living With Dinosaurs; Amy; Omnibus: Rape; The March; Cello; In the Border Country; The Doll's House.* **Address:** c/o Markham & Froggatt.

STEVENSON, *mat*

Matthew Stevenson. Actor. b. Melbourne, Australia, 15 April 1969. Studied at the Ensemble Theatre. **TV:** Mark Wheeler in *Breaking Up* (TV movie); Kevin Connor in *My Brother Tom* (mini-series); *Local Rag;* Jack Morrison in *Dusty* (mini-series); Skinner in *Neighbours;* Adam Cameron in *Home and Away* (1989-). TV commercials: National Australia Bank; Anti-Cancer Quit Campaign; Children's Anti-Smoking Old Cancer Fund. **Address:** c/o The Actors' Agency/Channel 7.

STEWART, *alastair*

Alastair James Stewart. Newscaster. b. Emsworth, Hampshire, 22 June 1952. **TV:** Southern TV reporter and industrial correspondent (1976–80); ITN industrial correspondent (1980–84), then presenter of *News At 5.40* and *Channel Four News* (1984–9), Washington correspondent (1990) and presenter of *News At Ten* (1989 and 1991-); presenter of ITV General Election and Budget programmes. **Address:** c/o ITN. Lives in Hampshire. m. TV production assistant Sally; 1 s. Alexander, 1 d. Clementine.

STEWART, *allan*

Allan Stewart. Entertainer. b. Garrow Hill, Glasgow, 30 July 1950. Made his first record at the age of 10 and started playing guitar and singing in Scottish clubs and theatres a year later. **TV:** *Hello, Good Afternoon, Welcome; The Allan Stewart Tapes; Copy Cats* (four series); *Hello, Good Evening, Welcome; Go for It; Live From...; Chain Letters.* **Address:** c/o International Artistes. m. Jane; 1 s. David.

STEWART, *jeff*

Jeffrey James Stewart. Actor. b. Aberdeen, Grampian, 28 October 1955. Trained at The Drama Centre. **TV:** *The Nightmare Man;* Harry Fellows in *Crossroads; Minder; Doctor Who; Angels; Hi-de-Hi Reilly – Ace of Spies; Roots;* PC Reg Hollis in *The Bill.* TV commercials: Guinness; Newcastle Exhibition Bitter; John Bull; Allied Dunbar; Elkie Brooks LP. *Pop videos:* Sam Brown's boyfriend in the Sam Brown video *Can I Get a Witness?* **Address:** c/o Darryl Brown Associates. Single; lives in London. Hobbies: food, music, theatre, lying on beaches, long-distance running (London Marathon twice and Moscow Marathon once). **Favourite TV programme:** *Rising Damp; Minder; The Sweeney; Doctor Who; Butterflies; The Good Life; The Price Is Right; Spender; The Bill.*

STILGOE, *richard*

Richard Stilgoe. Presenter/Writer/Performer. b. Camberley, Surrey, 28 March 1943. Former member of Cambridge Footlights Revue. **Theatre:** *Starlight Express; The Phantom of the Opera* (both as co-writer). **TV:** *Pssst...; Just Watch It; The Thumb of Barnaby Locke; A Class By Himself; Don't Ask Us; Nationwide; And Now the Good News; That's Life!; Finders Keepers; Stilgoe's Around; Royal Variety Performance* (1982). **Address:** c/o Noel Gay Artists. m. Annabel; 2 d. Jemima, Holly, 3 s. Rufus, Jack, Joe.

STOPPARD, *miriam*

Miriam Stoppard. Presenter. b. Newcastle upon Tyne, 12 May 1937. Worked in clinical medicine, specialising in dermatology, and became a research director in the pharmaceutical industry, before entering television. **TV:** *Where There's Life...; The Health Show; So You Want To Stop Smoking; Health Circuit* (Sky News); *People Today.* **Books:** *Miriam Stoppard's Book of Babycare; Miriam Stoppard's Book of Healthcare; The Face and Body Book; Marks & Spencer Book of Babycare; Marks & Spencer Book of Childcare.* **Address:** c/o Curtis Brown. m. playwright Tom Stoppard (sep); 2 step-s. Oliver, Barnaby, 2 s. William, Edmund.

STRACHAN, *michaela*

Michaela Strachan. Presenter. b. Ewell, Surrey, 7 April 1966. Trained at Arts Education School in dance, drama and singing. **Theatre:** *Seven Brides for Seven Brothers;* pantomimes. **TV:** *Wide Awake Club; Wacaday; Wac Extra* (all TV-am); *The Hit Man and Her; Owl TV; But Can You Do It On TV?; Boogie Box* (Music Box cable TV); *Freetime.* **Records:** *Happy Radio; Take Good Care of My Heart* (both singles). **Address:** c/o Michael Ladkin Personal Management/TV-am.

STRAULI, *christopher*

Christopher Strauli. Actor. b. Harpenden, Hertfordshire, 13 April 1946. Trained at RADA (won the Spotlight Award and William Poel Prize). **Theatre:** *The Taming of the Shrew; Death of a Salesman; London Assurance; Ticket of Leave Man; The Merchant of Venice; The Wizard of Oz; Absurd Person Singular.* **Films:** *SOS Titanic; Rising Damp.* **TV:** *A Family At War; Owen MD; Harriet's Back In Town; Angels; Warship; Edward VII; For Tea On Sunday;* Bunny in *Raffles; Eustace and Hilda Trilogy; Only When I Laugh; Gentle Folk; Romeo and Juliet; Measure for Measure; Aubrey Beardsley; Strangers and Brothers; Parlez Franglais; A Crack In the Ice; Dempsey and Makepeace; Lytton's Diary; Full House; Names and Games; Victoria Wood As Seen On TV; Fortunes of War; Bergerac.* **Address:** c/o Bryan Drew. m. Lesley; 2 d. Belinda, Hanneli, 2 s. Barnaby, Dominic.

STRIDE, *john*

John Stride. Actor. b. London, 11 July 1936. Trained at RADA. **Theatre:** Repertory theatre in Liverpool; Old Vic Theatre; National Theatre. **Films:** *Bitter Havest; Macbeth; Something To Hide; Juggernaut; Brannigan; The Omen; A Bridge Too Far; Macho; Innocent Heroes.* **TV:** *Scarlet Black; Knock On Any Door; Love Story; The Bonus; Detective; The Main Chance; The Heiress; Force of Circumstance; Papillons; Visit From a Stranger; Photograph; Wilde Alliance; Love Among the Artists; Hess; The Ice House; Henry VII; Diamonds; Lloyd George; Conversations With a Stranger; Thirteen At Dinner* (TV movie); *Lytton's Diary; Imaginary Friends; The Trial of Klaus Barbie; Jumping the Queue; Chelworth; Agatha Christie's Poirot; The Old Devils.* **Address:** c/o Richard Hatton. m. actress April Wilding; 3 d. Philippa, Lindsay, Eleanor.

STRINGER, *nick*

Nick Stringer. Actor. b. Torquay, Devon, 10 August 1948. **Films:** *The Shout; The Long Good Friday; Clockwise; Personal Services; Terence Davies Trilogy.* **TV:** *Pickersgill People; Devil's Crown; Playhouse: The Affront; The Sweeney; Minder; Butterflies; Shoestring; Squadron; The Professionals; Come To Mecca; Crown Court; Johnny Jarvis; Open All Hours; Lucky Jim; One By One; Dempsey and Makepeace; Auf Wiedersehen, Pet; The Collectors; C.A.T.S. Eyes; Only Fools and Horses; A Sort of Innocence; Blind Justice; About Face; Bergerac; Boon; Press Gang; The New Statesman; Black and Blue Lamp; Home Front; Shadow On the Sun; This Is David Lander;* PC Ron Smollett in *The Bill.* **Address:** c/o Kerry Gardner Management/The Bill. Lives in Kenilworth, Warwickshire. m.; 1 d. Pets: Two Welsh border collies. Hobbies: Drinking good wine.

STRONG, *gwyneth*

Gwyneth Strong. Actress. b. London, 2 December 1959. **Theatre:** *Live Like Pigs; Echoes From a Concrete Canyon; The Blood; Glad Hand* (all Royal Court Theatre); *Heroes; Woyzeck; Sugar and Spice; Shout Across the River* (RSC); *Favourite Nights; Care* (Royal Court Theatre); *Strangers In the Night; Loving Women; A Piece of My Mind.* **Films:** *Our Man From a Far Country; Horrid Intermission; Dark Water; Bloody Kids; Nothing But the Night; Cry Freedom.* **TV:** *Shadows; Edward VII; Jubilee: Age of Hypocrisy; The Story of Ruth; Breakaway Girls; The Ladies; Early Struggles; The Factory; Radio; Love Story: Mr Right;* Linda in *Rainy Day Women; It's a Lovely Day Tomorrow; Inside Out; Paradise Postponed;* Sadie in *King of the Ghetto;* Miss Dimmick in *Living With Dinosaurs;* Cassandra in *Only Fools and Horses.* **Address:** c/o Markham & Froggatt.

STUBBS, *imogen*

Imogen Stubbs. Actress. b. Rothbury, Northumberland, 20 February 1961. **Films:** *Nanou; A Summer Story; Fellow Traveller; Erik the Viking; True Colours.* **TV:** *The Browning Version; The Rainbow; Othello; Relatively Speaking.* **Address:** c/o ICM Duncan Heath Associates.

STUBBS, *una*

Una Stubbs. Actress. b. London, 1 May 1937. Trained as a dancer at La Roche Dancing School, Slough. **Theatre:** *A Midsummer Night's Dream; Norman Wisdom Show* (London Palladium); *Folies Bergere* revue; *Grab Me a Gondola; On the Brighter Side; The Knack...and how to get it; The Soldier's Tale* (both Young Vic Theatre); *Cowardly Custard; Oh, Mr Porter; Irma la Douce; Baggage; Secret Life of a Cartoon.* **Films:** *Summer Holiday; Wonderful Life.* **TV:** *Cool for Cats; Till Death Us Do Part; Fawlty Towers; Give Us a Clue;* Aunt Sally in *Worzel Gummidge* and *Worzel Gummidge Down Under; In Sickness and In Health; Happy Families; Morris Minor's Marvellous Motors.* **Address:** c/o Richard Stone Partnership. m. 1st actor Peter Gilmore (dis), 2nd actor actor Nicky Henson (dis); 3 s. Jason, Christian, Joe.

STUYCK, *joris*

Joris Stuyck. Actor. b. Orpington, Kent, 23 April 1952. Took part in productions while studying at McGill University, Montreal, Canada. **Theatre:** *The Normal Heart.* **Films:** *The Shooting Party; The Razor's Edge.* **TV:** *We'll Meet Again; Reilly – Ace of Spies; A Woman of Substance; Tender Is the Night.* **Address:** c/o Kate Feast Management.

SUCHET, *david*

David Suchet. Actor. b. London, 2 May 1946. Brother of newscaster John Suchet (qv). Trained at LAMDA. **Films:** *A Tale of Two Cities; The Hunchback of Notre Dame; The Falcon and the Snowman; Thirteen At Dinner; Harry and the Hendersons; The Last Innocent Man; To Kill a Priest; A World Apart.* **TV:** *Oppenheimer; Reilly – Ace of Spies; The Last Day; Being Normal; The Life of Freud;* title role in *Blott On the Landscape; The Muse; Playing Shakespeare; Oxbridge Blues; King and Castle; Time To Die; Murrow; Jackanory; Once In a Lifetime; Ulysses; Cause Célèbre; Bingo; Nobody Here But Us Chickens;* title role in *Agatha Christie's Poirot; Separation;* title role in *Timon of Athens.* Awards: RTS Best Actor, 1986; BAFTA Best Supporting Actor in a Film, 1989. **Address:** c/o The Brunskill Management. m. actress Sheila Ferris; 1 s. Robert, 1 d. Kate.

SUCHET, *john*

John Suchet. Newscaster. b. London, 29 March 1944. Brother of actor David Suchet (qv). A journalist with Reuters, before joining the BBC. **TV:** ITN since 1972 as reporter, Washington correspondent (1981–3), presenter of *News At One* and *News At 12.30.* Winner, Royal Television Society Journalist of the Year award, 1986–7. **Address:** c/o ITN. m. 1st Moya (dis), 2nd Bonnie; 3 s. Damian, Kieran, Rory (from 1st m.).

SUGDEN, *mollie*

Mollie Sugden. Actress. b. Keighley, West Yorkshire, 21 July 1922. Trained at Guildhall School of Music and Drama. **TV:** *Hugh and I; Please Sir!; Doctor In the House; For the Love of Ada; The Liver Birds;* Mrs Slocombe in *Are You Being Served?* and *Grace and Favour;* Nellie Harvey in *Coronation Street; Whodunnit?; Come Back Mrs Noah; Tea Ladies; That's My Boy; My Husband and I.* **Address:** c/o Joan Reddin. m. actor William Moore; 2 s. Robin, Simon (twins).

SULLIVAN, *dean*

Dean Sullivan. Actor/Director. b. Liverpool. Previously a teacher. **Theatre:** *On the Razzle; Cowardy Custard; Wild Oats; Gangs; Breezeblock Park; West Side Story; A Midsummer Night's Dream; Look Back In Anger; Bent; The Importance of Being Earnest; Soaplights; Road; The Northern Mystery Plays; Snow White; Babes In the Wood.* Formed the Liverpool Theatre Company (1989), directing: *The Importance of Being Earnest; Talent; Ghost Story; Hay Fever; Tons of Money.* **TV:** Jimmy Corkhill in *Brookside* (1986-); *All I Want for Christmas* (presenter). **Radio:** Sam Jackson in *The Merseysiders* (BBC Radio Merseyside serial, 1988–90). **Address:** c/o Mersey Television. Single; lives in Liverpool. Hobbies: The theatre, reading, writing, collecting modern paintings and ceramics. **Favourite TV programme:** *Question Time;* any TV election specials.

SUMMERS, *jill*

Jill Summers. Actress/Comedienne. b. Eccles, Lancashire, 10 December 1910. Father a circus tightrope walker, mother a revue artiste. **Theatre:** Acted in theatres throughout Britain and performed as a stand-up comedienne. **TV:** *Summers Here; Castlehaven; How We Used To Live; Agatha; Stay With Me Till Morning; This Year, Next Year; Coronation Street* (cleaner, then as Phyllis Pearce, 1982-); *Royal Variety Performance* (1989). **Address:** c/o Granada TV. m. 2nd Dr C Simpson-Smith (dec); 1 adopted-s. Hobbies: Cooking, entertaining, travel.

SWIFT, *clive*

Clive Swift. Actor. b. Liverpool, 9 February 1936. Experience in drama societies at Cambridge University. **TV:** *Compact; Dombey and Son; Love Story; South Riding; The Sailor's Return; Clayhanger; The Brothers; The Liver Birds; Chronicle; Romeo and Juliet; Henry IV; Dr Jekyll and Mr Hyde; Winston Churchill – The Wilderness Years; Tales of the Unexpected; Lucky Jim; Bless Me, Father; The Gentle Touch; The Barchester Chronicles; Pericles; Doctor Who; The Pickwick Papers; First Among Equals; Martin Luther – Heretic; Inspector Morse; Minder; Shelley; Laura and Disorder; Othello; Keeping Up Appearances; L P Hartley.* **Address:** c/o PTA. Lives in Liverpool. m. author Margaret Drabble (dis); 1 d., 2 s. Hobbies: Cricket, music (listening to it and playing), speaking and teaching poetry. **Favourite TV programme:** Good soccer.

SYKES, *eric, OBE*

Eric Sykes. Actor/Comedian/Writer. b. Oldham, Lancashire, 4 May 1923. Awarded the OBE, 1986. **Films:** *Watch Your Stern; Invasion Quartet; Village of Daughters; Kill Or Cure; Heavens Above; The Bargee; One-Way Pendulum; Those Magnificent Men In Their Flying Machines; Rotten To the Core; The Liquidator; Spy With a Cold Nose; The Plank; Shalako; Monte Carlo Or Bust; Rhubarb; Theatre of Blood; Ghost In the Noonday Sun; The Boys In Blue; Absolute Beginners.* **TV:** *Sykes; Sykes Versus ITV; Curry and Chips; Eric Sykes Spectacular; Charley's Aunt; Summer In Blackpool; The Plank* (Winner, Montreux Press Award); *If You Go Down To the Woods Today; It's Your Move; Mr H Is Late; The 19th Hole.* **Radio:** *Educating Archie; Variety Bandbox.* **Address:** c/o Norma Farnes. m. Edith Milbrandt; 3 d. Catherine, Susan, Julie, 1 s. David.

SYMONS, *emily*

Emily Symons. b. 10 August 1969. **TV:** *Hold the Circus* (TV movie); *The Investigators;* Anne Costello in *Richmond Hill;* Marilyn Chambers in *Home and Away* (1989-); *Video Smash Hits* (co-presenter). **Address:** c/o International Casting Service.

SYMS, *sylvia*

Sylvia May Laura Syms. Actress/Director. b. London, 6 January 1936. Trained at RADA. **TV**: *The Devil's Disciple; Love Story; The Saint; Danger Man; The Human Jungle; The Avengers; Love Story; Armchair Theatre; The Baron; The Adventurer; My Good Woman; The Movie Quiz; Murder Will Out; The Truth About Verity; Love and Marriage; Nancy Astor; Your Move; Crown Court; Nancy Astor; Sorry Darling; A Murder Is Announced; Murder At Lynch Cross; Intimate Contact; The Ruth Rendell Mysteries; Doctor Who; May To December; The Laughter of God; Intimate Contact; Countdown;* Margaret Thatcher in *Thatcher: The Final Days.* **Address:** c/o Barry Brown & Partner. Lives in London, m. Alan Edney (dis); 1 s. Ben, 1 d. actress Beatie (Edney). Pets: A dog. Hobbies: Gardening, walking. **Favourite TV programme:** Anything with David Jason, John Thaw or Patricia Hodge.

TAMM, *mary*

Mary Tamm. Actress. b. Dewsbury, West Yorkshire, 22 March 1950. Trained at RADA. **Films:** *The Odessa File; Witness Madness; The Likely Lads; Top Secret; The Doubt; Rampage.* **TV:** *Raging Calm; Whodunnit?; Hunter's Walk; Warship; Return of The Saint;* Pauline Ogden in *Coronation Street;* Romana in *Doctor Who; Assassination Run; The Treachery Game; Girls of Slender Means; The Donati Conspiracy; The Inheritors; Only When I Laugh; Quest for Love; Not the Nine O'Clock News; Jane Eyre; Bergerac; The Hello-Goodbye Man; Worlds Beyond; Three Kinds of Heat; Agatha Christie's Poirot; Perfect Scoundrels; The Bill; Casualty.* **Address:** c/o Langford Associates. Lives in London. m. Marcus Ringrose; 1 d. Lauren Zoe. Pets: One dog, three cats, two rabbits. Hobbies: Riding, computer Scrabble, painting, reading. **Favourite TV programme:** *Survival.*

TANDY, *donald*

Donald Tandy. Actor. b. London, 20 December 1918. Organised shows while a POW in the Second World War. **Theatre:** Repertory theatre; *The Dish Ran Away; Biggest Thief In Town.* **Films:** *The Captive Heart; The World of Suzy Wong; Jekyll and Hyde.* **TV:** Tom Clement in *EastEnders* (1985–88); *Timewatch.* **Address:** c/o Hamilton & Sydney. m. Diana Buckland; 1 s. Timothy.

TANDY, *mark*

Mark Tandy. Actor. b. Athlone, Westmeath, 8 February 1957. **Theatre:** Nicholas Nickleby (RSC); Major Barbara (National Theatre); *The Lucky Chance* (Royal Court Theatre); *Beauty and the Beast* (Old Vic Theatre); *Siblings; Study In Scarlet.* **Films:** *Defence of the Realm; Captive;* Lord Risley in *Maurice; Wings of Fame.* **TV:** *Aubrey Beardsley; The Jewel In the Crown; Nicholas Nickleby; Gems; Murder Not Proven; Call Me Mister; Hedgehog Wedding; Catherine; Pulaski; Hannay; Inspector Morse; Vote for Hitler; Saracen; Gibraltar Inquest; Tygo Road; Portrait of a Marriage; Prince* (TV movie). **Address:** c/o Julian Belfrage Associates.

TARBUCK, *jimmy*

Jimmy Tarbuck. Comedian/Entertainer/Quizmaster. b. Liverpool, 6 February 1940. Started as a compere with a rock 'n' roll show, then as a Butlin's Red Coat. **TV:** *Comedy Bandbox; Sunday Night At the London Palladium* (host); *It's Tarbuck; Tarbuck's Back; Winner Takes All; Live From Her Majesty's; Tarby and Friends; Bring Me Sunshine; Live From the Palladium; Live From the Piccadilly; The Frame Game.* **Books:** *Tarbuck On Golf.* **Address:** c/o Peter Prichard. m. Pauline; 2 d. actress Liza, Cheryl, s. James.

TARMEY, *william*

William Cleworth Piddington. Actor. b. Manchester, 4 April 1941. Worked in the building trade, singing in clubs by night, before entering TV as an 'extra'. **TV:** *Strangers; Crown Court; The Ghosts of Motley Hall; The Glamour Girls; Play for Today: Thicker Than Water; Rising Star* (sang with own group, Take Ten); *King Lear;* Jack Duckworth in *Coronation Street* (1979-); *Royal Variety Performance* (1989). **Records:** *I'll Be With You Soon* (single, with Elizabeth Dawn (qv), 1989). **Address:** c/o Granada TV. m. Alma; 1 s. Carl, 1 d. Sara.

TARRANT, *chris*

Chris Tarrant. Presenter. b. Reading, Berkshire, 10 October 1946. Studied for Central office of Information, taught English in a South London comprehensive school and took an ACTT director course degree. **TV:** *Tiswas; OTT; Saturday Stayback; The Six O'Clock Show* (LWT); *Prove It; PSI; Everybody's Equal; The Disney Christmas Special; Tarrant On TV; Crazy Comparisons.* **Radio:** Capital FM breakfast show. **Books:** *Ken's Furry Friends; Fishfriars Hall.* **Address:** c/o PVA Management. m. 1st Sheila (dis); 2 d. Helen, Jennifer (by 1st m.), Samantha.

TAYLFORTH, *gillian*

Gillian Taylforth. Actress. b. London, 14 August 1955. Trained at the Anna Scher Theatre School. **Films:** *The Long Good Friday.* **TV:** *Play for Today: Eleanor; Zigger Zagger; The One and Only Phyllis Dixey; The Rag Trade; Thunder Cloud; Little Girls Don't; Watch This Space; Hi-de-Hi!; Big Jim and the Figaro Club; Sink Or Swim; On Safari; The Gentle Touch; Minder; Fast Hand;* Kathy Beale in *EastEnders* (1985-). **Address:** c/o Saraband Associates/BBC Elstree Centre. Single; lives in Highbury, North London.

TAYLOR, *benedict*

Benedict Sean Taylor. Actor. b. London, 18 April 1960. Joined the RSC at the age of nine. **Films:** *The Watcher In the Woods.* **TV:** *Play for Today: The Other Woman; Union Castle; Mitch; The Gentle Touch; Barriers; Beau Geste; A Flame To the Phoenix; Jackanory; The Far Pavilions; The Facts of Life; Bergerac; The Dirty Dozen; Video Stars; The Last Days of Pompeii; The First Modern Olympics; The Corsican Brothers; My Brother Jonathan; Black Arrow; Thirteen At Dinner; 92 Grosvenor Street; Love Is Ever Young; Drums Along Balmoral Drive; The South Bank Show; A Perfect Spy; Vanity Fair; Tales of the Unexpected; An Actor's Life for Me; The Darling Buds of May; The Three Musketeers.* **Address:** c/o Hamper-Neafsey Associates. Hobbies: Travelling, reading, music, films, theatre, galleries, skiing, climbing, swimming, cycling, riding, scuba-diving.

TAYLOR, *dennis*

Dennis Taylor. Snooker commentator. b. Coalisland, County Tyrone, 19 January 1949. Won British Junior Billiards Championship in 1968; turned professional as a snooker player in 1972 and won the Rothman Grand Prix in 1984, World Snooker Championship in 1985 and Benson and Hedges Crown Masters in 1987. He, Alex Higgins and Eugene Hughes, representing Ireland, won the Tuborg World Cup. **TV:** BBC snooker commentator. **Address:** c/o Barry Hearn, 1 Arcade Place, South Street, Romford, Essex. m. Patricia; 2 s. Damian, Brendan, 1 d. Denise.

TAYLOR, *gwen*

Gwen Taylor. Actress. b. Derby, 19 February 1939. Worked for eight years as a bank clerk, before training at the East 15 Acting School. **Theatre:** *Top Girls* (Royal Court Theatre and New York). **Films:** *Monty Python's Life of Brian; Richard's Things.* **TV:** *Play for Today: The Land of Green Ginger; John Halifax, Gentleman; Play of the Month: The Common; Rutland Weekend Television; Pickersgill People; Play of the Week: Return Fare; Ripping Yarns; Sounding Brass; Only When I Laugh; Playhouse: Skirmishes; The Link Game; Forever Young; Billy 3; Antigone; Duty Free; Ties of Blood; Slip Up; Yes, Prime Minister; Colin's Sandwich; Sob Sisters; A Bit of a Do; Sauce for the Goose; Happy Christmas, I Love You.* **Address:** c/o James Sharkey Associates. Lives in North London with playwright Graham Reid. m. Fred (dis).

TAYLOR, *shirin*

Shirin Taylor. Actress. Trained at Bristol Old Vic Theatre School. **Theatre:** *Look Back In Anger; One Flew Over the Cuckoo's Nest; The Taming of the Shrew; Jumpers; Pygmalion;* title role in *Educating Rita* (Piccadilly Theatre); *Privates On Parade; Messiah; Alfie; The Dog In the Manger; Three Birds Alighting On a Field* (Royal Court Theatre). **TV:** *Cleopatra; Shine On Harvey Moon; Cockles; One By One; Boon; Ties of Blood;* Sue Kirk in *Crossroads; Love With a Perfect Stranger; Harold and Hiram; Give Us a Break; I Woke Up One Morning; Doctor Who; T-Bag Strikes Again; Soft Soap; Bust; Casualty; Mersey Stories; Private Practice; The Ruth Rendell Mysteries: The Best Man To Die; The Bill;* Jackie Ingram in *Coronation Street.* **Address:** c/o RKM. Single; lives in London.

TEALE, *owen*

Owen Teale. Actor. b. Swansea, West Glamorgan, 20 May 1961. Trained at the Guildford School of Acting. **Theatre:** *Cabaret; Charley's Aunt; Run for Your Wife; Waltzing Matilda;* John O'Brien in *The Fifteen Streets; When She Danced; The Comedy of Errors; Bérénice;* (National Theatre); Hotspur in *Henry VI, Pt I* (RSC); Mark Antony in *Julius Caesar* (RSC). **Films:** The Unknown Soldier in *War Requiem;* Will Scarlet in *Robin Hood.* **TV:** *Bowen; Doctor Who; Knights of God; David Copperfield; One By One; The Bureaucracy of Love; Way Out of Order; Strife;* John O'Brien in *The Fifteen Streets;* Det Sgt Mike McCarthy in *Waterfront Beat;* Bentley Drummle in *Great Expectations; Boon.* **Address:** c/o Markham & Froggatt. Lives in South London. m. actress Dilys Watling; 1 s. Ion-Rhys.

TENNANT, *victoria*

Victoria Tennant. Actress. b. London, 30 September 1950. Daughter of theatrical agent Cecil Tennant and Russian prima ballerina Irina Baronova. Trained at Elmhurst Ballet School and Central School of Speech and Drama. **Films:** *The Ragman's Daughter; Nullpunkt; Sphinx; Strangers Kiss; All of Me; The Holcroft Covenant; Flowers In the Attic; Best Seller; Foolsmate; The Handmaid's Tale; Whispers; LA Story.* **TV:** *The Speckled Band; The Winds of War; Tales of the Unexpected; Who's Got the Lady?; Dempsey; Chiefs; Funniest Guy In the World; Under Siege; George Burns Comedy Theatre; The Twilight Zone; Hitchcock; War and Remembrance; Maigret* (TV movie); *Voice of the Heart* (mini-series); *Tattingers; Act of Will* (mini-series). **Address:** c/o Richard Hatton. m. 1st Peppo Vanini (dis), 2nd actor-comedian Steve Martin.

TEWSON, *josephine*

Josephine Tewson. Actress. b. Hampstead, North London, 26 February. Trained at RADA. **Theatre:** Repertory theatre in Darlington, Salisbury and Bristol; *The Real Inspector Hound; Habeas Corpus; Rookery Nook; Noises Off; Woman In Mind; Last of the Red Hot Lovers; The Reluctant Debutante; The Spider's Web* (director); *Brighton Beach Memoirs* (director). **Films:** *The Hound of the Baskervilles; Wilt.* **TV:** *Lord Rustless Entertains; Son of the Bride; It's Tarbuck; Casanova 73; The Dick Emery Show; The Les Dawson Show; The Larry Grayson Show; Odd Man Out; Shelley; Terry and June; Clarence; Keeping Up Appearances.* **Address:** c/o International Artistes. m. 1st actor Leonard Rossiter (dis), 2nd (dec).

THAW, *john*

John Thaw. Actor. b. Manchester, 3 January 1942. Trained at RADA. **Theatre:** *A Shred of Evidence* (debut, Liverpool Playhouse, 1960); *The Fire Raisers* (Royal Court Theatre); *Night and Day; Henry VII; Pygmalion.* **Films:** *The Bofors Gun; The Last Grenade; The Sweeney; Sweeney 2; The Grass Is Singing; Cry Freedom; Business As Usual.* **TV:** *Redcap; The Younger Generation; Thick As Thieves;* Jack Regan in *Regan* and *The Sweeney; Drake's Venture; Killer Waiting; Mitch; Home To Roost;* title role in *Inspector Morse; Bomber Harris;* Stanley Duke in *Stanley and the Women.* **Address:** c/o John Redway Associates. m. 1st Sally Alexander (dis), 2nd actress Sheila Hancock; 2 d. Abigail (from 1st m.), Joanna.

THOMAS, *gareth*

Gareth Thomas. Actor. Trained at RADA. **Theatre:** RSC; Welsh Actors' Company; English Shakespeare Company; *King Lear.* **TV:** *Parkin's Patch; Stocker's Copper; Sutherland's Law; Country Matters; How Green Was My Valley; Children of the Stones; Fathers and Families; Gotcha; Who Pays the Ferryman?; Blake's 7; Hammer House of Horror; The Bell; The Citadel; Love and Marriage; The Adventures of Sherlock Holmes; Dog Food Dan and the Carmarthen Cowboy; By the Sword Divided; Morgan's Boy; Better Days; London's Burning; Chelworth; To Each His Own* (TV movie); *Maigret.* **Address:** c/o Julian Belfrage Associates.

THOMAS, *philip michael*

Philip Michael Thomas. Actor. b. Columbus, Ohio, USA, 26 May 1949. **Theatre:** *Reggae; Selling of the President; Hair.* **Films:** *Stigma; Sparkle Book of Numbers; Coonskin.* **TV:** *This Man Stands Alone; Starsky and Hutch; Medical Center; Roots: The Next Generation; Police Woman; Wonder Woman;* Det Ricardo Tubbs in *Miami Vice.* **Address:** c/o Kate Porter, Exclusive Artists, 2501 West Burbank Boulevard, Burbank, California 91505, USA. m. (dis); 8 children (3 from 1st m.).

THOMPSON, *emma*

Emma Thompson. Actress. b. London, 15 April 1959. Daughter of TV personality Eric Thompson. **Films:** *The Tall Guy; Henry V; Impromptu, Dead Again.* **TV:** *Tutti Frutti; Fortunes of War; The Emma Thompson Show; The Winslow Boy; Knuckle.* **Address:** c/o Noel Gay Artists. m. actor-director Kenneth Branagh.

THOMSON, *gordon*

Gordon Thomson. Actor. b. Ottawa, Canada, 2 March. Trained at the Shakespearian Festival, Ontario. **Theatre:** *The Fantasticks; King John; Godspell.* **Films:** *Explosion; Leopard In the Snow; Acts of Love; The Intruder.* **TV:** Adam Carrington in *Dynasty; Flappers; Fantasy Island; Ryan's Hope.* **Address:** c/o William Morris Agency (USA). m. Maureen (dis).

THOMSON, *marjorie*

Marjorie Thomson. Actress. b. Glasgow. **Theatre:** Unity Theatre, Glasgow; Edinburgh Festival; Citizens' Theatre, Glasgow; Perth Repertory; Royal Variety Performance (1958). **Films:** *The Gorbals Story.* **TV:** *Dr Finlay's Casebook; The McFlannels; Sutherland's Law; Skin Deep; High Living;* Grace Lachlan in *Take the High Road* (1980-). **Address:** c/o Scottish Television. Lives in Perth. m. actor Russell Hunter (dis).

THORNE, *barbara*

Barbara Thorn. Actress. **Theatre:** *Servant of Two Masters; Bedroom Farce; The Taming of the Shrew* (Theatre Royal, Stratford East); *The Black Hole of Calcutta; Four In a Million; The Ghost Train; Taking Steps; Just Between Ourselves; One for the Road; Wuthering Heights; Joseph and the Amazing Technicolor Dreamcoat; The Two of Us; Twelfth Night; Two Lads From London; Happy As a Sandbag* (Ambassadors Theatre); *French Without Tears; Time and Time Again; Frankenstein; The Hollow Crown; Rattle of a Simple Man; Creeps; Revels of Gargantua In Exile; Lottes Electric Opera Film; A Flea In Her Ear; The Cherry Orchard; Macbeth.* **Films:** Sheila Doel in *84 Charing Cross Road.* **TV:** *Game, Set & Match; Grange Hill; Tripods; Love and Marriage: Lucifer; Elizabeth Alone;* Inspector Frazer in *The Bill; TECX.* **Address:** c/o William Morris Agency.

THORNE, *angela*

Angela Thorne. Actress. b. Karachi, Pakistan, 25 January 1939. Trained at Guildhall School of Music and Drama. **Theatre:** *You Never Can Tell* (Haymarket Theatre); *The Rivals; The Merchant of Venice; Prometheus Bound; The Golden Age; Yahoo; Anyone for Denis?; Happy Families; London Assurance.* **Films:** *Oh! What a Lovely War; Yellow Dog.* **TV:** *Take a Sapphire; The Canterville Ghost; That Was the Week That Was; Ballet Shoes; Horizon; To the Manor Born; Three Up, Two Down; Paying Guests; Farrington of the FO; The Good Guys.* **Address:** c/o Michael Whitehall. m. Peter; 2 s. Rupert, Laurence.

THORP, *richard*

Richard Thorp. Actor. b. Purley, Surrey, 2 January 1932. Trained at Guildhall School of Music and Drama. **Theatre:** *Murder At the Vicarage; Moving.* **Films:** *The Dam Busters; The Barretts of Wimpole Street; The Good Companions.* **TV:** Dr John Rennie in *Emergency – Ward 10; Oxbridge 2000; Honey Lane; Public Eye; Maupassant; A Family At War; The Cedar Tree; To the Manor Born; Strangers; The Benny Hill Show; The Harry Worth Show;* Alan Turner in *Emmerdale* (1982-). **Address:** c/o Jean Drysdale Management/Yorkshire Television. Lives in Calderdale, West Yorkshire. m. 3rd TV floor manager Noola; 1 d. Emma, 1 step-d. Sarah, three children by previous marriages.

THRELFALL, *david*

David Threlfall. Actor. b. Manchester, 12 October 1953. Trained at Manchester Polytechnic School of Theatre. **Theatre:** *Bed of Roses; Not Quite Jerusalem.* RSC: *Julius Caesar; Nicholas Nickleby; The Party.* **Films:** *Red Monarch; When the Whales Came; The Russia House.* **TV:** *Scum; The Kiss of Death; Rolling Home; Nicholas Nickleby; Dog Ends; The Gathering Seed; King Lear; The Daughter-In-Law; Paradise Postponed; The Marksman; Murderers Among Us; Person To Person; Nightingales; Jumping the Queue; Casualty of War; Murder of Quality; Titmuss Regained.* **Address:** c/o James Sharkey Associates.

THROWER, debbie

Debbie Thrower. Presenter/Journalist. b. Nairobi, Kenya, 17 November 1957. Reporter on the *South London Guardian, Lynn News and Advertiser*, BBC Radio Leicester and BBC Radio Solent before entering television. **TV:** *South Today* (BBC South, reporter); *Hospital Watch* (reporter/presenter); reporter/newsreader with BBC TV News; *Out of Court; Lifeline; The Thrower Report; Coast To Coast* (TVS news magazine); *Songs of Praise; Fifteen Minutes From Now* (BSB). **Radio:** Guest presenter on BBC Radio 2 shows; *You and Yours; Nation of Shopkeepers; Soundtrack – Animal Hospital; Sunday.* **Address:** c/o Downes Presenters Agency. Lives near Alresford, Hampshire. m. Peter; 1 d. Pets: A labrador. Hobbies: Swimming, reading, cooking. **Favourite TV programme:** Any good cookery programme.

TIERNEY, malcolm

Malcolm Tierney. Actor. **Theatre:** *Measure for Measure; Macbeth* (both RSC). **Films:** *All Neat In Black Stockings; The Eagle Has Landed; Escape To Athena; The Medusa Touch; Star Wars; McVicar; Little Dorrit.* **TV:** *Love On the Dole; The Love School; Where Adam Stood; Family Life; The Main Chance; Collision Course; Poldark; Crime and Punishment;* Richard Warrington in *Spoils of War; Crown Court;* title role in *LS Lowry – A Private View* (drama-documentary); Garfield in *The Home Front; All the World's a Stage; Pope John Paul II; The Barretts of Wimpole Street; Spyship; The Gentle Touch; Bergerac; Lovejoy; C.A.T.S. Eyes; Room At the Bottom; Doctor Who;* Tommy McArdle in *Brookside;* Hannay Geoffrey Ellsworth-Smyth in *A Bit of a Do;* Patrick Woolton in *House of Cards;* Ivan Zoffany in *Put On By Cunning.* **Address:** c/o Hope & Lyne.

TILBROOK, paula

Paula Tilbrook. Actress. **Theatre:** *Kes; Breezeblock Park; Fur Coats and No Knickers; Spend, Spend, Spend; Effie's Burning; Noises Off; Last Tango In Whitby; Baths and Beds* (double-bill); *Stop the Children's Laughter; Chestnuts.* **Films:** *Wetherby; A Private Function; Yanks; Resurrected.* **TV:** *Pit Strike; Tales of the Unexpected; All Day On the Sands; Play for Today; Thicker Than Water; Stay With Me Till Morning; The Reason for Things; Open All Hours; Last of the Summer Wine; Walter* (TV movie); Mrs Tibbett in *Sharon and Elsie* (two series); *Cockles; Glorious Day; The New Statesman;* Betty Hunt in *Brookside; South of the Border; In Sickness and In Health; The Oldest Goose In the Business;* Aunt Flo in *Andy Capp;* title role in *Effie's Burning; The Final Frame* (Channel Four film); Mrs Barford in *Coronation Street.* **Address** c/o Tobias Management.

TILBURY, peter

Peter Tilbury. Actor/Writer. b. Redruth, Cornwall, 20 October 1945. Began as an assistant stage manager and actor at Chelmsford Rep. **Theatre:** RSC; National Theatre. **Films:** *Our Day Out; Breaking Glass; Those Glory, Glory Days.* **TV:** *The Expert; Perils of Pendragon; Dixon of Dock Green; My Son Reuben; Diamond Cracked Diamond; Whodunnit?; C.A.T.S. Eyes; Miss Marple; Fortunes of War; First Born; Casualty; It Takes a Worried Man; This Is David Lander; The Bill.* As writer: *Sprout; Shelley; Sorry, I'm a Stranger Here Myself; It Takes a Worried Man.* **Address:** c/o Scott Marshall.

TIMOTHY, christopher

Christopher Timothy. Actor. b. Bala, Gwynedd, 14 October 1940. Trained at Central School of Speech and Drama. **Theatre:** *Chips With Everything* (New York); *Macbeth; Rosencrantz and Guildenstern Are Dead; Peter Pan; The York Mystery Plays; The Real Thing; The Prisoner of Zenda; Henry VIII.* **Films:** *Othello; Here We Go Round the Mulberry Bush; Alfred the Great; The Virgin Soldiers.* **TV:** *Some Mothers Do 'Ave 'Em; Fly On the Wall; Kate; Spirit of Christmas; The Les Dawson Show; Jackanory Playhouse; See How They Run; The Kitchen; Three Sisters; The Moon Shines Bright On Charlie Chaplin; Twelfth Night; Julius Caesar; The Flaxborough Chronicles: Murder Most English;* James Herriot in *All Creatures Great and Small.* **Books:** *Vet Behind the Ears.* **Address:** c/o Markham & Froggatt. m. (dis); 2 d. Tabitha, Kate, 4 s. Simon, Nicholas, Robin, David.

TOBIN, *anny*

Anny Tobin. Actress. b. Clonmel, County Tipperary, Ireland, 30 March 1945. Brought up in Sevenoaks, Kent. Previously worked for the World Health Organisation and the United Nations Environment Programme. **Theatre:** *Oliver!; The Norman Conquests; The Vortex; Abigail's Party; Raffles; Once a Catholic; Cyrano de Bergerac; Taking Steps; Dandy Dick; The Elephant Man; Deathtrap; On the Razzle; Steaming; Cabaret; Over the Bar; Tom Jones; Bedroom Farce; The Merry Wives of Windsor; Night Must Fall; Passion Play; A Taste of Honey; Woman In Mind; Louisa; Judgement Day.* **TV:** *Play of the Week: Lifelike;* Sister Duffy in *Angels; The Life of Michael Faraday* (US TV); *Shadow of the Noose;* Diane Ellison in *Brookside;* Mary Ellen O'Brien in *The Fifteen Streets; Soldier, Soldier.* **Address:** c/o Hope & Lyne. Single; lives in South London.

TRAVANTI, *daniel j*

Daniel J Travanti. Actor. b. Kenosha, Wisconsin, USA, 7 March 1940. Trained at Yale Drama School and Bucks County Playhouse. **Theatre:** *Who's Afraid of Virginia Woolf?; Othello; Twigs; The Taming of the Shrew.* **TV:** *A Case of Libel; Adam; Aurora; Murrow; Midnight Crossing; Millenium* (all TV movies); Capt Frank Furillo in *Hill Street Blues; General Hospital; The Defenders; Route 66; Kojak; The FBI; Hart To Hart; Knots Landing.* **Address:** c/o William Morris Agency (USA).

TREACHER, *bill*

Bill Treacher. Actor. b. London, 4 June 1937. Trained at the Webber Douglas Academy. **Theatre:** Repertory theatre: *Shout for Your Life* (London West End debut, 1963); *Let Sleeping Wives Lie* (Brian Rix Theatre of Laughter Company); *Murder At the Vicarage* (London West End). **TV:** *Z-Cars; Bless This House; The Agatha Christie Hour; The Professionals; Angels; The Professionals; Maggie and Her; Grange Hill; Fanny By Gaslight; Sweet Sixteen; The Bright Side; Who Sir? Me Sir?;* Arthur Fowler in *EastEnders* (1985-). **Radio:** Sidney, the milkman, in *Mrs Dale's Diary.* **Address:** c/o BBC Elstree Centre. Lives in Suffolk. m. actress Kate Kessey; 1 s. Jamie, 1 d. Sophie. Pets: A dog called Toto and a cat called Lizzie. Hobbies: Sailing, gardening, reading.

TREVES, *frederick*

Frederick William Treves. Actor. b. Cliftonville, Margate, Kent, 29 March 1925. Trained at RADA. **TV:** *The Main Chance; Churchill's People; Z-Cars; The Brothers; The Naked Civil Servant; Softly, Softly; When the Boat Comes In; All Creatures Great and Small; Doctor Who; The Jewel In the Crown; The Invisible Man; My Brother Jonathan; Mountbatten, The Last Viceroy; Silas Marner; Yes, Prime Minister; Agatha Christie's Miss Marple; Inspector Morse; Game, Set & Match; Rumpole of the Bailey; Bomber Harris; Summer's Lease; The Return of Black Beauty; Bergerac; Agatha Christie's Poirot; Parnell and the Englishwoman; The Black Candle; God On the Rocks; Downtown Lagos.* **Address:** c/o April Young. Lives in London. m. Margaret; 2 s. Frederick, Patrick, 1 d. Jennet. Hobbies: Gardening, walking, reading. **Favourite TV Programme:** The Theban Plays.

TROTTER, *robert*

Robert Trotter. Actor. b. Dumbarton, Strathclyde, 7 March. Previously a drama lecturer. **Theatre:** *The Rising; Every Good Boy Deserves Favour; Ane Satyre of the Thrie Estayies: Waiting for Godot; Travesties; A Delicate Balance; I Have Been Here Before; The Boy Friend; Getting On; What Every Woman Knows; The Government Inspector; Hobson's Choice; Babes In the Wood; The Jungle Book; Schellenbrack.* **Films:** *John Paul Jones; The Hand of Adam; Children of Wax; Great Snake.* **TV:** *Clay, Smeddum and Greenden; Burgh Life; The Chiel Among Us; History Is My Witness; Annals of the Parish; The Haggard Falcon; The Omega Factor; Badger By Owl Light; City Sugar; The Fetch; John Ogilvy Saint and Martyr; Square Mile of Murder; The Scotched Earth Show;* Mr Murdoch in *Take the High Road* (1981-). **Address:** c/o Scottish Television. Lives in Glasgow.

TROUGHTON, *david*

David Troughton. Actor. b. Hampstead, North London, 9 June 1950. Son of actor Patrick Troughton; brother of actor Michael Troughton (qv). Performed with the Unicorn children's theatre. **Theatre:** Parents' Day; The Fool; Loot; The Wedding Feast; The Changeling; Terra Nova; A Midsummer Night's Dream; The Rover; Macbeth; Everyman In His Humour (RSC); Fool for Love; Don Juan (National Theatre). **Films:** Dance With a Stranger; The Chain. **TV:** The Regiment; Armchair Theatre; Wings; Man of Destiny; Molière; The Norman Conquests; Our Mutual Friend; Chips With Everything; David Copperfield; Wessex Tales; Backs To the Land; Crime and Punishment; Tales of Sherwood Forest; A Very Peculiar Practice; Performance: The Trials of Oz. **Address:** c/o David White Associates. m. actress Alison Groves; 3 s. Sam, Jim, William.

TROUGHTON, *michael*

Michael Troughton. Actor. b. Hampstead, North London, 2 March 1955. Son of actor Patrick Troughton; brother of actor David Troughton (qv). Began career as an ASM and actor at the Unicorn children's theatre, then ASM in Watford. **Theatre:** Young Vic Theatre; Hay Fever; The Taming of the Shrew (RSC national tour); Happy End; Teething Troubles (national tour). **TV:** Backs To the Land; The Mill On the Floss; Love Story; A Moment In Time; Testament of Youth; The Fatal Spring; Bless Me, Father; The Member for Chelsea; The Grudge Fight; Nancy Astor; Sorrell and Son; A Crack In the Ice; Minder; C.A.T.S. Eyes; Boon; The New Statesman; Singles; Woof!; The Chain. **Address:** c/o Joseph and Wagg. m. Caroline Rake; 1 s. Matthew, 1 d. Sally.

TUCKER, *michael*

Michael Tucker. Actor. b. Baltimore, Maryland, USA, 6 February 1944. Trained at Carnegie Tech Drama School. **Theatre:** Trelawney of the Wells; The Comedy of Errors; Measure for Measure; The Merry Wives of Windsor; Moonchildren; Modigliani; The Goodbye People; The Rivals; Mother Courage; Waiting for Godot; Oh! What a Lovely War; I'm Not Rappaport. **Films:** A Night Full of Rain; Eyes of Laura Mars; An Unmarried Woman; Diner; The Goodbye People; The Purple Rose of Cairo; Radio Days; Tin Men; Checking Out. **TV:** Concealed Enemies; Vampire; Assault and Matrimony; Day One; Spy; Too Young To Die? (all TV movies); The Quinns; Hill Street Blues; Stuart Markowitz in LA Law; Love, Sex...and Marriage; A Family Again. **Address:** c/o Writers & Artists Agency. m. actress Jill Eikenberry; 1 d. Alison (from 1st m.), 1 step-s. Max.

TULLY, *susan*

Susan Tully. Actress. b. Highgate, North London, 20 October 1967. Trained at the Anna Scher Theatre School. **Theatre:** A Little Bit Like Drowning. **Films:** Second To the Right and On Till Morning. **TV:** Our Show; The Saturday Banana (co-presenter, as a child); Why Can't I Go Home?; Never Never Land; Suzanne in Grange Hill; Michelle Fowler in EastEnders (1985-). **Address:** c/o Saraband Associates/BBC Elstree Centre.

ULLMAN, *tracey*

Tracey Ullman. Actress/Comedienne. b. Buckinghamshire, 30 December 1959. **Films:** Give My Regards To Broad Street; Plenty; I Love You To Death. **TV:** Three of a Kind; The Young Visiters (TV movie); Girls On Top; The Tracey Ullman Show (winner, two Emmy awards); A Class Act. **Address:** c/o ICM Duncan Heath Associates. m. TV executive Allan McKeown; 2 d.

URE, *gudrun*

Gudrun Ure. Actress. b. Campsie, Strathclyde, 12 March 1926. Started broadcasting while still at scho[...] and joined the Children's Theatre, before moving to the Citizens' Theatre, Glasgow. **Theatre:** Old V[...] Theatre; Edinburgh Festival; Royal Court Theatre; *Othello; The Comedy of Errors; The Kingfishe[...] Something Unexpected.* **Films:** *Doctor In the House; Million Pound Note; Thirty-Six Hours.* **TV:** *[...] Finlay's Casebook; Sutherland's Law; Going Holiday; Nanny;* title role in *Supergran.* **Address:** c/o Jc[...] Jameson. m. John.

USHER, *paul*

Paul Usher. Actor/Musician. b. Liverpool, 20 April 1961. Performed with rock group 20/20, then becam[...] a Blue Coat at Pontin's. **TV:** Barry Grant in *Brookside* (1982-). **Address:** c/o Mersey Television[...] Hobbies: Music, watching *Monty Python* films.

USTINOV, *sir peter, CBE*

Peter Ustinov. Actor/Writer/Director. b. London, 16 April 1921. Made CBE in 1975; knighted in 1990[...] Trained at the London Theatre Studio. **Films:** *One of Our Aircraft Is Missing; Private Angelo; One o[...] Our Dinosaurs Is Missing; Death On the Nile; Double Murder; Ashanti; Charlie Chan; Evil Under th[...] Sun; Memed My Hawk; Dead Man's Folly; Murder In Three Acts; Appointment With Death.* **TV:** *The Lif[...] of Samuel Johnson; Barefoot In Athens; The Well Tempered Bach; Peter Ustinov's Russia; Pete[...] Ustinov In China; Thirteen At Dinner; Around the World In 80 Days; The French Revolution; Glasnos[...] and Glamour.* **Books:** *Dear Me* (autobiography). **Address:** c/o William Morris Agency. m. 1st Isolde[...] Denham (dis), 2nd Suzanne Cloutier (dis), 3rd Helene de Lau d'Allermans; 3 d. Tamara (from 1st m.)[...] Pavia, Andrea, 1 s. Igor (all from 2nd m.).

VALENTINE, *anthony*

Anthony Valentine. Actor. b. Blackburn, Lancashire, 17 August 1939. Began acting as a child; trained[...] at the Valerie Glynn Stage School. **Films:** *Performance; To the Devil a Daughter; Escape To Athena.[...]* **TV:** *Whirligig; Vice Versa; Children of the New Forest; Rex Milligan; Billy Bunter; John Gabriel[...] Borkman; An Age of Kings; Armchair Theatre; The Avengers; Callan; Codename; The Donati[...] Conspiracy; Colditz; Justice; Raffles; The Dancing Years; Minder; Hammer House of Horror; Tales of the[...] Unexpected; I Have Been Here Before; Dangerous Corner; Robin of Sherwood; Airline; Bergerac[...] Lovejoy; Pulaski; Boon; Lime Street; The Fear; The Price of Fame; The Dirty Dozen; The Winds o[...] Change; Hannay; Boon; The Return of Sherlock Holmes; Trainer; The House of Eliott; Stay Lucky[...] Moon and Son; Van Der Valk.* **Address:** c/o London Management. m. actress Susan Skipper.

VAUGHAN, *matthew*

Matthew Vaughan. Actor. b. Mexborough, South Yorkshire, 17 September 1964. Theatre arts course at[...] Rotherham College of Arts; trained at Rose Bruford College of Speech and Drama. **Theatre:** *Mother Courage; Cloud Nine;* title role in *Macbeth; Ram Alley; Women; Beware Women; Breaking the Silence* (all at drama school); *The New House; Tibetan Inroads; The Public* (Theatre Royal, Stratford East); *The Way To Go Home* (national tour and Royal Court Theatre). **TV:** *Crimestrike; Missing Persons; The Final Frame* (Channel Four film); Michael Feldmann in *Emmerdale.* **Address:** c/o Tobias Management/Yorkshire Television. Single.

VAUGHAN, peter

ter Vaughan. Actor. b. Wem, Shropshire, 4 April 1924. **Films:** *Sapphire; The Naked Runner; ewitness; The Straw Dogs; The Pied Piper; The Savage Messiah; The Mackintosh Man; Valentino; Zulu wn; Time Bandits; The French Lieutenant's Woman; The Razor's Edge; Brazil; King of the Wind. :* Deadline Midnight; The Gold Robbers; Treasure Island; Oliver Twist; Great Expectations; Winston urchill – The Wilderness Years; Citizen Smith; Fox; Jamaica Inn; Czech Mate; Bleak House; Sins; nte Carlo; War and Remembrance; Coast To Coast; When We Are Married; Harry's Kingdom; dename Kyril; Strife; The Bourne Identity; Game, Set & Match; Our Geoff; Under a Dark Angel's e; Countdown To War; Chancer; The Return of Sherlock Holmes; Boon.* **Address:** c/o ICM. m. 1st ress Billie Whitelaw (dis), 2nd actress Lillias Walker; 1 s. David (from 2nd m.).

VERNON, richard

chard Vernon. Actor. b. Reading, Berkshire, 7 March 1925. Trained at Central School of Speech and ama. **Theatre:** *Peter Pan; A Friend Indeed; Hay Fever; Saturday, Sunday, Monday; The Passion of acula; Pack of Lies.* **Films:** *The Human Factor; Gandhi; Evil Under the Sun; Lady Jane; A Month In e Country.* **TV:** *A Friend Indeed; The Man In Room 17; Sextet; Sarah; Upstairs, Downstairs; Edward ; The Duchess of Duke Street; Aren't We All?; The Sandbaggers; Ripping Yarns; Suez; The Hitch-ker's Guide To the Galaxy; Something In Disguise; Nanny; Waters of the Moon; Roll Over ethoven; Paradise Postponed; The Return of the Antelope; Yes, Prime Minister; A Gentleman's Club.* **dress:** c/o Julian Belfrage Associates. m. actress Benedicta Leigh; 1 d. Sarah, 1 s. Tom.

VEZEY, pamela

amela Vezey. Actress. b. Bath, Avon, 19 September. Trained at Bristol Old Vic Theatre School. **heatre:** Repertory theatre in Birmingham, Leeds, Sheffield, Exeter, Oxford, Edinburgh, Coventry; *She toops To Conquer; The Cocktail Party; The Winter's Tale; A Man for All Seasons; Alphabetical Order; emi-Detached; Charley's Aunt; Sisters; Jimmie Dean, Hay Fever; The Pyjama Game; The Boy Friend; ancing Years; A Christmas Carol; Salad Days; Virtue In Danger; Oh, What a Lovely War!; The Wizard f Oz; The Ha Ha; The Threepenny Opera; When We Are Married.* **TV:** *Play of the Month: The ommon; Villains; Public Eye;* Mrs Fisher in *Billy Liar* (three series); *Grange Hill; Sounding Brass;* ath Brownlow in *Crossroads.* **Address:** c/o A.I.M.

VILLIERS, james

ames Villiers. Actor. b. London, 29 September 1933. Trained at RADA. **Theatre:** *Toad of Toad Hall; Vrite Me a Murder; The Burglar; The Happy Apple; Private Lives; The Little Hut; The Doctor's ilemma; The White Devil; Henry IV; St Joan; The Ghost Train; The Passion of Dracula; Peter Pan; The ast of Mrs Cheyney; The Way of the World.* **Films:** *The Entertainer; The Nanny; Otley; The Ruling lass; Saint Jack; Under the Volcano; Spectre; The Amazing Mr Blunden; For Your Eyes Only; King and ountry; Nothing But the Best; Scandal; Mountains of the Moon; King Ralph.* **TV:** *The First Churchills; ady Windermere's Fan; The Millionairess; Pygmalion; The Other 'Arf; The Good Doctor Bodkin dams; Fortunes of War; Chelworth; Anything More Would Be Greedy; House of Cards; A Perfect Hero; ovejoy.* **Address:** c/o ICM Duncan Heath Associates.

VINE, david

avid Vine. Sports presenter. b. Barnstaple, Devon, 3 January 1936. Began career as a newspaper ournalist, before moving into television. **TV:** Westward Television news and sports reporter (1962–6); BC TV sports presenter and commentator (1966–), including Olympic Games, Commonwealth Games, orse of the Year Show, World Ski Cup, Wimbledon Tennis Championships and bowls; *The Superstars.* **ddress:** c/o BBC TV. m. Mandy.

VINE, *john*

John Vine. Actor. b. Banbury, Oxfordshire, 20 February 1951. Trained at Rose Bruford College Speech and Drama. **Films:** *Richard's Things; Gandhi; Eureka; The Keep.* **TV:** *Knights of God; Bus Moneymen; The Seven Dials Mystery; King's Royal; Kate the Good Neighbour; Death of an Expe Witness; Shroud for a Nightingale; Cover Her Face; Murder Not Proven; QED; Not a Penny More; Th Franchise Affair; Rockliffe's Folly; Boon; The Ruth Rendell Mysteries: The Best Man To Di* **Address:** c/o Jeremy Conway. m. Alex; 2 s. Tom, Oliver.

VORDERMAN, *carol*

Carol Vorderman. Presenter/Writer. b. Bedford, 24 December 1960. Gained an MA (Cantab) honou degree in engineering from Cambridge University; worked as an engineer, before entering televisio **TV:** *Countdown; Take Nobody's Word for It; Software Show; Through the Keyhole; Wide Awake Clu Book Tower; So We Bought a Computer; Power Base; Search Out Science; Postcards From Dow Under; Drive My Car; Experiment!; Pick of the Week.* **Address:** c/o Jon Roseman Associates.

VOSBURGH, *tilly*

Tilly Vosburgh. Actress. b. London, 17 December 1960. **Theatre:** *Landmarks; Outskirts; Raspberry; La Summer In Chulimsk; Touch and Go; Up Against It; The Lower Depths; My Sister In This Hous* **Films:** *The Pirates of Penzance; The Missionary; Erik the Viking; Tight Trousers.* **TV:** *Two People Starting Out; Maria Martin; Minder; The Victoria Wood Show; Hold the Back Page; Treatment; File C Jill Hatch; Tears Before Bedtime; Meantime; You'll Never See Me Again; Raspberry; The Functi Room; Strong Poison;* Debbie in *Will You Love Me Tomorrow* (TV movie); *The Bill; A Perfect Sp Radical Chambers; Agatha Christie's Poirot; Morning Sarge; This Is David Lander; The House of Payn Inspector Morse;* Delia in *The Men's Room; The Darling Buds of May; Teenage Health Freak; The Goo Guys.* **Address:** c/o Annette Stone Associates.

WADDINGTON, *bill*

William J Waddington. Actor/Comedian. b. Oldham, Lancashire, 10 June 1916. **Theatre:** Stand-u comic on the same bill as Frankie Laine, Lena Horne, Dorothy Lamour, Billy Daniels and Sophi Tucker; Royal Variety Performance (1955); stage partnership with Sid James. **TV:** *A Family At War Dear Enemy; Talent; Fallen Hero; The Mating Season; Cousin Phyllis; Second Chance;* Perc Sugden in *Coronation Street* (1983-, after four bit-parts in the serial); *Royal Variety Performance* (1989 **Radio:** More than 800 comedy and variety broadcasts, starting with *Ack, Ack, Beer, Beer* (1940 **Address:** c/o Granada TV. Lives in High Lane, Cheshire. m. actress-singer Lillian Day (dec); 2 d. Denise actress Barbara. Pets: Eleven racehorses. Hobbies: Breeding thoroughbred racehorses. **Favourite TV programme:** *Coronation Street;* all sports programmes.

WAITE, *ralph*

Ralph Waite. Actor. b. White Plains, New York, USA, 22 June 1929. Social worker, publicity director assistant editor and minister before turning professional as an actor. **Theatre:** *Hogan's Goat; Th Watering Place; The Trial of Lee Harvey Oswald* (all Broadway); founder of the Los Angeles Actor Theater. **Films:** *Cool Hand Luke; Five Easy Pieces; Lawman; The Grissom Gang; Dime Box; Th Sporting Club; On the Nickel* (also wrote, produced and directed); *Crash and Burn.* **TV:** *The Waltons The Mississippi; Roots* (mini-series); *Red Alert; The Secret Life of John Chapman; OHMS; Angel City; Good Start; Crime of Innocence; Red Earth, White Earth.* **Address:** c/o Harris & Goldberg Talent Agency

WALDEN, brian

Alastair Brian Walden. Presenter/Journalist. b. 8 July 1932. Labour MP, Birmingham, All Saints (1964–74) and Birmingham, Ladywood (1974–77) before becoming a television presenter. **TV:** *Weekend World* (1977–86); *The Walden Interview* (1988, 1989); *Walden* (1990-); *Titmuss Regained* (playing himself). Winner, BAFTA Richard Dimbleby Award, 1985. **Address:** c/o LWT. Lives in Guernsey. m. 3rd Hazel; 1 s. (and 3 s. from previous marriages).

WALDHORN, gary

Gary Waldhorn. Actor. b. London, 3 July 1943. Trained at Yale University Drama School, USA. **Theatre:** National Theatre at the Old Vic; *Sleuth* (Australia, New Zealand and London West End); *Waiting for Godot; Two; Good; Joe Egg; Turning Over; Crime and Punishment.* **Films:** *Zeppelin; The Chain; Escape To Victory; Sir Henry At Rawlinson End; Chinese Whispers.* **TV:** *Outside Edge; All for Love; Love and Marriage; The Prisoner of Zenda; Drummonds; Mrs Capper's Birthday; All At No 20; Moving; Brush Strokes; After Pilkington; Minder; Mr Palfrey of Westminster; Campaign; Missing Persons; Rumpole of the Bailey; The Chief; Titmuss Regained.* **Address:** c/o London Management. m. (dis); 1 s. Joshua.

WALKER, roy

Roy Walker. Comedian/Entertainer. b. Belfast, 31 July 1940. Boy soprano, aged 14, with the Francis Langford Choir; entertained semi-professionally while an apprentice riveter at a shipyard, then turned professional. **Theatre:** *Dick Whittington; Snow White and the Seven Dwarfs; Cinderella; Catchphrase.* **TV:** *New Faces* (1977); *The Comedians; Licensed for Singing and Dancing* (own series); *Summertime Special* (host); *Live From Her Majesty's; Blankety Blank; Des O'Connor Tonight; The Bob Monkhouse Show; Tarby and Friends; The Paul Daniels Show; The Laughter Show; Live From the Palladium; Night of a Hundred Stars; Laugh Attack; The Russ Abbot Show; Catchphrase* (host, quiz show, seven series). **Address:** c/o Mike Hughes Entertainments/Clifford Elson Publicity. m. Jean (dec); 1 d. Joanne, 2 s. Mark, Phil. Hobbies: Golf, keeping fit.

WALLACE, juliet

Julie Therese Wallace. Actress. b. Wimbledon, South London, 28 May 1961. Trained at LAMDA. **Theatre:** *Billy the Kid; Barrel of Laughs; The House of Usher; Beauty and the Beast;* Anne in *The Worlds* (Royal Court Theatre). **Films:** Rosika in *The Living Daylights;* Coaxer in *The Threepenny Opera; Hawks; The Lunatic.* **TV:** Ruth in *The Life and Loves of a She-Devil; Morning Sarge; Selling Hitler; Stay Lucky; Time Riders.* **Address:** c/o Annette Stone Associates. **Favourite TV programme:** *Film* series with Barry Norman.

WALTER, harriet

Harriet Walter. Actress. Trained at LAMDA. **Theatre:** *The Ragged Trousered Philanthropists; Hamlet; Cloud Nine; The Seagull; The Merchant of Venice.* RSC: *Nicholas Nickleby; A Midsummer Night's Dream; The Twin Rivals; The Witch of Edmonton; Henry IV, Pts I and II; All's Well That Ends Well* (London and Broadway); *The Castle; Twelfth Night; The Duchess of Malfi.* Winner, Laurence Olivier Award for Actress of the Year In a Revival, 1988, for *Cymbeline, Three Sisters* and *A Question of Geography* (all RSC). **Films:** *Reflections; Turtle Diary; The Good Father; Milou En Mai; La Nuit Miraculeuse.* **TV:** *The Imitation Game; The Cherry Orchard;* Amy Johnson in *Amy; The Price; Girls On Top; Dorothy L Sayers Mysteries; Omnibus: Caryl Churchill; Benefactors; Timewatch; They Never Slept.* **Address:** c/o Richard Stone Partnership.

WALTERS, *julie*

Julie Walters. b. Birmingham, 22 February 1950. Trained at Manchester Polytechnic School of Theatre. **Theatre:** *Educating Rita* (RSC, winner Theatre Critics' and Variety Club awards for most promising new artist of 1980). **Films:** *Educating Rita* (winner, Golden Globe, BAFTA and Variety Club Best Actress awards); *She'll Be Wearing Pink Pyjamas; Car Trouble; Personal Services; Buster; Killing Dad; Mack the Knife; Prick Up Your Ears; Stepping Out.* **TV:** *Talent; Good Fun; Nearly a Happy Ending; Living Together; Happy Since I Met You; Say Something Happened; Intensive Care; Boys From the Blackstuff; Monologue; Wood and Walters; Unfair Exchanges; The Secret Diary of Adrian Mole Aged 13¾; Victoria Wood As Seen On TV; The Birthday Party; The Victoria Wood Show; Talking Heads; GBH; Julie Walters and Friends.* **Address:** c/o ICM.

WANAMAKER, *zoe*

Zoe Wanamaker. Actress. b. New York, USA, 13 May 1949. Daughter of actor-director Sam Wanamaker. Trained at Central School of Speech and Drama. **Theatre:** *Loot* (Broadway); *Bay At Nice; Wrecked Eggs; Wild Oats; Once In a Lifetime; Piaf* (London and New York); *Twelfth Night; The Comedy of Errors; Mother Courage; The Importance of Being Earnest; Mrs Klein; Othello; Guys and Dolls; Cabaret; The Crucible.* **Films:** *Hitler: The Last Ten Days; Inside the Third Reich; The Hunger; The Raggedy Rawney.* **TV:** *The Silver Mark; Village Hall; The Beaux' Stratagem; The Devil's Crown; Baal; Strike; All the World's a Stage; Richard III; Edge of Darkness; Paradise Postponed; Poor Little Rich Girl; Ball-Trap On the Cote Sauvage; The Dog It Was That Died; Othello; Inspector Morse; Prime Suspect; Love Hurts.* **Address:** c/o Jeremy Conway.

WARD, *tracy-louise*

Tracy-Louise Ward. Actress. b. London, 22 December 1958. Trained at the Drama Studio; performed in cabaret. **Theatre:** *Our Day Out; Intimacy* (London West End). **Films:** *Dance With a Stranger.* **TV:** *If Tomorrow Comes; Doctor Who; C.A.T.S. Eyes; Mussolini.* **Address:** c/o London Management. m. Harry Worcester.

WARING, *derek*

Derek Waring. Actor. b. London, 26 April 1930. Brother of TV scriptwriter Richard Waring. Trained at RADA. **Films:** *Dunkirk; I Accuse; Battle of Britain; Hitler: The Last Ten Days.* **TV:** *The Killers; Public Eye; The Informer; Not In Front of the Children; The Gold Watch Club; Sherlock Holmes; Callan; The Doctors; Z-Cars; Marked Personal; The Avengers; Carrington VC; Moody and Peg; Forget Me Not; She, And Mother Makes Three; Crown Court; An Unofficial Rose; Forget Me Not; Killers; The New Avengers; Two's Company; Miss Jones and Son; The Flaxborough Chronicles; Hi-Summer; Wings; George and Mildred; Thundercloud; Doctor Who; The Professionals; Partners; Don't Rock the Boat.* **Address:** c/o Barry Burnett Organisation. m. actress Dorothy Tutin; 1 d. Amanda, 1 s. Nicholas.

WARING, *george*

George Waring. Actor/Director. b. Eccles, Lancashire, 20 February 1927. Began acting with RAF Rep Company; various jobs before joining the Century Theatre. **Theatre:** Repertory theatre; *Emil and the Detectives; Alfie; The Fourth of June; The Bells; The Beaux' Stratagem; Noises Off; The Cherry Orchard; The Importance of Being Earnest; The Second Mrs Tanqueray; Lettice & Lovage; The Resistible Rise of Arturo Ui.* **Films:** *Squaring the Circle; God's Outlaw.* **TV:** *Z-Cars; Mrs Thursday; Doctor Who; Softly, Softly; Castlehaven; Crown Court; Armchair Thriller; Six Days of Justice; Arnold Swain in* Coronation Street; *Emmerdale Farm; Andy Capp; Mixed Blessings; No Place Like Home; After the War; The Bill; Forever Green; Agatha Christie's Poirot.* **Address:** c/o Joseph and Wagg. m. 1st (dis), 2nd actress Geraldine Gwyther; 1 d. Georgina, 1 s. Geoffry.

WARWICK, *james*

James Warwick. Actor. b. Broxbourne, Hertfordshire, 17 November 1947. Trained at Central School of Speech and Drama (Spotlight Award winner). **Theatre:** Vivat! Vivat Regina!; The Rocky Horror Show; Black Comedy; The Real Thing; Pride and Prejudice; Dr Faustus; Camelot; Night and Day. **Films:** The Secret Adversary. **TV:** Late Night Line-Up (TV debut, as an ostrich); The Onedin Line; Terracotta Horse; Rock Follies; Edward VII; Turtle's Progress; Doctor Who; Telford's Change; Lillie; Why Didn't They Ask Evans?; The Seven Dials Mystery; Nightmare Man; The Bell; Tales of the Unexpected: The Sound Machine; Tommy in Partners In Crime; Scarecrow & Mrs King; Dead Head; Howards' Way; Bergerac; Blore MP; Don't Wait Up; Perfect Scoundrels; Love Hurts. **Address:** c/o Barry Burnett Organisation. Single; lives in London. Hobbies: Travel, music, keeping fit.

WARWICK, *richard*

Richard Warwick. Actor. b. Dartford, Kent, 24 April 1945. Trained at RADA. **Theatre:** Higgins in My Fair Lady; In Praise of Love; The Real Thing. **Films:** Romeo and Juliet; If...; The Bed-Sitting Room; First Love; The Breaking of Bumbo; Alice's Adventures In Wonderland; Sebastiane; The Tempest. **TV:** The Vortex; Please Sir!; The Last of the Mohicans; Warship; Brensham People; School Play; A Fine Romance; It's My Pleasure. **Address:** c/o ICM.

WASHINGTON, *denzel*

Denzel Washington. Actor. b. Mount Vernon, New York, USA, 28 December 1954. Trained with the American Conservatory Theater. **Theatre:** Ceremonies In Dark Old Men; The Mighty Gents; Coriolanus; When Chickens Come Home To Roost; Malcolm X; A Soldier's Play. **Films:** Cry Freedom; Carbon Copy; For Queen and Country. **TV:** The George McKenna Story (TV movie); Dr Phillip Chandler in St Elsewhere; Wilma; Flesh and Blood. **Address:** c/o William Morris Agency (USA). m. Paulette Pearson; 1 s. John David, 1 d. Katia.

WATERS, *nick*

Nick Waters. Actor. b. Melbourne, Australia, 4 September 1951. Studied drama and mime at the Claremont Theatre, Melbourne. **Films:** The Great McCarthy; Strike-Bound; The Humpty-Dumpty Man; The Lighthorseman; Snowy River II. **TV:** Rush; Against the Wind; The Last Outlaw; The Sullivans; The Anzacs. **Address;** c/o Actors' Agency. m. Joanne; 2 s. Sean, Oliver. Hobbies: Cricket, horse-training, music, fishing, crosswords.

WATERMAN, *dennis*

Dennis Waterman. Actor. b. London, 24 February 1948. Began acting as a child; trained at the Corona Academy. **Films:** Up the Junction; A Smashing Bird I Used To Know; My Lover, My Son; The Belstone Fox; Fright; Man In the Wilderness; Sweeney; Sweeney 2. **TV:** Title role in Just William (as a child); Fair Exchange; Cry Baby Bunting; Journey Into the Unknown; The Right Attitude; Regan; The Sweeney; Terry in Minder; The World Cup – A Captain's Tale (also as co-producer); Mr H Is Late; Minder On the Orient Express; Sextet; The Life and Loves of a She-Devil; Thomas Gynn in Stay Lucky; Tony Carpenter in On the Up. **Records:** I Could Be So Good for You (Top 10 single). **Address:** c/o ICM. m. 1st Penny (dis), 2nd actress Patricia Maynard (dis), 3rd actrss Rula Lenska (sep); 2 d. Hannah, Julia (both from 2nd m.).

WATFORD, *gwen*

Gwen Watford. Actress. b. London, 10 September 1927. Trained at Embassy Theatre, Swiss Cottage. **Films:** *Never Take Sweets From a Stranger; The Very Edge; Cleopatra; Cry Freedom.* **TV:** *Fate and Mr Brown; Mr Brown Comes Home; Till Time Shall End; A Woman of No Importance; Take Care of Madam; Dangerous Corner; The Waters of Babylon; Second Time Around; The Train Now Standing . . .; A Bit of an Adventure; A Provincial Lady; A Suitable Case for Killing; Love Me To Death; Don't Forget To Write; Aren't We All?; The Shillingbury Tales; The Case of the Middle-Aged Wife; Present Laughter; Sorrell and Son; The Body In the Library; John David; Reluctant Chickens; Not That Kind of Person; Sharing Time; Elders and Betters; Behaving Badly; The Winslow Boy; Relatively Speaking.* **Address:** c/o Peters Fraser & Dunlop. m. actor Richard Bebb; 2 s. Mark, Owen.

WATSON, *ken*

Ken Watson. Actor/Writer. b. London. Trained at RADA. **Theatre:** Repertory theatre in Wolverhampton, Colchester, Oxford, Aberdeen and Edinburgh; *St Joan; Ticket of Leave Man.* **Films:** *Dr Who and the Daleks; Great White Hope; The Belstone Fox.* **TV:** *Diamond Run; The Undoing; King and Country; The Barretts of Wimpole Street; The Brothers;* Dr Dick Graham in *Emergency – Ward 10;* Ralph Lancaster in *Coronation Street; Crown Court; Darwin;* Brian Blair in *Take the High Road; Roll On Four O'Clock; Losing Her; Too Close To the Edge; Singles; Airline.* As writer or script editor: *From Inner Space; The Westerners; Fancy That.* **Address:** c/o Joan Gray. m. TV make-up artist Joan Watson; 1 d. Kate, 1 s. Jamie.

WATSON, *moray*

Moray Watson. Actor. b. Sunningdale, Berkshire, 25 June 1930. Trained at the Webber Douglas Academy. **Films:** *The Grass Is Greener; Every Home Should Have One; The Valiant; Operation Crossbow; The Sea Wolves; Crazy Like a Fox.* **TV:** Richard in *Compact; The Borderers; On Approval; Quiller; Upstairs, Downstairs; A Place In the Sun; The Pallisers; Murder Most English; Rumpole of the Bailey; Company and Co; Pride and Prejudice; Winston Churchill – The Wilderness Years; Doctor Who; Tales of the Unexpected; Nobody's Perfect; Union Castle; Yes Minister; Minder; Rude Health; Agatha Christie's Miss Marple: The Body In the Library; Star Cops; Flying Lady; Seal Morning; Campion; Norbert Smith – A Life; The House of Eliott;* the Brigadier in *The Darling Buds of May.* **Address:** c/o Ken McReddie. m. actress Pam Marmont; 1 d. Emma, 1 s. Robin.

WATT, *tom*

Thomas Watt. Actor. b. Wanstead, East London, 14 February 1956. Gained a BA hons degree in drama from Manchester University. **Theatre:** *Alberto y los Trios Paranoias;* performances with rep and improvisational companies; East West Co European tour; Graeae Theatre British and Indian tour; *The Foreigner; The Cherry Orchard* (both London West End). **TV:** *The Old Firm; A Kind of Loving; My Father's House; Never the Twain; Family Man;* Lofty Holloway in *EastEnders; Night Network; South of the Border; The Last Laugh; And a Nightingale Sang.* **Address:** c/o ICM Duncan Heath Associates.

WAX, *ruby*

Ruby Wax. Actress/Writer. b. Chicago, Illinois, USA, 19 April 1953. **TV:** *Girls On Top* (also as writer); *Don't Miss Wax* (chat-show); *Miami Beach; East Meets Wax; The Full Wax.* **Address:** c/o Peters Fraser & Dunlop.

WAXMAN, *al*

Al Waxman. Actor/Director. b. Toronto, Canada, 2 March 1935. Studied film technique in London and New York. **Films:** *Wild Horse Hank; Double Negative; Atlantic City; Tulips Deathbite; Class of '84.* **TV:** *The King of Kensington;* Lieutenant Bert Samuels in *Cagney and Lacey.* As director: *The Crowd Inside; The Littlest Hobo; Cagney and Lacey.* m. Sara; 1 d. Tobarone, 1 s. Adam.

WEBB, *lizzie*

Lizzie Webb. Fitness presenter. b. London, 12 August 1948. Trained as a teacher of English, drama and dance, then taught at a boys' school and spent a year teaching disturbed adolescents, before teaching at Richmond Ice Rink, Guildford School of Acting and stage schools, including the Italia Conti Academy. Also worked as a choreographer. **TV:** *Good Morning Britain* and *After Nine* (TV-am, 1983-). **Books:** *Lizzie Webb's Total Fitness Book.* **Address:** c/o TV-am. m. (dis); 1 s. Ben.

WEBSTER, *gary*

Gary Webster. Actor. b. Whitechapel, East London, 3 February 1964. Stage-door keeper and odd-job man at the Shaw Theatre, London, before training at LAMDA. **TV:** *Taggart; The Bill; London's Burning; Inspector Morse; EastEnders;* Ray Daley in *Minder.* **Address:** c/o Hope & Lyne. Single; lives in South London.

WEEKS, *alan*

Alan Frederick Weeks. Sports commentator. b. Bristol, Avon, 8 September 1923. Worked as public relations officer for Brighton Sports Stadium and secretary of the Brighton Tigers ice hockey club, before entering television. **TV:** BBC sports commentator since 1951, covering ice hockey, ice skating, soccer, gymnastics, swimming, World Cups, Olympic Games, Winter Olympics, athletics world championships and Commonwealth Games; *Grandstand; Pot Black.* **Address:** c/o Bagenal Harvey Organisation. Lives in Hove, East Sussex. m. former ice-skating champion (Barbara) Jane; 1 d. Beverly, 2 s. Nigel (dec), Roderick. **Favourite TV programme:** *Sportsnight.*

WEITZ, *bruce*

Bruce Weitz. Actor. b. Norwalk, Connecticut, USA, 27 May 1943. Trained with Long Wharf Repertory Theater. **Theatre:** *Death of a Salesman; Norman, Is That You?; Shakespeare In the Park.* **TV:** *Quincy; Kojak; One Day At a Time; The White Shadow; Lou Grant;* Det Mick Belker in *Hill Street Blues; Happy Days; Mork and Mindy; Kaz; The Rockford Files.* **Address:** c/o William Morris Agency (USA). m. (dis).

WELLAND, *colin*

Colin Welland. Actor/Writer. b. Leigh, Lancashire, 4 July 1934. **Films:** *Kes; Villain; The Straw Dogs; The Sweeney.* As writer: *Yanks; Chariots of Fire* (winner, Oscar); *Chaplin; The Yellow Jersey; Twice In a Lifetime; A Dry White Season.* **TV:** *North At Six; The Verdict Is Yours;* PC Graham in *Z-Cars* (1964–7) *United Kingdom; Man At the Top; Left; Passage To England; The Cost of Loving; Blue Remembered Hills; Jack Point; Cowboys; How To Stay Alive.* As writer-actor: *Banglestein's Boys; Slattery's Mounted Foot; Say Goodnight To Grandma; Roll On Four O'Clock.* As writer: *Catherine Wheel; The Hallelujah Handshake; A Room Full of Holes; Leeds United; Kisses At Fifty; The Wild West Show; Your Man From Six Counties.* **Address:** c/o Peter Charlesworth. m. former teacher Pat; 3 d. Genevieve, Catherine, Caroline, 1 s. Christie.

WELLING, *albert*

Albert Welling. Actor. b. London, 29 February 1952. Gained a BA hons degree in drama from Manchester University. **Theatre:** National Theatre; RSC; Royal Court Theatre; Young Vic Theatre. **TV:** *Lovejoy; EastEnders; Howards' Way; Tales of the Unexpected; Bulman; Telford's Change; Au Wiedersehen, Pet; The Gathering Seed; A Voyage Round My Father; Wish Me Luck; Inspector Morse; Boon; Casualty; Titmuss Regained; Moon and Son.* **Address:** c/o David White Associates. m. Judy Riley; 2 s. Benedict, Kaspar.

WELSBY, *elton*

Roger Elton Welsby. Presenter. b. St Helens, Lancashire, 28 May 1951. Sports editor of the *Liverpool Weekly News,* before entering radio and television. **TV:** *Kick Off; Match Time; Sportsweek; Soccer Night* (all Granada TV); *Results Service; Midweek Sport Special; The Match; The European Match;* anchorman for ITV's Olympics coverage, 1988, and World Cup coverage, 1990. **Radio:** Sports editor and commentator, Radio City, Liverpool (1974–8). **Address:** c/o Bagenal Harvey Organisation. Lives on the Wirral, Merseyside. m. Joyce, 1 s. Christopher, 1 d. Laura. Pets: A golden retriever called Jodie. Hobbies: Golf. **Favourite TV programme:** *Only Fools and Horses.*

WENDT, *george*

George Wendt. Actor. b. Chicago, Illinois, USA, 17 October. Trained with the Second City Comedy Workshop, Chicago. **Films:** *House; Gung Ho; Airplane II; Dreamscape; No Small Affair; Fletch; The Ratings Game; Glory Days.* **TV:** *Soap; Taxi; Alice; Hart To Hart; The Twilight Zone; St Elsewhere;* Norm Peterson in *Cheers.* **Address:** c/o Writers & Artists Agency. m. Bernadette; 1 d. Hilary, 2 step-s. Joshua, Andrew.

WENZEL, *brian*

Brian Wenzel. Actor. b. Adelaide, South Australia, 24 May 1929. Started as a chorus boy at the age of 17. **Films:** *The Death Train; Caddie; Alison's Birthday; The Odd Angry Shot.* **TV:** *Certain Women; Punishment;* Frank Gilroy in *A Country Practice; Division 4; Young Ramsey; Matlock Police; Homicide; Ryan; Boney.* **Address:** c/o June Cann Management. m. Linda.

WEST, *timothy*

imothy West. Actor. b. Bradford, West Yorkshire. Son of theatrical parents. Started as an ASM at Wimbledon Theatre. **TV:** *Big Breadwinner Hog; Richard II; Edward II; The Boswell and Johnson Show; Joy; Hine; Horatio Bottomley; Villains; The After Dinner Game; Cottage To Let; Hard Times; Henry VIII; Crime and Punishment; Churchill's Generals; Murder Is Easy; Oliver Twist; Brass; The Last Bastion; The Nightingale Saga; Tender Is the Night; The Monocled Mutineer; A Very Peculiar Practice; The Good Doctor Bodkin Adams; A Roller Next Year; What the Butler Saw; Harry's Kingdom; When We Are Married; The Garden of Evelyn; Weekend At Reykjavik; Strife; Shadow On the Sun; The Contractor; Campion; Blore MP; Beecham; Kennet and Avon.* **Address:** c/o James Sharkey Associates. m. actress Prunella Scales (qv); 1 d. Juliet, 2 s. actor Samuel, Joseph.

WESTBROOK, *danniella*

Danniella Westbrook. Actress. b. 5 November 1973. Trained at the Sylvia Young Theatre School. **Theatre:** *Joseph and the Amazing Technicolor Dreamcoat* (Royalty Theatre); *Jesus Christ Superstar* (Churchill Theatre, Bromley). **TV:** *To Have and To Hold; Grange Hill; Bad Boyes; Alfonso Bonzo; Agatha Christie's Miss Marple; The London Programme* (Thames Television); Sam Butcher (née Mitchell) in *EastEnders.* **Address:** c/o Sylvia Young Management.

WHATELY, *kevin*

Kevin Whately. Actor. b. Tyneside, 6 February 1951. **TV:** *Auf Wiedersehn Pet*, Det Sgt Lewis in *Inspector Morse; Night Voice* (TV movie). **Address:** c/o CDA.

WHICKER, *alan*

Alan Donald Whicker. TV broadcaster/writer. b. Cairo, Egypt, 2 August 1925. **TV:** *Tonight* (1957–64); *Whicker's World; Whicker Down Under; Whicker On Top of the World!; Whicker In Sweden; The Alan Whicker Report; Whicker's New World; Whicker In Europe; Broken Hill – Walled City; Gairy's Grenada; World of Whicker; Whicker's Orient; Whicker Within a Woman's World; Whicker's South Seas; Whicker Way Out West; Whicker's World – Down Under; Whicker's World Aboard the Orient Express; Around Whicker's World In 25 Years; Whicker's World – The First Million Miles; Whicker's World – A Fast Boat To China; Whicker; Whicker's World – Living With Uncle Sam; Whicker's World Down Under – Living With Waltzing Matilda; Whicker's World – Hong Kong.* Winner, BAFTA Richard Dimbleby Award, 1978. **Address:** Le Gallais Chambers, St Helier, Jersey.

WHITE, *betty*

Betty White. Actress. b. Oak Park, Illinois, USA, 17 January 1924. **TV:** *Life With Elizabeth; The Betty White Show; A Date With the Angels; Mama's Family;* Sue Ann Nivens in *The Mary Tyler Moore Show* (winner, Emmy Best Actress awards, 1975, 1976); *Just Men* (game-show, host, Emmy award, 1983); Rose in *The Golden Girls* (winner, Emmy Best Actress award, 1986). **Books:** Author of two books about animals. **Address:** c/o William Morris Agency (USA). Lives in Los Angeles. m. 1st Lane Allen (dis), 2nd TV game-show host Allen Ludden (dec); 2 step-d. Martha, Sarah, 1 step-s. David.

WHITE, *frances*

Frances White. Actress. b. Leeds, 1 November 1938. Trained at Central School of Speech and Drama. **Theatre:** *Fit To Print* (Duke of York's Theatre); *A Severed Head* (Criterion Theatre); *Appearances* (Mayfair Theatre). **Films:** *The Pumpkin Eater; Press for Time; Mary Queen of Scots.* **TV:** *The Victorian Chaise Longue; Armchair Theatre: Blue and White; Raging Calm; The Secret Agent; The Prince Regent; Wednesday's Child* (documentary); *Nobody's Perfect; Crossroads; I Claudius; Rumpole of the Bailey; Woke Up One Morning; Paradise Postponed; A Very Peculiar Practice; A Perfect Spy; Chelworth; Miss Flood* in *May To December* (three series). **Address:** c/o Bryan Drew. m. Anthony Hone (dis); 1 d. Kate.

WHITE, *mela*

Mela White. Actress. b. Woodford, Essex, 28 March. **Theatre:** *The Westwoods.* **TV:** *Shoestring; Angels; Bergerac; Casualty.* **Address:** c/o Thomas and Benda Associates. m. actor Ronald Lacey (dis); 1 d. Rebecca, 1 s. Jonathan.

WHITEHEAD, *amanda*

Amanda Whitehead. Actress. b. Oldham, Lancashire, 12 March 1965. Attended Oldham Theatre Workshop, took an A-level in theatre studies and trained at the Royal Scottish Academy of Music and Drama. **Theatre:** *No More Sitting On the Old School Bench; Alice In Wonderland; Beauty and the Beast; Wuthering Heights; Waving and Drowning; Snow White and the Seven Dwarfs.* **TV:** 'Extra' in *Tutti Frutti;* Emma Aitken in *Take the High Road* (1989-). **Address:** c/o Scottish Television. Single; lives in Oldham and Glasgow.

WHITEHEAD, *geoffrey*

Geoffrey Whitehead. Actor. b. Sheffield, South Yorkshire, 1 October 1939. Trained at RADA. **Films:** *The Rocking Horse Winner.* **TV:** *The Bulldog Breed; Z-Cars; The Avengers; Jane Eyre; The Sweeney; Some Mothers Do 'Ave 'Em; Affairs of the Heart; Upstairs, Downstairs; Crown Court; Hadleigh; Last of the Best Men; Robin's Nest; The Foundation;* title role in *The Rivals of Sherlock Holmes; Inside the Third Reich; The Kit Curran Radio Show; Who Dares Wins; Reilly – Ace of Spies; The Cleopatras; The Consultant; Alas Smith and Jones; Pinkerton's Progress; The Doll; Chelmsford 123; Scarecrow & Mrs King; Peter the Great; The Fourth Floor; War and Remembrance; A Strike Out of Time* (TV movie); *The Strauss Dynasty; Executive Stress; Red Fox; Second Thoughts.* **Address:** c/o Bryan Drew. m. actress Mary Hanefey; 1 d. Clare, 1 s. Jonty.

WHITEHOUSE, *christopher*

Christopher Whitehouse. Actor. Trained at Central School of Speech and Drama. **Theatre:** *Who's Afraid of Virginia Woolf?; Hamlet; Macbeth; Merchant of Venice; It's a Clean, Well Lighted Place; Endgame* (Royal Court Theatre); *Days of the Commune; The Bundle; That Good Between Us; Pillars of the Community* (all RSC); *A View From the Bridge; All My Sons; The Devils; The Old Order; Diary of a Hunger Strike; WCPC; Falling Prey.* **TV:** *Life of Shakespeare; Turtle's Progress; Harry's Game; Widows; Bleak House; Crossfire; Game, Set & Match; Bergerac;* Mervyn in *EastEnders; Casualty; Shoot To Kill; The Bill; Chimera; Soldier, Soldier.* **Address:** c/o Mary Arnold Management.

WHITELAW, *billie*

Billie Whitelaw. Actress. b. Coventry, Warwickshire, 6 June 1932. **Theatre:** National Theatre; RSC. **Films:** *Bobbikins; Hell Is a City; No Love for Johnnie; Payroll; The Comedy Man; Charlie Bubbles; Twisted Nerve; The Adding Machine; Eagle In a Cage; Leo the Last; Start the Revolution Without Me; Gumshoe; Frenzy; Nightwatch; The Omen; The Water Babies; An Unsuitable Job for a Woman; The Chain; Shadey; Old Girlfriends; Maurice; The Dressmaker; The Krays.* **TV:** *No Trams To Lime Street; Resurrection; The Poet Game; You and Me; Dr Jekyll and Mr Hyde; Wessex Tales; Beckett; Ghost Trio; Not I; Happy Days; Jamaica Inn; Committee; Private Schultz; The Secret Garden; The Picnic; Imaginary Friends; Camille; A Tale of Two Cities; The Fifteen Streets; Lorna Doone; Joyriders; The Cloning of Joanna May.* **Address:** c/o ICM Duncan Heath Associates.

WHITFIELD, *june, OBE*

June Rosemary Whitfield. Actress. b. London, 11 November. OBE, 1985. Trained at RADA. **Theatre:** *Ace of Clubs; South Pacific; Love From Judy* (all London West End); *A Bedful of Foreigners* (Victoria Palace and Duke of York's Theatres); *Not Now, Darling* (Savoy Theatre); *The Rivals; An Ideal Husband; Ring Round the Moon; Over My Dead Body* (Savoy Theatre). **Films:** *Carry On Abroad; Carry On Girls; Bless This House; The Spy With the Cold Nose.* **TV:** *Beggar My Neighbour; The Best Things In Life; Hancock's Half Hour; Scott On ...; Happy Ever After* (five series); *Terry and June* (10 series); *It Doesn't Have To Hurt* (presenter). **Radio:** *Take It From Here;* Eth in *The Glums; The News Huddlines.* **Address:** c/o April Young. Lives in London. m. Tim Aitchison; 1 d. actress Suzy. Pets: A dog named Rabbit.

WHITROW, *benjamin*

Benjamin Whitrow. Actor. b. Oxford, 17 February 1937. **Films:** *A Man for all Seasons; Quadrophenia; Brimstone and Treacle; A Shocking Accident; Clockwise; Personal Services; On the Black Hill; Hawks.* **TV:** *The Brontes of Howarth; Fathers and Families; The Merchant of Venice; The Kidnapping of James Cross; Abel's Will; Tales of the Unexpected; By George; Franklin and Jessica; King Lear; All for Love; A Moment In Time; Nanny; Minor Complications; Suez; Minutes and Men; On Approval; The Factory; Harry's Game; Hay Fever; Paying Guests; Bergerac; A Bit of Fry and Laurie; Ffizz; Chancer; The New Statesman.* **Address:** c/o Lou Coulson.

WHITTAKER, *sally*

Sally Whittaker. Actress. b. Middleton, Lancashire, 3 May 1963. Trained at Mountview Theatre School. **Theatre:** Toured as a dancer in *The Metal Mickey Road Show;* toured Britain and America with Abbadaba Theatre Company, including old-time music-hall and *Beauty and the Beast.* **TV:** *Juliet Bravo; The Practice; Hold Tight!;* Sally Webster (née Seddon) in *Coronation Street* (1986-); *Royal Variety Performance* (1989). **Address:** c/o Barry Brown & Partner/Granada TV. Single; lives in Altrincham, Cheshire, and North London. Hobbies: Horse-riding, keep-fit, walking.

WILBY, *james*

James Wilby. Actor. b. Rangoon, Burma, 20 February 1958. Attended public school in Britain, before graduating from Durham University and training at RADA. **Theatre:** *Another Country* (London West End); *As You Like It; Jane Eyre; The Tempest.* **Films:** *Privileged* (Oxford Film Foundation); *Dreamchild; A Room With a View; Maurice; A Handful of Dust; A Summer Story; Conspiracy.* **TV:** *The Adventures of Sherlock Holmes; The Bill; Dutch Girls; The Storyteller: Sapsorrow; A Tale of Two Cities; Mother Love; Adam Bede.* **Address:** c/o ICM Duncan Heath Associates. m. Shana; 1 s. Barnaby.

WILCOX, *paula*

Paula Wilcox. Actress. b. Manchester, 13 December 1949. Former member of the National Youth Theatre. **Theatre:** *Apprentices; My Fat Friend* (Australian tour); *Touch of Spring; Time To Kill; Bedroom Farce* (London West End); *Romeo and Juliet; The Cherry Orchard; The Birthday Party; Heartbreak House; Time and the Conways; Pygmalion; Hedda Gabler; Blithe Spirit; See How They Run; Shirley Valentine* (Manchester and London West End). **Films:** *The Lovers; Man About the House.* **TV:** *The Lovers; Coronation Street; The Dustbinmen; The Liver Birds; On Her Majesty's Pleasure; Man About the House;* title role in *Miss Jones and Son; The Cost of Loving; Kate; Hadleigh; Remember the Lambeth Walk?; Noel Gay; The Bright Side; Boon; Fiddlers Three; Crazy Comparisons* (team captain). **Address:** c/o Barry Burnett Organisation. m. actor Derek Seaton (dec).

WILLIAMS, *ian*

Ian Williams. Actor. b. 30 April 1968. Trained at the American Center for Musical Theater, Hollywood, USA. **Theatre:** *Godspell; Aladdin; Street Theatre; The Glory of Christmas; The Glory of Easter; Vulture Culture; Carousel.* **Films:** *Party of the Year; A University for Tomorrow; Hurricane Smith;* Kevin Lynch in *Bloodmoon.* **TV:** *Coast To Coast* (presenter); Ned Bowen in *Bony;* Adam Willis in *Neighbours* (1990-). **Address:** c/o James Laurie Management/Grundy Television.

WILLIAMS, *michael*

Michael Williams. Actor. b. Manchester, 9 July 1935. Trained at RADA. **Theatre:** *The Comedy of Errors; The Taming of the Shrew; The Merchant of Venice; As You Like It; Troilus and Cressida; Marat/Sade; London Assurance; Jingo; Too Good To Be True; The Winter's Tale; King Lear; Schweik In the Second World War* (all RSC); *Two Into One* (Theatre of Comedy). **Films:** *Marat/Sade; Eagle In a Cage; Dead Cert; Alexander the Great; Enigma; Educating Rita; Henry V.* **TV:** *Elizabeth R; Shadow On the Sun; A Raging Calm; The Hanged Man; The Comedy of Errors; My Son, My Son; Love In a Cold Climate; Ice Age; Turtle's Progress; Quest of Eagles; A Fine Romance; Amnesty; Shakespeare Master Class; Behaving Badly; Blunt; Double First; Angel Voices; Happy Christmas, I Love You; A Hell of a Road.* **Address:** c/o Michael Whitehall. m. actress Dame Judi Dench; 1 d. Tara.

WILLIAMS, *natasha*

Roselyn Agatha Williams. Actress. b. Trelawny, Jamaica, 18 July 1961. Trained at the Webber Douglas Academy. **Theatre:** *Fatherland; Romeo and Juliet; Resisters; Stamping, Shouting and Singing Home; Mainly After Dark; Body Cell; Leave Taking; Ambulance* (Royal Court Theatre); *Royal Borough* (Royal Court Theatre); *Panorama.* **Films:** *Nuns On the Run; A Connecticut Yankee In King Arthur's Court.* **TV:** *The Roughest Way; Three Kinds of Heat; Out of Order; Brookside; Fighting Back; South of the Border; The Ruth Rendell Mysteries – No Crying He Makes; London's Burning;* WPC Delia French in *The Bill.* **Address:** Barry Brown & Partner. Single; lives in Brixton, South London. Hobbies: Gardening. **Favourite TV programme:** *Panorama; 40 Minutes.*

WILLIAMS, *simon*

Simon Williams. b. Windsor, Berkshire, 16 June 1946. **Theatre:** *A Friend In Need; Hay Fever; His, Hers and Theirs; The Collector; No Sex, Please – We're British; Gigi; The Last Mrs Cheyney; See How They Run.* **Films:** *Katcho; Blue Haze; Breaking of Bumbo; Pace Good-bye; Joanna; The Touchables; Demon's Delight; The Incredible Sarah; Jabberwocky; No Longer Alone; The Uncanny; The Odd Job; The Prisoner of Zenda; The Fiendish Plot of Dr Fu Manchu.* **TV:** *The Regiment; Upstairs, Downstairs; Up School; Man In a Suitcase; Squash; Floreat Nilho; Romance; Wodehouse Playhouse; Mr Big; Liza; Agony; Company and Co; Strangers; Kinvig; Don't Wait Up; Artists In Crime; The Mixer; Crazy Comparisons* (team captain); *Bergerac; The Upper Hand.* **Address:** c/o Michael Whitehall. m. 1st actress Belinda Carroll, 2nd Lucy Fleming; 1 s. Tamlyn, 1 d. Amy.

WILLIAMSON, *trish*

Trish Williamson. Broadcast journalist. b. Newcastle upon Tyne, 3 January 1955. Magazine and newspaper journalist before entering TV as a researcher. **TV:** Researcher, reporter, presenter and weather forecaster with TV-am (1985–7); ITN reporter and weather presenter (1988–91); *Sailaway; Time for Christmas; Beat the Cheat.* **Address:** c/o Jacque Evans Management. m. David Devaux (dis); 1 s. Dominic (from previous relationship with TV floor manager Russell Wickens).

WILLIS, *bruce*

Bruce Willis. Actor. b. Germany, 19 March 1959. Attended Montclair State College. **Theatre:** *Fool for Love.* **Films:** *Blind Date; The Verdict; Prince of the City; Die Hard; Die Hard II.* **TV:** David Addison in *Moonlighting; Hart To Hart; The Return of Bruno.* **Address:** c/o Triad Artists. m. actress Demi Moore; 2 d. Rumer Glenn, Scout.

WILLITS, *adam*

Adam Charles Willits. Actor. b. Sydney, Australia, 18 February 1972. **Theatre:** *Badjelly the Witch; All My Sons; Home and Away* (British tour). **Films:** *Marbles; Anna; Damsels Be Damned; Weekend of the Lonesome Rustler* (all Australian Film and Television School); *The Maestro's Company;* Sgt Scratcher in *Mad Max: Beyond Thunderdome; The Perfectionist* (TV movie); Steven Matheson in *Home and Away* (1988–90); *Hampton House.* TV commercials: Colgate; Kraft singles. **Address:** c/o Bedford & Pearce Management.

WILMOT, *gary*

Gary Owen Wilmot. Actor. b. Kennington, London, 8 May 1954. Father was Harold Wilmot, lead singer with Fifties group The Southlanders. Various jobs on leaving school, including messenger, storeman, scaffolder and carpenter. Formed double act Gary Wilmot and Judy in 1976, touring theatres and clubs and making TV debut on *New Faces* (won three times). Went solo in 1979. **TV:** *New Faces; Royal Variety Performance; Royal Night of 100 Stars; Saturday Gang; Cue Gary; This Is Your Life* (subject). Winner, Variety Club Silver Heart Award for Most Promising Artiste of 1986. **Address:** c/o Dee O'Reilly Management. Lives in London. m. Carol Clark (sep); 2 d. Katie, Georgia. Hobbies: Sport, DIY. **Favourite TV programme:** *The Cosby Show.*

WILSON, *francis*

Francis Wilson. Weather presenter. b. Irvine, Ayrshire, 27 February 1949. Gained BSc from Imperial College, London University; trained at RAF Farnborough with the Met Research Flight. **TV:** *Thames News* (Thames Television); *Breakfast Time; BBC Breakfast News.* **Books:** *Spotter's Guide To Weather; Guide To Weather Forecasting; Weather Pop-Up Book.* **Address:** c/o BBC TV. m. Eva; 1 s. Joshua.

WILSON, *richard*

Richard Wilson. Actor/Director. b. Greenock, Renfrewshire, 9 July 1936. Worked as a research scientist, before training at RADA. **Films:** A Passage To India; Whoops Apocalypse; Prick Up Your Ears; A Dry White Season; Fellow Traveller; How To Get Ahead In Advertising. **TV:** Dr Finlay's Casebook; The Revenue Men; My Good Woman; Crown Court; Big Boy Now; Cilla's World of Comedy; Pickersgill People; A Sharp Intake of Breath; Through the Night; Some Mothers Do 'Ave 'Em; In Loving Memory; Chalk and Cheese; Under the Hammer (director); Only When I Laugh; Virginia Fly Is Drowning; Poppyland; Tutti Frutti; Whoops Apocalypse; Room At the Bottom; High and Dry; Victor Meldrew in One Foot In the Grave; Changing Step (director); Hot Metal; The Other Side of Paradise. Winner, Jester Best Comedy Actor award, 1991. **Address:** c/o Jeremy Conway.

WILSON, *sean*

Sean Wilson. Actor. b. Crumpsall, Manchester, 4 April 1965. Trained at the Oldham Theatre Workshop, then performed in cabaret. **Theatre:** The Gas Street Kids; The Mother; community theatre in Manchester area and at the Edinburgh Festival. **TV:** Crown Court; Travelling Man; title role in Mozart's Unfinished (Channel Four film); Martin Platt in Coronation Street (1985-). **Address:** c/o Julia MacDermot/Granada TV. Single; lives in Oldham. Pets: Goldfish, tropical fish, a budgie called Bill. **Favourite TV programme:** Twin Peaks; Inspector Morse.

WILTON, *penelope*

Penelope Wilton. Actress. b. Scarborough, North Yorkshire, 3 June 1946. Trained at The Drama Centre. **Theatre:** King Lear; Song of Songs; The Norman Conquests; Pearcross Girls; The Widowing of Mrs Holroyd; Othello; Country. **Films:** Joseph Andrews; The French Lieutenant's Woman; Laughterhouse; Cry Freedom; Clockwise. **TV:** King Lear; The Widowing of Mrs Holroyd; The Norman Conquests; Ever Decreasing Circles; Madly In Love; The Monocled Mutineer; The Sullen Sisters. **Address:** c/o Julian Belfrage Associates. m. actor Daniel Massey (sep); 1 d. Alice.

WINDING, *victor*

Victor Winding. Actor. b. London, 30 January 1929. Previously trained as a draughtsman and taught drama at night school. **Films:** Frightmare; The Confessional; Schizo; The System; The Medusa Touch. **TV:** Emergency – Ward 10; Probation Officer; No Hiding Place; The Informer; The Saint; Doctor Who; The Expert; The Flaxton Boys; Menace; Warship; Thriller; Sporting Tales; The Judas Goat; Z-Cars; Open House; Fall of Eagles; Crown Court; Tad Ryland in Emmerdale Farm; Private Diaries; Literary Profiles; Victor Lee in Crossroads; Turtle's Progress; Bognor; It Takes a Worried Man; Jemimah Shore Investigates; Shelley; Country Tales; Angels; Little & Large; Winter Harvest; Strike It Rich; Yes, Prime Minister; Menace Unseen; The Bill. **Address:** c/o Richard Stone Partnership. m. Rosalind (dis); 3 d. Celia, Kay, Jane, 1 s. Julian.

WINDSOR, *frank*

Frank Windsor. Actor. b. Walsall, Staffordshire, 12 July 1927. **Theatre:** Androcles and the Lion; Brand; Travesties (RSC); Old Vic Theatre; Middle-Aged Spread; Mr Fothergill's Murder; Every Good Boy Deserves Favour. **Films:** This Sporting Life; Spring and Port Wine; Sunday, Bloody Sunday; The Drop Out; Assassin; Someone Is Killing the Great Chefs of Europe; Dangerous Davies; Coming Out of the Ice. **TV:** Sgt John Watt in Z-Cars and Softly, Softly; An Age of Kings; A for Andromeda; Whodunnit?; Jack the Ripper; Headmaster; Middle Men; Crown Court; Kidnapped; The Union; Into the Labyrinth; Flying Lady; The Fifteen Streets; Boon. **Address:** c/o Scott Marshall. m. former dancer Mary Corbett; 1 d. Amanda, 1 s. David.

WING, *anna*

Anna Eva Lydia Catherine Wing. Actress. b. Hackney, London, 30 October 1914. Trained at Croydon School of Acting. **TV:** *Sons and Lovers; The Crucible; Smiley's People; The Woman In White; Skirmishes; Sink Or Swim; Making Good; The Chinese Detective; Sorry; Father's Day; The Old Men At the Zoo; Give Us a Break; Crown Court; The Witches of Grinnygog; The Invisible Man; Flying Lady; Play for Today: Picture Friend; Comrade Dad;* Lou Beale in *EastEnders* (1985–8); *Comedy Playhouse: Dowie and His Mates; I Like It Here; Collision Course;* Gran in *The Lime Grove Story: The Grove Family.* **Address:** c/o Darryl Brown Associates. Lives in London. m. 1st Peter Davey (dis), 2nd Philip O'Connor (dis); 2 s. actor Mark Wing-Davey (from 1st m.), Jon Wing O'Connor (from 2nd m.). Pets: Any strays. **Favourite TV programme:** Varied.

WINGETT, *mark*

Mark Wingett. Actor. b. Melton Mowbray, Lincolnshire, 1 January 1961. **TV:** *C.A.T.S. Eyes; The Professionals; Fords On Water; Private Schultz; Take Three Women; Woodentop* (pilot for *The Bill*); *Fox; The Ravelled Thread; Grudge Fight;* Det Con Jim Carver in *The Bill.* (1984-). **Address:** c/o London Management. Single; lives in London. Hobbies: Scuba-diving, underwater photography.

WINSTONE, *ray*

Ray Winstone. Actor. b. London. Former schoolboy international footballer. **Films:** *That Summer; Scum; Quadrophenia; All Washed Up; No 1; Tank Malling.* **TV:** *Sunshine Over Brixton; Scum; Mr Right; Death Angel; Minder; Fox; The Lonely Hearts Kid; A Fairly Secret Army; Bergerac; Robin of Sherwood; Ever Decreasing Circles; C.A.T.S. Eyes; Father Matthew's Daughter; Boon; Pulaski; Home To Roost; Blore MP; Birds of a Feather.* **Address:** c/o CAM.

WITCHELL, *nicholas*

Nicholas Witchell. Newsreader. b. Cosford, Shropshire, 23 September 1953. Joined the BBC on its news training scheme in 1976. **TV:** BBC Northern Ireland reporter; BBC TV News reporter and correspondent in Ireland, Beirut and the Falklands; *Six O'Clock News; BBC Breakfast News.* **Book:** *The Loch Ness Story.* **Address:** c/o BBC TV.

WITHINGTON, *shane*

Shane Withington. Actor. b. Toowoomba, Queensland, Australia, 22 August 1958. Trained at the Twelfth Night Theatre. **Theatre:** *Twelfth Night; How Does Your Garden Grow?; Rookery Nook; 1986 Casino Show; Everybody Makes Mistakes.* **Films:** *A Cry for Help; Dawn.* **TV:** *The Young Doctors; Glenview High; Timeless Land; Chopper Squad; A Country Practice; Willing & Abel.* Address: c/o Harry M Miller & Company Management, 153 Dowling Street, Kings Cross, Sydney, Australia.

WOGAN, *terry*

Terry Wogan. Presenter. b. Limerick, Ireland, 3 August 1938. Radio presenter before moving into television. **TV:** *Lunchtime With Wogan; Come Dancing; Miss World; Eurovision Song Contest; Song for Europe; Variety Club Awards; Carl-Allen Awards; Disco; Startown; Blankety Blank; What's On Wogan; You Must Be Joking; Wogan; Auntie's Bloomer*. Winner, *TVTimes* Most Popular TV Personality award for 10 successive years. **Books:** *Wogan on Wogan*. **Address:** c/o Jo Gurnett Management. Lives in Bray, Berkshire. m. former model Helen Joyce; 1 d. Katherine, 2 s. Alan, Mark.

WOLF, *rita*

Rita Wolf. Actress. b. Calcutta, India, 25 February 1960. Brought up in Camden Town, London; trained at the Royal Court Youth Theatre. **Theatre:** *Borderline; The Lion's Raj; Migrations; Wake; In Self-Defence; Divided and Ruled; Enemy of the People; Vigilantes;* Hermia in *A Midsummer Night's Dream; Heart Games; Othello; The Home Service; Song for a Sanctuary* (director). **Films:** *Majdhar; The Chain;* Tania in *My Beautiful Laundrette; Slipstream.* **TV:** *Arena; Romance, Romance;* Meena in *Albion Market;* Asha in *Tandoori Nights; Mohammed's Daughter; Rockliffe's Babies; One By One; Saracen; Shelley;* Felicity Khan in *Coronation Street; Kingdom Come; The Conversion of St Paul; Eye Contact; Out: Khush.* **Radio:** *Kaleidoscope* (twice); *Singing and Dancing In Kanpur; The Dragon Bone Man; The Deceivers.* **Address:** c/o Fletcher & Boyce. Lives in London.

WOLFENDEN, *stuart*

Stuart Wolfenden. Actor. b. Rochdale, Lancashire. 7 February 1970. Trained at Oldham Theatre Workshop. **Theatre:** *The Railway Children; Accrington Pals;* Billy Casper in *Kes* (Oldham Drama Festival); *A Talent To Endure.* **TV:** Hall in *Jossy's Giants; The Adventures of Sherlock Holmes;* Craig Russell and Mark Casey in *Coronation Street;* Craig in *Making Out;* Billy Shaw in *My Kingdom for a Horse; A Time To Dance.* **Address:** c/o Laine Management. Single; lives in Oldham.

WOOD, *janine*

Janine Wood. Actress. b. Bournemouth, Dorset, 30 December 1963. Trained at The Drama Centre. **Theatre:** *Romeo and Juliet; A Midsummer Night's Dream; The Kiss; The Hired Man; Black Coffee; Habeas Corpus; Mrs Warren's Profession; Dealing With Clair.* **TV:** Clare in *After Henry; Davro's Sketch Pad.* TV commercials: National Westminster Bank; Alliance & Leicester Building Society. **Address:** c/o Larry Dalzell Associates.

WOOD, *victoria*

Victoria Wood. Comedienne/Writer. b. Prestwich, Lancashire, 19 May 1953. Gained a degree in drama from Birmingham University. **Theatre:** *Talent; Good Fun; Funny Turns; Lucky Bag.* **TV:** *Talent; Happy Since I Met You; Wood and Walters; Victoria Wood As Seen On TV; Victoria Wood Now; An Audience With Victoria Wood; Victoria Wood; New Faces; Take the Stage; Cabbages and Kings; Jackanory; The Victoria Wood Show; Julie Walters and Friends.* **Address:** c/o Richard Stone Partnership. m. magician Geoffrey Durham; 1 d.

WOODCOCK, *steven*

Steven Woodcock. Actor. b. 23 February 1964. **Theatre:** *One Rule; The Taming of the Shrew; Antony and Cleopatra; Scrape Off the Black; O Babylon!; Blood, Sweat and Fears; By the Pool* (Edinburgh Festival); *Eden*. **Films:** *Keep Off the Grass; The Chain; Defence of the Realm; Claudia's Party*. **TV:** *Walcott; S.W.A.L.K.;* Rosta in *Grange Hill; The All Electric Amusement Arcade; Good Neighbours; Travellers By Night; Girls On Top; Paradise Postponed; The Lenny Henry Show; Rockliffe's Babies; Mixing In; Casualty; London's Burning; A Very Peculiar Practice; Only Fools and Horses;* Clyde Tavernier in *EastEnders*. **Address:** c/o Susan Angel Associates/BBC Elstree Centre.

WOODWARD, *edward*, OBE

Edward Woodward. Actor. b. Croydon, Surrey, 1 June 1931. Trained at RADA. **Films:** *Young Winston; Callan; Champions.* **TV:** *Sword of Honour;* title role in *Callan; Au Pair Swedish Style; Entertaining Mr Sloane; Murders In the Rue Morgue; Night of Talavera; Julius Caesar; The Listener; A Dream Divided; Scott Fitzgerald; Bit of a Holiday; Evelyn; The Bass Player and the Blonde; Saturday, Sunday, Monday; Cleo; Rod of Iron; The Trial of Lady Chatterley; Nice Work; Blunt Instrument; Wet Job; Winston Churchill – The Wilderness Years; Spice of Life; A Christmas Caroll; The Equalizer; Codename Kyril; Uncle Tom's Cabin; Sherlock Holmes; Over My Dead Body; World War 2l.* **Address:** c/o Eric Glass. m. 1st actress Venetia Barratt (dis), 2nd actress Michele Dotrice; 2 d. Sarah (from 1st m.), Emily Beth, 2 s. actor Tim (qv), Peter (both from 1st m.).

WOODWARD, *tim*

Tim Woodward. Actor. b. London, 24 April 1953. Son of actor Edward Woodward (qv). Trained at RADA. **Theatre:** *The Taming of the Shrew.* **Films:** *Galileo; The Europeans; Reds; King David; Salome; Personal Services; The Murder of Sir Harry Oakes.* **TV:** *Chips With Everything; Balzac; Within These Walls; French Without Tears; Wings; The Cost of Loving; Journals of Brigid Hitler; Cousin Phyllis; Tales of the Unexpected; Antonia White Quartet; Guests of the Nation; East Lynne; The Irish RM; The Affair of the Pink Pearl; The File On Jill Hatch; All the World's a Stage; The Case of the Frightened Lady; Pope John Paul II* (TV movie); *Lady Windermere's Fan; A Killing On the Exchange; Piece of Cake; Dark Angel; Ipiginea At Aulis; Greek Trilogy; Traitors;* John Thompson in *Families.* **Address:** c/o Larry Dalzell Associates.

WOODYATT, *adam*

Adam Woodyatt. actor. b. Woodford, Essex, 28 June 1968. Trained part-time at the Sylvia Young Theatre School. **Theatre:** *Oliver!* (London West End); Buttons in *Cinderella* (Rickmansworth 1987, Whitchurch 1988, St Albans 1990); *Silly Billy;* Ragamuffin in *On the Razzle* (National Theatre). **TV:** Shiner in *The Baker Street Boys;* Dave Firkettle in *The Witches of Grinnygog;* Ian Beale in *EastEnders* (1985-). **Address:** c/o Johnson's/BBC Elstree Centre. Single; lives in Borehamwood, Hertfordshire. Hobbies: Paint-ball, cricket, football, playing computer games. **Favourite TV programme:** Star Trek.

WOOLDRIDGE, *susan*

Susan Wooldridge. Actress. b. London. **Films:** *Loyalties; Hope and Glory; Bye Bye Blues; How To Get Ahead In Advertising.* **TV:** *The Jewel In the Crown; The Last Place On Earth; Hay Fever; Time and the Conways; Frankenstein; Night Mother; Dead Man's Folly; The Devil's Disciple; The Dark Room; Pastoral Care; The Small Assassin; Ticket To Ride; Changing Step* (TV movie); *The Pied Piper* (TV movie); *Crime Strike* (TV movie); *Bergerac; Broke; She-Play: Full Board.* **Address:** c/o Jonathan Altaras Associates.

WOOLLARD, *william*

William Woollard. Presenter/Producer. b. London, 20 August 1939. Worked for an oil company, learned Arabic and worked in social science before joining the BBC. **TV:** *Tomorrow's World; The Risk Business; Secret War; The History of the Fighter; The History of Flight; Cross Channel; Top Gear; Connections; Policing the Eighties; 2001 and All That; Rally Report.* **Address:** c/o Jon Roseman Associates. m. Isobel; 1 d. Jessica, 2 s. Julian, Alexander.

WORTH, *helen*

Helen Worth. Actress. b. Leeds, 7 January 1951. Grew up in Morecambe, Lancashire. Trained as a dancer at the Corona Academy. **Theatre:** *The Sound of Music* (London West End, aged 12); repertory theatre in Northampton, Hornchurch, Watford and Richmond-upon-Thames. **Films:** *Oliver!; The Prime of Miss Jean Brodie.* **TV:** Granada TV news magazine *Scene At 6.30; Z-Cars* (both aged 10); *Doctor Who; The Doctors;* Gail Platt (nee Potter, formerly Tilsley) in *Coronation Street* (1974-); *Royal Variety Performance* (1989). **Radio:** Two years in BBC radio repertory company. **Address:** c/o Julia MacDermot/Granada TV. Lives in London and Cheshire. m. actor Michael Angelis. Hobbies: Gardening, cooking, eating.

WRAY, *emma*

Jill Wray. Actress. b. Birkenhead, Cheshire, 22 March 1965. Trained at Rose Bruford College of Speech and Drama, then sang with three-part harmony group The Blooming Tulips. **TV:** Brenda in *Watching; Minder; Boon; Defrosting the Fridge;* Pippa in *Stay Lucky.* **Address:** c/o Burdett-Coutts Associates.

WYLIE, *frank*

Frank Wylie. Actor. Trained at the Royal Scottish Academy of Music and Drama. **Theatre:** Repertory theatre in Scotland and England; *Chips With Everything* (London West End and Broadway); *Volpone; A Flea In Her Ear; H; Oedipus; As You Like It; Three Sisters* (all National Theatre). **TV:** *Three Sisters; Blood Letting; Who'll Take the Low Road; Dog's Ransom; The Miser; Softly, Softly; The Rivals of Sherlock Holmes; Song of Songs; The Hanged Man; Churchill's People; Rooms; The Lost Tribe; Tales of the Unexpected; The Union; Doctor Who; King's Royal; Killer; Brigadista; Holy City;* Fergus Jamieson in *Take the High Road.* **Address:** c/o Howes and Prior/Scottish Television.

YARDLEY, *stephen*

Stephen Yardley. Actor. b. Ferrensby, North Yorkshire, 24 March 1942. Trained at RADA. **Films:** *Doctor and the Devils; The Shooting Party; Adolf Hitler – My Part In His Downfall.* **TV:** *Dr Finlay's Casebook; The XYY Man; Widows; Z-Cars; Secret Army; War and Peace; Roads To Freedom; Coronation Street; Harriet's Back in Town; Napoleon and Love; Remington Steele; Blood Money; Tom Gratton's War; Germinal; Nana; A Tale of Two Cities; Fanny By Gaslight;* Ken Masters in *Howards' Way.* **Address:** c/o Hilda Physick Agency. m. (sep); 1 d. Rebecca, 1 s. Joshua.

YATES, marjorie

Marjorie Yates. Actress. b. Birmingham, 13 April 1941. Trained at Guildhall School of Music and Drama. **Theatre:** *A Fair Quarrel; As You Like It; Small Change; Touched; Sea Anchor; Inner Voices; Outskirts; Good; Richard III; Thatcher's Woman* (last four with RSC). **Films:** *The Black Panther; Wetherby; Priest of Love; Stardust; The Optimists.* **TV:** *Kisses At Fifty; Connie; All Day On the Sands; Change In Time; Morgan's Boy; Lovely Day Tomorrow; Marya; Couples; The Sweeney; A Very British Coup; June.* **Address:** c/o Kate Feast Management. m. university administrator and councillor Michael Freeman; 1 d. Polly, 1 s. Carl.

YATES, pauline

Pauline Yates. Actress. b. St Helens, Lancashire, 16 June. **Theatre:** Oldham rep; *Pride and Prejudice; O'Malley's Talk of the Devil.* **Films:** *The Four Feathers; She'll Be Wearing Pink Pyjamas.* **TV:** *Cruise; Go On, It'll Do You Good; The Second Interview; Emma's Time; The Bridesmaid; Louise; Sentimental Education; A Room In Town; Bachelor Father; The Doctors; Crime of Passion; Home and Away* (Granada TV); *Harriet's Back In Town; Bootsie and Snudge; Nightingale's Boys; Going, Going, Gone; Free; Savages; My Honourable Mrs;* Elizabeth Perrin in *The Fall and Rise of Reginald Perrin; England's Green and Pleasant Land;The Emperor's New Hat; Rainbow; Rooms; Keep It In the Family; Hold the Dream; Touch of Danger; A Small Mourning.* **Address:** c/o Kate Feast Management. m. actor-writer Donald Churchill (dec); 2 d. Jemma, Polly.

YIP, david

David Yip. Actor. b. Liverpool, 4 June 1951. Trained at the East 15 Acting School. **Theatre:** *Hair* (London West End); *Jingo* (RSC); *Twelfth Night; Antony and Cleopatra; Romeo and Juliet; The Knack ...and how to get it; Made In Bangkok; Julius Caesar; The King and I.* **Films:** *Indiana Jones and the Temple of Doom; A View To a Kill; Ping Pong; Empire of the Sun; Hawks; Out of Order; Destiny San Francisco; Chinese Method.* **TV:** *The Cuckoo Waltz; 3–2–1–; It Ain't Half Hot Mum; Savages; Spies; Quatermass; Going To Work; Mystery of the Disappearing Schoolgirls; Doctor Who; The Chelsea Murders; Whodunnit?;* John Ho in *The Chinese Detective; The Caucasian Chalk Circle; King and Castle; Making Out; Murder On the Moon;* Dr Michael Choi in *Brookside; Wail of the Banshee.* **Address:** c/o Mayer Management. m. 1st Liz Bagley (dis), 2nd actress Lynn Farleigh.

YORK, susannah

Susannah York. Actress. b. London, 9 January 1942. Trained at RADA. **Films:** *A Man for All Seasons; Lock Up Your Daughters; The Killing of Sister George; Oh! What a Lovely War; The Battle of Britain; They Shoot Horses, Don't They?; Jane Eyre; Gold; Superman; Superman II; Yellowbeard; A Summer Story; Just Ask for Diamond; Melancholia.* **TV:** *The Crucible; The Creditors; La Grande Breteche; The Rebel and the Soldier; The First Gentleman; The Richest Man In the World; Fallen Angels; Prince Regent; Second Chance; A Christmas Carol; We'll Meet Again; The Other Side of Me; Agnes of God; Star Quality; The Two Ronnies; The Man From the Pru; The Haunting of New; Devices and Desires; Trainer.* **Books:** *In Search of Unicorns; Lark's Castle.* **Address:** c/o ICM Duncan Heath Associates. m. Michael Wells (dis); 1 d. Sasha, 1 s. Orlando.

YOUNG, paul

Paul Young. Actor. b. Edinburgh, 3 July 1944. Son of actor John Young (qv) and theatrical agent Winifred Young. Trained at the Royal Scottish Academy of Music and Drama. **Theatre:** *Willie Rough; The Revellers; The Passion; The Thrie Estaites.* **Films:** *Geordie; Submarine X–1; SOS Titanic; Another Time, Another Place; Chato's Land.* **TV:** *Sunset Song; Homework;* Gerald Parker in *Take the High Road; Holy City; Something Got To Give; Doom Castle; Taggart; Brond; House On the Hill; Brigadista; Extras; No Job for a Lady; Leaving; The Justice Game.* **Address:** c/o Hutton Management. m. journalist Sheila Duffy; 2 d. Kate, Hannah.

agents

A.I.M. (Associated International Management)
5 Denmark Street
London WC2H 8LP
Tel: 071–836 2001

AM Artists
Fourth Floor
23 Haymarket
London SW1Y 4DG
el: 071–839 8400

ATS Casting
26 St Michael's Road
Leeds LS6 3AW
Tel: (0532) 304300

Marjorie Abel
50 Maddox Street
London W1R 9PA
Tel: 071–499 1343

The Actors' Agency
197 Roden Street
West Melbourne
Victoria 3003
Australia
Tel: (010 61) 3 329 2488

Actors Alliance
Bon Marché Building
444 Brixton Road
London SW9 8EJ
Tel: 071–326 0070

The Agency
Suite 211
0351 Santa Monica Boulevard
Los Angeles
CA 90025
USA
Tel: (0101) 213 551 3000

Agency for the Performing Arts
Suite 1200
9000 Sunset Blvd
Los Angeles
CA 90069
USA
Tel: (0101) 213 273 0744

Jonathan Altaras Associates
2 Goodwins Court
London WC2N 4LL
Tel: 071–497 8878

Amor Reeves
80 Crawthew Grove
London SE22 9AB
Tel: 081–693 7733

Susan Angel Associates
First Floor
12 D'Arblay Street
London W1V 3FP
Tel: 071–439 3086

Arlington Enterprises
1/3 Charlotte Street
London W1P 1HD
Tel: 071–580 0702

Mary Arnold Management
12 Cambridge Park
East Twickenham
Middlesex TW1 2PF
Tel: 081–892 4860

The Artists Agency
Suite 305
10000 Santa Monica Boulevard
Los Angeles
CA 90067
USA
Tel: (0101) 213 277 7779

The Artists Group
Suite 403
1930 Century Park West
Los Angeles
California 90067
USA
Tel: (0101) 213 552 1100

Australian Creative Management
Second Floor
169 Phillip Street
Sydney
NSW 2000
Australia
Tel: (010 61) 2 232 4900

Aza Artists
652 Finchley Road
London NW11 7NT
Tel: 081–458 7288

Bagenal Harvey Organisation
141/143 Drury Lane
London WC2B 5TB
Tel: 071–379 4625

George Bartram Associates
Creative House
5 Commercial Street
Birmingham B1 1RS
Tel: 021–643 9346

Bauer Benedek Agency
Suite 716
9255 Sunset Boulevard
Los Angeles
CA 90069
USA
Tel: (0101) 213 275 2421

Bedford & Pearce Management
2 Portman Place
263/269 Alfred Street North
North Sydney
NSW 2060
Australia
Tel: (010 61) 2 929 4833

Julian Belfrage Associates
68 St James's Street
London SW1A 1LE
Tel: 071–491 4400

Terry Blamey Management
329 Montague Street
Albert Park
Victoria 3206
Australia
Tel: (010 61) 3 690 9663

Nina Blatt
The Coach House
1A Larpent Avenue
London SW15 6UP
Tel: 081–788 560⅔

Rebecca Blond Associates
52 Shaftesbury Avenue
London W1V 7DE
Tel: 071–434 2010

Ruth Boyle Management
Willow Dene
New Lane
Nun Monkton
York YO5 8EP
Tel: (0423) 331199

Michelle Braidman Associates
10/11 Lower John Street
London W1R 3PE
Tel: 071–437 0817

Barry Brown and Partner
47 West Square
London SE11 4SP
Tel: 071–928 1229

Darryl Brown Associates
Thornton House
Thornton Road
Wimbledon
London SW19 4NG
Tel: 081–944 6977

Peter Browne Management
Pebro House
13 St Martins Road
London SW9 0SP
Tel: 071–737 3444

Peter Browne Management Scotland
5 Queens Crescent
Glasgow G4 9BN
Tel: 041–332 4607

The Brunskill Management
Suite 8A
169 Queen's Gate
London SW7 5EH
Tel: 071–581 3388/071–584 8060

Burdett-Coutts Associates
Studio 132 Canalot
222 Kensal Road
London W10 5BN
Tel: 081–964 1122

Barry Burnett Organisation
Suite 42–43
Grafton House
2–3 Golden Square
London W1R 3AD
Tel: 071–437 7048/9

CAM
Suite 204
Garden Studios
11/15 Betterton Street
Covent Garden
London WC2H 9BP
Tel: 071–497 0448

CCA Personal Management
4 Court Lodge
48 Sloane Square
London SW1W 8AT
Tel: 071–730 8857

CDA (Caroline Dawson Associates)
Apartment 9
47 Courtfield Road
London SW7 4DB
Tel: 071–370 0708

CNA & Associates
Suite 1250
1801 Avenue of the Stars
Los Angeles
CA 90067
USA
Tel: (0101) 213 556 4343

CSM (Artistes)
49 Churchfield Road
Acton
London W3
Tel: 081–992 8668

Camden Artists
Suite 410
2121 Avenue of the Stars
Los Angeles
CA 90067
USA
Tel: (0101) 213 556 2022

Alexandra Cann Representation
68E Redcliffe Gardens
London SW10 9HE
Tel: 071–835 2200

June Cann Management
6/1 Ridge Street
North Sydney
NSW 2060
Australia
Tel: (010 61) 2 922 3066

Sara Cameron Management
1 Aberdeen Lane
Highbury
London N5 2EJ
Tel: 071–359 8178

Roger Carey Management
64 Thornton Avenue
Chiswick
London W4 1QQ
Tel: 081–995 4477

Century Artists
Suite 308
9744 Wilshire Boulevard
Beverly Hills
CA 90212
USA
Tel: (0101) 213 273 4366

Peter Charlesworth
Second Floor
68 Old Brompton Road
London SW7 3LQ
Tel: 071–581 2478

Charter Management
Suite 1112
9000 Sunset Boulevard
Los Angeles
California 90069
Tel: (0101) 213 278 1690

Chasin Agency
Suite 201
190 North Canon
Beverly Hills
California 90210
USA
Tel: (0101) 213 278 7505

Chatto and Linnit
Prince of Wales Theatre
Coventry Street
London W1V 7FE
Tel: 071–930 6677

Chiltern Casting
2A Eaton Road
West Derby
Liverpool L12 7JJ
Tel: 051–254 1686

Shane Collins Associates
24 Wardour Street
London W1V 3HD
Tel: 071–439 1976

Jeremy Conway
Eagle House
109 Jermyn Street
London SW1 6HB
Tel: 071–287 0077

Vernon Conway
5 Spring Street
London W2 3RA
Tel: 071–262 5506

Clive Corner Associates
Woodrow Business Centre
65–66 Woodrow
London SE18 5DH
Tel: 081–855 0025/081–854 1194

Lou Coulson
37 Berwick Street
London W1V 3RF
Tel: 071–734 9633

Creative Artists Agency
9830 Wilshire Boulevard
Beverly Hills
CA 90212
USA
Tel: (0101) 213 288 4545

Creative Talent Management
35 Harwood Road
London SW6 4QP
Tel: 071–371 5633

Crouch Associates
59 Frith Street
London W1V 5TA
Tel: 071–734 2167

Curtis Brown
162/168 Regent Street
London W1R 5TB
Tel: 071–437 9700

Daly Gagan Associates
68 Old Brompton Road
London SW7 3LQ
Tel: 071–581 0121

Larry Dalzell Associates
Suite 12
17 Broad Court
London WC2B 5QN
Tel: 071–379 0875

Isobel Davie
37 Hill Street
London W1X 8JY
Tel: 071–493 0343

Hazel de Leon
Hazeldene
248 Swakeleys Road
Ickenham
Middlesex UB10 8AU
Tel: (0895) 274077

Felix De Wolfe
Manfield House
376/378 Strand
London WC2R 0LR
Tel: 071–379 5767

Direct Line Personal Management
CHEL
Room 35
26 Roundhay Road
Leeds LS7
Tel: (0532) 444991

Downes Presenters Agency
96 Broadway
Bexleyheath
Kent DA6 7DE
Tel: 081–304 0541

Bryan Drew
Mezzanine
Quadrant House
80/82 Regent Street
London W1R 6AU
Tel: 071–437 2293

Jean Drysdale Management
Still Waters
Trolvercroft
Penpol
Feock
Nr Truro
Cornwall TR3 6RT
Tel: (0872) 865345

Joyce Edwards Representation
275 Kennington Road
London SE1 6BY
Tel: 071–735 5736

Ellison Combe Associates
16 Evelyn Gardens
Richmond-upon-Thames
Surrey TW9 2PL
Tel: 081–940 7863

Clifford Elson Publicity
233 Regent Street
London W1R 7DB
Tel: 071–495 4012

June Epstein Associates
Flat 1
62 Compayne Gardens
London NW6 3RY
Tel: 071–328 0864

Essanay
2 Conduit Street
London W1R 9TG
Tel: 071–409 3526

Evans and Reiss
221 New Kings Road
London SW6 4XE
Tel: 071–384 1843

Jacque Evans Management
11A St John's Wood High Street
London NW8
Tel: 071–722 4700

Norma Farnes
9 Orme Court
London W2 4RL
Tel: 071–727 1544

Kate Feast Management
43A Princess Road
London NW1 8JS
Tel: 071–586 5502

Alan Field
11 Arden Road
Finchley
London N3 2AB
Tel: 081–346 7861

Fletcher & Boyce
1 Kingsway House
Albion Road
London N16 0TA
Tel: 071–923 0606

Aida Foster
33 Abbey Lodge
Park Road
London NW8 7RJ
Tel: 071–262 2181

Jill Foster
3 Lonsdale Road
London SW13 9ED
Tel: 081–741 4910

Patrick Freeman Management
4 Cromwell Grove
London W6 7RG
Tel: 071–602 4035

French's
26 Binney Street
London W1Y 1YN
Tel: 071–629 4159

Frog Promotions
2a Armstrong Street
Middle Park
Victoria 3206
Australia
Tel: (010 61) 3 699 2488

GMM
Canonbury House
Canonbury Square
London N1 2NQ
Tel: 071–359 8152

Barbara Gange Management
40 Elizabeth Street
North Richmond
Victoria 3121
Australia
Tel: (010 61) 3 429 2650

Robyn Gardiner Management
5/30 Clarke Street
South Melbourne
Victoria 3205
Australia
Tel: (010 61) 3 696 2826

Kerry Gardner Management
15 Kensington High Street
London W8 5NP
Tel: 071–937 3142

Garricks
7 Garrick Street
London WC2 9AR
Tel: 071–240 0660

Jimmy Garrod Management
St Martins
Sandhills Meadow
Shepperton
Middlesex TW17 9HY
Tel: (0932) 246333

Noel Gay Artists
24 Denmark Street
London WC2H 8NJ
Tel: 071–240 0451

The Gersh Agency
232 North Canon Drive
Beverly Hills
CA 90210
USA
Tel: (0101) 213 274 6611

J Carter Gibson Agency
Suite 801
9000 Sunset Boulevard
Los Angeles
CA 90069
USA
Tel: (0101) 213 274 8813

Jo Gilbert's Associates
2 Silver Place
Soho
London W1R 3LL
Tel: 071–4378 6522/6682

Eric Glass
28 Berkeley Square
London W1X 6HD
Tel: 071–629 7162

Goodwin Associates
12 Rabbit Row
Kensington Church Street
London W8 4DX
Tel: 071–221 9364

Jimmy Grafton Management
9 Orme Court
London W2 4RL
Tel: 071–221 9364

David Graham Management
Designer Liner
Beckett's Wharf
Hampton Wick
Surrey KT1 4ER
Tel: 081–977 8707

Peter Graham Associates
59 Frith Street
London W1V 5TA
Tel: 071–734 2203

James Grant Management
42 Courtyard
42 Colwith Road
Hammersmith
London W6 9EY
Tel: 081–741 4484

Joan Gray Personal Management
29 Sunbury Court Island
Sunbury-on-Thames
Middlesex TW16 5PP
Tel: 081–979 1789

Green and Underwood
2 Conduit Street
London W1R 9TG
Tel: 071–493 0308

Sandra Griffin Management
6 Ryde Place
Richmond Road
East Twickenham
Surrey TW1 2EH
Tel: 081–891 5676

Jo Gurnett Personal Management
2 New Kings Road
London SW6 4SA
Tel: 071–736 7828

Eric Hall Management
26 Star Street
London W2
Tel: 071–723 9695

Hamilton and Sydney
21 Goodge Street
London W1P 1FD
Tel: 071–323 1162

Sue Hammer Personal Management
Otterbourne House
Chobham Road
Ottershaw
Chertsey
Surrey KT16 0QF
Tel: (0932) 874111/2

Hamper-Neafsey Associates
4 Great Queen Street
London WC2B 5DG
Tel: 071–734 1827/071–404 5255

Roger Hancock
Greener House
66/68 Haymarket
London SW1Y 4AW
Tel: 071–839 6753

Harbour & Coffey
9 Blenheim Street
London W1Y 9LE
Tel: 071–499 5548

Harris & Goldberg Talent Agency
Suite 950
2121 Avenue of the Stars
Los Angeles
CA 90067
USA
Tel: (0101) 213 553 5200

Richard Hatton
29 Roehampton Gate
London SW15 5JR
Tel: 081–876 6699

Stephen Hatton Management
The Basement
142a New North Road
London N1 7BH
Tel: 071–359 3593

George Heathcote Management
10 St Martin's Court
London WC2N 4AJ
Tel: 071–379 1081

David Higham Associates
5–8 Lower John Street
London W1R 4HA
Tel: 071–437 7888

Hindworth Management
235/241 Regent Street
London W1V 3AU
Tel: 071–434 3944

Hobson's Personal Management
Burlington House
64 Chiswick High Road
London W4 1SY
Tel: 081–747 8474

Elaine Holland & Associates
177 Virginia Avenue
Hawthorne
Brisbane
QLD 4171
Australia
Tel: (010 61) 7 399 3177

Hope & Lyne
108 Leonard Street
London EC2A 4RH
Tel: 071–739 6200

The Bill Horne Partnership
15 Exmoor Street
London W10 6BA
Tel: 081–960 8281

Howes and Prior
66 Berkeley House
Hay Hill
London W1X 7LH
Tel: 071–493 7570

Mark Hudson
Third Floor
146 Strand
London WC2R 1JH
Tel: 071–240 8851

Mike Hughes Entertainments
Prince of Wales Theatre
Coventry Street
London W1V 7FE
Tel: 071–930 9161

Bernard Hunter Associates
13 Spencer Gardens
London SW14 7AH
Tel: 081–878 6308

Hutton Management
200 Fulham Road
London SW10 9PN
Tel: 071–352 4825

ICM
388/396 Oxford Street
London W1N 9HE
Tel: 071–629 8080

ICM Duncan Heath Associates
Paramount House
162 Wardour Street
London W1V 3AT
Tel: 071–439 1471

IMG
23 Eyot Gardens
London W6 9TR
Tel: 081–846 8070/081–746 5311

Inter-City Casting
383 Corn Exchange
Manchester M4 3DH
Tel: 061–832 8848

International Artistes
Mezzanine Floor
235 Regent Street
London W1R 8AX
Tel: 071–439 8401

International Casting Service & Associates
Fourth Floor
Cornelius Court
147a King Street
Sydney
NSW 2000
Australia
Tel: (010 61) 2 232 6955

International Creative Management
8899 Beverly Boulevard
Los Angeles
CA 90048
USA
Tel: (0101) 213 550 4000

JLM
288 Munster Road
London SW6 6BQ
Tel: 071–386 9156

JR Management
9 Ashcroft Avenue
Lennoxtown
Glasgow G65 7EN
Tel: 041–954 7915

JY Publicity
100 Ebury Street
London SW1W 9QD
Tel: 071–730 9009

Maggie Jacques Promotions
Suite 2
182 Punt Road
Prahran
Melbourne
Vic 3181
Australia
Tel: (010 61) 3 529 5618

Carole James Management
2 Water Lane House
Water Lane
Richmond-upon-Thames
Surrey TW9 1TJ
Tel: 081–940 8154

Joy Jameson
19 The Plaza
535 Kings Road
London SW10 0SZ
Tel: 071–351 3971

Johnson's
Fifth Floor
Regent House
235/241 Regent Street
London W1R 8TL
Tel: 071–491 1551

Joseph and Wagg
Studio One
2 Tunstall Road
London SW9 8BN
Tel: 071–738 3026

Chuck Julian Agency
Third Floor
Cecil House
41 Charing Cross Road
London WC2H 0AR
Tel: 071–437 5380

Keane Management
1246 Pittwater Road
Narrabeen 2101
Australia
Tel: (010 61) 2 970 6311

Richard Kent Management
105 High Street
Milsons Point
New South Wales 2061
Australia
Tel: (010 61) 2 92 7684

Adrian King Associates
100 Fellows Road
London NW3 3JG
Tel: 071–722 1149

LWA
52 Wardour Street
London W1V 3HL
Tel: 071–434 3944

Michael Ladkin Personal Management
11 Southwick Mews
London W2 1JG
Tel: 071–402 6644

Laine Management
First Floor
Hampson Street Trading Estate
Hampson Street
Salford M5 4RL
Tel: 061–835 2122/2106

Langford Associates
Garden Studios
11/15 Betterton Street
London WC2
Tel: 071–379 7216/0344

James Laurie Management
39 Waterloo Street
Surry Hills 2010
Australia
Tel: (010 61) 2 690 1266

Leading Artists Penthouse
445 North Bedford Drive
Beverly Hills
California 90210
USA
Tel: (0101) 213 858 1999

Barbara Leane & Associates
261 Miller Street
North Sydney
NSW 2060
Tel: (010 61) 2 957 1847

Tessa Le Bars Management
18 Queen Anne Street
London W1M 9LB
Tel: 071–636 3191

Bernard Lee Management
Moorcroft Lodge
Farleigh Common
Warlingham
Surrey CR3 0PE
Tel: (0883) 625667

Jane Lehrer Associates
Third Floor
17 Nottingham Street
London W1M 3RD
Tel: 071–486 0888

Lemon, Unna and Durbridge
24/32 Pottery Lane
London W11 4LZ
Tel: 071–727 1346/071–229 9216

L'Epine Smith & Carney Associates
10 Wyndham Place
London W1H 1AS
Tel: 071–724 0739

Lee Leslie Management
72 Glebe Point Road
Glebe NSW 2037
Australia
Tel: (010 61) 2 660 4777

Tony Lewis Entertainments
235/241 Regent Street
London W1R 8TL
Tel: 071–734 7339

Lindsay Casting
22 Druids Cross Road
Liverpool L18 3EB
Tel: 051–722 5091

Linkside Agency
34 Glebe Road
Ashtead
Surrey KT21 2NT
Tel: (0372) 275577/378398

Lipson Tinker Associates
18–19 Warwick Street
London W1R 5RB
Tel: 071–439 8195

London Management
235/241 Regent Street
London W1R 7AG
Tel: 071–493 1610

Pat Lovett Agency
14 Broughton Place
Edinburgh EH1 3RX
Tel: 031–557 5565

Ian Lowe
200 Fulham Road
London SW10 9PN
Tel: 071–351 5442

MGA (Mahoney Gretton Associates)
Southbank House
Black Prince Road
London SE1 7SJ
Tel: 071–587 1463

MPC Artists and Management
MPC House
15 Maple Mews
London NW6 5UZ
Tel: 071–434 1861

Julia MacDermot
14 Leamore Street
London W6 0JZ
Tel: 081–741 0269

Lucinda Macdonald
32 Riverains
71 Vicarage Crescent
London SW11 3UN
Tel: 071–350 2364

Ricky McCabe Entertainments
26 Crosby Road
North Waterloo
Liverpool L22 4QF
Tel: 051–920 3322

McCartt-Oreck-Barrett
10390 Santa Monica Boulevard
Suite 310
Los Angeles
CA 90025
USA
Tel: (0101) 213 553 2600

Jane McIntyre
Suite 70
London House
271/273 King Street
London W6 9LZ
Tel: 081–748 1696

Ken McReddie
91 Regent Street
London W1R 7TB
Tel: 071–439 1456

Jennifer Maffini
32 Stafford Mansions
Stafford Place
London SW1E 6NL
Tel: 071–828 4595

Hazel Malone Associates
26 Wellesley Road
London W4 4BW
Tel: 081–994 1619

Markham & Froggatt
4 Windmill Street
London W1P 1HF
Tel: 071–636 4412

Marmont Management
Langham House
302/308 Regent Street
London W1R 5AL
Tel: 071–637 3183

Billy Marsh Associates
19 Denmark Street
London WC2H 8NA
Tel: 071–379 4004

Scott Marshall
44 Perryn Road
London W3 7NA
Tel: 081–749 7692

Carol Martin Personal Management
19 Highate
West Hill
London N6 6NP
Tel: 081–348 0847

Marina Martin Management
6A Danbury Street
London N1 8JU
Tel: 071–359 3646

Nigel Martin-Smith Personal Management
Half Moon Chambers
Chapel Walks
Manchester M2 1HN
Tel: 061–832 8259

Mayday Management
68A Delancey Street
London NW1 7RY
Tel: 071–284 0242

Mayer Management Suite
44 Grafton House
2–3 Golden Square
London W1R 3AD
Tel: 071–434 1242

Melbourne Artists Management
643 St Kilda Road
Melbourne
Vic 3004
Australia
Tel: (010 61) 3 515228

Barry Michael Artists
14a Nelson Street
Balaclava
Victoria 3183
Australia
Tel: (010 61) 3 534 2288

Miller Management
82 Broom Park
Teddington
Middlesex TW11 9RR
Tel: 081–943 1292

Al Mitchell Associates
5 Anglers Lane
Kentish Town Road
London NW5 3DG
Tel: 071–482 5113

Morgan and Goodman
1 Old Compton Street
London W1V 5PH
Tel: 071–437 1383

William Morris Agency
31–32 Soho Square
London W1V 5DG
Tel: 071–434 2191

William Morris Agency
151 El Camino Drive
Beverly Hills
CA 90212
USA
Tel: (0101) 213 274 7451

Elaine Murphy Associates
1 Aberdeen Lane
Highbury
London N5 2EJ
Tel: 071–704 9913

The Narrow Road Company
21–22 Poland Street
London W1V 3DD
Tel: 071–434 0406

Norman Murray & Anne Chudleigh
243/245 Regent Street
London W1R 5DD
Tel: 071–629 4817

Dee O'Reilly Management
112 Gunnersbury Avenue
London W5 4HV
Tel: 081–993 7441

PBAM
First Floor
37 Marshall Street
London W1V 1WL
Tel: 071–734 8346

PBR Management
138 Putney Bridge Road
London SW16 2NQ
Tel: 081–871 4139/4130

Otto Personal Management
Regency House
75/77 St Mary's Road
Sheffield S2 4AN
Tel: (0742) 752592

PBJ Management
47 Dean Street
London W1V 5HL
Tel: 071–434 0672

PTA
Bugle House
21a Noel Street
London W1V 3PD
Tel: 071–439 2282

PVA Management
Alpha Tower
Paradise Circus
Birmingham B1 1TT
Tel: 021–643 4011

Al Parker
55 Park Lane
London W1Y 3DD
Tel: 071–499 4232

Barbara Pemberton Associates
I-Mex House
40 Princess Street
Manchester M1 6DE
Tel: 061–228 6616

Ann Peters & Company
186a Pulteney Street
Adelaide
SA 5000
Australia
Tel: (010 61) 8 232 0560

Peters Fraser & Dunlop
Fifth Floor
The Chambers
Chelsea Harbour
Lots Road
London SW10 0XF
Tel: 071–376 7676/071–352 4446

Plunket Greene
4 Ovington Gardens
London SW3 1LS
Tel: 071–584 0688

Peter Prichard Mezzanine
Floor 235
Regent Street
London W1R 8AX
Tel: 071–352 6417

Probe One Enterprises
PO Box 545
Box Hill
Melbourne
Vic 3128
Australia
Tel: (010 61) 3 756 6543

Nina Quick Associates
Second Floor
12 Abingdon Road
London W8 6AF
Tel: 071–937 2117

RKM (Rolf Kruger Management)
121 Gloucester Place
London W1H 3PJ
Tel: 071–224 4493

Douglas Rae Management
28 Charing Cross Road
London WC2H 0DB
Tel: 071–836 3903

Joan Reddin
Hazel Cottage
Wheeler End
Common Lane End
Buckinghamshire HP14 3NL
Tel: (0494) 882729

John Redway & Associates
5 Denmark Street
London WC2H 8LP
Tel: 071–836 2001

Regency Agency
25 Carr Road
Calverley
Leeds LS28 5NE
Tel: (0532) 558980

John Reid Enterprises
32 Galena Road
London W6 0CT
Tel: 081–741 9933

Caroline Renton
23 Crescent Lane
London SW4 9PT
Tel: 071–498 7217

Stella Richards Management
42 Hazelbury Road
London SW6 2ND
Tel: 071–736 7786

Rogers, Coleridge & White
20 Powis Mews
London W11 1JN
Tel: 071–221 3717

Jon Roseman Associates
103 Charing Cross Road
London WC2H 0DT
Tel: 071–439 8245

Rossmore Associates
1A Rossmore Road
Marylebone
London NW1 6NJ
Tel: 071–258 1953

Royce Personal Management
44 Nasmyth Street
London W6 0HB
Tel: 071–741 4341

Gillian Russell
124 Mayfield Road
Wellington Court
London W12 9LU
Tel: 081–740 4807

STE Representation
9301 Wilshire
Boulevard Suite
312 Beverly Hills
CA 90210
USA
Tel: 213 550 3982

St James's Management
4 Bankside Drive
Thames Ditton
Surrey KT7 0AQ
Tel: 081–398 9799

Saraband Associates
365 Liverpool Road
London N1 1LX
Tel: 071–609 5313

Anna Scher Theatre Management
70/72 Barnsbury Road
London N1 0ES
Tel: 071–278 2101

Judy Schoen & Associates
606 North Larchmont
Boulevard Suite
309 Los Angeles
CA 90004
USA
Tel: (0101) 213 962 1950

Tim Scott Personal Management
Studio F
South Bank Business Centre
140 Battersea Park Road
London SW11 4NB
Tel: 071–978 1352/1358

Selected Artists
Agency Suite
204 13111 Ventura Boulevard
Studio City
California 91604
USA
Tel: (0101) 818 905 5744

Severn Management Services
36 Chadbrook Crest
Richmond Hill Road
Edgbaston
Birmingham B15 3RL
Tel: 021–454 6905

David Shapira & Associates
15301 Ventura Boulevard
Suite 345
Sharman Oaks
CA 91403
USA
Tel: (0101) 818 906 0322

James Sharkey Associates
Third Floor
Suite 15
Golden Square
London W1R 3AG
Tel: 071–434 3801

Philip Shaw Associates
Suite 204
Garden Studios
11/15 Betterton Street
London WC2H 9BP
Tel: 071–379 0344

Vincent Shaw Associates
20 Jay Mews
Kensington Gore
London SW7 2EP
Tel: 071–581 8215

Lew Sherrell Agency
1354 Los Robleg
Palm Springs
California 92262
USA
Tel: (0101) 619 323 9514

Silvester Management
30 Brewer Street
London W1R 3FW
Tel: 071–734 7232

Dorothy Solomon
94 Roebuck House
Palace Street
London SW1E 5BE
Tel: 071–828 8258

Spotlight 7
Leicester Place
London WC2H 7BP
Tel: 071–437 7631

Annette Stone Associates
9 Newburgh Street
London W1V 1LH
Tel: 071–734 0626

Richard Stone Partnership
25 Whitehall
London SW1A 2BS
Tel: 071–839 6421

Sutton, Barth & Vennari
145 South Fairfax Avenue
Suite 310
Los Angeles
CA 90036
USA
Tel: (0101) 213 938 6000

TAM Management
52 Stafford Street
Liverpool L3 8LX
Tel: 051–207 2868

Talent Artists
4 Mews House
Princes Lane
London N10 3LU
Tel: 081–444 4088

TalkBack
33 Percy Street
London W1P 9FG
Tel: 071–631 3940

Ruth Tarko Agency
50/52 Cecil Street
Hillhead
Glasgow G12 8RJ
Tel: 041–339 8037/041–334 0555

Stacey Testro Management
Second Floor
153 Park Street
South Melbourne
Vic 3205
Australia
Tel: (010 61) 3 690 7116/3991

The Agency
10351 Santa Monica
Boulevard Suite
211 Los Angeles
CA 90025
USA
Tel: (0101) 213 551 3000

Thomas and Benda Associates
361 Edgware Road
London W2 1BS
Tel: 071–723 5509

Nick Thomas Enterprises
Event House
Queen Margaret's Road
Scarborough YO11 2SA
Tel: (0723) 500038

Jim Thompson
Rivington House
82 Great Eastern Street
London EC2A 3JL
Tel: 071–739 8410

Tobias Management
Regency Court
62/66 Deansgate
Manchester M3 2EN
Tel: 061–832 5128

Triad Artists
10100 Santa Monica Boulevard
16th Floor
Los Angeles CA 90067
USA
Tel: (0101) 213 556 2727

Gary Trolan Management
30 Burrard Road
London NW6 1DB
Tel: 071–431 4367/071–794 4429

Twentieth Century Artists
Suite 303
3800 Barham Boulevard
Los Angeles
California 90068
USA
Tel: (0101) 213 850 5516

United Talent Agency
9560 Wilshire Boulevard
Beverly Hills
California 90212
USA
Tel: (0101) 213 273 6700

Adza Vincent
11A Ivor Place
London NW1 6HS
Tel: 071–262 9356

Janet Welch Personal Management
486 Chiswick High Road
London W4 5TT
Tel: 081–994 2696

David White Associates
2 Ormond Road
Richmond-upon-Thames
Surrey TW10 6TH
Tel: 081–940 8300

Michael Whitehall
125 Gloucester Road
London SW7 4TE
Tel: 071–244 8466

David Wilkinson Associates
115 Hazelbury Road
London SW6 2LX
Tel: 071–371 5188

Dave Winslett Entertainments
4 Cliff End
Purley
Surrey CR2 1BN
Tel: 081–668 0531

Writers & Artists Agency
11726 San Vicente Boulevard
Suite 300
Los Angeles CA 90049
USA
Tel: (0101) 213 820 2240

April Young
The Clockhouse
6 St Catherine's Mews
Milner Street
London SW3 2PU
Tel: 071–584 1274

Young Casting
7 Beaumont Gate
Glasgow G12 9EE
Tel: 041–334 2646

Sylvia Young Managment
Rossmore Road
London NW1 6NJ
Tel: 071–723 003543

Sonny Zahl Associates
57 Great Cumberland Place
London W1H 7LJ
Tel: 071–724 3684/071–723 5699

tv companies

Anglia Television
Anglia House
Norwich NR1 3JG
Tel: (0603) 615151

BBC TV
Television Centre
Wood Lane
London W12 7RJ
Tel: 081–743 8000

BBC Elstree Centre
Clarendon Road
Borehamwood
Hertfordshire WD6 1JF
Tel: 081–953 6100

The Bill
63 Windsor Avenue
Merton Abbey
London SW19 2SN
Tel: 081–540 0600

Border Television
Television Centre
Carlisle CA1 3NT
Tel: (0228) 25101

Central Television
Central House
Broad Street
Birmingham B1 2JP
Tel: 021–643 9898

Channel 7
Television Centre
Epping NSW 2121
Australia
Tel: (010 61) 2 877 7777

Channel Television
The Television Centre
St Helier
Jersey
Channel Islands
Tel: (0534) 59446

Channel Four Television
60 Charlotte Street
London W1P 2AX
Tel: 071–631 4444

Grampian Television
Queen's Cross
Aberdeen AB9 2XJ
Tel: (0224) 646464

Granada TV
Granada Television Centre
Quay Street
Manchester M60 9EA
Tel: 061–832 7211

Grundy Television
27 Church Street
Richmond
Victoria 3121
Australia
Tel: (010 61) 3 429 2533

HTV Wales
Television Centre
Culverhouse Cross
Cardiff CF5 6XJ
Tel: (0222) 590590

HTV West
Television Centre
Bath Road
Bristol BS4 3HG
Tel: (0272) 778366

ITN 200L
Grays Inn Road
London WC1
Tel: 071–833 3000

International Weather Productions
The Interchange
Oval Road
Camden Lock
London NW1
Tel: 071–284 3484

LWT
South Bank Television Centre
London SE1 9LT
Tel: 071–261 3434

Mersey Television
Campus Manor
Childwall Abbey Road
Childwall
Liverpool L16 0JP
Tel: 051–722 9122

Scottish Television
Cowcaddens
Glasgow G2 3PR
Tel: 041–332 9999

Thames Television
306/316 Euston Road
London NW1 3BB
Tel: 071–387 9494

TSW
Derry's Cross
Plymouth
Devon PL1 2SP
Tel: (0752) 663322

TV-am
Breakfast Television Centre
Hawley Crescent
London NW1 8EF
Tel: 071–267 4300/4377

TVS
Television Centre
Southampton SO9 5HZ
Tel: (0703) 634211

Tyne Tees Television
Television Centre
City Road
Newcastle upon Tyne NE1 2AL
Tel: 091–261 0181

Ulster Television
Haverlock House
Ormeau Road
Belfast BT7 1EB
Tel: (0232) 328122

Yorkshire Television
Television Centre
Leeds LS3 1JS
Tel: (0532) 438283

251

fan clubs

Send a stamped, self-addressed envelope with all enquiries

The A-Team Appreciation Society
'Xanth'
11 Somercotes
Laindon
Basildon
Essex SS15 5TZ

Auf Wiedersehen, Pet
David Beavis
Heatherley Cheshire Home
Effingham Lane
Copthorne
West Sussex RH10 3HS

The Avengers
Stay Tuned
114 Dartmouth Street
Burslem
Stoke-on-Trent
Staffordshire ST6 1HE

Overseas club:
Stay Tuned
64 Southampton Road
Carole Park
Queensland 4300
Australia

Battlestar Galactica
'The Thirteenth Tribe'
c/o 19 Woodlands Road
Stanton
Burton-on-Trent
Staffordshire DE15 9TH

Beauty and the Beast
UK Chamber
Sheila Waters
14 Judith Road
Kettering
Northamptonshire NN16 0NX

The Bill Fan Club
Sierra Oscar
PO Box 1816
Edmonton
London N18 2UZ

Crossroads:
The Noele Gordon and Crossroads Appreciation
Society
John Kavyo and Simon Cole
Flat 8 Harewood Apartments
9 Undercliff Road
Boscombe Bournemouth BH5 1BL

The Emmerdale Club
PO Box 330
St Albans
Hertfordshire AL4 0LF

Garrison's Gorillas Appreciation Society
4 Hedera Road
Southampton SO3 6SF

Home and Away UK Fan Club
PO Box 525
Maidenhead
Berkshire SL6 1YU

Poldark Appreciation Society
PO Box 24
St Just Nr Penzance
Cornwall TR19 7UR

The Prisoner:
Six of One
PO Box 60
Harrogate HG1 2TP

Prisoner: Cell Block H
Room 28
St James Chambers
St James Street
Derby DE1 1QZ

Randall and Hopkirk (Deceased) Appreciation Society (RAHDAS)
10 Brook Avenue
Edgware Middlesex HA8 9XF

The Saint Club
c/o Arbour Youth Centre
Shandy Street
Stepney
London E1

Scarecrow & Mrs King Fellowship
c/o Margaret Richardson
30 Kirkdale Green
Rye Hill
Newcastle upon Tyne NE4 6HU

The Sooty Fan Club
c/o Windhill Manor
Leeds Road
Shipley
West Yorkshire BD18 1BP

Take the High Road Fan Club
PO Box 24
St Just
Nr Penzance
Cornwall TR19 7UR

The TV Enthusiasts Club
(News and views about television)
64 Daisy Road
Brighouse
West Yorkshire HD6 3SX

'V' The Freedom League
c/o 30 Borodin Close
Brighton Hill
Basingstoke
Hampshire RG22 4EN

Westerns
Laramie Trail
196 Whitehouse Common Road
Sutton Coldfield
West Midlands B75 6DN

The Young Doctors
Appreciation Society
2 Marston Lane
Anchorage Park
Portsmouth PO3 5TW